C000228492

STREE'

Somerset

First published in 2002 by

Philip's, a division of
Octopus Publishing Group Ltd
2-4 Heron Quays, London E14 4JP

Second edition 2006
First impression 2006
SOMBA

ISBN-10   0-540-08843-9 (pocket)
ISBN-13   978-0-540-08843-0 (pocket)

© Philip's 2006

Ordnance Survey®

Contents

III   **Key to map symbols**

IV   **Key to map pages**

VI   **Route planning**

X   **Administrative and Postcode boundaries**

1   **Street maps** at 2⅔ inches to 1 mile

122   **Street maps** at 1⅓ inches to 1 mile

200   **Street maps** at 2⅔ inches to 1 mile

226   **Street maps of Bristol and Bath city centres** at 5⅓ inches to 1 mile

229   **Index** of towns and villages

233   **Index** of streets, hospitals, industrial estates, railway stations, schools, shopping centres, universities and places of interest

Digital Data

The exceptionally high-quality mapping found in this atlas is available as digital data in TIFF format, which is easily convertible to other bitmapped (raster) image formats.

The index is also available in digital form as a standard database table. It contains all the details found in the printed index together with the National Grid reference for the map square in which each entry is named.

For further information and to discuss your requirements, please contact Philip's on 020 7644 6932 or james.mann@philips-maps.co.uk

Motorway with junction number	
Primary route – dual/single carriageway	
A road – dual/single carriageway	
B road – dual/single carriageway	
Minor road – dual/single carriageway	
Other minor road – dual/single carriageway	
Road under construction	
Tunnel, covered road	
Rural track, private road or narrow road in urban area	
Gate or obstruction to traffic (restrictions may not apply at all times or to all vehicles)	
Path, bridleway, byway open to all traffic, road used as a public path	
Pedestrianised area	
DY7 **Postcode boundaries**	
County and unitary authority boundaries	
Railway, tunnel, railway under construction	
Tramway, tramway under construction	
Miniature railway	
Walsall **Railway station**	
Private railway station	
South Shields **Metro station**	
Tram stop, tram stop under construction	
Bus, coach station	

Ambulance station	
Coastguard station	
Fire station	
Police station	
Accident and Emergency entrance to hospital	
H **Hospital**	
Place of worship	
i **Information Centre** (open all year)	
Shopping Centre	
P P&R **Parking, Park and Ride**	
PO **Post Office**	
Camping site, caravan site	
Golf course, picnic site	
Prim Sch **Important buildings, schools, colleges, universities and hospitals**	
Built up area	
Woods	
River Medway **Water name**	
River, weir, stream	
Canal, lock, tunnel	
Water	
Tidal water	
Church **Non-Roman antiquity**	
ROMAN FORT **Roman antiquity**	
87 **Adjoining page indicators and overlap bands**	
237 The colour of the arrow and the band indicates the scale of the adjoining or overlapping page (see scales below)	

Enlarged mapping only

Railway or bus station building	
Place of interest	
Parkland	

Acad	**Academy**	Inst	**Institute**	Recn Gd	**Recreation**
Allot Gdns	**Allotments**	Ct	**Law Court**		**Ground**
Cemy	**Cemetery**	L Ctr	**Leisure Centre**	Resr	**Reservoir**
C Ctr	**Civic Centre**	LC	**Level Crossing**	Ret Pk	**Retail Park**
CH	**Club House**	Liby	**Library**	Sch	**School**
Coll	**College**	Mkt	**Market**	Sh Ctr	**Shopping Centre**
Crem	**Crematorium**	Meml	**Memorial**	TH	**Town Hall/House**
Ent	**Enterprise**	Mon	**Monument**	Trad Est	**Trading Estate**
Ex H	**Exhibition Hall**	Mus	**Museum**	Univ	**University**
Ind Est	**Industrial Estate**	Obsy	**Observatory**	W Twr	**Water Tower**
IRB Sta	**Inshore Rescue**	Pal	**Royal Palace**	Wks	**Works**
	Boat Station	PH	**Public House**	YH	**Youth Hostel**

■ The small numbers around the edges of the maps identify the 1 kilometre National Grid lines

■ The dark grey border on the inside edge of some pages indicates that the mapping does not continue onto the adjacent page

The scale of the maps on the pages numbered in blue is 4.2 cm to 1 km • 2⅔ inches to 1 mile • 1: 23810	0 ¼ ½ ¾ 1 mile 0 250m 500m 750m 1 kilometre
The scale of the maps on pages numbered in green is 2.1 cm to 1 km • 1⅓ inches to 1 mile • 1: 47620	0 ¼ ½ ¾ 1 mile 0 250m 500m 750m 1 kilometre
The scale of the maps on pages numbered in red is 8.4 cm to 1 km • 5⅓ inches to 1 mile • 1: 11900	0 220 yards 440 yards 660 yards ½ mile 0 125m 250m 375m ½ kilometre

IV

Key to map pages

227	Map pages at 5⅓ inches to 1 mile
113	Map pages at 2⅔ inches to 1 mile
141	Map pages at 1⅓ inches to 1 mile

Scale

0 — 5 — 10 — 15 — 20 km
0 — 5 — 10 miles

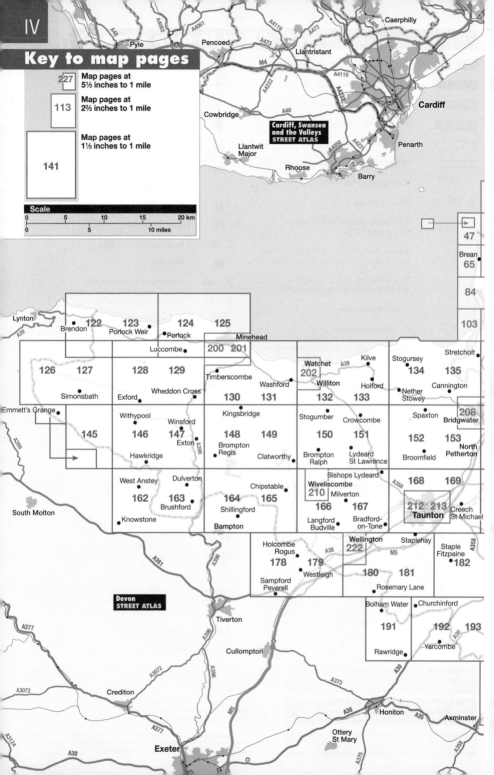

Pyle
Pencoed
A4119
Caerphilly
Llantristant
M4
A4119
Cardiff
Cowbridge
A48
Cardiff, Swansea and the Valleys STREET ATLAS
Llantwit Major
Penarth
Rhoose
Barry

47

Brean
65

84

103

Lynton
Brendon 122 123 Porlock Weir 124 125
Porlock
Minehead
Luccombe

126 127 128 129
Timberscombe 130 131 Washford
Watchet 202 Williton 132 133 Kilve
Holford
Stogursey 134 135 Stretcholt
Nether Stowey Cannington

Simonsbath Exford Wheddon Cross

Emmett's Grange
Withypool Winsford
145 146 147 Exton 148 149
Kingsbridge
Brompton Regis
Hawkridge Clatworthy
Stogumber 150 Crowcombe 151
Brompton Ralph Lydeard St Lawrence
Spaxton 152 153 Broomfield
Bridgwater 208
North Petherton

West Anstey Dulverton
162 163 164 165
Brushford Shillingford
Knowstone Bampton
Chipstable
Wiveliscombe 210 Milverton
166 Langford Budville 167 Bradford-on-Tone
Bishops Lydeard 168 169
212·213 Taunton Creech St Michael

Devon STREET ATLAS
Holcombe Rogus 178 179 Westleigh
Sampford Peverell
A38
Wellington 222
180 181 Rosemary Lane
Staplehay
Staple Fitzpaine 182

Tiverton
Cullompton
Bolham Water Churchinford
191 192 193 Yarcombe
Rawridge

Crediton
Honiton Axminster
Ottery St Mary
Exeter

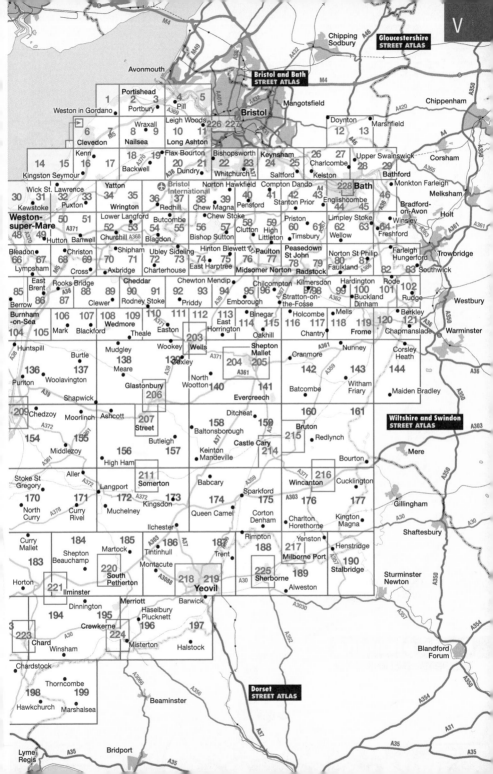

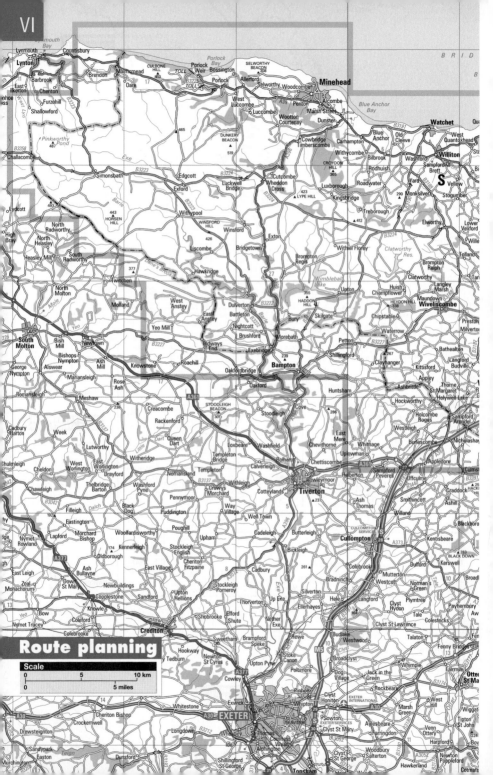

Route planning

Scale
0   5   10 km
0   5 miles

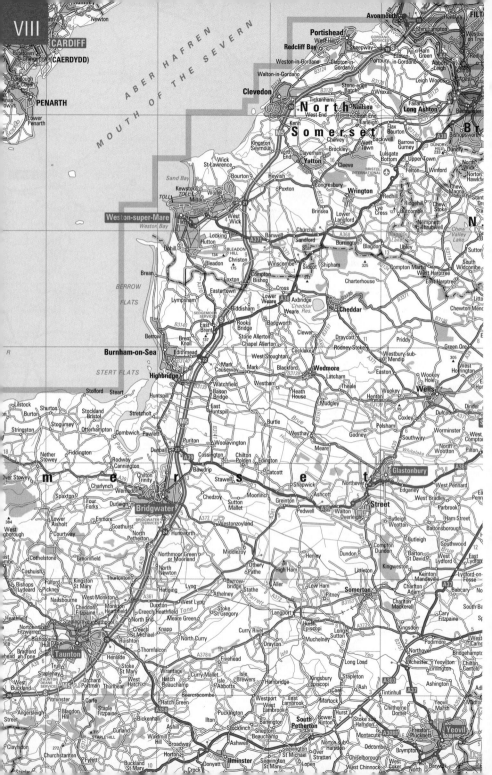

X

Major administrative and Postcode boundaries

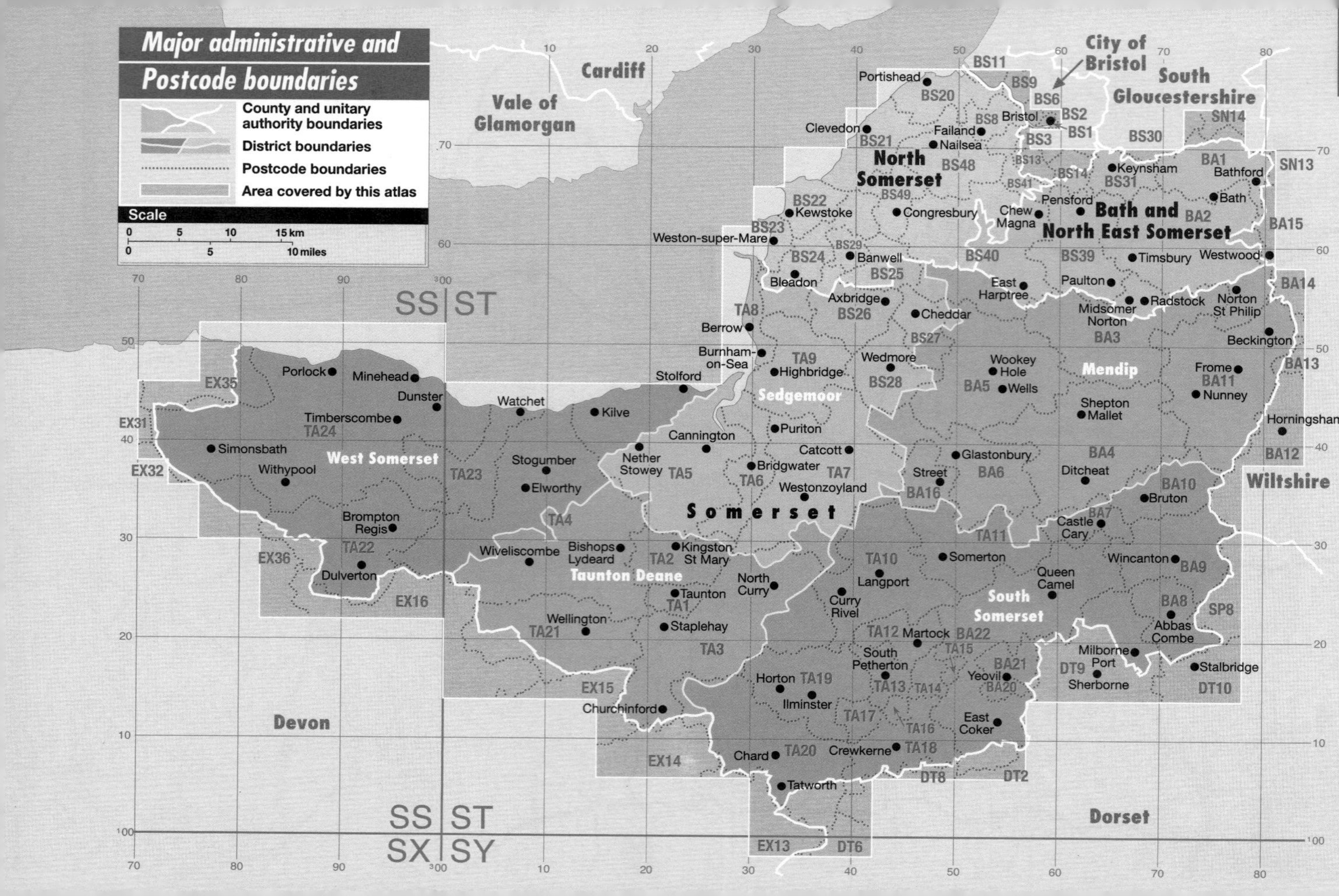

— County and unitary authority boundaries
— District boundaries
···· Postcode boundaries
☐ Area covered by this atlas

Scale
0   5   10   15 km
0   5   10 miles

City of Bristol
South Gloucestershire
Wiltshire
Dorset
Devon
North Somerset
Bath and North East Somerset
West Somerset
Sedgemoor
Mendip
South Somerset
Somerset
Taunton Deane
Cardiff
Vale of Glamorgan

SS | ST
SS ST
SX | SY
SX SY

Place names:
Portishead, Clevedon, Weston-super-Mare, Kewstoke, Bleadon, Burnham-on-Sea, Berrow, Stolford, Watchet, Dunster, Minehead, Porlock, Simonsbath, Withypool, Timberscombe, Brompton Regis, Dulverton, Kilve, Stogumber, Elworthy, Nether Stowey, Cannington, Bridgwater, Westonzoyland, Puriton, Catcott, Highbridge, Axbridge, Banwell, Congresbury, Nailsea, Failand, Keynsham, Bath, Bathford, Bathampton, Westwood, Beckington, Frome, Nunney, Norton St Philip, Radstock, Midsomer Norton, Timsbury, Paulton, Chew Magna, Pensford, East Harptree, Cheddar, Wedmore, Wookey Hole, Wells, Shepton Mallet, Glastonbury, Street, Langport, Somerton, Curry Rivel, North Curry, Kingston St Mary, Taunton, Staplehay, Bishops Lydeard, Wiveliscombe, Wellington, Churchinford, Chard, Tatworth, Crewkerne, Ilminster, Horton, South Petherton, Martock, Yeovil, East Coker, Queen Camel, Castle Cary, Ditcheat, Wincanton, Bruton, Abbas Combe, Milborne Port, Sherborne, Stalbridge, Hornsham

Postcode areas: SN13, SN14, BA15, BA14, BA13, BA12, BA1, BA2, BA3, BA4, BA5, BA6, BA7, BA8, BA9, BA10, BA11, BA16, BA20, BA21, BA22, BS30, BS31, BS14, BS13, BS41, BS40, BS48, BS8, BS3, BS1, BS2, BS6, BS9, BS11, BS20, BS21, BS22, BS23, BS24, BS25, BS26, BS27, BS28, BS29, BS49, BS39, SP8, DT10, DT9, DT2, DT8, DT6, DT5, TA1, TA2, TA3, TA4, TA5, TA6, TA7, TA8, TA9, TA10, TA11, TA12, TA13, TA14, TA15, TA16, TA17, TA18, TA19, TA20, TA21, TA22, TA23, TA24, EX13, EX14, EX15, EX16, EX32, EX35, EX36

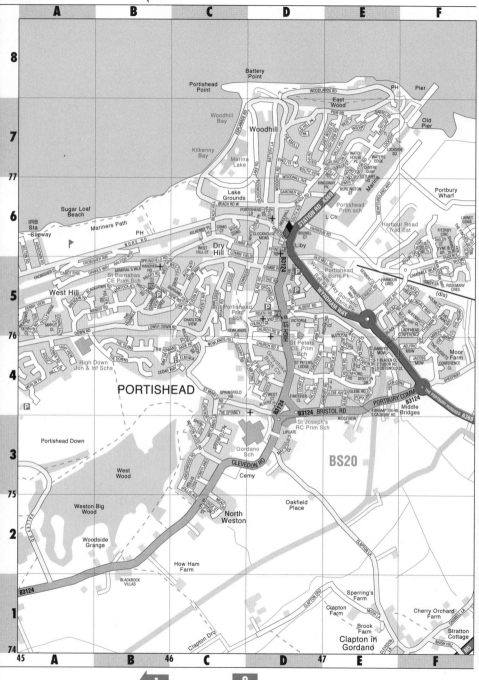

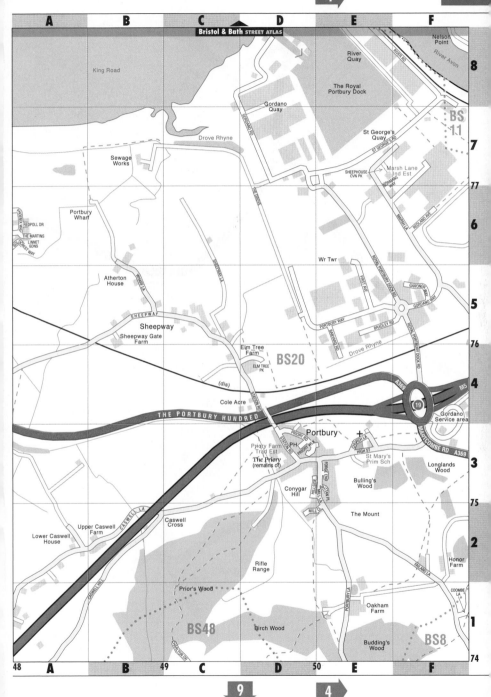

Bristol & Bath STREET ATLAS

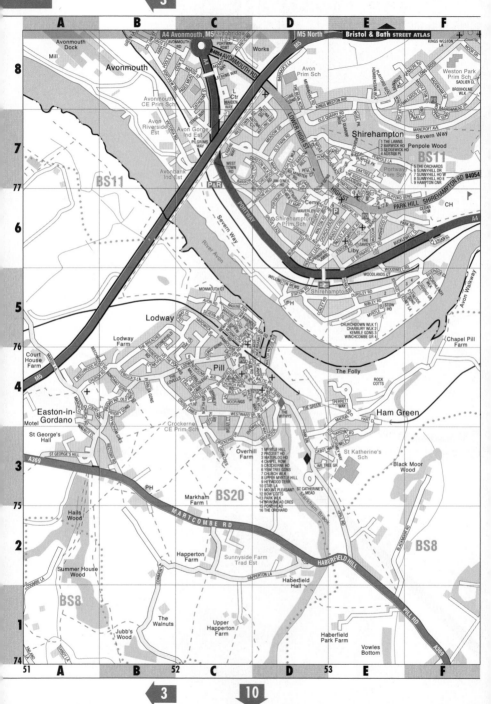

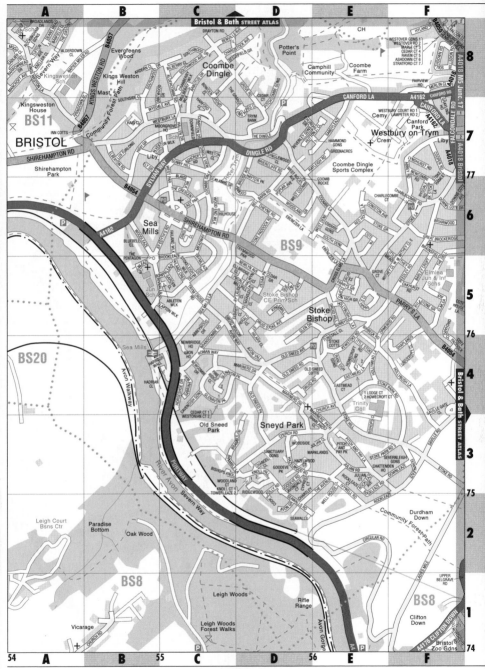

Bristol & Bath STREET ATLAS

BS11
BRISTOL
BS20
BS8
BS9
BS8

Kingsweston House
Kingsweston Sch
Evergreens Wood
Coombe Dingle
Kings Weston Hill
Potter's Point
Camphill Community
Coombe Farm
CH
WESTOVER GDNS 1
WESTOVER RD 2
MARIE CT 3
CEDAR CT 4
RAVEN CT 5
ASHDOWN CT 6
STRATFORD CT 7
FAIRVIEW HO
CANFORD LA
A4162
CANFORD RD
Cemy
Westbury Court Rd 1
Lampeter Rd 2
Canford Park
Westbury on Trym
Crem
Liby
Shirehampton Park
Shirehampton Rd
Dingle Rd
The Dingle
Hammond Gdns
Greenacres
Coombe Dingle Sports Complex
Charlecombe Ct
Great Brockeridge
Elmlea Jun & Inf Schs
Sea Mills
Bluebell Ho
The Pentagon
Stoke Bishop CE Prim Sch
Stoke Bishop
Grove Ct
Parrys La
B4054
Sea Mills
Avon Walkway
Hadrian Cl
Newbridge Ho
Roman Way
Mariners Dr
Old Sneed Cotts
Eastmead Ct
Eastmead
Stoke Park Rd
1 Lodge Ct
2 Howecroft Ct
Trinity Coll
Old Sneed Park
Sneyd Park
Church Rd
Woodside
Marklands
Pitch and Pay Pk
Severnleigh Gdns
Chattenden Ho
Julian Rd
Cedar Ct 1
Westonian Ct 2
Sanctuary Gdns
Hazelwood
Goodeve Pk
Bishops Knoll
Woodland Ct
Knoll Ct 1
Towerleaze 2
Ridgewood
Seawalls
Durdham Down
Community Forest Path
Circular Rd
Leigh Court Bsns Ctr
Paradise Bottom
Oak Wood
River Avon Severn Way
Portway
Leigh Woods
Rifle Range
Avon Gorge
Upper Belgrave Rd
Clifton Down
Vicarage
Church Rd
Leigh Woods Forest Walks
A4176 CLIFTON DOWN
Bristol Zoo Gdns

Bristol & Bath STREET ATLAS

54   55   56

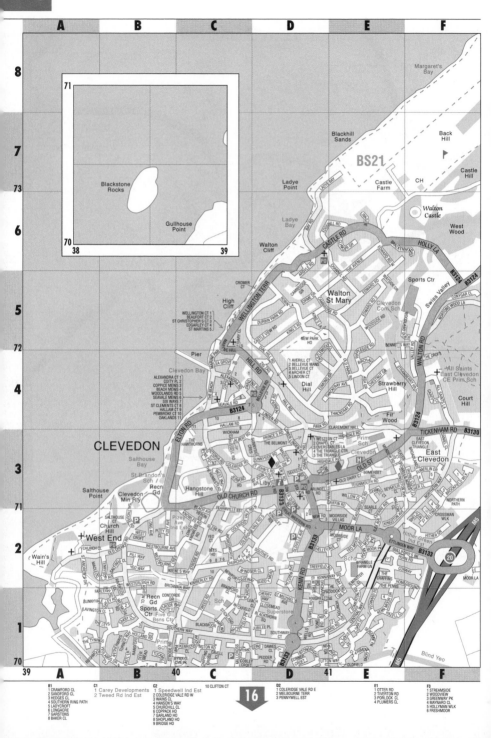

71

70

38   **39**

Blackstone
Rocks

Gullhouse
Point

Margaret's
Bay

Blackhill
Sands

Back
Hill

BS21

Castle
Hill

CH

Walton
Castle

West
Wood

Ladye
Point

Ladye
Bay

Walton
Cliff

CROMER
CT

High
Cliff

Walton
St Mary

Clevedon
Com Sch

Sports Ctr

Swiss Valley

NORTON WOOD LA

WELLINGTON CT 1
BEAUFORT CT 2
ST CHRISTOPHER'S 3
ST MARTINS 5

Pier

Clevedon Bay

ALEXANDRA CT 1
COITY PL 2
COPPICE MEWS 3
BEACH MEWS 4
WOODLANDS RD 5
SEAVALE MEWS 6
SIX WAYS 7
ST CLEMENTS CT 8
HALLAM CT 9
PEMBROKE CT 10
OAKLANDS 11

1 AVERILL CT
2 BELLEVUE MANS
3 BELLEVUE CT
4 ARCHER CT
5 LINDON CT

New Park
Ho

Dial
Hill

Strawberry
Hill

All Saints
East Clevedon
CE Prim Sch

Court
Hill

Fir
Wood

CLEVEDON

Salthouse
Bay

St Brandon's
Sch

Salthouse
Point

Clevedon Min Rly

Hangstone
Hill

Recn
Gd

The Hawthorns

HALLAM RD

WICKHAM

1 CHAPEL CT
2 WESTERN CT
3 DUNSTABLES LA
4 THE TRIANGLE STR
5 THE TRIANGLE

THE BELMONT

Prim
Sch

Clevedon

HIGHDALE

East
Clevedon
Triangle

East
Clevedon

TICKENHAM RD

B3130

Libry

CLAREMONT HALL

OLD CHURCH RD

Salthouse
Bay

West
Croft

Church
Hill

West End

Wain's
Hill

B3133

OLD DAIRY CT

OLD ST

Somerset

Northern
Path

CROSSMAN
WLK

MOOR LA

Moorside
Villas

B3133

Hither Green
Ind Est

M5

20

MOOR LA

THE
CHAFFINS
THE PENNIS

HOMEGROUND

Blind Yeo

M5

Recn
Gd

Sports
Ctr

Prim
Sch

Superstore

39   **A**   **B**   **40**   **C**   **D**   **41**   **E**   **F**

16

B1
1 CRAWFORD CL
2 SANDFORD CL
3 HEDGES CL
4 SOUTHERN RING PATH
5 LADYCROFT
6 LONGACRE
7 GARSTONS
8 BAKER CL

C1
1 Carey Developments
2 Tweed Rd Ind Est

C2
1 Speedwell Ind Est
2 COLERIDGE VALE RD W
3 WAINS CL
4 HANSON'S WAY
5 CHURCHILL CL
6 COPPACK HO
7 GARLAND HO
8 SHOPLAND HO
9 BRIDGE HO

10 CLIFTON CT

D2
1 COLERIDGE VALE RD E
2 MELBOURNE TERR
3 PENNYWELL EST

E1
1 OTTER RD
2 TIVERTON RD
3 PORLOCK CL
4 PLUMERS CL

F3
1 STREAMSIDE
2 WOODVIEW
3 GREENWAY PK
4 MAYNARD CL
5 HOLLYMAN WLK
6 FRESHMOOR

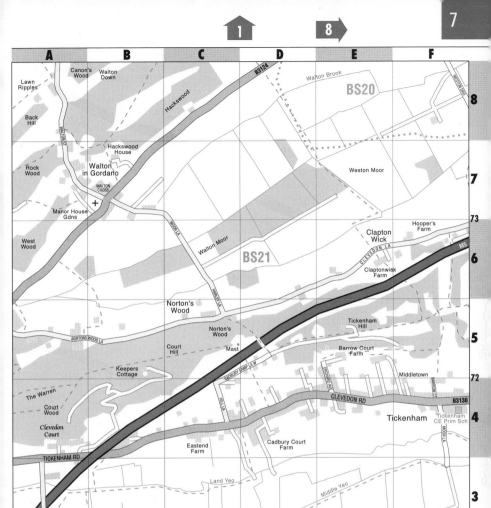

	A	B	C	D	E	F	

Lawn Ripples

Canon's Wood

Walton Down

Hackswood

B3124

Walton Brook

BS20

8

Back Hill

WESTON RD

Rock Wood

Hackswood House

Walton in Gordano

WALTON CROSS

Weston Moor

7

West Wood

Manor House Gdns

Walton Moor

BS21

73

Clapton Wick

Hooper's Farm

Clevedon La

M5

6

Norton's Wood

Claptonwick Farm

NORTONS WOOD LA

Norton's Wood

Tickenham Hill

5

Court Hill

Mast

Barrow Court Farm

Keepers Cottage

CADBURY CAMP LA W.

Middletown

72

The Warren

Court Wood

Clevedon Court

HILL LA

ORCHARD AVE

CLEVEDON RD

BARROW CT

B3130

4

Tickenham

Tickenham CE Prim Sch

TICKENHAM RD

Eastend Farm

Cadbury Court Farm

MOOR LA

Land Yeo

Middle Yeo

3

COURT LA

Clevedon Pottery

Clevedon Boundary Rhyne

Tickenham Drove

71

MOOR LA

Clevedon Moor

Tickenham Moor

2

MANMOOR LA

COOK'S LA

Clevedon Craft Ctr

Triangle Farm

Smeathyard Farm

North Drove

BS48

1

Old Smeath Farm

Nailsea Moor

Ten Feet Rhyne

70

| A | | B | 43 | C | | D | 44 | E | | F | |

A B C D E F

8

7

73

6

5

72

4

3

71

2

1

70

45 A B 46 C D 47 E F

BS20

BS21

BS21

BS48

NAILSEA

Clapton in Gordano

THE CAUSEWAY
SWANCOMBE
MORGANS BLDGS

NAISH HILL

Hillcrest

Nicholas Wood

Clapton Court

Clapton Moor

The Old Rectory

Morgans Buildings

Naish House

WOOD LA

Parsonage Wood

Clevedon Lane Farm

CLEVEDON LA

West Park Wood

New Farm

Cockheap Wood

Dunhill Wood

Naish Farm

West Park Wood

Upper Sidelands

CADBURY CAMP LA

Chummock Wood

Lime Breach Wood

M5

Cadbury Camp

Abbot's Horn

Mogg's Wood

Baye's Wood

High Wood

CH

Little Valley Farm

Round Wood

Summerhouse Wood

Hale's Farm

Longwood

CLEVEDON RD

B3128

ELM TREE AVE

Folly Farm House

OLD LA

Luggard's Cross

PH

Batch Farm

SUMMERHOUSE LA

TICKENHAM HILL

HOUSE LA

B3130

CLEVEDON RD

Luggard's Cross Farm

WAGGING BOUND LA

CHURCH LA

B3128

STONEHENGE LA

THE RIPPLE
STONEHENGE

Wellhouse Farm

Towerhouse Wood

Birdcombe Court Farm

Tickenham Court

Stone-edge Batch

Jacklands Bridge

Jacklands Farm

Milton's Farm

BIRDCOMBE CL

Southfield Rd Trad Est

Coates Est

Causeway Bridge

LIMEBREACH WOOD 1
MIDDLE YEO GN 2

Ravenswood Special Sch

GREENFIELD GDNS

MEADOW
SOUTHFIELD RD

SOUTHFIELD RD

WITHY CL

B3130

HIGH ST

Tickenham Boundary Rhyna

NORTH DRO

Kingshill CE Prim Sch

GLADE
SHADE RD

DROVE

Superstore
NAILSEA PARK
CL

GOLDEN VALLEY
PRIM SCH

CAUSEWAY VIEW

FRITH WAY
SILVER CT

NIGHTINGALE GDNS
MOORLANDS CL

BEECHWOOD RD

ABBOTS CL
EASTWAY

EASTWAY

TAVENERS WLK

HIGH OVERVIEW

FOSSE BARTON
FOSSE
SILVERBOW RD

SILVER ST

CRICKET FIELD

CHAPEL

STOCK WAY N

STOCK WAY N

P P

WATERY LA
HANNAH MORE RD

MOORFIELDS

SYCAMORE

Liby

P

SCOTCH HORN WAY

CHAPEL HILL

WOODVIELDS CL
GREENFIELD

MEADWAY AVE

Coll

STOCK WAY S

P P

ORCHARD RD
IVY CL

WYATT CL

VALLEY GDNS

Nailsea Com Sch

YEW TREE CL

RIDGEWAY

MIZZY CL

CLARKEN

POLDEN

Poplar Farm

LINKWOOD DR

GOSS CL
GOSS VIEW

Allot Gdns

COOMBE

POLLOCK GDNS

MANTON WAY

St Francis Prim Sch

Parish Brook

WEST END LA

BLACKFRIARS RD

YEO CL

TRINITY CL
TRINITY

PLOUGHED PADDOCK
WAREHAM CL

QUEENS RD

CORFE

SHAFTESBURY RD

CORFE

BURFORD

CHARTERHOUSE RD

West End Trad Est

1 AVALON HO
2 CROWN HO

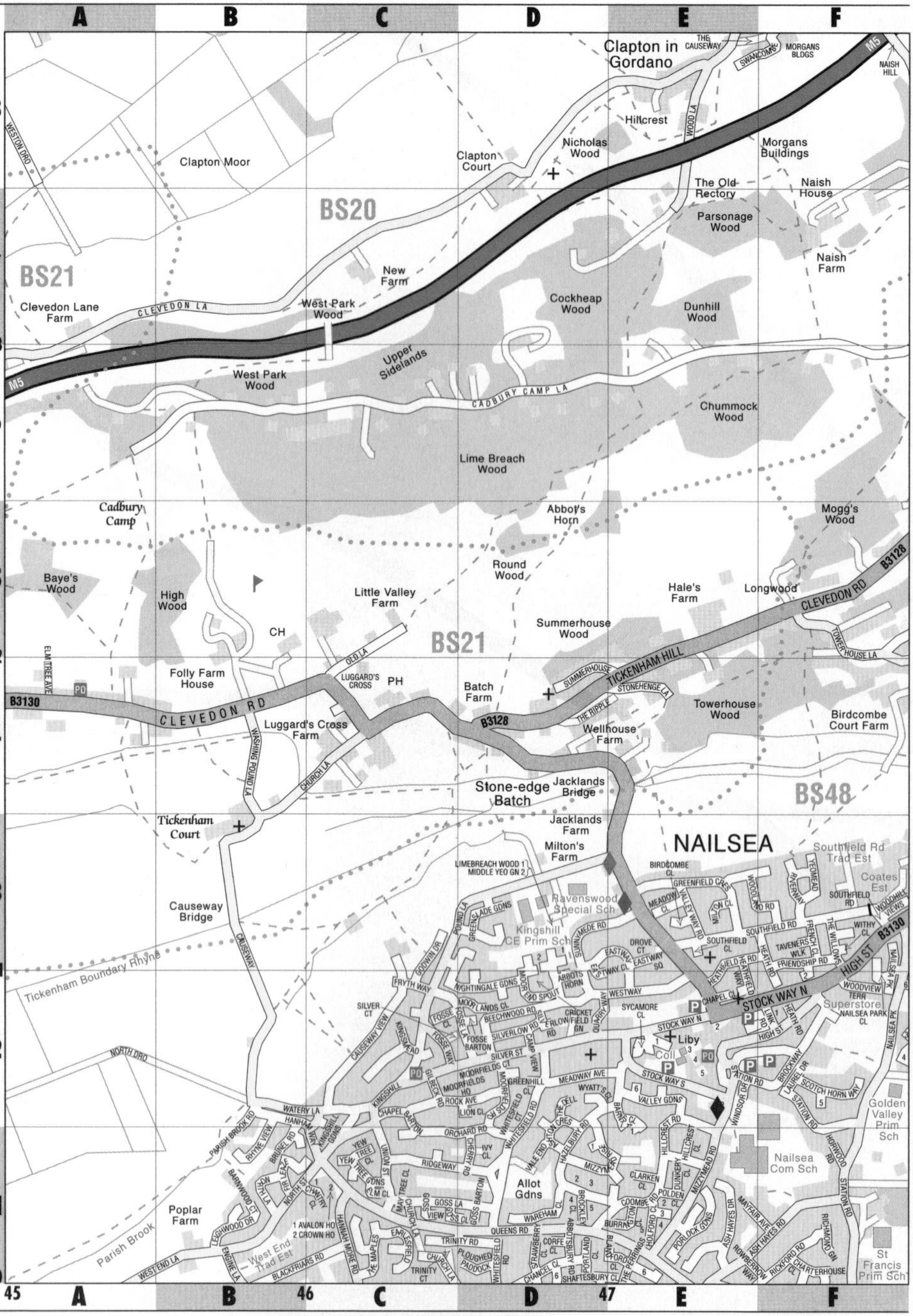

D1
1 MIZZYMEAD CL
2 BEAUFORT GDNS
3 AMBERLEY GDNS
4 CLAREMONT GDNS
5 DOWNLAND CL
6 DORCHESTER CL

E1
1 FARMHOUSE CT
2 BRENDON GDNS
3 MENDIP CL
4 SELWORTHY GDNS
5 DUNSTER GDNS
6 BIDDISHAM CL

E2
1 CHRIST CHURCH CL
2 CLEVEDON WLK
3 SOMERSET SQ
4 COLLIERS WLK
5 CROWN GLASS PL
6 VALLEY CL
7 FARMHOUSE CL

F2
1 HOBBS CT
2 FRIENDSHIP GR
3 SCOTS PINE AVE
4 HAWTHORN WAY
5 SCOTCH HORN CL
6 BLACKTHORN WAY

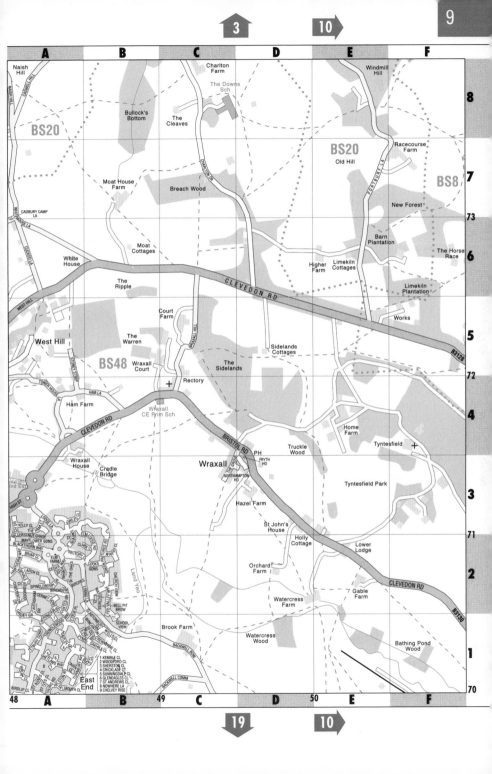

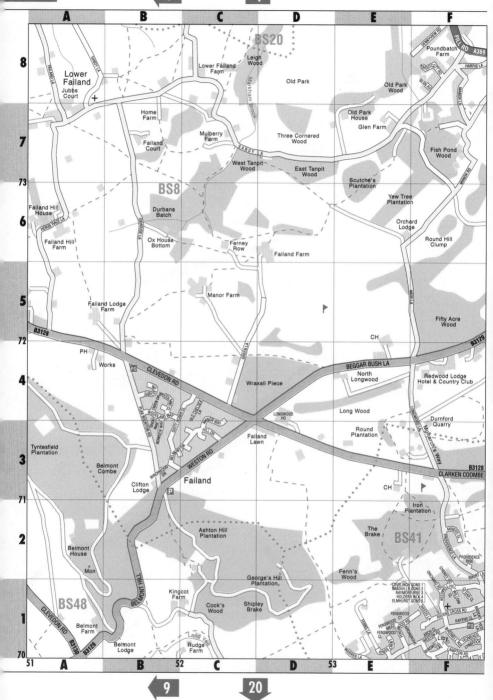

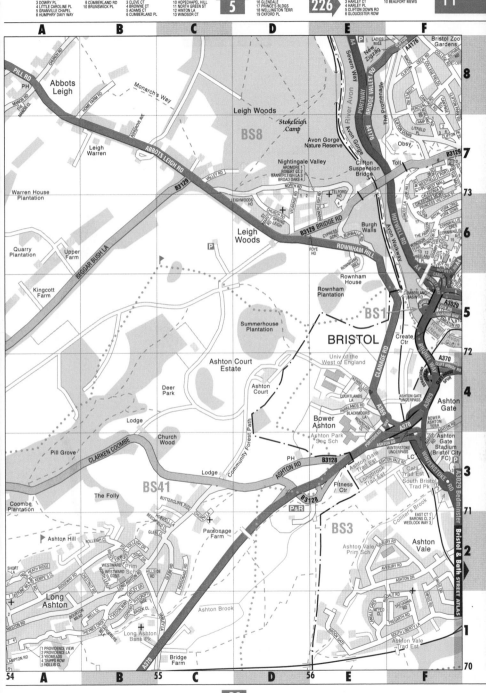

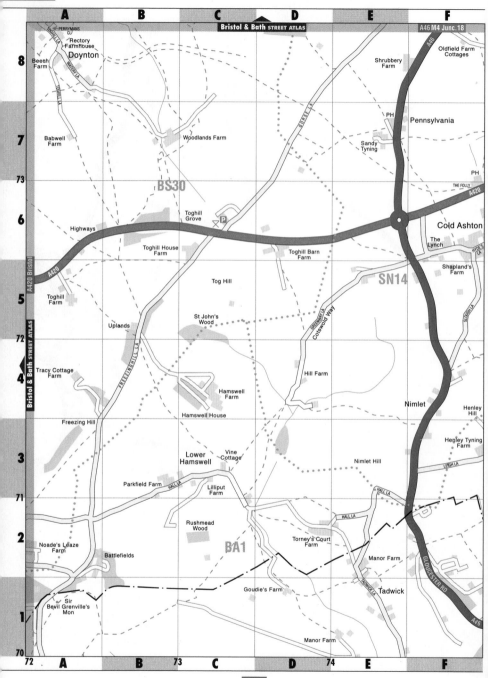

A46 M4 Junc.18

Doynton

PERRYMANS CL
Rectory Farmhouse
Beech Farm
YOGHILL LA
WATERS LA

Oldfield Farm Cottages

8

Shrubbery Farm

7

Babwell Farm

Woodlands Farm

PH

Pennsylvania

Sandy Tyning

PH

73

BS30

THE FOLLY

A420

6

Highways

Toghill Grove

P

Toghill Barn Farm

Cold Ashton

The Lynch

Toghill House Farm

A420 Bristol

A420

Tog Hill

SN14

Shapland's Farm

HIDES LA

5

Toghill Farm

St John's Wood

Cotswold Way
GREENHILL LA

SODBLE LA

Bristol & Bath STREET ATLAS

Uplands

72

FREEZINGHILL LA

Hill Farm

4

Tracy Cottage Farm

Hamswell Farm

Nimlet

Henley Hill

Freezing Hill

Hamswell House

Henley Tyning Farm

Lower Hamswell

Vine Cottage

LEIGH LA

3

Parkfield Farm

HALL LA

Lilliput Farm

Nimlet Hill

HALL LA

71

Rushmead Wood

HALL LA

2

Noade's Leaze Farm

BA1

Torney's Court Farm

Manor Farm

GLOUCESTER RD

Battlefields

HOWICK LA

Tadwick

Goudie's Farm

1

Sir Bevil Grenville's Mon

A46

70

Manor Farm

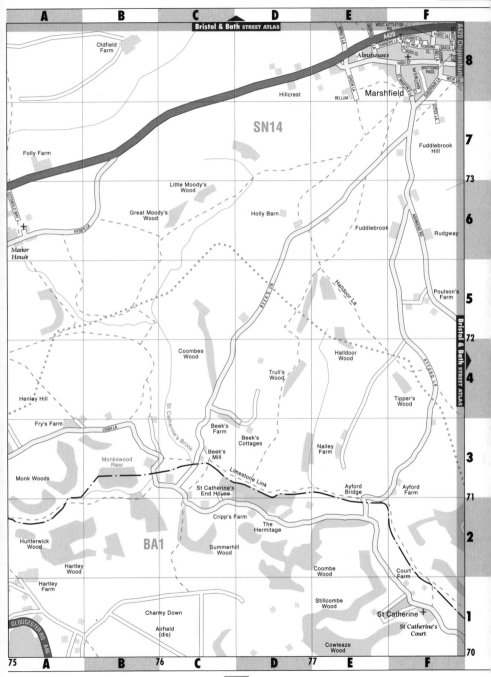

A B C D E F

8
7
73
6
5
72
4
3
71
2
1
70

SN14

Oldfield Farm

Hillcrest

WEST LITTLETON RD
A420
BOND LA
TREMES CL
VERS WLK
RINDES CL
BACK LA
GREENEAVES
HIBBS OLD LA
ROBBINS CL
HIGH ST
TANNERS LA

Almshouses

Marshfield

BELLUM
GREEN LA
ST MARTIN'S LA

WM SHUTTFIELD
BRITTONS PASS
WEIR LA
SHEEPFAIR LA

A420 Chippenham

A420

Folly Farm

Little Moody's Wood

Great Moody's Wood

Holly Barn

Fuddlebrook Hill

Fuddlebrook

Rudgway

Manor House

HYDE'S LA
COTSWOLD WAY

BEEK'S LN
ASHWICK RD

Halldoor La

Poulson's Farm

Coombes Wood

Trull's Wood

Halldoor Wood

Tipper's Wood

Henley Hill

St Catherine's Brook

AYFORD LA

Fry's Farm

LEIGH LA

Beek's Farm

Beek's Cottages

Nailey Farm

Monkswood Resr

Beek's Mill

Monk Woods

Limestone Link

St Catherine's End House

Ayford Bridge

Ayford Farm

Cripp's Farm

The Hermitage

Hunterwick Wood

BA1

Summerhill Wood

Coombe Wood

Court Farm

Hartley Wood

Stillcombe Wood

Hartley Farm

Charmy Down

Airfield (dis)

St Catherine

St Catherine's Court

GLOUCESTER RD A46

Cowleaze Wood

75 A B 76 C D 77 E F

Bristol & Bath STREET ATLAS

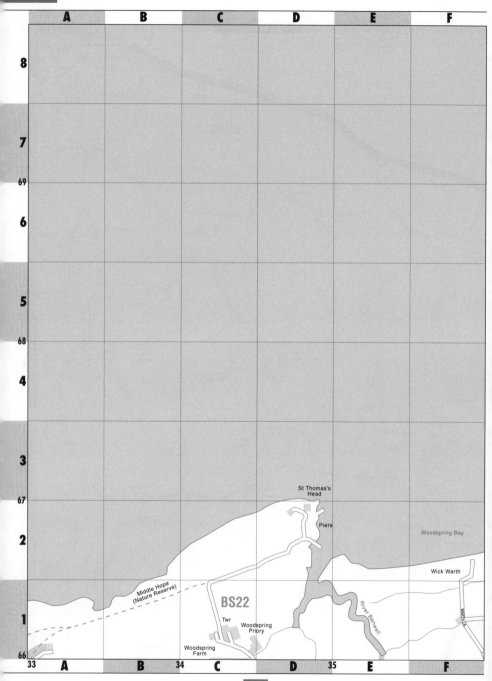

Dowlais Ditch

Kingston Pill

Hook's Ear

Seawall Farm

Treble House Farm

BACK LA

Sewage Works

Channel View Farm

BS21

Broadstone Rhyne

MIDDLE LA

MIDDLE LA

Broadstone Farm

BROADSTONE LA

Wharf Farm

HAM LA

New House Farm

Ham Farm

Pool Farm

Ham Rhyne

BS22

Sewage Works

MUDDICK

BS22

Yeo Bank Farm

Mendip View Farm

YEO BANK LA

Mill Leaze Rhyne

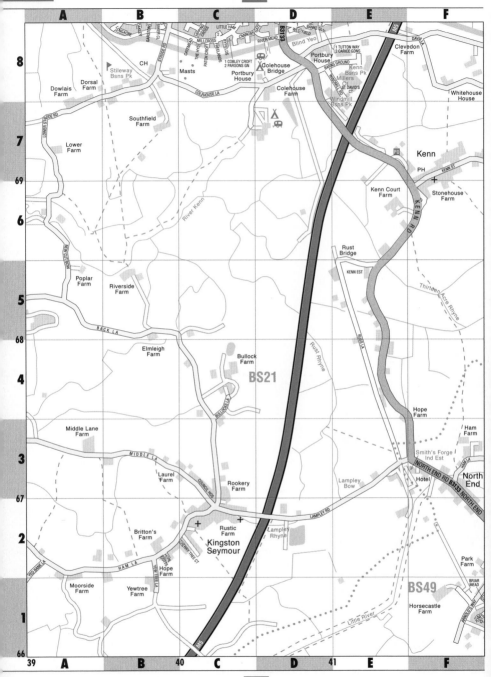

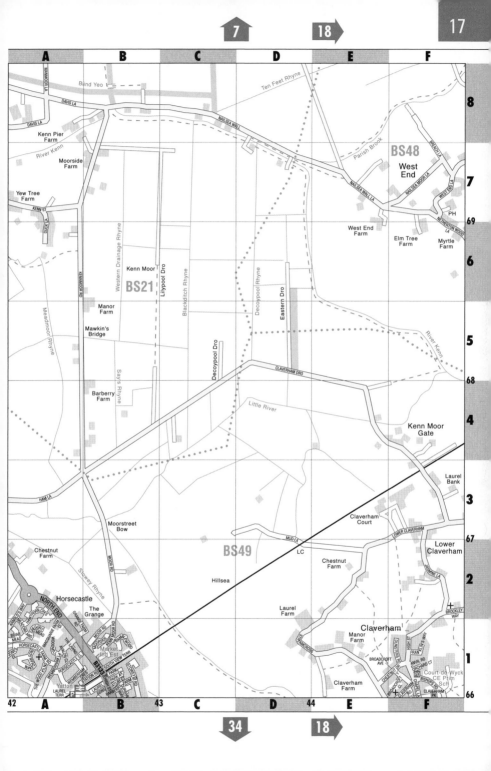

17
8

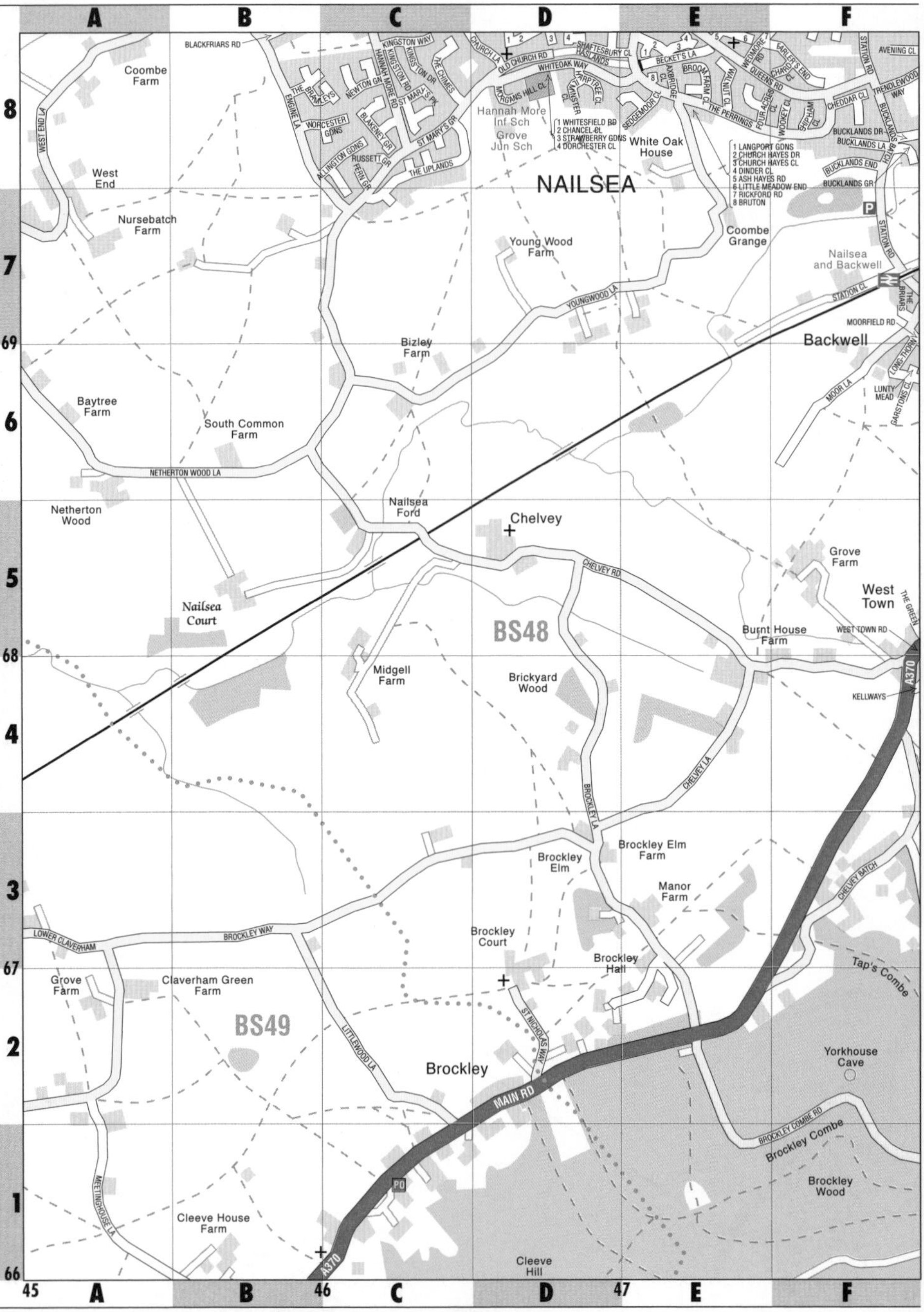
A
B
C
D
E
F
8
7
69
6
5
68
4
3
67
2
1
66
45
46
47
Coombe Farm
West End
Nursebatch Farm
BLACKFRIARS RD
WEST END LA
ENGINE LA
THE BRAMBLEYS
WORCESTER GDNS
ALLINGTON GDNS
NEWTON GN
KINGSTON WAY
KINGSTON RD
HANNAH MORE RD
KINGSTON DR
THE CHIMES
ST MARY'S PK
ST MARY'S GR
BLAKENEY GR
RUSSETT GR
FERN GR
THE UPLANDS
CHURCH LA
OLD CHURCH RD
SHAFTESBURY CL
HASLANDS
WHITEOAK WAY
MORGANS HILL CL
Hannah More Inf Sch
Grove Jun Sch
ILMINSTER CL
HARPTREE CL
1 WHITESFIELD RD
2 CHANCEL CL
3 STRAWBERRY GDNS
4 DORCHESTER CL
SEDGEMOOR CL
AXBRIDGE
BECKET'S LA
BROOM FARM CL
White Oak House
WALNUT CL
WEDMORE RD
QUEENS RD
FOUR ACRES CL
THE PERRINGS
EARLSTE'S END
CHARD CL
WOOKEY CL
SHIPHAM CL
CHEDDAR CL
STATION RD
AVENING CL
TRENDLEWOOD WAY
BUCKLANDS BATCH
BUCKLANDS DR
BUCKLANDS LA
BUCKLANDS END
BUCKLANDS GR
1 LANGPORT GDNS
2 CHURCH HAYES DR
3 CHURCH HAYES CL
4 DINDER CL
5 ASH HAYES RD
6 LITTLE MEADOW END
7 RICKFORD RD
8 BRUTON
NAILSEA
P
Young Wood Farm
Coombe Grange
Nailsea and Backwell
YOUNGWOOD LA
STATION CL
THE BRIARS
MOORFIELD RD
Backwell
Bizley Farm
LONG THORN
LUNTY MEAD
MOOR LA
GARSTONS CL
Baytree Farm
South Common Farm
NETHERTON WOOD LA
Netherton Wood
Nailsea Ford
Chelvey
CHELVEY RD
Grove Farm
West Town
THE GREEN
Nailsea Court
BS48
Burnt House Farm
WEST TOWN RD
Midgell Farm
Brickyard Wood
A370
KELLWAYS
BROCKLEY LA
CHELVEY LA
Brockley Elm Farm
Brockley Elm
Manor Farm
CHELVEY BATCH
LOWER CLAVERHAM
BROCKLEY WAY
Brockley Court
Brockley Hall
Tap's Combe
Grove Farm
Claverham Green Farm
BS49
LITTLEWOOD LA
ST NICHOLAS WAY
Yorkhouse Cave
Brockley
MAIN RD
BROCKLEY COMBE RD
Brockley Combe
Brockley Wood
MEETINGHOUSE LA
PO
Cleeve House Farm
Cleeve Hill
A370

17
35

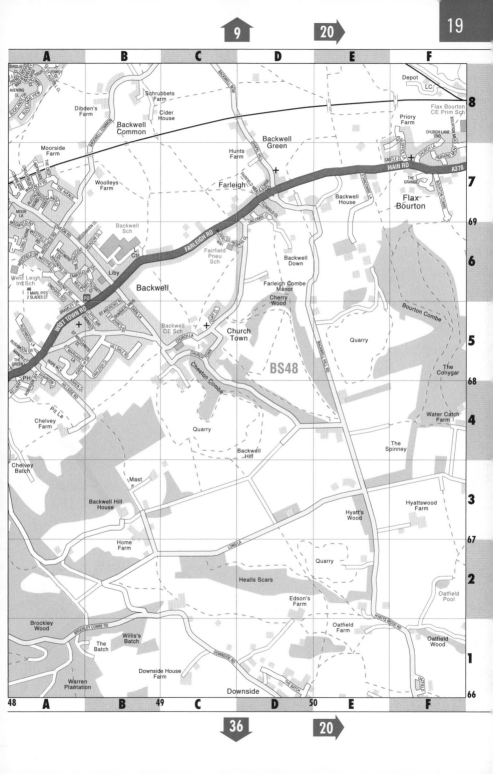

Map labels

Column A–F (top): A B C D E F

Row numbers (right): 8, 7, 69, 6, 5, 68, 4, 3, 67, 2, 1, 66

Depot
LC
Flax Bourton CE Prim Sch
Priory Farm
Schrubbets Farm
CHURCH LANE END
Dibden's Farm
Cider House
Backwell Common
Backwell Green
Hunts Farm
The GRANGE
Flax Bourton
Moorside Farm
MAIN RD
A370
Farleigh
Backwell House
Woolleys Farm
Backwell Sch
FARLEIGH RD
Fairfield Pneu Sch
Backwell Down
Ctr
Liby
Backwell
Farleigh Combe Manor
Cherry Wood
Bourton Combe
West Leigh Inf Sch
A6
1 MARL PITS
2 SLADES CT
WEST TOWN RD
Quarry
The Conygar
Church Town
Backwell CE Sch
BS48
PH
Cheston Combe
Water Catch Farm
Chelvey Farm
Pit La
Quarry
Backwell Hill
The Spinney
Chelvey Batch
Mast
Backwell Hill House
Hyattswood Farm
Home Farm
Hyatt's Wood
LONG LA
Quarry
Healls Scars
Brockley Wood
BROCKLEY COMBE RD
Edson's Farm
Oatfield Pool
Willis's Batch
The Batch
HYATTS WOOD RD
Oatfield Farm
Oatfield Wood
Downside House Farm
DOWNSIDE RD
THE BATCH
Downside
Warren Plantation

48 49 50

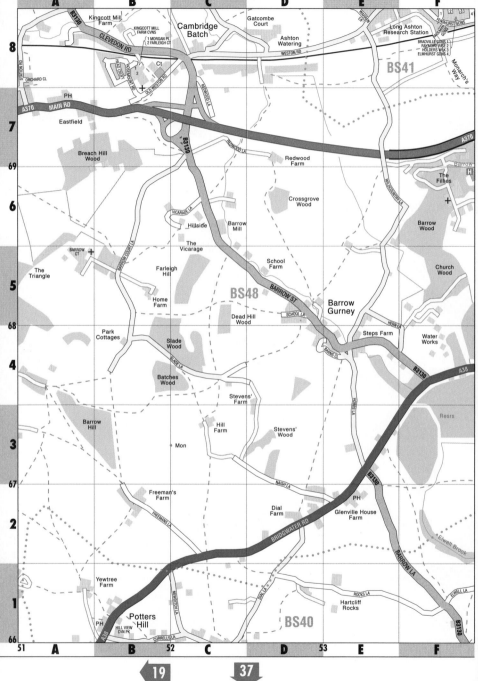

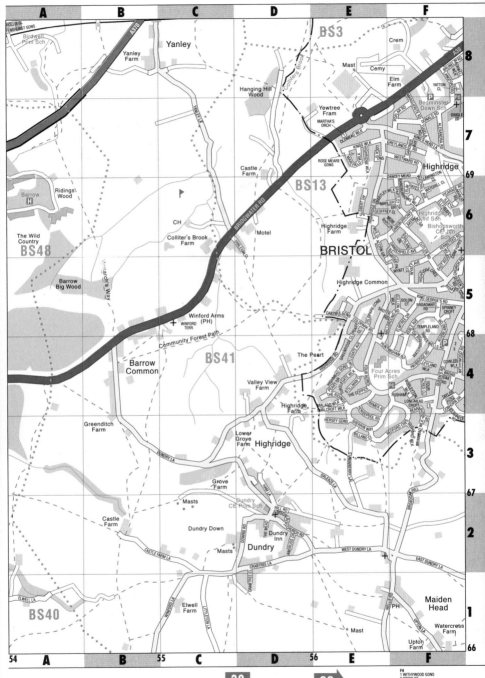

F4
1 WITHYWOOD GDNS
2 KINGS CT
3 LAKEMEAD GDNS
4 MARGARET RD
5 ROSSITER GRANGE

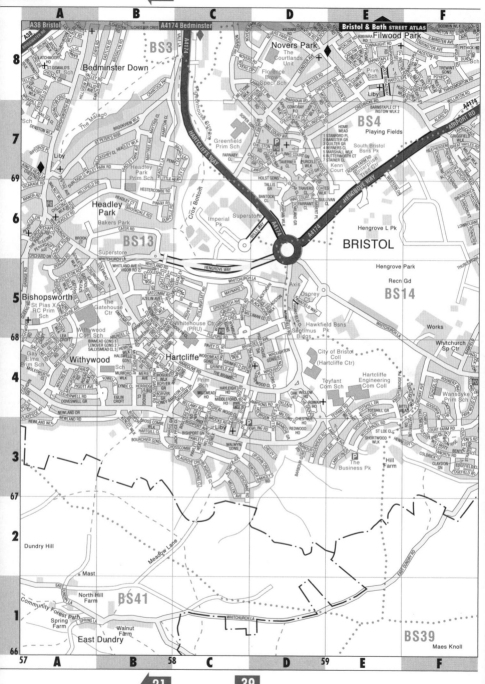

A   B   C   D   E   F

A38 Bristol   A4174 Bedminster   Bristol & Bath STREET ATLAS

BS3

Novers Park
The
Courtlands
Unit

Filwood Park

Bedminster Down

8

Florence
Brown
Spec! Sch

Prim
Sch

Liby

Greenfield
Prim Sch

BS4
Playing Fields

1 STANFORD PL
2 BANISTER GR
3 QUILTER GR
4 BERNERS CL
5 MARSHALL WLK
6 BUTTERWORTH CT
7 STAINER CL

South Bristol
Bsns Pk

7

The Malago

St PETER'S RISE

Enterprise
Trad Ctr

69

Headley
Park
Prim. Sch.

Kenn
Court

Imperial
Pk

Superstore

Hengrove L Pk

BRISTOL

6

Headley
Park

Bakers Park

Cra Bottom

BS13

Superstore

Hengrove Park
Recn Gd

BS14

5

Bishopsworth

St Pias X RC
RC Prim
Sch

The
Gatehouse
Ctr

Whitehouse Ctr
(PRU)

Osprey

Axis

Works

Whitchurch
Sp Ctr

68

Withywood
Com Sch

Hawkfield Bsns
Septimus
Bldgs

City of Bristol
Coll
(Hartcliffe Ctr)

Hartcliffe
Engineering
Com Coll

4

Gay
Elms
Prim Sch

Withywood

Hartcliffe

Prim
Sch

Teyfant
Com Sch

Wansdyke
Prim Sch

The
Brambles

3

Liby

The
Business Pk

Hill
Farm

67

2

Dundry Hill

Meadow Lane

1

Community Forest Path

Spring
Farm

North Hill
Farm

BS41

Walnut
Farm

WHITCHURCH LA

BS39
Maes Knoll

East Dundry

66

57   A   B   58   C   D   59   E   F

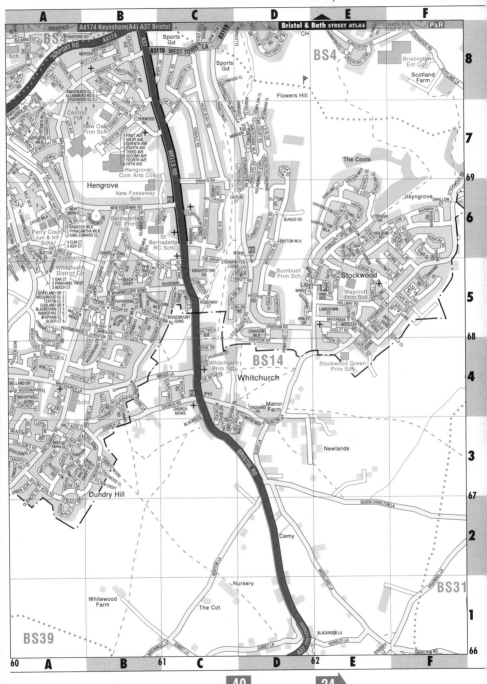

Bristol & Bath STREET ATLAS

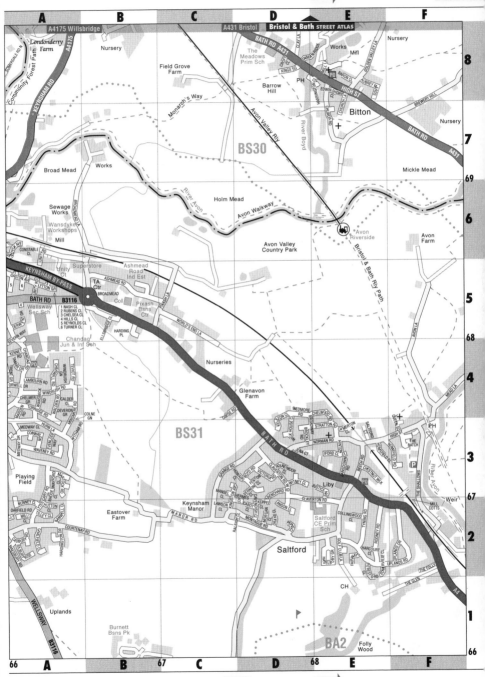

A4175 Willsbridge

A431 Bristol **Bristol & Bath** STREET ATLAS

Londonderry Farm

Nursery

Field Grove Farm

The Meadows Prim Sch

Works Mfl

Nursery

Monarch's Way

Barrow Hill

Bitton

Community Forest Path

KEYNSHAM RD

A4175

BATH RD A431

KINGS SQ

HIGH ST

BREWERY HILL

BATH RD

A431

Nursery

BS30

Avon Valley Rly

River Boyd

Broad Mead

Works

Mickle Mead

69

River Avon

Holm Mead

Avon Walkway

Sewage Works

Avon Riverside

Avon Farm

Wansdyke Workshops

Mill

Avon Valley Country Park

Bristol & Bath Rly Path

6

CONSTABLE CL

Superstore

Ashmead Road Ind Est

Unity Ct

KEYNSHAM BY-PASS

TA Ctr

BROADMEAD

ASHMEAD RD

AVON LA

5

GASTON AVE

BATH RD

B3116

Coll

Pixash Bsns Ctr

WORLD'S END LA

68

Wellsway Sec Sch

1 NASH CL
2 RUBENS CL
3 CHELSEA CL
4 HILLS CL
5 REYNOLDS CL
6 TURNER CL

HARDING PL

Nurseries

4

Chandag Jun & Inf Sch

Glenavon Farm

WEDMORE RD

CHELWOOD

STRATTON RD

SALTFORD

PH

THE BATCH

COLNE GN

BS31

BATH RD

NORMAN RD

CLAVERTON RD

River Avon

P

3

Playing Field

IFORD CL

Liby

67

Eastover Farm

Keynsham Manor

MANOR RD

GRANGE RD

VICTORIA

WITNEY CL

GLAVERTON RD

Saltford CE Prim Sch

COLLINGWOOD

MILL COTTS

Weir

2

Saltford

CH

THE GLEN

THE FOLLY

A4

Uplands

WELLSWAY

B3116

Burnett Bsns Pk

BA2

Folly Wood

1

66

66

A

B

67

C

D

68

E

F

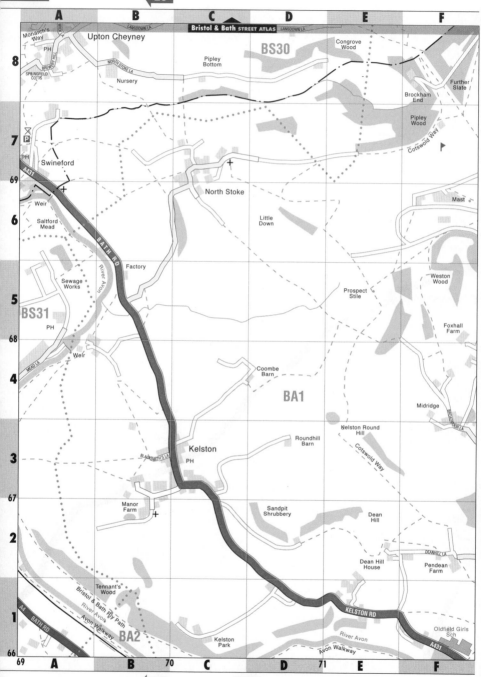

Bristol & Bath STREET ATLAS

BS30

Upton Cheyney

Monarch's Way

PH

SPRINGFIELD COTTS

LANSDOWN LA

NORTH STOKE LA

Pipley Bottom

Nursery

Congrove Wood

Brockham End

Pipley Wood

Further Slate

Cotswold Way

Swineford

A431

Weir

Saltford Mead

North Stoke

Little Down

Mast

BS31

Sewage Works

PH

Weir

Factory

River Avon

BATH RD

MEAD LA

Prospect Stile

Weston Wood

Foxhall Farm

Coombe Barn

BA1

Kelston Round Hill

Midridge

BRACKNELL LA

Cotswold Way

Kelston

PH

BLACKSMITH'S LA

Roundhill Barn

Manor Farm

Sandpit Shrubbery

Dean Hill

DEANHILL LA

Dean Hill House

Pendean Farm

Tennant's Wood

Bristol & Bath Rly Path

River Avon

Avon Walkway

A4

BATH RD

BA2

Kelston Park

River Avon

Avon Walkway

KELSTON RD

A431

Oldfield Girls Sch

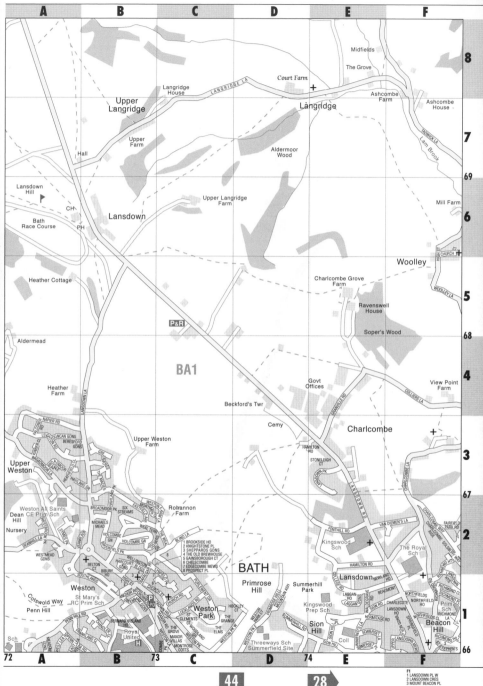

F1
1 LANSDOWN PL W
2 LANSDOWN CRES
3 MOUNT BEACON PL

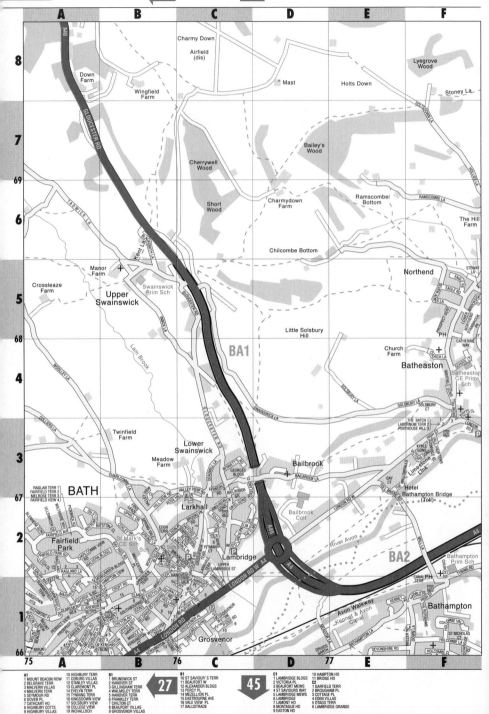

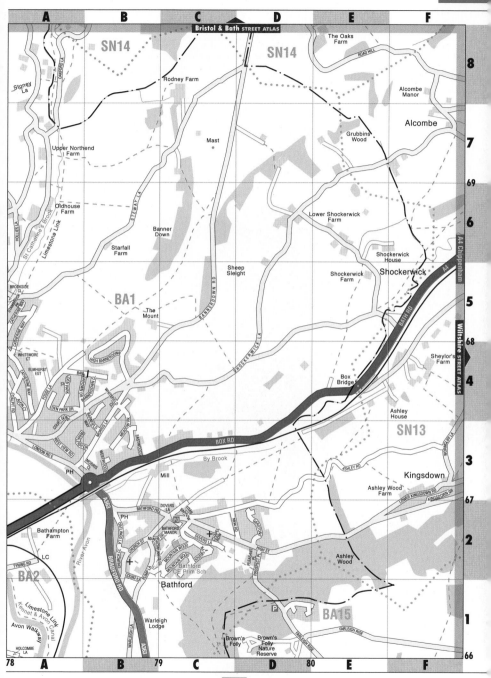

Bristol & Bath STREET ATLAS

SN14

SN14

The Oaks Farm

ROAD HILL

Alcombe Manor

Alcombe

Rodney Farm

Stoney La

Mast

Grubbins Wood

A4 Chippenham

Upper Northend Farm

St Catherine's Brook

Limestone Link

Oldhouse Farm

HOLLIES LA

STEWAY LA

Banner Down

Lower Shockerwick Farm

Starfall Farm

Sheep Sleight

Shockerwick House

A4

Wiltshire STREET ATLAS

BROOKSIDE

STARROOK LA

CATHERINE WAY

BA1

The Mount

Shockerwick Farm

Shockerwick

BANNERDOWN RD

WHITEMORE CT

ELMHURST EST

CATHERINE WAY

HIGH BANNERDOWN

SHOCKERWICK LA

Sheylor's Farm

Box Bridge

SN13

EDEN PARK DR

BANNERDOWN DR

WHITELE

Ashley House

BOX RD

By Brook

Ashley Wood Farm

Kingsdown

LONDON RD E

EARTHWOOD

MEANS LA

WESTWOOD

ASHLEY RD

LOWER KINGSDOWN RD

KINGSDOWN DR

PH

Mill

WORSALE LA

PROSPECT PL

PH

DOVERS LA

Ashley Wood

Bathampton Farm

BA2

A363

BATHFORD HILL

Bathford Manor

HIGH ST

GASTONS

Ashley Wood

LC

TYNING RD

BRADFORD RD

River Avon

CHURCH ST

MANOR RD

DOVERS LA

MOUNTAIN WOOD

Bathford CE Prim Sch

PLEASANT PL

Limestone Link
Kennet & Avon Canal

COURT LA

THORNBANK

Bathford

BA15

Avon Walkway

WARLEIGH VALE

Warleigh Lodge

Brown's Folly

Brown's Folly Nature Reserve

P

FARLEIGH RISE

HOLCOMBE LA

78   79   80

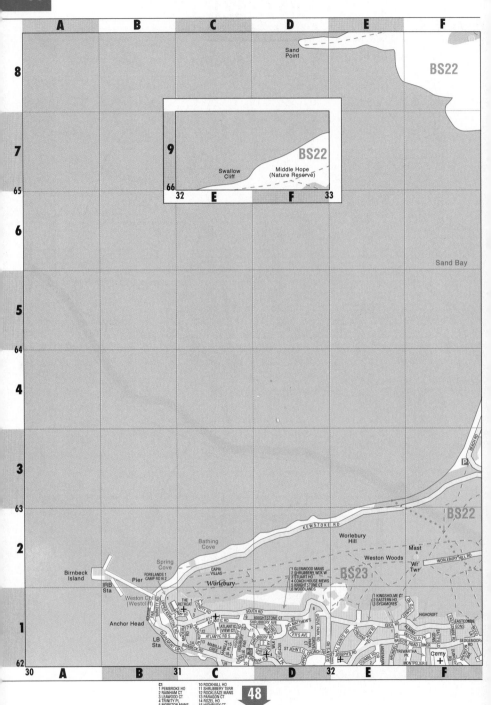

BS22

Sand Point

BS22

Swallow Cliff

Middle Hope (Nature Reserve)

Sand Bay

BS22

KEWSTOKE RD

Worlebury Hill

Bathing Cove

Spring Cove

Weston Woods

Mast

Wr Twr

WORLEBURY HILL RD

Birnbeck Island

Pier

FORELANDS 1 CAMP RD N 2

CAPRI VILLAS

Worlebury

1 GLENWOOD MANS
2 SHRUBBERY, WCK W
3 STUART HO
4 COACH HOUSE MEWS
5 KNIGHTSTONE CT
6 WOODLANDS

BS23

IRB Sta

Weston Coll (Westcliff)

THE RETREAT

Anchor Head

LB Sta

1 KINGSHOLME CT
2 EASTERN HO
3 SYCAMORES

HIGHCROFT

EASTCOMBE GDNS

SEDGEMOOR

Cemy

C1
1 PEMBROKE HO
2 RAINHAM CT
3 LEAWOOD CT
4 TRINITY PL
5 MORETON MANS
6 GOSFORD MANS
7 FRANKFORD MANS
8 HAMILTON RD
9 MAPLE CT
10 ROCKHALL HO
11 SHRUBBERY TERR
12 ROCKLEAZE MANS
13 PARAGON CT
14 ROZEL HO
15 HIGHBURY CT
16 VILLA ROSA
17 BADMINTON CT
18 CAIRO CT
19 GLENTWORTH CT
20 RAGLAN PL

48

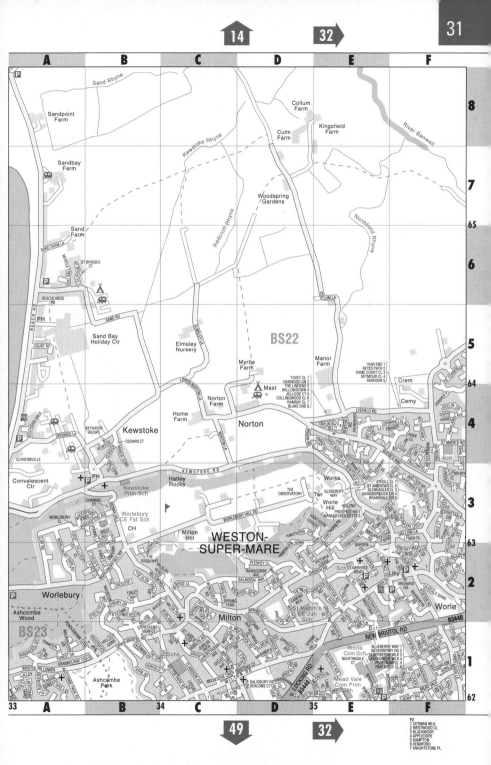

A2
1 KENNFORD
2 ST CLEMENTS CT
3 KINGSWEAR
4 BAMPTON
5 CREDITON
6 FENITON
7 INSTOW
8 IVYBRIDGE
9 HONITON
10 EXBOURNE
11 COLYTON
12 DALWOOD
13 DOWLAND
14 HARTLAND
15 EBDEN LO

B4
1 WELLARD CL
2 TYLER GN
3 TREMLETT MEWS
4 GARNER CT
5 WAINWRIGHT CL
6 EMLYN CL
7 THE SAFFRONS

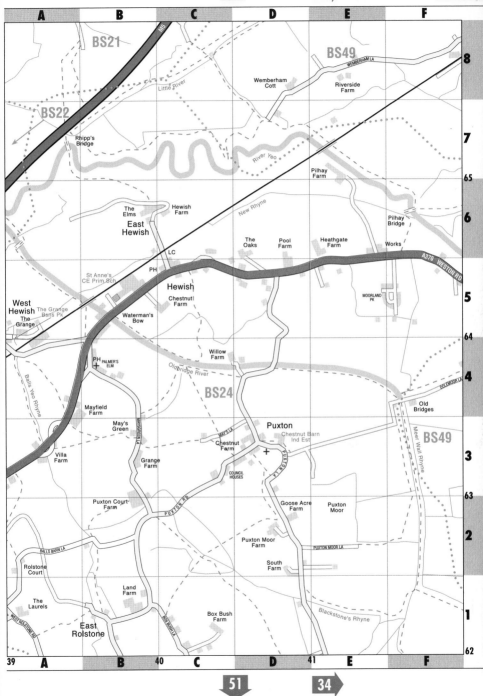

33 17

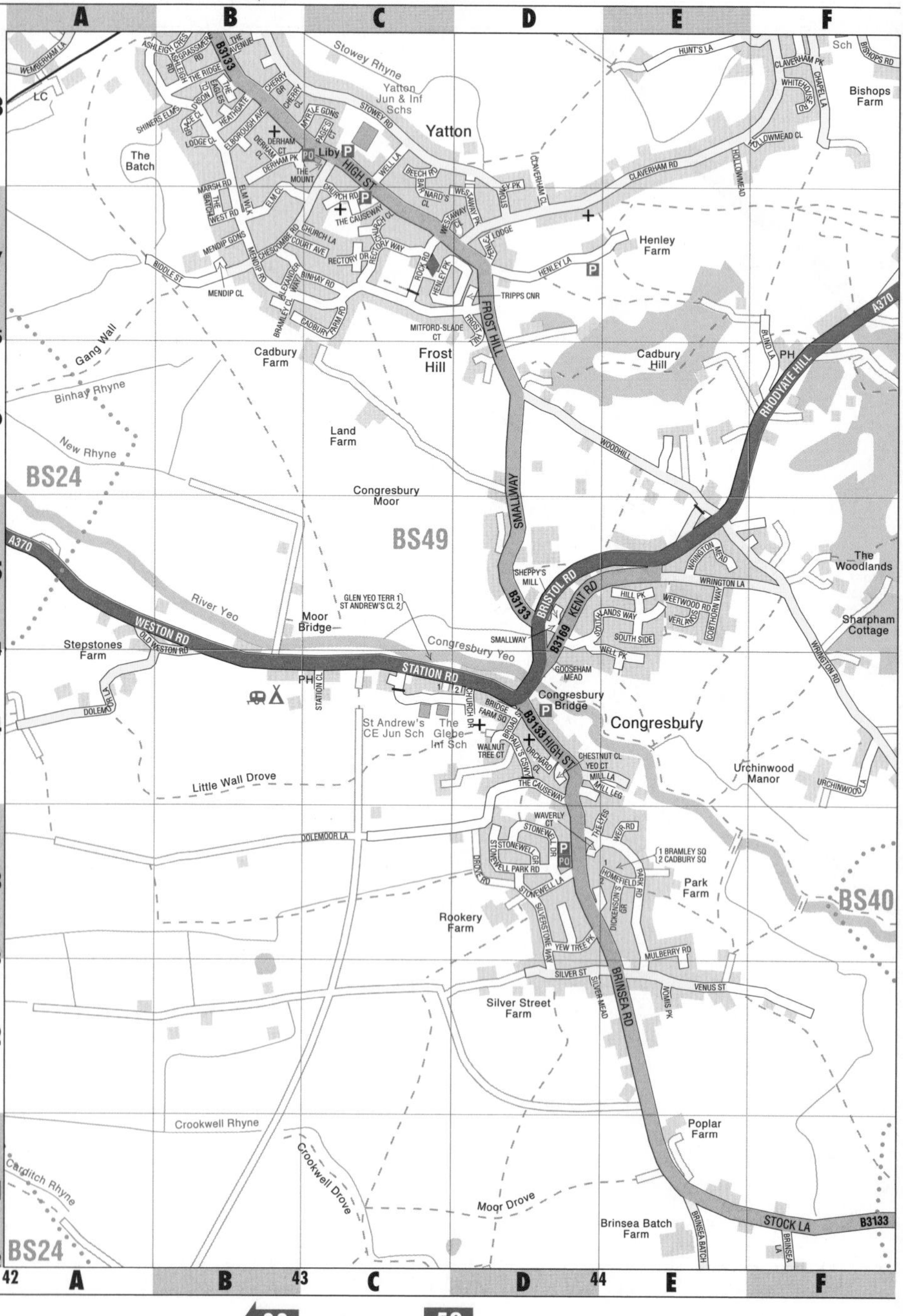

Yatton

The Batch

BS24

New Rhyne

Binhay Rhyne

Gang Wall

Cadbury Farm

Land Farm

Congresbury Moor

BS49

River Yeo

WESTON RD

A370

Stepstones Farm

Moor Bridge

Congresbury Yeo

GLEN YEO TERR 1
ST ANDREW'S CL 2

SMALLWAY

STATION RD

PH

Little Wall Drove

St Andrew's CE Jun Sch

The Glebe Inf Sch

WALNUT TREE CT

Congresbury Bridge

Congresbury

Urchinwood Manor

Park Farm

1 BRAMLEY SQ
2 CADBURY SQ

BS40

Rookery Farm

Silver Street Farm

Crookwell Rhyne

Crookwell Drove

Cadglitch Rhyne

BS24

Moor Drove

Brinsea Batch Farm

Poplar Farm

STOCK LA

B3133

BRINSEA RD

Stowey Rhyne

Yatton Jun & Inf Schs

Hunt's La

Claverham

Bishops Farm

LIby HIGH ST

The Mount

CHURCH LA

RECTORY DR

MENDIP CL

FROST HILL

TRIPPS CNR

MITFORD-SLADE CT

Frost Hill

Henley Farm

Cadbury Hill

Woodhill

SMALLWAY

BRISTOL RD

KENT RD

SHEPPY'S MILL

Wrington La

The Woodlands

Sharpham Cottage

RHODYATE HILL

A370

HILL PK

LANDS WAY

SOUTH SIDE

CHURCH RD

GOOSEHAM MEAD

B3133 HIGH ST

CHESTNUT CL

YEO CT

MILL LA

URCHINWOOD

WAVERLY

STONEWELL PARK RD

STONEWELL

YEW TREE CL

MULBERRY RD

SILVER ST

VENUS ST

BRINSEA RD

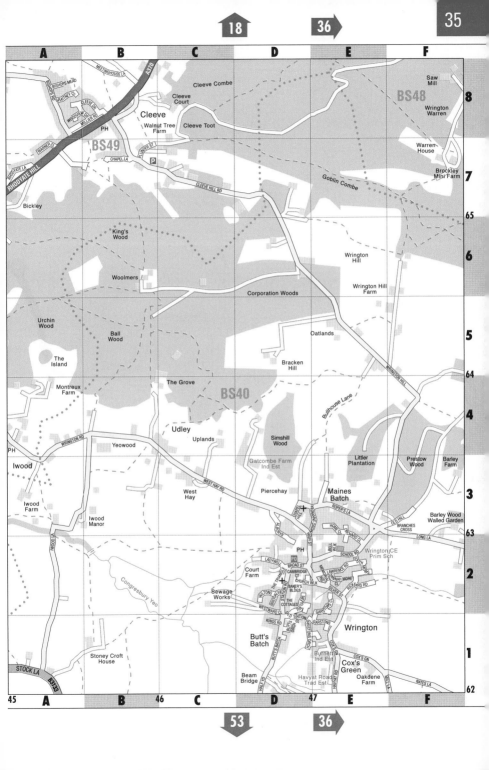

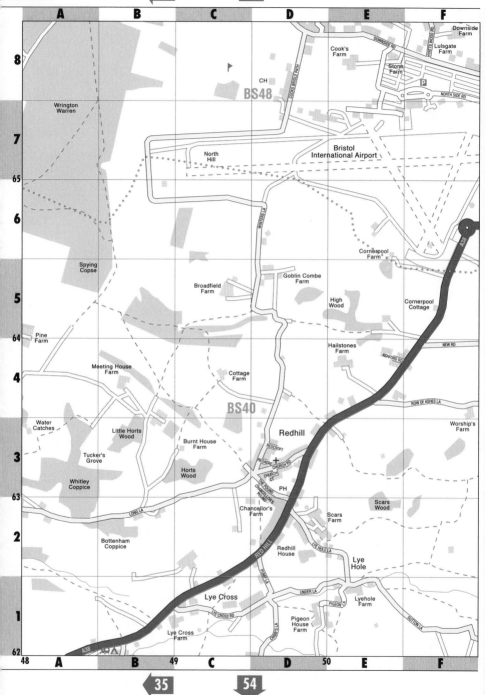

BS48

Wrington
Warren

CH

COOK'S BRIDLE PATH

Cook's
Farm

Downside
Farm

Lulsgate
Farm

DOWNSIDE RD

HYATTS WOOD RD

Stone
Farm

P

NORTH SIDE RD

Bristol
International Airport

North
Hill

WINTERS LA

Spying
Copse

Broadfield
Farm

Goblin Combe
Farm

High
Wood

Cornerpool
Farm

Cornerpool
Cottage

A38

Pine
Farm

Hailstones
Farm

NEW RD

ASHFORD RD

Meeting House
Farm

Cottage
Farm

BS40

ROW OF ASHES LA

Water
Catches

Little Horts
Wood

Burnt House
Farm

Redhill

Worship's
Farm

Tucker's
Grove

Horts
Wood

REDCROFT

CHURCH RD

Whitley
Coppice

REDACRE

CHURCH
CT

PH

Scars
Wood

THE ROUND
CHANCELLORS POUND

LONG LA

Chancellor's
Farm

Scars
Farm

Bottenham
Coppice

RED HILL

Redhill
House

LYE HOLE LA

Lye
Hole

Lye Cross

GIBBS LA

UNDER LA

PIGEON

Lyehole
Farm

LYE CROSS RD

Pigeon
House
Farm

SUTTON LA

Lye Cross
Farm

A38

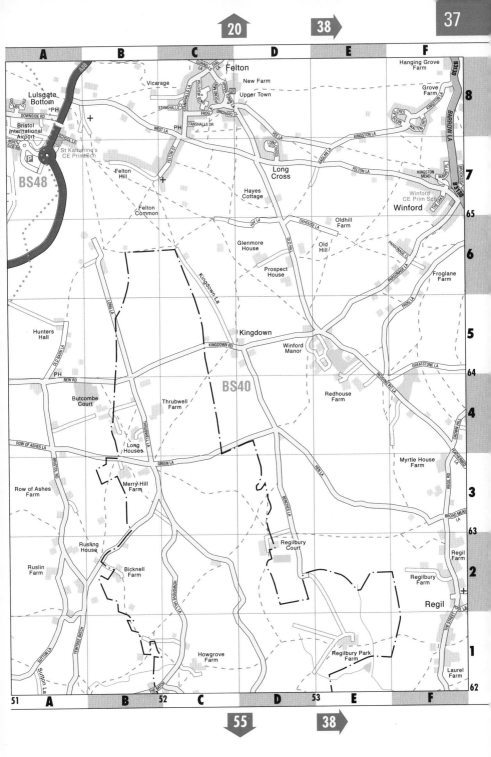

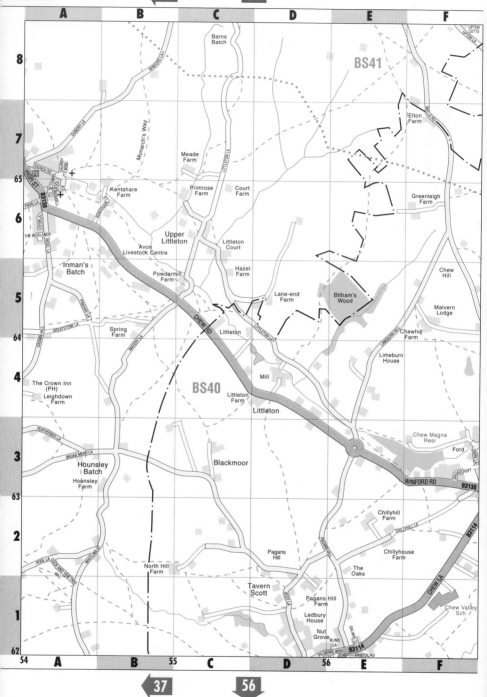

A B C D E F

8

BS41

UPTON COTTS
UPTON LA

7

Barns Batch

WINFORD LA

Monarch's Way

DUNBORY LA

Elton Farm

WELLS RD

Meade Farm

LITTLETON LA

CHURCH RD

65

HIGH ST

Primrose Farm

Court Farm

Greenleigh Farm

Kentshare Farm

FROG LA

B3130

THE RICKLANDS

CHAPEL

6

Upper Littleton

Littleton Court

Chew Hill

Avon Livestock Centre

Inman's Batch

Powdermill Farm

Hazel Farm

Bitham's Wood

Malvern Lodge

5

Lane-end Farm

Chewhill Farm

PRIORY LA

THE MAUNDS

GREATSTONE LA

WATERY LA

CHEW RD

Littleton

LITTLETON LA

Limeburn House

LIMEBURN RD

64

Spring Farm

The Crown Inn (PH)

Leighdown Farm

Mill

BS40

4

Littleton Farm

Littleton

FEATHERBED LA

BROAD MEAD LA

Chew Magna Resr

Ford

SHADCROFT

OAK LA

3

Hounsley Batch

Blackmoor

WINFORD RD

B3130

Hounsley Farm

Chillyhill Farm

CHILLYHILL LA

B3114

63

2

Chillyhouse Farm

POOL LA

OAK AND YEW TREE

WHITLEY ST

North Hill Farm

Pagans Hill

PAGANS HILL

The Oaks

CHEW LA

1

Tavern Scott

Pagans Hill Farm

SILVER ST

Ledbury House

Nut Grove

BLIND LA

Chew Valley Sch

62

PILGRIMS WAY

B3114

BRISTOL RD

54 A B 55 C D 56 E F

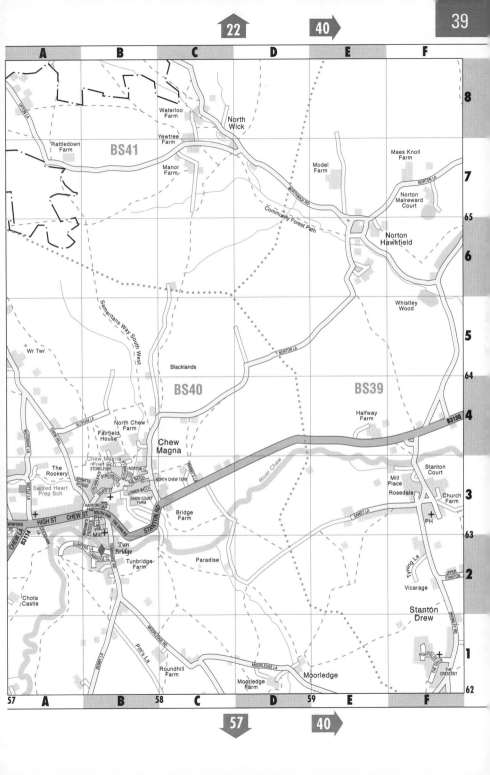

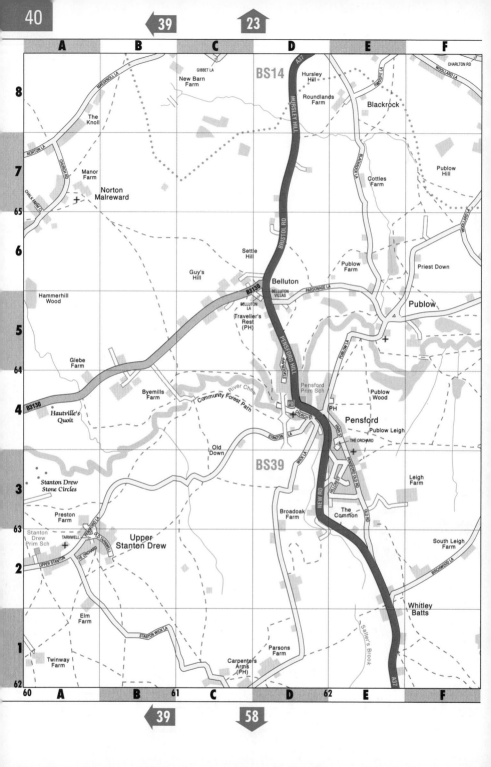

39

23

A   B   C   D   E   F

BS14

8

CHARLTON RD

WOOLLAND LA

New Barn
Farm

GIBBET LA

Hursley
Hill

Roundlands
Farm

Blackrock

The
Knoll

HURSLEY HILL

A37

7

NORTON LA

CHURCH RD

Manor
Farm

Norton
Malreward

65

CHALK HARE LA

BRISTOL RD

Cottles
Farm

Publow
Hill

BLACKROCK LA

RAMSPIT LA

6

Settle
Hill

Guy's
Hill

Publow
Farm

Priest Down

Belluton

5

Hammerhill
Wood

B3130

BELLUTON
VILLAS

BELLUTON
LA

Traveller's
Rest
(PH)

PARSONAGE LA

Publow

PUBLOW LA

Glebe
Farm

64

PENSFORD HILL

OLD HILL

Publow
Wood

B3130

Byemills
Farm

River Chew

Community Forest Path

Pensford
Prim Sch

4

Hautville's
Quoit

PO

PH

Pensford

Publow Leigh

CHURCH ST

STANTON LA

THE ORCHARD

Old
Down

WICK LA

HIGH ST

BS39

PENSFORD OLD RD

Leigh
Farm

3

Stanton Drew
Stone Circles

Preston
Farm

Broadoak
Farm

The
Common

NEW RD

OLD RD

63

Stanton
Drew
Prim Sch

TARNWELL

B3130 OLD TARNWELL

THE ORCHARD

Upper
Stanton Drew

South Leigh
Farm

BIRCHWOOD LA

2

UPPER STANTON

Whitley
Batts

1

Elm
Farm

STANTON WICK LA

Salter's Brook

A37

Twinway
Farm

Parsons
Farm

Carpenter's
Arms
(PH)

62

60   A   B   61   C   D   62   E   F

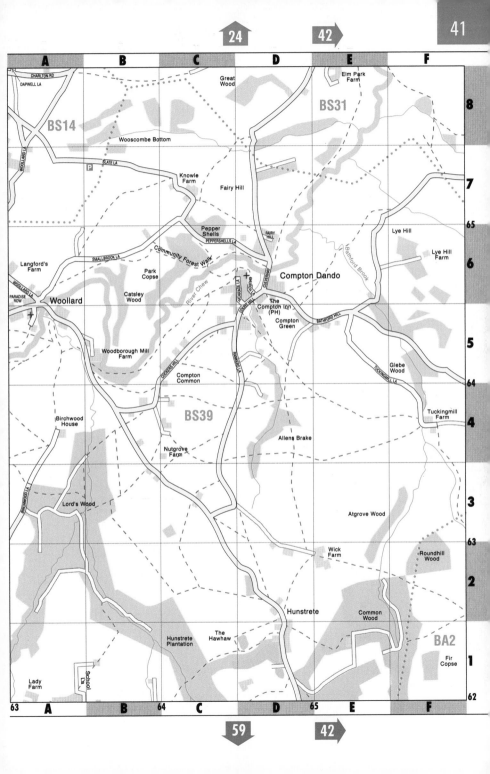

A **B** **C** **D** **E** **F**

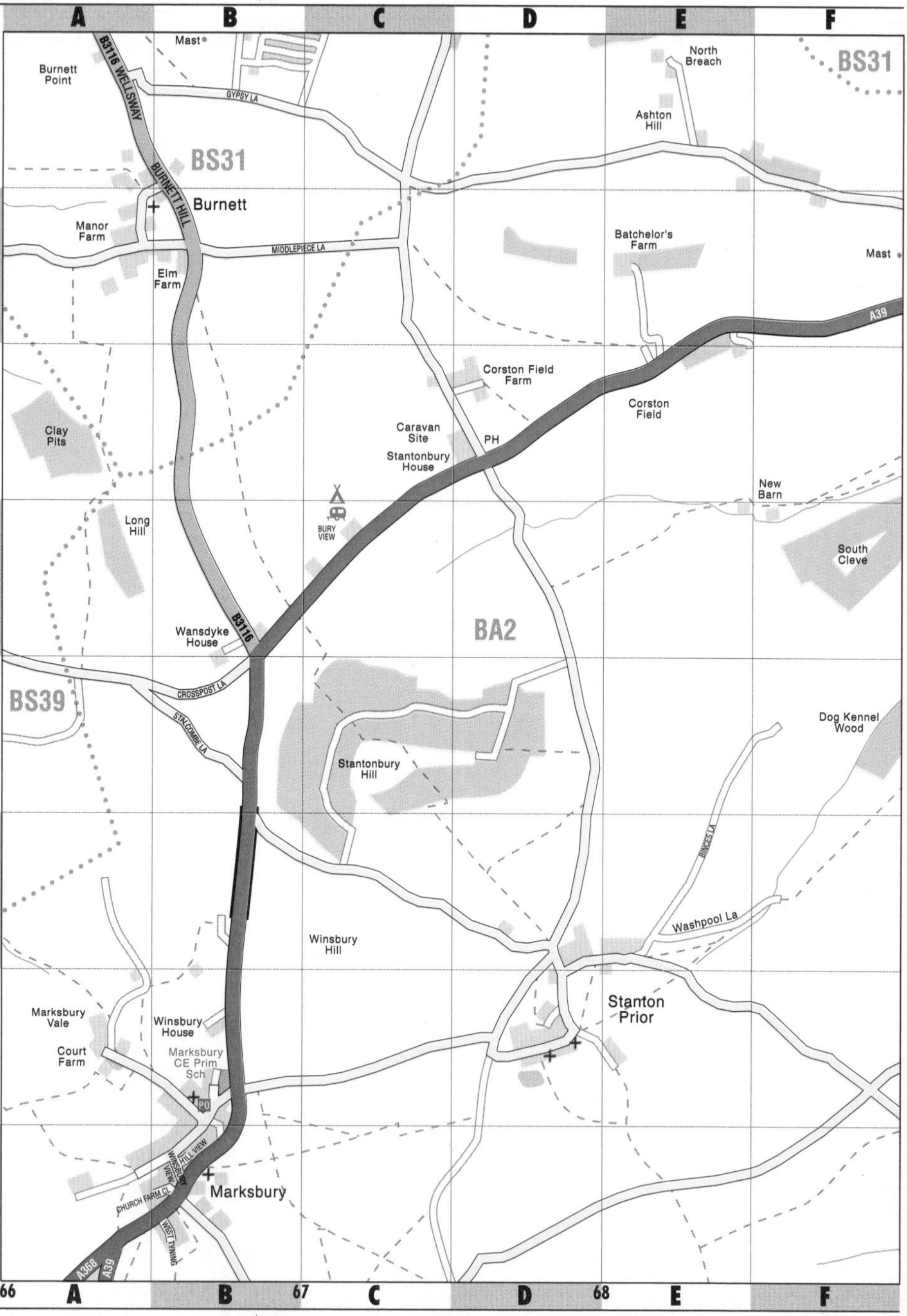

BS31

Burnett
Point

Mast

Mast

North
Breach

BS31

BS31

8

BS16 WELLSWAY

GYPSY LA

Ashton
Hill

Burnett

BURNETT HILL

Manor
Farm

Burnett

MIDDLEPIECE LA

Batchelor's
Farm

Mast

7

Elm
Farm

A39

65

Corston Field
Farm

Clay
Pits

Caravan
Site

Corston
Field

6

Stantonbury
House

PH

New
Barn

Long
Hill

BURY
VIEW

South
Cleve

5

B3116

BA2

Wansdyke
House

64

BS39

CROSSPOST LA

Dog Kennel
Wood

4

STACOMBE LA

Stantonbury
Hill

BINCES LA

3

Washpool La

Winsbury
Hill

63

Stanton
Prior

Marksbury
Vale

Winsbury
House

2

Court
Farm

Marksbury
CE Prim
Sch

A39

WELL VIEW

CHURCH FARM CL

Marksbury

WEST TYNING

1

A368

A39

62

66   A   **B**   67   **C**   **D**   68   **E**   **F**

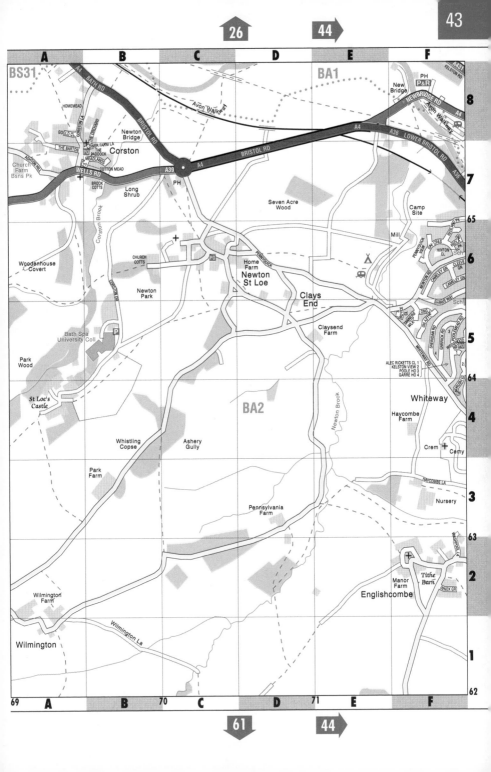

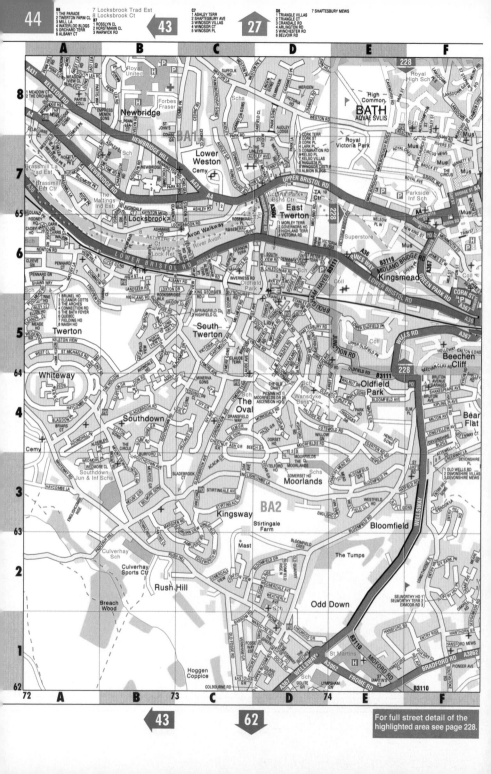

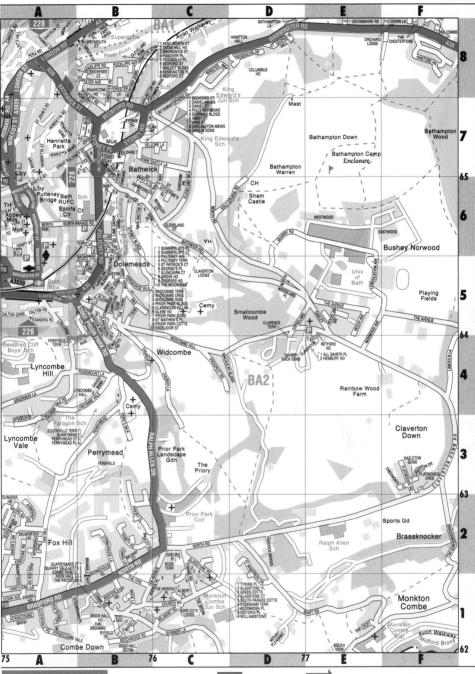

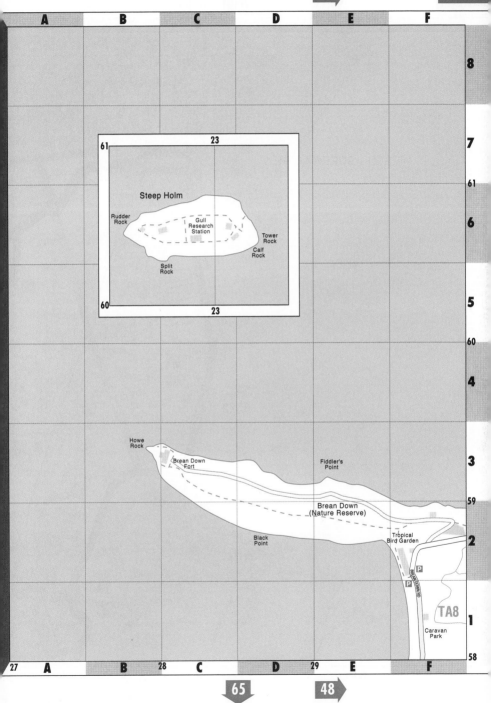

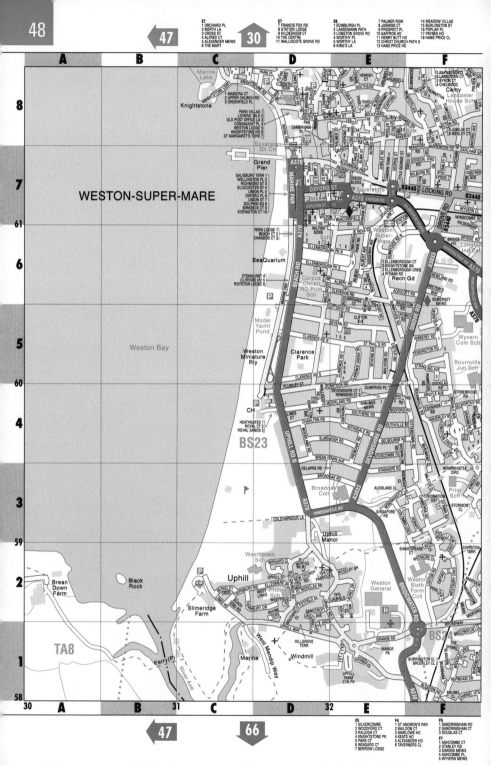

E7
1 ORCHARD PL
2 NORTH LA
3 CROSS ST
4 ALFRED CT
5 ALEXANDER MEWS
6 THE MART

E7
7 FRANCIS FOX RD
8 STATION LODGE
9 HILDESHIEM CT
10 THE CENTRE
11 WALLISCOTE GROVE RD

E8
1 EDINBURGH PL
2 LANDEMANN PATH
3 LONGTON GROVE RD
4 WORTHY PL
5 WORTHY LA
6 KING'S LA

7 PALMER ROW
8 JASMINE CT
9 PROSPECT PL
10 SAFFRON HO
11 HENRY BUTT HO
12 CHRIST CHURCH PATH S
13 HANS PRICE HO

14 MEADOW VILLAS
15 BURLINGTON ST
16 POPLAR PL
17 PAYNES HO
18 HANS PRICE CL

WESTON-SUPER-MARE

BS23

TA8

BS24

E5
1 SILVERCOMBE
2 WOODFORD CT
3 RALEIGH CT
4 KNIGHTSTONE PK
5 PARK CT
6 WINGARD CT
7 BERROW LODGE

F4
1 ST ANDREW'S PAR
2 BAILDON CT
3 MARLOWE HO
4 KEATS HO
5 ALEXANDER HO
6 TAVERNERS CL

F5
1 SANDRINGHAM RD
2 SANDRINGHAM CT
3 DOUGLAS CT

F7
1 ASHCOMBE CT
2 STANLEY RD
3 SIMONS MEWS
4 ASHCOMBE PL
5 WYVERN MEWS

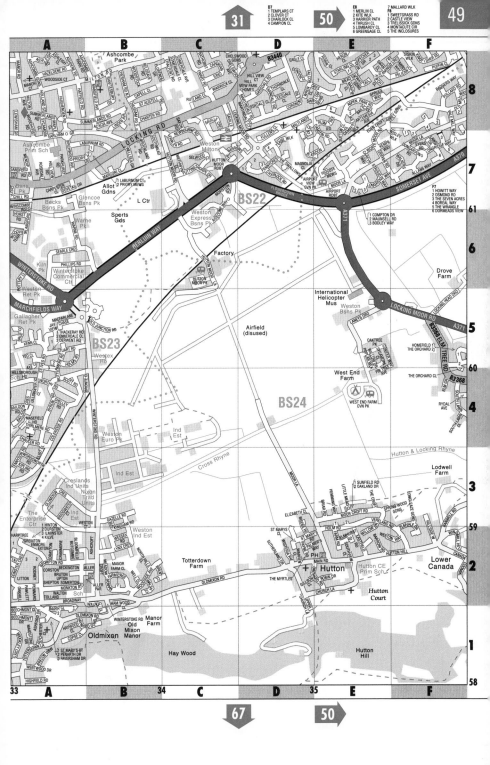

8

7

61

6

5

60

4

3

59

2

1

58

A   B   C   D   E   F

BS22

BS24

BS29

BS26   BS26

Liby
Superstore
Baytree Sch
Herons Moor
Prim Sch
SOMERSET AVE

1 LANTHONY CL
2 WALTHAM END
3 HONEYSUCKLE PL
4 HIGHGROVE WLK
5 LYPSTONE CL
6 CARBERRY VIEW
7 POLESTAR WAY
8 SWEETGRASS RD
9 BOUNDARY RD
10 CHESTER CL

1 MORGAN CL
2 HARVEST LA

WEST WICK
RDBT
CHURCHLAND WAY

Westacres
Farm

Ivy
Cottage

Locking Head
Cottages

Grumble Pill Rhyne

Wolvershill
Manor

Wolvershill
Ind Units

Waywick
Farm

Waterloo
Farm

Old Yeo Rhyne

Cannaway's
Farm

Ivy House
Farm

IVY
HOUSE
COTTS

EYER LA

SUMMER LA

Woolvers
Hill

Woolvers Hill
Batch

Pool
Farm

West Moor Rhyne

SILVER MOOR LA

WOLVERSHILL RD

Laurel
Farm

Park
Farm

Court
Farm
Park

Locking Head
Farm

Locking Farm
Ind Est

RAF
Locking

RUSSELL RD

LEEDHAM RD

McGRUE RD

LOWER PARADE
GROUND RD

POST OFFICE RD

PARRES RD

CRANWELL RD

A371

LOCKING MOOR RD

Homefield
Ind Est
Homefield
CL

PH

B3368

ELM TREE RD

PLUMLEY
CRES

GRANGE AVE

BARTLETTS

MANOR
CT

LIME CL

BIRCH CL

Locking
Prim Sch

TARNBOROUGH RD

SUNNY
RD

PINETREE RD

MENDIP RD

TOWER HILL

BROADWAY

ALTADALE
RD

OLD BANWELL RD   B3368

Locking

Church
Farm

THE GREEN
LYCHGATE LA

ELBOROUGH HILL

ELNDERDOWN RD

PORTAL
RD

SUMMER LANE
PARK HOMES

GROVE RD
PARK CVN
PK

SUMMER LANE
CVN PK

Cave
View

KNIGHTCOTT RD   A371

Knightcott
Ind Est

Knightcott

Knightcott

CHESTERFIELD
CL

HILLMER RISE

WELL LA

Perries

BANWELL RD

Elborough

FELNOUGH
CL

BEAFORT
RD

CEDERN
AVE

MEADOW WK

BLUE WATER

Hillend

HIGH ST

Mon

Banwell
Hill

Mast

Windmill
Farm

WINDMILL HILL

Wingfield
House

Manor
Farm

Benthills
Wood

Elborough
Hill

Whitley
Head

BRIDE-WELL LA

Upper
Canada

CANADA COOMBE

Christon
Hill

Christon
Plantation

Yarberry

36   37   38

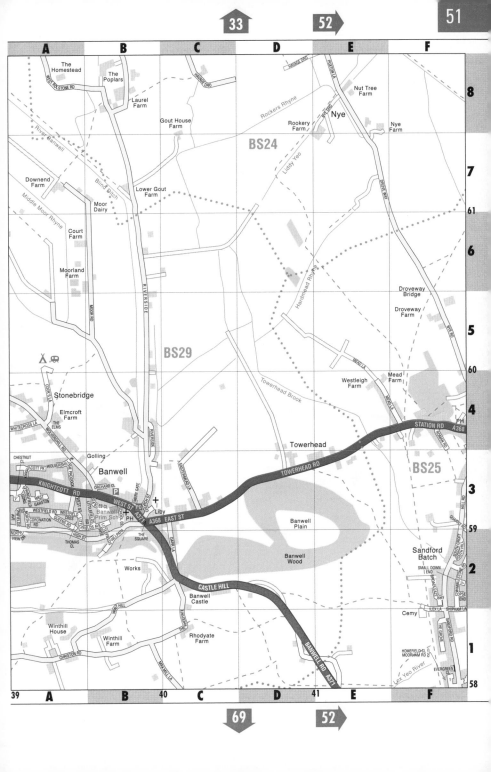

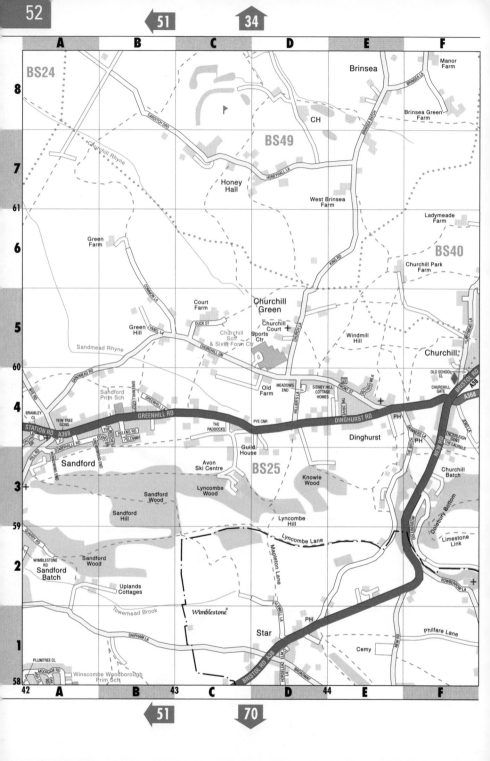

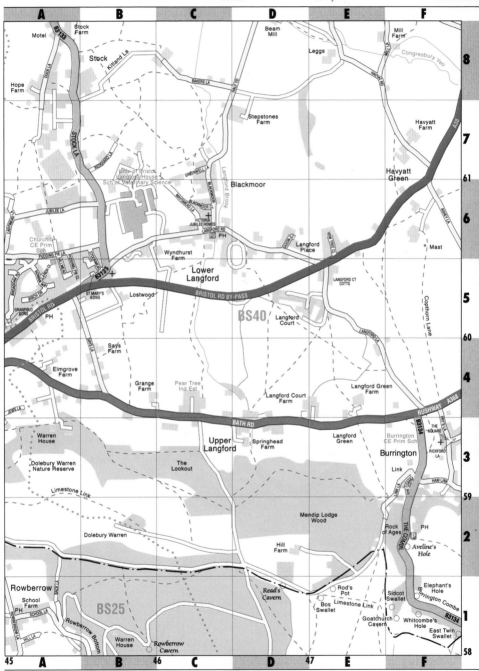

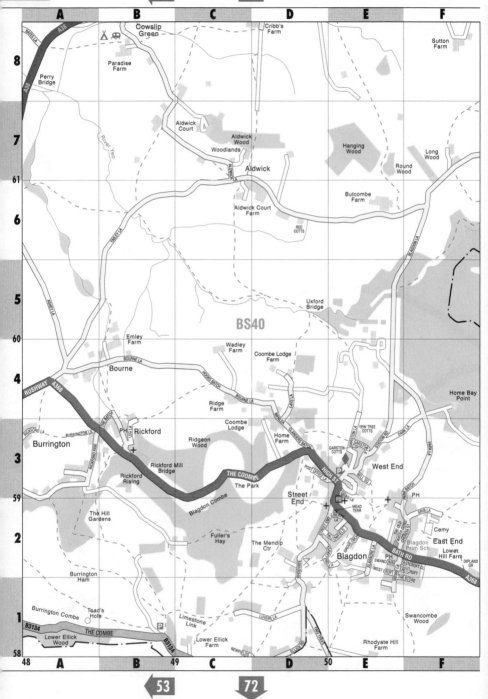

A **B** **C** **D** **E** **F**

8

Perry
Bridge

Cowslip
Green

Cribb's
Farm

Sutton
Farm

Paradise
Farm

7

River Yeo

Aldwick
Court

Aldwick
Wood
Woodlands

Aldwick

Hanging
Wood

Long
Wood

Round
Wood

61

Butcombe
Farm

6

Aldwick Court
Farm

RED
COTTS

5

Uxford
Bridge

BS40

60

Emley
Farm

Wadley
Farm

Coombe Lodge
Farm

4

RUSHWAY A368

BOURNE LA

Bourne

HOORS BATCH

BOURNE LA

Ridge
Farm

YEO LA

Coombe
Lodge

Home
Farm

YEW TREE
COTTS

Home Bay
Point

RICKFORD LA

BURRINGTON LA

ILE BATCH

PH

Rickford

Coombe

MEAD LA

FLANDERS BATCH

GARSTON
COTTS

BARSTOW

STATION RD

DARK LA

PARK LA

BLAGDON LA

Burrington

RICKFORD RISE

3

Rickford Mill
Bridge

Rickford
Rising

Ridgeon
Wood

THE COOMBE

The Park

POST OFFICE LA

HIGH ST

P

BELL SQ

P

West End

PH

59

The Hill
Gardens

Blagdon Combe

Street
End

LIBERY LA

MEAD
TERR

GRIB LA

Cemy

2

Fuller's
Hay

The Mendip
Ctr

STREET END LA

SCHOOL LA

BROOK LA

Blagdon

SWANCOMBE

BATH RD

SWANCOMBE

WEST CROFT
EASTCROFT

DIPLAND
GR

East End

Lower
Hill Farm

Blagdon
Prim Sch

PH

A368

Burrington
Ham

WEST CROFT

THE SCORE

1

Burrington Combe

Toad's
Hole

Limestone
Link

LUVERS LA

ELLICK RD

Swancombe
Wood

B3134

Lower Ellick
Wood

THE COMBE

B3134

Lower Ellick
Farm

NEWFIELDS

Rhodyate Hill
Farm

58

48 **A** **B** 49 **C** **D** 50 **E** **F**

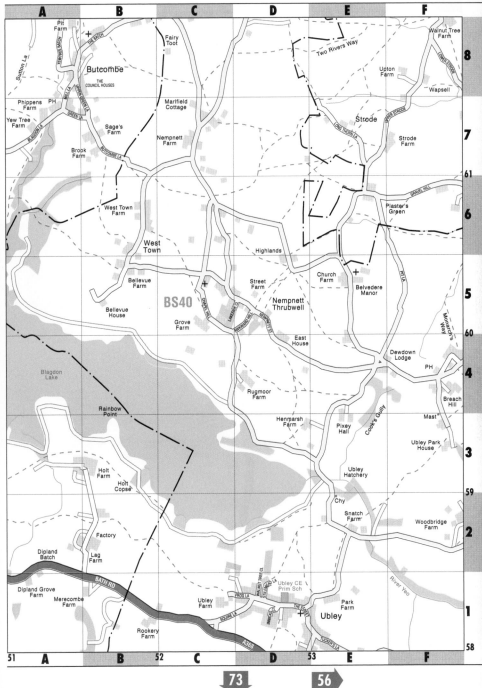

55
38

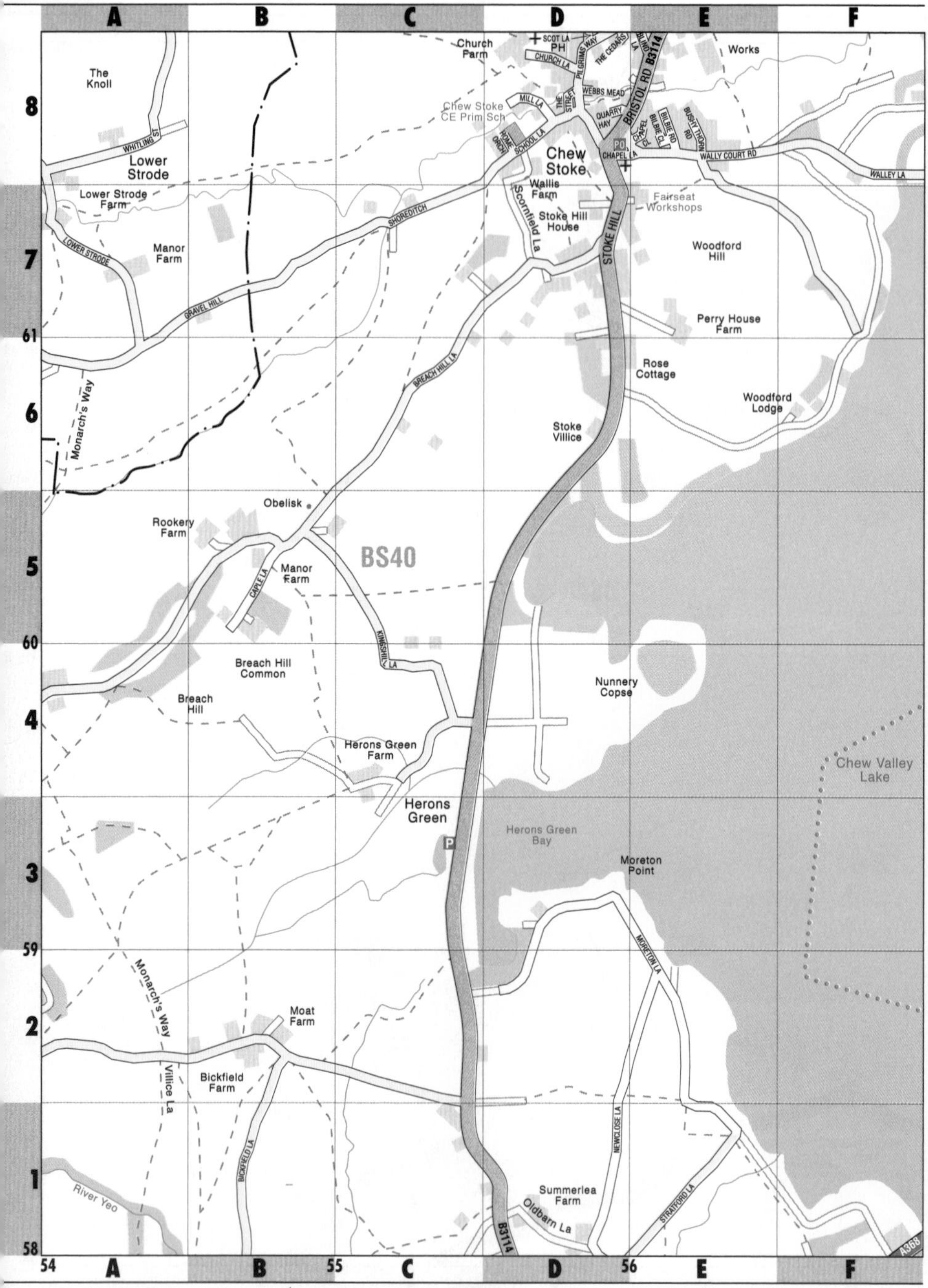
A
B
C
D
E
F
8
7
61
6
5
60
4
3
59
2
1
58
54
55
56
The Knoll
WHITLING ST
Lower Strode
Lower Strode Farm
LOWER STRODE
Manor Farm
GRAVEL HILL
SHOREDITCH
Church Farm
PH
SCOT LA
CHURCH LA
PILGRIMS WAY
THE CEDARS
THE STREET
WEBBS MEAD
MILL LA
BRISTOL RD B3114
QUARRY HAY
CHAPEL CL
BILBIE RD
BILBIE CL
BUSHY THORN RD
Works
Chew Stoke CE Prim Sch
HOME ORCH
SCHOOL LA
Chew Stoke
PO
CHAPEL LA
WALLY COURT RD
WALLEY LA
Wallis Farm
Scornfield La
Stoke Hill House
Fairseat Workshops
STOKE HILL
Woodford Hill
Perry House Farm
Rose Cottage
Woodford Lodge
BREACH HILL LA
Monarch's Way
Stoke Villice
Obelisk
Rookery Farm
BS40
Manor Farm
CAPLE LA
KINGSHILL LA
Breach Hill Common
Breach Hill
Nunnery Copse
Herons Green Farm
Herons Green
P
Herons Green Bay
Chew Valley Lake
Moreton Point
MORETON LA
Monarch's Way
Moat Farm
Bickfield Farm
Villice La
BICKFIELD LA
NEWCLOSE LA
STRATFORD LA
River Yeo
Summerlea Farm
Oldbarn La
B3114
A368

55
74

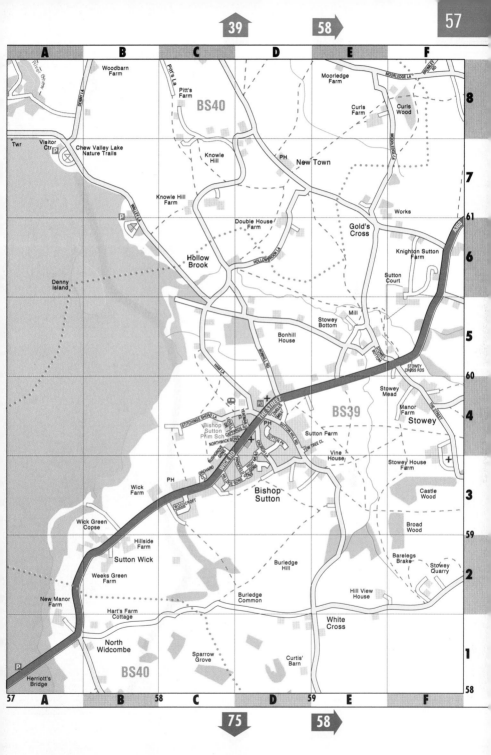

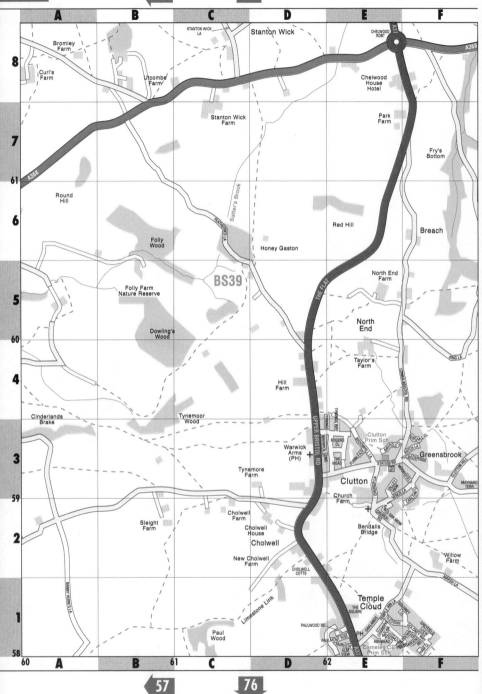

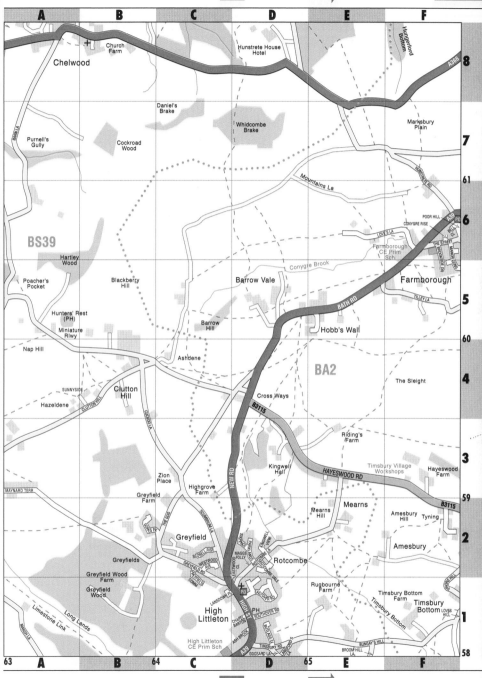

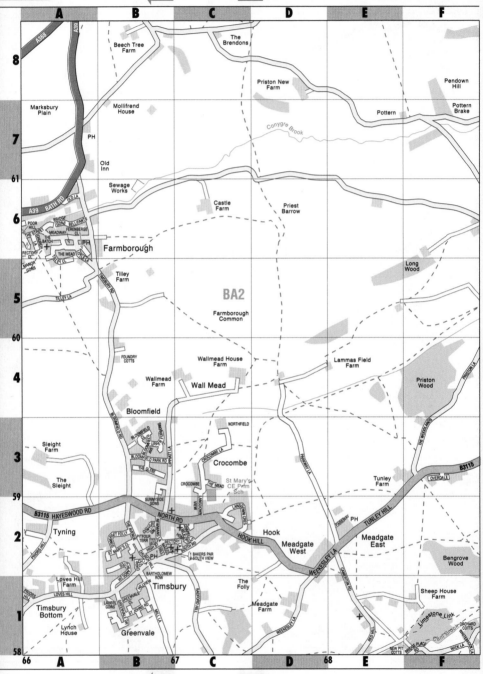

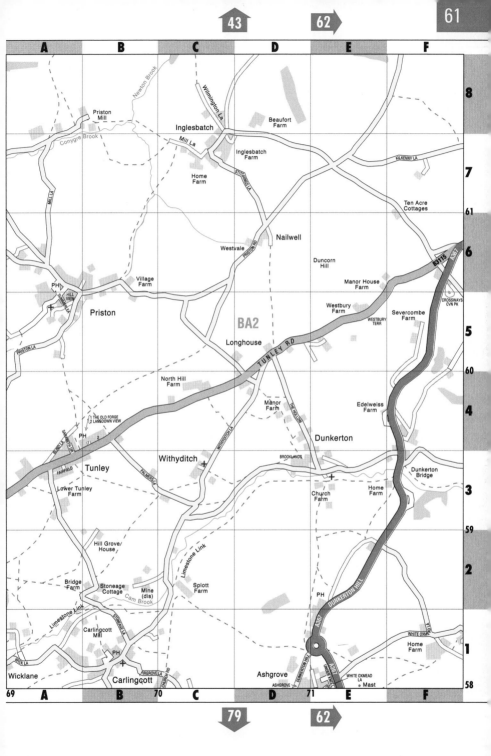

8

B3115

A367

7

61

6

60

5

4

59

3

2

1

58

A

B

C

D

E

F

Priston Mill

Inglesbatch

Mill La

Beaufort Farm

KILKENNY LA

Conygre Brook

Newton Brook

Wilmington La

Inglesbatch Farm

Home Farm

STILFUNGS LA

Ten Acre Cottages

MILL LA

Westvale

Nailwell

PRISTON RD

Duncorn Hill

PH

HILL VIEW

STOWBRUGH LA

Village Farm

Manor House Farm

CROSSWAYS CVN PK

Priston

BA2

Longhouse

Westbury Farm

WESTBURY TERR

Severcombe Farm

TUNLEY RD

PRISTON LA

North Hill Farm

Manor Farm

THE HOLLOW

Edelweiss Farm

1 THE OLD FORGE
2 LANSDOWN VIEW

SANDPIT DR

PH

1 2

Dunkerton

WITHYDITCH LA

Withyditch

BROOKLANDS

FAIRFIELD

PALMERS

BUNDLE LA

Tunley

Dunkerton Bridge

Lower Tunley Farm

Church Farm

Home Farm

Hill Grove/ House

Limestone Link

Bridge Farm

Stoneage Cottage

Mine (dis)

Cam Brook

Splott Farm

PH

DUNKERTON HILL

A367

59

Limestone Link

Carlingcott Mill

STONEAGE LA

A367

A367

Home Farm

WICK LA

PH

CHURCH RD

FIRGROVE LA

WHITE OXMD

Wicklane

Carlingcott

Ashgrove

DUNKERTON HILL

ASH LA

WHITE OXMEAD LA

ASHGROVE

Mast

61
44

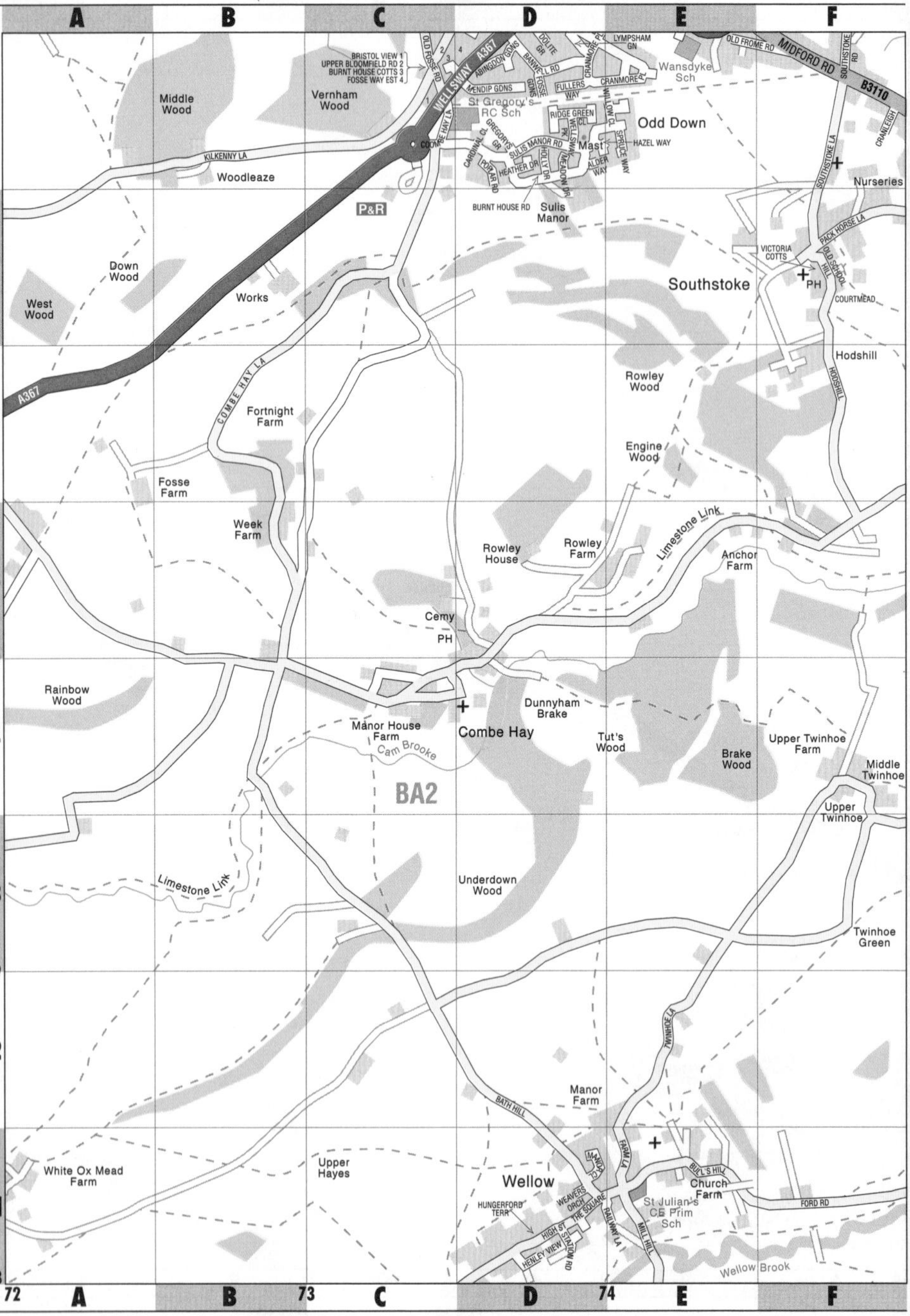

	A	B	C	D	E	F

8

Middle Wood

Vernham Wood

BRISTOL VIEW 1
UPPER BLOOMFIELD RD 2
BURNT HOUSE COTTS 3
FOSSE WAY EST 4

St Gregory's RC Sch

Wansdyke Sch

Odd Down

Mast

HAZEL WAY

LYMPSHAM GN

OLD FROME RD

MIDFORD RD

B3110

Nurseries

Woodleaze

KILKENNY LA

Sulis Manor

BURNT HOUSE LA

Victoria Cotts

PACK HORSE LA

Southstoke

7

Down Wood

Works

West Wood

A367

61

P&R

PH

COURTMEAD

Hodshill

6

Fortnight Farm

COMBE WAY LA

Rowley Wood

Engine Wood

Fosse Farm

Week Farm

Rowley House

Rowley Farm

Limestone Link

Anchor Farm

5

Cemy
PH

60

Rainbow Wood

Manor House Farm

Cam Brooke

Combe Hay

Dunnyham Brake

Tut's Wood

Brake Wood

Upper Twinhoe Farm

Middle Twinhoe

4

BA2

Upper Twinhoe

Limestone Link

3

Underdown Wood

Twinhoe Green

59

2

BATH HILL

Manor Farm

TWINHOE LA

White Ox Mead Farm

Upper Hayes

HUNGERFORD TERR

Wellow

WEAVERS ORCH

St Julian's CE Prim Sch

Church Farm

BULL'S HILL

FORD RD

1

HENLEY VIEW

HIGH ST

THE ISLAND

MILL LA

Wellow Brook

58

72	A		73	B		C		73		D		74	E		F

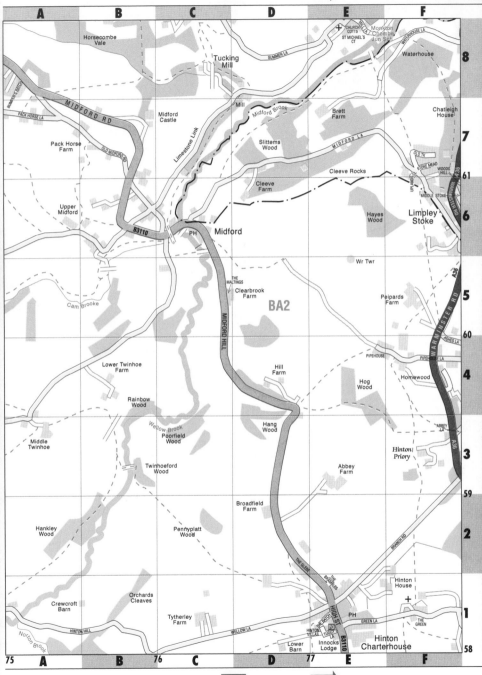

63 46

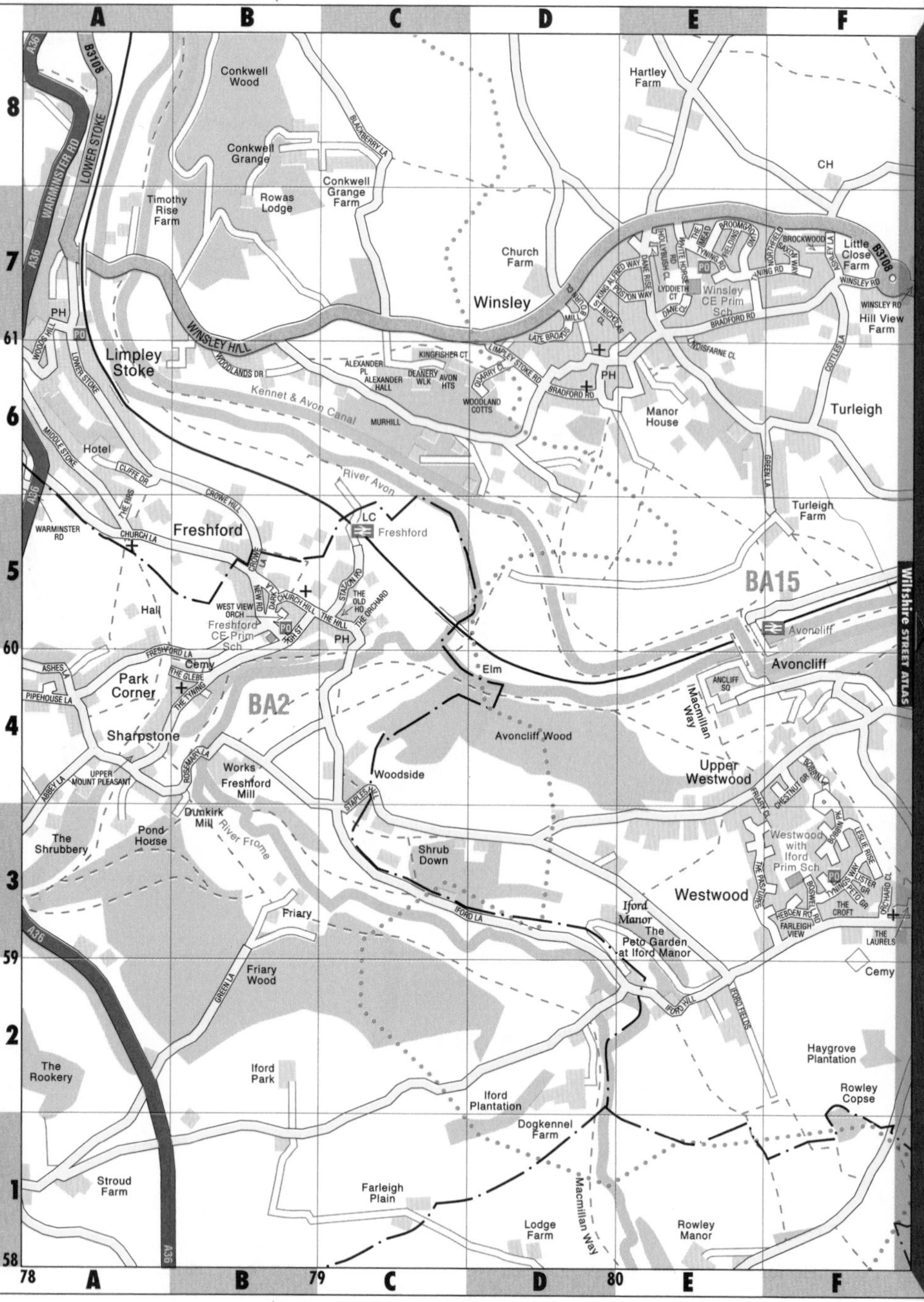

A B C D E F

8

Conkwell Wood

Conkwell Grange

Rowas Lodge

Conkwell Grange Farm

Timothy Rise Farm

Hartley Farm

CH

BLACKBERRY LA

7

Church Farm

Winsley

Winsley CE Prim Sch

Little Close Farm

Winsley Rd Hill View Farm

WINSLEY RD

61

LOWER STOKE

WARMINSTER RD

B3108

A36

B3108

PH

PO

Limpley Stoke

WINSLEY HILL

WOODLANDS DR

ALEXANDER PL
ALEXANDER HALL

KINGFISHER CT

DEANERY WLK AVON HTS

LIMPLEY STOKE RD

MILL

LATE BROAD

ST

BRADFORD RD

PH

LISFARNE CL

Turleigh

6

Kennet & Avon Canal

MURHILL

WOODLAND COTTS

Manor House

Hotel

CLIFFE DR

MIDDLE STOKE

THE HILL

River Avon

Turleigh Farm

5

WARMINSTER RD

CHURCH LA

Freshford

LC
Freshford

BA15

Avoncliff

Hall

WEST VIEW ORCH
Freshford CE Prim Sch

CHURCH HILL

THE OLD RD

CROWE HILL

NEW RD

THE HILL

HIGHFIELD

PO
PH

Elm

ANCLIFF SQ

Avoncliff

60

ASHES LA

PIPEHOUSE LA

Cemy

FRESHFORD LA

THE GLEBE

THE TYNING

Park Corner

BA2

Macmillan Way

Upper Westwood

4

Sharpstone

UPPER MOUNT PLEASANT

GREEN LA

ROSS LA

Works Freshford Mill

Woodside

Avoncliff Wood

Westwood with Iford Prim Sch

Westwood

THE CROFT

THE LAURELS

Dunkirk Mill

Pond House

River Frome

STOKE LA

3

The Shrubbery

Shrub Down

Iford Manor
The Peto Garden at Iford Manor

FARLEIGH VIEW

Cemy

Priary

FORD LA

59

A36

Friary Wood

GREEN LA

2

Iford Park

Iford Plantation

FORD HILL

FORD LANE

Macmillan Way

Haygrove Plantation

The Rookery

Rowley Copse

1

Stroud Farm

A36

Farleigh Plain

Dogkennel Farm

Lodge Farm

Rowley Manor

Macmillan Way

58

78 A B 79 C D 80 E F

Wiltshire STREET ATLAS

63 82

A B C D E F

8

Brean Farm

7

57

Brean Down Inn

HILLTOPS

6

WARREN FARM CVN PK & CAMP SITE

Caravan Park

PH

WESTON RD

Brean

PO

TA8

ST BRIDGET'S CL.

SOUTHFIELD FARM CVN PK & CAMP SITE

56

5

Caravan Park

Caravan Parks

4

CROSS RD

NORTHAM FARM CVN PK & CAMP SITE

Northam Farm

BREAN COURT HO

HUETT CL.

FIRS WOOD CL.

Caravan Parks

Caravan Park

3

The Seagull (PH)

Caravan Park

55

5 KNOLL PK 4 3 2 1

ASH HO 1 BIRCH HO 2 CHESTNUT HO 3 ELDER HO 4 OAK HO 5

Caravan Parks

SOUTH RD

Brean Sands Holiday Ctr

PH

HILL VIEW

2

L Ctr

CH Brean Leisure Park

Caravan Parks

COAST RD

NAPHTHA LA

CH Brean Leisure Park

1

Caravan Parks

54

27 A B 28 C D 29 E F

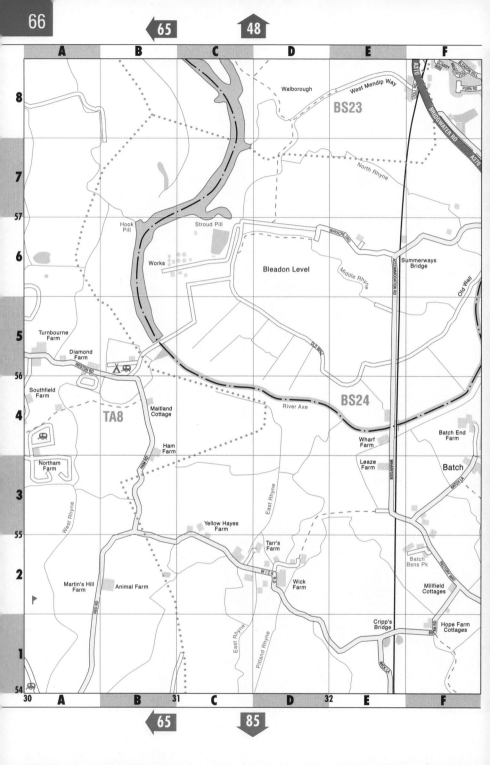

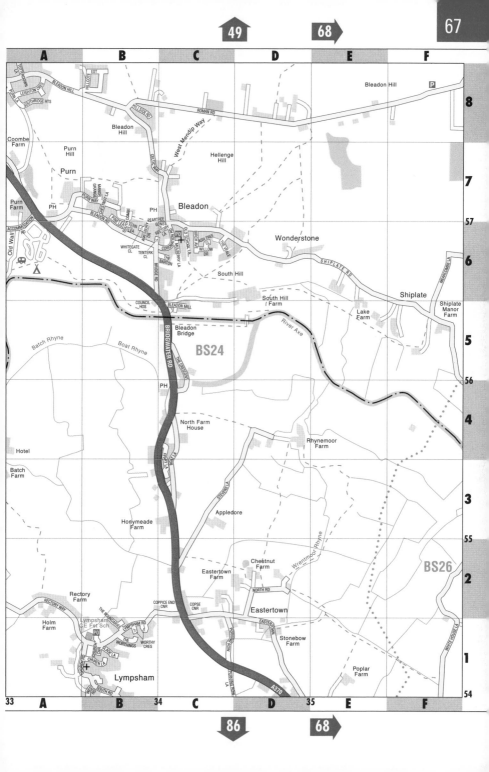

67
50

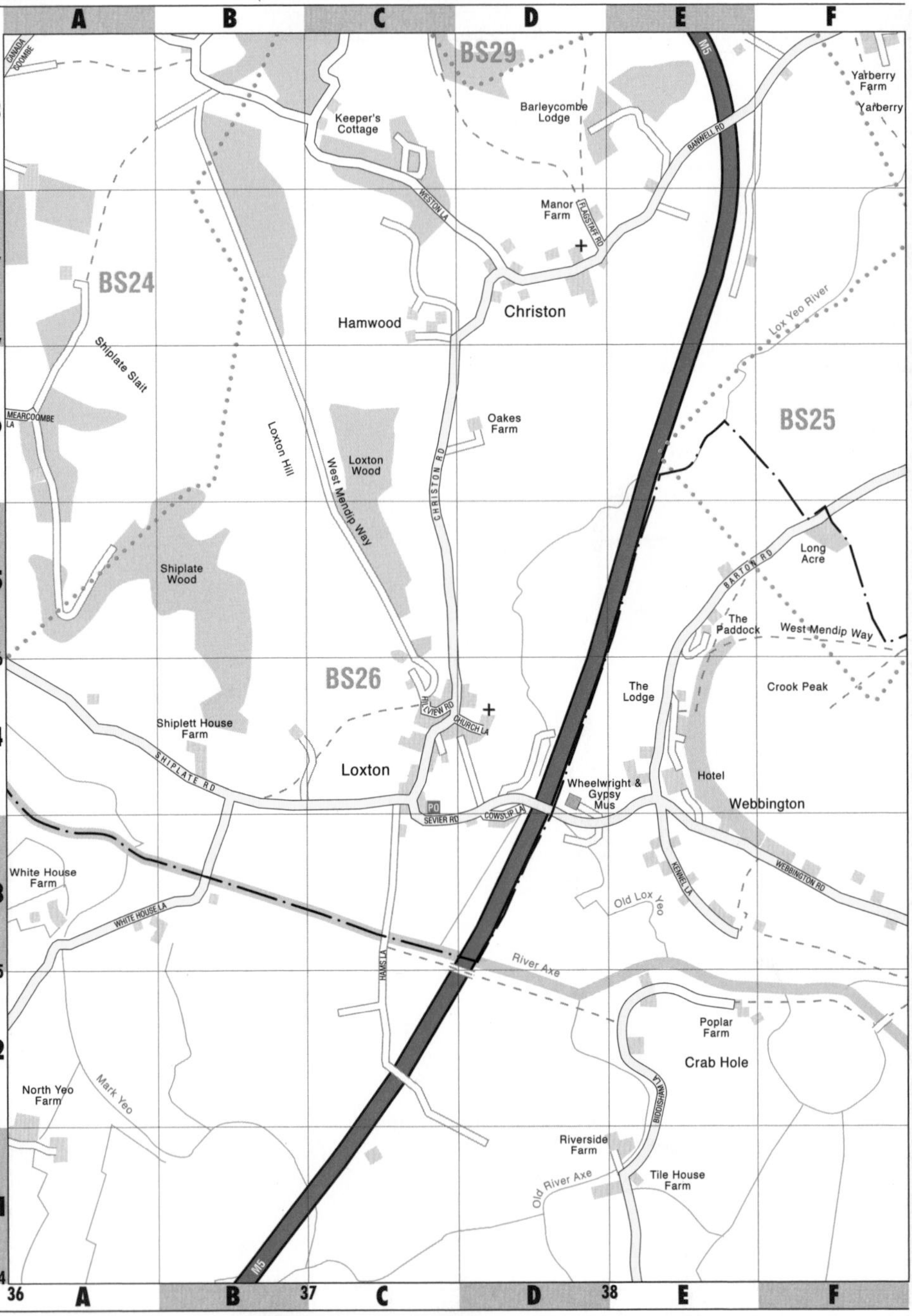

A B C D E F

BS29

8

Keeper's
Cottage

Barleycombe
Lodge

Yatberry
Farm
Yatberry

7

BS24

Manor
Farm

Christon

57

Hamwood

BS25

6

Oakes
Farm

Loxton Hill

Loxton
Wood

Shiplate Slait

MEARDCOMBE LA

West Mendip Way

CHRISTON RD

WESTON LA

EASTER RD

BANWELL RD

M5

Lox Yeo River

Long
Acre

BARTON RD

5

Shiplate
Wood

The
Paddock

West Mendip Way

56

BS26

The
Lodge

Crook Peak

4

Shiplett House
Farm

Loxton

Wheelwright &
Gypsy
Mus

Hotel

Webbington

SHIPLATE RD

HILLVIEW RD

CHURCH LA

COWSLIP LA

SEVIER RD

BENNELL LA

WEBBINGTON RD

PO

White House
Farm

3

Old Lox Yeo

River Axe

WHITE HOUSE LA

HAM LA

55

Poplar
Farm

2

Crab Hole

North Yeo
Farm

Mark Yeo

RIVERSIDE LA

1

Riverside
Farm

Tile House
Farm

Old River Axe

M5

54

36 A B 37 C D 38 E F

67
87

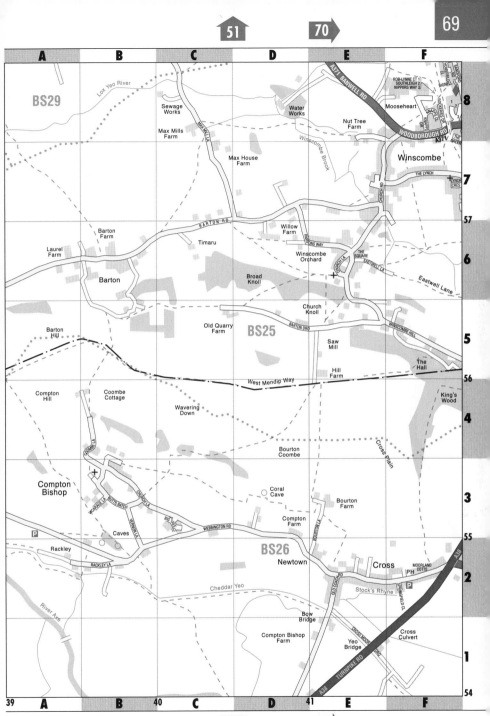

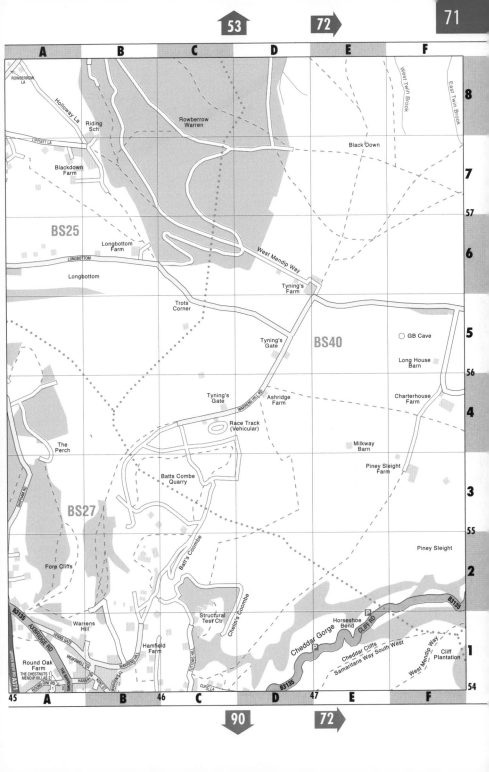

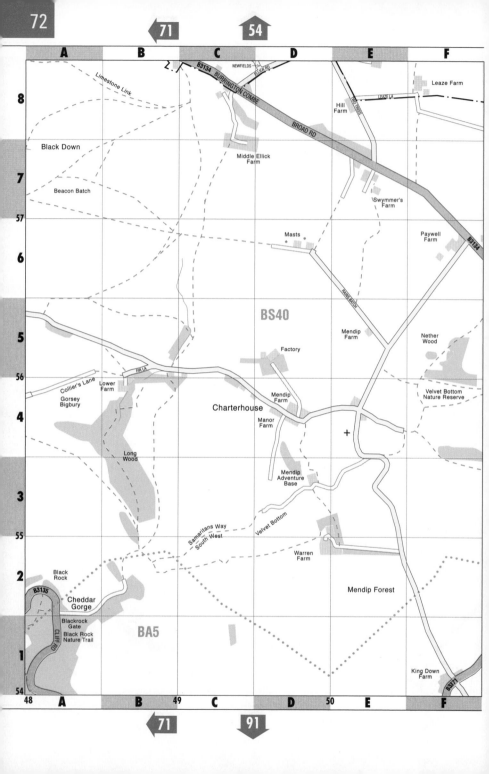

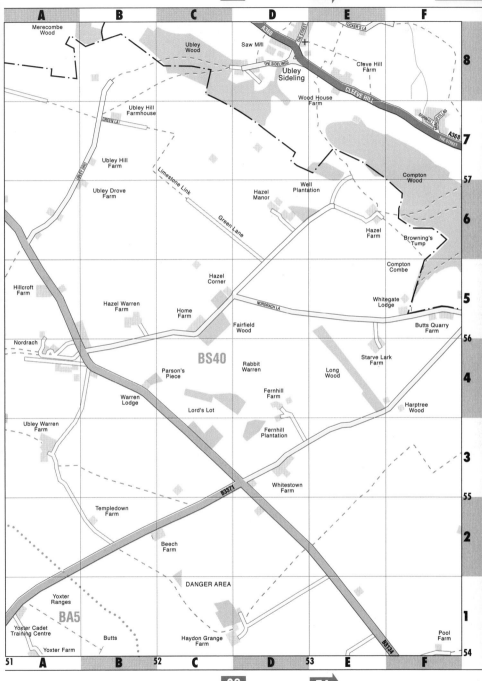

Merecombe
Wood

Ubley
Wood

Saw Mill

Tucker's La

8

Cleve Hill
Farm

Ubley
Sideling

A368

The Sidelings

The Street

CLEVE HILL

Wood House
Farm

A368
The Street

Dunhill Villas

7

Ubley Hill
Farmhouse

Green La

Compton
Wood

57

Ubley Hill
Farm

Ubley La Dro

Limestone Link

Ubley Drove
Farm

Hazel
Manor

Well
Plantation

Green Lane

Hazel
Farm

6

Browning's
Tump

Compton
Combe

Hillcroft
Farm

Hazel
Corner

Whitegate
Lodge

5

Hazel Warren
Farm

Home
Farm

Fairfield
Wood

Nordrach La

Butts Quarry
Farm

56

Nordrach

BS40

Parson's
Piece

Rabbit
Warren

Long
Wood

Starve Lark
Farm

4

Warren
Lodge

Lord's Lot

Fernhill
Farm

Harptree
Wood

Ubley Warren
Farm

Fernhill
Plantation

3

Templedown
Farm

B3371

Whitestown
Farm

55

Beech
Farm

2

DANGER AREA

Yoxter
Ranges

BA5

Pool
Farm

1

Yoxter Cadet
Training Centre

Butts

Haydon Grange
Farm

B3134

54

Yoxter Farm

A
B
C
D
E
F

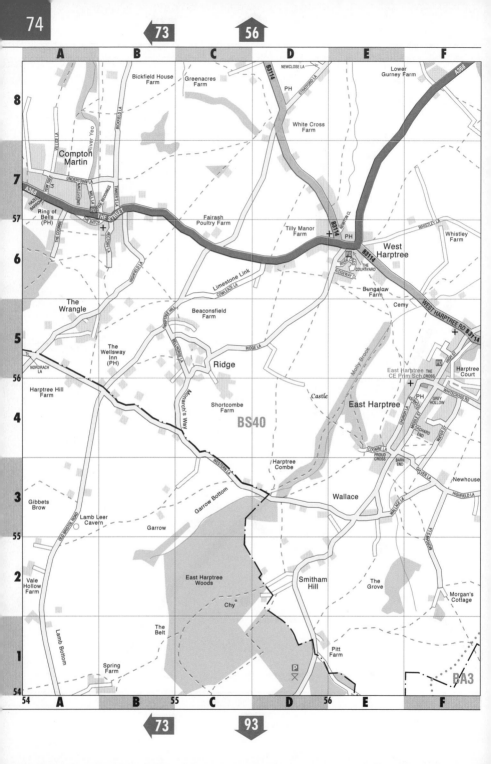

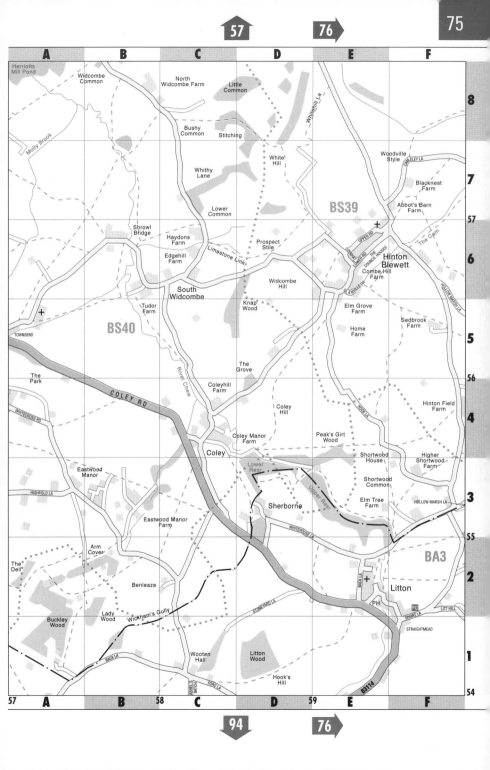

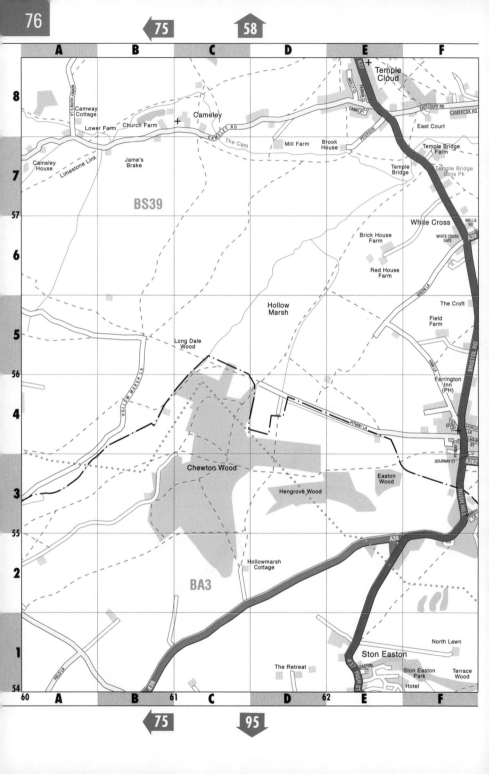

77
60

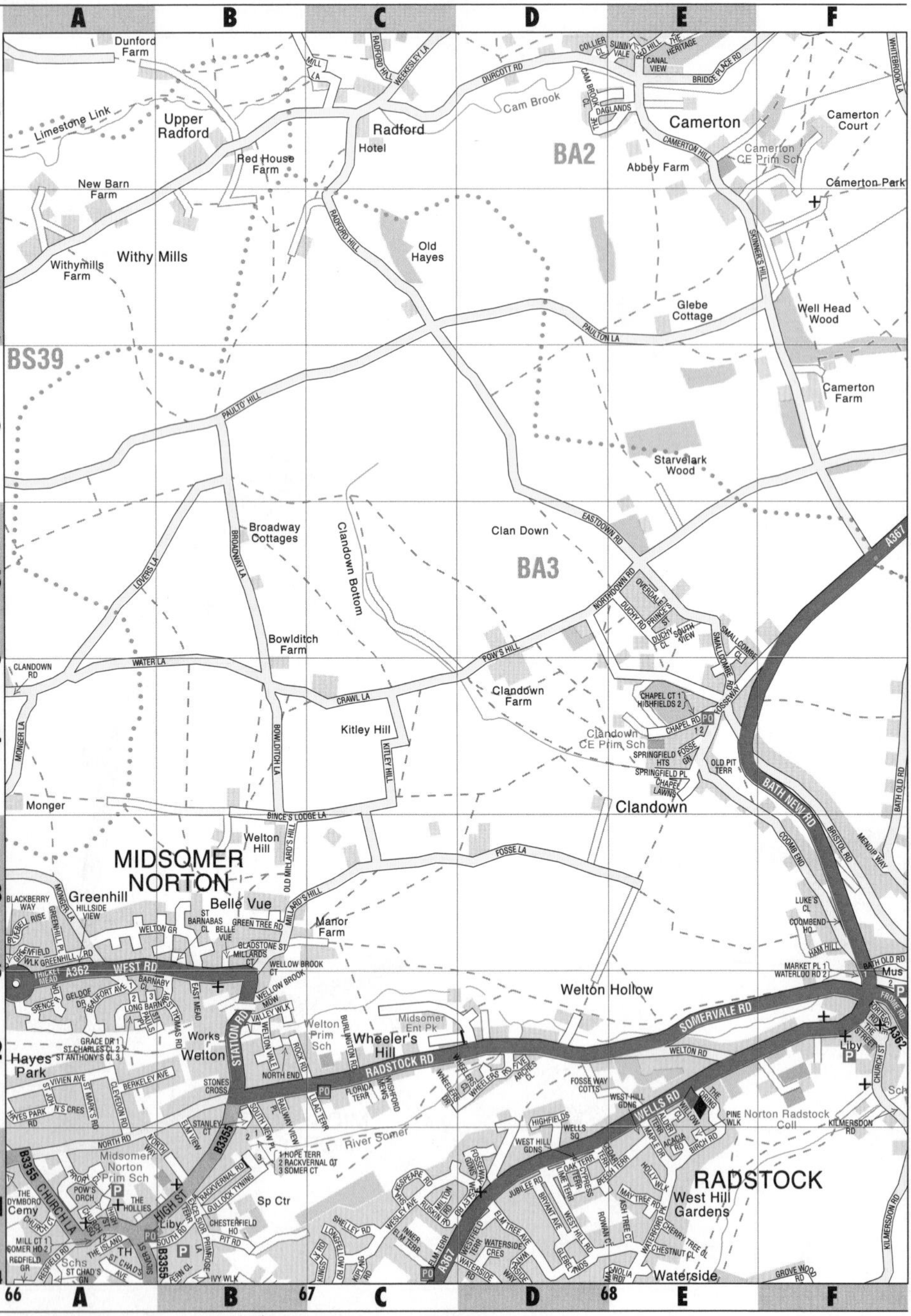
A
B
C
D
E
F
8
7
57
6
5
56
4
3
55
2
1
54
66
67
68
Dunford Farm
Limestone Link
Upper Radford
Red House Farm
Radford
Hotel
MILL LA
RADFORD HILL
WEEKESLEY LA
DURCOTT RD
Cam Brook
COLLIER CL
SUNNY VALE
RED HILL
THE HERITAGE
CANAL VIEW
BRIDGE PLACE RD
CAM BROOK CL
THE DAGLANDS
Camerton
Camerton Court
BA2
CAMERTON HILL
Camerton CE Prim Sch
Abbey Farm
Camerton Park
WHITEBROOK LA
New Barn Farm
Withy Mills
Withymills Farm
Old Hayes
SKINNER'S HILL
Glebe Cottage
Well Head Wood
PAULTON LA
BS39
PAULTON HILL
Camerton Farm
Starvelark Wood
Broadway Cottages
BROADWAY LA
Clandown Bottom
Clan Down
EASTDOWN RD
BA3
A367
LOVERS LA
NORTHDOWN RD
OVERDALE
DUCHY RD
PRINCE'S ST
DUCHY CL
SOUTH VIEW
SMALLCOMBE CL
SMALLCOMBE RD
Bowlditch Farm
POW'S HILL
CLANDOWN RD
WATER LA
CRAWL LA
Clandown Farm
CHAPEL CT 1
HIGHFIELDS 2
FOSSEWAY
CHAPEL RD
PO
MONGER LA
Kitley Hill
BOWLDITCH LA
KITLEY HILL
Clandown CE Prim Sch
SPRINGFIELD HTS
FOSSE GN
OLD PIT TERR
SPRINGFIELD PL
CHAPEL LAWNS
BATH NEW RD
BATH OLD RD
Monger
BINCE'S LODGE LA
Clandown
Welton Hill
OLD MILLARD'S HILL
FOSSE LA
COOMB END
BRISTOL RD
MENDIP WAY
MIDSOMER NORTON
BLACKBERRY WAY
Greenhill
HILLSIDE VIEW
BLUEBELL RISE
GREENHILL PL
Belle Vue
MILLARD'S HILL
ST BARNABAS CL
BELLE VUE
GREEN TREE RD
Manor Farm
LUKE'S CL
COOMBEND HO
WELTON GR
GLADSTONE ST
MILLARDS CT
GREENFIELD WLK
GREENHILL RD
HAM HILL
THICKET MEAD
A362
WEST RD
WELLOW BROOK CT
MARKET PL 1
WATERLOO RD 2
Mus
BARNABY CL
WELLOW BROOK MDW
Welton Hollow
SPENCER DR
GELDOF DR
BEAUFORT AVE
LONG BARN RD
ST THOMAS RD
EAST MEAD
VALLEY WLK
SOMERVALE RD
FROME RD
Midsomer Ent Pk
STATION RD
Welton Prim Sch
Works
Welton
Wheeler's Hill
GRACE DR 1
ST CHARLES CL 2
ST ANTHONY'S CL 3
WELTON VALE
ROCK RD
BURLINGTON RD
WELTON RD
Liby
CHURCH ST
Hayes Park
VIVIEN AVE
BERKELEY AVE
NORTH END
RADSTOCK RD
WHEELERS CL
WHEELERS DR
WHEELERS RD
FIVE ARCHES CL
ST MARK'S RD
CLEVEDON RD
STONES CROSS
PO
FLORIDA TERR
WISHFORD MEWS
LILAC TERR
FOSSE WAY COTTS
WEST HILL GDNS
WELLS RD
THE DRING
WILLOW
Sch
HAYES PARK RD
ST JOHN'S CRES
STANLEY CT
RAILWAY VIEW
SOUTH VIEW PL
PINE WLK
Norton Radstock Coll
KILMERSDON RD
NORTH RD
ELM VIEW
B3355
River Somer
HIGHFIELDS
WELLS SQ
ALDER TERR
ASH CL
ACACIA RD
BIRCH RD
1 HOPE TERR
2 RACKVERNAL CT
3 SOMER CT
WEST HILL GDNS
MAPLE DR
CEDAR TERR
OAK TERR
BEECH TERR
Midsomer Norton Prim Sch
RACKVERNAL RD
GULLOCK TYNING
LIME TERR
CYPRESS TERR
HOLLY WLK
CHURCH LA
PRIORY RD
POW'S ORCH
THE HOLLIES
Sp Ctr
SHAKESPEARE RD
FOSSEWAY GDNS
WESLEY AVE
RUSKIN RD
MILTON RD
WESTFIELD RD
JUBILEE RD
BRYANT AVE
WEST HILL RD
ROWAN CT
ASH TREE CT
MAY TREE RD
RADSTOCK
West Hill Gardens
THE DYMBORO
Cemy
HIGH ST
Liby
EXCELSIOR TERR
CHESTERFIELD HO
SHELLEY RD
LONGFELLOW RD
INNER ELM TERR
ELM TREE AVE
WATERFORD PK
CHERRY TREE CL
CHESTNUT CL
MILL CT 1
SOMER HO 2
THE ISLAND
TH
SOUTH RD
PIT RD
P
WATERSIDE CRES
REDFIELD GR
REDFIELD RD
Schs
ST CHAD'S GN
ST CHAD'S AVE
SILVER ST
B3355
FERN CL
PRIMROSE LA
IVY WLK
KINGS RD
KIPLING RD
ELM TERR
A367
WESTFIELD TERR
WATERSIDE RD
WATERSIDE WAY
GLEBELANDS
MAGNOLIA RD
Waterside
GROVE WOOD RD

77
97

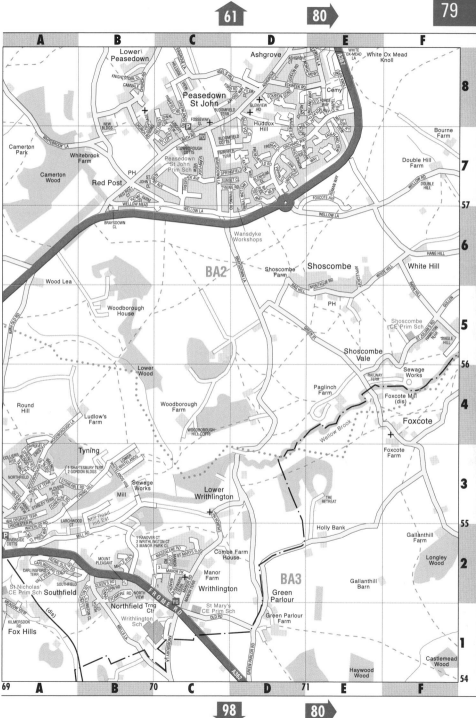

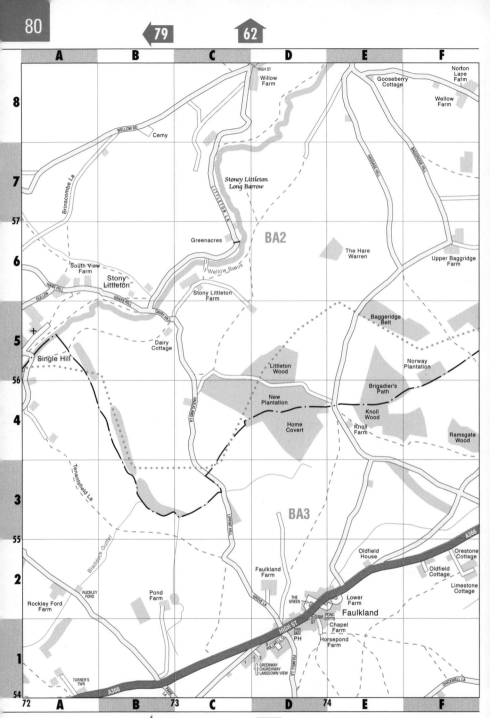

A   B   C   D   E   F

8

WELLOW RD
Cemy

7

57

BA2

6

HIGH ST
Willow
Farm

Gooseberry
Cottage

Norton
Lane
Farm

Wellow
Farm

Stoney Littleton
Long Barrow

BRINSCOMBE LA

LITTLETON LA

Greenacres

Wellow Brook

The Hare
Warren

Upper Baggridge
Farm

South View
Farm

Stony
Littleton

HANG HILL

GULLEN

GRAYS HILL

DAIRY HILL

Stony Littleton
Farm

Baggeridge
Belt

HASSAGE HILL

BAGGRIDGE HILL

+

5

Single Hill

Dairy
Cottage

56

Littleton
Wood

Norway
Plantation

4

FAULKLAND LA

New
Plantation

Brigadier's
Path

Tenantsfield La

Home
Covert

Knoll
Wood

Knoll
Farm

Ramsgate
Wood

3

Bladdock Gutter

UPPER HILL

BA3

55

Rockley Ford
Farm

RUCKLEY
FORD

Pond
Farm

Faulkland
Farm

Oldfield
House

A366

Orestone
Cottage

2

GROVE LA

THE
GREEN

BISHOP
ST

Lower
Farm

Oldfield
Cottage

Limestone
Cottage

PILL WELL LA

HIGH ST

PO
PH

POND
COTTS

Faulkland

Chapel
Farm

FLIWELL LA

Horsepond
Farm

1

TURNER'S
TWR

A366

PARK
LA

1 GREENWAY
2 CHURCHWAY
3 LANSDOWN VIEW

CHICKWELL LA

54

72   A   B   73   C   D   74   E   F

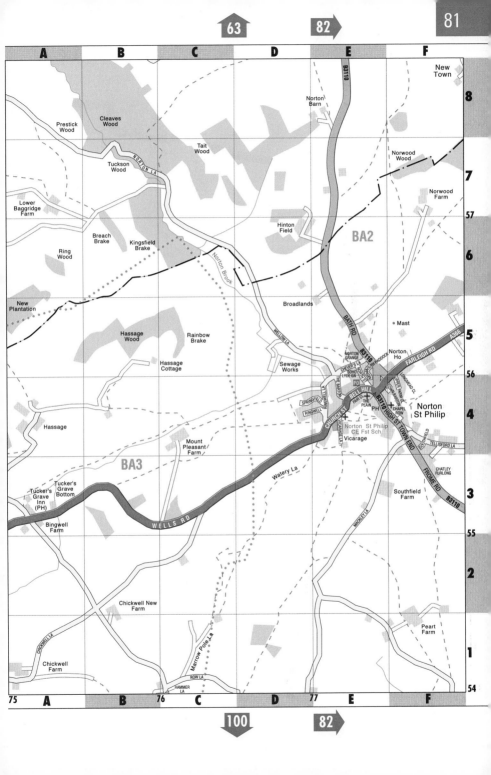

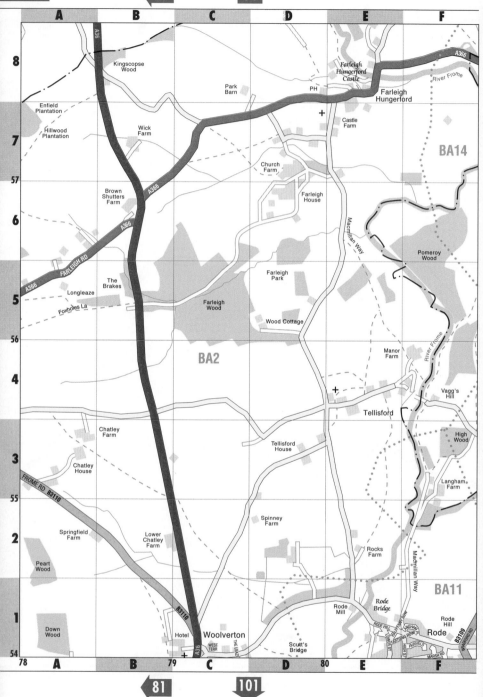

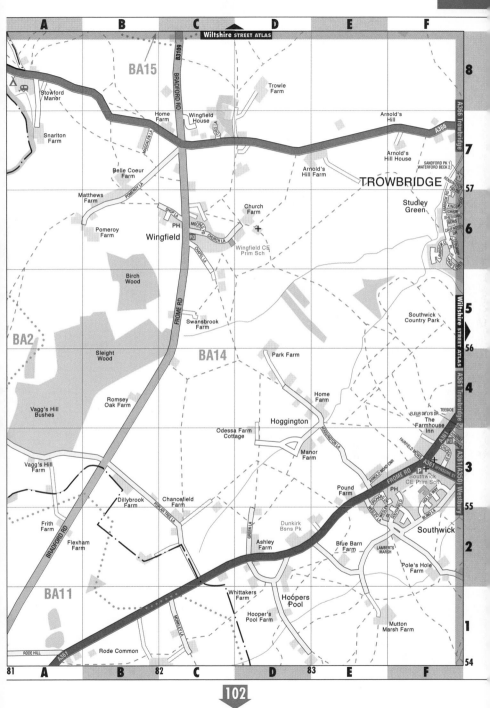

	A	B	C	D	E	F

Unity Farm

SHRUBBERY CL

HERON PK

Hurn Farm

COAST RD

Mead Farm

Berrow Manor

MANOR CL
MANOR DR
MANOR WY

CLAREMONT CVN PK

RED RD

BRAMBLE DR
ROWAN DR

Rose Farm

PARSONAG

PIMPERNE

PADDOCK CROFT

Westcroft Nurseries

TA8

LITTLE PEN
PENMOOR PEMB

CHURCH HOUSE RD

BARTON CL

Berrow

Sch

BARTON CL

JUBILEE ACRES

ST AUBYNS RD

BRISTOL RD

FAIRWAY CL

ROSE TREE PADDOCK

ROSENEATH AVE

BEACH RD

SANDIHALS

PH

P

PO

LARK GDNS

Lark Spit

THE RETREAT CVN PK

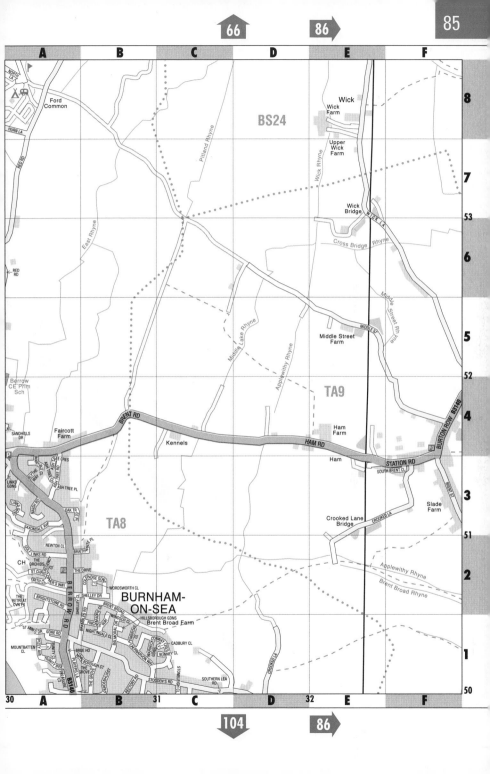

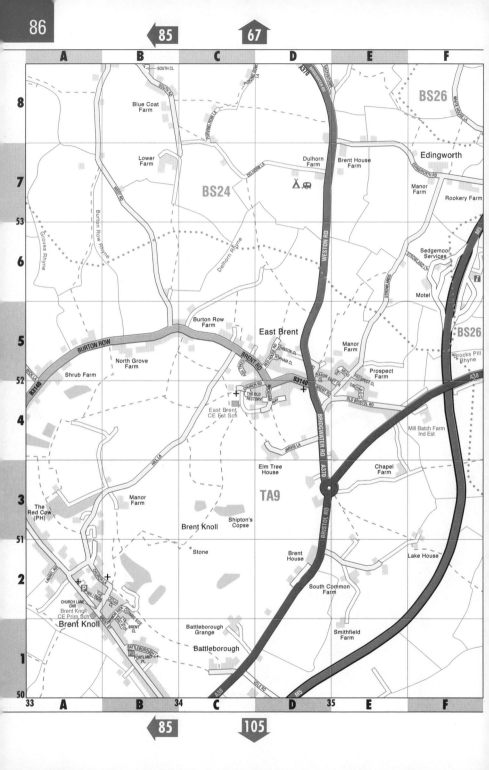

A   B   C   D   E   F

8

SOUTH CL

Blue Coat
Farm

BS26

Edingworth

WHITE HOUSE LA

Lower
Farm

EDINGWORTH RD

Manor
Farm

Dulhorn
Farm

Brent House
Farm

Rookery Farm

7

BS24

53

Burton Row Rhyme

Delhorn Rhyne

WEST RD

DELHORN LA

WESTON RD

Sedgemoor
Services

Groves Rhyne

6

Motel

M5

BS26

Burton Row
Farm

East Brent

Manor
Farm

Brocks Pill
Rhyne

5

BURTON ROW

North Grove
Farm

BRENT RD

JOHNSON CL
POPHAM CL

Prospect
Farm

A38

52

Shrub Farm

B3140

B3140

CHURCH RD

MANOR CL

OLD BRISTOL RD

BRENT RD

A370

The Old
Rectory

4

East Brent
CE Fst Sch

Mill Batch Farm
Ind Est

JARVIS LA

Elm Tree
House

BRIDGWATER RD

Chapel
Farm

HILL LA

3

Manor
Farm

TA9

The
Red Cow
(PH)

Brent Knoll

Shipton's
Copse

BRISTOL RD

51

Stone

Brent
House

Lake House

2

LABEL RD

CHURCH LA

P

THE
WILLOWS

CEDAR RD

BRENT CL

South Common
Farm

CHURCH LANE
CNR
Brent Knoll
CE Prim Sch

Brent Knoll

BATTLEBOROUGH RD
PORTLAND PL

Battleborough
Grange

Smithfield
Farm

1

Battleborough

A38

GOLF RD

M5

50

33   A   B   34   C   D   35   E   F

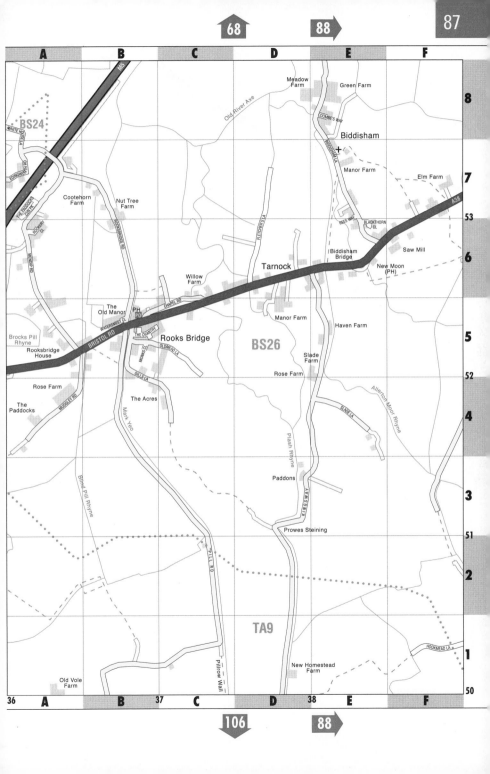

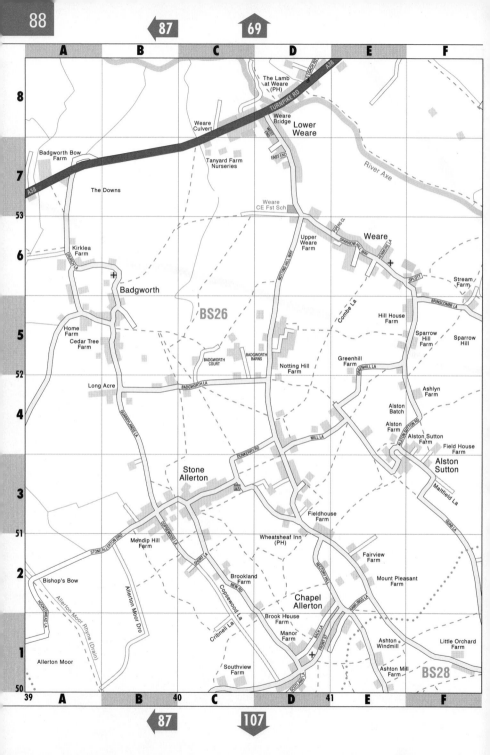

| | A | B | C | D | E | F |

8

The Lamb
at Weare
(PH)

TURNPIKE RD

Weare
Culvert

Weare
Bridge

Lower
Weare

EAST END

Badgworth Bow
Farm

7

River Axe

A38

Tanyard Farm
Nurseries

The Downs

Weare
CE Fst Sch

53

Upper
Weare
Farm

Weare

Kirklea
Farm

6

SPARROW HILL WAY

Stream
Farm

CHURCH LA

NOTTING HILL WAY

SPLOTT

BRINSCOMBE LA

Badgworth

BS26

Combe La

Hill House
Farm

Sparrow
Hill
Farm

Sparrow
Hill

5

Home
Farm

Cedar Tree
Farm

BADGWORTH
COURT

BADGWORTH
BARNS

Notting Hill
Farm

Greenhill
Farm

GRENHILL LA

Ashlyn
Farm

52

Long Acre

BADGWORTH LA

QUABBS LANES LA

4

Alston
Batch

Alston
Farm

Alston Sutton
Farm

ALSTON SUTTON RD

Field House
Farm

MILL LA

DUNKERRY RD

Stone
Allerton

Alston
Sutton

3

P.O.

Maltfield La

QUAR LA

51

Mendip Hill
Farm

STONE ALLERTON DRO

COPSEWOOD LA

Fieldhouse
Farm

Wheatsheaf Inn
(PH)

Fairview
Farm

Mount Pleasant
Farm

2

Bishop's Bow

Allerton Moor Dro

SHORT LA

Brookland
Farm

Chapel
Allerton

BECKINGS HILL

HARPLINES LA

Allerton Moor Rhyne (Drain)

MOORHEAD LA

NEW RD

Copsewood La

Brook House
Farm

1

Allerton Moor

Cribnell La

Manor
Farm

BECK LA

FRONT ST

Ashton
Windmill

Little Orchard
Farm

BS28

Southview
Farm

SOUTH RD

Ashton Mill
Farm

50

| 39 | A | B | 40 | C | D | 41 | E | F |

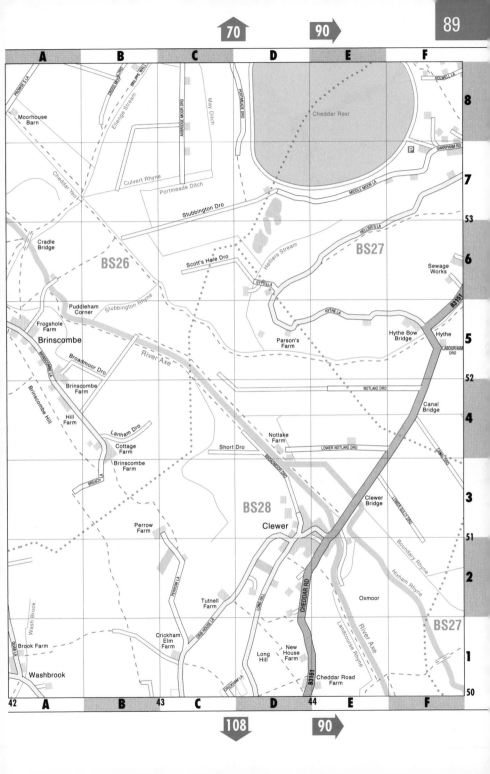

89
71

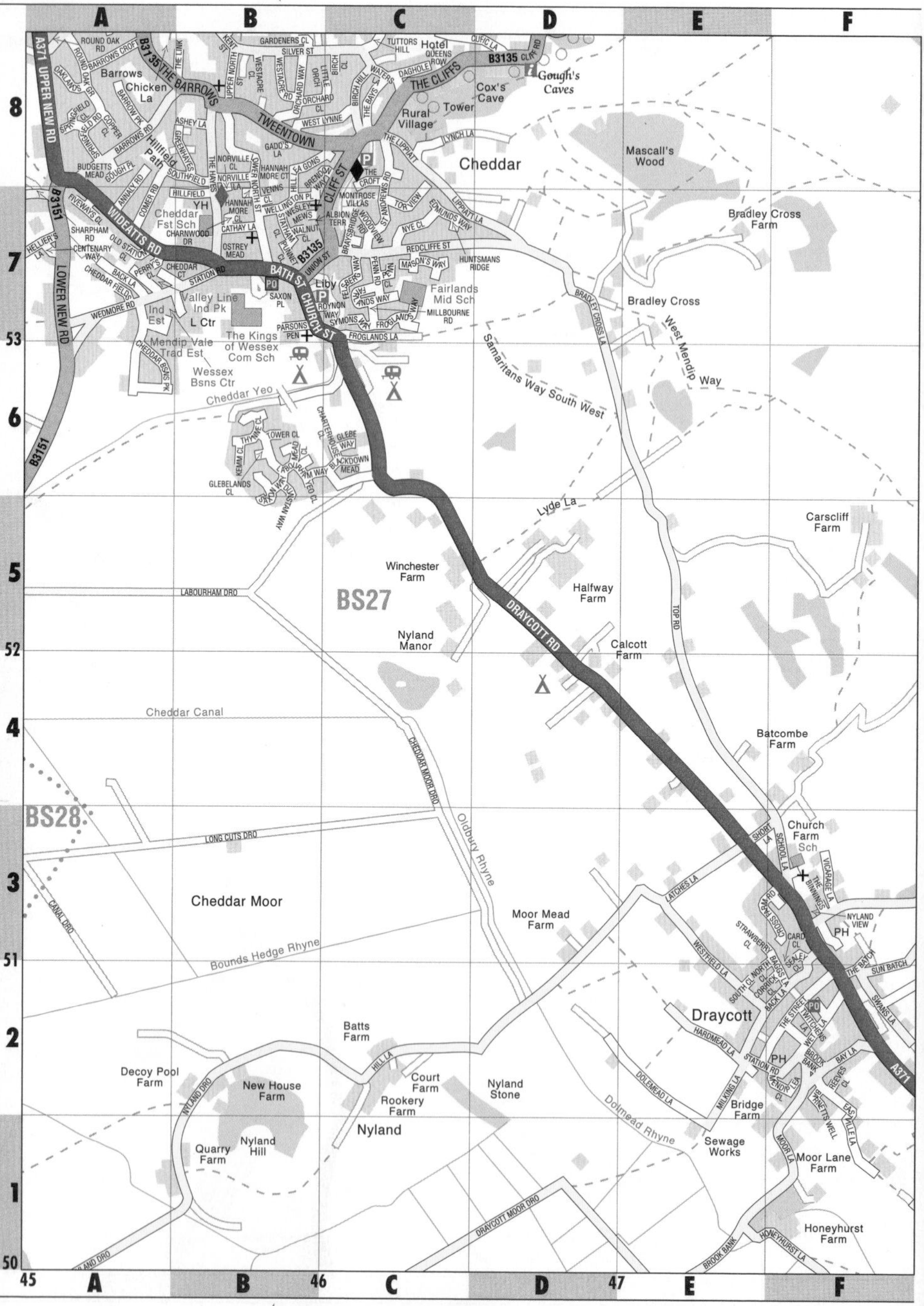
A
B
C
D
E
F
8
7
53
6
5
52
4
3
51
2
1
50
45
46
47
A371 UPPER NEW RD
ROUND OAK RD
BARROWS CROFT
B3135 THE BARROWS
Barrows
Chicken La
Hillfield Path
GARDENERS CL
SILVER ST
TUTTORS HILL
Hotel
QUEENS ROW
CUFIC LA
CLIFF RD
B3135
Gough's Caves
THE CLIFFS
Cox's Cave
Tower
Rural Village
TWEENTOWN
WEST LYNNE
LYNCH LA
THE LIPPIATT
Cheddar
Mascall's Wood
B3151
WIDEATTS RD
Cheddar Fst Sch
YH
CHARNWOOD DR
OSTREY MEAD
CATHAY LA
B3135
CLIFF ST
MONTROSE VILLAS
ALBION TERR
TOR VIEW
EDMUNDS WAY
LIPPIATT LA
NYE CL
REDCLIFFE ST
MASON'S WAY
HUNTSMANS RIDGE
Bradley Cross Farm
BATH ST
CHURCH ST
PO
Liby
P
SAXON PL
ROYNON WAY
SYMONS WAY
FROGLANDS LA
FROGLANDS WAY
Fairlands Mid Sch
MILLBOURNE RD
Bradley Cross
BRADLEY CROSS LA
West Mendip Way
WEDMORE RD
Valley Line Ind Pk
Ind Est
L Ctr
The Kings of Wessex Com Sch
Mendip Vale Trad Est
Wessex Bsns Ctr
CHEDDAR BSNS PK
PARSONS PEN
LOWER NEW RD
Cheddar Yeo
Samaritans Way South West
GLEBE WAY
BLACKDOWN MEAD
CHARTERHOUSE CL
GLEBELANDS CL
Lyde La
Carscliff Farm
Winchester Farm
Halfway Farm
LABOURHAM DRO
BS27
DRAYCOTT RD
TOP RD
Nyland Manor
Calcott Farm
Cheddar Canal
CHEDDAR MOOR DRO
Batcombe Farm
BS28
Oldbury Rhyne
LONG CUTS DRO
Church Farm
Sch
SHORT LA
SCHOOL LA
VICARAGE LA
THE BINNINGS
CANAL DRO
Cheddar Moor
LATCHES LA
Moor Mead Farm
NYLAND VIEW
PH
Bounds Hedge Rhyne
WESTFIELD LA
STRAWBERRY CL
THE BATCH
SUN BATCH
SWANS LA
Draycott
HARDMEAD LA
THE STREET
PO
Batts Farm
HILL LA
STATION RD
PH
BAY LA
A371
Decoy Pool Farm
New House Farm
Court Farm
Rookery Farm
Nyland Stone
DOLEMEAD LA
MILKING LA
Bridge Farm
NYLAND DRO
Nyland
Quarry Farm
Nyland Hill
Dolmead Rhyne
Sewage Works
MOOR LA
Moor Lane Farm
DRAYCOTT MOOR DRO
Honeyhurst Farm
BROOK BANK
HONEYHURST LA
NYLAND DRO

89
109

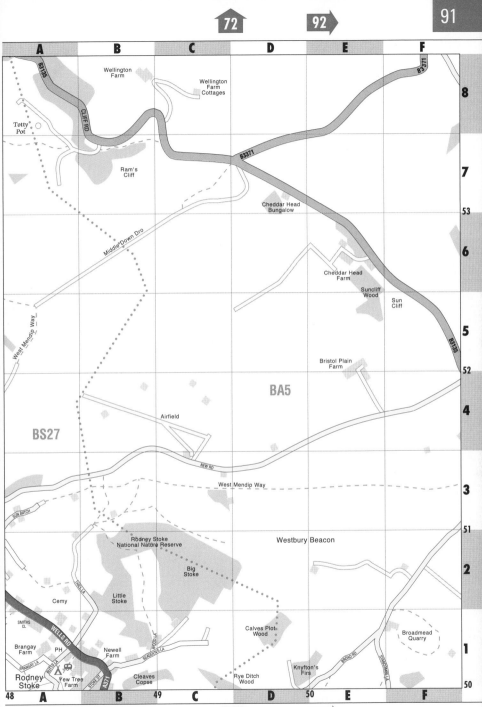

8
7
53
6
5
52
4
3
51
2
1
50

BA5

BS27

B3135

CLIFF RD

Totty Pot

Wellington Farm

Wellington Farm Cottages

B3371

Ram's Cliff

Cheddar Head Bungalow

Middle Down Dro

West Mendip Way

Cheddar Head Farm

Suncliff Wood

Sun Cliff

B3135

Bristol Plain Farm

Airfield

NEW RD

West Mendip Way

SUN BATCH

Rodney Stoke National Nature Reserve

Westbury Beacon

Big Stoke

Cemy

Little Stoke

Calves Plot Wood

Broadmead Quarry

SMITHS CL

WELLS RD

Brangay Farm

PH

BRANGAY LA

STOKE ST

A371

Newell Farm

SCADDENS LA

STOCKHILL LA

Cleaves Copse

Rye Ditch Wood

Knyfton's Firs

BROAD RD

STANCOMBE LA

Rodney Stoke

Yew Tree Farm

91 73

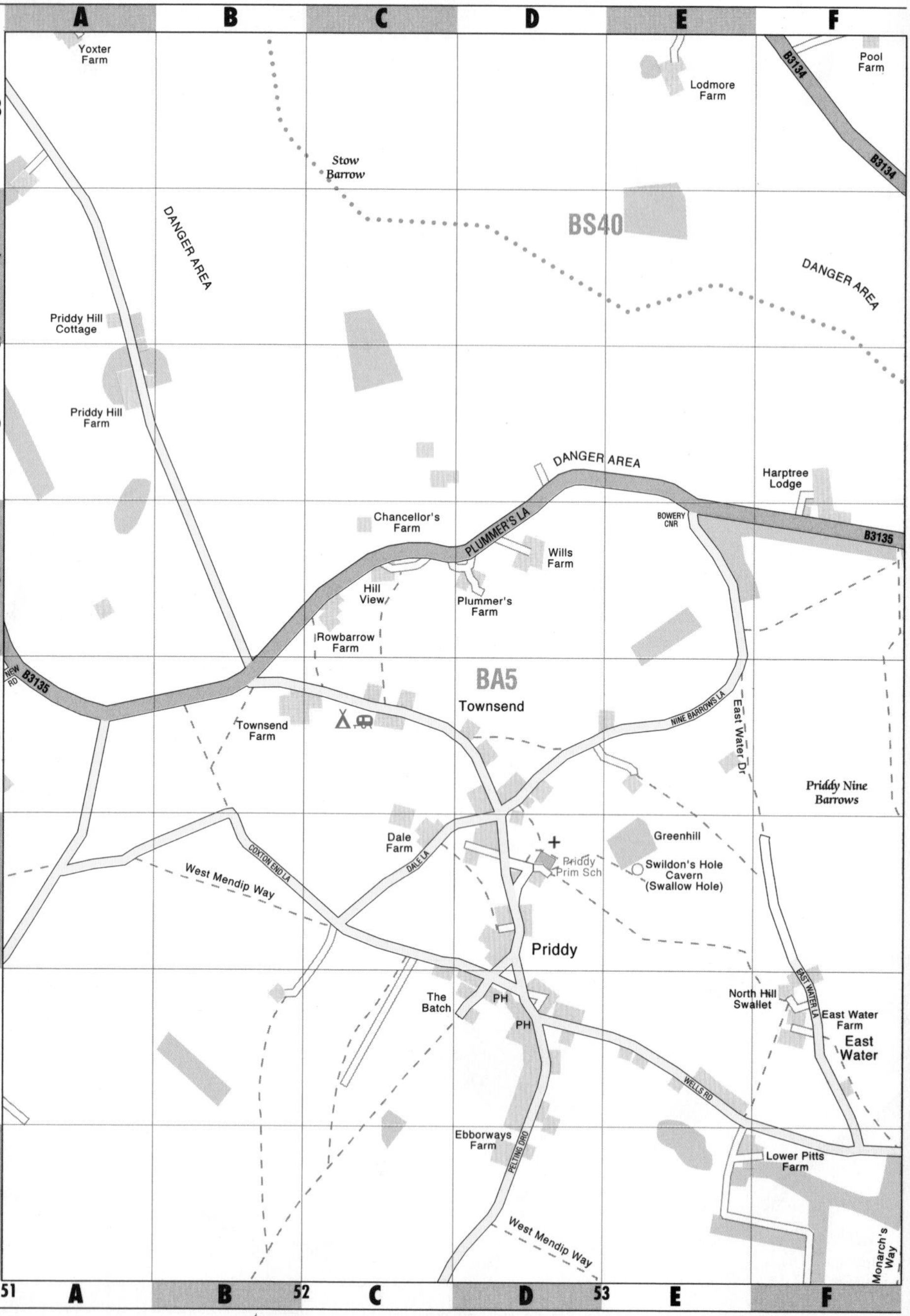

	A	B	C	D	E	F

8

Yoxter Farm

Stow Barrow

B3134

Pool Farm

Lodmore Farm

BS40

7

DANGER AREA

DANGER AREA

53

Priddy Hill Cottage

B3134

6

Priddy Hill Farm

Harptree Lodge

DANGER AREA

5

Chancellor's Farm

PLUMMER'S LA

Wills Farm

BOWERY CNR

B3135

Hill View

Plummer's Farm

Rowbarrow Farm

52

VIEW RD

B3135

BA5

Townsend

NINE BARROWS LA

East Water Dr

4

Townsend Farm

Priddy Nine Barrows

3

West Mendip Way

COXTON END LA

Dale Farm

DALE LA

Priddy Prim Sch

Greenhill

Swildon's Hole Cavern (Swallow Hole)

EAST WATER LA

51

Priddy

North Hill Swallet

East Water Farm

2

The Batch

PH

PH

WELLS RD

East Water

1

Ebborways Farm

PELTING DRO

Lower Pitts Farm

West Mendip Way

Monarch's Way

50

51	A	B	52	C	D	53	E	F

91 111

A | B | C | D | E | F

8

Devil's Punch Bowl

Swallet Farm

Mast

Hill Grange

OLD BRISTOL RD

B3134

Hill Farm

BS40

Roadside Clump

Wurt Pit (dis)

Big Clump

Nett Wood Farm

Monarch's Way

Greendown Batch

Niver Hill

7

53

Castle of Comfort (PH)

Priddy Circles

Castle Farm

The Belt

Wigmore Farm

Monarch's Way

Eaker Hill Farm

Bendall's Grove

West End

BA3

6

Cranmore View

Miners' Arms

B3134

Eaker Hill

5

Red Quarr Farm

52

TORHOLE BOTTOM

BA5

4

North Hill

Monarch's Way

P

3

Priddy Mineries

Bendalls Farm

B3135

51

Under Barrow Farm

Stockhill

2

Nursery

Cuckoo Cleeves

Tower Hill

1

Ash Plantation

Hunters Lodge Inn

HILLGROVE RD

50

54 | A | B | 55 | C | D | 56 | E | F

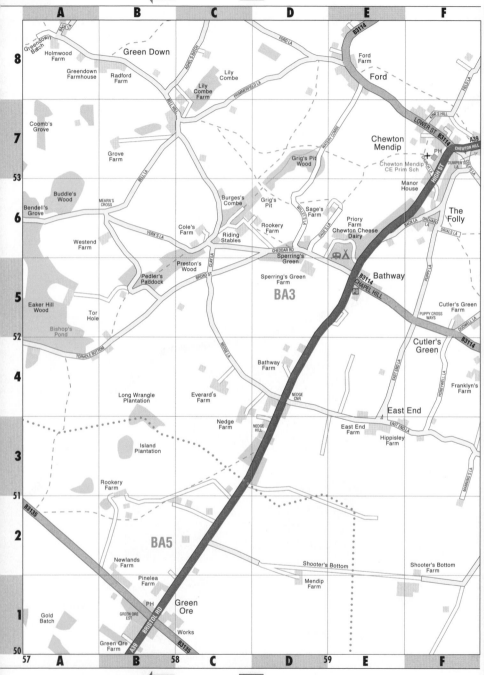

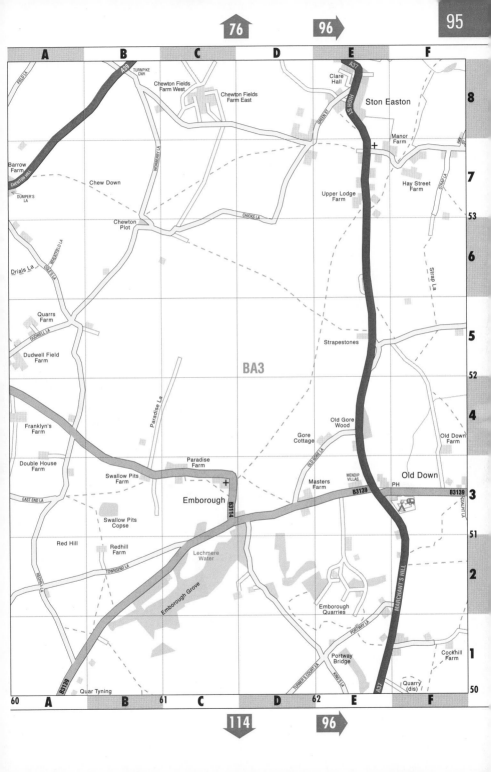

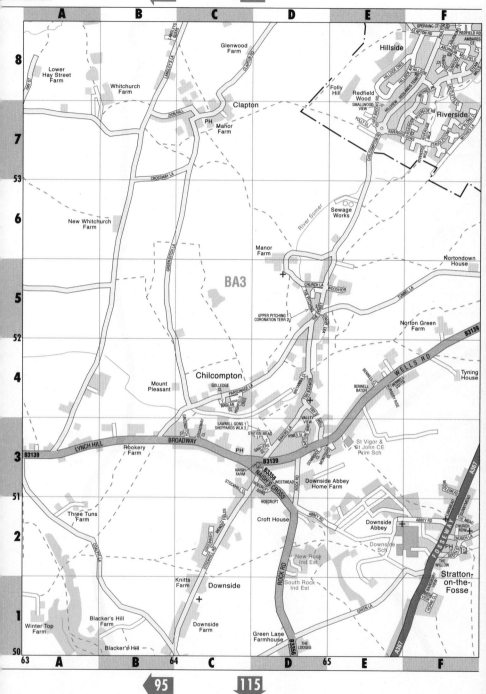

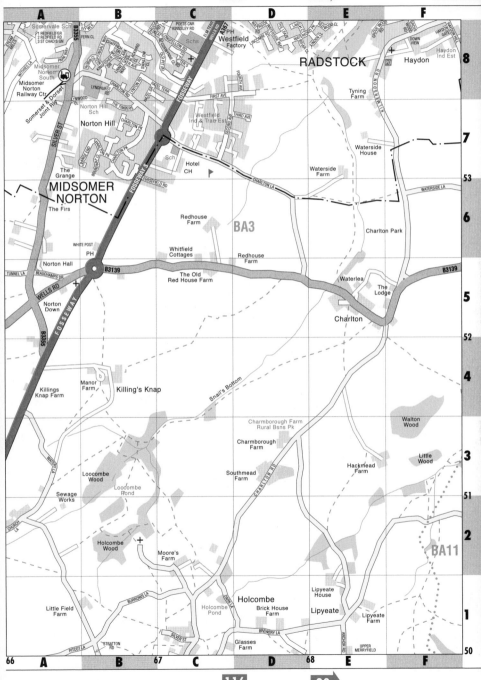

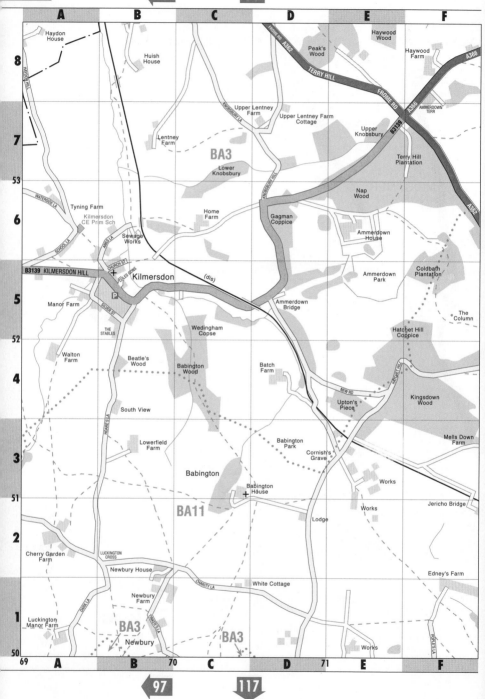

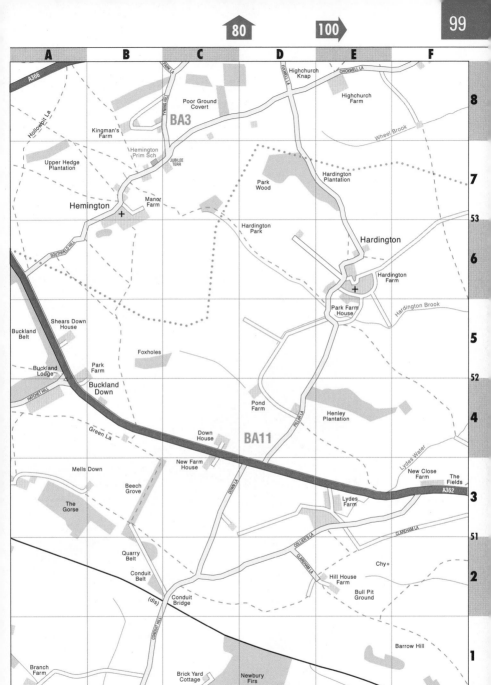

Map labels (as shown on the map):

A366

Hollowpit La

Upper Hedge Plantation

Kingman's Farm

PARK LA

THINING HILL

Poor Ground Covert

BA3

Hemington Prim Sch

JUBILEE TERR

Highchurch Knap

COLWELL LA

CHICKWELL LA

Highchurch Farm

Wheel Brook

8

7

53

Hemington

Manor Farm

Park Wood

Hardington Plantation

SOUTHFIELD HILL

Hardington Park

Hardington

Hardington Farm

6

Shears Down House

Buckland Belt

Buckland Lodge

HATCHET HILL

Park Farm

Buckland Down

Foxholes

Park Farm House

Hardington Brook

5

52

Green La

Mells Down

The Gorse

Beech Grove

Down House

New Farm House

Pond Farm

Henley Plantation

PILLAR LA

BA11

DOWN LA

Lydes Water

New Close Farm

The Fields

A362

4

3

51

Quarry Belt

Conduit Belt

(dis)

Conduit Bridge

CONDUIT HILL

Lydes Farm

COLLIER'S LA

CLAREHAM LA

Hill House Farm

OLDFORD LA

Chy

Bull Pit Ground

2

Branch Farm

Brick Yard Cottage

Newbury Firs

Barrow Hill

1

50

72

73

74

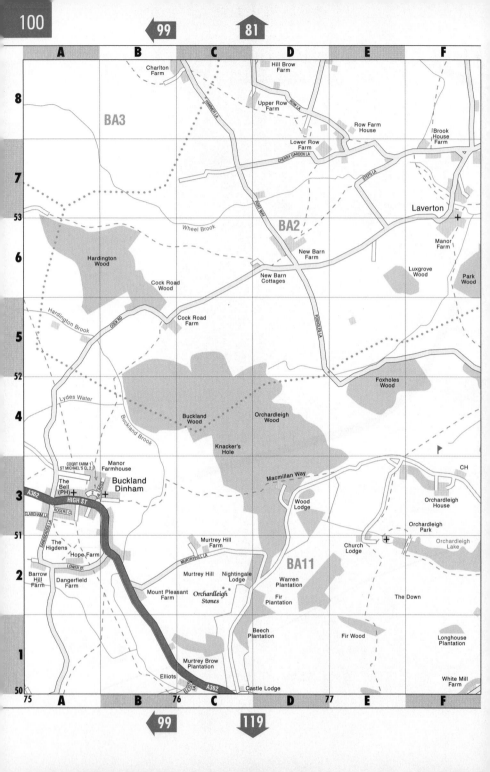

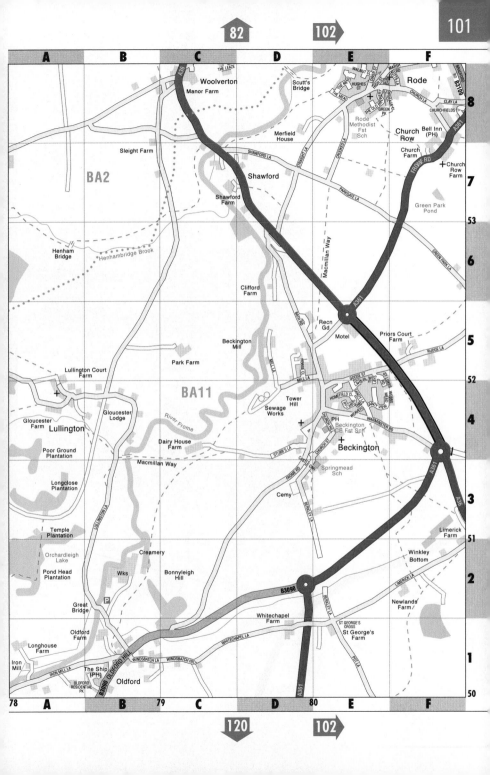

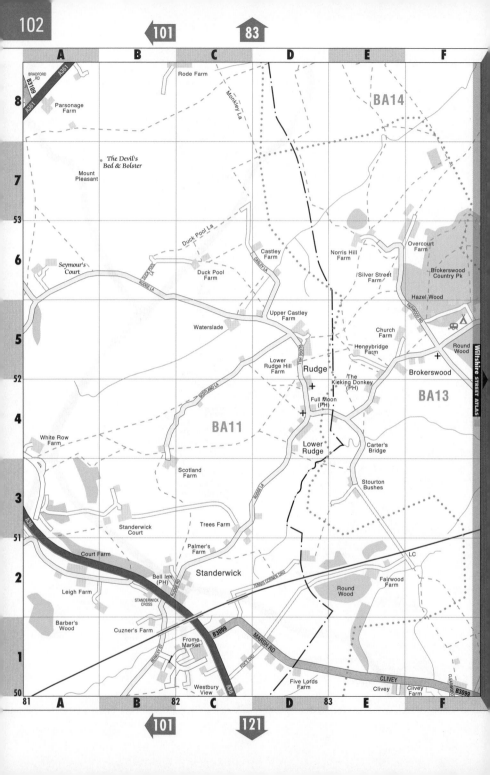

	A	B	C	D	E	F

8

BRADFORD RD
B3109
A361

Rode Farm

Monkley La

BA14

Parsonage
Farm

7

The Devil's
Bed & Bolster

Mount
Pleasant

53

6

Seymour's
Court

Duck Pool La

RUDGE LA

DUCK POOL

Duck Pool
Farm

Castley
Farm

CASTLEY LA

Norris Hill
Farm

Silver Street
Farm

Overcourt
Farm

Brokerswood
Country Pk

Hazel Wood

FAIRWOOD RD

5

Waterslade

Upper Castley
Farm

RUDGE HILL

Church
Farm

Honeybridge
Farm

Round
Wood

Wiltshire STREET ATLAS

52

SCOTLAND LA

Lower
Rudge Hill
Farm

Rudge

The Kicking Donkey
(PH)

Brokerswood

4

White Row
Farm

BA11

Full Moon
(PH)

Lower
Rudge

Carter's
Bridge

BA13

3

Scotland
Farm

Stourton
Bushes

Standerwick
Court

Trees Farm

RUDGE LA

51

Court Farm

A36

Palmer's
Farm

LC

2

Leigh Farm

Bell Inn
(PH)

RUDGE RD

Standerwick

TENNIS CORNER DRO

Round
Wood

Fairwood
Farm

STANDERWICK
CROSS

Barber's
Wood

Cuzner's Farm

BERKLEY LA

Frome
Market

B3099

TOYS DRO

MARSH RD

A36

CLIVEY

Clivey

Clivey
Farm

CLIVEWOOD

B3099

1

Westbury
View

Five Lords
Farm

50

81

	A		B		C		D		E		F

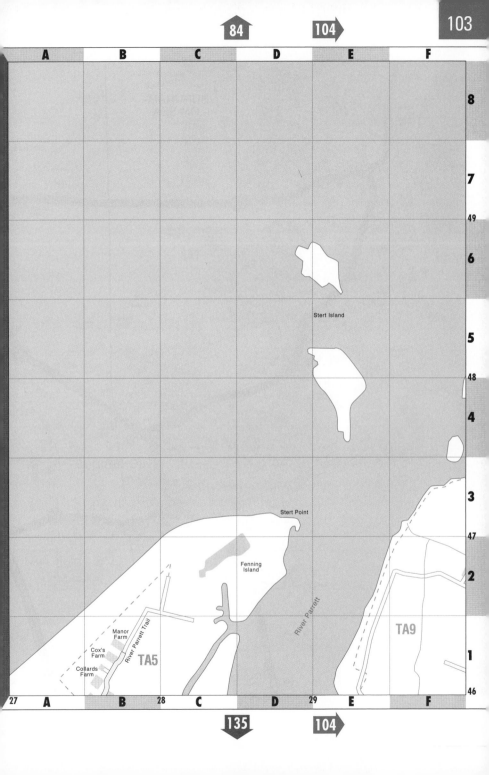

A   B   C   D   E   F

8

7

49

6

Stert Island

5

48

4

3

Stert Point

47

Fenning
Island

2

River Parrett

Manor
Farm

Cox's
Farm   TA9

Collards
Farm   River Parrett Trail   TA5

1

46

27   A   B   28   C   D   29   E   F

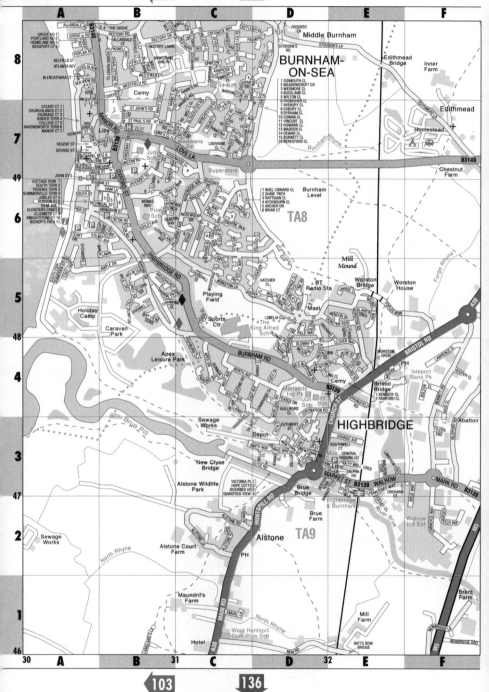

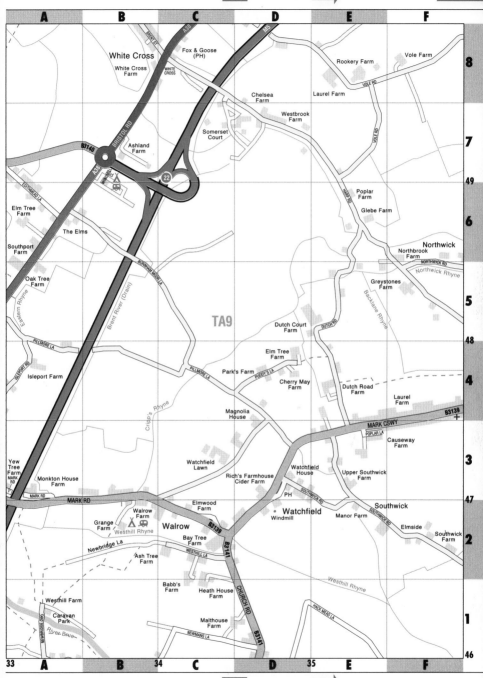

White Cross
White Cross Farm
Fox & Goose (PH)
WHITE CROSS
Chelsea Farm
Rookery Farm
Vole Farm
Laurel Farm
Westbrook Farm
Somerset Court
Ashland Farm
B3140
A38
BRISTOL RD
BRENT ST
M5
VOLE RD

22

49

Poplar Farm
Glebe Farm

Elm Tree Farm
The Elms
Southport Farm
Oak Tree Farm
EDITHMEAD LA
A38
Eastern Rhyne
Brent River (Drain)
BURNHAM MOOR LA
HARP RD
VOLE RD

Northwick
Northbrook Farm
NORTHWICK RD
Northwick Rhyne

6

Greystones Farm
Backlane Rhyne

TA9

5

48

Dutch Court Farm
DUTCH RD

Isleport Farm
ISLEPORT RD
PILLMORE LA
Cripp's Rhyne

Elm Tree Farm
Park's Farm
PUDDY'S LA
Cherry May Farm
Dutch Road Farm
Laurel Farm

Magnolia House

B3139
MARK CSWY
POPLAR LA
Causeway Farm

4

Yew Tree Farm
MARK RD
Monkton House Farm
MARK RD
Watchfield Lawn
Rich's Farmhouse Cider Farm
Watchfield House
Upper Southwick Farm

3

47

PH
SOUTHWICK RD
Southwick
Manor Farm
SOUTHWICK RD
Elmside
Southwick Farm

Grange Farm
Walrow Farm
Walrow
Westhill Rhyne
Elmwood Farm
B3139
Watchfield
Windmill

2

Newbridge La
Bay Tree Farm
Ash Tree Farm
WESTHILL LA
B3141
CHURCH RD
Westhill Rhyne

Babb's Farm
Heath House Farm
HACK MEAD LA

Westhill Farm
Caravan Park
NEWBRIDGE DRO
River Brue
Malthouse Farm
NEWMANS LA
B3141

1

46

105
87

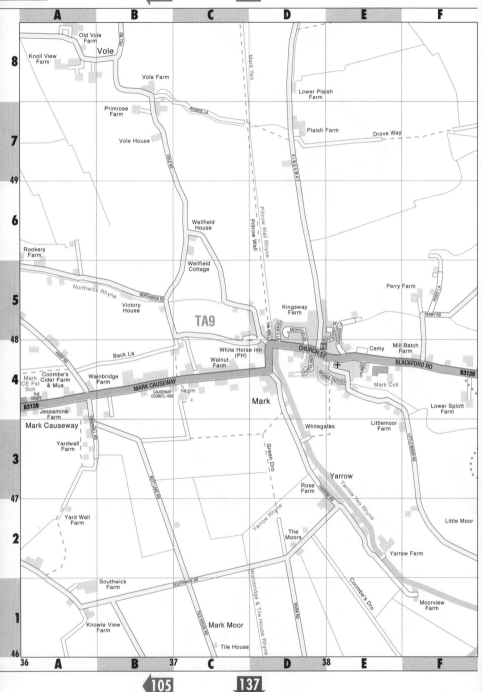

105
137

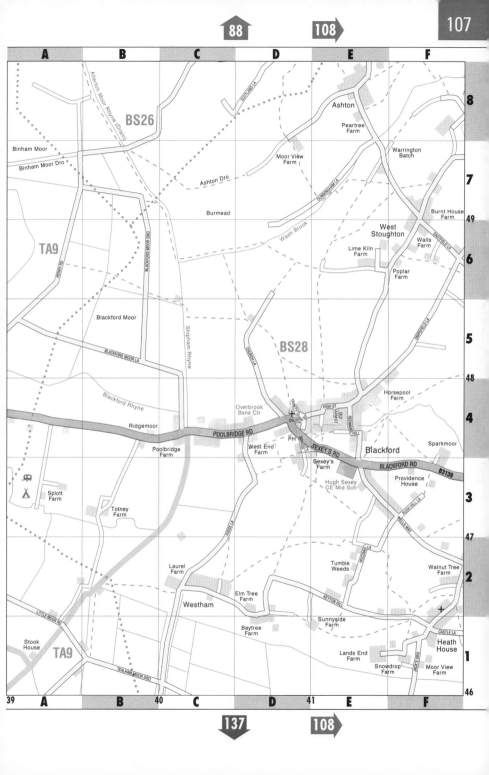

88
108

A   B   C   D   E   F

8

Ashton

Peartree Farm

Warrington Batch

7

Binham Moor

Binham Moor Dro

Ashton Dro

Moor View Farm

Burnt House Farm

49

BS26

Allerton Moor Rhyne (Drain)

TA9

Burmead

Wash Brook

West Stoughton

Walls Farm

CASTLEFIELD LA

6

Lime Kiln Farm

Poplar Farm

BLACKFORD MOOR DRO

PENNY RD

Blackford Moor

BLACKFORD MOOR LA

Shipham Rhyne

BS28

Horsepool Farm

5

48

Blackford Rhyne

Ridgemoor

POOLBRIDGE RD

Overbrook Bsns Ctr

CHURCH LA

HIGH ST

OLD FARM CT

REDHAM HILL

SWIPFIELD LA

4

Poolbridge Farm

West End Farm

PH

CHURCH

TRINITY ST

SEXEY'S RD

Blackford

Sparkmoor

BLACKFORD RD

B3139

Sexey's Farm

Providence House

Hugh Sexey CE Mid Sch

RUSHHILL LA

3

Splott Farm

Totney Farm

FOSSE LA

47

WELLS WAY

Laurel Farm

Tumble Weeds

Walnut Tree Farm

2

Westham

Elm Tree Farm

HUZARD LA

KEYTON HILL

Sunnyside Farm

CASTLE LA

LITTLE MOOR RD

Stook House

TA9

Baytree Farm

Lands End Farm

Heath House

JACK'S DRO

1

TEALHAM MOOR DRO

Snowdrop Farm

Moor View Farm

46

39   A   B   40   C   D   41   E   F

137
108

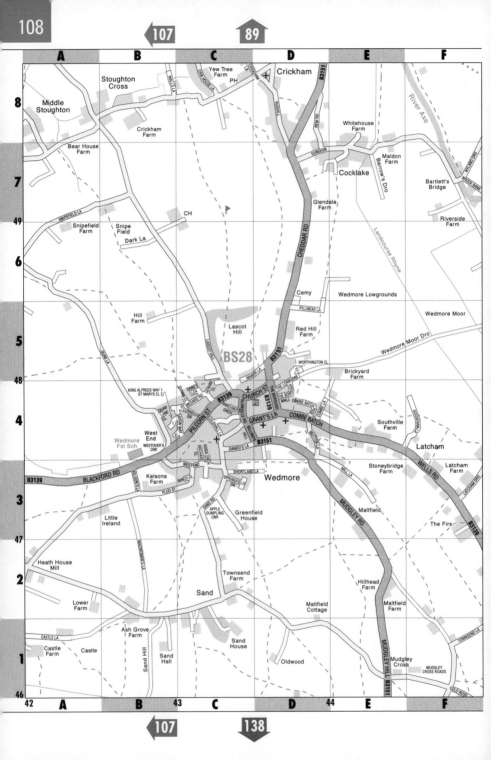

A   B   C   D   E   F

8

Middle Stoughton

Stoughton Cross

Crickham Farm

Bear House Farm

Yew Tree Farm
PH

Crickham

Whitehouse Farm

Maldon Farm

Cocklake

River Axe

7

Snipefield Farm

CH

Glendale Farm

Bartlett's Bridge

49

Snipe Field

Dark La

Riverside Farm

6

Hill Farm

Lascot Hill

Cemy

Red Hill Farm

Wedmore Lowgrounds

Wedmore Moor

Landcourse Rhyne

5

BS28

PILLMEAD LA

Wedmore Moor Dro

WORTHINGTON CL

Brickyard Farm

48

KING ALFREDS WAY 1
ST MARYS CL 2

CHURCH ST

COMBE BATCH

Southville Farm

4

West End

Wedmore Fst Sch
WESTOVER'S CNR

GRANT'S LA

B3151

COMBE BATCH

Stoneybridge Farm

Latcham

Latcham Farm

WELLS RD

B3139   BLACKFORD RD

Kelsons Farm

PLUD ST

DANDO'S LA

Wedmore

Maltfield

The Firs

3

47

Little Ireland

APPLE DUMPLING CNR

Greenfield House

MUDGLEY RD

2

Heath House Mill

Lower Farm

Townsend Farm

Sand

Hillhead Farm

Maltfield Farm

1

CASTLE LA

Castle Farm

Castle

Ash Grove Farm

Sand Hill

Sand Hall

Sand House

Oldwood

Maltfield Cottage

MUDGLEY HILL

Mudgley Cross

MUDGLEY CROSS ROADS

46

42   A   B   43   C   D   44   E   F

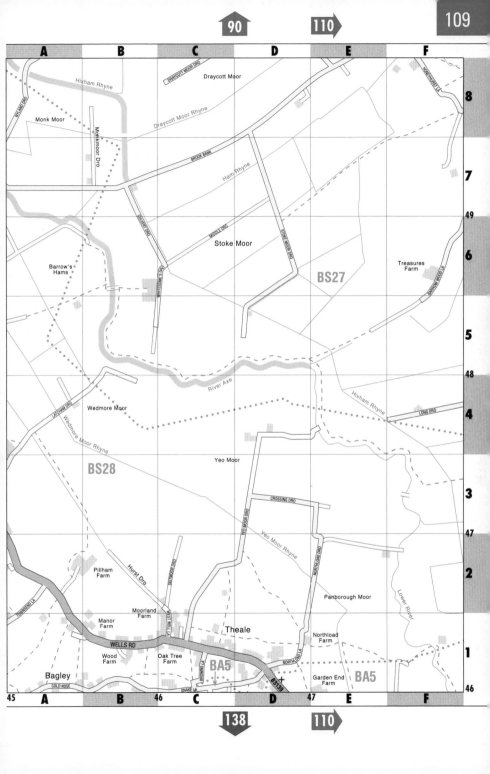

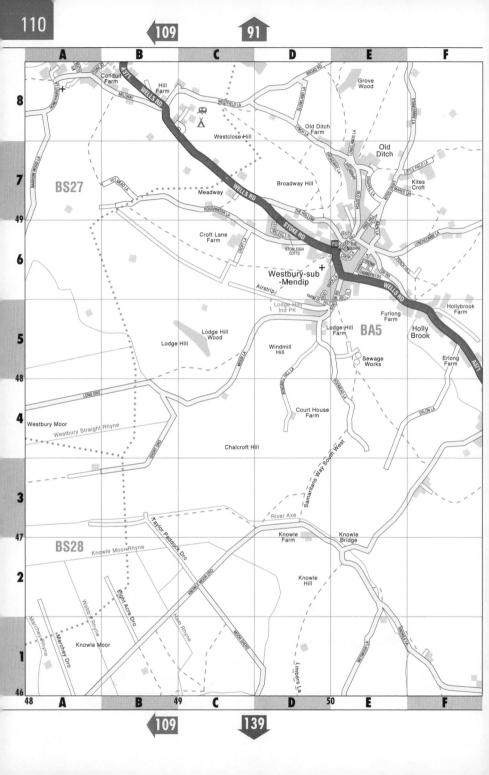

109

91

A   **B**   **C**   **D**   **E**   **F**

8

Conduit Farm

Hill Farm

Grove Wood

STOKE ST

A371

WELLS RD

MILLWAY

WESTFIELD LA

Westclose Hill

Old Ditch Farm

Old Ditch

BARROW WOOD LA

HORRINGTON HILL

BUTTS

LYNCH LA

ST. LOW'S HILL LA

BROAD RD

LONG MEAD LA

BROOK LA

FRAPPLE LA

OLD DITCH

STANCOMBE LA

LITTLE FIELD LA

ST. MARES LA

7

BS27

YET MEAD LA

Meadway

WELLS RD

Broadway Hill

ROUGHMOOR LA

THE HOLLOW

Kites Croft

KITES CROFT

49

Croft Lane Farm

STOKE RD

Sch

LYNCHCOMBE LA

CROFT LA

EDGE LA

FREE HILL

BACK LA

6

STONLEIGH COTTS

PO

THE SQUARE

PERCH HILL

Westbury-sub-Mendip

CHURCH LA

HOME ST

THOMEFIELDS

COW RD

WELLS RD

Airstrip

Lodge Hill Ind PK

BUCKLE LA

BELL LA

FARM LA

Furlong Farm

Hollybrook Farm

5

Lodge Hill

Lodge Hill Wood

Windmill Hill

Lodge Hill Farm

BA5

Holly Brook

MOOR LA

Sewage Works

Erlong Farm

A371

48

LONG DRO

WINDMILL HILL LA

BROOK LA

ERLON LA

4

Westbury Moor

Westbury Straight Rhyne

Court House Farm

ERLON LA

SHORT DRO

Chalcroft Hill

Samaritans' Way South West

3

River Axe

47

BS28

Taylor Paddock Dro

Knowle Moore Rhyne

Knowle Farm

Knowle Bridge

2

Eight Acre Dro

Webb's Rhyne

KNOWLE MOOR DRO

Ham Rhyne

MOOR SIDE RD

Knowle Hill

KNOWLE LA

WETMOOR LA

1

Marchey Rhyne

Marchey Dro

Knowle Moor

Limbers La

46

48   **A**   **B**   49   **C**   **D**   50   **E**   **F**

109

139

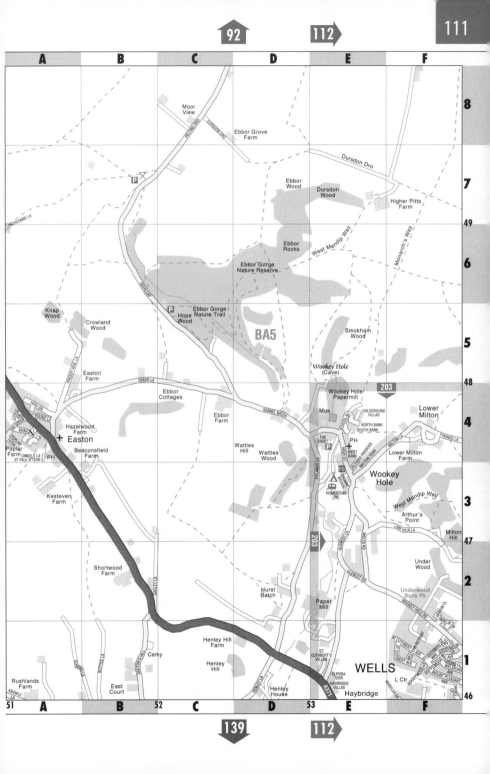

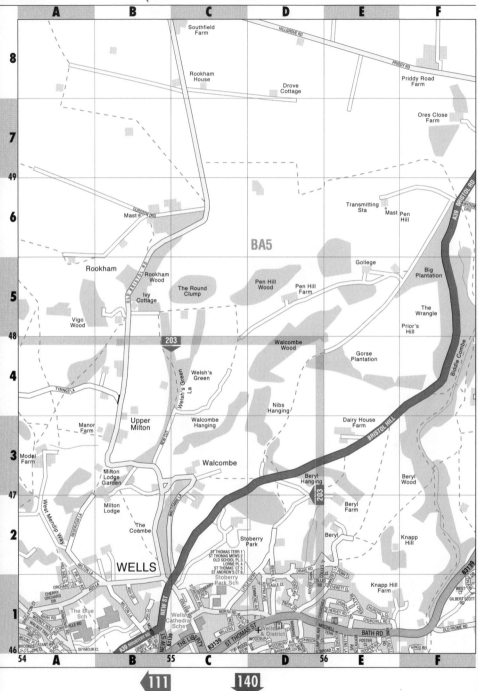

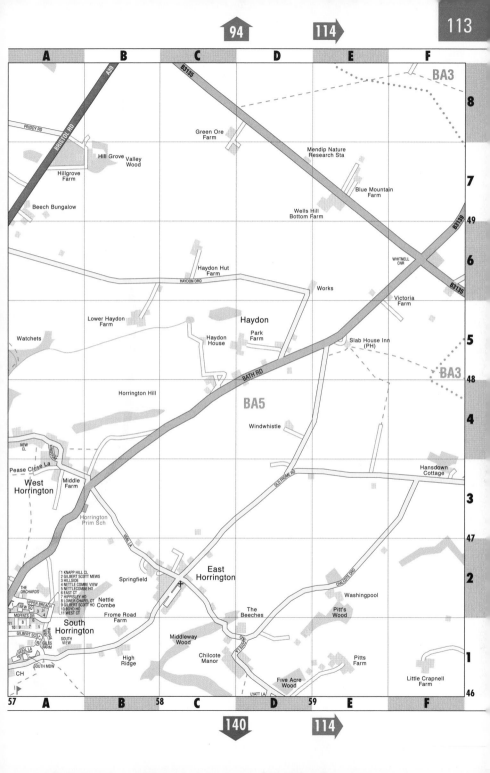

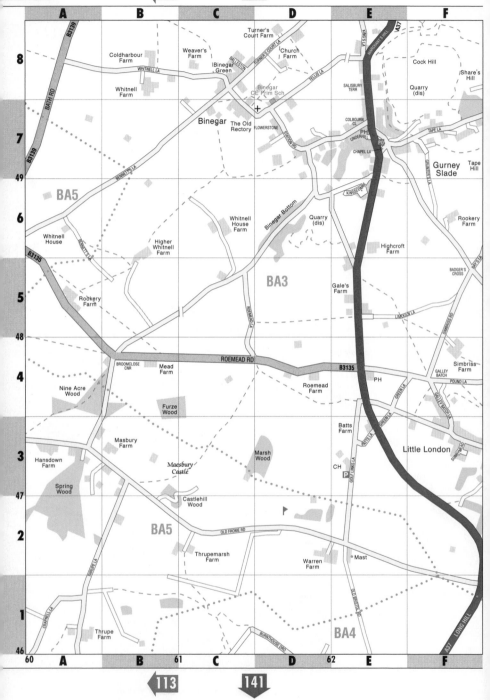

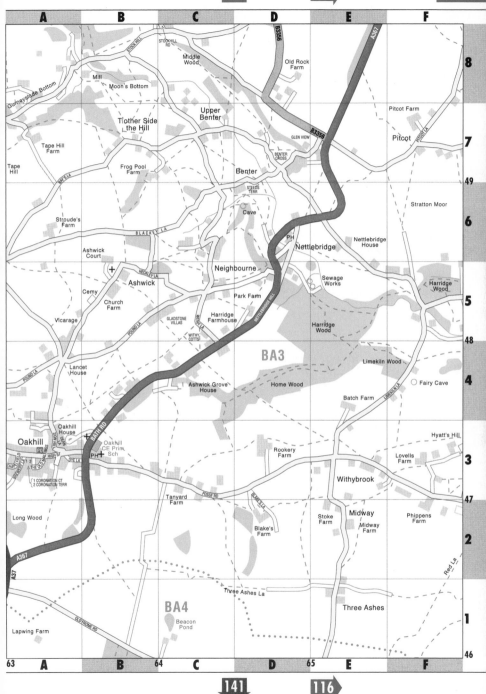

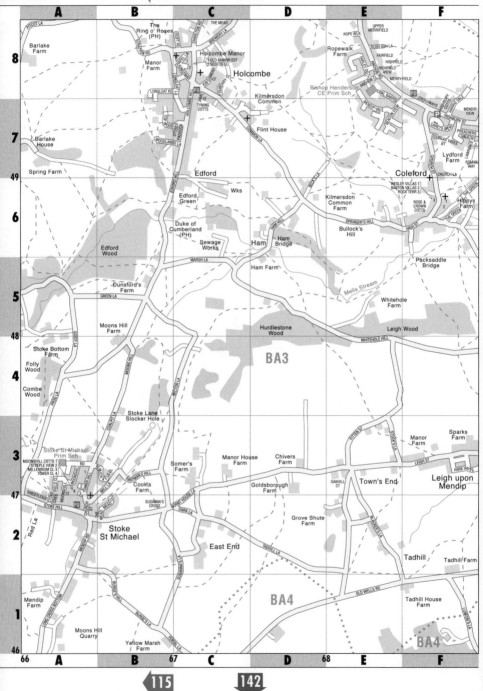

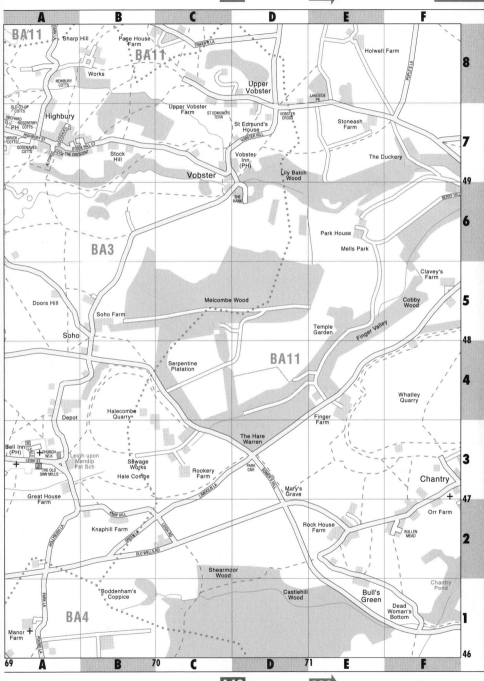

A   B   C   D   E   F

BA11
Sharp Hill
Page House Farm
TINKER'S LA
BA11
Holwell Farm
PYLE'S LA   8

NEWBURY COTTS
Works
Upper Vobster
LAKESIDE PK

OLD CO-OP COTTS
ORCHARD CL PH
ROSEBERRY COTTS
Highbury
Upper Vobster Farm
ST EDMUND'S TERR
St Edmund's House
VOBSTER CROSS
Stoneash Farm
7

BRICK COTTS
HIGHBURY ST
LIFFORD HOUSE STOCK HILL CT THE CRESCENT
VOBSTER HILL
Vobster Inn (PH)
The Duckery

GOODEAVES COTTS
Stock Hill
Vobster
Lily Batch Wood
49

THE RANK
BERRY HILL
6

BA3
Park House
Mells Park

Doors Hill
Melcombe Wood
Clavey's Farm
5

Soho Farm
Cobby Wood

Soho
Temple Garden
Finger Valley
48

Serpentine Platation
BA11
4

Whatley Quarry

Depot
Halecombe Quarry
Finger Farm

Bell Inn (PH)
CHURCH WLK
LEIGH ST
Leigh upon Mendip Fst Sch
The Hare Warren
3

THE OLD SAW MILLS
Sewage Works
Rookery Farm
PARK CNR
Mary's Grave
Chantry
47

Great House Farm
Hale Combe
SOMERSET HILL
Orr Farm

KNAP HILL
LIMEKILN LA
Rock House Farm
BULLEN MEAD
2

HOLWELL BUSH LA
Knaphill Farm
GREEN LA
LEIGH RD
OLD WELLS RD

PARK LA
Boddenham's Coppice
Shearmoor Wood
Castlehill Wood
Bull's Green
Chantry Pond
1

POUND LA
Manor Farm
BA4
Dead Woman's Bottom
46

69   A   B   70   C   D   71   E   F

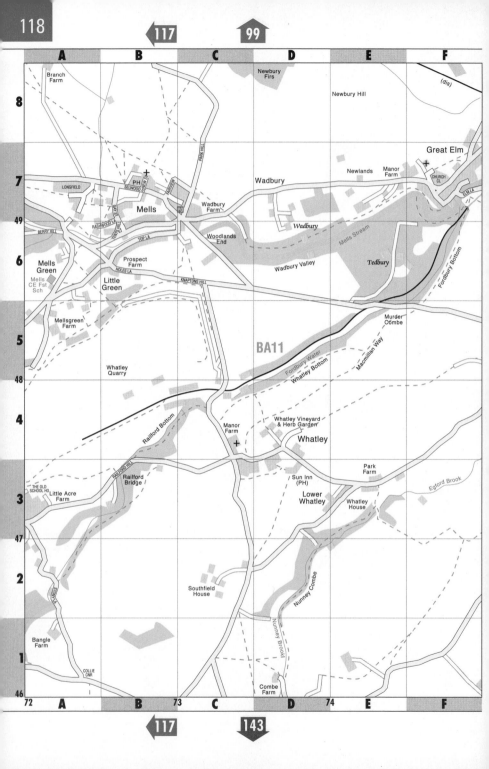

117
99

A B C D E F

8

Branch Farm

Newbury Firs

Newbury Hill

(dis)

Great Elm

7

LONGFIELD

PH
SELWOOD ST

PARK HILL

PARKVIEW

Wadbury

Newlands

Manor Farm

CHURCH CL

ELM LA

Mells

GAY ST

RASHWOOD LA

Wadbury Farm

49

BERRY HILL

TOP LA

Woodlands End

Wadbury

Mells Stream

6

Mells Green

Prospect Farm

HOLES LA

KNAPTONS HILL

Wadbury Valley

Tedbury

Fordbury Bottom

Mells CE Fst Sch

Little Green

5

Mellsgreen Farm

Murder Combe

BA11

Fordbury Water

Macmillan Way

48

Whatley Quarry

Whatley Bottom

4

Railford Bottom

Manor Farm

Whatley Vineyard & Herb Garden

Whatley

RAILFORD HILL

Railford Bridge

Sun Inn (PH)

Park Farm

Eglord Brook

3

THE OLD SCHOOL HO

Little Acre Farm

Lower Whatley

Whatley House

47

LA ANGLE

2

Southfield House

Nunney Combe

Nunney Brook

1

Bangle Farm

COLLIE CNR

46

Combe Farm

72 A B 73 C D 74 E F

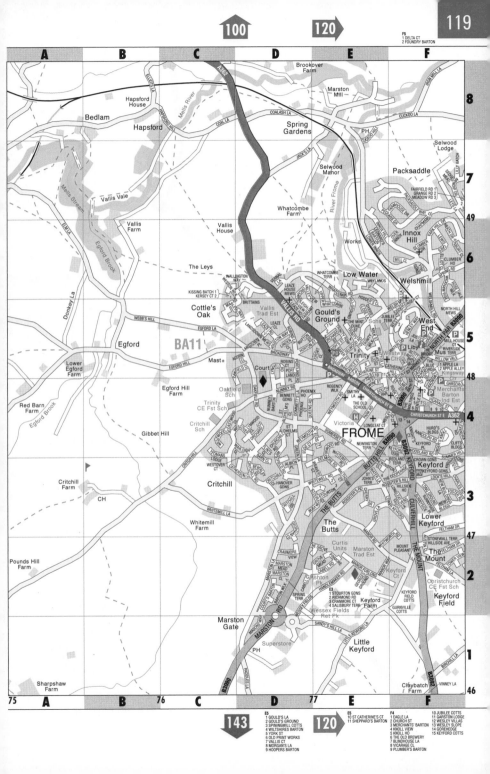

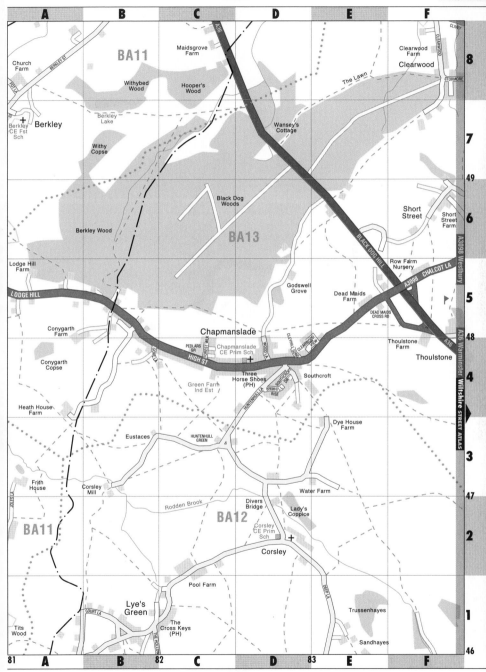

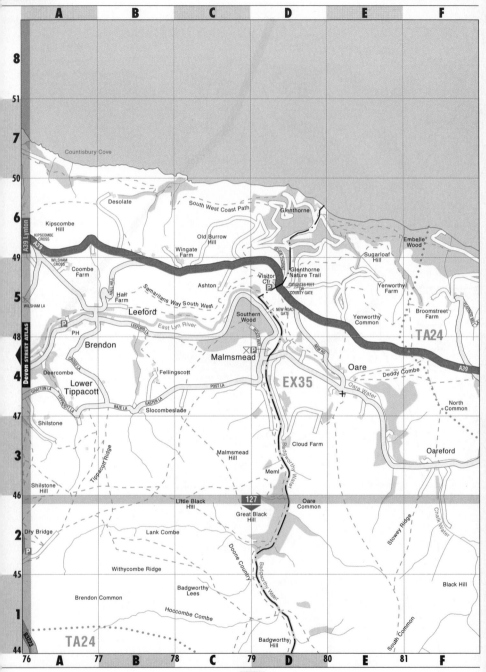

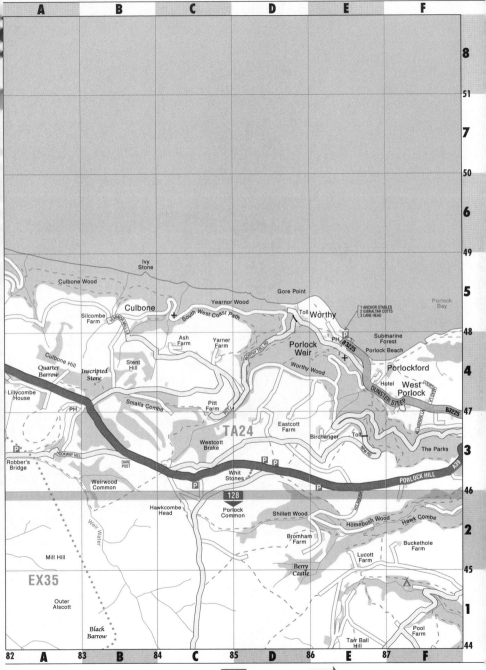

Scale: 1⅓ inches to 1 mile

0   ¼   ½ mile
0   250m 500m 750m 1 km

124

| | A | B | C | D | E | F |

8
51
7
50
6
49
5
48
4
47
3
46
2
45
1
44

Ivy Stone
Culbone Wood
Yearnor Wood
Gore Point
Porlock Bay
Culbone
Silcombe Farm
South West Coast Path
Toll
Worthy
1 ANCHOR STABLES
2 GIBRALTAR COTTS
3 LANE HEAD
LEMMONS MILL LN
Ash Farm
Yarner Farm
PH
Submarine Forest
Porlock Beach
Cullbone Hill
Stent Hill
Porlock Weir
Porlockford
Quarter Barrow
Inscripted Stone
Worthy Wood
WORTHY TOLL RD
B3225
West Porlock
Lillycombe House
Hotel
DUNSTER STEEP
PH
Smalla Combe
Pitt Farm
PITT LN
B3225
COURTNEY CL
TA24
Eastcott Farm
Westcott Brake
Birchanger
Toll
The Parks
COOKWAY HILL
OARE POST
P
P
P
NEW RD
A39
Robber's Bridge
P
Whit Stones
P
PORLOCK HILL
Weirwood Common
128
Hawkcombe Head
Porlock Common
Shillett Wood
Homebush Wood
Hawk Combe
INKDINBUSH
Weir Water
Bromham Farm
Bucكethole Farm
Mill Hill
Berry Castle
Lucott Farm
EX35
Tarr Ball Hill
Pool Farm
Outer Alscott
Black Barrow

128   124

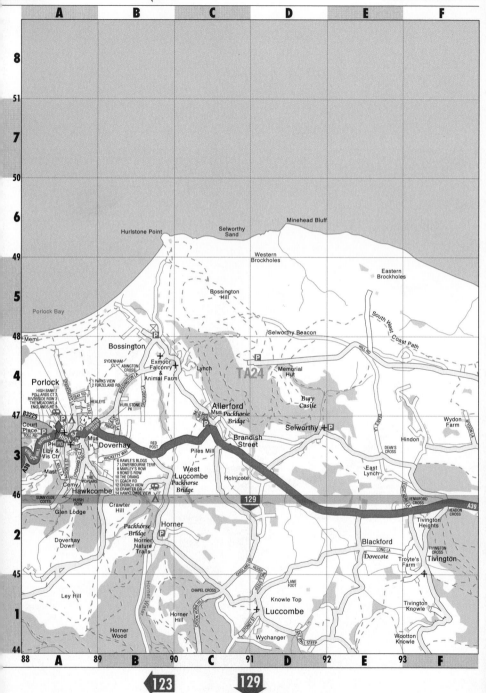

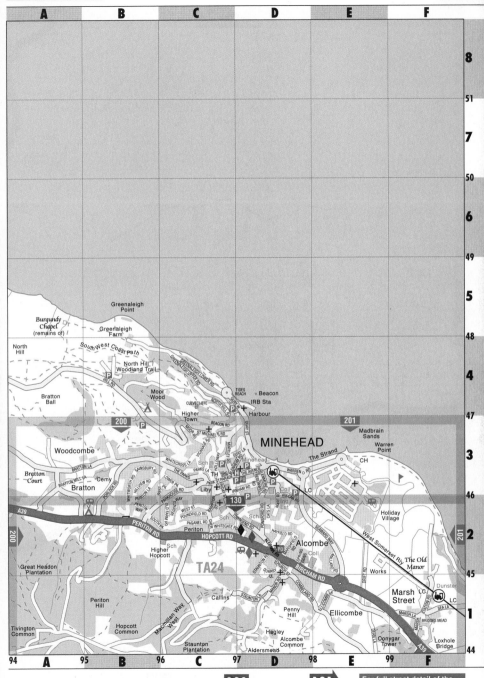

Scale: 1⅓ inches to 1 mile

| 0 | ¼ | ½ mile |
| 0 | 250m | 500m 750m | 1 km |

A B C D E F

8
51
7
50
6
49
5
48
4
47
3
46
2
45
1
44

Greenaleigh
Point

Burgundy
Chapel
(remains of)

Greenaleigh
Farm

North
Hill

South West Coast path

North Hill
Woodland Trail

HILL RD

GREENALEIGH LOWER RD
GREENALEIGH UPPER RD

Bratton
Ball

Moor
Wood

Higher
Town

CULVECLIFFE
CT

NORTH HILL RD

TIDES
BEACH

Beacon

IRB Sta

Harbour

BEACON RD

ST MICHAEL S RD

200

201

Madbrain
Sands

MINEHEAD

Warren
Point

Woodcombe

WHITECROSS LA

SAINSBURY RD

Sch

Minehead

PANKS LA

THE PARKS

The Strand

WARREN RD

CH

Bratton
Court

BRATTON LA

BRATTON MILL LA

Bratton

Cemy

WHITWORTH RD

PERITON LA

HILLVIEW RD

TOWER PK

PERNDOUSE RD

WEST ST

REDWAY

PARK ST

THE AVENUE

WOLLOWAY

MART RD

QUAY ST

Liby

TH

Coll

Est

LC

Holiday
Village

A39

PERITON RD

SOUTH RD

OLD PARK RD

PAGANEL RD

POUNDFIELD RD

Sch

Periton

Sch

HOPCOTT RD

WHITEGATE RD

ST PARAM RD

TOWNSEND RD

CATS LA

Sch

HAYFIELD RD

130

Alcombe

Coll

BIRCHAM RD

SEAWARD TER

VALIRD

SANDY LA

West Somerset Rly

The Old
Manor

Works

Great Headon
Plantation

200

Higher
Hopcott

TA24

STAUNTON RD

QUARRY

BURGUNDY RD

MOOR LA

PO

Callins

STAUNTON LA

DONIFORD RD

LONGLANDS RD

Penny
Hill

Ellicombe

DRIFT RD

BEACH RD

MARSH LA

Marsh
Street

LC

Dunster

LC

SEA LA

201

Periton
Hill

Macmillan Way West

Hopcott
Common

Staunton
Plantation

Hagley

Alcombe
Common

Conygar
Tower

BRIDGES MEAD

Loxhole
Bridge

Tivington
Common

Aldersmead

A39

130 **131**

For full street detail of the
highlighted areas see pages
200 and 201.

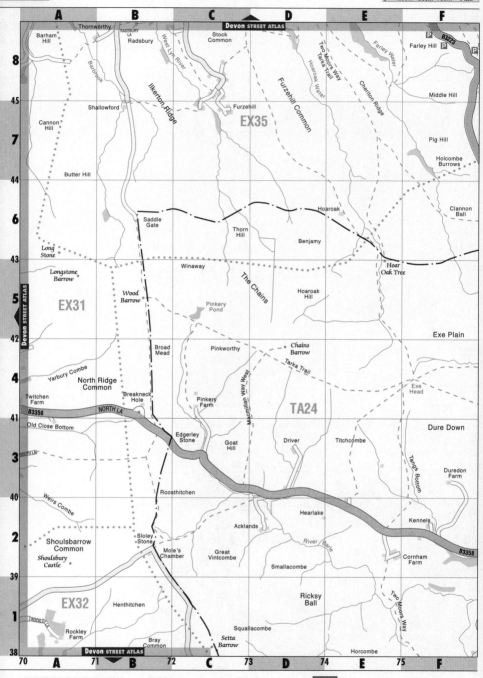

Scale: 1⅓ inches to 1 mile

0   ¼   ½ mile
0   250m 500m 750m 1 km

Devon STREET ATLAS

A   B   C   D   E   F

Thornworthy
Barham Hill
RADSBURY LA
Radsbury
Stock Common
West Lyn River
Two Moors Way
Tarka Trail
Hoaroak Water
Farley Water
P Farley Hill P
P
B3223

Shallowford
Ilkerton Ridge
Furzehill
Furzehill Common
Cheriton Ridge
Middle Hill

Cannon Hill
Barbrook
EX35
Pig Hill

Butter Hill
Holcombe Burrows

Saddle Gate
Thorn Hill
Hoaroak
Benjamy
Clannon Ball

Long Stone
Winaway
The Chains
Hoar Oak Tree

Longstone Barrow
EX31
Wood Barrow
Pinkery Pond
Hoaroak Hill
Exe Plain

Broad Mead
Pinkworthy
Chains Barrow
Tarka Trail

Yarbury Combe
North Ridge Common
Breakneck Hole
Pinkery Farm
Millennium Way West
TA24
Exe Head

Twitchen Farm
B3358
NORTH LA
Old Close Bottom
Edgerley Stone
Goat Hill
Driver
Titchcombe
Dure Down

SOUTH LA
Roosthitchen
Tangs Bottom
Duredon Farm

Weirs Combe
Hearlake
Kennels

Shoulsbarrow Common
Sloley Stone
Acklands
River Barle
B3358

Shoulsbury Castle
Mole's Chamber
Great Vintcombe
Smallacombe
Cornham Farm

EX32
Henthitchen
Ricksy Ball
Two Moors Way

ROCKLEY LA
Rockley Farm
Bray Common
Squallacombe
Setta Barrow
Horcombe

Devon STREET ATLAS

70   A   71   B   72   C   73   D   74   E   75   F

145

Devon STREET ATLAS

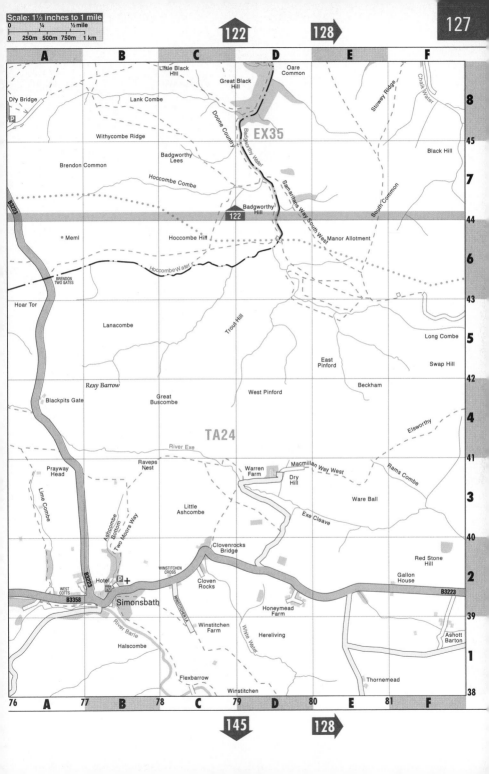

Scale: 1⅓ inches to 1 mile

0   ¼   ½ mile
0 250m 500m 750m 1 km

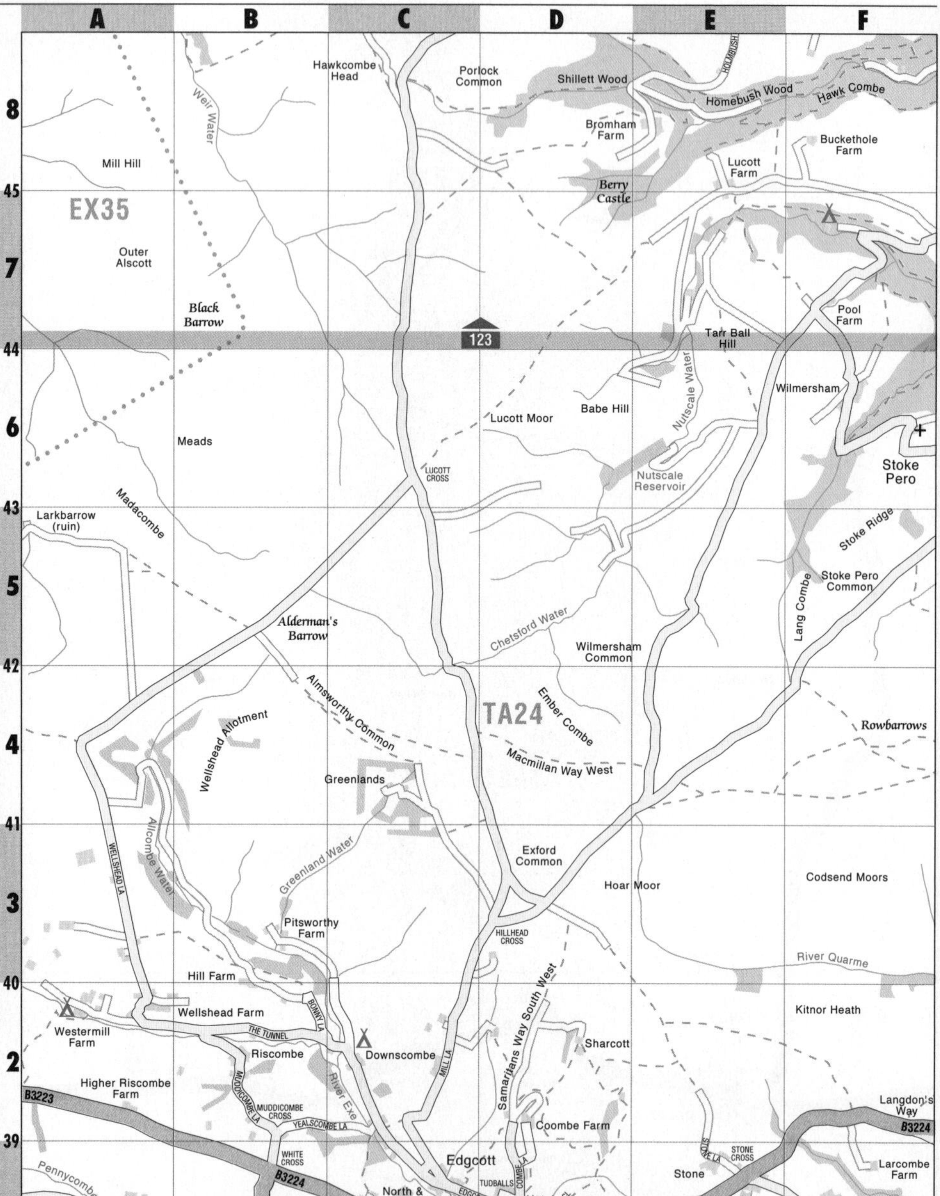

8

A **B** **C** **D** **E** **F**

Hawkcombe Head
Porlock Common
Shillett Wood
Homebush Wood
Hawk Combe
Mill Hill
EX35
Bromham Farm
Lucott Farm
Buckethole Farm
Outer Alscott
Berry Castle
45
7
Black Barrow
Pool Farm
44
123
Tarr Ball Hill
6
Lucott Moor
Babe Hill
Nutscale Water
Wilmersham
Meads
Stoke Pero
Madecombe
Lucott Cross
Nutscale Reservoir
43
Larkbarrow (ruin)
Stoke Ridge
5
Stoke Pero Common
Alderman's Barrow
Chetsford Water
Lang Combe
42
Almsworthy Common
Wilmersham Common
Ember Combe
Rowbarrows
4
Wellshead Allotment
TA24
Greenlands
Macmillan Way West
41
Greenland Water
Exford Common
Codsend Moors
3
Pitsworthy Farm
Hoar Moor
River Quarme
HILLHEAD CROSS
40
Hill Farm
Kitnor Heath
Westermill Farm
Wellshead Farm
Riscombe
Downscombe
Sharcott
2
Higher Riscombe Farm
THE TUNNEL
MUDDICOMBE CROSS
Langdon's Way
B3223
YEALSCOMBE LA
Coombe Farm
B3224
39
WHITE CROSS
Stone
Larcombe Cross
Pennycombe Water
B3224
Edgcott
STONE CROSS
1
Newland
NEWLAND CROSS
North & South Ley
TUDBALLS
Hotel
Stetfold Rocks
Higher Thorne
Kennels
Exford
Higher Combe
Withycombe
Lower Thorne
Exford CE Fst sch
MONK CROSS
CHURCH HILL
38
B3223
82 **A** **83** **B** **84** **C** **85** **D** **86** **E** **87** **F**

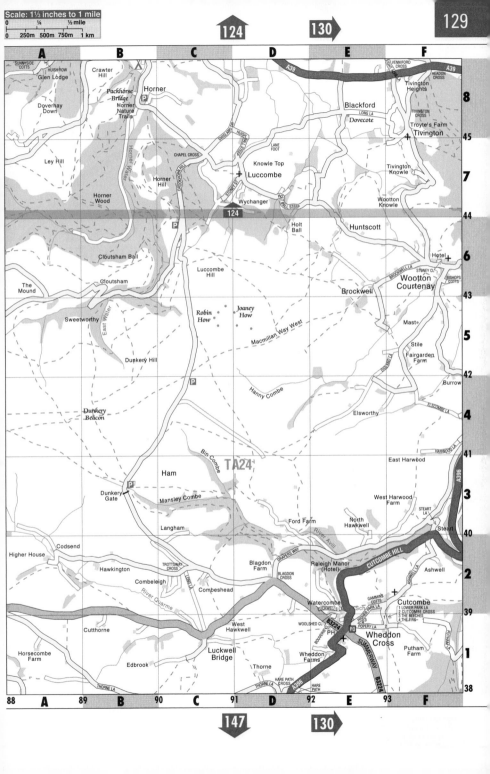

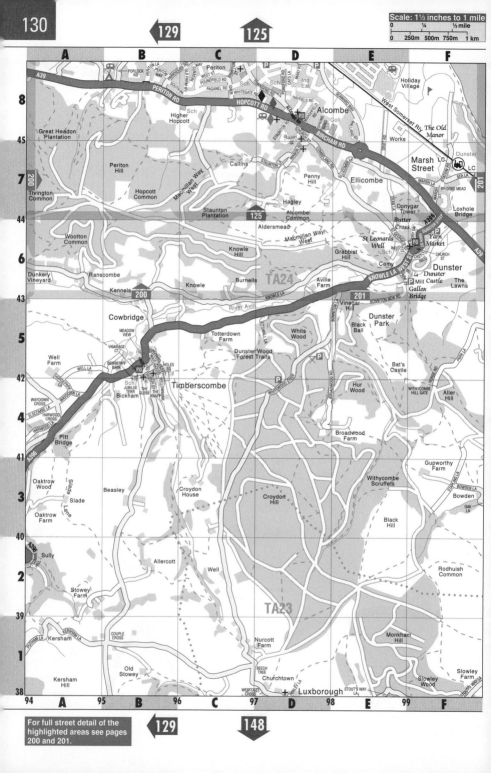

Scale: 1⅓ inches to 1 mile

129
125

A **B** **C** **D** **E** **F**

A39 PORLOCK LA
PERITON RD
South Ed
Periton
Alcombe
HOPCOTT RD
BIRCHAM RD
West Somerset Rly
Holiday Village
The Old Manor
Works
Marsh Street
Dunster
LC
LC
Great Headon Plantation
Higher Hopcott
8
Periton Hill
Callins
STAUNTON
Penny Hill
Ellicombe
Conygar Tower
Loxhole Bridge
45
Hopcott Common
Staunton Plantation
Hagley
Butter Cross
Yarn Market
7
Tivington Common
200
125
Aldermead
Alcombel Common
Macmillan Way West
St Leonards Well
Grabbist Hill
CHURCH ST
Dunster
44
Wootton Common
Knowle Hill
Cemy
Dunster
The Lawns
Mill Castle
6
Dunkery Vineyard
Ranscombe
Knowle
Burnells
TA24
Aville Farm
KNOWLE LA WEST ST
Gallox Bridge
Kennels
200
Knowle
River Avill
KNOWLE LA
201
Vinegar Hill
Dunster Park
43
Cowbridge
MEADOW VIEW
VICARAGE CT.
Totterdown Farm
Dunster Wood Forest Trails
Whits Wood
Black Ball
Bat's Castle
5
Well Farm
BEMBERRY BANK
WELL LA
Timberscombe
Bickham
THE GLEBE THE KNAPPS
Hur Wood
WITHYCOMBE HILL GATE
Aller Hill
42
WAYDOWN CROSS
ELSCOMBE LA
HARWOOD CROSS
HARWOOD LA
Pitt Bridge
Broadwood Farm
Gupworthy Farm
4
A396
Slade Lane
Beasley
Croydon House
Croydon Hill
Withycombe Scruffets
Bowden
OAK LA
41
Oaktrow Wood
Slade
Oaktrow Farm
Black Hill
3
A396
Sully
Allercott
Well
Rodhuish Common
40
Stowey Farm
COUPLE CROSS
TA23
Monkham Hill
Slowley Farm
2
Kersham
Nurcott Farm
Churchtown
Slowley Wood
39
Kersham Hill
Old Stowey
BEECH TREE
Luxborough
STOUT'S WAY LA
1
94 **A** 95 **B** 96 **C** 97 **D** 98 **E** 99 **F**
38

129
148

For full street detail of the highlighted areas see pages 200 and 201.

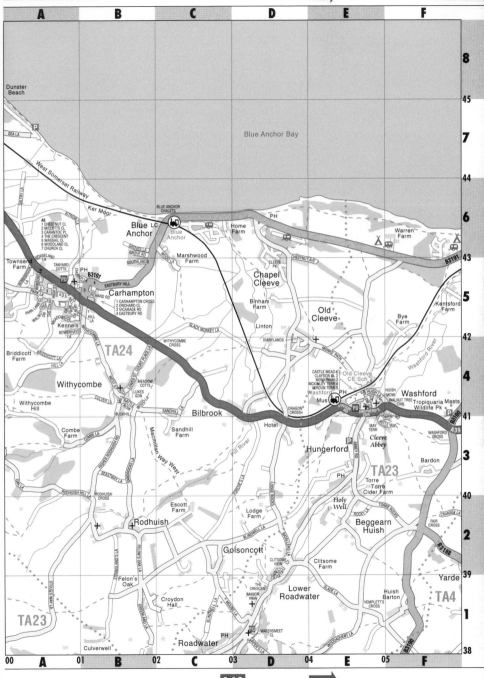

Scale: 1½ inches to 1 mile

0   ¼   ½ mile

0   250m 500m 750m 1 km

132

| A | B | C | D | E | F |

8

45

Dunster Beach

7

Blue Anchor Bay

44

West Somerset Railway

Ker Moor

6

43

BLUE ANCHOR CHALETS

Blue Anchor

Home Farm

PH

Warren Farm

SEA LA

SALTRY LA

KITNOR LA

HORSELAND LA

STROLES LA

GROVE RD

ROSS LA

SOUTHLANDS

Marshwood Farm

CLEEVE PK

CHESTNUT AVE

Chapel Cleeve

Kentsford Farm

Townsend Farm

WINNIFORD LA

TANYARD COTTS

PO PH

B3191

EASTBURY HILL

Carhampton

ORCHARD RD

1 CHESTNUT CL
2 MILEETTS CL
3 CARANTOC PL
4 THE CRESCENT
5 WASSAIL CL
6 WOODLAND CL
7 CHURCH CL

A5

1 CARHAMPTON CROSS
2 ORCHARD CL
3 VICARAGE RD
4 EASTBURY RD

Binham Farm

Old Cleeve

Bye Farm

B3191

5

42

PARK LA

WALNUT LA

BRIDGE ST

THE COURT

4 5

1 2 3

HILL LA

KENNELS

BOWERHAYES LA

WINDSOME LA

Linton

BLACK MONKEY LA

WITHYCOMBE CROSS

DIARYLANDS

MONKS PATH

Washford River

TA24

Briddicott Farm

BRIDICOTT LA

HILL LA

MEADOW COTTS

LUKES GDN

Withycombe

LOWER ST. BEGGET CLOSE LA

4

Withycombe Hill

CULVER LA

SANDHILL

BUCKHILL

Bilbrook

DRAGON CROSS

CASTLE MEAD
CLAYDON
MCKINLEY TERR
VERDUN TERR
Washford

Old Cleeve CE Sch

HUISH MDW

WALNUT TREE CNR

Washford

Tropiquaria Masts
Wildlife Pk

41

Combe Farm

COMBE LA

Sandhill Farm

Hotel

Mus

THE HUGLETS

QUARRY RD

MAY TERR

BELLE VUE

WASHFORD CROSS

B3190

A39

Macmillan Way West

Pill River

Hungerford

P

ABBEY RD

Cleeve Abbey

TA23

Bardon

3

40

HIGHER RODHUISH RD

BEASTWAY LA

RODHUISH HILL LA

RODHUISH CROSS

Escott Farm

Lodge Farm

LODGE ROCKS

LOWBER LA

PH

Torre
Torre
Cider Farm

Holy Well

ROCKY LA

TORRE ROCKS

Beggearn Huish

FAIR CROSS

CRANDER LA

Rodhuish

FELON'S OAK LA

BLINDWELL LA

BRATTLE LA

Golsoncott

CLITSOME VIEW

Clitsome Farm

SLADE LA

B3188

2

39

SKA LA

STRINGLAND'S LA

GREEN ALLER LA

Felon's Oak

Croydon Hall

THE CRESCENT
MANOR VIEW

Lower Roadwater

Huish Barton

VEMPLETT'S CROSS

Yarde

TA4

1

38

TA23

STOULES WAY LA

BLINDWELL LA

MOUNT LA

HARPERS LA

WATERSMEET CL

WOODADVENT LA

B3190

PH

Culverwell

Roadwater

| 00 | A | 01 | B | 02 | C | 03 | D | 04 | E | 05 | F |

149   132

131

Scale: 1⅓ inches to 1 mile

A	B	C	D	E	F

8

45

7

44

202

WATCHET

6

West St. Audrie's Bay

43

B3191

Mill

BREADON RD

WATCHFORD HILL

St Decumans

Watchet

P

P

Watchet Sch

DONIFORD RD

Doniford Beach Halt

NORMANDY AVE

Holiday Park

The Belt

Holiday Village

Perry Farm

The Home Farm

5

Five Bells

Liddymore Farm

TA23

Doniford

Rydon Farm

St Audrie's House

West Wood

A39

42

B3190

B3191 FIVE BELLS

LIDDYMORE LA

UNION LA

Williton

SEA LA

202

Wibble Farm

STAPLE CL

Stowborrow Hill

PH

4

B3190

SMITHAM LA

NORTH RD

WARD'S LA

B3191

Williton & District H

LONG ST

STATION RD

LC

High Bridge

West Somerset Railway

Castle Hill

Torweston Farm

TA4

West Quantoxhead

BRACKEN EDGE

STAPLE LA

CRIDLANDS LA

LUCKES LA

Staple Plantation

P

41

A39

PRIEST ST

HALFACRE LA

BATH

BRIDGE ST

HIGH ST

Williton

P

TOWER HILL

A358

Mus

Burrow Rocks

Sampford Brett

Woolston

Lower Weacombe

Weacombe

HOLT LA

KENT ROAD LA

3

40

202

Orchard Wyndham

Macmillan Way West

DASHWOODS LA

Bicknoller Hill

Bickholler

GATCHELLS LA

Trendle Ring

2

Stream

CHARSEY

Black Down Wood

Capton

CAPTON CROSS

YELLOW WOOD CROSS

PH

TRENDLE LA

CHILOMBE LA

Quantock Moor Farm

Chilcombe

39

B3188

Yarde

YELLOW WOOD LA

Yellow Wood Farm

Lower Yellow

YELLOW WOOD LA

Newton

HALSWAY HILL A358

Culverhays

1

WOODFORD GOTTS

NETTLECOMBE PARK LA

Cemy

Woodford

B3188

BEECH TREE CROSS

COMBECROSS LA

Rowdon Farm

ESCOTT LA

ESCOTT LA

Yard Farm

COOKLEY LA

CULVERHAYS LA

38

06	07	08	09	10	11
A	B	C	D	E	F

131 150

For full street detail of the highlighted area see page 202.

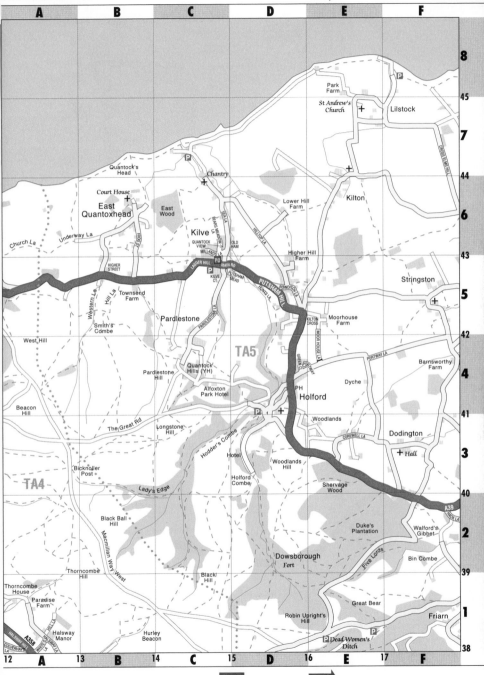

Scale: 1⅓ inches to 1 mile

0   ¼   ½ mile
0   250m 500m 750m   1 km

8

45

7

44

6

43

5

42

4

41

3

40

2

39

1

38

Park Farm

St Andrew's Church

Lilstock

P

Kilton

Quantock's Head

Court House

East Quantoxhead

East Wood

Chantry

Lower Hill Farm

Kilve

Underway La

Church La

Higher Hill Farm

Stringston

Moorhouse Farm

Kilton Cross

Higher Street

Townsend Farm

Pardlestone

Smith's Combe

West Hill

TA5

Putsham Hill

Barnsworthy Farm

Portway La

Quantock Hills (YH)

Pardlestone Hill

Alfoxton Park Hotel

Dyche

Holford

PH

Dodington

Hall

Beacon Hill

The Great Rd

Longstone Hill

Woodlands

Corewell La

Hodder's Combe

Hotel

Woodlands Hill

Holford Combe

Shervage Wood

Bicknoller Post

Lady's Edge

Black Ball Hill

Macmillan Way West

Dowsborough Fort

Duke's Plantation

Five Lords

Walford's Gibbet

Bin Combe

TA4

Thorncombe Hill

Black Hill

Great Bear

Thorncombe House

Paradise Farm

Halsway Manor

Hurley Beacon

Robin Upright's Hill

Dead Women's Ditch

Friarn

A39

A358

12   A   13   B   14   C   15   D   16   E   17   F

151   134

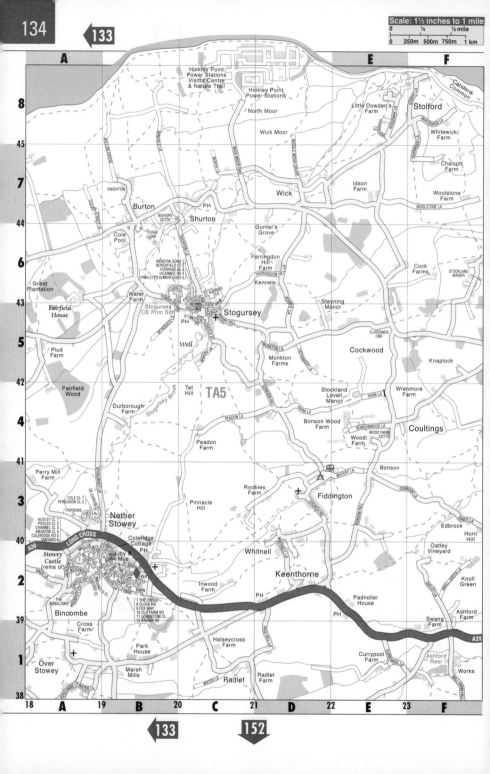

Scale: 1⅓ inches to 1 mile

0 ¼ ½ mile
0 250m 500m 750m 1 km

103
136

A **B** **C** **D** **E** **F**

Steart
River Parrett Trail
Stockland Reach
The Island
Huntspill River
CADWELL B LA
TA9

8
Wall Common
45

Marsh Farm
STERT DRO
Yearsley Farm
7
STRETHOLM LA
44
Dodds Farm
Stretcholt
STEART DRO

Stockland Bristol
Cobb's Leaze Rhyne
TA6
MOUNT VIEW TERR
CHAPEL RD
MANOR PK
BRISTOL RD
6
Otterhampton
Hill House
White House Rhyne
WHITE HOUSE RD
GAUNTS RD
Pawlett Hill
Pawlett Prim Sch
43

Hill Farm
Combwich
PH
WITHYCOMBE HILL
SCHOOL LA
CHURCH LA
Otterhampton Prim Sch
BROOKSIDE RD
ESTUARY PK
Pawlett Hams
Gaunt's Farm
MONMOUTH FARM CL 1
OLD MAIN RD 2
SCOT CL 3
GRANGE WAY 4
RIVER RD
CARMEL LA
5

DAME WITHYCOMBE VILLAS
TA5
Combwich Reach
River Parrett
1 NURSERY CL
2 FENDER CL
3 RIVER VIEW
4 MARTYN CL
5 HARBOUR VIEW
6 HARBOUR CT
7 KILN CL
42

Beere Manor Farm
Bolham House
Putnell Farm
River Parrett Trail
4

Castle Hill Quarry
Rodway Farm
Shark's La
Hallicks Farm
41

Fort
Cannington Park
STRAW MEA S HILL
Cannington Quarry
Rodway
Cannington Brook
River Parrett Trail
Dairy House Farm
CHINEHORN DRO
3
40

SANDY LA
PARK LA
RODWAY
Cannington
Cannington CE Prim Sch
1 SCHOOL FIELDS
2 RYDON CRES
3 SOUTHBROOK
Perry Court Farm
SQUARES RD 2
COLES COTTS 3
CHURCH COTTS 4
MEADOW CL 1
STRAIGHT DRO
Chilton Trinity
2

Bower Hill
Bridgwater Coll Cannington Ctr
Vst Ctr
Cemy
Withiel Farm
WITHIEL DR
CLIFFORD
ROSE VILLAS
MILL CT
OAK TREE
BROWNINGS
Gdns
FORE ST
EAST ST
Perry Moor
Sewage Works
Perry Green
Manor Farm
208
39

Brymore Sch
Blackmore Farm
PH
BLACKMORE LA
Bradley Green
MAIN RD
The Grange
Chiltern Trivett
QUANTOCK RD
NEW RD
208
Barton Farm
CHARLYNCH LA
LIMESTONE
A39 B3339
MOORES LA
MOTWAY
BLAKES LA
ARCHSTONE LA
WESTERN WAY
Chilton Trinity Tech Coll
CHILTON RD
TA6
208
1
38

A 24 25 **B** 26 **C** 27 **D** 28 **E** 29 **F**

153
136

B2
1 TOLL HOUSE RD
2 HENRY ROGERS HO
3 CLIFFORD LODGE
4 LOVERS' WLK
5 CHURCH ST
6 BROOK LA
7 DUKE AVE
8 TEALS ACRE
9 HAWKERS CL
10 BOWLING GN

For full street detail of the highlighted area see page 208.

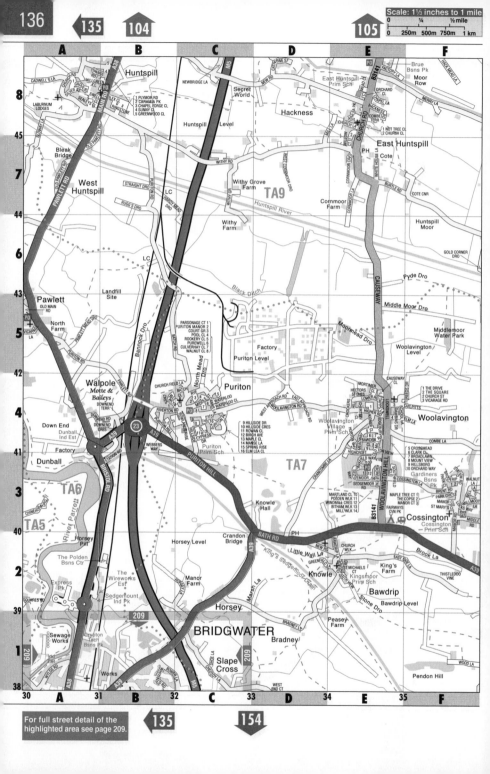

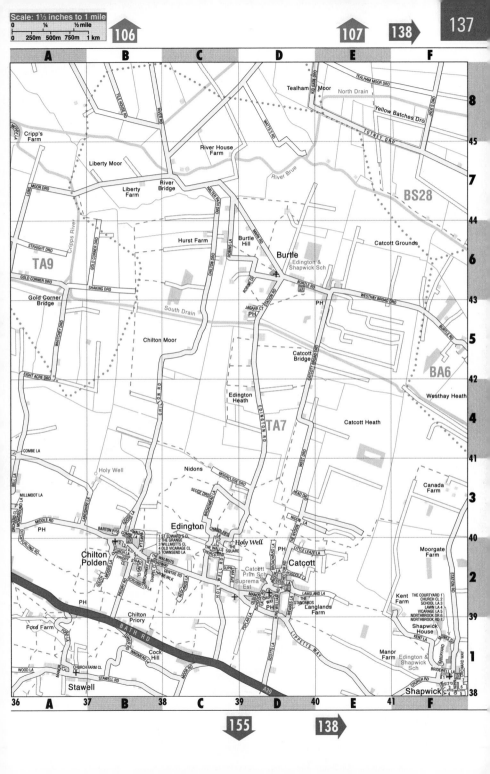

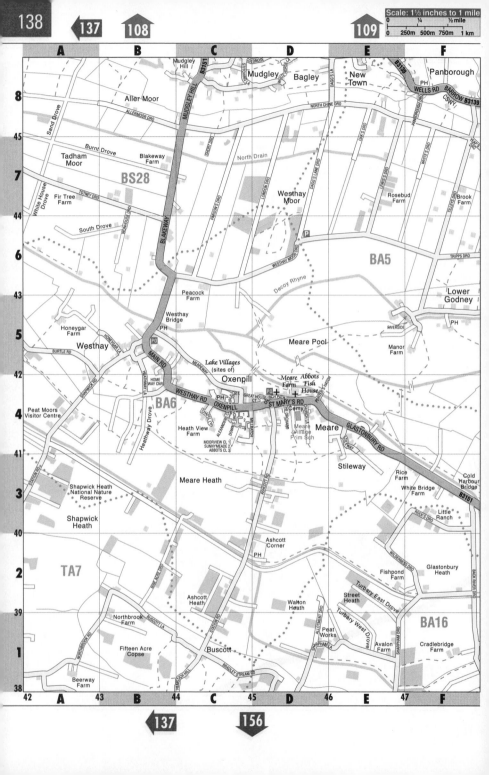

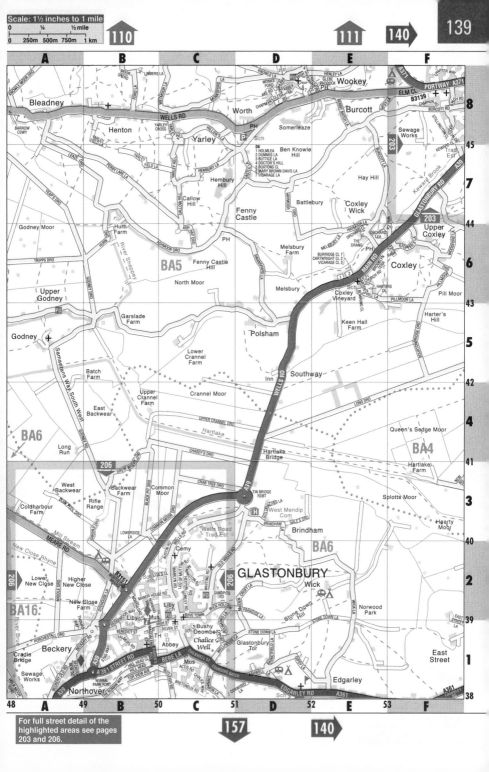

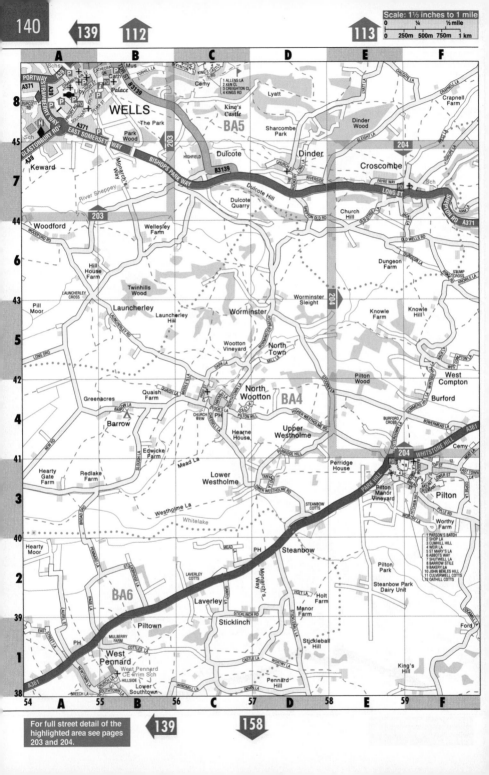

Scale: 1⅓ inches to 1 mile

0   ¼   ½ mile
0   250m 500m 750m 1 km

8

PORTWAY
A371
STRAWBERRY WAY
BURCOTT RD
A39
Schs
CATHEDRAL GN
Liby
Mus
CATH ST
TORHILL LA
BECKYNTON
Cemy
King's Castle
1 ALLENS LA
2 KEN CL
3 CREIGHTON CL
4 KINGS RD
Lyatt
UATT LA
CRANNEL LA
Crapnell Farm
CRAPNELL LA
SILVER ST
WELLS
Cath
Palace
The Park
Park Wood
BA5
Sharcombe Park
Dinder Wood
CHELOTTE LA
45
EAST SOMERSET
A371
WAY
PARK
HIGHFIELD
Dulcote
Dinder
Croscombe
A39
Sch
H
203
FAYRE WAY
Sch
PO
204
7
Keward
Monarch's Way
BISHOPS PARK WAY
B3139
Dulcote Hill
CHURCH
RIVERSIDE
LONG ST
SHEPTON RD
A371
River Sheppey
Dulcote Quarry
SHEPTON OLD RD
Church Hill
OLD ST REET
JACK
SHEPTON
HILL
44
203
Woodford
Wellesley Farm
WOODFORD RD
OLD WELLS RD
DUNGEON LA
STUMP CROSS
KNOWLE LA
6
Hill House Farm
Twinhills Wood
Dungeon Farm
43
Pill Moor
LAUNCHERLEY CROSS
Launcherley
Launcherley Hill
Worminster
Worminster Sleight
204
Knowle Farm
Knowle Hill
LONG DRO
LAUNCHERLEY RD
DARK LA
WORMINSTER SLEIGHT
Wootton Vineyard
North Town
MILL LA
West Compton
5
MOORE'S LA
HOLT
TANYARD LA
DUNSTONE LA
Pilton Wood
COOMBE LA
Burford
42
Greenacres
QUAISH LA
Quaish Farm
North Wootton
BA4
SIMMERS MEAD
BURFORD CROSS
ROWMEAD LA
A361
4
Barrow
COW LA
CHURCH VIEW
STOCK'S LA
PH
Pilton Hill
Hearne House
HIGHER WESTHOLME RD
Upper Westholme
COTTERCOMBE LA
WHITSTONE HILL
Cemy
41
Hearty Gate Farm
Redlake Farm
Edwicke Farm
SLOUGH LA
Mead La
PERRIDGE HILL
Lower Westholme
LOWER WESTHOLME RD
TAN LA
Perridge House
PARK HILL
Pilton Manor Vineyard
204
PO
Pilton
UPPER ST
EAST TOWN
1 PARSON'S BATCH
2 SHOP LA
3 CUMHILL HILL
4 WEIR LA
3
NEW RD
BROAD DRO
Westholme La
Whitelake
STEANBOW COTTS
WORTHY LA
PYLLE RD
Worthy Farm
5 ST MARY'S LA
6 ABBOTS WAY
7 SHUTWELL LA
8 BARROW STILE
9 BAKERY LA
10 JOHN BEALES HILL
11 CULVERWELL COTTS
12 OATHILL COTTS
40
Hearty Moor
FERNBRIDGE LA
MEAD
PH
Steanbow
Pilton Park
Steanbow Park Dairy Unit
2
BA6
LAVERLEY COTTS
Monarch's Way
HOLT LA
Holt Farm
STOCKBRIDGE LA
STG BRIDGE LA
PAGE LA
39
Piltown
MULBERRY FARM
COTTLES LA
Laverley
STICKLINCH RD
Sticklinch
STICKLEBALL LA
Manor Farm
Stickleball Hill
Ford
COCKMILL LA
EAST STREET LA
AMBER LA
1
West Pennard
PH
West Pennard CE Prim Sch
HILLSIDE
Lower Southtown
BREECH LA
SOUTHTOWN LA
CASTLE LA
WINDMILL LA
WORTHY LA
Pennard Hill
King's Hill
A361

54   55   56   57   58   59
A   B   C   D   E   F

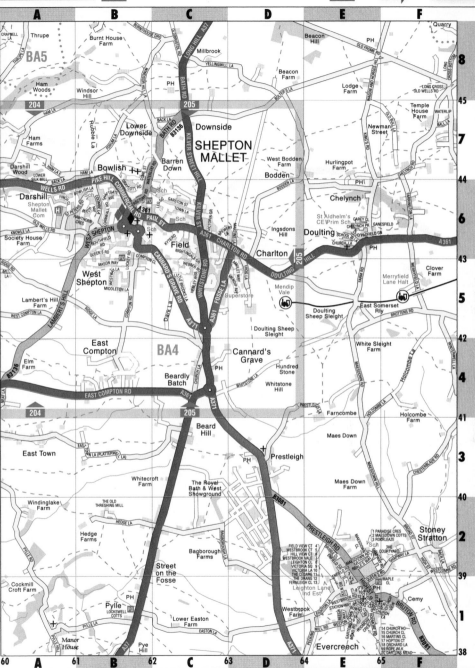

A   B   C   D   E   F

CRANMELL LA
Thrupe
BA5
Burnt House Farm
Millbrook
Beacon Hill
Quarry
8

BURNT HOUSE DRO
YELLINGMILL LA
OLD FROME RD
PH
45

Ham Woods
Windsor Hill
PH
BATH RD
205
Beacon Farm
Lodge Farm
BOX'S LA
Temple House Farm
WATERLIP
BALL LA
LONG CROSS OLD WELLS RD
7

Ham Farms
HAM LA
204
Rubble La
Lower Downside
BACK RD
B3136
Downside
SHEPTON MALLET
West Bodden Farm
Hurlingpot Farm
Newman Street
KING'S RD

Darshill Wood
LOWER SILK MILL
Bowlish
Barren Down
Bodden
Chelynch
44

Darshill
PIKE HILL COMMERCIAL RD
A361
PAUL ST
Sch
Sch
TOWN LA
KILVER ST
BODDEN LA
St Aldhelm's CE Prim Sch
CAREY PK
CHELYNCH RD
Doulting
6

Shepton Mallet Com
H
WELLS RD
Field
Ingsdons Hill
CHURCH LA
GANESFIELD
CHIPPADFIELD GN
PH
A361

Society House Farm
WEST SHEPTON
QUEEN'S RD
CHARLTON RD
Charlton
DOULTING HILL
205
43

West Shepton
MASON WAY
CANNARD'S GRAVE RD
WHITSTONE RD
FOSSE LA
Superstore
Mendip Vale
Doulting Sheep Sleight
East Somerset Rly
Merryfield Lane Halt
Clover Farm
5

Lambert's Hill Farm
LAMBERT'S HILL
MIDDLETON LA
A371
PARK LA
Doulting Sheep Sleight
White Sleight Farm
BROTTENS RD
42

East Compton
BA4
Cannard's Grave
Hundred Stone
HOLCOMBE LA
4

Elm Farm
B3136
204
EAST COMPTON RD
205
Beardly Batch
A361
A371
PH
WHITSTONE LA
Whitstone Hill
Farncombe
Holcombe Farm
41

East Town
EAST COMPTON RD
Beard Hill
Maes Down
3

Whitecroft Farm
PH
Prestleigh
PRESTLEIGH RD
Maes Down Farm
CHESTERBLADE
40

Windinglake Farm
THE OLD THRESHING MILL
HEDGE LA
The Royal Bath & West Showground
B3081
Stoney Stratton
2

Hedge Farms
Bagborough Farms
Street on the Fosse
PRESTLEIGH RD
1 PARADISE CRES
2 MAESDOWN COTTS
3 RODKLEAZE
THE COURTYARD
WESTCOMB RD
39

Cockmill Croft Farm
PILLER RD
PH
Pylle
LOCKSWELL COTTS
PYLLE LA
Lower Easton Farm
EASTON LA
FIELD VIEW CT 4
WESTBROOK CT 5
HILL VIEW CL 6
WESTBROOK VALE 3
LEIGHTON CL
VICTORIA SQ 9
VICTORIA CL 10
THE CEDARS 11
THE DRANG 12
FERNLEIGH CL 13
Leighton Lane Ind Est
Westbrook Farm
MAPLE CL
Cemy
1

Manor House
Pye Hill
A37
A371
STATION WAY
14 CHURCH HO
15 CHURCH CL
16 MARTINS CL
17 HOPTON CT
18 ORCHARD LA
19 ROPE WLK
20 DARTONS MEAD
Evercreech
B3081
38

60   A   61   B   62   C   63   D   64   E   65   F

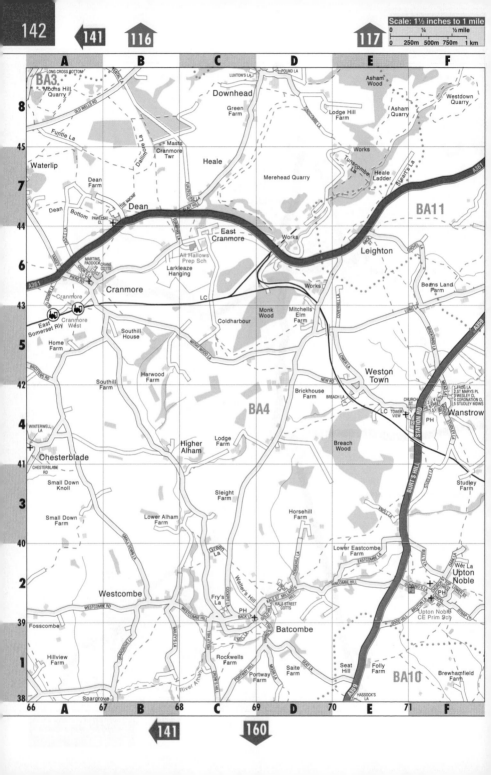

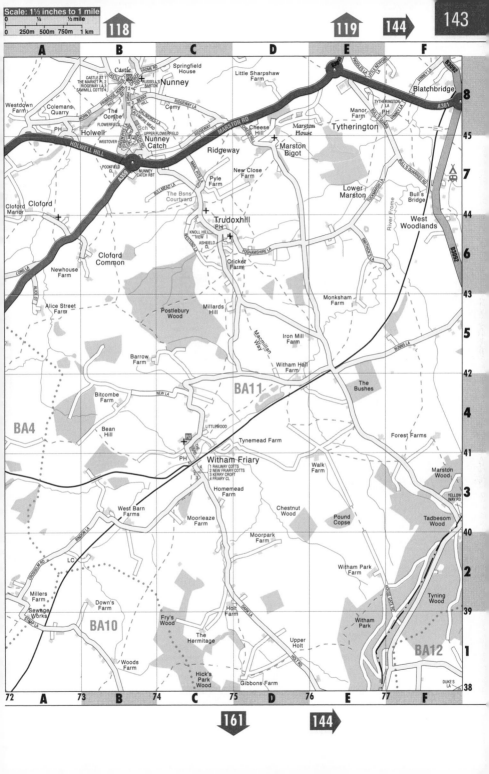

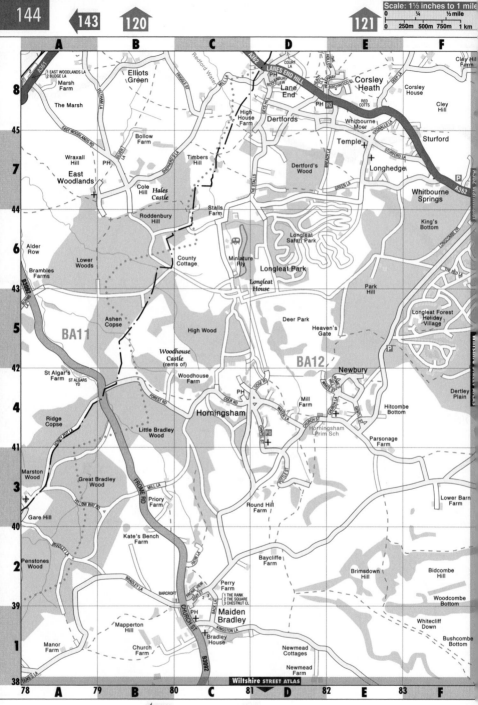

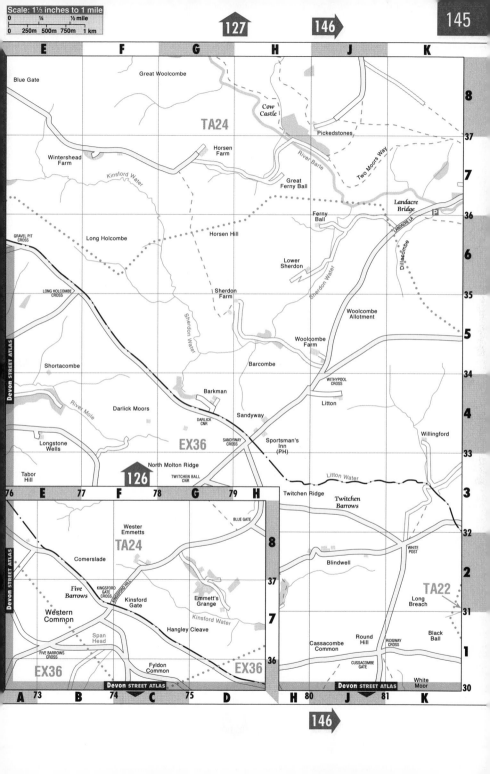

Scale: 1⅓ inches to 1 mile
0 ¼ ½ mile
0 250m 500m 750m 1 km

E F G H J K

Blue Gate

Great Woolcombe

Cow Castle

TA24

Pickedstones

Two Moors Way

8

37

Wintershead Farm

Horsen Farm

River Barle

Great Ferny Ball

Landacre Bridge

P

7

Kinsford Water

Ferny Ball

LANDACRE LA

36

GRAVEL PIT CROSS

Long Holcombe

Horsen Hill

Lower Sherdon

Dillacombe

6

LONG HOLCOMBE CROSS

Sherdon Water

Woolcombe Allotment

35

Sherdon Farm

Shortacombe

Sherdon Water

Woolcombe Farm

5

River Mole

Barcombe

WITHYPOOL CROSS

34

Longstone Wells

Darlick Moors

Barkman

DARLICK CNR

Sandyway

SANDYWAY CROSS

Litton

4

Tabor Hill

EX36

North Molton Ridge

TWITCHEN BALL CNR

Sportsman's Inn (PH)

Litton Water

Willingford

33

126

Twitchen Ridge

Twitchen Barrows

3

76 E 77 F 78 G 79 H

BLUE GATE

32

WHITE POST

Western Emmetts

TA24

Comerslade

KINGSFORD GATE CROSS

Kinsford Gate

KINGSFORD HILL

Emmett's Grange

Blindwell

TA22

2

Five Barrows

Western Common

Kinsford Water

Long Breach

31

Span Head

Hangley Cleave

Cassacombe Common

Round Hill

RIDGWAY CROSS

Black Ball

1

FIVE BARROWS CROSS

EX36

Fyldon Common

EX36

CUSSACOMBE GATE

White Moor

30

A 73 B 74 C 75 D

H 80 J 81 K

Devon STREET ATLAS

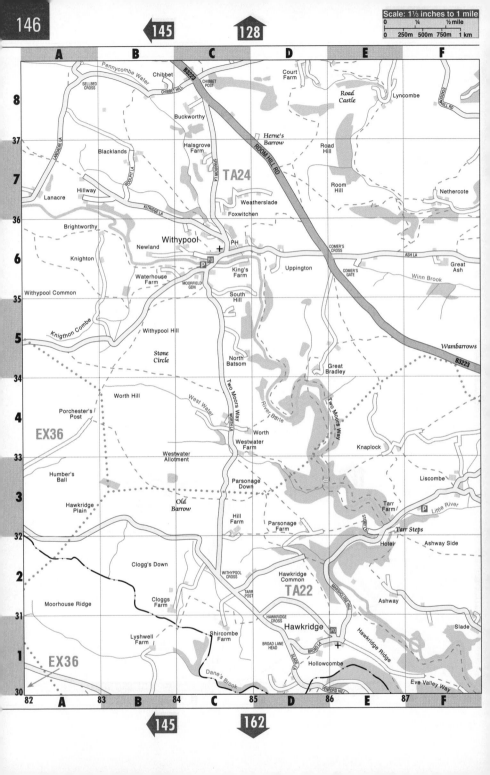

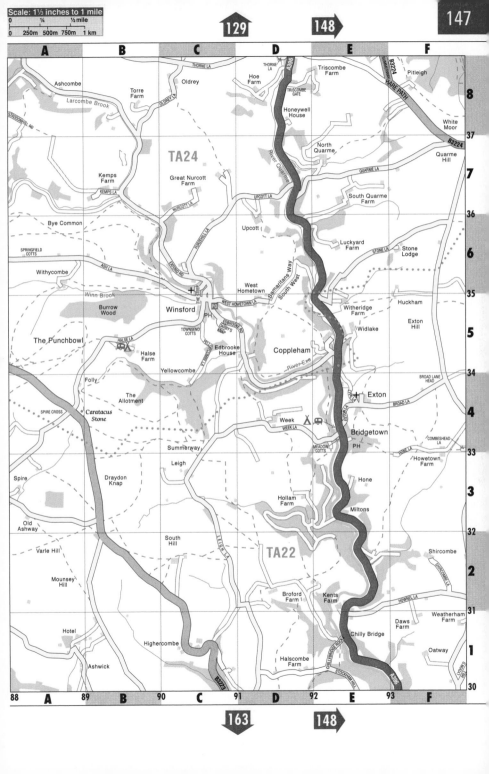

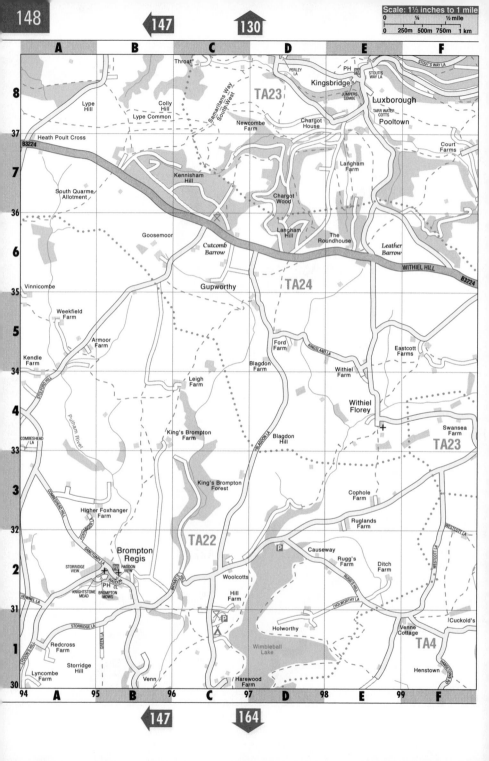

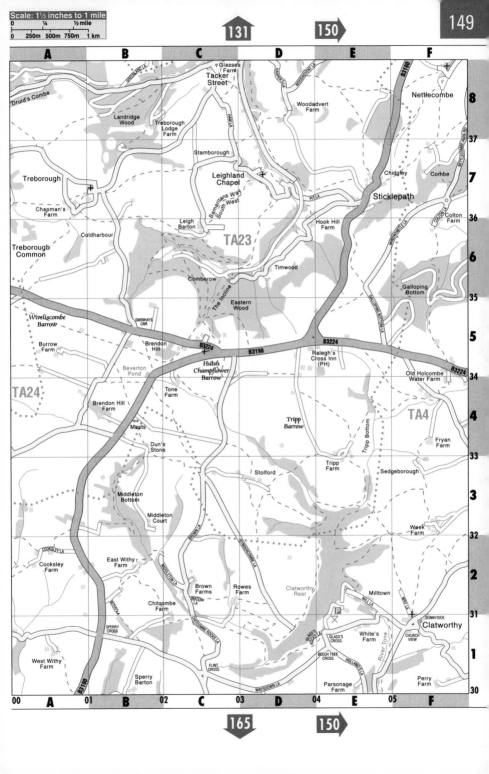

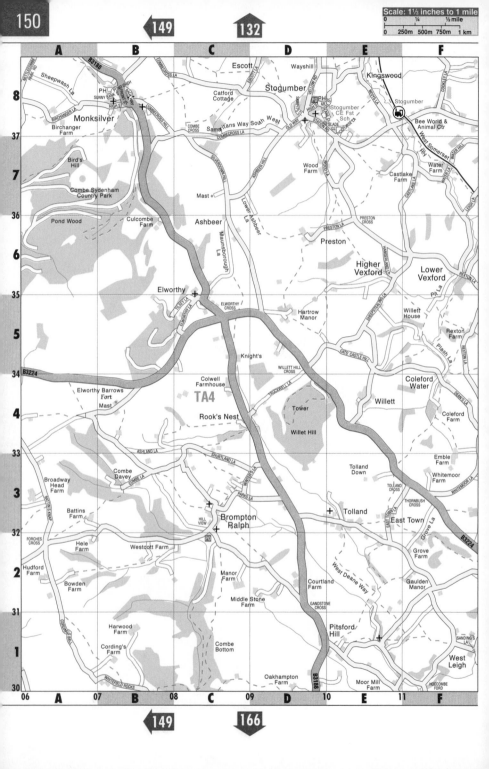

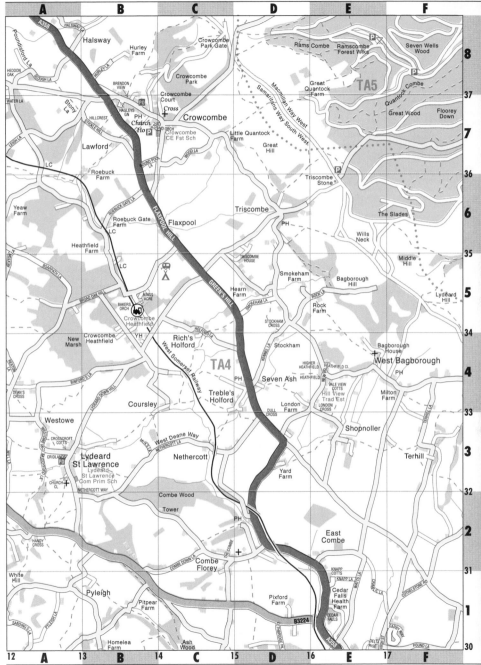

Scale: 1⅓ inches to 1 mile

0   ¼   ½ mile
0 250m 500m 750m 1 km

133   152

A **B** **C** **D** **E** **F**

A358

Halsway
HALSWAY

Hurley
Farm

Heddon Oak

Water La

Story La

Brendon View

Crowcombe
Park Gate

Crowcombe
Park Gate

Crowcombe
Park

Crowcombe
Court

PH

Church
Ho

Crowcombe
CE Fst Sch

Rams Combe

Ramscombe
Forest Wks

Seven Wells
Wood

Great
Quantock
Farm

TA5

Quantock Combe

Great Wood

Floorey
Down

8

37

Samaritans Way South West

Macmillan Way West

Cross

Crowcombe

Little Quantock
Farm

Great
Hill

7

Lawford

Roebuck
Farm

Triscombe
Stone

36

Yeaw
Farm

Heathfield
Farm

Roebuck Gate
Farm

LC

Flaxpool

Flaxpool

Triscombe

PH

Wills Neck

The Slades

Middle
Hill

Lydeard
Hill

6

35

BOARPATH LA

LC

TRISCOMBE
HOUSE

Smokeham
Farm

Bagborough
Hill

5

Hearn
Farm

KINGS
ACRE

BAKERS
ORCH

Crowcombe
Heathfield

West Somerset Railway

Rock La

Rock
Farm

Bagborough
House

34

New
Marsh

Crowcombe
Heathfield

YH

Rich's
Holford

STOCKHAM
CROSS

Stockham

HIGHER
HEATHFIELD

Heathfield Cl

West Bagborough

TA4

PH

Seven Ash

HEATHFIELD

VALE VIEW
COTTS

Hill View
Trad Est

Milton
Farm

4

33

DEAN'S
CROSS

Coursley

Treble's
Holford

London
Farm

LONDON
CROSS

DULL
CROSS

Shopnoller

Terhill

3

Westowe

CROSSCROFT
COTTS

CRIDLANDS

West Deane Way

Nethercott

NETHERCOTT LA

Yard
Farm

32

Lydeard
St Lawrence

Lydeard
St Lawrence
Com Prim Sch

CHURCH CL

NETHERCOTT WAY

Combe Wood

Tower

East
Combe

KNAPP
COTTS

KNAPP LA

31

Handy
Cross

White
Hill

Pyleigh

Pitpear
Farm

COMBE DOWN LA

PH

Combe
Florey

Pixford
Farm

Cedar Falls
Health
Farm

CEDAR
FALLS

2

1

SANDING LA

PYLEIGH LA

Homelea
Farm

Ash
Wood

B3224

A358

POUND LA

DARBY WAY

COTTLESTONE RD

30

12 A 13 B 14 C 15 D 16 E 17 F

167   152

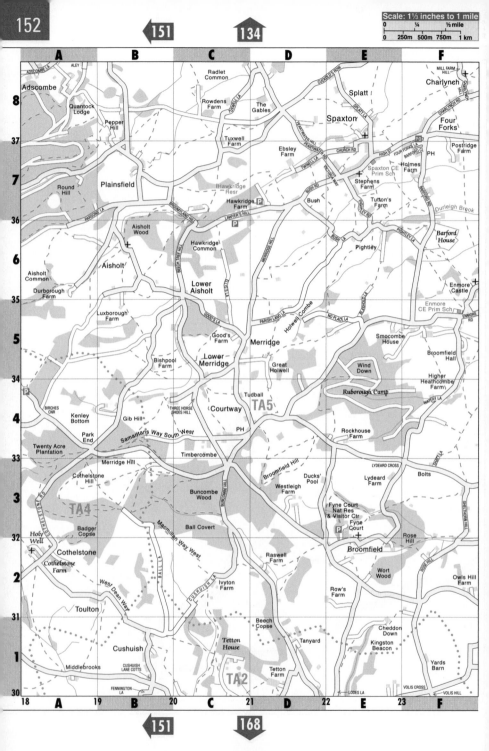

Scale: 1⅓ inches to 1 mile

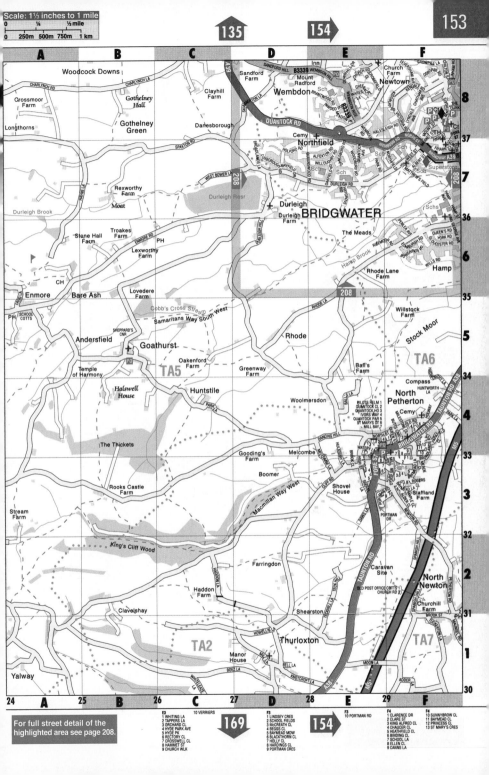

	A		B		C		D		E		F	

Woodcock Downs

CHARLYNCH RD   CHARLYNCH LA

Crossmoor Farm

Gothelney Hall

Clayhill Farm

Sandford Farm
Sandford Hill   B3339   WEMBDON HILL
Mount Radford   Inn

Church Farm
Newtown

Longthorns

Gothelney Green

Danesborough

SPAXTON RD

Wembdon   Sch

QUANTOCK RD

Cemy   Northfield

8

37

Durleigh Resr

WEST BOWER LA

208

Durleigh
Durleigh Farm   BRIDGWATER

Rexworthy Farm

Moat

Durleigh Brook

Stone Hall Farm

Troakes Farm

ENMORE RD   PH

Lexworthy Farm

The Meads

7

36

CH

Enmore   Bare Ash

Lovedere Farm

Cobb's Cross Stream

Samaritans Way South West

Rhode Lane Farm

Hamp

208

6

35

PH   SCHOOL COTTS

Andersfield

SHEPPARD'S CNR

Goathurst

PO

TA5

Oakenford Farm

Greenway Farm

Rhode

Baff's Farm

Willstock Farm

Stock Moor

TA6

5

Temple of Harmony

Halswell House

Huntstile

PARK LA

Woolmersdon

Compass
HUNTWORTH LA

North Petherton

PILOTS RELM 1
QUANTOCK CL 2
QUANTOCK HO 3
IVORS WAY 4
QUANTOCK PK 5
ST MARYS CT 6
MILL BAY 7

Cemy

34

The Thickets

Gooding's Farm

Melcombe

DANCING HILL

Boomer

FORE ST

BRIDGWATER RD

4

33

Rooks Castle Farm

Macmillan Way West

CLIFF RD

Shovel House

Staffland Farm

PORTMAN DR

ROGERS

3

32

Stream Farm

King's Cliff Wood

Farringdon

Caravan Site

OLD POST OFFICE COTTS
CHURCH RD 2

North Newton

TAUNTON RD

2

Haddon Farm

HADDON LA   TECH LA

Shearston

Churchill Farm   BROOK ST   PH

31

Clavelshay

HOWELL'S LA

Thurloxton

TA7

TA2

WHITEFIELD RD

Manor House   BOEZ LA   BELL LA

KNOTCROFT LA   MOOR LA

ADDER LA

1

Yalway

30

	A		B		C		D		E		F	

For full street detail of the highlighted area see page 208.

169   154

E3
1 WHITING LA
2 TAPPERS LA
3 ORCHARD CL
4 HYDE PARK AVE
5 HYDE PK
6 RECTORY CL
7 CROSSWELL CL
8 HAMMET ST
9 CHURCH WLK

10 VERRIERS

F3
1 LINDSEY CRES
2 SCHOOL FIELDS
3 McCREATH CL
4 BEGGS CL
5 BAYMEAD MDW
6 BLACKTHORN CL
7 HOLLY CL
8 HARDINGS CL
9 PORTMAN CRES

F3
10 PORTMAN RD

F4
1 CLARENCE DR
2 CLARE ST
3 KING ALFRED CL
4 CHAUCER CL
5 HEATHFIELD CL
6 BINDING CL
7 SCHOOL LA
8 ELLEN CL
9 CANNS LA

F4
10 SUNNYBROW CL
11 BAYMEAD CL
12 PRINCESS CL
13 ST MARY'S CRES

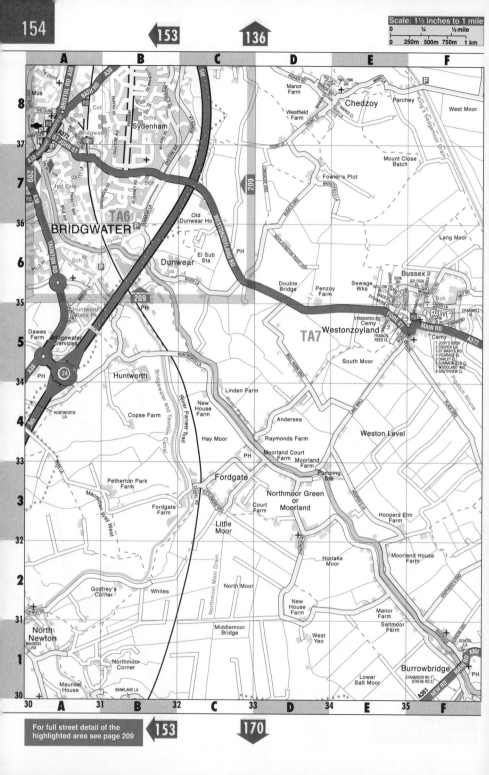

Scale: 1⅓ inches to 1 mile

0   ¼   ½ mile
0 250m 500m 750m 1 km

A **B** **C** **D** **E** **F**

8

THE GROVE

Mus

THE CLINK

Coll

Sch

Bridgwate

37

EASTOVER

Sydenham

7

209

Ind Ests

36

TA6

BRIDGWATER

Old Dunwear Ho

6

Dunwear

El Sub Sta

PH

Sch

River La

Double Bridge

Penzoy Farm

Sewage Wks

Bussex

Chedzoy

Manor Farm

Westfield Farm

Willow Gn

Parchey

West Moor

Mount Close Batch

Fowler's Plot

Lang Moor

Cemy

Standards Rd

TA7

Westonzoyland

35

209

PH

Huntworth Bsns Pk

Dawes Farm

Bridgwater Services

5

PH

24

Huntworth

HUNTWORTH LA

Copse Farm

Hay Moor

Linden Farm

Andersea

Raymonds Farm

South Moor

Weston Level

1 JUDY'S ORCH
2 CHURCH LA
3 ST MARYS RD
4 VICARAGE CL
5 OAKLEY CL
6 SUMMERFIELD CL
7 WOODLAND AVE
8 SOUTHVIEW CL

Cemy

34

River Parrett

New House Farm

Moorland Court Farm

Moorland Farm

PH

4

Petherton Park Farm

Macmillan Way West

Fordgate

Fordgate Farm

Northmoor Green or Moorland

Court Farm

Pumping Sta

Hoopers Elm Farm

33

3

Little Moor

Horlake Moor

Moorland House Farm

Northmoor Main Drain

32

2

Godfrey's Corner

Whites

North Moor

New House Farm

Manor Farm

Saltmoor Farm

31

North Newton

Middlemoor Bridge

West Yeo

Burrowbridge

1

Northmoor Corner

Lower Salt Moor

STANMOOR RD 1
STATHE RD 2

PH

Maunsel House

BANKLAND LA

NEW RD

30

30 **A** **31** **B** **32** **C** **33** **D** **34** **E** **35** **F**

For full street detail of the highlighted area see page 209

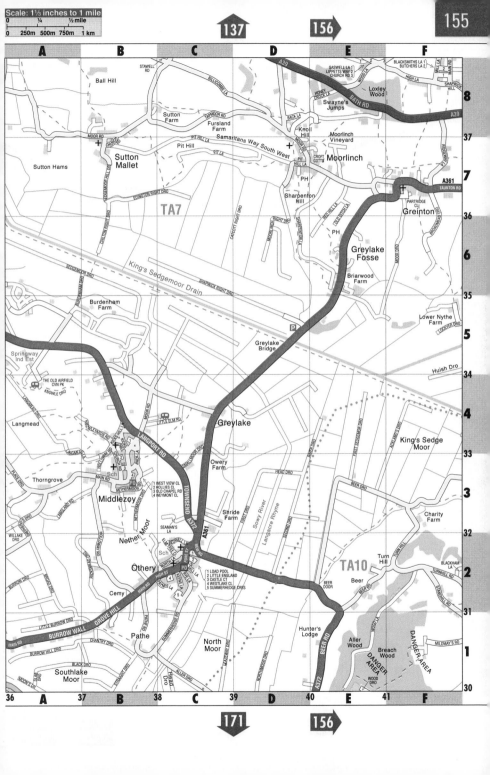

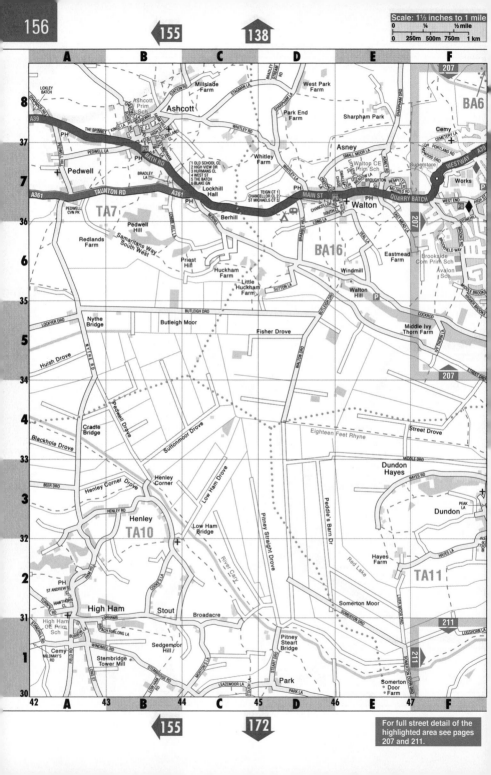

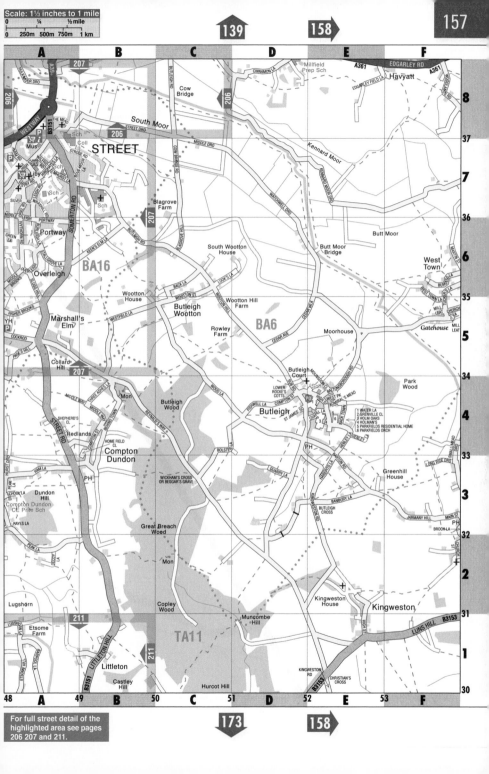

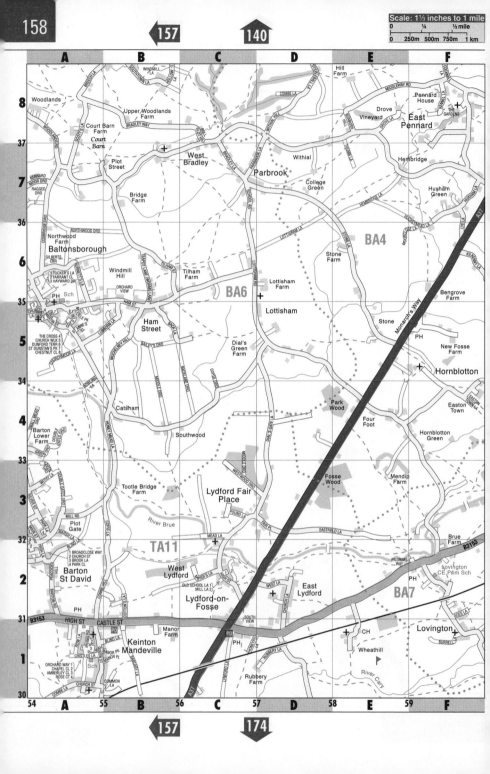

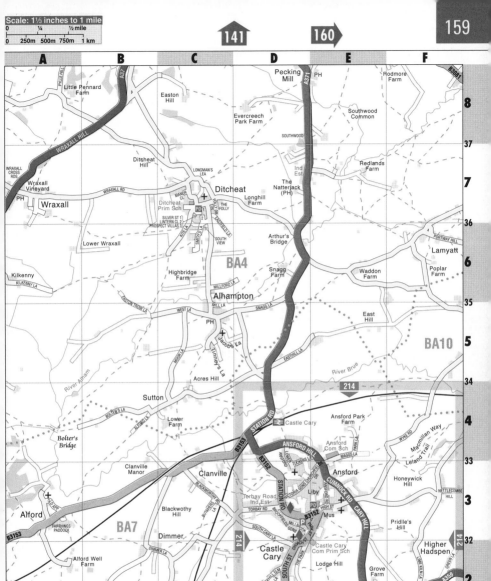

175   160

For full street detail of the highlighted area see page 214.

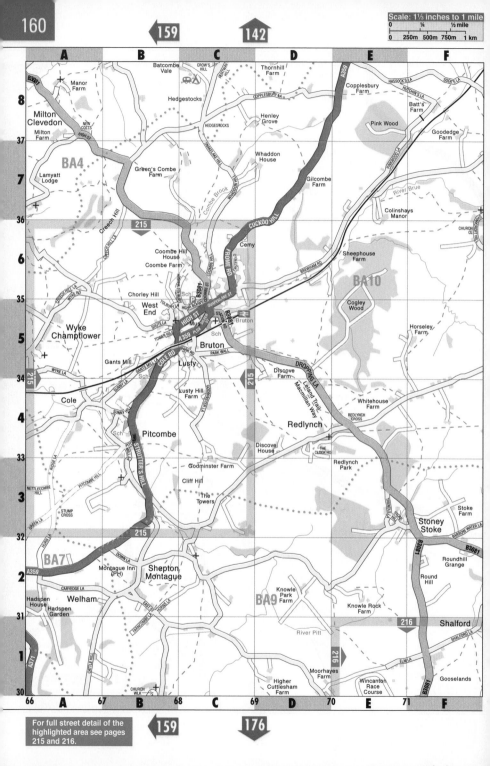

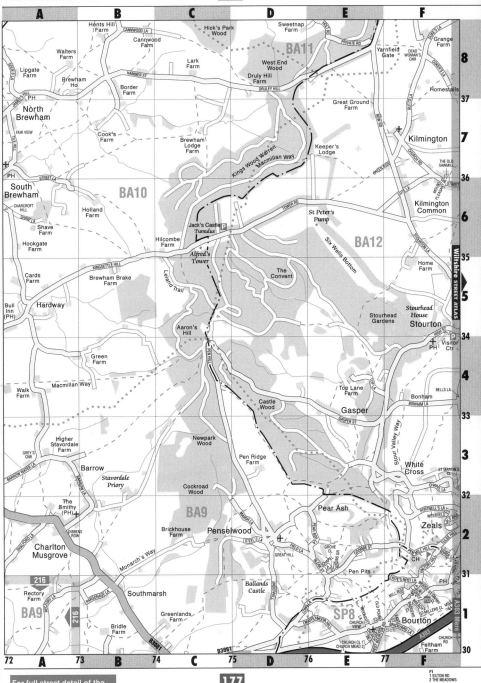

Scale: 1⅓ inches to 1 mile

0   ¼   ½ mile
0   250m 500m 750m 1 km

143

Wiltshire STREET ATLAS

177

For full street detail of the
highlighted area see page 216.

F1
1 SILTON RD
2 THE MEADOWS

A 72 **B** 73 74 **C** 75 **D** 76 **E** 77 **F**

Hent's Hill Farm
Walters Farm
Lipgate Farm
Brewham Ho
North Brewham
FAIR VIEW
PH
South Brewham
CHARCROFT HILL
Shave Farm
SHAVE LA
Hookgate Farm
Cards Farm
Bull Inn (PH)
Hardway
Green Farm
Walk Farm
Macmillan Way
Higher Stavordale Farm
GREY'S CNR
Barrow
Stavordale Priory
The Smithy (PH)
DIBBENS ROW
Charlton Musgrove
216
Rectory Farm
BA9
Southmarsh
Bridle Farm
Greenlands Farm
B3081

Cannwood Farm
CANNWOOD LA
Border Farm
HAMMER ST
Cook's Farm
BA10
Holland Farm
Brewham Brake Farm
KINGSETTLE HILL

Hick's Park Wood
Lark Farm
Brewham Lodge Farm
Hilcombe Farm
Alfred's Tower
Leland Trail
Aaron's Hill
PEN HILL
Newpark Wood
Pen Ridge Farm
Cockroad Wood
Brickhouse Farm
BA9
Penselwood
MARSH LA
STEEL'S LA
GREAT HILL
Ballands Castle

Sweetnap Farm
West End Wood
Druley Hill Farm
DRULEY HILL
BA11
Kings Wood Warren
Macmillan Way
Jack's Castle Tumulus
The Convent
Castle Wood

HILL RD
NEW RD
PRIVATE RD
Yarnfield Gate
Great Ground Farm
Keeper's Lodge
SWEET RIDGE
TOWER RD
St Peter's Pump
Six Wells Bottom
BA12
Stourhead Gardens
Top Lane Farm
Stourhead House
Stourton
Bonham
BONHAM LA
Gasper
GASPER ST
Stour Valley Way
White Cross
ST MARTIN'S CL
CHASE LA
Pear Ash
PEAR ASH LA
GROVE
COOMBE ST
Pen Pits

COLE ST LA
Grange Farm
DEAD WOMAN'S CNR
Homestalls
Kilmington
THE OLD SAWMILL
MOUNT PLEASANT LA
Kilmington Common
COLE LA
Home Farm
STOURTON LA
HIGH ST
PH
Visitor Ctr
P
BELLS LA
PORTNELL'S LA
WESTFIELD
Zeals
A303
KITE'S NEST LA
PH
MILL RISE
MILLERS CL
SP8
Bourton
OLD POUND
BRICKYARD LA
CHURCH RD
Feltham Farm
A303 Mere
CHURCH CL
CHURCH MEAD 2
B3081

8
37
7
36
6
35
5
34
4
33
3
32
2
31
1
30

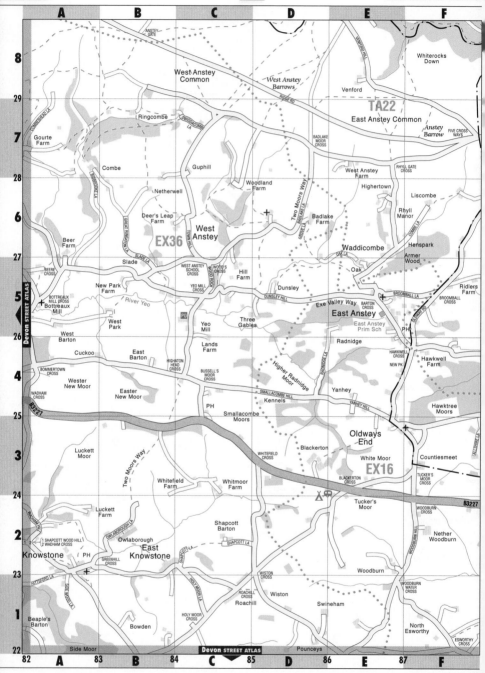

146

Scale: 1½ inches to 1 mile

0   ¼   ½ mile
0 250m 500m 750m 1 km

Scale: 1⅓ inches to 1 mile

0   ¼   ½ mile
0 250m 500m 750m 1 km

147

164

163

A   B   C   D   E   F

Brewer's Castle
Mounsey Castle
Hinam Farm
Draydon Farm
Court Down
Stockham
Oxgrove Farm

8

Marsh Hill House
Northcombe
Barlynch Farm

29

New Invention
MARSHBRIDGE CROSS
Northmoor
Hollam Cross
LOUISA GATE

CHILCOTT CROSS
SNOWBALL HILL
NEWGATE CROSS
Hollam House
Barlynch Woods

7

HINAM CROSS
Old Shute
Oldberry Castle
WEIR HEAD COTTS
HANOVER CT
TOWN MARSH

1 EXMOOR GDNS
2 THE PADDOCK
3 BANK SQ
4 FORE ST
5 UNION ST
6 CHURCH LA
7 VICARAGE HILL
8 BRIDGE ST
9 BARNSCLOSE N
10 HERBERT RD
11 BARNSCLOSE
12 BARNSCLOSE W

Bury Hill

BEECH TREE CROSS
Old Berry Farm
PH
Hele Bridge

28

Chilcott
Liby & Visitor Ctr
JURY RD
JURY HILL
B3222
MACHINE CROSS

Cawkett Farm
Wilway
WILNA LA
ANDREW'S HILL CROSS
KING'S CLM
Dulverton

6

Streamcombe
THREE GATES CROSS
Clayford
COMBE LA
BATTLETON
Barns Close Ind Est
Pixton Park

27

Bere
Knowle Farm
Gulland
CLAYFORD LA
Ashill
Beasley Farm
Combe
TA22
Allers Wood
Pixton Hill
Bury Castle

5

Beer Moors
IRON POST
Mast
Weir House
DYEHOUSE CROSS
Pixy Copse

Venn
Nightcott
Brockey River
Exe Valley Way
Brushford
THE GREEN
BRUSHFORD NEW RD
Perry Farm

26

West Knowle
DENNINGTON LA
LANGALLER HILL
Langaller Farm
ELLERSDOWN LA
TYERDALE CL
MARKET CL
PERRY NEW RD

4

TWELVE ACRE POST
Upcott
CROFT LA
Kents Hill
1 NICHOLAS CL
2 POUNDSCLOSE
Hulverton Hill
Exebridge Ind Est

25

ALLSHIRE LA
Wind Pump
TRACKFORDMOOR CROSS
Croft
Rocks
Riphay Barton
RIPHAY CROSS
Poole Farm

Sowerhill
Langridge
Fishery
RIVER VIEW
Exebridge

3

Den Brook
Hele Manor Farm
PH
B3227
Wilsons Farm

West Tapps
Higher Grants Farm
BLUEATS HILL

24

Western Farm
Red Deer Farm
East Tapps
Great Highleigh
Combe Head

2

Combe Water
EAST TAPPS LA
BLACKALLER LA
EX16
Mast
NEW LA

23

East Mildon
Newhouse Farm
Hutswell Farm
East Loosemoor
Benshayes Farm

1

West Mildon
Ford Farm
HIGH BOLHAM
A3227
A396
GRANTS HILL
Westbrook Farmhouse
B3227

22

88   A   89   B   90   C   91   D   92   E   93   F

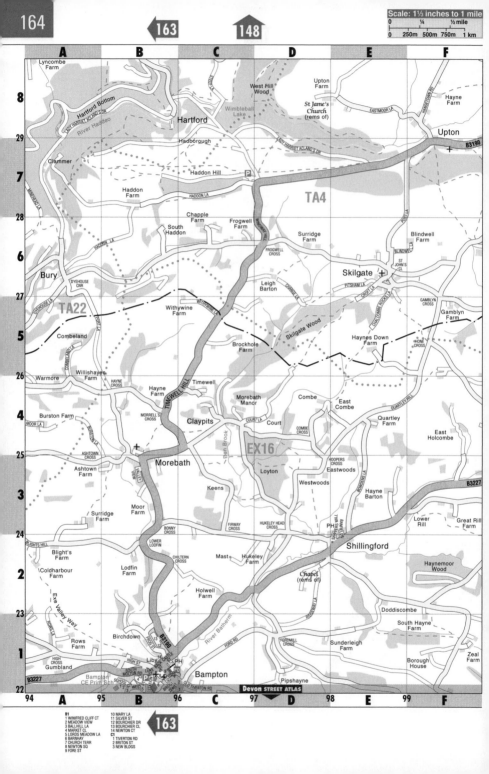

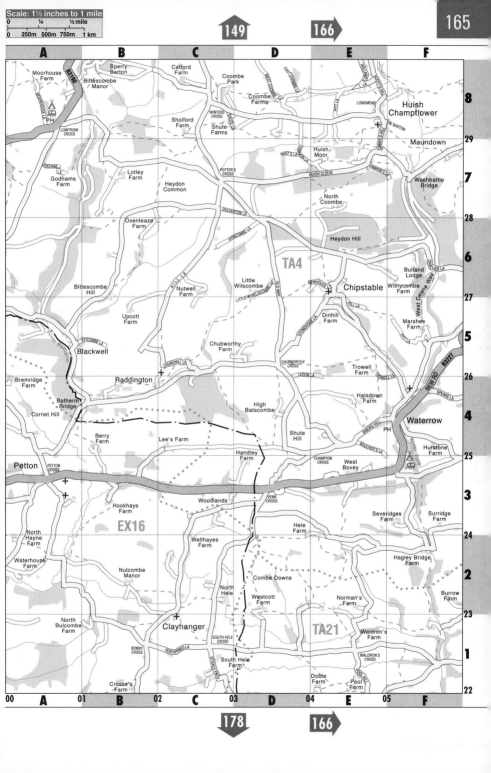

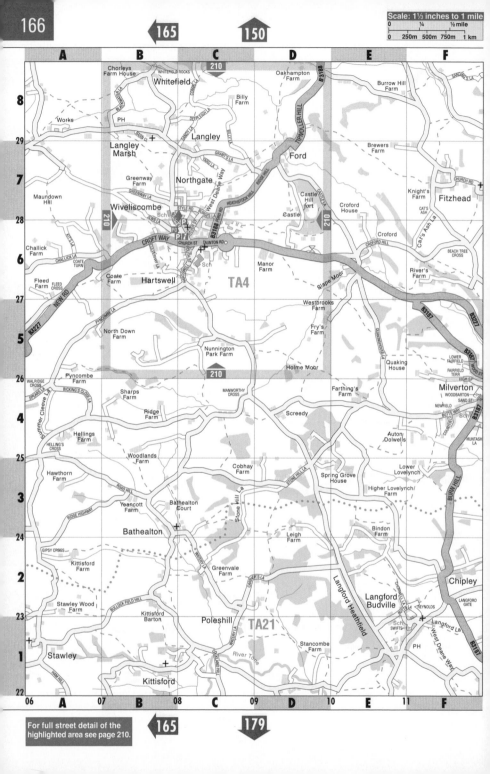

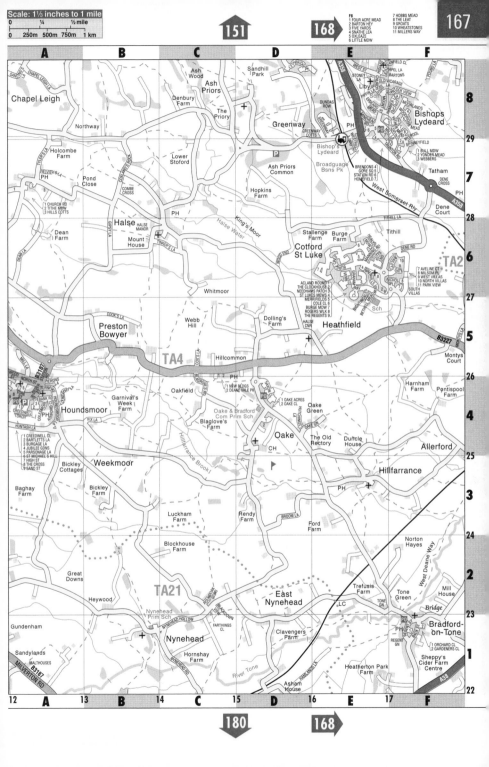

Scale: 1⅓ inches to 1 mile

For full street detail of the highlighted area see pages 212 and 213.

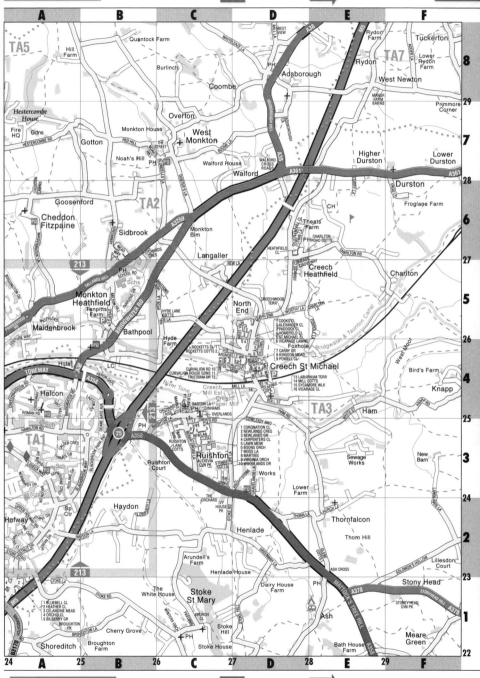

TA5
Quantock Farm
Hill Farm
Burlinch
Coombe
Hestercombe House
Fire HQ
Gdns
Gotton
Monkton House
Overton
West Monkton
Noah's Hill
RED HILL
THE STREET
BOONE LA
HESTERCOMBE RD
CHEDDON LAWNS
Goosenford
Cheddon Fitzpaine
TA2
Sidbrook
A3259
Monkton Elm
Langaller
Monkton Heathfield
Tanpitts Farm
Maidenbrook
Bathpool
Hyde Farm
Schs
PH
SCHOOL RD
BRIDGWATER RD
YALLANDS HILL
213
VENTURE WAY
PROGRESS DR
WATERLEZE
TONEWAY
Halcon
ROMAN RD
HAMILTON RD
A38
A358
Hotel
LC
TA1
Hofway
Sp Ctr
Haydon
HAYDON LA
213
Shoreditch
Broughton Farm
Cherry Grove
The White House
STOKE RD
STOKE LA
1 BLUEBELL CL
2 HEATHER CL
3 CELANDINE MEAD
4 ORCHID CL
5 BILBERRY GR
BROUGHTON PK
BROUGHTON LA
Stoke St Mary
Stoke Hill
Stoke House
PH
CHURCH CL
WEST VIEW
MILL LA
WHITELEAZE LA
A38
Adsborough
PH
ADSBOROUGH HILL
WALFORD CROSS ROADS
A361
Walford
Walford House
WALFORD HILL
Langaller
NEW LA
HEATHFIELD CL
North End
Creechwood Terr
CREECHWOOD TERR
SOUTH END
WEST END
WORTHY LA
Foxhole
Creech St Michael
CURVALION RD
CURVALION HOUSE GDNS
TRISTRAM DR
River Tone
Creech Mill Est
Creech Paper Mill
MILL LA
BULL ST
OVERLANDS
CHEATS RD
RUISHTON LANE COTTS
25
A358
Ruishton
Ruishton Court
THE ORCHARD
IVY HOUSE PK
OLD BRICK CL
GRANGE LA
STEART GDNS
ALEXEVIA CVN PK
THE GROVE
Works
Lower Farm
Henlade
THORN LA
Arundell's Farm
Henlade House
Dairy House Farm
PATTENS
WHITES OROL
CHURCH OROL
PH
TA7
Tuckerton
Lower Rydon Farm
Rydon Farm
Rydon
West Newton
MANOR FARM BARNS
Primmore Corner
Higher Durston
Lower Durston
Durston
A361
Froglane Farm
CH
Theats Farm
Charlton PH Road Cotts
CHARLTON RD
Creech Heathfield
FRANCIS CROSSWAY
EMERSON CROSSWAY
Charlton
West Moor
Bridgwater & Taunton Canal
Bird's Farm
Knapp
KNAPP RD
Ham
HAM HILL
TA3
COWLEAZE DRO
1 CORONATION CL
2 NEWLANDS CRES
3 NEWLANDS GR
4 CARPENTERS CL
5 LAWN MDW
6 BOONS ORCH
7 MOSS LA
8 MARTINS
9 VIRGINIA ORCH
10 WOODLANDS DR
Sewage Works
New Barn
Thornfalcon
Thorn Hill
ASH CROSS
Stony Head
PH
MATTOCK'S TREE HILL
A378
STONEYHEAD CVN PK
STONEYHEAD
Lillesdon Court
SOLOMON'S HOLLOW
Ash
Bath House Farm
Meare Green
A358

Creech St Michael area:
1 COOKS CL
2 ALEXANDER CL
3 PADDOCK CL
4 HOMEFIELD CL
5 ST MICHAEL CL
6 VICARAGE LAWNS
7 CARAY GR
8 KINGDON MEAD
9 POWELL CL
13 LABURNUM TERR
14 MILL COTTS
15 SYCAMORE WLK
16 VICARAGE CL

For full street detail of the highlighted area see page 213.

182 170

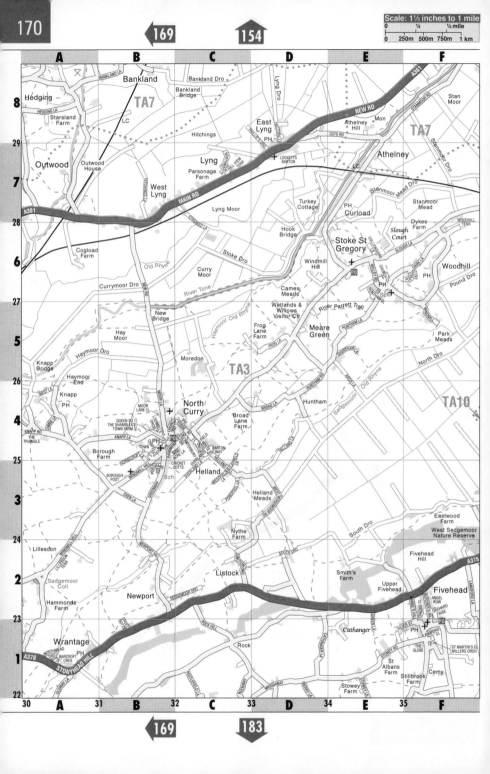

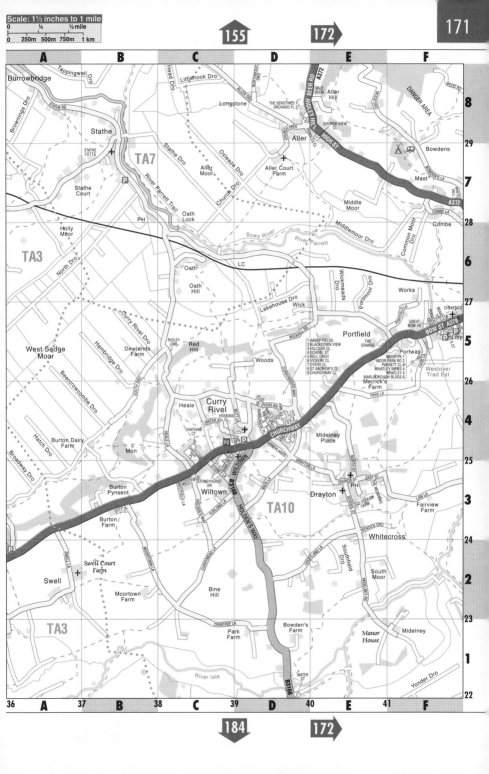

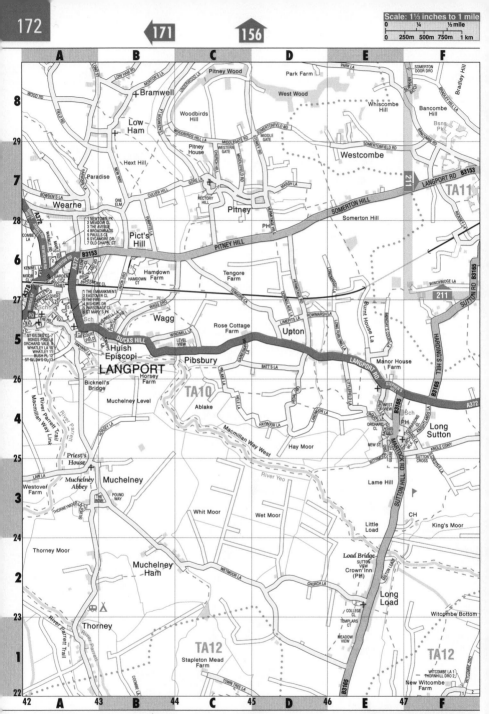

Scale: 1⅓ inches to 1 mile

171
156

A B C D E F

8
29
7
28
6
27
5
26
4
25
3
24
2
23
1
22

Bramwell

Low Ham

Pitney Wood
Woodbirds Hill
Pitney House
Hext Hill
Paradise
Wearhe
Pict's Hill
Pitney
Rectory Hill

Park Farm
West Wood
Whiscombe Hill
Bancombe Hill
Westcombe

Langport Rd
TA11
B3153
211

Somerton Hill
Somerton Hill

PH

One Elm

1 NEWTOWN PK
2 MEADOW GL
3 THE AVENUE
4 BROADMEADS
5 PAULS CE
6 SYCAMORE DR
7 OLD CHAPEL CT

B3153

Pitney Hill

Hamdown Farm
Tengore Farm

Wagg
Rose Cottage Farm
Upton

Windyridge La
B3165
211

Sutton Rd

Harding's Hill
B3165

Huish Episcopi
LANGPORT
Pibsbury
Bicknell's Bridge
Horsey Farm

Ducks Hill

Muchelney Level
Ablake
TA10

Manor House Farm
West View
Long Sutton
Sutton Cross

A372

Priest's House
Muchelney Abbey
Muchelney

Macmillan Way West
Hay Moor
Lame Hill

CH
King's Moor

Westover Farm

Thorney Moor
Muchelney Ham

Whit Moor
Wet Moor

River Yeo

Little Load

Load Bridge
Sutton View
Crown Inn (PH)

Long Load

Witcombe Bottom

Thorney

TA12
Stapleton Mead Farm

COLLEGE CL
TEMPLARS CT
MEADOW VIEW

New Witcombe Farm
TA12
WITCOMBE LA 1
THORNHILL DRO 2

42 A 43 B 44 C 45 D 46 E 47 F

171
185

For full street detail of the highlighted area see page 211.

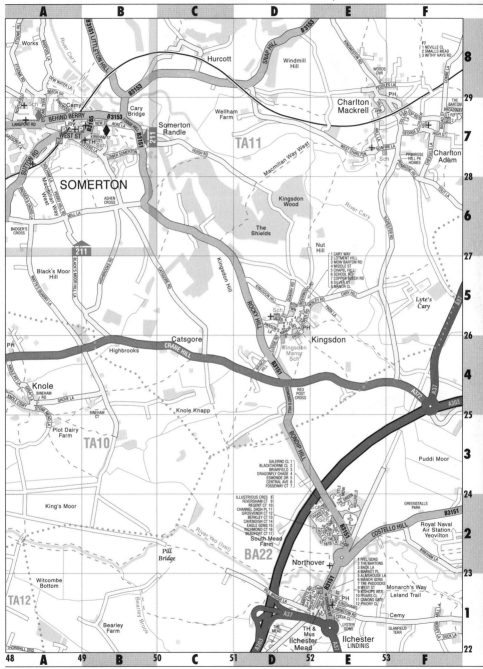

Scale: 1⅓ inches to 1 mile

157
174

SOMERTON

Hurcott

Windmill Hill

Snap Hill

Charlton Mackrell

Charlton Adam

Cary Bridge

Somerton Randle

TA11

Wellham Farm

Macmillan Way West

Kingsdon Wood

River Cary

Lyte's Cary

The Shields

Nut Hill

1 CARY WAY
2 LOTMENT HILL
3 MOW BARTON RD
4 MIDDLE ST
5 CHAPEL HILL
6 SCHOOL RD
7 COPPER BEECH RD
8 SILVER ST
9 MANOR CL

Black's Moor Hill

211

Catsgore

CRANE HILL

Kingsdon Hill

ROCKY HILL

Kingsdon

Kingsdon Manor Sch

Highbrooks

Knole

Knole Knapp

RED POST CROSS

A37

A372

A303

TA10

Plot Dairy Farm

Bineham CT

BONDIP HILL

SALERNO CL 1
BLACKTHORNE CL 2
BRIARFIELD 3
DRAGONFLY CHASE 4
ESMONDE DR 5
CENTRAL AVE 6
FOSSEWAY CT 7

Puddi Moor

King's Moor

ILLUSTRIOUS CRES 8
FEVERSHAM CT 9
REGENT CT 10
CHANNEL DASH PL 11
GROSVENOR CT 12
BERKLEY CT 13
CAVENDISH CT 14
EAGLE GDNS 15
RICHMOND CT 16
BEAUFORT CT 17

GREENSTALLS PARK

B3151

Royal Naval Air Station Yeovilton

River Yeo (Ivel)

South Mead Farm

BA22

Northover

1 IVEL GDNS
2 THE BARTONS
3 BACK LA
4 MARKET PL
5 ALMSHOUSE LA
6 MANOR GDNS
7 THE PADDOCKS
8 WEST ST
9 BISHOPS WTX
10 FRIARS CL
11 CANONS GATE
12 PRIORY CL

Monarch's Way
Leland Trail

Pill Bridge

Witcombe Bottom

Bearley Brook

TA12

Cemy

Ilchester LINDINIS

Ilchester Mead

TH & Mus

Bearley Farm

THORNHILL DRO

186
174

For full street detail of the highlighted area see page 211.

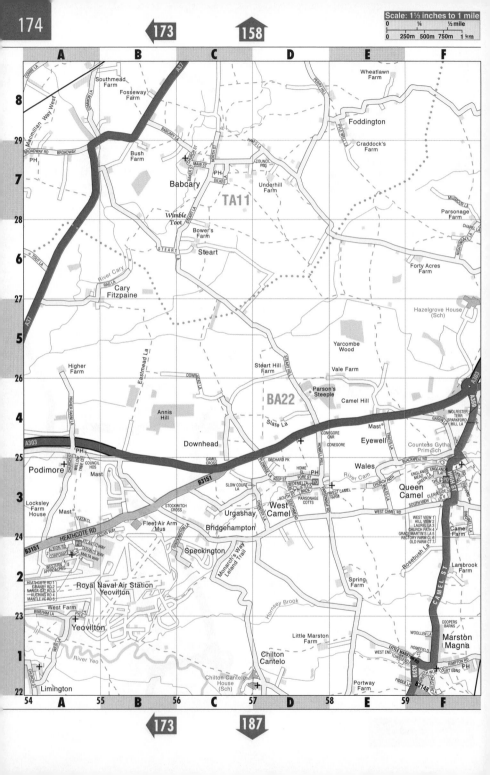

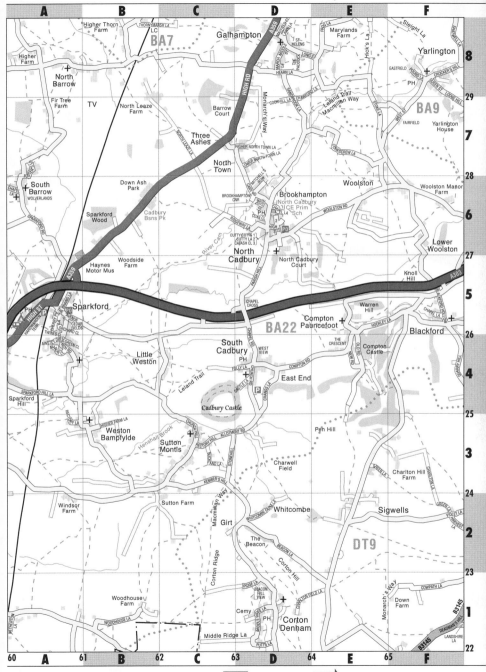

Higher Thorn Farm
THORNY MARSH LA
LC
BA7
Galhampton
ST HELENS
HIGH RD
Maryland's Farm
Sleight La
Yarlington
Higher Farm
North Barrow
Fir Tree Farm
TV
North Leaze Farm
Barrow Court
Monarch's Way
COOKHILL LA
HEARN LA
LONG ST
PADDOCK
Hick's La
CROCKER'S HILL
EASTFIELD
POUND LA
WEST ST
PH
GREEN ST / LOOSE HILL
BA9
Yarlington House
FAIRFIELD
8
29
7
Three Ashes
NORTH CADBURY LA
HIGHER NORTH TOWN LA
North Town
OVER NORTH TOWN LA
Leland Trail
Macmillan Way
CORKSCREW LA
Woolston
28
6
Down Ash Park
Sparkford Wood
Cadbury Bsns Pk
BROOKHAMPTON CNR
ST MITCHELL'S PATH
Brookhampton
North Cadbury CE Prim Sch
PH
PO
North Cadbury
CUTTY COTTS 1
CUTTY LA 2
CATASH CL 3
RIDGEWAY LA
River Cam
HIGH LA
WOOLSTON RD
Woolston Manor Farm
Lower Woolston
27
5
Haynes Motor Mus
A359
Woodside Farm
North Cadbury Court
Knoll Hill
A303
Sparkford
PH ST
HIGH ST
CEDAR FIELDS
CHURCH HILL
GREEN CL
TWINES
AINSLEY RD
CHAPEL CROSS
North Cadbury Court
Warren Hill
Compton Pauncefoot
HOCKLEY LA
BLACKFORD LA
CHAPEL LA
Blackford
26
4
Little Weston
AVENUE
South Cadbury
WEST VIEW
PH
FULLY LA
Leland Trail
East End
COMPTON RD
THE CRESCENT
Compton Castle
OLD RD
HIGH RD
Sparkford Hill LA
Sparkford Hill
RECTORY LA
Weston Bampfylde
HIGHER FARM LA
CHURCH HILL
Henshall Brook
Sutton Montis
Cadbury Castle
RECTORY HILL
ALLOTMENT RD
CASTLE LA
CHAPEL LA
Pen Hill
25
3
LAND LA
STONEHILL
KEMBER'S HILL
Charwell Field
SPEEN LA
Charlton Hill Farm
CHARLTON RD
24
2
Windsor Farm
Sutton Farm
Macmillan Way
WHITCOMBE FITTN LA
Girt
Whitcombe
Sigwells
GREEN LA
VIOLET LA
SWEET ST
DT9
23
1
Woodhouse Farm
Corton Ridge
The Beacon
RIDGE LA
BEACON LA
Corton Hill
Cemy
BEACON HILL VIEW
PH
CORTON FIELD LA
Corton Denham
Monarch's Way
COWPATH LA
Down Farm
B3145
DEADMAN'S LA
LANDSHIRE LA
22
WOODHOUSE LA
Middle Ridge La
PUTTS LA

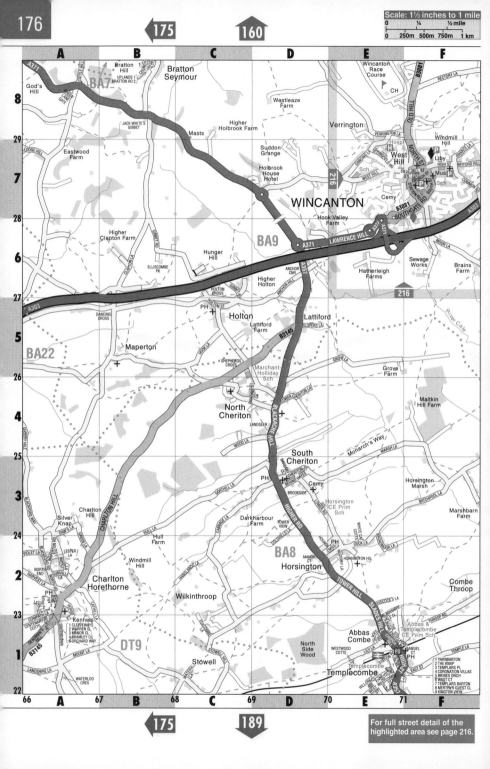

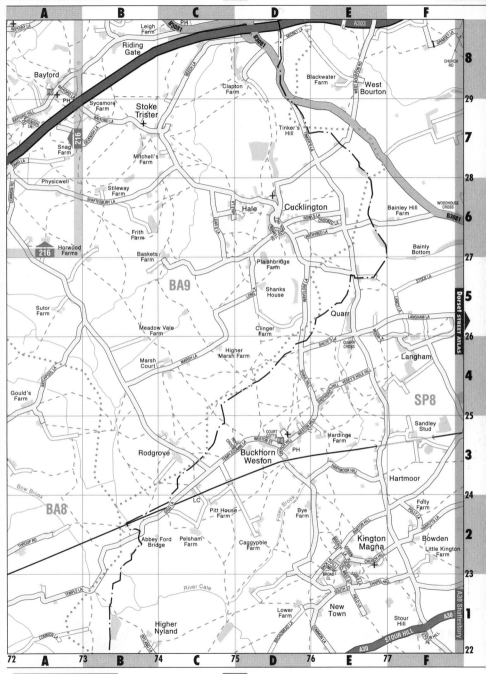

Scale: 1⅓ inches to 1 mile

0   ¼   ½ mile
0   250m 500m 750m 1 km

A B C D E F

8
29
7
28
6
27
5
26
4
25
3
24
2
23
1
22

RECTORY LA

Bayford

PO
PH

BAYFORD HILL
DEVENISH LA

Snag Farm

SNAG LA

Physicwell

COMMON RD

216

216
Horwood Farms

Sutor Farm

Gould's Farm

BATCOOL LA

BA8

Bow Brook

THROOP RD

TEMPLE LA

COMMON LA

Leigh Farm

Riding Gate

B3081
PH

Sycamore Farm

Stoke Trister

BAYFORD LA
DEVENISH LA

BEECH LA

Mitchell's Farm

Stileway Farm

SHAFTESBURY LA

Frith Farm

EARS LA

Baskets Farm

Meadow Vale Farm

Marsh Court

MARSH LA

Rodgrove

Abbey Ford Bridge

GIBB LA

Pelsham Farm

INCHES LA

Higher Nyland

Clapton Farm

B3081

Hale

LANE LA

HALE LA

Plaishbridge Farm

Shanks House

LONG LA

Clinger Farm

Higher Marsh Farm

WHITCLOSE LA

LC

Pitt House Farm

Caggypole Farm

River Cale

BROADMEAD LA

A303

MIDKEY LA

Blackwater Farm

Tinker's Hill

TINKER'S LA

West Bourton

WINTERTON RD

Cucklington

ROWLS LA
CROOKED LA
WITHYRED LA

Quarr

SHUTE'S LA

QUARR CROSS

SHEPHERD'S HILL
STOKE HILL

SHUTE HILL
VESEY'S HOLE LA

COURT COTTS
WESTON ST
PO

Buckhorn Weston
CHURCH LA
PH

Hardings Farm

WESTON RD

HARTMOOR HILL

Filley Brook

Bye Farm

BARTON HILL

Lower Farm

COMMON LA

New Town

Kington Magna
BLACK LA
SOUTH ST
CHURCH HILL
CHAPEL LA
FRED LA
PURSE LA
BROAD CL

GRANGE LA

CHURCH RD

BAINLEY HILL FARM

WOODHOUSE CROSS
B3081

Bainly Bottom

STOCK LA

LARCH LA

LANGHAM LA

Langham

MOOR LA

SP8

Sandley Stud

Hartmoor

Folly Farm
FOLLY LA
HARPITRE LA

Bowden

Little Kington Farm

Stour Hill

STOUR HILL
A30

COW HILL
COW PK

A30 Shaftesbury

Dorset Street Atlas

190

For full street detail of the highlighted area see page 216.

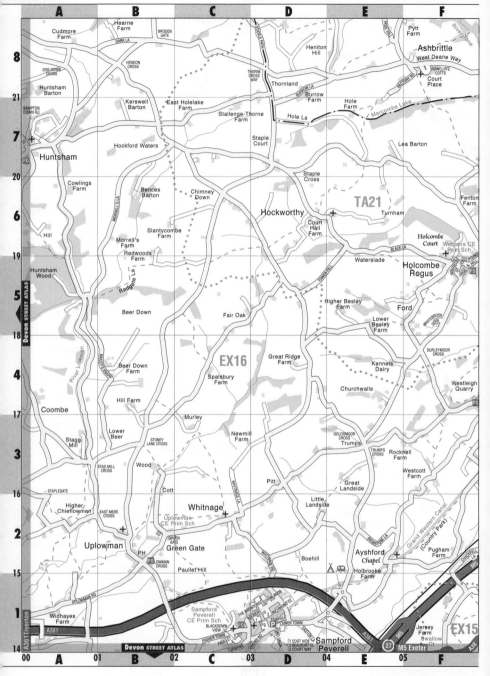

Scale: 1⅓ inches to 1 mile

0   ¼   ½ mile
0   250m   500m   750m   1 km

165

Scale: 1⅓ inches to 1 mile

0   ¼   ½ mile
0 250m 500m 750m 1 km

166

180

179

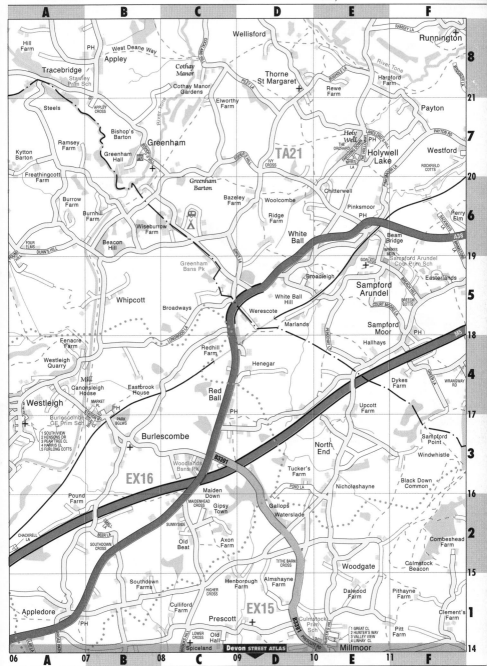

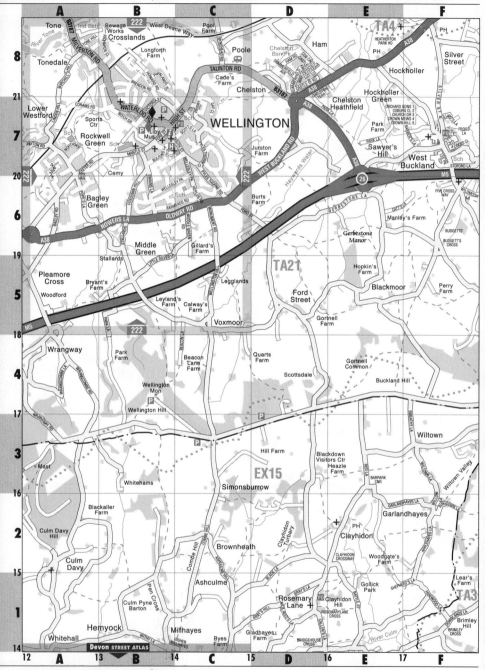

Devon STREET ATLAS

For full street detail of the highlighted area see page 222.

Scale: 1½ inches to 1 mile

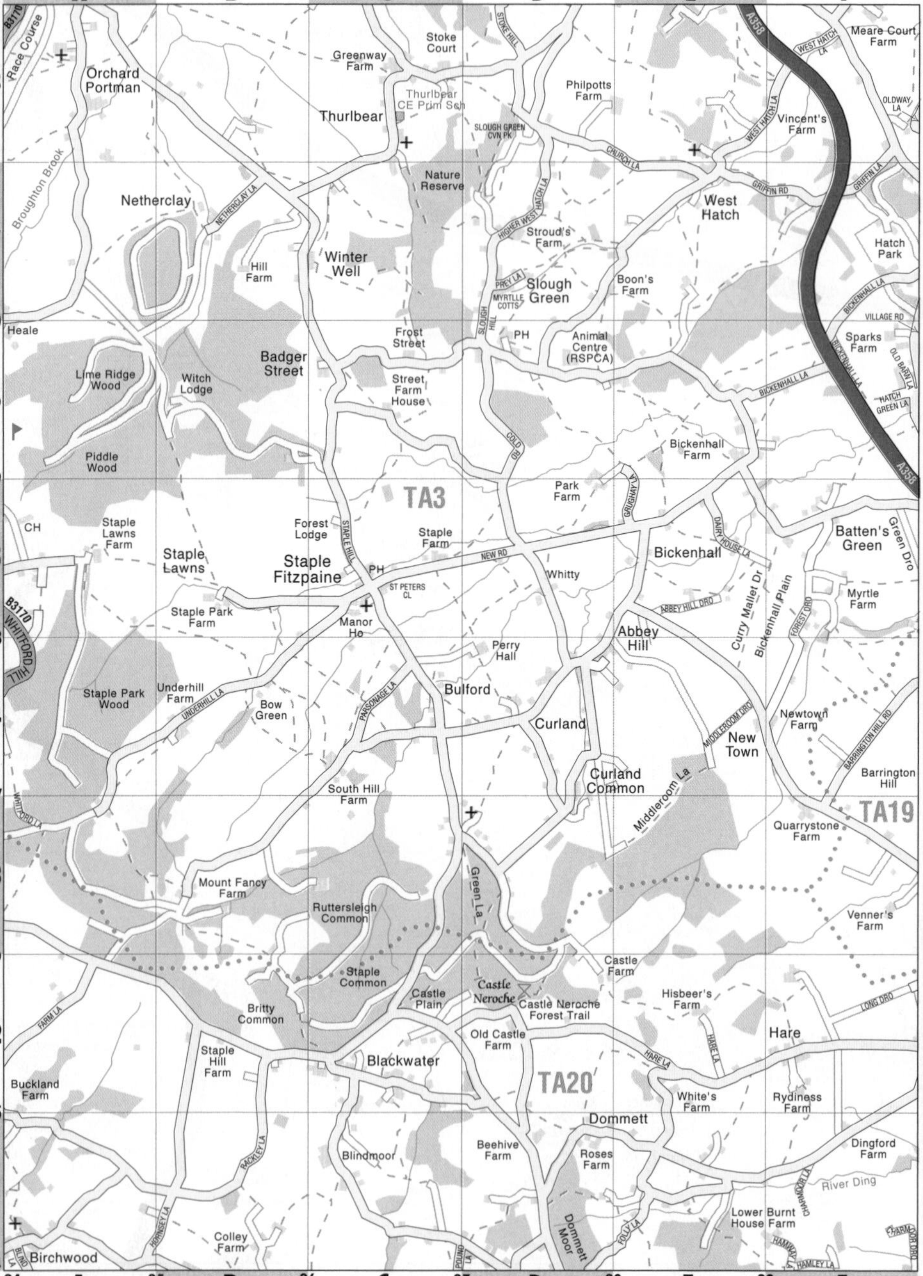

0   ¼   ½ mile
0   250m   500m   750m   1 km

A   B   C   D   E   F

Race Course
Orchard Portman
Greenway Farm
Stoke Court
Thurlbear CE Prim Sch
Philpotts Farm
Meare Court Farm
WEST HATCH LA
OLDWAY LA
Vincent's Farm
Thurlbear
8
SLOUGH GREEN CVN PK
Netherclay
NETHERCLAY LA
Nature Reserve
21
West Hatch
GRIFFIN RD
GRIFFIN LA
Hill Farm
Winter Well
Stroud's Farm
UPPER WEST HATCH LA
CHURCH LA
Hatch Park
7
Slough Green
Boon's Farm
PREY LA
MYRTLE COTTS
Frost Street
SLOUGH HILL
PH
Animal Centre (RSPCA)
Sparks Farm
VILLAGE RD
BICKENHALL LA
OLD MANOR LA
20
Heale
Badger Street
Street Farm House
HATCH GREEN LA
6
Lime Ridge Wood
Witch Lodge
COLD BDY
Bickenhall Farm
BICKENHALL LA
19
Piddle Wood
Park Farm
PARKHOUSE LA
TA3
Batten's Green
GREEN DRO
CH
Staple Lawns Farm
Forest Lodge
Staple Farm
NEW RD
Bickenhall
DAIRY HOUSE LA
5
Staple Fitzpaine
STAPLE HILL LA
PH
St Peters CL
Whitty
CURRY MALLET DR
BICKENHALL PLAIN
Myrtle Farm
18
Staple Lawns
Staple Park Farm
Manor Ho
ABBEY HILL DRO
Abbey Hill
FOREST DRO
B3170 WHITFORD HILL
UNDERHILL LA
Perry Hall
Newtown Farm
BARRINGTON HILL RD
4
Staple Park Wood
Underhill Farm
Bow Green
PASSAGE LA
Bulford
Curland
MIDDLEROOM DRO
New Town
Barrington Hill
South Hill Farm
Curland Common
17
Middleroom La
TA19
Quarrystone Farm
WHITTY LA
3
Mount Fancy Farm
Ruttersleigh Common
GREEN LA
Venner's Farm
LONG DRO
16
Staple Common
Castle Plain
Castle Farm
Castle Neroche
Hisbeer's Farm
FARM LA
2
Britty Common
Castle Neroche Forest Trail
Hare
Staple Hill Farm
Old Castle Farm
TA20
HARE LA
White's Farm
Rydiness Farm
Dingford Farm
15
Buckland Farm
BADGER LA
Blackwater
Dommett
CHARD RD
River Ding
Blindmoor
Beehive Farm
Roses Farm
Lower Burnt House Farm
HAMLEY LA
1
Birchwood
Colley Farm
FOLLY LA
Dommett Moor
PRY LA
HAMLEY LA
14

24   A   25   B   26   C   27   D   28   E   29   F

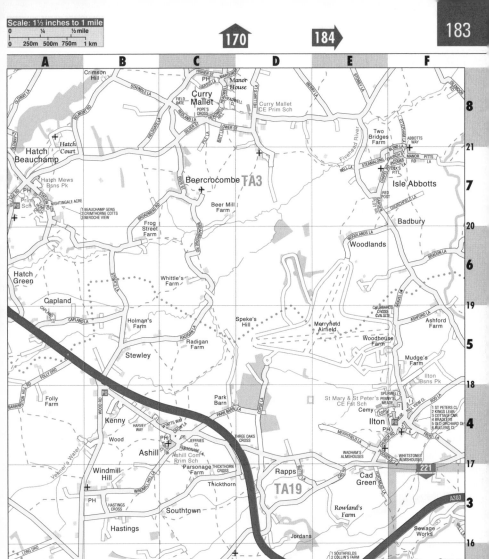

Scale: 1⅓ inches to 1 mile

0   ¼   ½ mile
0   250m 500m 750m 1 km

170

184

183

A   B   C   D   E   F

8

Crimson Hill

HIGHER ST
HARRIS LA
MARSHWAY
BERRY LA

Curry Mallet
PH
Manor House
POPE'S CROSS
FIELD GATE
HASWELL

BEDLAND LA
SILVER ST
LOWER ST

Curry Mallet CE Prim Sch

BEERLEY LA
STONELL LA

Two Bridges Farm

LITTERHILL LA
ABBOTTS WAY
BLIND LA
MANOR RD
PITTS LA

21

Hatch Beauchamp
Hatch Court

Hatch Mews Bsns Pk
Prim Sch
PH
PO
NIGHTINGALE ACRE
1 BEAUCHAMP GDNS
2 CRIMTHORNE COTTS
3 NEROCHE VIEW

STANDLE LA

BEERCROMBE RD

Beercrocombe
Beer Mill Farm

Fivehead River
BELL LA
STEAMALONG LA
CHURCH LA
PROMES
FOX'S PITTS
POT HILL
RED POST

Isle Abbotts

CHURCHELS LA

TA3

7

Frog Street Farm

BROADWEY RD

Badbury

WOODLANDS LA
BRADON LA

20

Hatch Green

Capland

CAPLAND LA

Holman's Farm

Whittle's Farm

RADIGAN LA

Speke's Hill

Woodlands

Merryfield Airfield

Woodhouse Farm

CHURCH LA
ASHFORD LA

CURBRAKO'S CROSS CVN SITE

Ashford Farm

6

19

Stewley

Radigan Farm

Mudge's Farm

Ilton Bsns Pk

5

18

Folly Farm

BARRINGTON HILL RD

Vehno's Water

WOOD RD

Kenny

HARVEY WAY

Wood

WYATTS WAY
DREWS LA

PH
JEFFRIES CL
PARSONAGE
Ashill Com Prim Sch

Park Barn

PARK BARN LA

COLLEY LA

THREE OAKS CROSS

St Mary & St Peter's CE Fst Sch

Cemy

MERRYFIELD LA

WADHAM'S ALMSHOUSES

SPURWELL LA
PENNY B. MEADE
HILL VIEW RD

CROSS

Ilton
PH
PO

1 ST PETERS CL
2 KINGS LEAB
3 COTTAGE CNR
4 BRADLEYS
5 OLD ORCHARD CL
6 BUCLENS CL

FROST LA

WHETSTONE'S ALMSHOUSES

4

17

Windmill Hill

PH

HASTINGS CROSS

WINDMILL HILL LA

Ashill

Parsonage Farm

THICKTHORN CROSS

Thickthorn

Southtown

Rapps

TA19

Cad Green

BUTT LA

221

3

Hastings

Jordans

Rowland's Farm

A303

Sewage Works

16

LONG DRO

Hare Farm

Newhouse Farm

HARE LA

Broadway

Neroche Prim Sch

STOFORD LA
SOUTH VIEW
ELM ST
CLARKS LA

BROADWAY RD

1 SOUTHFIELDS
2 COLLIN'S FARM

Horton Cross

A358

Motel

PH

RIVER ISLE

HOME FARM PK
GREEN LA
HOLWAY
HOLWAY HOUSE

221

B3168

Winterhay Green

BEACON
NEW RD
B3168

Cemy

2

15

Hermitage Farm

TORS MILL LA

LANG'S CNR

FIVE DIALS

TROTTS LA

BROOKSIDE
TANYARD
1 CARLAN STEPPS
2 HANNING PK
3 STANDERWICK ORCH
4 RIVERSIDE

Horton
PH
PO

POTTERY VIEW

SHAVE LA

Puddlebridge

CHESHAY'S HILL

PH

Rose Mills Ind Est

STATION RD

PH

Ind Est
Westcombe Trad Est

Cold Harbour

Hotel
P

CANAL WAY

THE MEAD

1

14

Two Waters Farm

TA20

A303

DUALS

Shave Farm

Almshouses 1 Church St 2

DONYATT HILL EST

Donyatt

A358

PARK LA

1 BROADOAK
2 ST PETER'S CL
3 SWELL CL
4 HANNING RD
5 SLADYS ORCH
6 LANGWORTHY ORCH

DONYATT HILL

PH

ILMINSTER

30   A   31   B   32   C   33   D   34   E   35   F

193

For full street detail of the highlighted area see page 221.

194

184

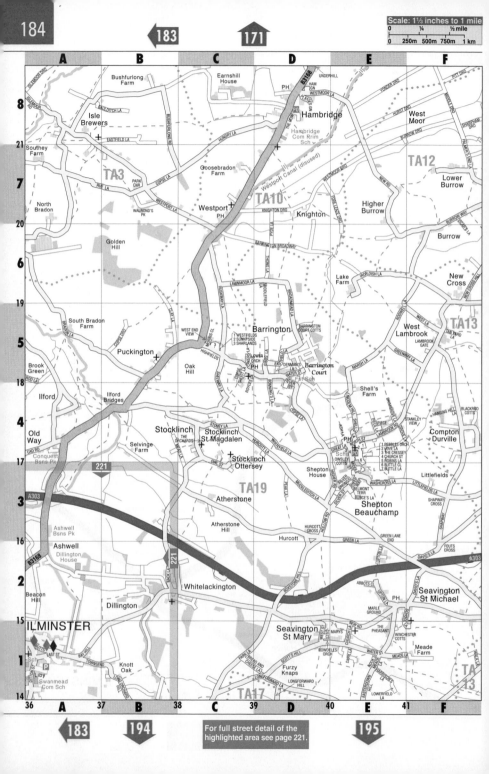

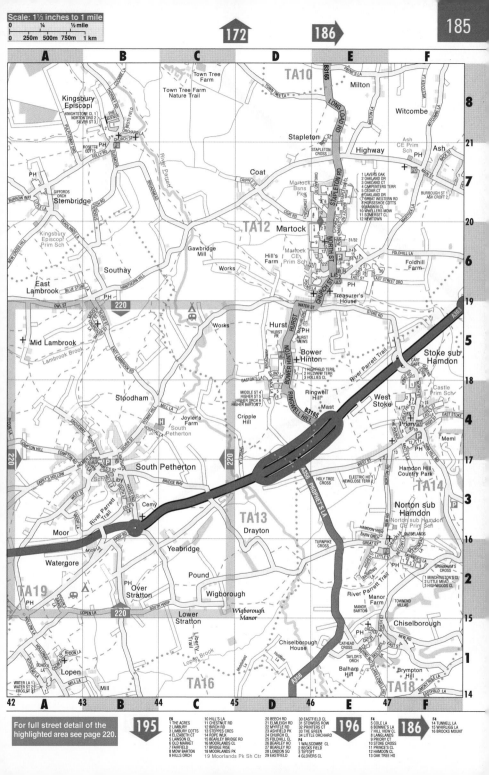

Scale: 1½ inches to 1 mile

0 ¼ ½ mile

0 250m 500m 750m 1 km

172

186

185

TA10

Milton

Witcombe

Kingsbury Episcopi

KNIGHTSTONE CL 1
NORTON ORD 2
SILVER ST 3

ORCHARD LA
CHURCH ST

PH

ROSETTE COTTS

PH

Town Tree Farm

Town Tree Farm Nature Trail

Stapleton

Coat

Highway

Ash CE Prim Sch

Ash

PH

BURROUGH ST 1
ASH CROFT 2

GIFFORDS ORCH

Stembridge

PH

East Lambrook

BLUE STONE LA

Southay

Gawbridge Mill

Works

Kingsbury Episcopi Prim Sch

TA12

Martock

Martock Bsns Pk

Hill's Farm

Martock CE Prim Sch

Liby

1 LAVERS OAK
2 OAKLAND DR
3 OAKLAND CT
4 CARPENTERS TERR
5 CEDAR CT
6 OAKLAND DR
7 GREAT WESTERN RD
8 HORSESHOE COTTS
9 BARWIN CL
10 WHEELERS MDW
11 SOMERSET CL
12 NEWTOWN

31/32

34

Foldhill La

Foldhill Farm

Treasurer's House

220

Mid Lambrook

Lambrook Brook

Stoodham

Works

Joyler's Farm

South Petherton

H

Cripple Hill

HURST PK

Hurst

PH

HURST MEWS

Bower Hinton

1 HIGHFIELD TERR
2 HILTMEW TERR
3 HOLLIES CL

MIDDLE ST 4
HIGHER ST 5
HIGHER ORCH 6
HIGHER BARTON 7

Ringwell Hill

B3165

Mast

River Parrett Trail

Stoke sub Hamdon

West Stoke

Castle Prim Sch

EAST STOKE

Priory

PH

Meml

A303

220

220

Sch

Liby

P

BRIDGE WAY

Cemy

River Parrett Trail

Moor

TA13

Drayton

Yeabridge

Pound

HOLY TREE CROSS

ELECTRIC HO 1
NEWCLOSE TERR 2

Hamdon Hill Country Park

TA14

Norton sub Hamdon

Norton sub Hamdon CE Prim Sch

BLEBLANDS

HAMDON VIEW
BARN ORCH

TURNPIKE CROSS

GREAT ST

TA19

PH

Watergore

Over Stratton

PH

Wigborough

Lower Stratton

220

SOUTH HARP

Wigborough Manor

1 MINCHINGTON'S CL
2 LITTLE MEAD
3 HIGHWOODS CL

GREENHAM'S CROSS

Manor Farm

MANOR BARTON

River Parrett Trail

TOWNEND VILLAS

Chiselborough

CHISELBOROUGH CROSS

CATHEAD CROSS

TAYLOR'S ORCH

NEW RD

Lopen

SCHOOL LA

MILL RD

WATER LA 1
WATER ST 2
FROG ST 3

Mill

TA16

Chiselborough House

Holdfast La

Liberty Trail

Lopen Brook

Balham Hill

Brympton Hill

TA18

42 A 43 B 44 C 45 D 46 E 47 F

195

196

186

E6
1 THE ACRES
2 LIMBURY
3 LIMBURY COTTS
4 ELIZABETH CT
5 LAWSON CL
6 OLD MARKET
7 FAIRFIELD
8 MOW BARTON
9 HILLS ORCH

10 HILL'S LA
11 CHESTNUT RD
12 BIRCH RD
13 STEPPES CRES
14 ROPE WLK
15 BEARLEY BRIDGE RD
16 MOORLANDS CL
17 BRIDGE RISE
18 MOORLANDS PK
19 Moorlands Pk Sh Ctr

20 BEECH RD
21 ELMLEIGH RD
22 MYRTLE RD
23 ASHFIELD PK
24 CHURCH CL
25 FOLDHILL CL
26 BEARLEY HO
27 BEARLEY RD
28 LONDON SQ
29 EASTFIELD

30 EASTFIELD CL
31 STOWERS ROW
32 PRINTERS CT
33 THE GREEN
34 LITTLE ORCHARD
F4
1 WALSCOMBE CL
2 BECKS FIELD
3 TIPTOFT
4 GLOVERS CL

F4
5 COLE LA
6 BONNIE'S LA
7 HILL VIEW CL
8 LANGLANDS
9 PRIORY CT
10 STOKE CROSS
11 PRINCE'S CL
12 HAMDON CL
13 OAK TREE HO

F4
14 TUNNELL LA
15 WHIRLIGIG LA
16 BROOKS MOUNT

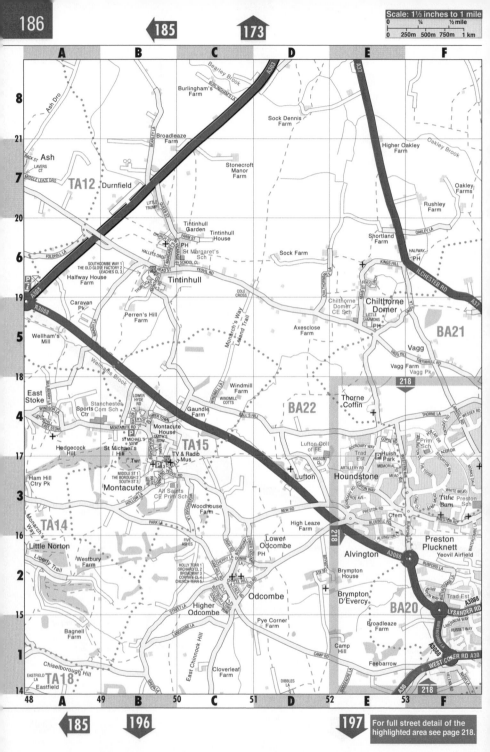

185
173

Scale: 1⅓ inches to 1 mile

0 ¼ ½ mile
0 250m 500m 750m 1 km

8

21

7

20

6

19

5

18

4

17

3

16

2

15

1

14

A 48 B 49 50 C 51 D 52 E 53 F

Ash Dro

Bearley Brook

Burlingham's Farm

BURLINGHAM LA

A303

Sock Dennis Farm

Higher Oakley Farm

Oakley Brook

BEARLEY LA

Broadleaze Farm

Stonecroft Manor Farm

Oakley Farms

BACK ST

Ash

LAVERS CT

MIDDLE LEAZE DRO

TA12 Durnfield

LITTLE TRUMPS

Rushley Farm

Tintinhull Garden

FARM ST

Tintinhull House

Shortland Farm

OAKLEY LA

CHURCH ST

PH

St Margaret's Sch

Sock Farm

ILCHESTER RD

HALFWAY

PH

Kings Hill

A37

FOLDHILL LA

HALLETS ORCH

SCHOOL CL

YEOVIL RD

FOX LUCH

SOUTHCOMBE WAY 1
THE OLD GLOVE FACTORY 2
LEACHES CL 3

HEAD ST

Tintinhull

CHILTHORNE RD

Chilthorne Domer CE Sch

Chilthorne Domer

Halfway House Farm

THORNELL A

COLE CROSS

LITTLE SAMMONS

PH

BA21

A3088

A303

Caravan Pk

Perren's Hill Farm

Axesclose Farm

Vagg

FROGS HILL

TINTINHULL RD

A37

Wellham's Mill

Monarch's Way
Leland Trail

Vagg Farm
Vagg Pk

Wellhams Brook

Windmill Farm

218

East Stoke

MULBERRY LA

Stanchester Sports Com Sch

LOWER HYDE RD

Windmill Cotts

BALL'S HILL

BA22

Thorne Coffin

THORNE LA

WESSEX RD

WINDSOR LA
EAST STOKE

MONTACUTE RD

HYDE RD

Gaundle Farm

Prim Sch

ACER DR

STOURTON WAY

Hedgecock Hill

St Michael's View

ST MICHAEL'S Montacute House
SMITH'S ROW

TA15

Lufton Coll of FE

BOUNDARY WAY

Huish Park

MEMORIAL

St Michael's Hill

Twr

TV & Radio Mus

HIGSON CL

Trad Est
ARTILLERY RD

MEAD

WHITE MEAD

Tithe Barn

Preston Sch

Ham Hill Ctry Pk

MIDDLE ST 1
THE BOROUGH 2
CORRATE ST 3

P

Lufton

Houndstone

LONG CL

Preston

Montacute

All Saints CE Prim Sch

LUFTON WAY

MONROE AVE

Preston RD

J T PRESTON WAY

HOLLOW LA

Woodhouse Farm

PARK LA

NEW RD

218

Preston RD

Crem

WATERCOMBE LA

TA14

Monarch's Way

FIVE ASHES

High Leaze Farm

Preston Plucknett

Little Norton

Liberty Trail

Westbury Farm

HOLLY TERR 1
ORCHARD CL 2
BROADWAY 3
CORRATE CL 4
CHURCH TERR 5

CHERRY LA

DONNE LA

CHAPEL HILL

Lower Odcombe

PH

Brympton House

Alvington

A3088

ALVINGTON

Yeovil Airfield

BLUMFORD LA

Trad Est

BA20

A3088

Bagnell Farm

STREET LA

LANGDON LA

Higher Odcombe

Odcombe

Pye Corner Farm

Brympton D'Evercy

Camp Hill

Broadleaze Farm

LYSANDER RD

LARBINUM WAY

RUSSET WAY

WATERCOMBE LA

A30

A3088

Chiselborough Hill

EASTFIELD LA

TA18

Eastfield

East Chinnock Hill

GREEN LA

Cloverleaf Farm

DIBBLES LA

CAMP RD

Feebarrow

WEST COKER RD A30

A30

HELYAR RD

218

185
196
197

For full street detail of the highlighted area see page 218.

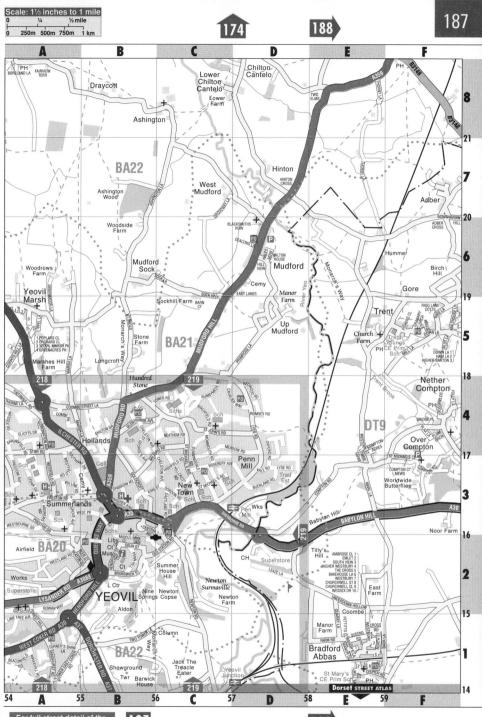

A **B** **C** **D** **E** **F**

8
21
7
20
6
19
5
18
4
17
3
16
2
15
1
14

PH
BORELAND LA
FAIRVIEW TERR

Draycott

Ashington

BA22

Ashington Wood

Woodside Farm

Woodrows Farm

Yeovil Marsh

1 POPLARS CL
2 ORCHARD CL
3 YEOVIL MARSH PK
4 GREENACRES PK

Marshes Hill Farm

Stone Farm

Longcroft

Monarch's Way

Mudford Sock

Sockhill Farm

BARN CT

BA21

Hundred Stone

218   **219**

Lower Chilton Cantelo

Lower Farm

West Mudford

Blacksmiths Row

DEACONS LA

DROVEWAY LA

SOCK HILL

EAST LANES

Cemy

Milton House

HILL VIEW

Mudford

Up Mudford

Manor Farm

River Yeo

Monarch's Way

Chilton Cantelo

TWO ELMS

A359

THORNE LA

Hinton

HINTON CROSS

Hummer

Birch Hill

Gore

Trent

Church Farm

Trent Youngs CE Prim Sch

PH

DOWN LA

RIGG LANE COTTS

DOWN LA 1
HAM LA 2
HIGHER BARTON 3

Adber

ROWBARROW HILL

ADBER CROSS

Nether Compton

PH

DT9

Over Compton

ST MICHAELS CL

COMPTON CT MEWS

Worldwide Butterflies

Trent Brook

BRIDGE PL

PLATTS PLUM

B3148

PH

Hollands

Summerlands

BA20

Airfield

Works

Superstore

New Town

Penn Mill

LYDE RD Trad Est

Pen MLN

Wks

Newton Surmaville

Newton Farm

Summer House Hill

Nine Springs

Newton Copse

YEOVIL

Aldon

Column

Showground

Twr

Barwick House

Jack The Treacle Eater

Yeovil Junction

BA22

218   **219**

CH

Superstore

Babylon Hill

A30

BABYLON HILL

219

Noor Farm

Tilly's Hill

AMBROSE CL 1
EMLET 2
SOUTH VIEW 3
HIGHER WESTBURY 4
THE CROSS 5
BAKEHOUSE LA 6
WESTBURY 7
CHURCHWELL ST 8
CHURCHWELL CL 9
WESSEX DR 10

Coombe

Manor Farm

Bradford Abbas

St Mary's CE Prim Sch

PH

East Farm

Dorset STREET ATLAS

54   **A**   55   **B**   56   **C**   57   **D**   58   **E**   59   **F**

For full street detail of the highlighted area see pages 218 and 219.

197

188

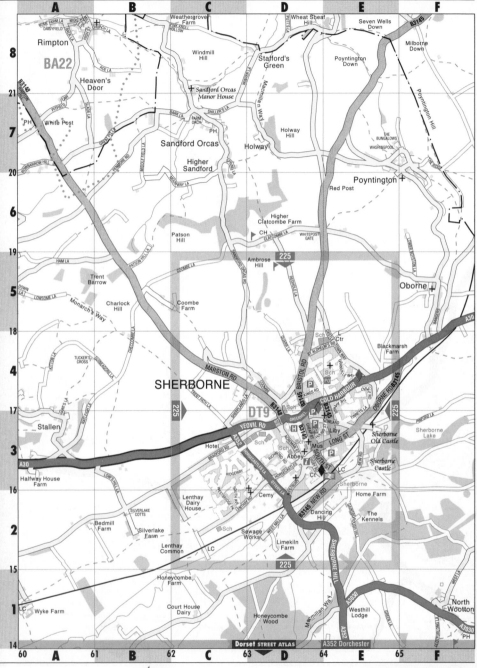

Scale: 1½ inches to 1 mile

For full street detail of the highlighted area see page 225.

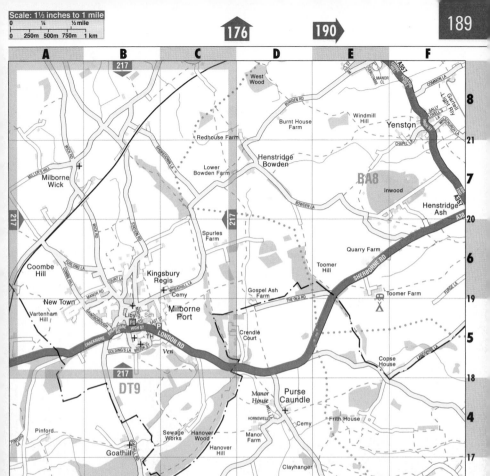

For full street detail of the highlighted area see page 217.

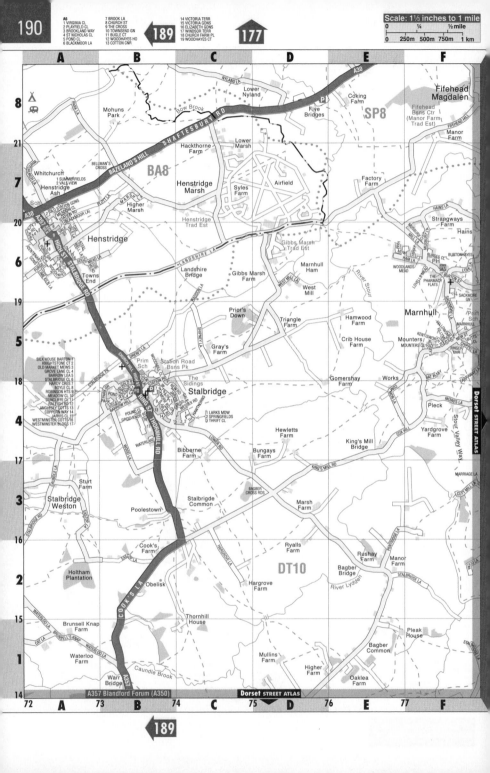

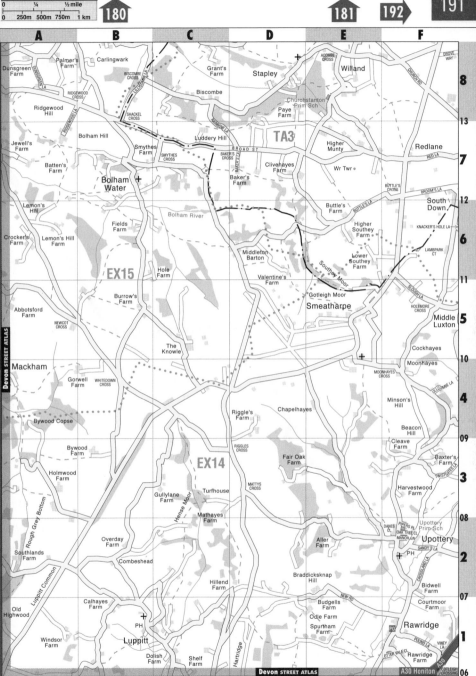

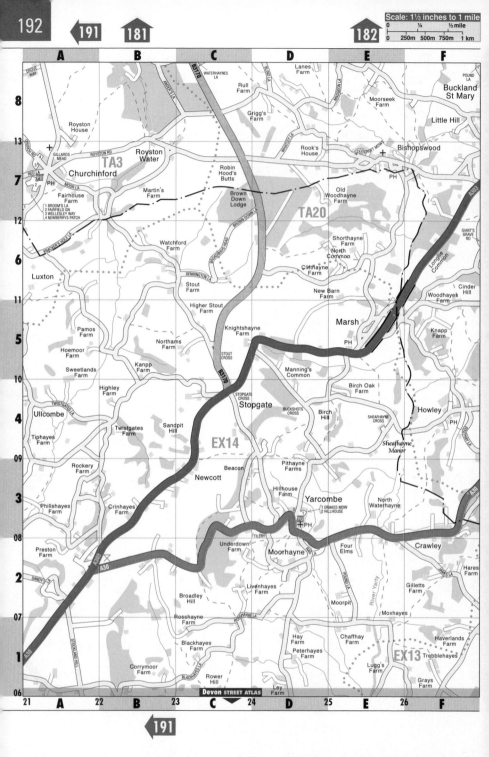

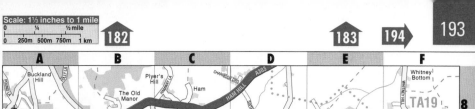

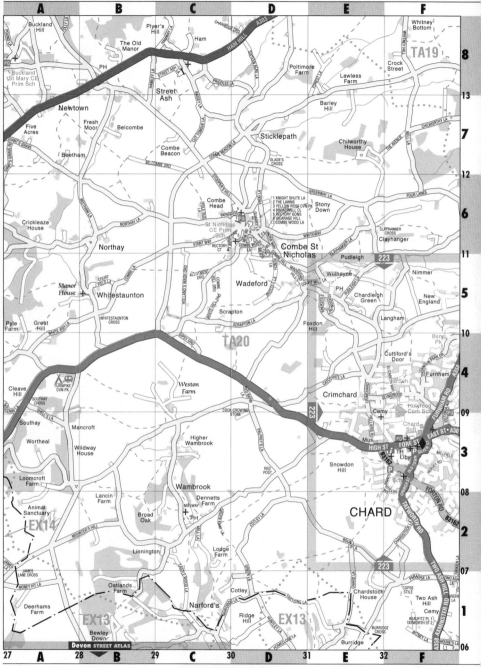

For full street detail of the highlighted area see page 223.

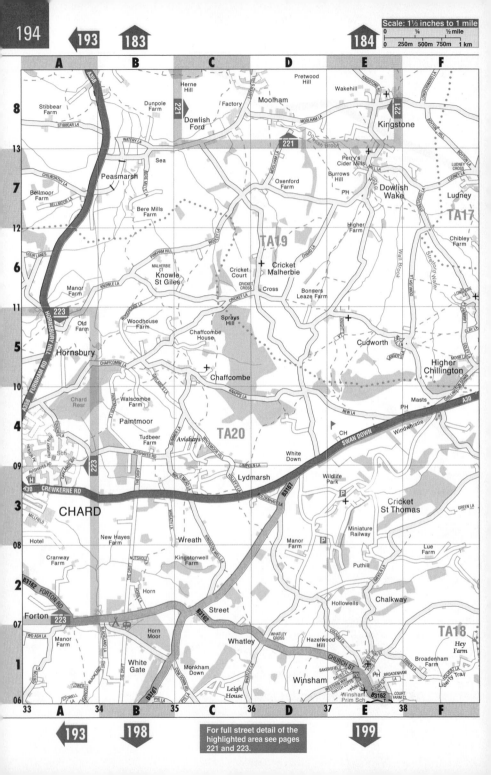

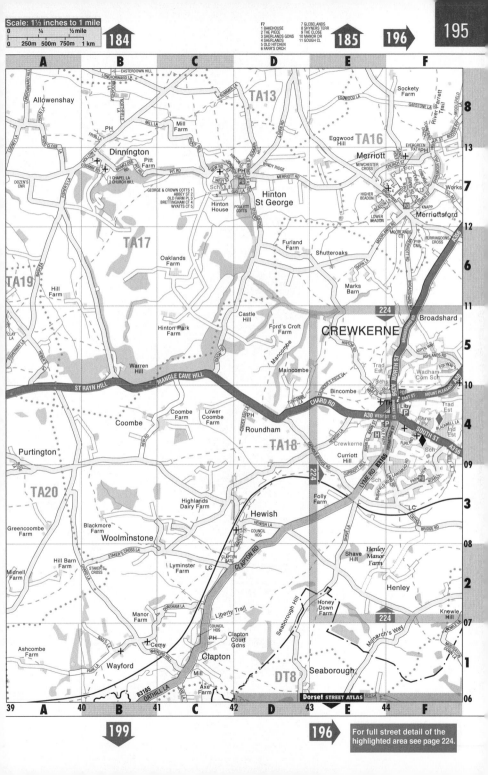

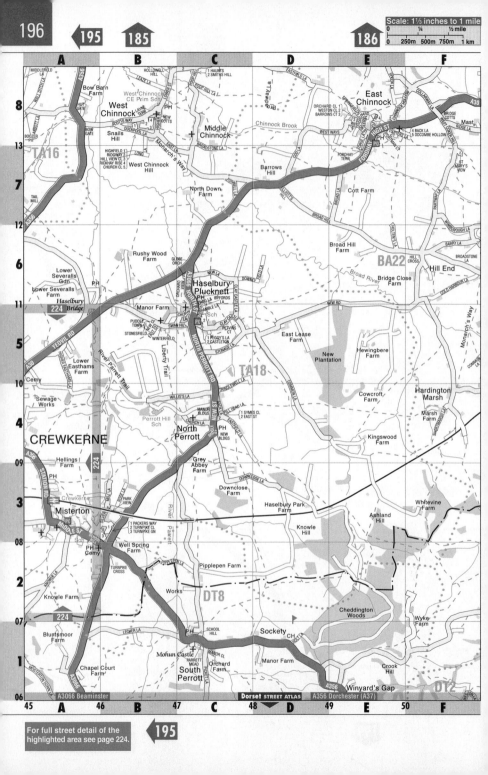

For full street detail of the highlighted area see page 224.

195

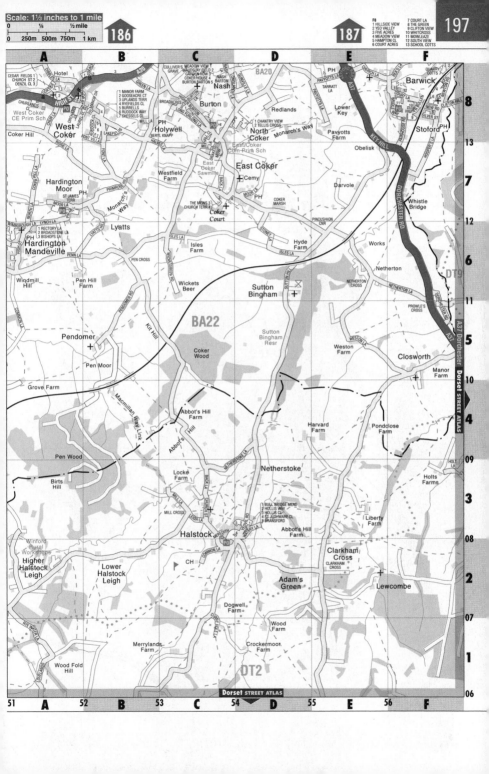

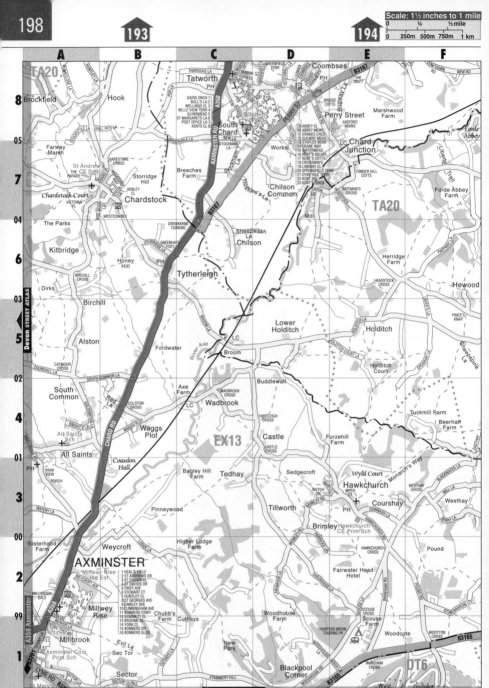

A1
1 MILLBROOK CROSS
2 CATNIP CL
3 JEFFS WAY
4 NEWBERY CL
5 LORETTO GDNS
6 MONKSTONE GDNS
7 CRIDLAKE
8 VALLEY VIEW
9 PRESTOR
10 ST MARY'S CL
11 SALWAY GDNS

Devon STREET ATLAS

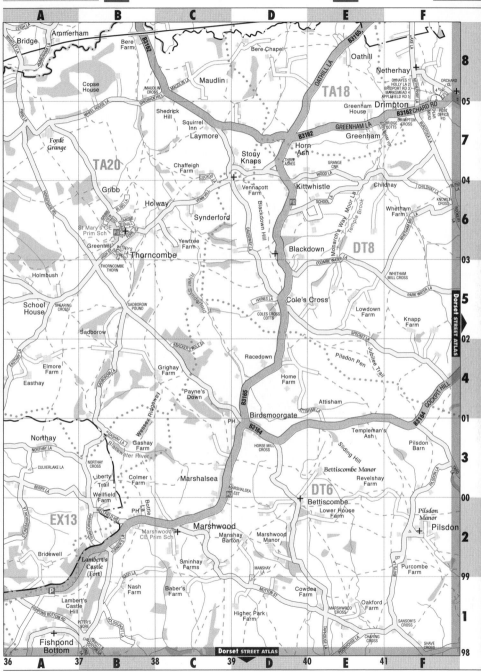

Scale: 1⅓ inches to 1 mile

194 195

Dorset STREET ATLAS

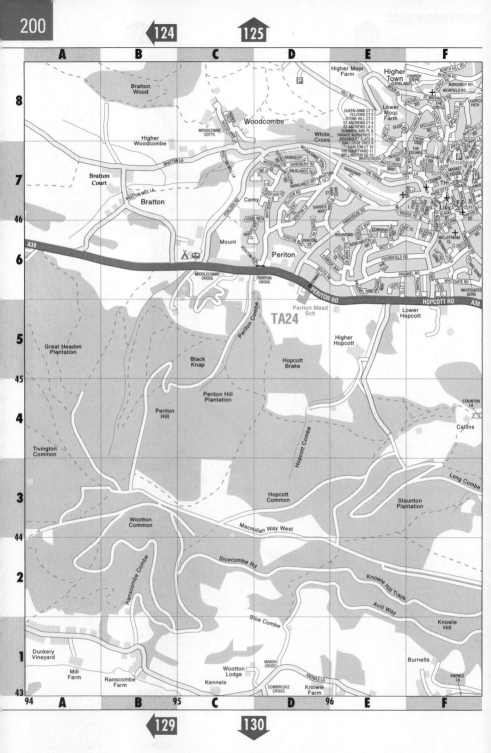

124
125

A   B   C   D   E   F

8

7

46

6

5

45

4

3

44

2

1

43

94   A   B   95   C   D   96   E   F

129
130

Bratton Wood

Woodcombe

WOODCOMBE COTTS

Higher Woodcombe

Higher Moor Farm

Higher Town

Lower Moor Farm

White Cross

Bratton Court

Bratton

Cemy

Mount

Periton

Middlecombe Cross

Periton Cross

A39

PERITON RD

HOPCOTT RD   A39

Great Headon Plantation

Black Knap

Periton Hill Plantation

Periton Hill

Periton Combe

Peritan Mead Sch

TA24

Hopcott Brake

Higher Hopcott

Lower Hopcott

Tivington Common

Hopcott Combe

Callins

STAUNTON LA

Long Combe

Wootton Common

Hopcott Common

Staunton Plantation

Ranscombe Combe

Macmillan Way West

Sloecombe Rd

Knowle Hill Track

Avill Way

Knowle Hill

Stoe Combe

Dunkery Vineyard

Mill Farm

Ranscombe Farm

Wootton Lodge

Kennels

MARSH CROSS

COWBRIDGE CROSS

KNOWLE LA

Knowle Farm

Burnells

KNOWLE LA

QUEEN ANNE CT 1
FULFORD CT 2
STONE HILL CT 3
ST ANDREWS CT 4
ST ANDREWS LA 5
SUMMERLAND PL 6
PARADE NURSERIES 7
BOSANQUET FLATS 8
OAK LODGE CRES 9
CARLTON CT 10
THE COURTYARD 11
WELLINGTON SQ 12
WHITECROSS

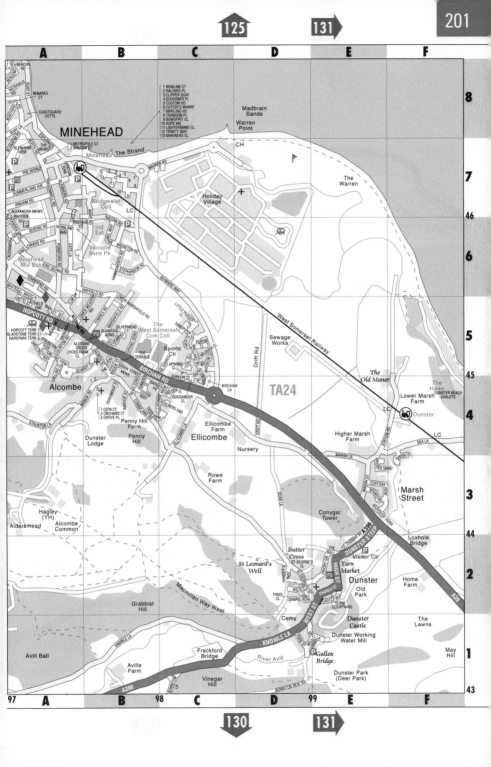

MINEHEAD

1 BOWLINE CT
2 HALYARD PL
3 CLIPPER QUAY
4 SCHOONER PL
5 CUSTOM HO
6 CUTTER'S WHARF
7 MARLING CL
8 TRANSOM PL
9 BOWSPRIT CL
10 ROPE WK
11 LIGHTERMANS CL
12 TRINITY WAY
13 MARINERS CL

Madbrain Sands
Warren Point

The Warren

1 METROPOLE CT
2 WALTON CT
The Strand
Minehead

Holiday Village

BEACON RD
WESTFIELD
BENARES CT
COASTGUARD COTTS
QUAY LA
BLENHEIM VIEW
THE MEWS
The Avenue
SUMMERLAND AVE
IRNHAM RD
ALEXANDRA MEWS WARDEN
QUEENS RD
LOWARD RD
Minehead Mid Sch
KING GEORGE RD
WHITBY
WHITEA FIELD
HOPCOTT RD
HOPCOTT TERR 1
GLADSTONE TERR 2
HAREPARK TERR 3
STAUNTON LA

Bridgwater Coll
LC
Ind Est
PEERAGE CT
VENLAND WAY
Venland Bsns Pk
OATS LA
BRERETON RD
STEPHENSON RD
HAYFIELD RD
MARSHFIELD RD
LITTLE PUXLEY
PUXLEY CL
SAMPFORD
TOWNE SEND RD
QUANTICK CT
SILVERMEAD CT
ALCOMBE CROSS
CROSS FARM CL
ALCOMBE RD
QUARRY LA
BIRCHAM RD
The Terrace
LAPWING LA
CURLEW CL
BADGER CL
GOOSANDER CL
POACHERS END
ALCOMBE LA
EDGARLEY RD
Sports Ctr
The West Somerset Com Coll
BIRCHAM LA

Alcombe

West Somerset Railway

Sewage Works

Drift Rd

TA24

The Old Manor

The Hawn
DUNSTER BEACH CHALETS
Lower Marsh Farm
LC
Dunster

LC
SEA LA
LC

Penny Hill Farm
Dunster Lodge
Penny Hill
Ellicombe Farm
Ellicombe
Nursery

Higher Marsh Farm

MARSH LA

Marsh Street

Hagley (YH)
Aldersmead
Alcombe Common

Rowe Farm

Conygar Tower

DRIFT RD
TICKA LA

Loxhole Bridge

Home Farm

Grabbist Hill

Macmillan Way West

KNOWLE LA

St Leonard's Well
Butter Cross
ST GEORGE'S
HAMBERS
HIGH ST
ST THOMAS ST
DUNSTER STEEP
Visitor Ctr
Yarn Market
Dunster
Old Park

The Lawns

Avill Ball

Aville Farm
Freckford Bridge
Vinegar Hill
A396
River Avill
KNOWLE LA
CHURCH ST
PIKES CL
CHAPEL ROW
WEST ST
Cemy
THE BALL
PARK ST
Dunster Castle
Dunster Working Water Mill
Gallox Bridge
Dunster Park (Deer Park)

May Hill

BONNITON NEW RD

A B C D E F

8

Warren Bay

7

Western Pier
Mus
Eastern Pier
Watchet Harbour
Watchet
Caravan Park
PH
Helwell Bay
WEST ST
GREENWAY
Daw's Castle
CLEEVE HILL
SAXON RD
SAXON CL
MARKET ST
MILL LA
WHITEHALL
WARREN CL
High Bank
Liby
1 PORTLAND TERR
2 ALMYR TERR
3 SEVERN TERR
4 LITTLE SILVER CT
5 THE CROFT
6 THE ROPE WLK
7 PEEL CT
West Somerset Railway

43
B3191
Tuck's Brake
Paper Mill
SCHOOL CL
WRIETLAND RD
DONIFORD RD
Doniford Beach Halt
Court Farm
SWRIDGE CVN PK
DONIFORD MDW
DONIFORD ORCH

6
Snailholt Farm
Holy Well
Buckland Sch
QUANTOCK RD
WYNDHAM
Knights Templar CE Meth Com Sch
CHERRY TREE WAY
Doniford
WATCHET
St Decumans
BRENDON RD
Parsonage Farm
INGRAMS MDW
CHURCHILL WAY
WOODLAND RD
TA23
NORMANDY AVE

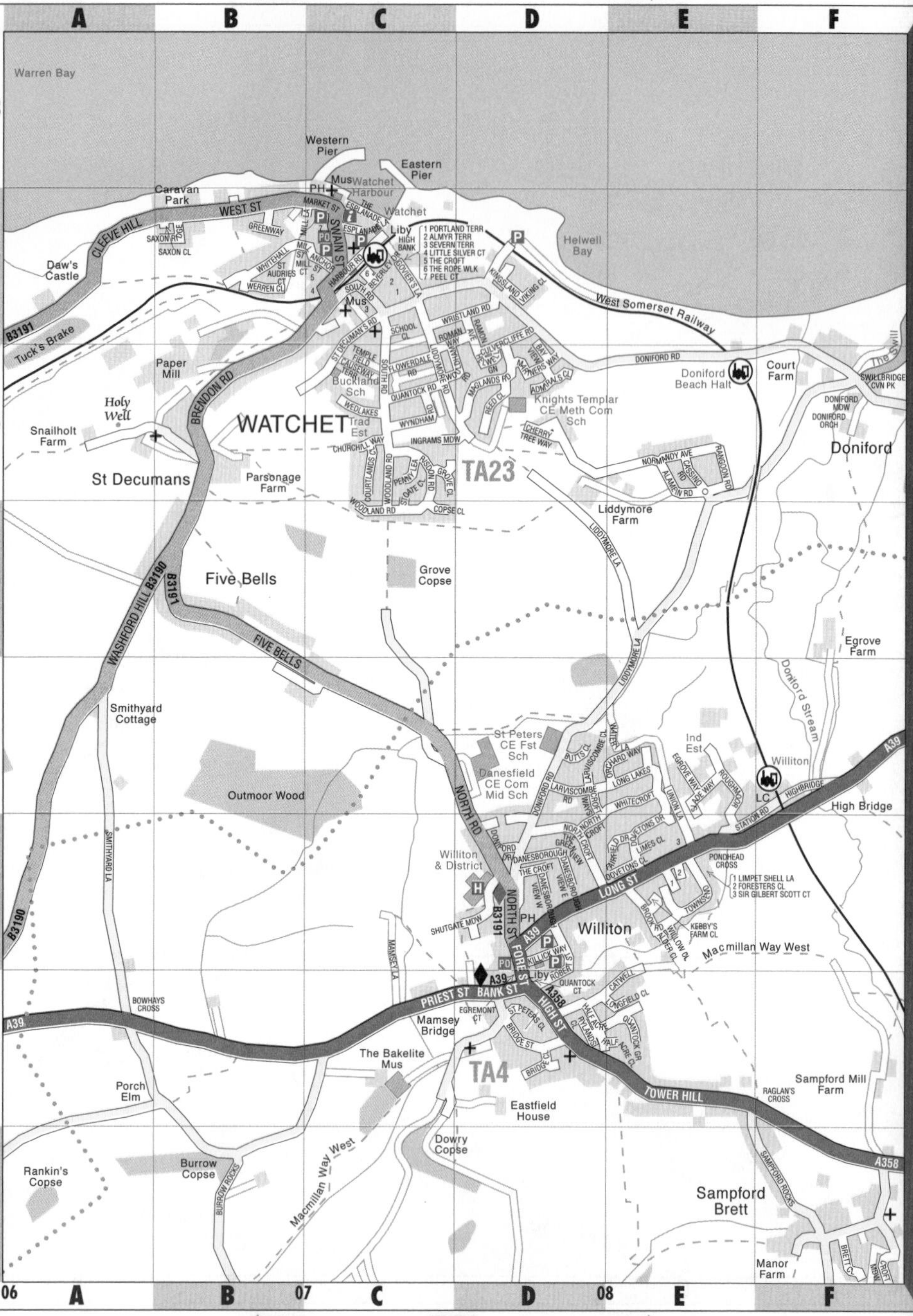

5
Five Bells
WASHFORD HILL
B3190
Grove Copse
Liddymore Farm

42
FIVE BELLS
LIDDYMORE LA

4
Smithyard Cottage
Outmoor Wood
St Peters CE Fst Sch
Danesfield CE Com Mid Sch
LARKSCOMBE RD
ORCHARD WAY
LONG LANES
Ind Est
Williton
LC
HIGHBRIDGE
A39
High Bridge
NORTH RD
STATION RD
Doniford Stream
Egrove Farm

3
SMITHYARD LA
B3190
Williton & District
DANESBOROUGH RD
THE CROFT
LONG ST
Williton
PONDHEAD CROSS
1 LIMPET SHELL LA
2 FORESTERS CL
3 SIR GILBERT SCOTT CT
KEBBY'S FARM CL

41
MARSH LA
SHUTGATE MDW
NORTH ST
B3191
FORE ST
PH
Liby
QUANTOCK CT
ORCHARD CL
CATWELL
Macmillan Way West

2
BOWHAYS CROSS
A39
EGREMONT RD
Mamsey Bridge
The Bakelite Mus
TA4
PRIEST ST
BANK ST
ST PETERS CL
BROOK ST
HIGH ST
Eastfield House
TOWER HILL
RAGLAN'S CROSS
Sampford Mill Farm
Porch Elm

1
Rankin's Copse
Burrow Copse
BURROW DOCKS
Macmillan Way West
Dowry Copse
Sampford Brett
A358
SAMPFORD CROSS
BRETT
Manor Farm

40
06 A B 07 C D 08 E F

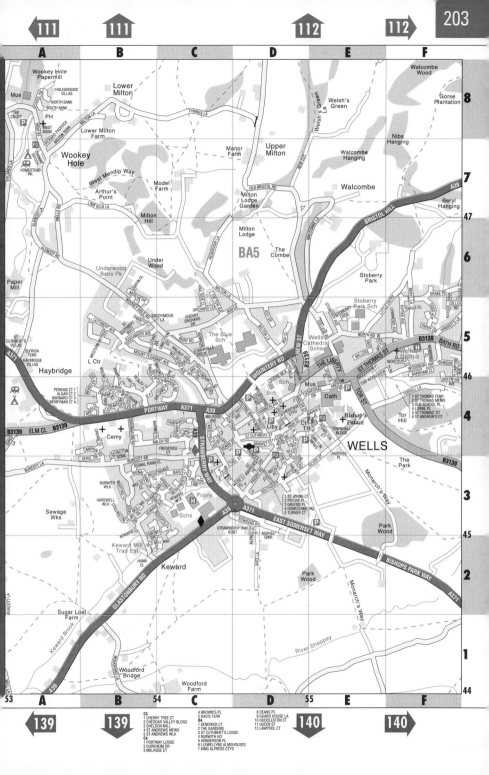

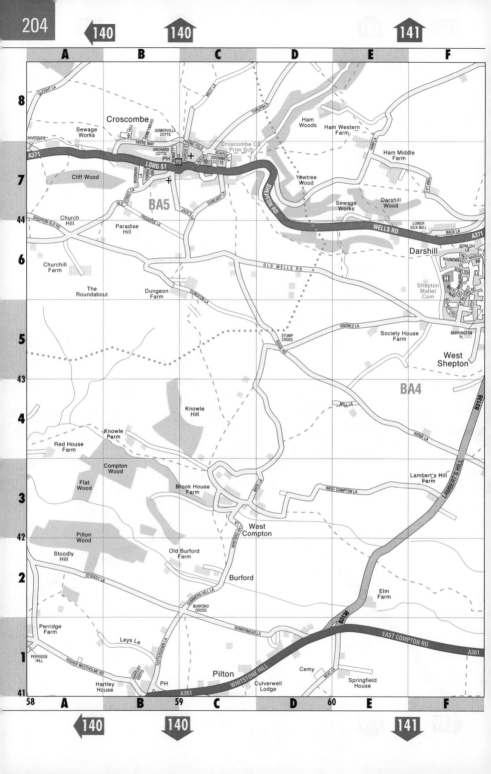

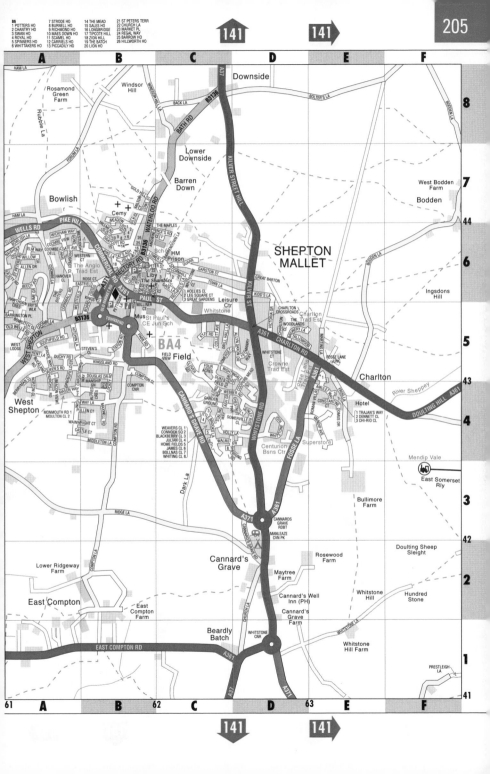

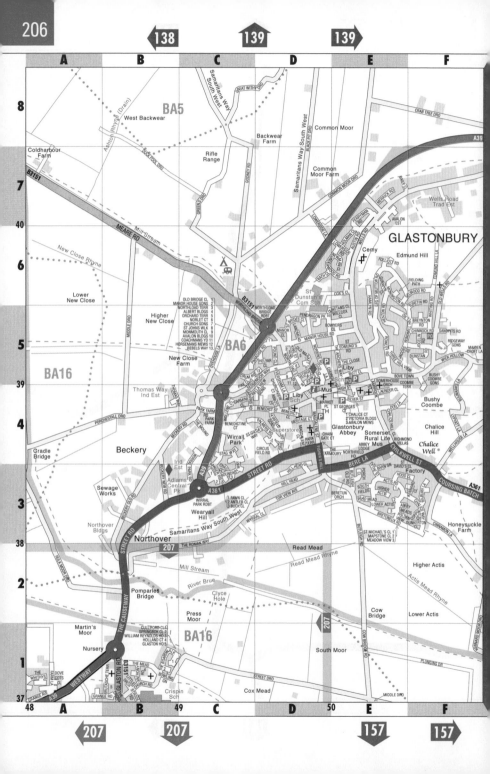

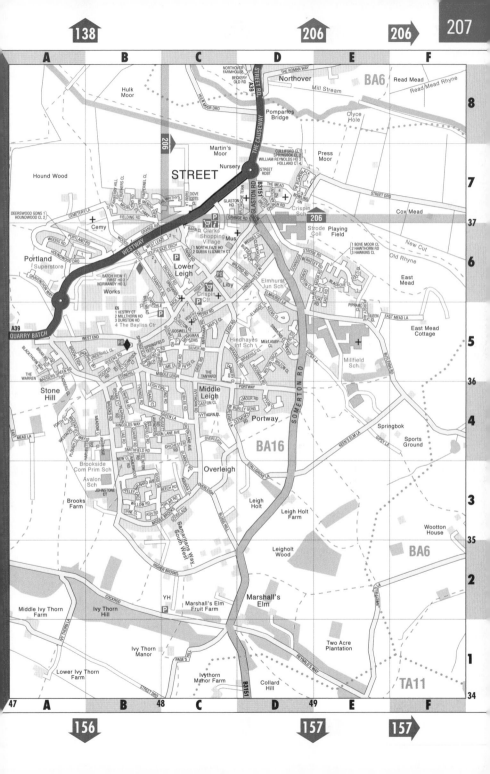

135 135

A B C D E F

8
7
38
6
5
37
4
3
36
2
1
35

27 A B 28 C D 29 E F

153 153

Perrycroft
Perry Green
Perry Green Farm
Perrymoor Brook
Manor Lodge
Grabhams Cottage
Chilton Trinity Tech Coll
CHILTON PK
RICHMOND
Sports Ctr
Barton Farm
Grabhams Farm
WESTERN WAY
CRESTFIELD AVE
CAMDEN PL
BALTLANDS
BALTLANDS AVE
Moores
Blakes Farm
NAYLES VIEW
POSITANO
DUCHESS CL
EARLS CT
COLMER CT
CROWPILL
B3339
SANDFORD HILL
Wembdon Farm
BLAKES LA
WEMBDON HILL
Inn
Wembdon
WATERMANS
Church Farm Newtown
MORAVIA CT
TRINITY
ESCOTT
Sandford Farm
Mount Radford
Cokerhurst Farm
A39
THE PIPPINS
THE LAURELS
Wembdon St George's CE Prim Sch
GREENWAY
WARES LA
OAK APPLE
BERKELEY
CROWPILL COTTS
RIVER VIEW
BRUNEL
Marina Dock
ADMIRALS
SKIMMERTON LA
Greenway Farm
SILVERDALE CL
INWOOD
OAK
BRAMBLE
COLERIDGE GN
CHURCH PATH
HILLGROVE
WAVERLEY RD
COLLINGWOOD
THE CLINK
RIVER PARRETT
WEST QUAY
BOND
QUANTOCK RD
QUANTOCK WAY
PORTLAND PL
HALESLEIGH RD
WASHINGTON GDNS
BLACKLANDS
YORK Ct
BLDGS
SQUIBBS HO
CAMDEN
KING S
ST
TA5
Queenswood Farm
Cemy
Cemy
WEMBDON RD
WEMBDON CT
NORTH ST
ST MARY'S
WESTERCOMBE
WIND MILL
PENARTH
ASPEN
CLASSIC BLDGS
FENEL CT
ORIFL
TRIARS CT
P
WEST BOWER LA
Northfield
ALFOXTON RD
WOODBURY RD
WILLOUGHBY
ASHMAN WAY
FURZE CL
BROADWAY
A39
RHINE CL
GEORGE WILLIAM
Superstore
CHARTER
Durleigh Elms
COTHELSTONE CL
St Mary's CE Prim Sch
Haygrove Sch
St Joseph's RC Prim Sch
Westover Green Com Sch
THE PARKS
GRANGE DR
TRIARN LAWN
Penrose Sch
River Parrett Trail
Bridgwater & Taunton Canal
Browne's Pond
Durleigh Brook Farm
DURLEIGH RD
Durleigh CL
SOUTHBOURNE HO 1
WEST BOW HO 2
WESTFIELD HO 3
ALBERT CT 4
ELEVEN CT 5
ELMWOOD AVE
FERNLEIGH
Durleigh Reservoir
ROMAN LA
SPRINGFIELD AVE
Haygrove House
TA6
Haygrove Farm
BRIDGWATER
Robert Blake Science Coll
MEADS CT
Hamp Inf Sch
ASHLEIGH AVE 1
ASHLEIGH TERR 2
GREENFIELDS 3
ELMSIDE HO
ELMWOOD Sch
Durleigh
Durleigh Farm
DURLEIGH RD
SUNNYBANK
Hamp Com Jun Sch
CURLANDS AVE
PARKSTONE AVE
SUNNYSIDE
THE GREEN
GRENVILLE RD
QUEEN'S RD
YORK RD
PHILLIP
The Meads
HAMP BROOK WAY
RSDNR
PENEL CT
GARTON
MILLWOOD CT
MAPLE RD
Hamp
GLOUCESTER RD
DUKES MEAD
BROOKE LA
RHODE LA
Hamp Brook
Broadmeadow Farm
South Lea
Rhode Lane Farm
SPILLERS CL 1
WOLMER CL 2
MILNE CL
SHELLTHORN GR 1
BAGBOROUGH DR 2
REED CL
PALMER
WILLS RD
HAGGET CL
Poultry Farm
Samaritans Way South West
Shortlands Farm
BROOK LA

F4
1 ST MARY'S CT
2 BLAKE ST
3 OLD TAUNTON RD
4 GREEN DRAGON CT

F5
1 CHALICE MEWS
2 HOMECASTLE HO
3 THE AVENUE
4 CHURCH PASS
5 COURT ST
6 Angel Place Sh Ctr
7 Bridgwater Ent Ctr
8 MARKET CT

B4
1 PARKSIDE CT
2 STEAM PACKET TERR
3 PATHFINDER TERR
4 OXFORD TERR
5 THE MEWS
6 HUGHES CL
7 GRAVES CL
8 MOONRAKER CL

C4
1 NIGHTINGALE CL
2 HERON HO
3 DUNWEAR HO

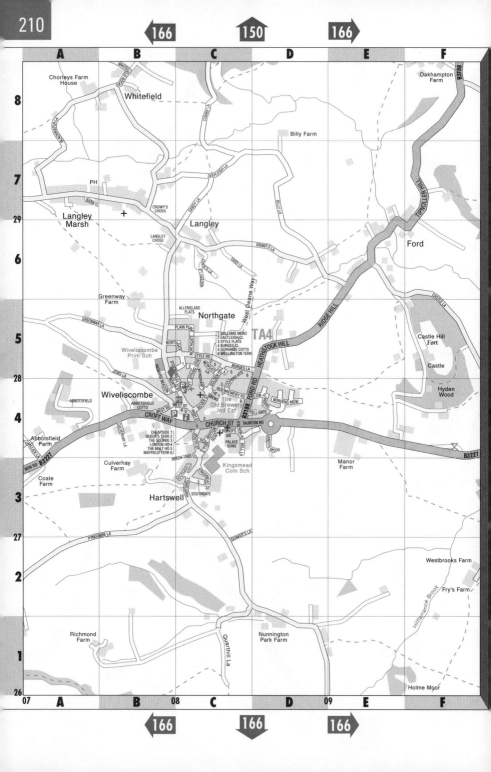

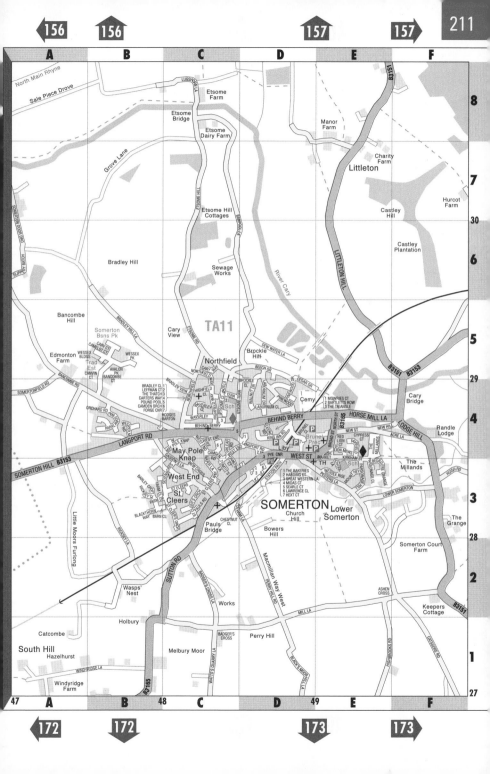

A   B   C   D   E   F

North Main Rhyne

Sale Piece Drove

Lugshorn La

Etsome
Farm

Etsome
Bridge

Manor
Farm

8

Grove Lane

Etsome
Dairy Farm

Charity
Farm

Littleton

7

Etsome Hill
Cottages

Castley
Hill

Hurcot
Farm

30

Bradley Hill

Sewage
Works

River Cary

Castley
Plantation

6

Bancombe
Hill

Somerton
Bsns Pk

Cary
View

TA11

Brockle
Hill

Cary
Bridge

5

Edmonton
Farm

Northfield

Dew Water La

B3151 B3153

29

Cemy

Randle
Lodge

1 MGWRIES CT
2 BARTLETTS ROW
3 THE TRIANGLE

Horse Mill La
Lodge Hill

4

Behind Berry

Brunel
Prec

West St

The
Millands

Langport Rd

May Pole
Knap

Lib

Market

TH

1 THE BAKERIES
2 HARDING CL
3 GREAT WESTERN LA
4 MIDAS CT
5 SEARLE CT
6 LAWRENCE CL
7 HEXT CT

3

West End

St
Cleers

SOMERTON

Lower
Somerton

The
Grange

Somerton Hill B3153

Church
Hill

28

Pauls
Bridge

Bowers
Hill

Somerton Court
Farm

Little Moors Furlong

Sutton Rd

Chestnut
Cl

Macmillan Way West

2

Wasps'
Nest

Works

Ashen
Cross

Keepers
Cottage

B3151

Holbury

Badger's
Cross

Perry Hill

Mill La

1

Catcombe

South Hill

Hazelhurst

Melbury Moor

27

Windyridge
Farm

B3165

47   A   B   48   C   D   49   E   F

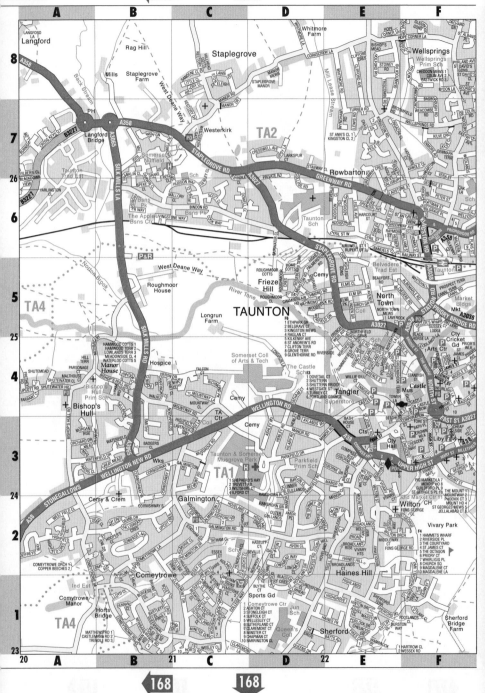

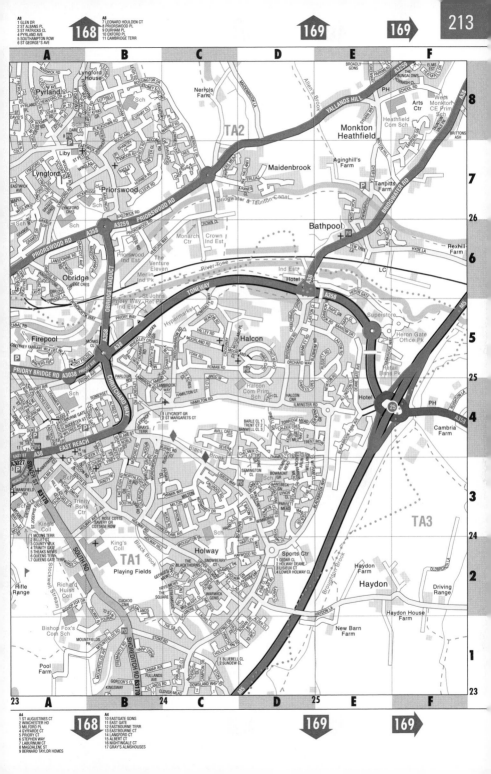

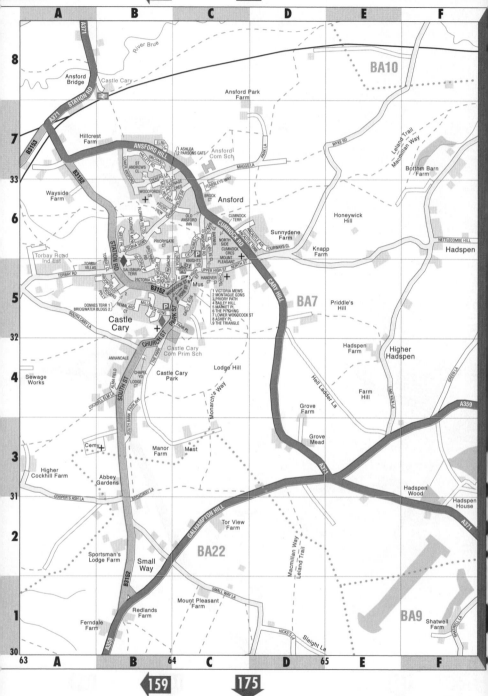

159
159

BA10

River Brue

Ansford Park Farm

Ansford Bridge

Castle Cary

STATION RD

Hillcrest Farm

ANSFORD HILL

1 ASHLEA
2 PARSONS GATE

Ansford Com Sch

ELM

ORCHARD
ST ANDREWS CL

TUCKERS LA

LOWER GDNS

MAGGS LA

WYKE RD

Leland Trail
Macmillan Way

Bottom Barn Farm

Wayside Farm

B3153

B3152

WOODFORDS GN

Ansford

GARAGE
CRES

BROCK CT

YEARLEYS WAY

Honeywick Hill

NETTLECOMBE HILL

Hadspen

CUMNOCK
TERR

CUMNOCK RD

OLD ANSFORD INN

Sunnydene Farm

Knapp Farm

Torbay Road Ind Est

STATION RD

GAITHER AV

FLORIDA FIELDS

VICTORIA GDNS

WEST ST

PRIORYGATE CT

GREENACRE

DYBENHAM

CATHERINE ST

FLORIDA ST

FORE ST

BARNES CL

UPPER HIGH ST

NORTH SIDE

KNIGHTS DR

CUMNOCK CRES

MOUNT PLEASANT

NORTH ST

BA7

Priddle's Hill

Torbay Villas

TORBAY LA

SALISBURY TERR

VICTORIA RD

WOODCOCK ST

CHAPEL

HANOVER CT

1 VICTORIA MEWS
2 MONTAGUE GDNS
3 PRIORY PATH
4 BAILEY HILL
5 MARKET PL
6 THE PITCHING
7 LOWER WOODCOCK ST
8 ASHBY
9 THE TRIANGLE

Mus

Castle Cary

BEMALARD

DONNES TERR 1
BRIDGWATER BLDGS 2

B3152

MILL LA

MANOR GDNS

THE PARK

PARK ST

PARK PL

CARY HILL

Hadspen Farm

Higher Hadspen

SOUTH CARY LA

CHURCH ST

Castle Cary Com Prim Sch

ANNANDALE

ALMA FIELD

SOUTH ST

CHAPEL
LODGE CT

Castle Cary Park

Lodge Hill

Monarch's Way

Hell Ladder La

Farm Hill

THE KILN LA

GREEN LA

Sewage Works

COCKHILL ELM LA

SOUTH HAWK PARK AVE

Manor Farm

Mast

Grove Farm

Grove Mead

A359

Higher Cockhill Farm

Cemy

Abbey Gardens

BROADWAY LA

A371

Hadspen Wood

Hadspen House

COOPER'S ASH LA

GALHAMPTON HILL

BA22

Tor View Farm

Macmillan Way

Leland Trail

A371

BA9

Sportsman's Lodge Farm

B3152

Small Way

SMALL WAY LA

Mount Pleasant Farm

Redlands Farm

Shatwell Farm

Ferndale Farm

A359

HICKS LA

Sleight La

SHATWELL LA

159
175

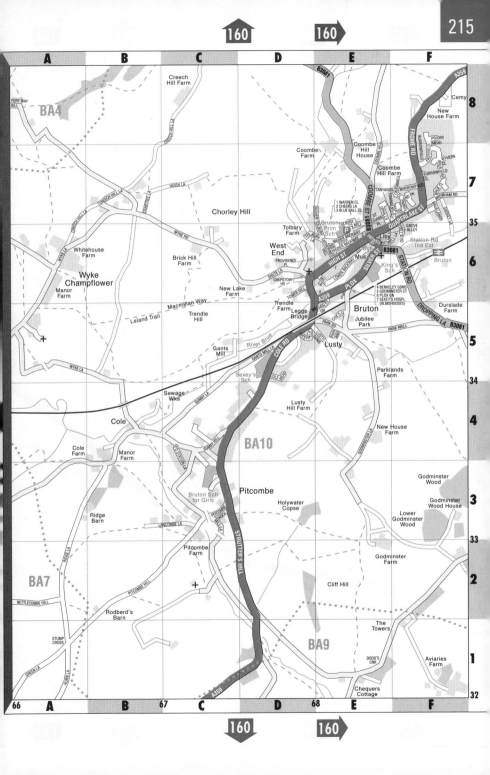

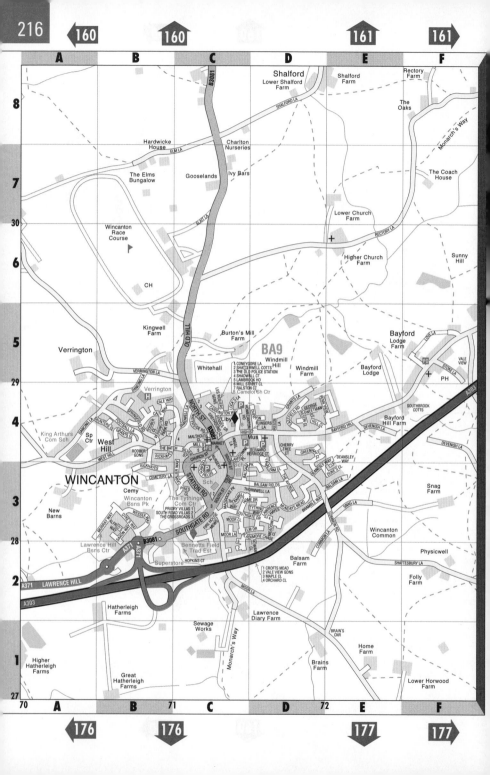

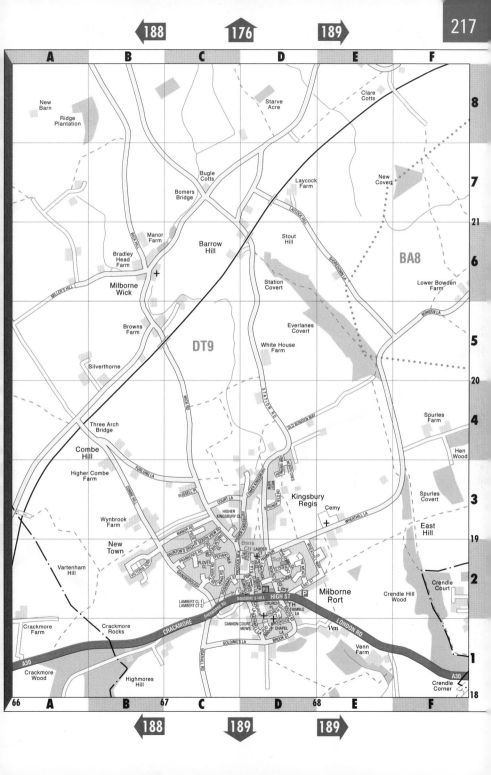

A B C D E F

8 7 21 6 5 20 4 3 19 2 1 18

66 67 68

New Barn
Ridge Plantation
Starve Acre
Clare Cotts
Bugle Cotts
Bomers Bridge
Laycock Farm
New Covert
Manor Farm
Barrow Hill
Stout Hill
Bradley Head Farm
BA8
Milborne Wick
Station Covert
Lower Bowden Farm
Browns Farm
Everlanes Covert
Silverthorne
White House Farm
DT9
Three Arch Bridge
Spurles Farm
Combe Hill
Hen Wood
Higher Combe Farm
Spurles Covert
Wynbrook Farm
Kingsbury Regis
Cemy
East Hill
New Town
Vartenham Hill
Higher Kingsbury Cl
Bsns Ctr LAUDER
Sch
Liby
Crackmore Farm
Crackmore Rocks
Lambert Cl 1
Lambert Ct 2
Sansome's Hill
HIGH ST
Milborne Port
Crendle Hill Wood
Crendle Court
Church Pl
Thimble La
Ven
Cannon Court Mews
Chapel
Crackmore Wood
Highmores Hill
Golding's La
Brook St
London Rd
Venn Farm
A30
Crackmore
A30
Crendle Corner

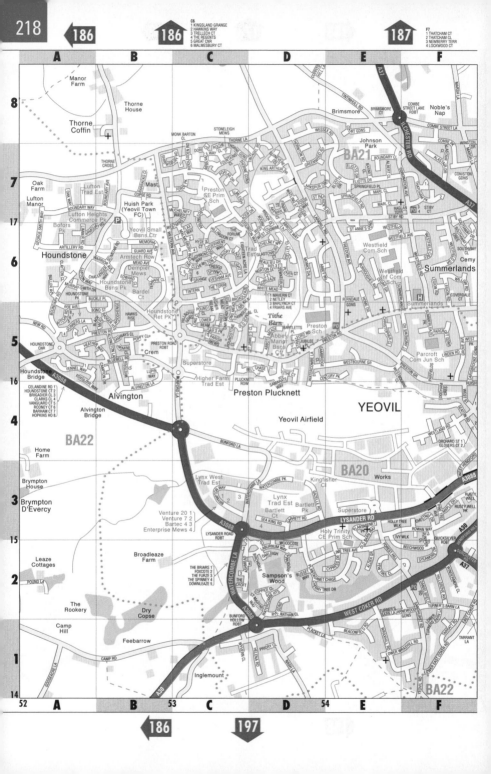

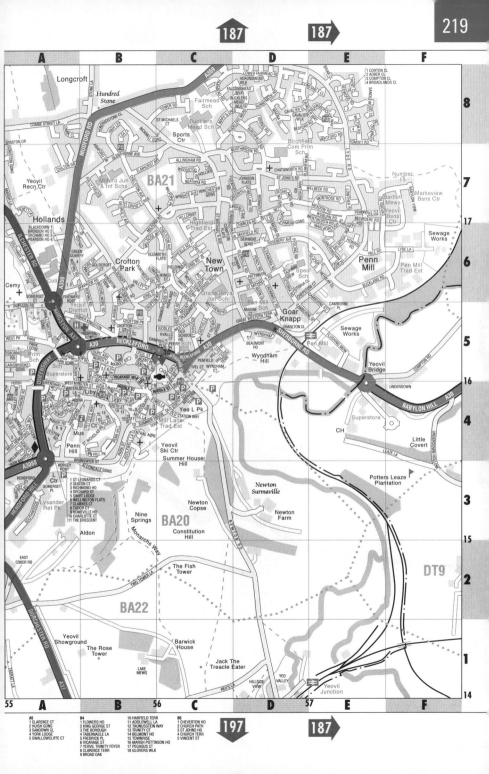

187

187

197

187

A5
1 CLARENCE CT
2 HUISH GDNS
3 SANDOWN CL
4 YORK LODGE
5 SWALLOWCLIFFE CT

B4
1 FLOWERS HO
2 KING GEORGE ST
3 THE BOROUGH
4 TABERNACLE LA
5 FREDRICK PL
6 VICARAGE ST
7 YEOVIL TRINITY FOYER
8 TUDOR CT
9 BROAD OAK

10 HARFIELD TERR
11 ADDLEWELL LA
12 TAUNUSSTEIN WAY
13 TRINITY CT
14 BELMONT HO
15 TOWNRISE
16 MARSH POTTINSON HO
17 PEGASUS CT
18 GLOVERS WLK

B5
1 CHEVERTON HO
2 CHURCH PATH
3 ST JOHNS HO
4 CHURCH TERR
5 VINCENT ST

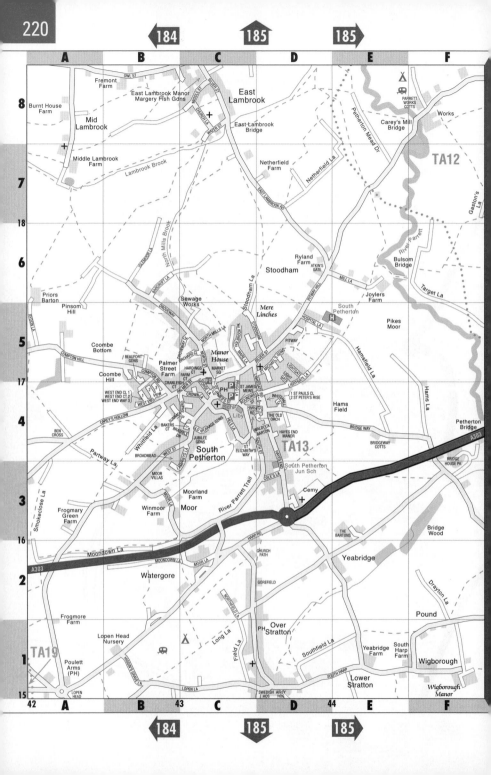

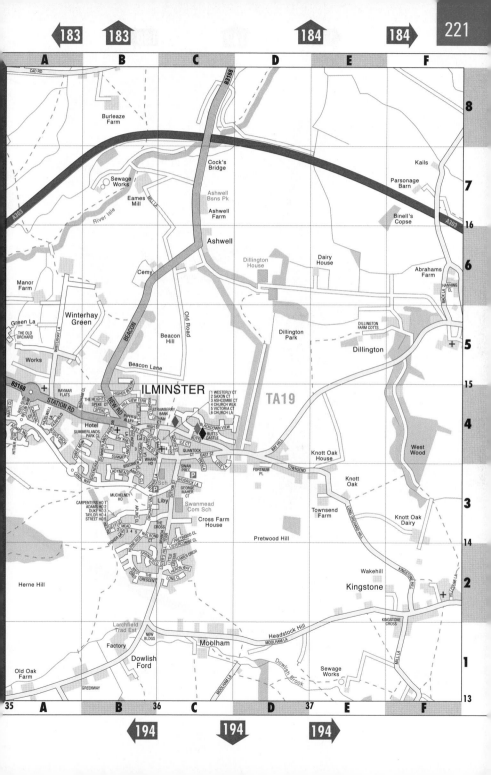

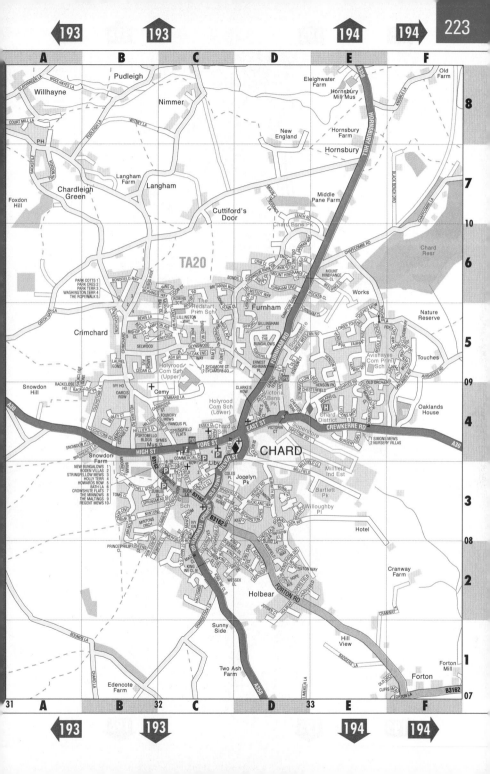

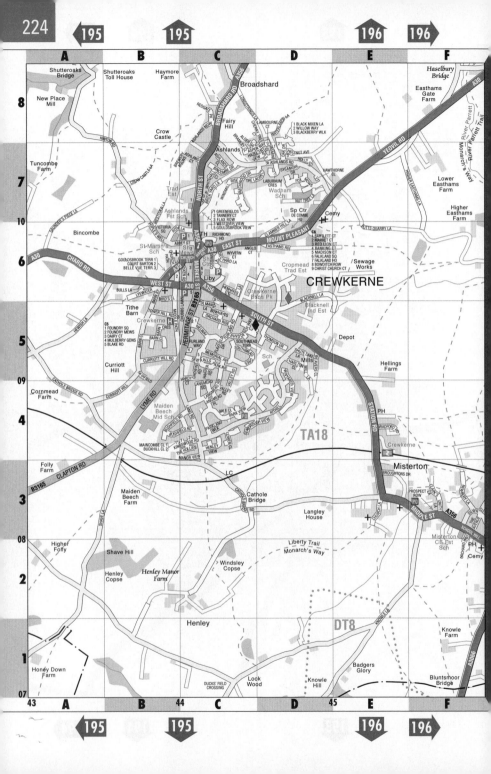

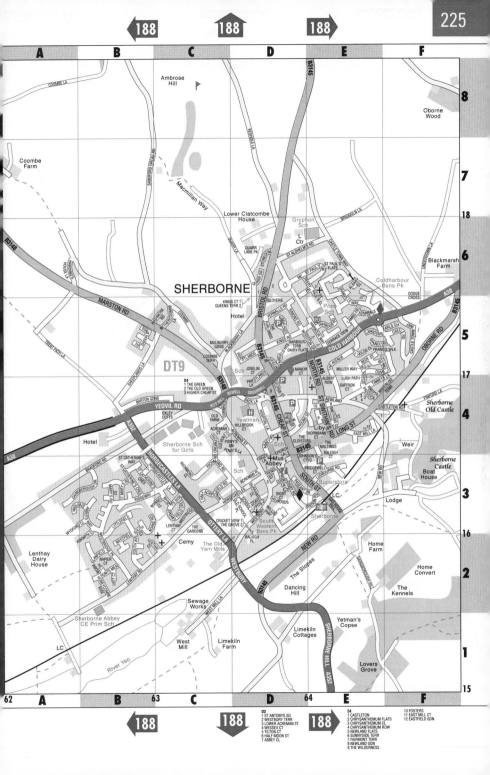

A   B   C   D   E   F

8

Oborne
Wood

Ambrose
Hill

COOMBE LA

Coombe
Farm

18

B3148

Macmillan Way

Lower Clatcombe
House

Gryphon
Sch

Blackmarsh
Farm

7

6

UNDERDOWN LA

DODGE
CROSS

Coldharbour
Bsns Pk

St ALDHELM'S RD

St PAUL'S
FLATS

Quarr
Lane Pk

L
Ctr

SHERBORNE

Hotel

KINGS CT 1
QUEENS TERR 2

GLOVERS

MARSTON RD

B3148

COLD HARBOUR

OBORNE RD

B3145

A30

5

17

DT9

D4
1 THE GREEN
2 THE OLD GREEN
3 HIGHER CHEAP ST

MULBERRY
GDNS

COOMBE
TERR

JOSELIN
CT

PRIESTLANDS

MANOR
CT

ALBERT
ROW

NORTH RD

MILLER WAY

LUSH PATH

SAFFRON
CT

Sherborne
Old Castle

CASTLETON RD

PINFORD LA

Weir

4

YEOVIL RD

OXLEY
COTTS

OLD
FARM

BARTON GDNS

Hotel

Yeatman
HILLBROOK

A352

ACREMAN
ST

Sherborne Sch
for Girls

ST SWITHIN ST

LONG ST

CHEAP ST

B3145

EAST MILL LA

Sherborne
Castle
Boat
House

3

16

ST CATHERINE'S
WAY

HORSECASTLES LA

Bradford Rd

Abbey

Mus

The
Cloisters

RALEIGH

THE
MALTINGS

BRIDGEWELL

SOUTH ST

Superstore

LC

Lodge

Cemy

Lenthay
Dairy
House

Cricket View 1
The Grove 2

THE
GARDENS

OTTERY LA

Lenthay
Ct

RALEIGH
PL

South
Western
Bsns Pk

Sherborne

Home
Farm

Home
Convert

The
Kennels

2

NEW RD

WESTBURY

B3145

The Slopes

Dancing
Hill

Lovers
Grove

Sewage
Works

Sherborne Abbey
CE Prim Sch

The Old
Yarn Mills

West
Mill

Limekiln
Farm

Limekiln
Cottages

Yetman's
Copse

SHERBORNE HILL

A352

1

15

LC

River Yeo

62   A   B   63   C   D   64   E   F

D3
1 ST ANTONYS SQ
2 WESTBURY TERR
3 LOWER ACREMAN ST
4 WESSEX CT
5 TILTON CT
6 HALF MOON ST
7 ABBEY CL

E4
1 CASTLETON
2 CHRYSANTHEMUM FLATS
3 CHRYSANTHEMUM CL
4 CHRYSANTHEMUM ROW
5 NEWLAND FLATS
6 SUNNYSIDE TERR
7 FAIRMONT TERR
8 NEWLAND GDN
9 THE WILDERNESS

10 FOSTERS
11 EAST MILL CT
12 EASTFIELD GDN

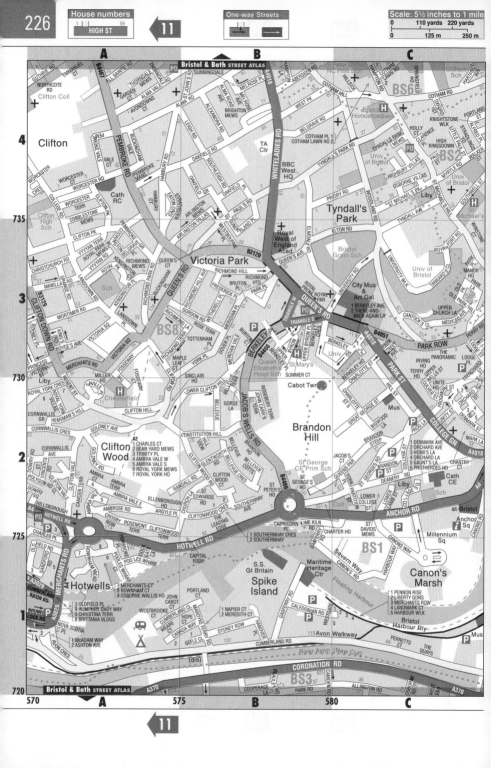

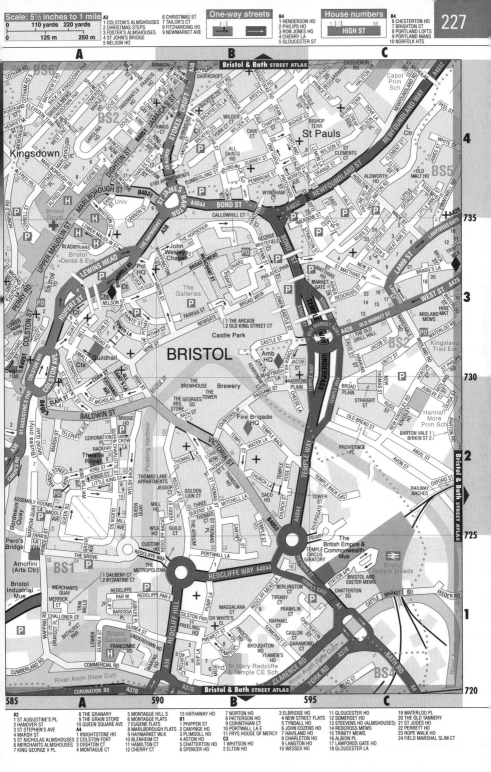

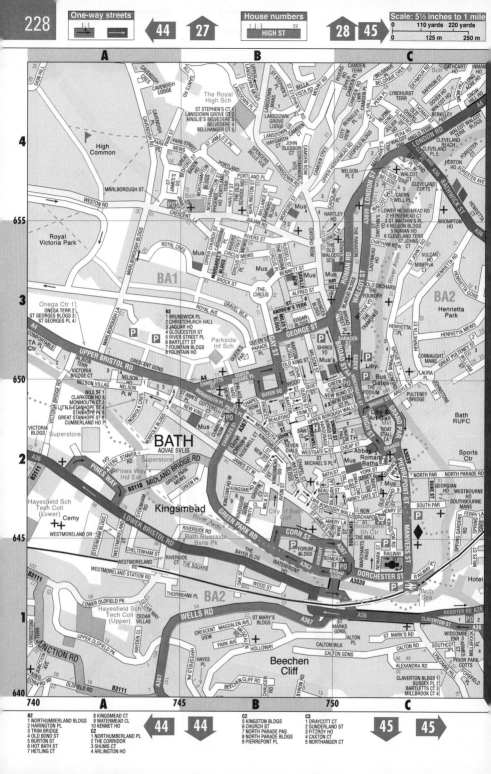

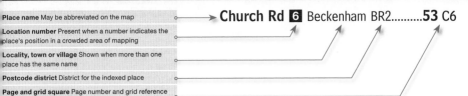

Place name May be abbreviated on the map

Location number Present when a number indicates the place's position in a crowded area of mapping

Locality, town or village Shown when more than one place has the same name

Postcode district District for the indexed place

Page and grid square Page number and grid reference for the standard mapping

Church Rd 6 Beckenham BR2.........53 C6

Public and commercial buildings are highlighted in magenta Places of interest are highlighted in blue with a star ★

Abbreviations used in the index

Acad	Academy	Comm	Common	Gd	Ground	L	Leisure	Prom	Promenade
App	Approach	Cott	Cottage	Gdn	Garden	La	Lane	Rd	Road
Arc	Arcade	Cres	Crescent	Gn	Green	Liby	Library	Recn	Recreation
Ave	Avenue	Cswy	Causeway	Gr	Grove	Mdw	Meadow	Ret	Retail
Bglw	Bungalow	Ct	Court	H	Hall	Meml	Memorial	Sh	Shopping
Bldg	Building	Ctr	Centre	Ho	House	Mkt	Market	Sq	Square
Bsns, Bus	Business	Ctry	Country	Hospl	Hospital	Mus	Museum	St	Street
Bvd	Boulevard	Cty	County	HQ	Headquarters	Orch	Orchard	Sta	Station
Cath	Cathedral	Dr	Drive	Hts	Heights	Pal	Palace	Terr	Terrace
Cir	Circus	Dro	Drove	Ind	Industrial	Par	Parade	TH	Town Hall
Cl	Close	Ed	Education	Inst	Institute	Pas	Passage	Univ	University
Cnr	Corner	Emb	Embankment	Int	International	Pk	Park	Wk, Wlk	Walk
Coll	College	Est	Estate	Intc	Interchange	Pl	Place	Wr	Water
Com	Community	Ex	Exhibition	Junc	Junction	Prec	Precinct	Yd	Yard

Index of localities, towns and villages

A

Abbas Combe..........176 E1
Abbey Hill............182 E5
Abbots Leigh...........11 A8
Adam's Green..........197 D2
Adber................187 F7
Adderwell............120 A3
Adsborough...........169 D8
Adscombe............152 A8
Aisholt..............152 B6
Alcombe
  Kingsdown............29 F7
  Minehead............201 A4
Aldwick...............54 D7
Alford...............159 A3
Alhampton...........159 C6
Aller................171 D8
Allerford
  Porlock.............124 C4
  Taunton.............167 F4
Allowenshay.........195 A8
All Saints...........198 A4
Alston...............198 A5
Alston Sutton.........88 F3
Alvington...........218 B4
Alweston............189 A1
Amesbury.............199 A8
Ammerham............199 A8
Andersfield.........153 B5
Angersleigh.........181 C5
Ansford.............214 C6
Appledore...........179 A1
Appley..............179 B8
Ash
  Martock.............185 F7
  Taunton.............169 E1
Ashbeer..............150 C6
Ashbrittle...........178 F8
Ashcott.............156 B8
Ashculme............180 C1
Ashgrove.............79 D8
Ashill...............183 B4
Ashington...........187 B8
Ash Priors..........167 C8
Ashton..............107 E8
Ashton Gate..........11 F4
Ashton Vale..........11 F2
Ashwell.............221 C6
Ashwick.............115 B5
Asney...............156 E7
Atherstone..........184 C3
Avoncliff............64 F4
Avonmouth............4 B8
Axbridge.............70 B1
Axminster...........198 B2

B

Babcary.............174 C7
Backwell.............19 B6
Backwell Common.......19 B8
Backwell Green........19 D8
Badbury.............183 F7
Badger Street........182 B6
Badgworth............88 B6
Bagley..............109 A1
Bagley Green........222 A3
Bailbrook............28 D3
Baltonsborough......158 A6
Bampton............164 C1
Banwell..............51 B3
Bare Ash............153 B6
Barr................168 B3
Barren Down.........205 C7
Barrington..........184 D5
Barrow
  Wells..............140 B4
  Wincanton..........161 B3
Barrow Common.........21 B4
Barrow Gurney........20 C5
Barrow Vale..........59 D5
Barton...............69 B6
Barton St David......158 A2
Barwick.............197 F8
Batch................66 F3
Batcombe............142 D1
Bath................228 A2
Bathampton...........28 F1
Bathealton..........166 B3
Batheaston...........28 F4
Bathford.............29 C1
Bathpool............213 E6
Bathway.............94 E5
Bathwick.............45 B7
Batten's Green.......182 F5
Battleborough........86 C1
Bawdrip............136 C2
Bayford.............216 F5
Beacon Hill..........27 F1
Beard Hill..........141 C3
Beardly Batch.......205 C1
Bear Flat............44 F4
Beckery.............206 B4
Beckington..........101 E4
Bedlam..............119 B8
Bedminster Down......22 B8
Beechen Cliff.......228 B1
Beggearn Huish......131 E2
Belle Vue............78 B3
Belluton.............40 D6

Benter...

Benter..............115 D7
Berkley.............121 A7
Berkley Down........120 C5
Berkley Marsh.......120 F7
Berrow...............84 E5
Bettiscombe.........199 E2
Bickenhall..........182 E5
Bicknoller..........132 F2
Biddisham............87 E8
Bilbrook............131 C4
Bincombe............134 A2
Binegar.............114 C7
Birchill............198 A5
Birchwood...........182 A1
Birdsmoorgate.......199 D4
Bishop's Hull.......212 A4
Bishops Lydeard.....167 F8
Bishop Sutton........57 D3
Bishopswood........192 F7
Bishopsworth.........22 A5
Bitton..............25 E7
Blackdown...........199 D6
Blackford
  Minehead...........129 E8
  Wedmore............107 E4
  Wincanton..........175 F5
Blackmoor
  Chew Stoke..........38 C3
  Churchill...........53 D6
  Wellington.........180 E5
Blackpool Corner....198 D1
Blackrock............40 E8
Blackwater..........182 C2
Blackwell...........165 B5
Blagdon..............54 E2
Blagdon Hill........181 D5
Blatchbridge........143 F8
Bleadney............139 A8
Bleadon..............67 C7
Bloomfield
  Bath...............44 E3
  Timsbury...........60 B4
Blue Anchor.........131 B6
Bodden..............205 F7
Bolham Water........191 B7
Bossington..........124 B4
Bourne...............54 B4
Bourton
  Gillingham.........161 F1
  Weston-super-Mare...32 E6
Bowden..............177 F2
Bower Ashton........11 E4
Bower Hinton........185 D5
Bowlish.............205 A7
Bradford Abbas......187 E1
Bradford on Tone....167 F1
Bradley Green.......135 B1

Bradney...

Bradney.............136 D1
Bramwell............172 B8
Brandish Street.....124 C3
Brandon Hill........226 B2
Brassknocker.........45 F2
Bratton.............200 B7
Bratton Seymour.....176 C8
Breach...............58 F6
Brean................65 F5
Brendon.............122 A4
Brent Knoll..........86 A1
Bridge..............199 A8
Bridgehampton.......174 C3
Bridgetown..........147 E4
Bridgwater..........208 E3
Brimley.............198 D3
Brindham............139 D3
Brinscombe...........89 A5
Brinsea..............52 E8
Bristol.............227 B3
Brittens.............77 F6
Broadway............183 B2
Brockfield..........198 A8
Brockley.............18 C2
Brockwell...........129 E6
Brokerswood.........102 F5
Brompton Ralph......150 C3
Brompton Regis......148 B2
Brookhampton........175 D6
Broomfield..........152 E2
Brownheath..........180 C2
Brushford...........163 D4
Bruton..............215 E5
Brympton D'Evercy...218 A3
Buckhorn Weston.....177 D3
Buckland Dinham.....100 A3
Buckland Down........99 B4
Buckland St Mary....192 F8
Buckton..............92 C4
Bulford.............182 C4
Bull's Green........117 E3
Burcott.............139 E8
Burford.............204 C2
Burlands............168 C6
Burlescombe.........179 B3
Burnett..............42 B7
Burnham-on-Sea......104 D8
Burrington...........53 F3
Burrow..............184 F6
Burrowbridge........154 F1
Burtle..............137 D6
Burton
  Stogursey..........134 B7
  Yeovil.............197 C8
Bury................164 A6
Buscott.............138 C1
Bushey Norwood.......45 F6
Bussex..............154 F6

Butcombe...

Butcombe.............55 B8
Butleigh............157 D4
Butleigh Wotton.....157 C5
Butt's Batch.........35 D1

C

Cad Green...........183 E3
Cambridge Batch......20 C8
Cameley..............76 C8
Camerton.............78 E8
Cannard's Grave.....205 D2
Cannington..........135 C2
Cannon's Marsh......226 C1
Capland.............183 A6
Capton..............132 C2
Carhampton..........131 B5
Carlingcott..........61 B1
Cary Fitzpaine......174 B6
Castle..............198 D4
Castle Cary.........214 B5
Catcott.............137 D2
Catsgore............173 C4
Chaffcombe..........194 C5
Chalkway............194 E2
Chantry.............117 F3
Chapel Allerton......88 D2
Chapel Cleeve.......131 D5
Chapel Leigh........167 A8
Chapmanslade........121 C5
Chard...............223 D4
Chard Junction......198 E7
Chardleigh Green....223 A7
Chardstock..........198 B7
Charlcombe..........27 E3
Charlton
  Creech St Michael..169 F5
  Radstock............97 E5
  Shepton Mallet.....205 E5
Charlton Adam.......173 F7
Charlton Horethorne.176 B2
Charlton Mackrell...173 E7
Charlton Musgrove...161 A2
Charlynch...........152 F8
Charterhouse.........72 C4
Cheddar..............90 D8
Cheddon Fitzpaine...169 A6
Chedzoy.............154 E8
Chelston............180 D8
Chelston Heathfield.180 E7
Chelvey..............18 D5
Chelwood.............59 A8
Chelynch............141 E6
Chesterblade........142 A4
Chew Magna..........39 C4
Chew Stoke...........56 D8

Chewton Keynsham 24 E2
Chewton Mendip 94 E7
Chilcombe 132 F1
Chilcompton 96 C4
Chilson 198 C6
Chilson Common 198 D7
Chilthorne Domer 186 E5
Chilton Cantelo 174 D1
Chilton Polden 137 B2
Chilton Trinity 135 F2
Chipley 166 F2
Chipstable 165 E6
Chiselborough 185 F1
Cholwell 58 F1
Christon 68 D7
Churchill 52 F5
Churchill Green 52 D5
Churchinford 192 A7
Church Row 101 F8
Churchstanton 181 B1
Church Town 19 C5
Clandown 78 E4
Clanville 159 C3
Clapton
  Crewkerne 195 C1
  Midsomer Norton 96 C2
Clapton In Gordano 2 E1
Clapton Wick 7 E6
Clarkham Cross 197 E2
Clatworthy 149 F1
Claverham 17 E1
Claverton 46 C2
Claverton Down 45 F3
Clayhanger 165 C1
Clayhidon 180 E2
Claypits 164 C4
Clays End 43 D6
Clearwood 121 F8
Cleeve 35 B8
Clevedon 6 B3
Clewer 89 D3
Clifton 226 A4
Clifton Wood 226 A2
Clink 120 C6
Cloford 143 A7
Cloford Common 143 B6
Closworth 197 F5
Clutton 58 E3
Clutton Hill 59 B4
Coat 185 D7
Cocklake 108 E7
Cockwood 134 E5
Cold Ashton 12 F6
Coleford 116 F7
Coleford Water 150 F4
Cole's Cross 199 D5
Coley 75 C4
Combe Down 45 B1
Combe Florey 151 C2
Combe Hay 62 D4
Combe Hill 217 A4
Combe St Nicholas 193 D6
Combe Throop 176 F2
Combwich 135 B5
Comeytrowe 212 B1
Compton Bishop 69 A3
Compton Dando 41 D6
Compton Dundon 157 B4
Compton Durville 184 F4
Compton Martin 74 A7
Compton Pauncefoot 175 E5
Congresbury 34 E4
Conkwell 46 C1
Coombe
  Crewkerne 195 B4
  Sampford Peverell 178 A4
  Taunton 169 C8
Coombe Dingle 5 C8
Coppleham 147 D5
Corfe 181 F6
Corsley 121 D2
Corsley Heath 144 E8
Corston 43 B7
Corton Denham 175 D1
Cossington 136 F3
Cotford St Luke 167 E6
Cothelstone 152 A2
Cottle's Oak 119 C5
Coultings 134 F4
Courshay 198 E3
Coursley 151 B4
Courtway 152 C4
Cowbridge 130 B5
Cowslip Green 54 B8
Coxley 139 F6
Coxley Wick 139 E7
Cox's Green 35 E1
Cranmore 142 B6
Crawley 192 F2
Creech Heathfield 169 E5
Creech St Michael 169 D4
Crewkerne 224 D6
Cricket Malherbie 194 D6
Cricket St Thomas 194 E3
Crickham 108 D8
Crimchard 223 B5
Critchill 119 C3
Crocombe 60 C3
Crofton Park 219 B6
Croscombe 204 B8
Cross 69 E2
Crosslands 222 C8
Crowcombe 151 C7
Cucklington 177 D6
Cudworth 194 E5
Culbone 123 B5
Culm Davy 180 A2
Culverhays 132 F1

Curland 182 D4
Curland Common 182 D4
Curload 170 E7
Curry Mallet 183 C8
Curry Rivel 171 C4
Cushuish 152 B1
Cutcombe 129 F2
Cutler's Green 94 F4
Cuttiford's Door 223 C7

D

Darshill 204 F6
Deacons 168 C7
Dean 142 B7
Dertfords 144 D8
Dillington 221 E5
Dimmer 159 C3
Dinder 140 D7
Dinghurst 52 E4
Dinnington 195 B7
Ditcheat 159 C7
Dodhill 168 D7
Dodington 133 F3
Dolemeads 45 B5
Dommett 182 D1
Doniford 202 F6
Donyatt 183 D1
Doulting 141 E6
Doverhay 124 B3
Dowlish Ford 221 B1
Dowlish Wake 194 E7
Downhead
  Stoke St Michael 142 C8
  Yeovilton 174 C4
Downside
  Chilcompton 96 C1
  Felton 19 D1
  Shepton Mallet 205 D8
Dowslands 168 F1
Doynton 12 A8
Draycott
  Cheddar 90 E2
  Yeovil 187 B8
Drayton
  Curry Rival 171 E3
  Southerton 185 D3
Drimpton 199 F7
Dry Hill 2 C6
Duddlestone 181 F8
Dulcote 140 C7
Dulverton 163 E6
Dunball 136 A3
Dundon 156 F3
Dundon Hayes 156 E3
Dundry 21 D2
Dundry Hill 23 B3
Dunkerton 61 E4
Dunster 201 E2
Dunwear 209 D1
Durleigh 208 B3
Durnfield 186 B7
Durston 169 F6

E

East Anstey 162 E5
East Bower 209 E6
East Brent 86 D5
Eastbrook 168 E1
East Chinnock 196 E8
East Clevedon 6 F3
East Coker 197 D7
East Combe 151 E2
East Compton 205 A2
East Cranmore 142 C6
East Dundry 22 A1
East End
  Blagdon 54 F2
  Chewton Mendip 94 E4
  Nailsea 9 A1
  South Cadbury 175 D4
  Stoke St Michael 116 C2
Eastertown 67 D2
East Harptree 74 E4
East Hewish 33 B6
Easthill 120 B4
East Huntspill 136 E7
East Knowstone 162 B2
East Lambrook 220 C8
East Lydford 158 D2
East Lyng 170 D8
East Nynehead 167 D2
Easton 111 A4
Easton-in-Gordano 4 A4
Eastover 209 B5
East Pennard 158 F8
East Quantoxhead 133 B6
East Rolstone 33 B1
East Stoke 186 A4
East Street 139 F1
East Town
  Lydeard St Lawrence 150 E3
  Shepton Mallet 141 A3
East Twerton 44 D7
East Water 92 F2
East Woodlands 144 A7
Ebdon 32 B6
Edford 116 C7
Edgarley 139 E3
Edgcott 128 C1
Edington 137 C3
Edingworth 86 F7
Edithmead 104 F7
Egford 119 B5
Ellicombe 201 E4

Elliots Green 144 B8
Elworthy 150 C6
Emborough 95 C3
Englishcombe 43 F2
Enmore 153 A6
Escott 150 C8
Evercreech 141 E1
Exebridge 163 F3
Exford 128 D1
Exton 147 E4
Eyewell 174 E4

F

Failand 10 C3
Fairfield Park 28 A2
Farleigh 19 D7
Farleigh Hungerford 82 E8
Farleigh Wick 46 E4
Farley 1 B1
Farmborough 60 B6
Farrington Gurney 77 A3
Faulkland 80 E2
Felton 37 C8
Fennington 168 B8
Fenny Castle 139 D7
Fiddington 134 D3
Field 205 C5
Fifehead Magdalen 190 F8
Filwood Park 22 E8
Firepool 213 A5
Fishpond Bottom 199 A1
Fitzhead 166 F7
Fitzroy 168 A6
Five Bells 202 B5
Fivehead 170 F2
Flax Bourton 19 F7
Flaxpool 151 C6
Foddington 174 E8
Ford
  Chewton Mendip 94 E4
  Holcombe Rogus 178 F5
  Wiveliscombe 210 F6
Fordgate 154 C3
Ford Street 180 D5
Forton 223 F1
Four Forks 152 F1
Foxcote 79 F4
Fox Hill 45 A1
Fox Hills 79 A1
Freshford 64 B5
Friarn 133 F1
Frieze Hill 212 D5
Frome 119 E4
Fromefield 120 A6
Frost Hill 34 C5
Fulford 168 C8
Furnham 223 D1

G

Galhampton 175 D8
Galmington 212 C2
Garlandhayes 180 F2
Gasper 161 E4
Girt 175 C2
Glastonbury 206 F5
Goar Knapp 219 D5
Goathill 189 B4
Goathurst 153 B5
Godney 139 A5
Gold's Cross 57 E6
Golsoncott 131 D2
Goosenford 169 A6
Gore 187 F6
Gothelney Green 153 B8
Gotton 169 B7
Gould's Ground 119 E5
Great Elm 118 F7
Green Down 94 B8
Green Gate 178 B2
Greenham
  Drimpton 199 E7
  Wellington 179 B7
Greenhill 78 A3
Green Ore 94 C1
Green Parlour 79 D2
Greensbrook 58 F3
Greenvale 60 B1
Greenway 167 D8
Greinton 155 F7
Greyfield 59 C2
Greylake 155 C4
Greylake Fosse 155 C6
Gribb 199 B6
Grosvenor 28 C1
Gupworthy 148 C6
Gurney Slade 114 F7

H

Hackness 136 C8
Hadspen 214 F6
Haines Hill 212 E2
Halcon 213 D5
Hale 177 D6
Hallatrow 77 B7
Halse 167 B6
Halstock 197 C5
Halsway 151 B4
Ham
  Creech St Michael 169 E4
  Holcombe 116 D6
  Paulton 77 F5
  Wellington 180 D8

Hambridge 184 D8
Ham Green 4 E4
Hamp 208 F2
Ham Street 158 B5
Hamwood 68 C7
Hapsford 119 B8
Hardington 99 E6
Hardington Mandeville 197 A3
Hardington Marsh 196 F4
Hardington Moor 197 A4
Hardway 161 A5
Hare 182 F2
Hartcliffe 22 C4
Hartford 164 C8
Hartmoor 177 F3
Hartswell 210 B3
Haselbury Plucknett 196 C6
Hastings 183 B3
Hatch Beauchamp 183 A7
Hatch Green 183 A6
Havyatt 157 F8
Havyatt Green 53 F7
Hawkchurch 198 E3
Hawkcombe 124 A3
Hawkridge 146 D1
Haybridge 203 A5
Haydon
  Milborne Port 189 B2
  Radstock 97 F8
  Taunton 213 E2
  Wells 113 D5
Hayes Park 78 B2
Headley Park 22 B6
Heale 142 C7
Heathfield 167 E5
Heath House 107 F1
Heaven's Door 188 A8
Hedging 170 A8
Hele 168 A3
Helland 170 C3
Hemington 99 B7
Hemyock 180 B1
Hengrove 23 B6
Henlade 169 D2
Henley 156 B3
Henstridge 190 A6
Henstridge Ash 189 F7
Henstridge Bowden 189 D7
Henstridge Marsh 190 C7
Henton 139 B8
Herons Green 56 C3
Hewish
  Crewkerne 195 D3
  Weston-super-Mare 33 C5
Hicks Gate 24 B8
Highbridge 104 E3
Highbury 117 A7
Higher Alham 142 C4
Higher Burrow 184 E7
Higher Chillington 194 F5
Higher Durston 169 E7
Higher Hadspen 214 E3
Higher Halstock Leigh 197 A2
Higher Nyland 177 C1
Higher Odcombe 186 C2
Higher Sandford 188 C7
Higher Town 200 E8
Higher Vexford 150 E6
High Ham 156 A2
High Littleton 59 C1
Highridge
  Bristol 21 F7
  Dundry 21 D3
Highway 185 E7
Hillcommon 167 E8
Hill Corner 120 E6
Hill End 196 F6
Hillfarrance 167 E3
Hillside
  Axbridge 70 C2
  Midsomer Norton 96 E8
Hinton 187 D7
Hinton Blewett 75 E4
Hinton Charterhouse 63 E1
Hinton St George 195 D7
Hobb's Wall 59 E5
Hockholler 180 E8
Hockholler Green 180 D8
Hockworthy 178 D6
Hoggington 83 D1
Holbear 223 D2
Holcombe 116 C8
Holcombe Rogus 178 F5
Holford 151 F8
Hollands 219 A7
Hollow Brook 57 C6
Holly Brook 110 F5
Holman Clavel 181 E3
Holton 176 C5
Holway
  Sherborne 188 D7
  Taunton 213 C2
  Thorncombe 199 C6
Holwell 143 B8
Holywell 197 C8
Holywell Lake 179 E7
Honey Hall 52 C7
Hook
  Chard 198 B8
  Timsbury 60 D2
Hoopers Pool 83 D1
Horn Ash 199 D7
Hornblotton 158 F5
Horner 129 B8
Horningsham 144 C4
Hornsbury 223 E2
Horrington 113 A1
Horsecastle 17 A2
Horsey 136 C2

Horsington 176 D2
Horton 183 C1
Horton Cross 183 D2
Hotwells 226 A1
Houndsmoor 167 A4
Houndstone 218 A6
Hounsley Batch 38 A3
Howley 192 F4
Huish Champflower 165 F8
Huish Episcopi 172 B5
Hungerford 131 E3
Hunstrete 41 D2
Huntscott 129 E6
Huntsham 178 A7
Huntspill 136 B8
Huntstile 153 C4
Huntworth 154 B5
Hurcott 173 C8
Hurst 185 D5
Hutton 49 E2

I

Icelton 32 C8
Ilchester 173 E1
Ilchester Mead 173 D1
Ilford 184 A4
Ilminster 221 C4
Ilton 183 E4
Inglesbatch 61 C8
Inman's Batch 38 A5
Innox Hill 119 F6
Isle Abbotts 183 F7
Isle Brewers 184 A8
Ivood 35 A3

K

Keenthorne 134 D2
Keinton Mandeville 158 B1
Kelston 26 C3
Kenn 16 F7
Kenn Moor Gate 17 F4
Kenny 183 B4
Keward 203 C2
Kewstoke 31 B4
Keyford 119 F3
Keyford Field 119 F2
Keynsham 24 E3
Killing's Knap 97 B4
Kilmersdon 98 B5
Kilmington 161 F7
Kilmington Common 161 F6
Kilton 133 E6
Kilve 133 C6
Kingdown 37 D5
Kingsbridge 148 E8
Kingsbury Episcopi 185 A8
Kingsbury Regis 217 D3
Kingsdon 173 E4
Kingsdown
  Box 29 F3
  Bristol 227 A4
Kingsmead 228 A2
Kingstone 221 E2
Kingston St Mary 168 E8
Kingston Seymour 16 C2
Kingsway 44 C3
Kingswood 150 E6
Kington Magna 177 E2
Kingweston 157 E2
Kitbridge 198 A6
Kittisford 166 B1
Kittwhistle 199 D6
Knapp 169 F4
Knightcott 50 F3
Knighton 184 D7
Knole 173 A4
Knowle 136 D2
Knowle St Giles 194 B6
Knowstone 162 A2

L

Lambridge 28 C2
Lamyatt 159 F6
Lane End 144 D8
Langaller 169 C6
Langford 212 A8
Langford Budville 166 E2
Langham
  Chard 223 C7
  Gillingham 177 A8
Langley 210 C6
Langley Marsh 210 A7
Langport 172 B5
Langridge 27 E7
Lansdown
  Bath 27 E1
  Langridge 27 B6
Larkhall 28 C2
Latcham 108 F4
Lattiford 176 D5
Launcherley 140 D5
Laverley 140 C2
Laverton 100 F7
Lawford 151 B7
Laymore 199 C7
Leeford 122 B5
Leighland Chapel 149 C2
Leighton 142 E6
Leigh upon Mendip 116 F3
Leigh Woods 11 D4
Lewcombe 197 E2
Lilstock 133 C7

Limington 174 A1
Limpley Stoke 64 A6
Lipyeate 97 E1
Listock 170 C2
Little Green 118 B6
Little Hill 192 F8
Little Keyford 119 E1
Little London 114 F3
Little Norton 186 A2
Littleton 38 D4
Little Weston 175 B4
Litton 75 F2
Locking 50 A4
Locksbrook 44 B6
Lodway 4 B5
Longaller 168 B4
Long Ashton 11 A1
Longcroft 219 A8
Long Cross 37 D7
Longhedge 144 E7
Longhouse 61 D5
Long Load 172 E2
Long Sutton 172 F4
Lopen 185 A1
Lottisham 158 D5
Lovington 158 F1
Lower Aisholt 152 C6
Lower Burrow 184 F7
Lower Canada 49 F2
Lower Chilton Cantelo 187 C8
Lower Claverham 17 F2
Lower Downside 205 C7
Lower Durston 169 F7
Lower Failand 10 A8
Lower Godney 138 F5
Lower Halstock Leigh 197 B2
Lower Harmswell 12 C3
Lower Holditch 198 D5
Lower Keyford 119 F3
Lower Langford 53 C5
Lower Leigh 207 C6
Lower Marston 143 E7
Lower Merridge 152 C5
Lower Milton 203 B8
Lower Odcombe 186 D2
Lower Peasedown 79 B8
Lower Roadwater 131 D1
Lower Rudge 102 D4
Lower Somerton 211 E3
Lower Stratton 220 E1
Lower Strode 56 A8
Lower Swainswick 28 C3
Lower Tippacott 122 A4
Lower Vellow 132 D1
Lower Vexford 150 F6
Lower Weacombe 132 E3
Lower Weare 88 D8
Lower Westford 222 A6
Lower Westholme 140 C3
Lower Weston 44 C7
Lower Whatley 118 D3
Lower Woolston 175 F6
Lower Writhlington 79 C3
Low Ham 172 B8
Lowton 181 B5
Low Water 119 E6
Loxton 68 C4
Luccombe 129 D7
Luckwell Bridge 129 C1
Ludney 194 F7
Lufton 186 D3
Lullington 101 A4
Lulsgate Bottom 37 A8
Luppitt 191 B1
Luxborough 148 E8
Luxton 192 A6
Lyatts 197 B6
Lydeard St Lawrence 151 B3
Lydford Fair Place 158 C3
Lydmarsh 194 C3
Lye Cross 36 C1
Lye Hole 36 E2
Lye's Green 121 B1
Lympsham 67 B1
Lyncombe Hill 45 A4
Lyncombe Vale 45 A3
Lynford-on-Fosse 158 C2
Lyng 170 C7
Lyngford 213 A7

M

Mackham 191 A4
Maiden Bradley 144 C1
Maidenbrook 213 D7
Maiden Head 21 F1
Maines Batch 35 E3
Malmsmead 122 C4
Maperton 176 B5
Mark 106 D4
Mark Causeway 106 A3
Marksbury 42 B1
Marnhull 190 F5
Marsh 192 E5
Marshall's Elm 207 D2
Marshalsea 199 C3
Marshfield 13 E8
Marsh Street 201 F3
Marshwood 199 C2
Marston Bigot 143 D7
Marston Gate 119 C1
Marston Magna 174 F1
Martock 185 D6
Maudlin 199 C8
Maundown 165 F7
May Pole Knap 211 C4
Meadgate East 60 E2
Meadgate West 60 D2
Meare 138 D4
Meare Green
Hatch Beauchamp 169 F1
Stoke St Gregory 170 D5
Mearns 59 E2
Mells 118 B7
Mells Green 118 A6
Merridge 152 D5
Merriott 195 E7
Merriottsford 195 F7
Middle Burnham 104 D8
Middle Chinnock 196 C8
Middle Green 222 D3
Middle Leigh 207 C4
Middle Luxton 191 F5
Middle Stoughton 108 A8
Middlezoy 155 B3
Midford 63 C6
Mid Lambrook 220 A8
Midsomer Norton 78 B3
Midway 115 E2
Milborne Port 217 E2
Milborne Wick 217 B6
Millbrook 198 A1
Millhayes 180 C1
Millmoor 179 E1
Millwey Rise 198 A2
Milton
Martock 185 E8
Weston-Super-Mare 31 C2
Milton Clevedon 160 A8
Milverton 166 F4
Minehead 201 A8
Misterton 224 E3
Monksilver 150 A8
Monkton Combe 45 F1
Monkton Farleigh 46 F7
Monkton Heathfield 213 E8
Montacute 186 B3
Moolham 221 C1
Moor 220 C3
Moorhayne 192 D2
Moorlands 44 D3
Moorledge 39 E1
Moorlinch 155 E7
Morebath 164 B3
Mount Radford 208 C6
Muchelney 172 B3
Muchelney Ham 172 B2
Mudford 187 D6
Mudford Sock 187 B6
Mudgley 138 D8

N

Nailsbourne 168 D7
Nailsea 8 E3
Nailwell 61 D6
Narford's 193 C1
Nash 197 C8
Neighbourne 115 C5
Nempnett Thrubwell 55 D5
Netherclay 182 B7
Nether Compton 187 F4
Nethercott 151 C3
Netherhay 199 F8
Netherstoke 197 D3
Nether Stowey 134 B3
Nettlebridge 115 D6
Nettlecombe 149 F8
Newbridge 44 B8
Newbury
Coleford 98 B1
Horningsham 144 E4
Newcott 192 C3
New Cross 184 F6
Newport 170 B2
Newton
Combe St Nicholas 193 A7
Watchet 132 E1
Newton St Loe 43 D6
Newtown
Axbridge 69 D2
Bridgwater 208 E6
New Town
Bishop Sutton 57 D7
Freshford 81 F8
Hatch Beauchamp 182 E4
Kington Magna 177 E1
Milborne Port 217 B2
Paulton 77 D6
Wedmore 138 E8
Yeovil 219 C6
Nimmer 223 C8
Northay
Combe St Nicholas 193 B6
Hawkchurch 199 A3
North Barrow 175 A8
North Brewham 161 A7
North Cadbury 175 D6
North Cheriton 176 C4
North Coker 197 D8
North Curry 170 C4
Northend 28 F5
North End
Clutton 58 E5
Millmoor 179 E3
Taunton 169 D5
Yatton 16 F3
Northfield
Bridgwater 208 C4
Radstock 79 B1
Somerton 211 C5
Northgate 210 C5
North Newton 153 F2
Northover Glastonbury 206 B3
Ilchester 173 E2
North Perrott 196 C4
North Petherton 153 F4
North Stoke 26 C6
North Town
North Cadbury 175 C7
North Wootton 140 D5
Taunton 212 E5
North Weston 2 C2
Northwick 105 F6
North Wick 39 D8
North Widcombe 57 B1
North Wootton
Sherborne 188 F1
Wells 140 C4
Norton 31 D4
Norton Fitzwarren 168 B4
Norton Hawkfield 39 F6
Norton Hill 97 B7
Norton Malreward 40 B7
Norton St Philip 81 F4
Norton Sub Hamdon 185 F3
Norton's Wood 7 C5
Novers Park 22 D8
Nunney 143 C8
Nunney Catch 143 B7
Nye 51 E8
Nyland 90 C1
Nynehead 167 C1

O

Oake 167 D4
Oakhill 115 A3
Oare 122 E4
Oareford 122 F3
Oathill 199 E8
Obridge 213 A6
Odcombe 186 D2
Odd Down 44 D2
Old Cleeve 131 E5
Old Ditch 110 E7
Old Down 95 F3
Oldfield Park 44 E4
Oldford 101 B1
Old Mills 77 D3
Oldmixon 49 B1
Old Way 184 A4
Oldways End 162 E3
Orchard Common 182 A8
Othery 155 B2
Otterford 181 E1
Otterhampton 135 A6
Over Compton 187 F4
Overleigh 207 C3
Over Stowey 134 A1
Over Stratton 220 D1
Overton 169 C7
Oxenpill 138 C4

P

Packsaddle 119 F7
Paintmoor 194 B4
Panborough 138 F8
Parbrook 158 D7
Pardlestone 133 C5
Park 156 D1
Park Corner 64 A4
Paulton 77 F5
Pawlett 136 A5
Payton 179 F7
Pear Ash 161 E2
Peasedown St John 79 C8
Peasmarsh 194 B7
Pecking Mill 159 D8
Pedwell 156 A7
Pendomer 197 B5
Penn Mill 219 E6
Pennsylvania 12 F7
Penselwood 161 C2
Pensford 40 E4
Periton 200 D6
Perry Green 208 B8
Perrymead 45 B3
Perry Street 198 E8
Petton 165 A3
Pibsbury 172 C5
Pickney 168 B8
Pict's Hill 172 B6
Pill 4 C4
Pilsdon 199 F2
Pilton 140 F3
Pitcombe 215 D3
Pitcot 115 F7
Pitminster 181 E6
Pitney 172 C7
Pitsford Hill 150 E1
Plainsfield 152 B7
Pleamore Cross 222 A2
Plummer's Hill 77 E6
Podimore 174 A3
Poleshill 166 C1
Polsham 139 D5
Poole 222 F8
Pooltown 148 E8
Porlock 124 A4
Porlockford 123 F4
Porlock Weir 123 D4
Portbury 3 D3
Portfield 171 E5
Portishead 2 B4
Portland 207 A6
Portway 207 D4
Potters Hill 20 B1
Pound 220 F2
Poyntington 188 E6
Prescott 179 C1
Prestleigh 141 D3
Preston 150 E6
Preston Bowyer 167 B5
Preston Plucknett 218 D4
Priddy 92 D3
Primrose Hill 27 D1
Priorswood 213 B7
Priston 61 B5
Providence Place 77 F1
Publow 40 F5
Puckington 184 B5
Pudleigh 223 B8
Puriton 136 C4
Purn 67 A7
Purse Caundle 189 D4
Purtington 195 A4
Puxton 33 D3
Pyleigh 151 B1
Pylle 141 B1
Pyrland 213 A8

Q

Quarr 177 E5
Queen Camel 174 F3
Queen Charlton 24 B3

R

Raddington 165 B4
Radford 78 C8
Radlet 134 C1
Radstock 78 E1
Rapps 183 D3
Rawridge 191 F1
Red Ball 179 C4
Redcliffe Bay 1 E4
Redhill 36 D3
Redlane 191 F7
Redlynch 160 D4
Red Post 79 B7
Regil 37 F2
Rhode 153 D5
Rich's Holford 151 C4
Rickford 54 B3
Ridge 74 C5
Ridgeway 143 C7
Riding Gate 177 B8
Rimpton 188 A8
Riverside
Midsomer Norton 96 F7
Wellington 222 B6
Roadwater 131 C1
Rockwell Green 222 B5
Rode 101 F8
Rodgrove 177 C3
Rodhuish 131 B2
Rodney Stoke 91 A1
Rodway 135 B3
Rolstone 32 F2
Rookham 112 B5
Rooks Bridge 87 C5
Rook's Nest 150 C4
Rosemary Lane 180 D1
Rotcombe 59 D2
Roundham 195 D4
Rowbarton 212 E7
Rowberrow 53 A1
Rowford 168 F6
Royston Water 192 B7
Rudge 102 D5
Ruishton 169 C3
Rumwell 168 B2
Runnington 179 F8
Rush Hill 44 B2
Rydon 169 E8

S

St Catherine 13 F1
St Cleers 211 C3
St Decumans 202 B6
St Georges 32 D3
St Pauls 227 C4
Saltford 25 D2
Sampford Arundel 179 E5
Sampford Brett 202 E1
Sampford Moor 179 F5
Sampford Peverell 178 E1
Sand 108 C2
Sandford 52 A3
Sandford Batch 51 F2
Sandford Orcas 188 C7
Sawyer's Hill 180 E7
School House 199 A5
Seaborough 195 E1
Sea Mills 5 B6
Seavington St Mary 184 D1
Seavington St Michael 184 F2
Sector 198 B1
Selworthy 124 D3
Seven Ash 151 D4
Shalford 216 D8
Shapwick 137 F1
Sharpstone 64 A4
Shawford 101 D7
Sheepway 3 B5
Shepton Beauchamp 184 E3
Shepton Mallet 205 D6
Shepton Montague 160 B2
Sherborne
Litton 75 D3
Milborne Port 225 C6
Sherford 212 E1
Shillingford 164 E2
Shipham 70 F7
Shiplate 67 F6
Shirehampton 4 E7
Shockerwick 29 F5
Shopnoller 151 E3
Shoreditch 169 A1
Short Street 121 F6
Shoscombe 79 E6
Shoscombe Vale 79 E5
Shurton 134 C7
Sidbrook 169 B6
Sidcot 70 C7
Sigwells 175 E2
Silver Street 180 F8
Simonsbath 127 B2
Simonsburrow 180 C3
Single Hill 80 A5
Sion Hill 27 E1
Skilgate 164 E6
Slape Cross 209 F6
Slough Green 182 D7
Small Way 214 B2
Smeatharpe 191 E5
Smitham Hill 74 D2
Sneyd Pk 5 D3
Sockety 196 D1
Soho 117 A5
Somerdale 24 E7
Somerton 211 D3
Somerton Randle 173 C7
Southay 185 B6
South Barrow 175 A6
South Brewham 161 A6
South Cadbury 175 C4
South Chard 198 C8
South Cheriton 176 D3
South Common 198 A4
Southdown 44 B4
South Down 191 F6
Southfield 79 A2
South Hill 211 A1
Southmarsh 161 B1
South Perrott 196 C1
South Petherton 220 C4
Southstoke 62 E7
Southtown 183 C3
South Twerton 44 C5
Southway 139 D5
Southwick
Trowbridge 83 F2
Watchfield 105 E2
South Widcombe 75 C6
Sparkford 175 A5
Spaxton 152 E8
Speckington 174 C2
Spike Island 226 B1
Splatt 152 E8
Spring Gardens 119 D8
Stafford's Green 188 D8
Stalbridge 190 C4
Stalbridge Weston 190 A3
Stallen 188 A3
Standerwick 102 C2
Stanton Drew 39 F2
Stanton Prior 42 E2
Stanton Wick 58 D8
Staple Fitzpaine 182 C5
Staplegrove 212 C8
Staplehay 181 D8
Staple Lawns 182 B5
Stapleton 185 E8
Stapley 191 D8
Star 52 D1
Stathe 171 B8
Stawell 137 A1
Stawley 166 A1
Steanbow 140 D2
Steart
Babcary 174 C6
Combwich 135 D8
Stembridge 185 A7
Stewley 183 B5
Sticklepath
Combe St Nicholas 193 D7
Monksilver 149 E7
Sticklinch 140 C1
Stileway 138 E3
Stock 53 B8
Stockland Bristol 135 A6
Stocklinch 184 B4
Stocklinch Ottersey 184 C4
Stocklinch St
Magdalen 184 C4
Stockwood 23 E5
Stockwood Vale 24 C6
Stoford 197 F8
Stogumber 150 D8
Stogursey 134 C5
Stoke Bishop 5 E5
Stoke Pero 128 F6
Stoke St Gregory 170 E6
Stoke St Mary 169 C1
Stoke St Michael 116 B2
Stoke sub Hamdon 185 F5
Stoke Trister 177 B7
Stolford 134 F8
Stone Allerton 88 C3
Ston Easton 95 E8
Stonebridge
Banwell 51 A4
Frome 120 A7
Stone-edge Batch 8 D4
Stone Hill 207 A4
Stoney Stoke 160 F3
Stoney Stratton 141 F2
Stony Head 169 F1

Stony Knaps ... 199 D7
Stony Littleton ... 80 B6
Stoodham ... 220 D6
Stopgate ... 192 C4
Stoughton Cross ... 108 B8
Stourton ... 161 F5
Stourton Caundle ... 189 F2
Stout ... 156 B2
Stowell ... 176 C1
Stowey ... 57 F4
Stratton-on-the Fosse ... 96 F1
Stream ... 132 A2
Street
  Chard ... 194 C2
  Glastonbury ... 207 C7
Street Ash ... 193 C8
Street End ... 54 D3
Street on the Fosse ... 141 C2
Stringston ... 133 F5
Strode ... 55 E7
Studley Green ... 83 F6
Sturford ... 144 F7
Summerlands ... 218 F6
Sutton ... 159 B4
Sutton Bingham ... 197 D6
Sutton Mallet ... 155 B7
Sutton Montis ... 175 C3
Sutton Wick ... 57 B2
Swell ... 171 A2
Swineford ... 26 A7
Sydenham ... 209 C5
Synderford ... 199 C6

T

Tacker Street ... 149 C8
Tadhill ... 116 F2
Tadwick ... 12 E1
Tangier ... 212 E4
Tarnock ... 87 D6
Tatworth ... 198 C8
Taunton ... 212 D5
Tavern Scott ... 38 D1
Tellisford ... 82 E4
Temple ... 144 E7
Temple Cloud ... 58 E1
Templecombe ... 176 E1
Terhill ... 151 F3
Theale ... 109 C1
The Butts ... 119 E3
The Folly ... 94 F6
The Mount ... 119 F2
The Oval ... 44 C4
The Wrangle ... 74 A5
Thicket Mead ... 77 F3
Thorncombe ... 199 B6
Thorne Coffin ... 218 A8
Thorne St Margaret ... 179 D8
Thorney ... 172 A1
Thornfalcon ... 169 E2
Thoulstone ... 121 F4
Three Ashes
  North Cadbury ... 175 C7
  Oakhill ... 115 E1
Thurlbear ... 182 C8
Thurloxton ... 153 D1
Tickenham ... 7 F4
Tillworth ... 198 D3
Timberscombe ... 130 C4
Timsbury ... 60 B1
Timsbury Bottom ... 60 A1
Tintinhull ... 186 C6
Tivington ... 129 F8
Tolland ... 150 E3
Tone ... 222 A8
Tonedale ... 222 B7
T'other Side the Hill ... 115 B7
Toulton ... 152 A2
Towerhead ... 51 D4

Townsend ... 92 D4
Towns End ... 77 E4
Town's End ... 116 E3
Tracebridge ... 179 A8
Treble's Holford ... 151 C4
Treborough ... 149 A7
Trent ... 187 F5
Trinity ... 119 E5
Triscombe ... 151 D6
Trowbridge ... 83 F7
Trudoxhill ... 143 C6
Trull ... 168 D1
Tuckerton ... 169 F8
Tucking Mill ... 63 C8
Tudhay ... 198 C3
Tunley ... 61 B3
Turleigh ... 64 F6
Twerton ... 44 A5
Tyndall's Park ... 226 C4
Tyning
  Radstock ... 79 B3
  Timsbury ... 60 A2
Tytherington ... 143 E8
Tytherleigh ... 198 C6

U

Ubley ... 55 E1
Ubley Sideling ... 73 D8
Udley ... 35 C4
Ullcombe ... 192 A4
Upcott ... 168 B3
Uphill ... 48 C2
Uplowman ... 178 B2
Up Mudford ... 187 D5
Upottery ... 191 F2
Upper Benter ... 115 C7
Upper Cheddon ... 168 F7
Upper Coxley ... 139 F6
Upper Godney ... 139 A6
Upper Langford ... 53 C3
Upper Langridge ... 27 B7
Upper Littleton ... 38 B6
Upper Milton ... 203 D7
Upper Radford ... 78 B8
Upper Stanton Drew ... 40 B2
Upper Swainswick ... 28 B5
Upper Vobster ... 117 D8
Upper Westholme ... 140 D4
Upper Weston ... 27 A3
Upper Westwood ... 64 E4
Uppotery ... 191 F2
Upton
  Langport ... 172 D5
  Skilgate ... 164 F8
Upton Cheyney ... 26 B8
Upton Noble ... 142 F2
Urgashay ... 174 C3

V

Vagg ... 186 F5
Verrington ... 216 A5
Victoria Park ... 226 B3
Vobster ... 117 C7
Vole ... 106 B8
Voxmoor ... 222 F1

W

Wadbrook ... 198 C4
Wadbury ... 118 D7
Waddicombe ... 162 E6
Wadeford ... 193 D5
Wagg ... 172 B5
Waggs Plot ... 198 B4
Walcombe ... 203 E7

Wales ... 174 E3
Walford ... 169 D7
Wallace ... 74 E3
Wall Mead ... 60 C4
Walpole ... 136 B4
Walrow ... 105 C2
Walton ... 156 E7
Walton in Gordano ... 7 B7
Walton St Mary ... 6 E5
Wambrook ... 193 C3
Wanstrow ... 142 F4
Warleigh ... 46 C6
Washbrook ... 89 A1
Washford ... 131 F4
Watchet ... 202 B6
Watchfield ... 105 D2
Watergore ... 220 B2
Waterlip ... 142 A7
Waterrow ... 165 F4
Waterside ... 78 E1
Wayford ... 195 B1
Way Wick ... 32 E1
Weacombe ... 132 F3
Weare ... 88 E6
Wearne ... 172 A7
Webbington ... 68 E4
Wedmore ... 108 D3
Weekmoor ... 167 B3
Welham ... 160 A2
Wellington ... 222 D7
Wellisford ... 179 D8
Wellow ... 62 D1
Wells ... 203 E4
Wellsprings ... 212 F8
Welshmill ... 119 F6
Welton ... 78 B2
Welton Hollow ... 78 D2
Wembdon ... 208 C6
West Anstey ... 162 C6
West Bagborough ... 151 F4
West Bourton ... 177 E8
West Bradley ... 158 C7
West Buckland ... 180 F7
Westbury on Trym ... 5 F7
Westbury-sub-Mendip ... 110 D6
West Camel ... 174 D3
West Chinnock ... 196 B8
West Coker ... 197 A8
Westcombe
  Batcombe ... 142 B2
  Somerton ... 172 E7
West Compton ... 204 C3
West End
  Blagdon ... 54 E3
  Chewton Mendip ... 93 F6
  Clevedon ... 6 B2
  Frome ... 119 F5
  Nailsea ... 17 F7
  Somerton ... 211 C3
Westfield ... 97 C8
Westford ... 179 F7
Westham ... 107 C2
West Harptree ... 74 E6
West Hatch ... 182 E7
Westhay ... 138 A5
West Hewish ... 33 A5
West Hill
  Nailsea ... 9 A5
  Portishead ... 2 A5
  Wincanton ... 216 B4
West Hill Gardens ... 78 E1
West Huntspill ... 136 A7
West Lambrook ... 184 F5
Westleigh ... 179 A4
West Leigh ... 150 F1
West Luccombe ... 124 C3
West Lydford ... 158 C2
West Lyng ... 170 B7
West Monkton ... 169 C7
West Mudford ... 187 C7

West Newton ... 169 F8
Weston ... 27 B1
Weston Bampfylde ... 175 B3
Weston in Gordano ... 1 F1
Weston Park ... 27 C1
Weston-Super-Mare ... 48 B7
Weston Town ... 142 E5
Westonzoyland ... 154 E5
Westowe ... 151 A3
West Pennard ... 140 B1
West Porlock ... 123 F4
Westport ... 184 C7
West Quantoxhead ... 132 E4
West Shepton ... 205 A4
West Stoke ... 185 E4
West Stoughton ... 107 E6
West Town
  Backwell ... 18 F5
  Baltonsborough ... 157 F6
  Ubley ... 55 B6
West Wick ... 32 C1
Westwood ... 64 E3
West Woodlands ... 143 F6
Weycroft ... 198 B2
Whatley
  Frome ... 118 D4
  Winsham ... 194 C1
Wheddon Cross ... 129 E1
Wheeler's Hill ... 78 C2
Whipcott ... 179 B5
Whitbourne Springs ... 144 F7
Whitchurch ... 23 D4
Whitcombe ... 175 D2
White Ball ... 179 D6
Whitecross ... 171 E3
White Cross
  Bishop Sutton ... 57 E1
  Burnham-on-Sea ... 105 B8
  Hallatrow ... 76 F6
  Zeals ... 161 F3
Whitefield ... 210 B8
White Gate ... 194 B1
Whitehall ... 180 A1
White Hill ... 79 F6
Whitelackington ... 184 C2
Whitestaunton ... 193 B5
Whiteway ... 44 A4
Whitley Batts ... 40 F2
Whitnage ... 178 C2
Whitnell ... 134 D2
Wick
  Burnham-on-Sea ... 85 E8
  Glastonbury ... 139 E2
  Stogursey ... 134 D7
Wick St Lawrence ... 32 B7
Widcombe ... 45 C4
Wigborough ... 220 F1
Wilkinthroop ... 176 C2
Willand ... 191 E8
Willett ... 150 E4
Willhayne ... 223 A8
Williton ... 202 D3
Wilmington ... 43 A1
Wilton ... 212 F2

Witcombe ... 185 F8
Witham Friary ... 143 C3
Withiel Florey ... 148 E4
Withybrook ... 115 E3
Withycombe ... 131 B4
Withyditch ... 61 C3
Withypool ... 146 C6
Withywood ... 22 A4
Wiveliscombe ... 210 B4
Wonderstone ... 67 D6
Woodborough ... 70 B8
Woodcombe ... 200 C8
Woodford
  Watchet ... 132 A1
  Wells ... 140 A6
Woodgate ... 179 E2
Woodhill
  Portishead ... 2 D7
  Stoke St Gregory ... 170 F6
Woodlands ... 183 E6
Wookey ... 139 E8
Wookey Hole ... 203 A7
Woolavington ... 136 F4
Woollard ... 41 A6
Woolley ... 27 F5
Woolminstone ... 195 B3
Woolston
  North Cadbury ... 175 E6
  Watchet ... 132 D2
Woolverton ... 82 C1
Wootton Courtenay ... 129 F6
Worle ... 31 F2
Worlebury ... 31 A2
Worminster ... 140 C5
Worth ... 139 D8
Worthy ... 123 E5
Wrangway ... 180 A4
Wrantage ... 170 A1
Wraxall
  Ditcheat ... 159 A7
  Nailsea ... 9 C3
Wreath ... 194 C3
Wrington ... 35 E1
Writhlington ... 79 C2
Wyke Champflower ... 215 A6

Y

Yalway ... 153 A1
Yanley ... 21 C8
Yarcombe ... 192 D3
Yarde ... 132 A2
Yarford ... 168 C8
Yarrow ... 106 E3
Yarlington ... 175 F8
Yatton ... 34 C8
Yeabridge ... 220 E2
Yenston ... 189 F8
Yeovil ... 218 E4
Yeovil Marsh ... 187 A6
Yeovilton ... 174 A1

Z

Zeals ... 161 F2

Index of streets, hospitals, industrial estates, railway stations, schools, shopping centres, universities and places of interest

510–Ash 233

5102 Appartments BS1 . . 227 B4

A

Abbas & Templecombe CE Prim Sch BA8 . . . 176 E1
Abbey Cl
Curry Rivel TA10 . . . 171 D4
Keynsham BS31 . . . 24 F6
7 Sherborne DT9 . . . 225 D3
Tatworth TA20 . . . 198 D8
Wookey BA5 . . . 139 D8
Abbey Ct BA2 . . . 45 B7
Abbey Fields TA10 . . . 171 D4
Abbey Gate St BA1 . . . 228 C2
Abbey Gdns BS22 . . . 49 E8
Abbey Gn BA1 . . . 228 C2
Abbey Hill Dro TA3 . . . 182 E5
Abbey La BA3 . . . 64 A4
Abbey Lodge BA6 . . . 206 E4
Abbey Manor Bsns Ctr BA21 . . . 218 D5
Abbey Meads BA6 . . . 206 E3
Abbey Mews TA20 . . . 198 D8
Abbey Pk BS31 . . . 24 F6
Abbey Rd
Bristol BS9 . . . 5 F7
Chilcompton BA3 . . . 96 D2
Sherborne DT9 . . . 225 D4
Stratton-on-t F BA3 . . . 96 F2
Washford TA23 . . . 131 E3
Yeovil BA21 . . . 218 D6
Abbey St
Bath BA1 . . . 228 C2
Crewkerne TA18 . . . 224 C6
Hinton St George TA17 . . . 195 C7
Abbey Trad Est BA21 . . . 218 D6
Abbey View
Bath BA2 . . . 45 B5
Radstock BA3 . . . 79 A3
Abbey View Gdns BA2 . . . 45 B5
Abbeywood Dr BS9 . . . 5 C5
Abbot's Cl BS22 . . . 32 A3
Abbotsbury Rd BS48 . . . 8 D1
Abbots Cl
Bristol BS14 . . . 23 A3
Burnham-on-S TA8 . . . 104 B6
Ilminster TA19 . . . 221 B3
Oxenpill BA6 . . . 138 C4
Seavington St Michael TA19 . . . 184 E2
Abbots Ct BA6 . . . 206 D4
Abbotsfield TA4 . . . 210 A4
Abbotsfield Cotts TA4 . . . 210 B4
Abbots Fish Ho* BA6 . . . 138 D4
Abbots Horn BS48 . . . 8 D2
Abbots Leigh Rd BS8 . . . 11 C7
Abbots Meade BA21 . . . 218 D5
Abbots Way
Minehead TA24 . . . 200 C6
Pilton BA4 . . . 140 E3
Sherborne DT9 . . . 225 B3
Yeovil BA21 . . . 218 D6
Abbott's Wootton La DT6 . . . 199 B1
Abbott La TA16 . . . 196 A8
Abbotts Farm Cl BS39 . . . 77 D5
Abbotts Rd BA22 . . . 173 D1
Abbotts Way TA3 . . . 183 F7
Abels La DT9 . . . 187 F5
Aberdeen Rd BS6 . . . 226 B4
Abingdon Gdns BA2 . . . 62 D8
Abingdon St TA8 . . . 104 B6
Abington Cross TA24 . . . 124 B4
Ablake La TA10 . . . 172 C5
Ableton Wlk BS9 . . . 5 C5
Abon Ho BS9 . . . 5 C4
Acacia Ave BS23 . . . 49 B8
Acacia Ct BS31 . . . 24 C4
Acacia Dr BA11 . . . 120 C7
Acacia Gdns TA2 . . . 213 E7
Acacia Gr BA2 . . . 44 C3
Acacia Rd BA3 . . . 79 E1
Accommodation Rd BS24 . 66 E6
Acer Dr BA21 . . . 218 C7
Ackland's Dro TA10 . . . 155 F4
Acland Round TA4 . . . 167 E6
Acombe Cross TA3 . . . 191 E8
Aconite Cl BS22 . . . 32 B5
Acorn Cl
Frome BA11 . . . 119 D5
Highbridge TA9 . . . 104 D4
Acorn Gr BS13 . . . 21 E6
Acre Cotts TA21 . . . 222 E6
Acre La TA11 . . . 211 F4
Acreman Ct DT9 . . . 225 C4
Acreman Pl DT9 . . . 225 D3
Acreman St DT9 . . . 225 D4
Acresbush Cl BS13 . . . 22 A5
Acres Ct BA22 . . . 197 F8
Acres The 1 TA12 . . . 185 E6
Actis Rd BA6 . . . 206 E3
Adam's La TA5 . . . 134 D6
Adams Cl
Highbridge TA9 . . . 104 C2
Peasedown St John BA2 . . . 79 D8
Adams Ct 5 BS8 . . . 11 F6
Adams Ho TA19 . . . 221 B3
Adams Mdw TA19 . . . 221 A4
Adam St TA8 . . . 104 B6
Adastral Rd BS24 . . . 50 D4
Adber Cl BA21 . . . 219 E8
Adber Cross DT9 . . . 187 F6
Adcombe Cl TA3 . . . 181 D5
Adcombe Rd TA2 . . . 213 B8
Adder La TA7 . . . 169 F8
Adderwell BA11 . . . 120 A3
Adderwell Cl BA11 . . . 120 A3
Addicott Rd BS23 . . . 48 E6
Addiscombe Rd
Bristol BS14 . . . 23 B5
Weston-Super-Mare BS23 . . . 48 E4
Addison Gr TA2 . . . 212 E6
Addlewell La 11 BA20 . . . 219 B4
Adlams Central Pk BA6 . . . 206 B3
Admiral's Mead BA6 . . . 157 E4
Admiral's Wlk BS20 . . . 2 B5
Admiral Blake Mus* TA6 . . . 209 A4
Admirals Cl
Sherborne DT9 . . . 225 E5
Watchet TA23 . . . 202 D6
Admirals Ct TA6 . . . 208 F5
Admiralty Way TA1 . . . 213 C5
Adsborough Hill TA2 . . . 169 D7
Adsborough La TA2 . . . 169 D7
Adscombe Ave TA6 . . . 209 C6
Adscombe La TA5 . . . 134 A1
Aelfric Mdw BS20 . . . 2 F4
Ainslie's Belvedere BA1 . . 228 B4
Ainstey Dr BA22 . . . 175 A4
Airey Hos TA13 . . . 220 D1
Airport Rd BS14 . . . 23 A8
Airport Rdbt BS24 . . . 49 E7
Airport View Cvn Pk BS24 . 49 D7
Aisecome Way BS22 . . . 49 C6
Akeman Cl BA21 . . . 218 D7
Akeman Way BS11 . . . 4 C8
Alamein Rd TA23 . . . 202 E6
Alard Rd BS4 . . . 22 F7
Alastair Cl BA21 . . . 218 F7
Alastair Dr BA21 . . . 218 F7
Albany BS23 . . . 30 F1
Albany Cl DT9 . . . 225 E6
Albany Ct 6 BA1 . . . 44 B6
Albany Rd BA2 . . . 44 C6
Albemarle Rd TA1 . . . 212 F5
Albermarle Row 9 BS8 . . . 11 F6
Albert Ave
Peasedown St John BA2 . . . 79 C7
Weston-Super-Mare BS23 . . . 48 E6
Albert Bldgs BA6 . . . 206 D5
Albert Cl BA21 . . . 218 E7
Albert Ct
Bridgwater TA6 . . . 208 E4
15 Taunton TA1 . . . 213 A4
Weston-Super-Mare BS23 . . . 48 E6
Albert Pl
Bath BA2 . . . 45 C1
Portishead BS20 . . . 2 D4
Albert Quadrant BS23 . . . 48 E8
Albert Rd
Clevedon BS21 . . . 6 C3
Keynsham BS31 . . . 24 E5
Portishead BS20 . . . 2 D5
Weston-Super-Mare BS23 . . . 48 E6
Albert Row DT9 . . . 225 E4
Albert St TA6 . . . 208 E4
Albert Terr BA2 . . . 44 C6
Albion Bldgs BA1 . . . 44 D7
Albion Cl TA6 . . . 209 B5
Albion Pl
16 Bristol BS2 . . . 227 C3
Frome BA11 . . . 119 D3
Albion Rd BA22 . . . 174 A2
Albion Terr
Bath BA1 . . . 228 A3
Cheddar BS27 . . . 90 B7
Alburys BS40 . . . 35 D3
Alcombe Cross TA24 . . . 201 B5
Alcombe Rd TA24 . . . 201 A5
Aldeburgh Pl BA14 . . . 83 F6
Alder Cl
North Petherton TA6 . . . 153 F3
Taunton TA1 . . . 213 D1
Williton TA4 . . . 202 E3
Aldercombe Rd BS9 . . . 5 C8
Alder Ct BS14 . . . 23 B5
Alderdown Cl BS11 . . . 5 A8
Alder Gr
Crewkerne TA18 . . . 224 C7
Yeovil BA20 . . . 218 E2
Alderley Rd BA2 . . . 44 B4
Alderney Rd TA6 . . . 209 C3
Alder Terr BA3 . . . 78 E2
Alder Way BA2 . . . 62 D8
Alder Wlk BA11 . . . 120 B7
Aldondale Gdns BA20 . . . 219 B3
Aldwick Ave BS13 . . . 22 C3
Aldwick La BS40 . . . 54 C7
Aldworth Ho BS2 . . . 227 C4
Aldwych Cl TA8 . . . 104 C6
Alec Ricketts Cl BA2 . . . 43 F5
Alexander Bldgs 12 BA1 . . . 28 B1
Alexander Cl TA3 . . . 169 D5
Alexander Hall BA3 . . . 64 C6
Alexander Ho 5 BS23 . . . 48 F4
Alexander Mews 5 BS23 . . 48 E7
Alexander Pl BA3 . . . 64 C6
Alexanders Cl BA6 . . . 138 C4
Alexander Way BS49 . . . 34 B7
Alexandra Ct BS21 . . . 6 C4
Alexandra Gdns TA24 . . . 201 A6
Alexandra Mews TA24 . . . 201 A7
Alexandra Par BS23 . . . 48 E7
Alexandra Pk BS39 . . . 77 E5
Alexandra Pl BA2 . . . 45 C1
Alexandra Rd
Bath BA2 . . . 228 C1
Bridgwater TA6 . . . 208 E5
Bristol BS8 . . . 226 B4
Bristol, Highridge BS13 . . . 21 F7
Clevedon BS21 . . . 6 C4
Frome BA11 . . . 119 F4
Minehead TA24 . . . 201 A6
Wellington TA21 . . . 222 D6
Yeovil BA21 . . . 219 D6
Alexandra Terr BS39 . . . 77 E5
Alexevia Cvn Pk TA3 . . . 169 C3
Aley TA5 . . . 152 A8
Alford La BA4, BA7 . . . 159 B4
Alfords Ridge BA3 . . . 117 A7
Alfoxton Rd TA6 . . . 208 C4
Alfred's Twr* BA10 . . . 161 C6
Alfred's Way BA9 . . . 216 B3
Alfred Cres BA4 . . . 205 B4
Alfred Ct 4 BS23 . . . 48 E7
Alfred Hill BS2 . . . 227 A4
Alfred Par BS2 . . . 227 A4
Alfred Pl BS2 . . . 226 C4
Alfred St
Bath BA1 . . . 228 B3
Taunton TA1 . . . 213 B4
Wells BA5 . . . 203 D3
Weston-Super-Mare BS23 . . . 48 E8
Algar Ct BA5 . . . 203 B4
Alice St BA11 . . . 143 A6
Alison Gdns BS48 . . . 19 A7
Allandale Ct TA8 . . . 104 B8
Allandale Rd TA8 . . . 104 A8
Allanmead Rd BS14 . . . 23 B8
Allans Way BS24 . . . 49 F7
Allen Dr BA4 . . . 205 A6
Allen Rd TA6 . . . 208 F1
Allens La
Shipham BS25 . . . 70 F8
Wells BA5 . . . 112 E1
Allenslade Flats TA4 . . . 210 C5
Aller BS24 . . . 49 B2
Aller Dro
Aller TA10 . . . 171 D8
Othery TA7 . . . 155 C1
Allermoor Dro BS28 . . . 138 B8
Aller Par BS24 . . . 49 B2
Allerpark La TA24 . . . 123 F3
Allerton Cres BS14 . . . 23 B4
Allerton Gdns BS14 . . . 23 B5
Allerton Rd
Bridgwater TA6 . . . 209 B7
Bristol BS14 . . . 23 B4
All Hallows Prep Sch BA4 . . . 142 C6
Allingham Rd BA21 . . . 219 C7
Allington Cl TA1 . . . 213 E4
Allington Gdns BS48 . . . 18 C8
Allington Rd BS3 . . . 226 C1
Allotment Dro
Combe St Nicholas TA20 . . 193 C5
Glastonbury BA16 . . . 138 D1
Allotment Rd BA22 . . . 175 C3
All Saints' La BS1 . . . 227 A2
All Saints' Rd
Bristol BS8 . . . 226 A4
Weston-Super-Mare BS23 . . . 30 E1
All Saints' St BS1 . . . 227 A3
All Saints' Terr TA6 . . . 209 B4
All Saints CE Prim Sch
Dulverton TA22 . . . 163 D6
Montacute TA15 . . . 186 B3
All Saints CE Sch EX13 . . 198 A4
All Saints East Clevedon CE Prim Sch BS21 . . . 6 F4
All Saints Ho BS2 . . . 227 B4
All Saints La BS21 . . . 6 F4
All Saints Pl BA2 . . . 45 E4
All Saints Rd BA1 . . . 228 B4
Allshire La EX16 . . . 162 F3
Allyn Saxon Dr BA4 . . . 205 D5
Alma Field BA7 . . . 214 B4
Alma Rd BS8 . . . 226 B4
Alma Road Ave BS8 . . . 226 B4
Alma St
Taunton TA1 . . . 213 A3
Weston-Super-Mare BS23 . . . 48 E7
Alma Vale Rd BS8 . . . 226 A4
Almond Cl BS22 . . . 32 A1
Almond Tree Cl TA6 . . . 209 D4
Almshouse La BA22 . . . 173 E1
Almshouses
Donyatt TA19 . . . 183 D1
Marshfield SN14 . . . 13 E8
Almyr Terr TA23 . . . 202 C7
Alpha Cotts TA2 . . . 168 E8
Alpha Ho TA9 . . . 104 E3
Alpine Cl BS39 . . . 77 F4
Alpine Gdns BA1 . . . 228 C4
Alpine Rd BS39 . . . 77 F4
Alston Cl TA1 . . . 212 C1
Alstone Gdns TA9 . . . 104 C2
Alstone La TA9 . . . 104 C2
Alstone Rd TA9 . . . 104 C2
Alstone Wildlife Pk* TA9 . . . 104 C3
Alston Sutton Rd BS26 . . . 88 F4
Alton Pl BA2 . . . 228 C1
Alun Rees Way TA20 . . . 223 B3
Alverstoke BS14 . . . 22 F7
Alveston Wlk BS9 . . . 5 B7
Alvington La BA22 . . . 218 B5
Alweston DT9 . . . 189 A1
Ambares Ct BA3 . . . 96 F8
Amberd La TA3 . . . 181 D8
Amberey Rd BS23 . . . 48 F5
Amberlands Cl BS48 . . . 19 A7
Amberley Cl
Keinton Mandeville TA11 . . 158 A1
Keynsham BS31 . . . 24 E4
Amberley Gdns 8 BS48 . . . 8 D1
Amber Mead TA1 . . . 213 D3
Ambleside Rd BA2 . . . 44 C2
Ambra Ct BS8 . . . 226 A2
Ambra Terr BS8 . . . 226 A2
Ambra Vale BS8 . . . 226 A2
Ambra Vale E BS8 . . . 226 A2
Ambra Vale S 5 BS8 . . . 226 A2
Ambra Vale W 4 BS8 . . . 226 A2
Ambridge Cl BA16 . . . 207 B4
Ambrose Cl DT9 . . . 187 E1
Ambrose Rd BS8 . . . 226 A2
Ambury BA1 . . . 228 B1
Amercombe Wlk BS14 . . . 23 D7
American Mus in Britain* BA2 . . . 46 A5
Amery La BA1 . . . 228 C2
Amesbury Dr BS24 . . . 67 B6
Ames La BA3 . . . 98 B6
Ammerdown Terr BA3 . . . 98 F7
Ammerham La TA20 . . . 199 A8
Amor Pl TA1 . . . 212 D2
Amory Rd TA22 . . . 163 D6
Amulet Way BA4 . . . 205 E4
Ancastle Ave BA7 . . . 214 D6
Ancastle Terr BA7 . . . 214 C6
Anchor Cl BA3 . . . 116 E8
Anchor Cnr BA9 . . . 176 D6
Anchor Hill BA9 . . . 176 D6
Anchor Rd
Bath BA1 . . . 27 B1
Bristol BS1 . . . 226 C2
Coleford BA3 . . . 116 E8
Anchor Sq BS1 . . . 226 C2
Anchor St TA23 . . . 202 C7
Anchor Stables TA24 . . . 123 E4
Anchor Way BS20 . . . 4 D4
Ancliff Sq BA15 . . . 64 E4
Ander's La TA3 . . . 192 B8
Andereach Cl BS14 . . . 23 B8
Andersfield Cl TA6 . . . 208 A4
Andrew's Hill TA22 . . . 163 D6
Andrew's Hill Cross TA22 . . . 163 C6
Andrew Allan Rd TA21 . . . 222 B4
Andruss Dr BS41 . . . 21 D2
Angela Cl TA1 . . . 212 D2
Angel Cres TA6 . . . 208 F5
Angel La BA9 . . . 216 C4
Angel Place Sh Ctr 6 TA6 . . . 208 F5
Angel Row TA3 . . . 170 F2
Anglesey Cotts DT10 . . . 190 B4
Anglo Ct TA18 . . . 224 C6
Anglo Terr BA1 . . . 228 C4
Anglo Trad Est The BA4 . . 205 B6
Angwin Cl BA4 . . . 205 B6
Animal Farm* TA8 . . . 66 B2
Annaly Rd BS27 . . . 90 A7
Annandale BA7 . . . 214 B4
Annandale Ave BS22 . . . 31 E1
Anseres Pl BA5 . . . 203 E4
Ansford Com Sch BA7 . . 214 C7
Ansford Hill BA7 . . . 214 B7
Ansford Rd BA7 . . . 214 C6
Anson Cl BS31 . . . 25 D2
Anson Rd
Locking BS24 . . . 50 B6
Weston-Super-Mare BS22 . . . 31 D4
Anson Way TA6 . . . 208 F5
Anstey Gate TA22 . . . 162 B8
Anthony Rd BA16 . . . 207 D7
Antler Cl BA6 . . . 206 C3
Antona Ct BS11 . . . 4 D7
Antona Dr BS11 . . . 4 D7
Anvil Rd BS49 . . . 17 F1
Anvil St BS2 . . . 227 C2
Apex Dr TA9 . . . 104 C4
Aplins Cl TA19 . . . 221 B3
Apple Alley BA11 . . . 119 F5
Apple Bsns Ctr The TA2 . . 212 B6
Appleby Wlk BS4 . . . 22 D7
Apple Cl TA19 . . . 194 F7
Applecroft BA2 . . . 79 E6
Appledore 4 BS22 . . . 31 F2
Appledore Cl BS14 . . . 23 B8
Apple Dumpling Cnr BS28 . . . 108 C3
Applefield Rd DT8 . . . 199 F8
Applehayes La EX15 . . . 180 F2
Apple La BA11 . . . 119 F5
Apple Tree Cl TA6 . . . 209 D4
Appletree Ct BS22 . . . 32 B2
Apple Tree Dr BS25 . . . 70 A8
Appletree Mews BS22 . . . 32 B2
Appley Cross TA21 . . . 179 B7
Appsley Cl BS22 . . . 31 C1
Apricot Tree Cl TA6 . . . 209 D5
Apsley Rd BA1 . . . 44 A7
Aquara Cl BA16 . . . 207 C3
Arbutus Dr BS9 . . . 5 C8
Arcade The BS1 . . . 227 B3
Archbishop Cranmer CE Com Prim Sch TA1 . . . 213 A4
Arch Cl BS41 . . . 10 F1
Archer Ct BS21 . . . 6 D4
Archer Dr TA8 . . . 104 C6
Archers Way The BA6 . . . 206 E5
Archer Wlk BS14 . . . 23 E6
Arches The BA2 . . . 44 A6
Archgrove BS41 . . . 10 F1
Arch La TA3 . . . 170 E4
Archstone Ave TA5 . . . 135 F2
Archway St BA2 . . . 45 B5
Arden Cl BS22 . . . 31 F3
Ardern Cl BS9 . . . 5 B8
Ardmore BS8 . . . 11 D7
Ardwyn TA21 . . . 222 D4
Arena The BA20 . . . 219 A4
Argyle Ave BS23 . . . 48 F4
Argyle Pl BS8 . . . 226 A2
Argyle Rd
Bristol BS2 . . . 227 B4
Clevedon BS21 . . . 6 D6
Argyle St BA2 . . . 228 C2
Argyle Terr BA2 . . . 44 C6
Arlington Cl
Bridgwater TA6 . . . 209 A2
Yeovil BA21 . . . 218 C7
Arlington Ho 4 BA1 . . . 228 C2
Arlington Mans BS8 . . . 226 B4
Arlington Rd 4 BA2 . . . 44 D5
Arlington Villas BS8 . . . 226 B3
Armada Ho BS2 . . . 227 A4
Armada Pl BS1 . . . 227 B4
Armada Rd BS14 . . . 23 A6
Armes Ct BA2 . . . 228 C1
Armoury Rd BA22 . . . 218 A6
Armoury The BA6 . . . 206 D4
Armstrong Rd BA11 . . . 120 B5
Armtech Row BA22 . . . 218 B6
Arnewood Gdns BA20 . . . 218 F2
Arnold's Way BS49 . . . 17 A2
Arnold Cl TA2 . . . 212 F7
Arnold Noad Cnr BA14 . . . 83 E3
Arnolfini (Arts Ctr)* BS1 . . . 227 A1
Arnor Cl BS22 . . . 32 A4
Arrowfield Cl BS14 . . . 23 A2
Artemesia Ave BS22 . . . 49 E8
Arthurswood Rd BS13 . . . 22 A4
Artillery Rd BA22 . . . 218 A6
Arundel Cl BS13 . . . 22 B5
Arundel Ct BS23 . . . 48 E8
Arundell Rd BS23 . . . 30 E1
Arundells Way TA3 . . . 169 D4
Arundel Rd
Bath BA1 . . . 28 A1
Clevedon BS21 . . . 6 D3
Yeovil BA21 . . . 219 E6
Arundel Wlk BS31 . . . 24 D5
Arun Gr TA1 . . . 213 D4
Ascension Ho BA2 . . . 44 D4
Ashbeer Hill TA4 . . . 150 D7
Ashbourne Cres TA1 . . . 213 D3
Ash Brook BS39 . . . 59 D1
Ashbrooke House Sch BS23 . . . 48 D6
Ashbury Dr BS22 . . . 31 B2
Ashby Pl BA7 . . . 214 C5
Ash CE Prim Sch TA12 . . . 185 F7
Ash Cl
Bridgwater TA6 . . . 209 D4
Wells BA5 . . . 203 D5
Weston-Super-Mare BS22 . . . 32 D2
Winscombe BS25 . . . 52 A1
Ashcombe Ct
Ilminster TA19 . . . 221 B4
1 Weston-Super-Mare BS23 . . . 48 F7
Ashcombe Gdns BS23 . . . 49 A8
Ashcombe La
Alweston DT9 . . . 189 B2
Ilminster TA19 . . . 221 B4
Ashcombe Park Rd BS23 . . 31 A1
Ashcombe Pl 4 BS23 . . . 48 F7
Ashcombe Prim Sch BS23 . 49 A7
Ashcombe Rd BS23 . . . 48 F7
Ashcott BS14 . . . 22 F7
Ashcott Cl TA8 . . . 104 C6
Ashcott Dr TA8 . . . 104 C6
Ashcott Pl TA8 . . . 104 C6
Ashcott Prim Sch TA7 . . . 156 B8
Ashcott Rd BA6 . . . 138 D3
Ash Cres TA1 . . . 212 B2
Ashcroft
Chard TA20 . . . 223 D2
Weston-Super-Mare BS24 . . . 49 B2
Ash Croft TA12 . . . 185 F7
Ashcroft Ave BS31 . . . 24 D5
Ashcroft Rd BS9 . . . 5 C7
Ash Cross TA3 . . . 169 E2
Ash Ct BS14 . . . 23 A6
Ashculme Hill EX15 . . . 180 C2
Ashdene Rd BS23 . . . 49 A8
Ashdown Ct BS9 . . . 5 F8
Ashdown Rd BS20 . . . 2 A6
Ashel's Batch BA3 . . . 94 C8
Ashen Cross TA11 . . . 211 E2

Ash End BA8 189 F7
Asher La BS2 227 C3
Ashes La BA3 64 A4
Ashey La
Burrington BS40 54 A5
Cheddar BS27 90 B8
Ashfield TA20 223 D2
Ashfield Cl BA11 143 C6
Ashfield Pk 23 TA12 185 E6
Ashford Cl
Bridgwater TA6 208 E2
Milverton TA4 167 A4
Ashford Dr BS24 49 A1
Ashford Gr BA21 219 B7
Ashford La TA19 183 F5
Ashford Rd
Bath BA2 44 D4
Redhill BS40 36 E4
Taunton TA1 212 C2
Wellington TA21 222 D4
Ash Gr
Bath BA2 44 C4
Chard TA20 223 C5
Clevedon BS21 6 E4
Minehead TA24 200 D7
Shepton Mallet BA4 205 C4
Wells BA5 203 D5
Weston-Super-Mare BS23 48 E2
Ashgrove BA2 79 D8
Ashgrove Ave BS8 11 B7
Ashgrove Ct BA2 79 D8
Ash Grove Way TA6 209 D7
Ash Hay Dro BA5 139 C6
Ash Hayes Dr BS48 8 E1
Ash Hayes Rd BS48 8 F1
Ash Ho TA8 65 F2
Ashill Cl TA1 212 E1
Ashill Com Prim Sch
TA19 183 C4
Ashington La BA21 187 B7
Ash La
Shepton Beauchamp
TA19 184 E4
Wells BA5 203 C5
Winsford TA24 147 B6
Ashland Ct TA18 224 C7
Ashland La TA4 150 B4
Ashland Rd BS13 22 A4
Ashlands Cl TA18 224 C7
Ashlands Fst Sch TA18 224 C7
Ashlands Mdw TA18 224 C8
Ashlands Rd TA18 224 D7
Ashlea BA7 214 B6
Ashlea Pk TA9 136 E8
Ashleigh Ave TA6 209 A3
Ashleigh Cl
Paulton BS39 77 E6
Weston-Super-Mare BS23 49 A8
Ashleigh Cres BS49 34 B8
Ashleigh Gdns TA1 212 E5
Ashleigh Rd
Weston-Super-Mare BS23 49 A8
Yatton BS49 34 B8
Ashleigh Terr TA6 209 A3
Ashley Ave
Bath BA1 44 C7
Burnham-on-S TA8 104 B6
Ashley Cl BS25 70 A7
Ashley La BA15 64 F7
Ashley Rd
Bathford BA1 29 E3
Clevedon BS21 6 B1
Taunton TA1 212 D3
Ashley Terr 1 BA1 44 C7
Ashmans Ct BA1 44 B6
Ashmans Gate BS39 77 E5
Ashmans Yd BA1 44 B6
Ashman Way TA6 208 D4
Ashmead
Temple Cloud BS39 58 E1
Yeovil BA20 218 C2
Ashmead Rd BS31 25 B5
Ashmead Road Ind Est
BS31 25 B5
Ashmead Way 8 BS1 11 F5
Ashmoor Dro BA5 139 C6
Ash Rd
Banwell BS29 50 E4
Street BA16 207 B3
Ashton Ave BS1 226 A1
Ashton Cl
Ashill TA19 183 C4
Clevedon BS21 6 B1
Ashton Court Est* BS41 11 C4
Ashton Cres BS48 8 D1
Ashton Ct TA1 212 C1
Ashton Dr BS3 11 F2
Ashton Gate Stadium (Bristol
City FC)* BS3 11 F3
Ashton Gate Trad Est BS3 11 E3
Ashton Gate Underpass
BS3 11 F3
Ashton Hill BA2 43 A7
Ashton Park Sec Sch BS3 11 E3
Ashton Pk BA11 119 E2
Ashton Rd
Bridgwater TA6 208 F2
Bristol, Ashton Gate BS3 11 F4
Bristol, Bower Ashton BS3 11 D3
Ashton Vale Prim Sch
BS3 11 F2
Ashton Vale Rd BS3 11 E3
Ashton Vale Trad Est BS3 11 F1
Ashton Way BS31 24 E6
Ashton Windmill* BS28 88 E1
Ashtown Cross EX16 164 A3
Ash Tree Cl
Bleadon BS24 67 C6
Burnham-on-S TA8 85 A3
Ash Tree Cres TA8 85 A3
Ash Tree Ct BA3 78 E1
Ash Tree Pl TA8 85 A3
Ashtree Rd BA11 120 A6
Ash Tree Rd TA8 85 A3
Ash Trees TA9 86 C5
Ashvale Cl BS48 9 A2
Ashwell Bsns Pk TA19 221 C7
Ashwell Cl BS14 23 E6
Ashwell La
Glastonbury BA6 139 D1
Wheddon Cross TA24 129 F2
Ashwicke BS14 23 A6
Ash Wlk BA8 190 A6
Ashwood BS40 74 F4
Ashwood Dr BA21 219 E8
Askwith Cl DT9 225 B3
Asney Rd BA16 156 E7
Aspen Cl BA11 120 B7
Aspen Ct TA6 208 E4
Aspen Park Rd BS22 49 E8
Aspen Way TA18 224 D7
Aspley Cl BA1 44 B7
Asquith St TA2 212 E6
Assembly Rooms La BS1 227 A2
Aston Ho 4 BS1 227 B1
at-bristol* BS1 226 C1
Athelney Way BA21 218 D6
Athlone Rd TA6 209 A2
Atholl Cl BS22 31 F3
Atkin's Gate TA13 220 D6
Atkins Cl BS14 23 E6
Atlanta Key TA8 104 A8
Atlantic Cres TA8 104 B5
Atlantic Rd
Bristol BS11 4 C8
Weston-Super-Mare BS23 30 C1
Atlantic Rd S BS23 30 C1
Atlantic View Ct BS23 30 C1
Atlantic Way BA22 174 A2
Atlay Ct BS49 17 B1
Atrium The BS1 227 B2
Attewell Ct BA2 44 F4
Attisham La DT6 199 D4
Atyeo Cl
Bristol BS3 11 E1
Burnham-on-S TA8 104 C8
Aubrey Meads BS30 25 E8
Auckland Cl BS23 48 F3
Auckland Way TA20 223 D3
Audley Ave BA1 44 D7
Audley Cl
Bath BA1 44 D7
Nether Stowey TA5 134 A2
Audley Gr BA1 44 C7
Audley Lodge BA1 44 D7
Audley Park Rd BA1 44 C7
Augusta Pl BA1 44 D7
Augustine's Cl BS20 1 E4
Austen Dr BS22 32 B4
Austen Pl BS11 4 E7
Austin Cl BA11 119 F2
Austin Rd BA6 206 E6
Autumn Mews BS24 50 A8
Avalon Bldgs BA6 206 D5
Avalon Cl BS49 17 A1
Avalon Est BA6 206 E7
Avalon Ho BS48 8 C1
Avalon Mews BA6 206 E4
Avalon Pk TA11 211 B5
Avalon Rd
Bridgwater TA6 209 D5
Highbridge TA9 104 E4
Avalon Sch BA16 207 B3
Avebury Cl TA8 104 D8
Avebury Dr TA6 209 D5
Avebury Rd BS3 11 F2
Aveline Ct TA4 167 F6
Avening Cl BS48 19 A8
Avenue Pl BA2 45 B1
Avenue Rd BA11 120 A4
Avenue The
Backwell BS48 19 A7
Bath, Bushey Norwood BA2 45 E4
Bath, Combe Down BA2 45 C1
Bicknoller TA4 132 F4
3 Bridgwater TA6 208 F5
Bristol, Sneyd Park BS9 5 E3
Chard TA20 193 F7
Clevedon BS21 6 E6
Keynsham BS31 24 E6
Kingsbury Episcopi TA12 185 B8
Langport TA10 172 A6
Minehead TA24 201 A7
Misterton TA18 224 F3
Sherborne DT9 225 E5
Sparkford BA22 175 A5
Stoke sub Hamdon TA14 185 F4
Taunton TA1 212 E5
Timsbury BA2 60 B2
Weston-Super-Mare BS22 32 C3
Wincanton BA9 216 D3
Winscombe BS25 70 C8
Yatton BS49 34 B8
Yeovil BA21 219 B5
Averill Ct BS21 6 D4
Avill Cres TA1 213 C4
Avishayes Com Prim Sch
TA20 223 E5
Avishayes Rd TA20 223 E4
Avonbank Ind Est BS11 4 B7
Avonbridge Trad Est BS11 4 C8
Avon Cl
Keynsham BS31 24 F6
Avon Cl *continued*
Taunton TA1 212 D2
Weston-Super-Mare BS23 48 F2
Yeovil BA21 219 D6
Avoncliff Halt BA15 64 F5
Avon Cres BS1 226 A1
Avon Ct BA1 29 A4
Avondale Bldgs BA1 28 B2
Avondale Ct
Bath BA1 44 B7
Bristol, Sneyd Park BS9 5 D3
Avondale Ho
Bath BA2 44 B5
Bridgwater TA6 209 A2
Avondale Rd BA1 44 B6
Avondowns Ct BS8 226 A4
Avon Gorge Ind Est BS11 4 C7
Avon Gorge Nature Reserve*
BS8 11 E7
Avon Gr BS9 5 D2
Avon Hts BA3 64 C6
Avon La BS31 25 F5
Avonleaze BS9 5 B5
Avonmead BS2 227 B4
Avon Mill La BS31 24 F6
Avonmouth CE Prim Sch
BS11 4 C8
Avonmouth Rd BS11 4 C8
Avon Pk BA1 44 A7
Avon Prim Sch BS11 4 D8
Avon Rd
Bristol BS13 22 A6
Keynsham BS31 24 F5
Pill BS20 4 C5
Avon Riverside Est BS11 4 B7
Avon Riverside Sta* BS30 25 E6
Avon Ski Ctr* BS25 52 C3
Avon & Somerset Pol HQ
BS20 1 F3
Avon St
Bath BA1 228 B2
Bristol BS2 227 C2
Avon Vale BS9 5 D4
Avonvale Pl BA1 28 F3
Avon Valley Ctry Pk*
BS31 25 D6
Avon Valley Rly* BS30 25 D7
Avon Way
Bristol, Sneyd Park BS9 5 C4
Portishead BS20 2 C5
Avonwood Cl BS11 4 E6
Awkward Hill BS40 55 D5
Axbridge CE Fst Sch BS26 70 C1
Axbridge Cl
Burnham-on-S TA8 104 C8
Nailsea BS48 18 E8
Axbridge Moor Dro BS26 70 C1
Axbridge Mus* BS26 70 C2
Axbridge Rd
Bath BA2 45 A2
Cheddar BS27 70 F2
Axe Cl BS23 49 A5
Axeford TA20 198 E8
Axeford Mdws TA20 198 E8
Axe La
Clapton DT8 195 C1
Drimpton DT8 199 F8
Axe Rd
Bridgwater TA6 209 B3
Wookey BA5 139 D8
Axe Valley Com Coll The
EX13 198 A1
Axford Way BA2 79 D8
Axis BS14 22 D5
Axminster Com Prim Sch
EX13 198 A1
Axminster Rd TA20 198 C7
Ayckbourn Cl TA8 104 C6
Aycote Cl BS22 31 C2
Ayford La SN14 13 F4
Aylands Rd TA1 212 D3
Aylmer Cres BS14 23 B6
Ayr St BA2 44 D6
Azalea Rd BS22 32 A5
Azelin Ave BS13 22 B5

B

Babcary La BA22 174 B8
Babwell Rd BA9 177 D6
Babylon Hill
Sherborne DT9 188 A3
Yeovil BA21 219 F4
Babylon View BA21 219 F7
Backfields BS2 227 B4
Backfields Ct BS2 227 B4
Backfields La BS2 227 B4
Back La
Axbridge BS26 70 C2
Baltonsborough BA6 158 B5
Batcombe BA4 142 C2
Bradford Abbas DT9 187 F1
Chapel Allerton BS26 88 D1
Cheddar BS27 90 A7
Chewton Mendip BA3 75 B1
Curry Rivel TA10 171 D3
Draycott BS27 90 F2
East Chinnock BA22 196 E8
East Coker BA22 197 C7
Halstock BA22 197 C3
Ilchester BA22 173 E1
Keynsham BS31 24 E6
Kington Seymour BS21 16 A5
Kington Magna SP8 177 E2
Litton BA3 75 E2
Maiden Bradley BA12 144 C2
Marshfield SN14 13 F8
Back La *continued*
Martock TA12 185 D4
Middlezoy TA7 155 B3
Montacute TA15 186 B3
Moorlinch TA7 155 D8
North Perrott TA18 196 C4
Pill BS20 4 C5
Pilton BA4 204 D3
Rimpton BA22 188 A8
Rowberrow BS25 53 A1
Shepton Mallet, Darshill
BA4 204 F6
Shepton Mallet, Downside
BA4 205 C8
Sherborne DT9 225 D4
Stoney Stratton BA4 141 F2
Street BA16 207 C6
Street, Butleigh Wootton
BA6 157 C6
Westbury-sub-Mendip BA5 110 E6
Whitelackington TA19 221 F6
Backlane Dro BA6 158 C5
Back Of Kingsdown Par
BS6 227 A4
Back River Dro BA16 138 F2
Back St
Ash TA12 186 A7
Bampton EX16 164 B1
Bradford On Tone TA4 167 F1
Leighton BA11 142 E6
Long Sutton TA10 172 E4
Martock TA12 185 F7
West Camel BA22 174 D3
Weston-Super-Mare BS23 48 E7
Winsham TA20 194 E1
Back Stoke La BS9 5 F6
Back Town BA6 157 E4
Back Way TA4 150 B8
Backways La TA21 179 F6
Backwell Bow BS48 9 C1
Backwell CE Jun Sch
BS48 19 C5
Backwell Comm BS48 19 B8
Backwell Hill Rd BS48 19 E5
Backwell Sch BS48 19 B6
Backwell Wlk BS13 21 F8
Bacon Dr TA1 213 D3
Badcox BA11 119 E4
Badenham Gr BS11 4 F8
Baden Ho BA1 228 B4
Badger's Cross
Oakhill BA3 114 F5
Somerton TA11 211 C1
Badger's Cross La TA11 211 C2
Badger Hts BA22 218 B5
Badger Pk TA24 201 C4
Badger Rise BS20 1 F3
Badgers' La TA20 223 E1
Badgers Cl
Bourton SP8 161 F1
Street BA16 207 A5
Taunton TA1 212 B3
Badgers Folly BA7 214 B5
Badgers Green Rd BA16 207 A5
Badgers Hill BA11 120 A5
Badgers Holt BS14 23 C6
Badgers The BS22 32 D3
Badgers Way BS24 49 F8
Badgworth Barns BS26 88 D5
Badgworth Ct BS26 88 C5
Badgworth La BS26 88 C4
Badlake La EX36 162 D6
Badlake Moor Cross
TA22 162 D7
Badman Cl BS39 77 D5
Badminton Ct 17 BS23 30 C1
Badminton Gdns BA1 44 C8
Bagber Cross Rds DT10 190 D3
Bagborough Dr TA6 208 F2
Bagborough La BA4 141 C2
Bagborough Rd TA2 212 F7
Baggridge Hill BA2 80 F7
Baggs La BS27 90 F2
Bagley Rd TA21 222 A3
Bagnell Cl BS14 23 E5
Bagnell Rd BS14 23 E5
Bailbrook Coll BA1 28 D2
Bailbrook Gr BA1 28 C3
Bailbrook La BA1 28 D3
Baildon Cres BS23 49 A4
Baildon Ct 2 BS23 48 F4
Baildon Rd BS23 49 A4
Bailey's Dro BA6 158 B5
Bailey's Knapp EX16 178 B4
Bailey's La BA4 142 B1
Bailey Cl BS22 49 E8
Bailey Ct BS20 2 F6
Bailey Hill BA7 214 C5
Baileys Gate TA4 167 F6
Bailey St TA6 209 B5
Bailiffs' Wall BS26 70 B1
Bailiffs Cl BS26 70 C1
Baily Cl BA6 206 E7
Bainsbury View BA3 96 F1
Bakehouse 1 TA16 195 F7
Bakehouse La DT9 187 E1
Bakelite Mus The* TA4 202 C2
Baker's Bldgs BS40 35 D2
Baker's Cross TA3 191 D7
Baker's La
Churchinford TA3 191 D7
Wellington TA21 222 E6
Baker Cl 8 BS21 6 B1
Bakeries The TA11 211 D3
Bakers Cl TA1 212 A3
Bakers Ct TA13 220 C4
Bakersfield TA20 194 E1
Bakers La
Barrington TA19 184 C5
Chilcompton BA3 96 D3
Lower Langford BS40 53 C8
Bakers Orch TA4 151 B5
Bakers Par BA2 60 B2
Bakers Pk BS13 22 B6
Baker St
Babcary TA11 174 C7
Frome BA11 119 E5
Weston-Super-Mare BS23 48 E8
Bakery La BA4 140 F3
Balch Rd BA5 203 C4
Baldwin Rd TA1 213 B5
Baldwin St BS1 227 A2
Ball's Hill BA22, TA15 186 C4
Ball's La TA5 153 E4
Ballance St BA1 228 B4
Ballfield Rd TA24 200 F8
Ballhill La EX16 164 B1
Ball La
Doulting BA4 141 F7
Isle Abbotts TA3 183 E7
Spaxton TA2, TA5 152 B2
Balls Barn La BS24 33 A2
Ball The
Dunster TA24 201 E2
Minehead TA24 200 F8
Balmoral Dr TA8 85 B1
Balmoral Ho TA6 209 C4
Balmoral Rd
Keynsham BS31 24 E4
Yeovil BA21 219 E6
Balmoral Way BS22 31 D2
Balsam Cl BA9 216 D3
Balsam Fields BA9 216 D3
Balsam La BA9 216 E3
Balsam Pk BA9 216 C3
Baltic Pl BS20 4 D4
Baltonsborough CE Prim Sch
BA6 158 A6
Baltonsborough Rd BA6 157 E4
Balustrade 17 BA1 28 B1
Bamfield BS14 23 A6
Bampton 5 BS22 31 F2
Bampton Ave TA20 223 B5
Bampton Cl BS13 22 B7
Bampton Down Rd EX16 178 A7
Bampton Prim Sch EX16 164 B1
Bampton St TA24 200 F6
Banbury La BA6 157 E3
Bancks St TA24 200 F7
Bancombe Ct TA11 211 B5
Bancombe Rd TA11 211 A4
Banfield Cl BS11 5 A8
Bangers DT9 188 F5
Bangrove Wlk BS11 4 E8
Banister Gr BS4 22 D7
Banking Ct 4 TA18 224 C6
Bankland La TA7 154 B1
Bank Pl BS20 4 D4
Banks Cl BS21 16 D8
Bank Sq TA22 163 D6
Bank St
Highbridge TA9 104 D3
Williton TA4 202 D2
Bannerdown Cl BA1 29 B4
Bannerdown Dr BA1 29 A4
Bannerdown Rd BA1 29 C5
Bannerleigh La BS8 11 E6
Bannerleigh Rd BS8 11 E6
Banneson Rd TA5 134 B2
Bantock Cl BS4 22 D6
Bantry Rd BS4 22 E8
Banwell Cl
Bristol BS13 22 A8
Keynsham BS31 25 A2
Taunton TA1 213 D4
Banwell Prim Sch BS29 51 B3
Banwell Rd
Banwell BS26, BS29 68 E8
Bath BA2 62 D8
Locking BS24 50 B3
Winscombe BS25, BS29 69 E8
Banyard Rd BS20 3 E5
Barbary Cl BA8 176 D3
Barber's La TA21 180 F7
Barberry Dr TA20 223 F5
Barberry Farm Rd BS49 17 B1
Barbers Mead TA2 213 C7
Barbour Gdns BS13 22 D3
Barbour Rd BS13 22 D3
Barclay St TA6 209 A5
Barcroft BA12 144 B2
Barcroft Cres TA3 170 A1
Barcroft La TA13 220 B6
Bardel Ct BA22 218 B6
Barford Cl TA5 152 F7
Barford Ho* TA5 152 F6
Barford Rd TA5 152 F7
Barham Ct BA22 218 A5
Barhams Cl TA6 209 A7
Barkham Cl BA5 203 F5
Barle Cl TA1 213 D4
Barley Cl BA5 203 C3
Barley Croft
Bristol BS9 5 F5
Somerton TA11 211 B3
Barley Cross BS22 32 A5
Barley Wood Walled Gdn*
BS40 35 F3
Barlinch Cl TA2 213 B7
Barlynch Ct BA21 218 D6
Barnabas Cl BS26 70 D2
Barnaby Cl BA3 78 B2
Barnard's Cl BS49 34 C7
Barnard Ave BA16 207 B3
Barnard Ct BA5 203 B4

Barnard Wlk BS31 ....24 D4
Barn Cl
Crewkerne TA18 ....224 B5
Frome BA11 ....119 D3
Nether Stowey TA5 ....134 B2
Somerton TA11 ....211 B3
Street BA16 ....207 C6
Wiveliscombe TA4 ....210 A7
Barn Cres TA18 ....224 B5
Barn Ct BA21 ....187 C5
Barn End BS40 ....74 E3
Barnes Cl
Castle Cary BA7 ....214 C6
Wells BA5 ....203 B4
Barnes Close Mead
TA22 ....163 D6
Barnet Cl BA21 ....218 E7
Barnetts Well BS27 ....90 F2
Barnfield Way BA1 ....29 B3
Barn Gn BA6 ....206 E3
Barnhay 6 EX16 ....164 B1
Barn Hill BA2 ....79 F5
Barn La
Clutton BS39 ....59 A7
Crewkerne TA18 ....195 E6
Barn Meads Rd TA21 ....222 E4
Barn Orch TA14 ....185 E3
Barn Pool BS25 ....70 F8
Barns Cl
Barrow Gurney BS48 ....20 E4
Nailsea BS48 ....8 E2
Barnsclose TA22 ....163 D6
Barns Close Ind Est
TA22 ....163 D6
Barnsclose N TA22 ....163 D6
Barnsclose W TA22 ....163 D6
Barns Gd BS21 ....16 E8
Barn St TA18 ....224 B6
Barnstaple Ct BS4 ....22 E8
Barnstaple Rd BS4 ....22 E8
Barnstaple Wlk BS4 ....22 F8
Barnwood Ct BS48 ....8 B1
Baron Cl BS30 ....25 E8
Barons Cl BS3 ....11 F3
Barossa Pl BS1 ....227 A1
Barpark Cnr EX15 ....180 E3
Barpool La TA11 ....211 D6
Barrack's La BS11 ....4 D8
Barracks Cl BA22 ....218 B7
Barrendown La BA4 ....205 C6
Barrie Way TA8 ....104 C6
Barrington Broadway
TA10 ....184 D6
Barrington Cl TA1 ....212 C1
Barrington Court Cotts
TA19 ....184 D5
Barrington Ct* TA19 ....184 D5
Barrington Hill Rd TA19 ....182 F4
Barrington Pl BA4 ....204 F5
Barrington Rd TA8 ....104 C8
Barrow Court La BS19 ....20 B5
Barrow Cswy BA5 ....138 F8
Barrow Ct
Barrow Gurney BS48 ....20 A5
Tickenham BS21 ....7 F4
Barrow Dr TA1 ....213 E5
Barrow Hill
Stalbridge DT10 ....190 B4
Stourton Caundle DT10 ....189 F1
Barrow Hill Cres BS11 ....4 C7
Barrow Hill Rd BS11 ....4 D6
Barrow Ho 25 BA4 ....205 B6
Barrow Hospl
Barrow Gurney BS48 ....20 F6
Dundry BS48 ....21 A6
Barrow La
Charlton Musgrove BA9 ....161 B3
North Wootton BA4 ....140 B4
Pilton BA4 ....140 F3
Winford BS40 ....20 F1
Barrow Lea DT10 ....190 B4
Barrowmead Dr BS11 ....4 F7
Barrow Pk BS27 ....90 A8
Barrow Rd
Bath BA2 ....44 C1
Hutton BS24 ....49 E2
Barrows Cl TA6 ....208 E2
Barrows Croft BS27 ....90 A8
Barrows Ct BA22 ....196 E8
Barrows La TA14 ....185 E2
Barrows Rd BS27 ....90 A8
Barrow St BS48 ....20 D5
Barrows The
Cheddar BS27 ....90 A8
Weston-Super-Mare BS22 ....49 C7
Barrow Stile BA4 ....140 F3
Barrow Water La BA9 ....161 A3
Barrow Wood La BS27 ....110 A7
Barry Cl BS24 ....49 A1
Barry La BA22 ....196 F6
Barrymore Cl TA10 ....172 A6
Barstable Ho BS2 ....227 C3
Bartec 4 BA20 ....218 C3
Bartholomew Row BA2 ....60 B2
Bartlett Cl
Frome BA11 ....120 C6
Taunton TA1 ....212 B1
Bartlett Ct
1 Crewkerne TA18 ....224 C6
Yeovil BA20 ....218 D3
Bartlett Mews BA21 ....219 F7
Bartlett Pk
Chard TA20 ....223 E3
Yeovil BA20 ....218 D3
Bartletts Ct BA2 ....228 C1
Bartletts La TA4 ....167 A4
Bartletts Pl BA21 ....218 D5
Bartletts Row TA11 ....211 D4
Bartlett St 6 BA1 ....228 B3
Bartletts Way BS24 ....50 A4
Barton Bldgs BA1 ....228 B3
Barton Cl
Berrow TA8 ....84 F5
Taunton TA1 ....212 D3
Barton Cross EX16 ....162 E5
Barton Dro BS25 ....69 D5
Barton Gdns DT9 ....225 B4
Barton Gn TA3 ....168 D1
Barton Hey 2 TA4 ....167 F8
Barton Hill SP8 ....177 E2
Barton La TA3 ....169 C4
Barton Rd
Barton St David TA11 ....158 A2
Berrow TA8 ....84 F4
Bristol BS2 ....227 C2
Butleigh BA6 ....157 E3
Minehead TA24 ....201 B4
Winscombe BS26 ....69 C6
Barton Rise TA7 ....137 B3
Barton St
Bath BA1 ....228 B2
Bristol BS1 ....227 A4
Bartons The
Bishops Lydeard TA4 ....167 E8
Ilchester BA22 ....173 E1
South Petherton TA13 ....220 E3
Barton The
Bleadon BS24 ....67 C6
Charlton Adam TA11 ....173 F7
Corston BA2 ....43 A7
Huish Champflower TA4 ....165 E8
Norton St Philip BA2 ....81 E4
Barton Vale BS2 ....227 C2
Barton Villas BA3 ....116 F6
Barton Way TA3 ....170 C4
Barton Wlk BA11 ....119 D2
Barwick Ho BS11 ....4 E7
Barwick & Stoford Com Prim
Sch BA22 ....197 F8
Basketfield La BA6 ....139 D1
Batallers La TA23 ....131 D2
Bat Alley DT10 ....190 F5
Batch Bsns Pk BS24 ....66 F2
Batch Cl TA7 ....136 C4
Batch La
Clutton BS39 ....58 F3
Lympsham BS24 ....66 F3
Batchpool La BA8 ....176 F3
Batch Rd TA7 ....136 B5
Batch The
Ashcott TA7 ....156 B7
Backwell BS48 ....19 D1
Batheaston BA1 ....28 F3
Burrington BS40 ....54 B3
Butcombe BS40 ....55 B8
Chew Magna BS40 ....39 B3
Churchill BS25 ....52 F4
Draycott BS27 ....90 F2
Farmborough BA2 ....60 A6
Hinton Charterhouse BA2 ....63 E1
Saltford BS31 ....25 F3
19 Shepton Mallet BA4 ....205 B6
Wincanton BA9 ....216 B4
Yatton BS49 ....34 B7
Batch View BA16 ....207 B6
Bateman's Cross TA20 ....198 E7
Bath Abbey* BA1 ....228 C2
Bathampton La BA2 ....28 E1
Bathampton Prim Sch
BA2 ....28 F2
Bath Bridge Bsns Pk
TA6 ....209 B6
Bath Cl BA6 ....206 D6
Batheaston CE Prim Sch
BA1 ....28 F4
Bathford CE Prim Sch
BA1 ....29 C2
Bathford Hill
Bathford BA1 ....29 B2
Compton Dando BS39 ....41 E5
Bathford Manor BA1 ....29 C2
Bath Foyer The BA2 ....44 A6
Bath Hill
Keynsham BS31 ....24 F5
Wellow BA2 ....62 D2
Bath House Ct TA1 ....212 E3
Bath La TA20 ....223 C3
Bath Meadow Dr TA22 ....163 E6
Bath New Rd BA3 ....78 F4
Bath Old Rd BA3 ....78 F4
Bath Pl TA1 ....212 F3
Bath Postal Mus* BA1 ....228 C3
Bath Race Course* BA1 ....27 A6
Bath Rd
Ashcott TA7 ....156 B7
Bawdrip TA7 ....136 D2
Beckington BA11 ....101 D5
Bitton BS30 ....25 D8
Blagdon BS40 ....55 B1
Bridgwater TA6 ....209 C7
Bristol BS2 ....227 C1
Farmborough BA2 ....59 E5
Frome BA11 ....120 A7
Horrington BA3, BA5 ....113 D5
Kelston BA1, BS30 ....26 B6
Kingsdown SN13 ....29 F5
Moorlinch TA7 ....155 E8
Norton St Philip BA2 ....81 E5
Oakhill BA3 ....115 B3
Paulton BS39 ....77 F6
Peasedown St John BA2 ....79 C7
Saltford BS31 ....25 D3
Shepton Mallet BA4 ....141 C8
Stawell TA7 ....137 B1
Upper Langford BS40 ....53 D3
Wells BA5 ....112 E1
Bath Riverside Bsns Pk
BA2 ....228 B1
Bath Spa Sta BA1 ....228 C1
Bath Spa Univ Coll BA1 ....27 E1
Bath Spa University Coll
(Newton Pk Campus)
BA2 ....43 B5
Bath Sq TA20 ....223 C3
Bath St
Bath BA1 ....228 C2
Bristol BS1 ....227 B2
Chard TA20 ....223 C3
Cheddar BS27 ....90 B7
Frome BA11 ....119 F4
Bathurst Cl TA8 ....104 D8
Bathurst Par BS1 ....227 A1
Bathurst Rd BS22 ....49 C8
Bath View BA3 ....96 F1
Bathwell La DT9 ....217 D1
Bathwick Hill BA2 ....45 C6
Bathwick Rise BA2 ....45 B7
Bathwick St BA1, BA2 ....228 C4
Batstone Cl BA1 ....28 B2
Batt's La TA10 ....172 D5
Battery La BS20 ....2 D7
Battery Rd BS20 ....2 D6
Battin's Knap TA4 ....150 A3
Batt La TA3 ....183 C8
Battleborough La TA9 ....86 B1
Battle La BS40 ....39 A3
Battle St EX15 ....180 E1
Battleton TA22 ....163 D6
Batts Bow Bridge TA9 ....104 E1
Batts La
Oakhill BA3 ....114 E3
Pilsdon DT6 ....199 F2
Battson Rd BS14 ....23 E4
Batts Pk TA1 ....212 E1
Baulditch La TA3 ....184 B8
Baunton's Orch DT9 ....217 C2
Bauntons Cl DT9 ....217 C2
Bawden Cl TA7 ....136 E4
Bawdrip La TA7 ....136 E2
Bawler's La TA10 ....171 C3
Bay's La BA3 ....115 A7
Bayer Bldg The BA2 ....228 B1
Bayford Hill BA9 ....216 E4
Bayford La BA9 ....177 B7
Bayford Rd TA6 ....209 C6
Bay Hill TA19 ....221 D4
Bay La BS27 ....90 F2
Bayliss Ctr The 4 BA16 ....207 C5
Baymead Cl 11 TA6 ....153 F4
Baymead La TA6 ....153 F3
Baymead Mdw 5 TA6 ....153 F3
Baynes Cl TA21 ....222 E7
Bay Rd
Clevedon BS21 ....6 D6
Porlock TA24 ....124 A4
Bays The BS27 ....90 C8
Baytree Ct BS22 ....31 D1
Baytree Rd BS22 ....31 C1
Bay Tree Rd
Bath BA1 ....28 B2
Clevedon BS21 ....6 E1
Baytree Sch BS24 ....50 A8
Baytree View BS22 ....31 D1
Bay Tree View BS22 ....31 D1
Bay View TA23 ....202 D6
Bay View Gdns TA8 ....104 B5
Baze La EX35 ....122 B4
Bazelands Hill BA8 ....190 B7
Beach Ave BS21 ....6 C2
Beach Ct BS23 ....48 D6
Beach End Rd BS23 ....48 C2
Beach Hill BS20 ....2 C6
Beachlands Pk BS22 ....31 A6
Beachley Wlk BS11 ....4 D7
Beach Mews BS21 ....6 C4
Beach Rd
Weston-Super-Mare BS23 ....48 D6
Weston-Super-Mare, Kewstoke
BS22 ....31 A5
Beach Rd E BS20 ....2 D6
Beach Rd W BS20 ....2 C6
Beach The BS21 ....6 C4
Beach Tree Cross TA4 ....166 F6
Beacon TA19 ....221 B5
Beaconfield Ho TA6 ....209 A2
Beaconfield Rd BA20 ....218 E1
Beacon Hill View DT9 ....175 D1
Beacon La
Corton Denham DT9 ....175 D2
Wellington TA21 ....180 C4
Beacon Rd
Bath BA1 ....28 A1
Minehead TA24 ....200 F8
Beaconsfield Rd
Clevedon BS21 ....6 E3
Weston-Super-Mare BS23 ....48 E7
Beaconsfield Way BA11 ....120 B7
Beacon View
Coleford BA3 ....116 E7
Shepton Mallet BA4 ....205 A4
Beadon La TA16 ....195 F7
Beadon Rd TA1 ....213 C5
Beafort Ct BS24 ....50 C3
Beale Cl BS14 ....23 E6
Beale Way TA8 ....104 D5
Bean Acre The BS11 ....4 D8
Bearbridge Rd BS13 ....21 F4
Beard's Yd TA10 ....171 F5
Bearley Bridge Rd 15
TA12 ....185 E6
Bearley Ho 26 TA12 ....185 E6
Bearley La BA22 ....186 B7
Bearley Rd 27 TA12 ....185 E6
Bears Meadow La TA5 ....133 C6
Bear Yard Mews 2 BS8 ....226 A2
Beasley Ct TA20 ....223 B5
Beastway La TA24 ....131 B3
Beatty Way TA8 ....104 C7
Beauchamp Gdns TA3 ....183 A7
Beauchamps Dr BA3 ....97 A5
Beaufitz Pl TA20 ....193 F1
Beauford Pk TA2 ....168 B4
Beauford Sq BA1 ....228 B2
Beaufort Ave BA3 ....78 A2
Beaufort Bldgs 7 BS8 ....11 F7
Beaufort Cl EX16 ....178 D1
Beaufort Ct
Clevedon BS21 ....6 C5
Ilchester BA22 ....173 E2
Beaufort E BA1 ....28 C1
Beaufort Gdns
2 Nailsea BS48 ....8 D1
South Petherton TA13 ....220 B5
Beaufort Mews
3 Bath BA1 ....28 C1
10 Bristol BS8 ....11 F7
Beaufort Pl BA1 ....28 C1
Beaufort Rd
Taunton TA1 ....212 E5
Weston-Super-Mare BS23 ....48 F7
Beaufort Villas 8 BA1 ....28 B1
Beaufort W 11 BA1 ....28 B1
Beauley Rd BS3 ....226 B1
Beaulieu Dr BA21 ....218 D6
Beaumont BA1 ....27 F1
Beaumont Cl BS23 ....48 F4
Beaumont Ho BA21 ....219 D5
Beau St BA1 ....228 B2
Beavor La EX13 ....198 A1
Beck's La BA3 ....116 D6
Beckery New Rd BA6 ....206 B3
Beckery Old Rd BA6 ....206 B3
Beckery Rd BA6 ....206 B4
Becket's La BS48 ....18 E8
Becket Dr BS22 ....32 A3
Becket Pl BA5 ....203 D3
Becket Prim Sch BS22 ....32 A2
Becket Rd BS22 ....32 A4
Beckford's Twr* BA1 ....27 D4
Beckford Ct BA2 ....45 B7
Beckford Gdns
Bath BA2 ....45 B8
Bristol BS14 ....23 A3
Beckford Rd BA2 ....45 B7
Beckhampton Rd BA2 ....44 D5
Beckington BS24 ....49 A2
Beckington CE Fst Sch
BA11 ....101 E4
Beckington Cres TA20 ....223 D3
Becks Bsns Pk BS23 ....49 A7
Becks Field 2 TA14 ....185 F4
Beckworth Cl TA6 ....209 C3
Bector La BA3 ....116 C4
Bede St DT9 ....225 E5
Bedford Cl TA6 ....209 C3
Bedford Ct BA1 ....45 B8
Bedford Rd
Wells BA5 ....112 E1
Weston-Super-Mare BS23 ....48 E4
Yeovil BA21 ....219 D8
Bedford St BA1 ....45 B8
Bedminster Down Sch
BS13 ....21 F7
Bedwell La TA7 ....155 C2
Bedwin Cl BS20 ....1 F4
Beech Ave
Bath BA2 ....45 E5
Shepton Mallet BA4 ....205 A6
Beech Cl
Doulting BA4 ....141 E6
Shipham BS25 ....70 F8
Taunton TA2 ....212 F8
Beechcroft BS41 ....21 D2
Beech Croft BS14 ....23 B5
Beech Ct
Bristol BS14 ....23 A5
Frome BA11 ....120 B7
Taunton TA1 ....212 E3
2 Wellington TA21 ....222 D6
Beech Dr
Bridgwater TA6 ....209 D5
Nailsea BS48 ....9 A3
Shipham BS25 ....70 E8
Beechen Cliff Boys' Sch
BA2 ....45 A4
Beechen Cliff Rd BA2 ....228 B1
Beeches The
Bath BA2 ....44 D1
Langport TA10 ....172 A6
Sandford BS25 ....52 B4
Wheddon Cross TA24 ....129 E1
Beechfield Cl BS41 ....11 C2
Beechfield Gr BS9 ....5 C8
Beechfield Inf Sch TA9 ....104 D4
Beech Gr
Bath BA2 ....44 D4
Somerton TA11 ....211 D5
Wellington TA21 ....222 C6
Beech Grove Prim Sch
TA21 ....222 C6
Beech Hill TA21 ....222 F5
Beeching Cl TA20 ....223 E6
Beech La
Axminster EX13 ....198 E1
Stoke Trister BA9 ....177 C8
Beechmont Dr BS24 ....49 A1
Beechmount Cl BS24 ....48 F1
Beechmount Ct BS14 ....23 B8
Beechmount Gr BS14 ....23 B8
Beech Rd
Bridgwater TA6 ....209 D5
20 Martock TA12 ....185 E6
Beech Rd continued
Saltford BS31 ....25 E3
Shipham BS25 ....70 F8
Street BA16 ....207 C3
Yatton BS49 ....34 C8
Beech Terr BA3 ....78 E1
Beech Tree TA23 ....130 D1
Beech Tree Cl TA4 ....210 C4
Beech Tree Cross
Clatworthy TA4 ....149 E1
Dulverton TA22 ....163 C7
Monksilver TA4 ....132 B1
Beech Tree Hill TA5 ....152 C6
Beech Way BA4 ....141 E1
Beechwood
Bridgwater TA6 ....208 E2
Yeovil BA20 ....218 F2
Beechwood Ave
Frome BA11 ....120 A5
Locking BS24 ....50 A5
Beechwood Cl
Bristol BS14 ....23 C8
Frome BA11 ....120 A5
Beechwood Dr
Crewkerne TA18 ....224 C7
Portishead BS20 ....1 E5
Beechwood Rd
Bath BA2 ....45 B1
Easton-in-G BS20 ....4 A4
Nailsea BS48 ....8 D2
Portishead BS20 ....1 E5
Beehive Yd BA1 ....228 C3
Beek's La SN14, BA1 ....13 D5
Beer Door TA10 ....155 E2
Beer Dro TA10 ....155 E3
Beere Cross EX36 ....162 A5
Beer La
Burlescombe EX16 ....179 B2
Dulverton TA22 ....163 B5
Beer Rd TA10 ....155 E1
Beer St
Curry Mallet TA3 ....183 C7
Yeovil BA20 ....219 A4
Bees Ho BS21 ....6 C2
Beetham La TA20 ....193 B6
Bee World & Animal Ctr*
TA4 ....150 F8
Beggar Bush La BS8 ....11 B6
Beggarswell Cl BS2 ....227 C4
Beggs Cl 4 TA6 ....153 F3
Behind Berry TA11 ....211 D4
Behind Butts TA14 ....185 E1
Behind Hayes BA8 ....176 D3
Behind Town TA11 ....157 B4
Bekynton Ave BA5 ....203 F4
Belcombe Dro TA20 ....193 B7
Belfast Wlk BS4 ....22 E8
Belfield Ct TA8 ....104 A8
Belgrave Cres BA1 ....228 C4
Belgrave Ct 2 TA2 ....212 F6
Belgrave Pl
Bath BA1 ....228 C4
Bristol BS8 ....226 A3
Taunton TA2 ....212 F6
Belgrave Rd
Bath BA1 ....28 B1
Bristol BS8 ....226 B4
Weston-Super-Mare BS22 ....49 B8
Belgrave Terr 2 BA1 ....28 A1
Bellamy Ave BS13 ....22 C4
Belland Dr BS14 ....22 F4
Bella View Gdns BA6 ....206 D4
Bella Vista Rd BA1 ....228 B4
Bell Barn Rd BS9 ....5 D6
Bell Chase BA20 ....218 D5
Bell Cl
Bridgwater TA6 ....208 F6
Farmborough BA2 ....59 F6
Westbury-sub-Mendip BA5 ....110 E6
Belle View Terr TA20 ....198 C8
Bellevue BS8 ....226 B2
Belle Vue
Midsomer Norton BA3 ....78 B3
Washford TA23 ....131 E3
Belle Vue Cl BA2 ....79 D7
Bellevue Cotts BS8 ....226 B2
Bellevue Cres BS8 ....226 B2
Bellevue Ct
Bristol BS8 ....226 B2
Clevedon BS21 ....6 D4
Bellevue Mans BS21 ....6 D4
Bellevue Rd BS21 ....6 D4
Bellevue Terr BS8 ....226 B2
Belle Vue Terr TA18 ....224 B6
Bellfield BA3 ....117 A3
Bellhanger Ct BA1 ....228 B4
Bell Hill
Chewton Mendip BA3 ....94 B7
Norton St Philip BA2 ....81 E4
Bellhorse La BS40 ....74 C5
Bellifants BA2 ....60 A6
Bell La
Bristol BS1 ....227 A3
Chard TA19, TA20 ....193 F7
Chewton Mendip BA3 ....94 B7
Cossington TA7 ....137 A3
Thurloxton TA2 ....153 D1
Bell Language Sch The
BA1 ....44 C8
Bellman's Cross BA8 ....190 B7
Bellmoor La TA19 ....194 A7
Bell Orch TA10 ....171 D4
Bellotts Rd BA2 ....44 C6
Bell Pit Brow BS48 ....9 B2
Bell Sq BS40 ....54 E3

Bellum SN14 .... 13 E8
Belluton La BS39 .... 40 D5
Belluton Villas BS39 .... 40 D5
Bell Wlk BS40 .... 35 E2
Belmont Cl TA6 .... 208 B4
Belmont Dr
Failand BS8 .... 10 B3
Taunton TA1 .... 212 E2
Belmont Hill BS48 .... 10 B1
Belmont Ho 14 BA20 .... 219 B4
Belmont Rd
Bath BA2 .... 45 C1
Hatch Beauchamp TA3 .... 183 A8
Taunton TA1 .... 212 C3
Winscombe BS25 .... 70 A8
Belmont Terr TA19 .... 184 E3
Belmont The BS21 .... 6 D3
Belmore Gdns BA2 .... 44 B3
Belstone Wlk BS4 .... 22 C8
Belton Ct BA1 .... 27 B2
Belton Rd BS20 .... 2 A6
Belvedere BA1 .... 228 B4
Belvedere Cl TA5 .... 135 B2
Belvedere Cres BS22 .... 31 C1
Belvedere Ct 3 TA21 .... 222 D6
Belvedere Grange TA11 .... 211 E3
Belvedere Rd
Taunton TA1 .... 212 F5
Yeovil BA21 .... 219 E7
Belvedere Trad Est TA1 .... 212 E5
Belvoir Rd 6 BA2 .... 44 D5
Bemberry Bank TA24 .... 130 B5
Benares Ct TA24 .... 201 A8
Bences Cl SN14 .... 13 F8
Benches La BS40 .... 37 D3
Bench La TA20 .... 193 D5
Ben Cross TA13 .... 220 A4
Benedictine Ct BA6 .... 206 C4
Benedict St BA6 .... 206 D4
Benhole La TA5 .... 134 B8
Bennell Batch BA3 .... 96 E4
Bennell Cl BA3 .... 96 E4
Bennell Cotts BA3 .... 96 E4
Bennett's Cl BA5 .... 204 B7
Bennett's La BA3, BA5 .... 114 B7
Bennett's Rd BA1 .... 28 C3
Bennett Gdns BA11 .... 119 D4
Bennett La BA1 .... 28 A1
Bennett Rd TA9 .... 104 F4
Bennetts Field Trad Est
BA9 .... 216 C2
Bennett St BA1 .... 228 B3
Bennetts Way BS21 .... 6 E5
Bennett Way BS1, BS8 .... 11 F5
Benter Cross BA3 .... 115 D7
Bentley Cl BS14 .... 22 F3
Bentley Rd BS22 .... 32 B3
Ben Travers Way TA8 .... 104 C6
Benville Ave BS9 .... 5 C8
Bere La BA6 .... 206 E4
Bere Mills La TA19 .... 194 B7
Beresford Cl
Burnham-on-S TA8 .... 104 C7
Saltford BS31 .... 25 E2
Beresford Gdns BA1 .... 27 A3
Beretun Orch BA6 .... 206 E3
Berhill TA7 .... 156 C7
Berkeley Ave
Bristol BS8 .... 226 C3
Midsomer Norton BA3 .... 78 A2
Berkeley Cres
Bristol BS8 .... 226 B3
Weston-Super-Mare BS23 .... 48 C2
Berkeley Ct BA2 .... 45 C6
Berkeley Gdns
Bruton BA10 .... 215 E6
Keynsham BS31 .... 24 E4
Berkeley Ho
Bath BA1 .... 228 C4
Bristol BS1 .... 226 C3
Berkeley Pl
Bath BA1 .... 228 C4
Bristol BS8 .... 226 B3
Berkeley Rd
Street BA16 .... 207 E6
Yeovil BA20 .... 219 A4
Berkeley Sq BS8 .... 226 B3
Berkley Ave BS8 .... 226 B3
Berkley CE Fst Sch BA11 .... 121 A7
Berkley Cross BA11 .... 120 F6
Berkley Ct BA22 .... 173 E2
Berkley La
Beckington BA11 .... 101 D3
Frome BA11 .... 120 D8
Berkley Rd BA11 .... 120 B6
Berkley St BA11 .... 121 A8
Berlington Ct BS1 .... 227 B1
Bernard Cres TA24 .... 200 F6
Bernard Herridge Ct
BA9 .... 216 D4
Bernard Ireland Ho BA1 .... 27 B1
Bernard Taylor Homes 9
TA1 .... 213 A4
Berners Cl BS4 .... 22 D7
Berrow CE Prim Sch TA8 .... 84 F4
Berrow Lodge 7 BS23 .... 48 E5
Berrow Rd TA8 .... 85 A2
Berry Cl TA6 .... 208 E2
Berrydale Ave TA6 .... 208 F6
Berry Hill
Mells BA11 .... 118 A6
Nunney BA11 .... 143 B8
Berry La EX13 .... 198 F3
Berryman Cl BA4 .... 205 A5
Berryman Ct BA5 .... 203 B4
Bertha Terr TA9 .... 104 D3
Berwick Cl TA1 .... 212 C1
Beryl Gr BS14 .... 23 C8
Beryl Knapp BA22 .... 197 B8
Beryl La BA5 .... 203 F6
Besley Ct BA5 .... 203 B4
Bests Field TA12 .... 185 B8
Bethell Mead TA4 .... 167 E6
Beverley Cl
Frome BA11 .... 119 D3
Taunton TA2 .... 212 E6
Beverley Dr TA23 .... 202 C7
Beverley Gdns BS9 .... 5 D7
Bewdley Rd BA2 .... 45 B4
Bewley Ct TA20 .... 223 B4
Bews La TA20 .... 223 B5
Bibors Hill TA4 .... 165 E4
Bibury Cl BS48 .... 9 A1
Bibury Ho BA1 .... 27 B2
Bickenhall La TA3 .... 182 F6
Bickfield La BS40 .... 74 B8
Bicking's Close La TA4 .... 166 A4
Bicknell Gdns BA21 .... 219 B8
Bidbrooke La EX36 .... 162 A6
Biddiscombe Cl TA6 .... 208 E1
Biddisham Cl 6 BS48 .... 8 E1
Biddisham La BS26 .... 87 E7
Biddlesden Rd BA21 .... 218 C7
Biddle St BS49 .... 34 B7
Bideford Cres BS4 .... 22 F8
Bideford Rd BS22 .... 31 F2
Bifield Cl BS14 .... 23 F5
Bifield Gdns BS14 .... 23 E5
Bifield Rd BS14 .... 23 F5
Bignal Rand Cl BA5 .... 203 B3
Bignal Rand Dr BA5 .... 203 B3
Bignell Cl BS25 .... 69 F8
Big Tree Cl BS26 .... 69 C3
Bigwood La BS1 .... 226 C2
Bilberry Cl BS9 .... 5 C8
Bilberry Gr TA1 .... 168 F1
Bilbie Cl BS40 .... 56 E8
Bilbie Rd
Chew Stoke BS40 .... 56 E8
Weston-Super-Mare BS22 .... 32 B3
Bilbury La
Bath BA1 .... 228 B2
Glastonbury BA6 .... 206 F3
Billand Cl BS13 .... 21 E3
Billetfield TA1 .... 212 F3
Billet St TA1 .... 212 F3
Billicombe La TA7 .... 155 C8
Billing's Hill BS28 .... 108 C4
Billy La TA4 .... 210 D7
Bince's Lodge La BA3 .... 78 B3
Binces La BA2 .... 42 E3
Bincombe Dr TA18 .... 224 C7
Bincombe Rd TA6 .... 209 C4
Binding Cl 6 TA6 .... 153 F4
Bindon La BA11 .... 143 B2
Bindon Rd TA2 .... 212 C6
Bindwell La BA22 .... 174 F3
Binegar CE Prim Sch
BA3 .... 114 D8
Bineham Ct TA10 .... 173 B4
Bineham La
Ilchester BA22 .... 173 F2
Yeovilton BA22 .... 174 A2
Bineham Rd TA10 .... 173 A4
Binford's La TA4 .... 151 A4
Binford Pl TA6 .... 209 A5
Binhay Rd BS49 .... 34 C7
Binley Gr BS14 .... 23 D5
Binmead Gdns BS13 .... 22 B4
Binnings The BS27 .... 90 F3
Birbeck Rd BS9 .... 5 E5
Bircham Cl TA6 .... 208 C4
Bircham La TA24 .... 201 C4
Bircham Rd
Minehead TA24 .... 201 B5
Taunton TA2 .... 213 B8
Birchanger La TA4 .... 150 A8
Birch Ave
Bleadon BS24 .... 67 C6
Clevedon BS21 .... 6 E4
Puriton TA7 .... 136 C4
Birch Cl
Bridgwater TA6 .... 209 D5
Cannington TA5 .... 135 B2
Cheddar BS27 .... 90 C8
Locking BS24 .... 50 B4
Wedmore BS28 .... 108 C3
Birch Croft BS14 .... 23 A3
Birch Ct BS31 .... 24 C4
Birchdale BA20 .... 218 D2
Birchdale Rd BS14 .... 23 A8
Birchdene BS48 .... 9 A2
Birch Dr BS40 .... 53 A5
Birches Cnr TA4 .... 152 A4
Birches The BS48 .... 9 A2
Birchfield Com Prim Sch
BA21 .... 219 D7
Birchfield Rd BA21 .... 219 D8
Birch Gr
Portishead BS20 .... 2 C4
Taunton TA1 .... 212 E5
Birch Hill BS27 .... 90 C8
Birch Ho TA8 .... 65 F2
Birchill Cross EX13 .... 198 A6
Birchill La BA11 .... 120 A1
Birch Lawn TA8 .... 104 B6
Birch Rd
12 Martock TA12 .... 185 E6
Radstock BA3 .... 78 E1
Wellington TA21 .... 222 E5
Birch Wlk BA11 .... 120 B7
Birchwood Ave BS23 .... 49 A7
Birchwood Cl BA12 .... 144 E8
Birchwood Dr BS8 .... 10 B3
Birchwood La BS39 .... 40 F2
Bird's Cl TA18 .... 224 B6
Birdcombe Cl BS48 .... 8 E3
Birdlip Cl BS48 .... 9 A1
Birdwell La BS41 .... 10 F1
Birdwell Prim Sch BS41 .... 21 A8
Birdwell Rd BS41 .... 10 F1
Birkbeck Ct BS23 .... 48 D7
Birkett Rd BS23 .... 30 B1
Birkin St BS2 .... 227 C2
Birnbeck Rd BS23 .... 30 C1
Biscay Dr BS20 .... 2 F6
Biscombe Cross TA3 .... 191 B8
Bisdee Rd BS24 .... 49 D2
Bishop's Hill TA21 .... 179 B7
Bishop's Hull Hill TA1 .... 212 B4
Bishop's Hull Prim Sch
TA1 .... 212 B4
Bishop's Hull Rd TA1 .... 212 A3
Bishop's La DT9 .... 187 E1
Bishop's Lydeard Sta
TA4 .... 167 E7
Bishop's Mead TA2 .... 212 E8
Bishop's Pal* BA5 .... 203 E4
Bishop's Path TA8 .... 104 B6
Bishop Ave BS22 .... 32 A3
Bishop Cl TA20 .... 223 B5
Bishop Cres BA4 .... 204 F5
Bishop Fox's Com Sch
TA1 .... 213 A1
Bishop Fox Dr TA1 .... 213 A2
Bishop Henderson CE Prim
Sch
Coleford BA3 .... 116 E8
Taunton TA1 .... 212 C2
Bishop Rd TA5 .... 134 B2
Bishops Cl BS9 .... 5 E3
Bishops Cotts
Stogursey TA5 .... 134 B7
Wootton Courtenay TA24 .... 129 F6
Bishops Cove BS13 .... 21 F5
Bishops Ct 4 TA21 .... 222 D6
Bishops Dr TA10 .... 172 A5
Bishops Gn TA4 .... 210 C4
Bishops Knoll BS9 .... 5 C3
Bishops La BA22 .... 197 A6
Bishopslea Cl BA5 .... 203 C3
Bishops Lydeard CE Prim
Sch TA4 .... 167 E8
Bishops Mead BS49 .... 35 A8
Bishops Park Way BA5 .... 203 F2
Bishops Rd BS49 .... 35 A8
Bishop St
Bristol BS2 .... 227 B4
Faulkland BA3 .... 80 D2
Bishopston TA15 .... 186 B4
Bishop Sutton Prim Sch
BS39 .... 57 D4
Bishops Wlk BA22 .... 173 D1
Bishopsworth CE Jun Sch
BS13 .... 21 F6
Bishopsworth Rd BS13 .... 22 A7
Bishop Terr BS2 .... 227 C4
Bishport Ave BS13 .... 22 C3
Bishport Cl BS13 .... 22 B4
Bishport Gn BS13 .... 22 C3
Bitham Wlk TA7 .... 136 E3
Bittern Cl BS22 .... 31 F1
Bittlemead BS13 .... 22 F4
Black's Moor Hill La
TA11 .... 173 A5
Blackacre BS14 .... 23 C4
Blackacre Hill BA8 .... 176 D4
Blackaller La EX16 .... 163 C1
Black Bench Dro TA20 .... 223 F7
Blackberry Cl BA4 .... 205 C4
Blackberry Ct TA21 .... 222 D4
Blackberry Dr BS22 .... 32 A2
Blackberry La
Portishead BS20 .... 1 F2
Sherborne DT9 .... 225 D5
Winsley BA3, BA15 .... 64 C8
Blackberry Way BA3 .... 77 F3
Blackberry Wlk TA18 .... 224 D7
Blackbird Cl BA3 .... 97 B8
Blackbird Way BA11 .... 120 B6
Blackbrook Park Ave
TA1 .... 213 E4
Blackbrook Prim Sch
TA1 .... 213 D3
Blackbrook Rd TA1 .... 213 E5
Blackbrook Way TA1 .... 213 E3
Black Dog Hill BA13 .... 121 E6
Blackdown BA21 .... 219 A6
Blackdown Bsns Pk
TA21 .... 222 E6
Blackdown Ct BS14 .... 23 B5
Blackdown Mead BS27 .... 90 C6
Blackdown Rd
Bridgwater TA6 .... 209 D4
Portishead BS20 .... 2 B5
Rockwell Green TA21 .... 222 B4
Taunton TA2 .... 213 B8
Blackdown View
Curry Rivel TA10 .... 171 D4
Ilminster TA19 .... 221 C4
Norton Fitzwarren TA2 .... 168 B5
Nynehead TA21 .... 167 C2
Sampford Peverell EX16 .... 178 C1
Blackdown Visitors Ctr*
EX15 .... 180 D3
Black Dro TA7 .... 155 A1
Blacker's La BA3 .... 116 E2
Blackerton Cross EX16 .... 162 E3
Blackey La BA3 .... 115 B6
Blackford Hollow BA22 .... 175 F5
Blackford Moor Dro BS26,
BS28 .... 107 B6
Blackford Moor La TA9,
BS28 .... 107 B5
Blackford Rd
Charlton Horethorne
DT9 .... 176 A2
Mark TA9 .... 106 F4
Wedmore BS28 .... 108 A3
Blackford Way DT9 .... 176 A3
Blackfriars BS1 .... 227 A3
Blackfriars Rd BS48 .... 8 B1
Blackham La TA10 .... 155 F2
Blackhayes La EX14 .... 192 C1
Black Horse La TA1 .... 212 F5
Black La
Axbridge BS26 .... 70 E2
Hemyock EX15 .... 180 D2
Holcombe Rogus TA21 .... 178 E6
Blackland Dro TA20 .... 194 A1
Blackland La TA20 .... 194 B1
Blacklands TA6 .... 208 F5
Black Mere BA22 .... 218 B5
Black Mixen La TA18 .... 224 C7
Black Monkey La TA24 .... 131 C5
Blackmoor
Clevedon BS21 .... 6 C1
Lower Langford BS40 .... 53 C6
3 Weston-Super-Mare
BS22 .... 31 F2
Blackmoor Cl BS40 .... 53 C6
Blackmoor La 6 BA8 .... 190 A6
Blackmoor Rd
Abbots Leigh BS8 .... 4 E2
Taunton TA2 .... 213 B7
Wellington TA21 .... 222 F4
Blackmoors La BS3 .... 11 E4
Blackmore Chase BA9 .... 216 D3
Blackmore Dr BA2 .... 44 C5
Blackmore La TA5 .... 135 B1
Blackmore Rd DT10 .... 190 B4
Blackmore Vale Cl BA8 .... 176 E1
Blacknell Ind Est TA18 .... 224 D5
Blacknell La TA18 .... 224 D6
Black Nore Point BS20 .... 1 F5
Black Pit Dro BA6 .... 206 D8
Blackrock La BS39 .... 40 E7
Black Rock Nature Trail*
BA5 .... 72 A1
Blackrock Villas BS20 .... 2 B1
Blackrod Cotts TA13 .... 184 F4
Blacksmith's La BA1 .... 26 B3
Blacksmith La BA1 .... 28 B6
Blacksmiths La TA7 .... 155 F8
Blacksmiths Row BA21 .... 187 D6
Blackthorn Cl
Biddisham BS26 .... 87 E6
Bristol BS13 .... 22 D5
6 North Petherton TA6 .... 153 F3
Blackthorn Dr BS20 .... 2 E5
Blackthorne Cl BA22 .... 173 E2
Blackthorn Gdns
Taunton TA2 .... 168 F6
Weston-Super-Mare BS22 .... 32 A1
Blackthorn Rd BS13 .... 22 D5
Blackthorn Sq BS21 .... 6 D1
Blackthorns The TA1 .... 213 C2
Blackthorn Terr BS22 .... 32 A1
Blackthorn Way
Nailsea BS48 .... 9 A2
Somerton TA11 .... 211 B3
Street BA16 .... 207 A5
Blackwater La
Axminster EX13 .... 198 F3
Wiveliscombe TA4 .... 210 A8
Blackwell Rd BA22 .... 174 F3
Blackworthy Rd BA7 .... 159 C3
Bladen Cl BS20 .... 2 E4
Bladud Bldgs BA1 .... 228 C3
Blagdon Cl BS24 .... 48 F1
Blagdon Cres TA1 .... 212 D1
Blagdon Cross TA24 .... 129 D2
Blagdon Hill Prim Sch
TA3 .... 181 C5
Blagdon La
Blagdon BS40 .... 54 F6
Brompton Regis TA22,
TA24 .... 148 D4
Blagdon Pk BA2 .... 44 A4
Blagdon Prim Sch BS40 .... 54 F2
Blagdon Wlk BA11 .... 120 D7
Blagrove's Rd TA4 .... 167 C4
Blagrove Cl
Bristol BS13 .... 22 C3
Street BA16 .... 207 E6
Blagrove Cres BS13 .... 22 C3
Blagrove Hill BA6 .... 157 C6
Blaisdon BS22 .... 49 D7
Blaise Wlk BS9 .... 5 C6
Blake's Cres TA9 .... 104 E5
Blake's La BA3 .... 115 D2
Blake End BS22 .... 31 E4
Blake Gn TA7 .... 156 B7
Blake Ind Est TA6 .... 209 A3
Blakeney Gr BS48 .... 18 C8
Blake Pl TA6 .... 209 A5
Blake Rd
5 Crewkerne TA18 .... 224 C5
Wells BA5 .... 203 C5
Blakes La TA5, TA6 .... 208 C7
Blakes Rd TA6 .... 208 D6
Blake St
2 Bridgwater TA6 .... 208 F4
Taunton TA1 .... 213 B4
Blakeway BS28 .... 138 B6
Blandford Cl BS48 .... 8 E1
Blaxhold La TA5 .... 152 E5
Bleadon Hill BS23, BS24 .... 67 A8
Bleadon Mill BS24 .... 67 C5
Bleadon Rd BS24 .... 67 B7
Bleak St BA9 .... 161 E2
Blencathara Ct TA8 .... 104 A8
Blenheim Cl
Peasedown St John BA2 .... 79 D7
Weston-Super-Mare BS22 .... 32 A2
Blenheim Ct 10 BS1 .... 227 A4
Blenheim Gdns BA1 .... 28 A2
Blenheim Mews TA24 .... 200 F7
Blenheim Rd
Bridgwater TA6 .... 209 D7
Minehead TA24 .... 201 A7
Street BA16 .... 207 B4
Taunton TA1 .... 213 D5
Yeovil BA21 .... 219 D7
Blenheim View TA24 .... 201 A7
Blenheim Way BS20 .... 2 E5
Blights Hill EX16, TA22 .... 163 F3
Blindhouse La 7 BA11 .... 119 F4
Blind La
Barton St David TA11 .... 158 A2
Bath BA1 .... 27 C2
Buckland St Mary TA20 .... 182 A1
Chard TA20 .... 223 D2
Chew Stoke BS40 .... 56 E8
Congresbury BS49 .... 34 F6
Drimpton DT8 .... 199 F6
Isle Abbotts TA3 .... 183 F8
Keinton Mandeville TA11 .... 158 B1
Martock TA12 .... 185 D5
Southwick BA14 .... 83 F2
Thorncombe TA20 .... 199 B6
Tunley BA2 .... 61 A4
Blindwell La
Golsoncott TA23, TA24 .... 131 C1
Skilgate TA4 .... 164 E6
Bloomfield BS24 .... 49 A2
Bloomfield Ave
Bath BA2 .... 44 E4
Timsbury BA2 .... 60 B3
Bloomfield Cl
Taunton TA1 .... 213 C5
Timsbury BA2 .... 60 B3
Bloomfield Cotts BA2 .... 79 C7
Bloomfield Cres BA2 .... 44 D2
Bloomfield Dr BA2 .... 44 D2
Bloomfield Gr BA2 .... 44 E3
Bloomfield La BS39 .... 77 E5
Bloomfield Park Rd BA2 .... 60 B3
Bloomfield Pk BA2 .... 44 E3
Bloomfield Rd
Bath BA2 .... 44 E3
Timsbury BA2 .... 60 B3
Bloomfield Rise BA2 .... 44 D2
Bloomfield Rise N BA2 .... 44 D2
Bloomfield Terr BA2 .... 79 C7
Bloom Row TA6 .... 209 D5
Blossom Cl TA6 .... 209 C5
Blue Anchor Chalets
TA24 .... 131 C6
Blue Anchor Sta TA24 .... 131 C6
Blue Ball Cl BA10 .... 215 E6
Bluebell Cl
Bristol BS9 .... 5 B6
Taunton TA1 .... 213 C1
Bluebell Rd
Weston-Super-Mare BS22 .... 32 A6
Yeovil BA22 .... 218 B5
Bluebell Rise BA3 .... 77 F3
Blueberry Way BS22 .... 31 F1
Blue Gate TA24 .... 145 D8
Blue Ho The BA11 .... 119 F5
Blue Sch The BA5 .... 203 C5
Blue Stone La TA13 .... 185 B6
Bluett Rd TA21 .... 222 D4
Blue Water Dr BS24 .... 50 D3
Blundells La TA2 .... 169 C7
Blythe Ct TA1 .... 212 D1
Blythe Gdns BS22 .... 32 A3
Blythe Way TA8 .... 85 A3
Board Cross BA4 .... 205 B6
Boards La BA5 .... 204 C7
Boards Rd TA6 .... 209 A6
Boardwalk The BA16 .... 207 D7
Boarpath La TA4 .... 151 A5
Boat La BS24 .... 67 C3
Boat Stall La BA2 .... 228 C2
Bobbin La BA15 .... 64 F4
Bobbin Pk BA15 .... 64 F3
Bodden La BA4 .... 205 E6
Boden St TA20 .... 223 C3
Boden Villas TA20 .... 223 C3
Bodley Way BS24 .... 49 E7
Bodmin Rd TA2 .... 213 A8
Bodmin Wlk BS4 .... 22 F8
Boez La TA2 .... 153 D1
Bofors Pk BA22 .... 218 A6
Bollams Mead TA4 .... 210 C5
Bollnas Cl BA4 .... 205 C4
Bolster La BA6 .... 157 C4
Bolter's La
Alhampton BA4, BA7 .... 159 B4
Shepton Mallet BA4 .... 141 D8
Bolton Cl TA9 .... 104 F4
Bommertown Cross
EX36 .... 162 A4
Bond's La SN14 .... 13 E8
Bond's Row TA24 .... 124 A3
Bondfield Way TA20 .... 223 B6
Bondip Hill BA22, TA11 .... 173 D3
Bonds Cl TA20 .... 223 D6
Bonds Pool TA10 .... 172 A5
Bond St
Bridgwater TA6 .... 208 F5
Bristol BS1 .... 227 B3
Yeovil BA20 .... 219 B4
Yeovil, Houndstone BA22 .... 218 B5

Bonfire Cl TA20 .... 223 C2
Bonfire La TA11 .... 173 E7
Bonham La BA12 .... 161 F4
Bonhill Rd BS39 .... 57 D5
Boniface Wlk TA8 .... 104 B6
Bonners Cswy EX13 ..... 198 A2
Bonners Dr EX13 .... 198 A1
Bonners Glen EX13 .... 198 A1
Bonnie's La 6 TA14 ...... 185 F4
Bonning's La TA19 .... 184 D4
Bonniton La TA24 .... 130 E5
Bonniton New Rd TA24 .. 201 D1
Bonny Cross
Clayhanger EX16 .... 165 B1
Morebath EX16 .... 164 B3
Bonny La TA24 .... 128 B2
Bonson Hill TA5 .... 134 E3
Bonsonwood La TA5 ..... 134 E4
Boobery EX16 .... 178 D1
Boome La TA2 .... 169 C7
Boons Orch TA3 .... 169 C3
Booth Way TA6 .... 208 D5
Boozer Pit TA16 .... 195 F8
Borden Gate EX16 .... 178 B8
Bordesley Rd BS14 .... 23 A3
Boreal Way 4 BS24 .... 49 F7
Boreland La BA22 .... 187 A8
Borgie Pl BS22 .... 31 F3
Borleyton Wlk BS13 .... 21 F4
Borough Mall The BS28 . 108 D4
Borough Post TA3 .... 170 B3
Borough The
Montacute TA15 .... 186 B3
Wedmore BS28 .... 108 D4
3 Yeovil BA20 .... 219 B4
Borver Gr BS13 .... 22 B4
Bosanquet Flats TA24 .... 200 F7
Bossington Dr TA2 .... 213 B8
Bossington La TA24 .... 124 B4
Boswell Rd BA15 .... 64 F3
Botham Cl BS22 .... 32 A4
Bottreaux Mill Cross
EX36 .... 162 A5
Boucher's La TA4 .... 165 E4
Boulevard BS23 .... 48 E8
Boulters Rd BS13 .... 22 C4
Boundaries The BS24 ..... 67 B1
Boundary Ave
Frome BA11 .... 120 B5
Yeovil BA22 .... 218 B7
Boundary Cl
Holcombe BA3 .... 116 C8
Midsomer Norton BA3 .... 97 B7
Weston-Super-Mare BS23 .. 48 E3
Yeovil BA21 .... 218 E7
Boundary Rd
Weston-Super-Mare BS24 .. 50 A7
Yeovil BA22 .... 218 A5
Boundary Way
Glastonbury BA6 .... 206 C3
Yeovil BA22 .... 218 A7
Boundhay BA22 .... 186 C2
Bounds La TA20 .... 223 A1
Bourchier Cl 13 EX16 ..... 164 B1
Bourchier Dr 12 EX16 .... 164 B1
Bourchier Gdns BS13 ..... 22 B3
Bourne Gr TA1 .... 213 D4
Bourne La
Blagdon BS40 .... 54 C4
Burrington BS40 .... 54 B4
Bournville Inf Sch BS23 ... 49 A4
Bournville Jun Sch BS23 .. 48 F5
Bournville Rd BS23 .... 48 F4
Bourtonbridge Dro BA5 .. 139 F5
Bourton Combe BS48 ..... 19 F7
Bourton La
Cross BS26 .... 69 E3
Weston-Super-Mare BS22 .. 32 D4
Bourton Mead
Flax Bourton BS48 .... 19 F8
Long Ashton BS41 .... 11 A1
Bourton Wlk BS13 .... 22 A8
Bouverie Cl TA24 .... 129 E1
Bouverie Rd TA6 .... 208 D5
Bove Moor Cl BA16 .... 207 E6
Bove Moor Rd BA16 ...... 207 E6
Bovet Cl TA1 .... 212 B1
Bove Town BA6 .... 206 E5
Bovet St TA21 .... 222 C6
Bow Cotts BS20 .... 4 C4
Bowden's La TA10 .... 171 F7
Bowden Cl BS9 .... 5 C8
Bowden Hill BA3 .... 96 D4
Bowden La
Milborne Port BA8 .... 217 F5
Rodhuish TA24 .... 130 F3
Yenston BA8 .... 189 D7
Bowden Rd BA8 .... 189 D8
Bowdens La EX16 .... 164 E3
Bowden Way BS8 .... 10 B3
Bowditch Cl BA4 .... 205 A5
Bowditch Row 8 TA18 .. 224 C6
Bowen Rd BS24 .... 50 C5
Bower Ashton Terr BS3 ... 11 F4
Bower Ave TA6 .... 209 C6
Bower Fields TA6 .... 209 D6
Bowerhayes La TA24 ..... 131 A5
Bower Hinton TA12 .... 185 D5
Bowerings Rd TA6 .... 208 E2
Bower La TA6 .... 209 E6
Bowerleaze BS9 .... 5 C5
Bower Manor Sh Ctr
TA6 .... 209 D6
Bowermead La BA4 .... 204 C1
Bowery Cnr BA5 .... 92 E5
Bowfell Cl TA1 .... 212 C1
Bow Gate TA18 .... 196 A8
Bowhayes TA18 .... 224 C5
Bowhays Cross TA4 ..... 202 A2
Bowlditch La BA3 .... 78 B4
Bowleaze BA21 .... 218 D6
Bowline Cl TA6 .... 208 E7
Bowline Ct TA24 .... 201 B7
Bowling Gn
10 Cannington TA5 .... 135 B2
Street BA16 .... 207 D7
Bowlish Inf Sch BA4 .... 205 A6
Bowlish La BA4 .... 205 A6
Bowmont Gr TA1 .... 213 D3
Bowns Cl BA4 .... 141 E1
Bowood Rd TA2 .... 213 A6
Bowring Cl
Bristol BS13 .... 22 C3
Coxley BA5 .... 139 E6
Bowsprit Cl TA24 .... 201 B7
Bow St TA10 .... 171 F5
Bowyers Cl BA6 .... 206 E5
Boxbury Hill BS39 .... 77 F3
Boxbush Hill BA4 .... 158 E8
Box Bush La BS24 .... 33 C1
Box Rd BA1 .... 29 C3
Boxstone Hill TA19 .... 184 D2
Box Wlk BS31 .... 24 C4
Boyce's Ave BS8 .... 226 A3
Boyce Cl BA2 .... 43 F5
Boyd Ho BA5 .... 113 A1
Boyd Rd BS31 .... 25 D3
Boyle Cl DT10 .... 190 B4
Boyton Hill TA19 .... 194 F8
Boyton La TA19 .... 194 F7
Bracey Rd TA12 .... 185 E7
Bracken Edge TA4 .... 132 E4
Bracken Way TA20 .... 223 F5
Brackenwood Gdns* BS20 . 1 F5
Brackenwood Rd BS21 ..... 6 E6
Bracton Dr BS14 .... 23 A5
Bradbeers TA3 .... 181 D8
Bradfield Cl TA6 .... 208 E1
Bradfield Way TA20 ..... 223 C3
Bradford Cl
Clevedon BS21 .... 6 C1
Taunton TA1 .... 168 D1
Bradford Pk BA2 .... 45 A2
Bradford Rd
Bath BA2 .... 45 A1
Bathford BA1 .... 29 B2
Misterton TA18 .... 224 E4
Rode BA11, BA14 .... 83 A2
Sherborne DT9 .... 225 B3
Wingfield BA14, BA15 ...... 83 C8
Winsley BA15 .... 64 D6
Winsley BA15 .... 64 E7
Bradley Ave BS11 .... 4 E6
Bradley Cl TA11 .... 211 C4
Bradley Cres BS11 .... 4 E6
Bradley Cross La BS27 .... 90 D7
Bradley Hill La TA11 ...... 211 B5
Bradley La
Ashcott TA7 .... 156 B7
Maiden Bradley BA11,
BA12 .... 144 B2
Parbrook BA6 .... 158 C7
Bradley Rd BS20 .... 3 E5
Bradleys TA19 .... 183 F4
Bradley Stream Rd BA16,
TA7 .... 138 C1
Bradley View TA11 .... 211 C4
Bradley Way BA6 .... 158 B8
Bradney La TA7 .... 136 D1
Bradon La
Isle Abbotts TA3 .... 183 F6
Stocklinch TA19 .... 184 A5
Bradville Gdns BS41 ...... 20 F8
Brae Rd BS25 .... 70 B8
Brae Rise BS25 .... 70 A8
Bragg's La BS2 .... 227 C3
Braikenridge Cl BS21 ...... 6 C1
Brain's Cnr BA9 .... 216 E1
Brainsfield BS9 .... 5 F6
Brains La BA22 .... 175 A5
Braithwaite Pl TA8 .... 85 A2
Braithwaite Way BA11 .. 120 C6
Brakewell Gdns BS14 ..... 23 A4
Bramble Dr
Berrow TA8 .... 84 F5
Bristol BS9 .... 5 D3
South Petherton TA13 .... 220 C4
Bramble Hill BA16 .... 156 D6
Bramble La
Bristol BS9 .... 5 C3
Haselbury Plucknett TA18 . 196 C5
Bramble Pk TA1 .... 213 C2
Brambles Rd TA8 .... 85 B1
Brambles The
Bristol BS13 .... 22 C4
Hinton Charterhouse BA2 ... 63 E1
Keynsham BS31 .... 24 D3
Wellington TA21 .... 222 D4
Weston-Super-Mare BS22 ... 32 D2
Bramble Way BA2 .... 45 B1
Bramblewood BS49 .... 17 B1
Bramblewood Rd BS22 .... 31 E3
Bramley Cl
Charlton Horethorne
DT9 .... 176 A2
Crewkerne TA18 .... 224 C7
Locking BS24 .... 50 A5
Peasedown St John BA2 .... 79 D7
Pill BS20 .... 4 C4
Sandford BS25 .... 52 A4
Yatton BS49 .... 34 B7
Bramley Dr
Backwell BS48 .... 19 A5
Frome BA11 .... 120 C6
Bramley Rd
Street BA16 .... 207 B4
Bramley Rd *continued*
Taunton TA1 .... 213 D5
Bramley Sq BS49 .... 34 E3
Bramleys The
Nailsea BS48 .... 18 B8
Portishead BS20 .... 2 F5
Brampton Ho BS20 .... 2 E4
Brampton Way BS20 .... 2 E4
Bramshill Dr BS22 .... 31 F3
Branche Gr BS13 .... 22 D3
Branches Cross BS40 ..... 35 E3
Branch Rd BA2 .... 63 F2
Brandon Ho BS8 .... 226 B2
Brandon St BS1 .... 226 C2
Brandon Steep BS1 .... 226 C2
Brangay La BS27 .... 91 A1
Brangwyn Sq BS22 .... 31 F2
Branksome Ave TA6 ...... 209 B5
Bransby Way BS24 .... 50 A8
Branscombe Rd BS9 .... 5 C4
Branscombe Wlk BS20 ...... 1 F3
Bransford BA22 .... 197 D3
Brantwood Rd TA6 .... 208 C5
Brassknocker Hill BA2 .... 45 F2
Brassmill Ent Ctr BA1 ..... 44 A7
Brassmill La BA1 .... 44 A7
Brassmill Lane Trad Est
BA1 .... 44 A7
Bratton Cl TA24 .... 200 D7
Bratton Ho BA9 .... 176 B8
Bratton La TA24 .... 200 B7
Bratton Mill La
Minehead, Bratton TA24 ... 200 B7
Minehead, Woodcombe
TA24 .... 200 C7
Bratton Rd BS4 .... 22 D7
Bray Cl EX16 .... 179 B3
Braysbridge BS27 .... 90 C7
Braysdown Cl BA2 .... 79 B6
Braysdown La BA2 .... 79 C7
Breach Cl SP8 .... 161 F1
Breaches The BS20 .... 4 B5
Breach Furlong La TA10 . 156 A1
Breach Hill TA21 .... 179 F5
Breach Hill La BS40 .... 56 C6
Breach La
Brinscombe BS26 .... 89 B3
Corsley Heath BA12 .... 144 E7
Kington Magna SP8 .... 177 E2
Nailsea BS48 .... 17 F7
Weston Town BA4 .... 142 E4
Bread & Cheese La TA19 184 C1
Bread St BA4 .... 140 F3
Brean Court Ho TA8 .... 65 F3
Brean Ct TA8 .... 65 F3
Brean Down Ave BS23 ..... 48 E4
Brean Down Rd TA8 .... 47 F1
Brean Leisure Pk* TA8 .... 65 F1
Brean Rd BS24 .... 66 F1
Brecon View BS24 .... 49 A1
Breech Cotts TA21 .... 179 F5
Breech La BA6 .... 158 A8
Bree Cl BS22 .... 32 A4
Bremis Rd TA24 .... 201 E3
Brendon Ave BS23 .... 48 F8
Brendon Cl TA23 .... 131 D2
Brendon Gdns 2 BS48 ...... 8 E1
Brendon Ho BA21 .... 219 A6
Brendon Rd
Bridgwater TA6 .... 208 F6
Portishead BS20 .... 2 A5
Watchet TA23 .... 202 B6
Wellington TA21 .... 222 D7
Brendons TA4 .... 167 E8
Brendons The EX16 .... 178 D1
Brendon Two Gates
TA24 .... 127 A6
Brendon View TA4 .... 151 B7
Brendon Way
Bridgwater TA6 .... 208 F6
Cheddar BS27 .... 90 C8
Brent Broad TA8 .... 85 B2
Brent Cl
Brent Knoll TA9 .... 86 B1
Weston-Super-Mare BS24 ... 49 B2
Brent Knoll CE Prim Sch
TA9 .... 86 A2
Brent Rd
Burnham-on-S TA8, TA9 ..... 85 B4
Cossington TA7 .... 136 F3
East Brent TA9 .... 86 C5
Brentsfield La TA7 .... 154 E7
Brent St TA9 .... 86 A2
Breowen Cl TA19 .... 221 B3
Brereton Rd TA24 .... 201 B6
Bretoneux Rd BA6 .... 206 E3
Brett Cl TA4 .... 202 F1
Brettingham Ct TA17 ..... 195 C7
Brewery Bglws TA18 ..... 224 C7
Brewery Hill BS30 .... 25 F7
Brewery La
Holcombe BA3 .... 97 D1
Ilminster TA19 .... 221 B4
Oakhill BA3 .... 115 A3
Shepton Mallet BA4 .... 205 D5
Brewham Rd BA10 .... 160 D6
Brewhouse The BS1 ...... 227 B2
Brewhouse Theatre & Arts
Ctr* TA1 .... 212 F4
Breynton Rd BA6 .... 206 F5
Brian Mooney Cl TA20 .... 223 B3
Briant Cl TA1 .... 212 B1
Briar Cl
Burnham-on-S TA8 .... 104 C6
Frome BA11 .... 120 B7
Nailsea BS48 .... 9 A2
Radstock BA3 .... 97 D8
Yeovil BA21 .... 219 E8
Briar Ct
Bridgwater TA6 .... 208 E5
Burnham-on-S TA8 .... 104 C6
Pill BS20 .... 4 C4
Briarfield BA22 .... 173 E2
Briar Mead BS49 .... 17 A1
Briar Rd
Hutton BS24 .... 49 E3
Street BA16 .... 207 A5
Briars Ct BA2 .... 44 A4
Briars The
Backwell BS48 .... 18 F7
Yeovil BA20 .... 218 C2
Briarwood BS9 .... 5 F6
Briary Rd BS20 .... 2 C5
Brick Cotts BA3 .... 117 A7
Brickkiln La DT9 .... 225 E7
Brick St BS2 .... 227 C3
Brickyard La
Bourton SP8 .... 161 F1
Wanstrow BA4 .... 142 F5
Brick Yard La TA18 .... 224 C7
Briddicott La TA24 .... 131 A4
Bridewell La
Bath BA1 .... 228 B2
Hutton BS24, BS26, BS29 ... 50 D1
Shapwick TA7 .... 137 F1
Bridewell St BS1 .... 227 A3
Bridge Bldgs BS39 .... 77 B3
Bridge Cl
Evercreech BA4 .... 141 E2
Whitchurch BS14 .... 23 C4
Williton TA4 .... 202 D2
Bridge Cotts
Chard Junction TA20 ..... 198 D8
Drimpton DT8 .... 199 F7
East Chinnock BA22 .... 196 F8
Bridge Farm Cl BS14 ...... 23 A3
Bridge Farm Inf Sch BS14 23 A4
Bridge Farm Jun Sch
BS14 .... 23 A4
Bridge Farm Sq BS49 ..... 34 D4
Bridge Gdns BA2 .... 60 A6
Bridge Hill BA4 .... 142 F4
Bridge Ho
11 Bath BA1 .... 28 C1
Bristol BS1 .... 227 A2
9 Clevedon BS21 .... 6 C2
Weston-Super-Mare BS23 ... 48 F6
Bridgehouse Cross EX15 180 D1
Bridge House Pk TA13 ... 220 F4
Bridge Pl DT9 .... 187 F4
Bridge Place Rd BA2 ...... 78 E8
Bridge Rd
Bath BA2 .... 44 C5
Bleadon BS24 .... 67 B6
Leigh Woods BS8 .... 11 E6
Weston-Super-Mare BS23 ... 48 F6
Bridge Rise 17 TA12 ...... 185 E6
Bridges Mead TA24 .... 201 E3
Bridge St
Bath BA2 .... 228 C2
Bourton SP8 .... 161 F1
Bristol BS1 .... 227 A2
Dulverton TA22 .... 163 D6
Frome BA11 .... 119 F5
Taunton TA1 .... 212 F4
Williton TA4 .... 202 D2
Bridge Terr EX16 .... 164 B1
Bridge The
Frome BA11 .... 119 F5
Taunton TA1 .... 212 F4
Bridge Valley Rd BS8 ...... 11 E8
Bridgwater Coll Cannington
Ctr TA5 .... 135 B2
Bridgwater Ent Ctr 7
TA6 .... 208 F5
Bridge Way TA13 .... 220 E4
Bridgeway Cotts TA13 .... 220 E4
Bridgewell Ct DT9 .... 225 E3
Bridgwater TA6 .... 208 F4
Bridgwater Bldgs BA7 ... 214 B5
Bridgwater Coll
Bridgwater TA6 .... 209 B5
Minehead TA24 .... 201 A7
Bridgwater Ct BS24 .... 49 A3
Bridgwater General Hospl
TA6 .... 209 A5
Bridgwater Rd
Dundry BS41, BS13, BS48 .. 21 D6
East Brent TA9 .... 86 D4
Lympsham BS24 .... 67 C5
North Petherton TA6 .... 153 F4
Taunton, Bathpool TA2 ..... 213 F7
Taunton TA1 .... 213 D5
Weston-Super-Mare BS23,
BS24 .... 48 F2
Winscombe BS25 .... 70 A5
Bridgwater Sta TA6 .... 209 B4
Bridle Way BA22 .... 197 F8
Bridport Rd DT8 .... 199 F8
Briercliffe Rd BS9 .... 5 D7
Briery Leaze Rd BS14 ..... 23 A4
Brigadier Cl BA22 .... 218 A5
Brigg Cl TA6 .... 208 E7
Brighton Mews BS8 .... 226 B4
Brighton Rd BS23 .... 48 E6
Brighton St 7 BS2 .... 227 B4
Brightstowe Rd TA8 .... 85 A2
Brigstocke Rd BS2 .... 227 B4
Brimble Cotts DT10 .... 189 F1
Brimbleworth La BS22 ..... 32 C3
Brimclose Rd TA17 .... 195 B7
Brimgrove La TA19 .... 184 E4
Brimhill Rise BA13 .... 121 D4
Brimley Cross TA3 .... 180 F1
Brimley Hill EX13 .... 198 D2
Brimley Rd EX13 .... 198 D3
Brimridge Rd BS25 .... 70 A8
Brimsmore Ct BA21 .... 218 E8
Brimstone La
Rockwell Green TA21 ..... 222 A2
Sampford Arundel TA21 ... 179 F6
Sampford Peverell EX16 ... 178 E2
Brincil Hill TA11 .... 173 D4
Brindham La BA6 .... 139 D3
Brindle Cl TA2 .... 212 C7
Brines Orch BA8 .... 176 E1
Brinmead Wlk BS13 .... 21 F3
Brinscombe La BS26 ...... 89 A5
Brinsea Batch BS49 .... 52 E8
Brinsea La BS49 .... 52 F8
Brinsea Rd BS49 .... 34 E2
Brinsmead Cres BS20 ...... 4 D4
Briscoes Ave BS13 .... 22 D4
Brislington Ent Coll BS4 .. 23 F8
Bristol Cathedral Sch
BS1 .... 226 C2
Bristol Dental Hospl
BS1 .... 227 A3
Bristol & Exeter Mews
BS1 .... 227 C1
Bristol Eye Hospl BS1 .... 227 A3
Bristol Gate 1 BS8 .... 11 F5
Bristol General Hospl
BS1 .... 227 A1
Bristol Gram Sch BS8 ... 226 C3
Bristol Harbour Rly*
BS1 .... 226 C1
Bristol Hill BA5 .... 112 E3
Bristol Homeopathic Hospl
BS8 .... 226 C4
Bristol Ind Mus* BS1 ... 227 A1
Bristol International Airport
BS48 .... 36 E7
Bristol Rd
Bridgwater TA6 .... 209 B7
Chew Stoke BS40 .... 56 E8
Chewton Mendip BA5 .... 113 A8
Churchill BS25 .... 53 A5
Congresbury BS49 .... 34 D5
Farrington Gurney BS39 .... 76 F5
Highbridge TA9 .... 104 F4
Horrington BA5 .... 112 F6
Keynsham BS31 .... 24 E6
Newton St Loe BA2 .... 43 D7
Paulton BS39 .... 77 E7
Pensford BS39 .... 40 D6
Portishead BS20 .... 2 E4
Radstock BA3 .... 78 F3
Redhill BS40 .... 37 A3
Rooks Bridge BS26, TA9 .... 87 B5
Sherborne DT9 .... 225 D5
Walpole TA6 .... 136 B3
Weston-Super-Mare BS22 ... 32 C2
Whitchurch BS14 .... 23 D3
Winscombe BS25 .... 70 C8
Wraxall BS48 .... 9 D4
Bristol Rd By-pass BS40 .. 53 C5
Bristol Rd Lower BS23 .... 30 F1
Bristol Road Lower BS23 .. 30 E1
Bristol Royal Infmy BS2 . 227 A4
Bristol Temple Meads Sta
BS1 .... 227 C1
Bristol View BA2 .... 62 C8
Bristol Zoo Gdns* BS8 ..... 5 F1
Britannia Cl BA3 .... 96 D4
Britannia Way
Chard TA20 .... 223 C6
Clevedon BS21 .... 6 C1
British Empire &
Commonwealth Mus The*
BS1 .... 227 C1
Briton St 2 EX16 .... 164 C1
Brittains BA11 .... 119 D6
Brittania Bldgs BS8 ..... 226 A1
Brittan Pl BS20 .... 3 E3
Britten's Cl BS39 .... 77 F6
Britten's Hill BS39 .... 77 F6
Brittons Ash TA2 .... 213 F8
Brittons Pass SN14 .... 13 F8
Broadacres BA22 .... 197 C8
Broadbridge Rd TA3 ..... 183 C6
Broadbury Rd BS4 .... 22 E8
Broad Cl
Kington Magna SP8 .... 177 E1
Wells BA5 .... 112 E1
Broadclose Way TA11 .... 158 A2
Broadcroft BS40 .... 38 F3
Broadcroft Ave BS49 ...... 17 F1
Broadcroft Cl BS49 .... 17 F1
Broad Dro
Burrowbridge TA7 .... 155 A2
North Wootton BA4 .... 140 A3
Broadenham La TA20 ..... 194 E1
Broadfield Rd BS4 .... 23 A8
Broadguage Bsns Pk
TA4 .... 167 E7
Broadhay BA5 .... 110 E7
Broad Hill BA22 .... 196 D7
Broadhurst Gdns TA8 .... 104 B5
Broad La
East Chinnock BA22 .... 196 E7
Hawkridge TA22 .... 146 D1
North Curry TA3 .... 170 D4
Winsford TA22 .... 147 F4
Broadlands BS21 .... 6 F3
Broadlands Ave
Keynsham BS31 .... 24 D6
North Petherton TA6 .... 153 F4
Broadlands Cl BA21 ...... 219 E8
Broadlands Ct TA1 .... 212 E2
Broadlands Dr BS11 .... 5 A8

Broadlands La TA5 208 A4
Broadlands Rd TA1 212 E2
Broadlands Rise TA1 212 E2
Broadlands Sch BS31 24 D6
Broadlands Way TA1 212 E2
Broad Lane Head
  Hawkridge TA22 146 D1
  Winsford TA22 147 F4
Broadlawn TA7 136 E4
Broadleas BS13 22 C7
Broadleaze
  Bristol BS11 4 E7
  Yeovil BA21 218 C6
Broadleaze Way BS25 51 F2
Broadly Gdns TA2 213 E8
Broadmead
  Bristol BS1 227 B3
  Keynsham BS31 25 B5
  Kingsbury Episcopi TA12 185 B7
  South Petherton TA13 220 B4
Broadmead Dro TA7 155 F6
Broadmead La
  Barrington TA19 184 D6
  Catcott TA7 137 D2
  Edington TA7 137 C3
  Keynsham BS31 25 A6
  Kington Magna SP8 177 D1
  Norton Sub Hamdon TA14 185 F2
Broad Mead La BS40 38 A3
Broadmead Rd TA3 183 B7
Broadmeads TA10 172 A6
Broadmoor Dro BS28 89 D3
Broadmoor La
  Bath BA1 27 A3
  Horsington BA8 176 E2
Broadmoor Pk BA1 27 B2
Broadmoor Vale BA1 27 A3
Broadoak TA19 183 C1
Broad Oak 9 BA20 219 B4
Broadoak Hill BS41 21 F2
Broad Oak Hill TA4 151 B5
Broadoak Mathematics & Computing Coll BS23 48 E3
Broadoak Rd
  Bridgwater TA6 209 D5
  Churchill BS40 53 A5
  Weston-Super-Mare BS23 48 D3
Broad Oak Rd BS13 21 F4
Broad Oaks BS8 11 E6
Broad Path EX15 179 A1
Broad Plain BS2 227 C2
Broad Quay
  Bath BA1 228 C1
  Bristol BS1 227 A2
Broad Rd
  Blagdon BS40 72 D8
  Rodney Stoke BA5 91 E1
Broadshard Rd TA18 224 C8
Broad St
  Bath BA1 228 C3
  Bristol BS1 227 A3
  Charlton Adam TA11 173 F7
  Chewton Mendip BA3 94 C5
  Churchinford TA3 191 D7
  Congresbury BS49 34 D4
  Somerton TA11 211 E4
  Stoney Stratton BA4 141 F2
  Wells BA5 203 D4
  Wrington BS40 35 D2
Broadstone TA7 154 E6
Broadstone La
  Hardington Mandeville BA22 197 A6
  Kingston Seymour BS21 15 F3
  West Chinnock TA18 196 C7
Broad Stones BA15 46 E7
Broadstone Wlk BS13 22 D5
Broad Street Pl BA1 228 C3
Broadway
  Bath BA2 45 B6
  Bridgwater TA6 208 F4
  Charlton Adam TA11 174 A7
  Chilcompton BA3 96 C3
  Chilton Polden TA7 137 B2
  Frome BA11 119 D5
  Locking BS24 50 D4
  Merriott TA16 195 F7
  Odcombe BA22 186 C2
  Saltford BS31 25 D3
  Shipham BS25 70 E8
  Weston-Super-Mare BS24 49 A2
Broad Way TA12 185 D5
Broadway Acres BS27 70 F1
Broadway Ave TA7 137 B2
Broadway Cl BA3 96 C3
Broadway Hill TA19 183 B1
Broadway La
  Castle Cary BA22 214 B3
  Midsomer Norton BA3 78 B5
  Westbury-sub-Mendip BA5 110 D7
Broadway Rd
  Bristol, Bishopsworth BS13 21 F5
  Charlton Adam TA11 173 F7
  Horton TA19 183 C2
Broadways Head EX14, TA20 192 C6
Broad Weir BS1 227 B3
Broadwell Cl TA20 193 D6
Broadwood Rd TA24 130 D4
Brock Ct BA7 214 C6
Brock End BS20 1 F3
Brockhole La
  Dinnington TA17 195 B8
Brockhole La continued
  Tatworth EX13, TA20 198 B7
Brockle Cl TA11 211 D4
Brockley Cl
  Nailsea BS48 8 D1
  Weston-Super-Mare BS24 48 F1
Brockley Combe Rd BS48 19 B1
Brockley Cres BS24 48 F1
Brockley La BS48 18 D4
Brockley Mini Farm (Open Farm)* BS48 35 F7
Brockley Rd BS31 25 D3
Brockley Way BS49 18 B3
Brockley Wlk BS13 22 A8
Brocks La BS41 10 F1
Brocks Mount 16 TA14 185 F4
Brocks Rd BS13 22 C3
Brock St BA1 228 B3
Brockway BS48 8 F2
Brockwell La TA24 129 F6
Brockwood BA15 64 F7
Brocole La TA20 193 D5
Broderip TA7 136 F3
Brokerswood Country Pk* BA13 102 F6
Bromes La TA3 183 F7
Bromley Rd BS39 39 F1
Brompton Ho BA2 228 C4
Brompton Mdws TA22 148 B2
Brompton Rd BS24 49 A2
Bronte Cl BS23 49 B4
Brook's Hill EX15 179 C1
Brook Bank
  Draycott BS27 90 F2
  Rodney Stoke BS27 109 C7
Brook Cl
  Long Ashton BS41 11 B1
  Minehead TA24 200 F7
  North Petherton TA6 153 E3
  Yeovil BA21 218 D7
Brook Cotts
  Corfe TA3 181 F6
  Corston BA2 43 B7
Brook Ct BS13 22 A6
Brookdale Rd BS13 22 B6
Brooke Rd
  Berrow TA8 84 F4
  Taunton TA1 213 B4
Brookes Ct BA5 203 C5
Brookfield Pk BA1 27 B2
Brookfields BA7 214 B5
Brookfield Way BA16 207 A4
Brookfield Wlk BS21 6 F3
Brook Gate BS3 11 E1
Brookhampton Cnr BA22 175 D6
Brook La
  Barton St David BA6 157 F3
  6 Cannington TA5 135 B2
  Catcott TA7 137 D2
  7 Henstridge BA8 190 A6
Brookland Rd
  Langport TA10 172 A6
  Weston-Super-Mare BS22 49 B7
Brooklands
  Bridgwater TA6 209 C5
  Dunkerton BA2 61 D3
Brooklands Rd TA21 222 B5
Brookland Way 3 BA8 190 A6
Brookleaze BS9 5 C5
Brookleaze Bldgs BA1 28 B2
Brookleigh BA16 207 A5
Brooklyn BS40 35 D2
Brooklyn Rd
  Bath BA1 28 C2
  Bristol BS13 22 B8
Brooklyn Terr BA5 139 E6
Brook Rd
  Bath BA2 44 D6
  Williton TA4 202 E3
Brookside
  Broadway TA19 183 C2
  Milborne Port DT9 217 D1
  Paulton BS39 77 E6
  Pill BS20 4 D3
  South Cheriton BA8 176 D3
  West Coker BA22 197 A8
Brookside Cl
  Batheaston BA1 28 F5
  Paulton BS39 77 E6
  Taunton TA3 168 D1
Brookside Com Prim Sch BA16 207 B4
Brookside Dr BA2 59 F6
Brookside Ho BA1 27 B1
Brookside Rd TA5 135 B5
Brooks Pl TA21 222 E6
Brooks Rd BA16 207 B4
Brook St
  Bampton EX16 164 B1
  Cannington TA5 135 B2
  Milborne Port DT9 217 D1
  Minehead TA24 201 B5
  North Newton TA7 153 F1
  Timberscombe TA24 130 B5
Brook Street Mews TA24 201 B5
Brookview Wlk BS13 22 B7
Broom's La TA3 191 F7
Broomball Cross TA22 162 F5
Broomball La EX16 162 E5
Broomclose Cnr BA3 114 B4
Broome Cl EX13 198 A1
Broom Farm Cl BS48 18 E8
Broomfield Ho TA2 212 E7
Broomground BA15 64 E7
Broomhill La BS39 58 E3
Broom Hill La BS39 77 E8
Broom La
  Chardstock EX13 198 C5
  Oake TA4 167 D3
Broomyland Hill TA5 152 C7
Brottens Rd
  Cranmore BA4 142 A5
  Doulting BA4 141 F5
Brougham Hayes BA2 44 D6
Brougham Pl 2 BA1 28 C2
Broughton Cl
  Taunton TA1 213 C2
  Walton BA16 156 E7
Broughton Ho BS1 227 B1
Broughton La TA3 169 B1
Broughton Pk TA3 169 A1
Broughtons Dr TA18 224 E3
Brow Hill BA2 28 F4
Brown's Folly Nature Reserve BA15 29 D1
Brown's Pl 4 BA5 203 C4
Brown Down La TA20 192 C7
Browne Ct 4 BS8 11 F6
Brownings Rd TA5 135 B2
Brown La TA4, TA23 149 C3
Brownlow Rd BS23 48 E4
Browns Ct BS23 48 E6
Browns La BS28 109 C1
Brow The
  Bath BA2 44 B5
  Bath, Combe Down BA2 45 C1
Broxholme Wlk BS11 4 F8
Brue Ave
  Bridgwater TA6 209 B3
  Bruton BA10 215 F7
Brue Bsns Pk TA9 136 E8
Brue Cl
  Bruton BA10 215 F7
  Weston-Super-Mare BS23 49 A5
Brue Cres TA8 104 B5
Brue Ho TA8 85 A1
Bruelands BA10 215 F7
Brue Way TA9 104 F3
Bruford Cl TA1 212 E3
Brummel Way BS39 77 C6
Brunel's Way TA9 104 E5
Brunel Cl
  Somerton TA11 211 D4
  Weston-Super-Mare BS24 48 F1
Brunel Ct
  Bridgwater TA6 208 F6
  Portishead BS20 2 D6
Brunel Ho BA2 44 A6
Brunel Lock Rd BS1 11 F5
Brunel Prec TA11 211 D4
Brunel Rd
  Bristol BS13 22 A8
  Nailsea BS48 8 B1
Brunel Way
  Bristol BS1, BS3 11 F4
  Frome BA11 120 C7
  Minehead TA24 201 B6
Brunsell's Knap DT10 190 A1
Brunswick Pl
  1 Bath BA1 228 B3
  10 Bristol BS1 11 F5
Brunswick Sq BS2 227 B4
Brunswick St
  1 Bath BA1 28 B1
  Bristol BS2 227 B4
  Yeovil BA20 219 A4
Brushford New Rd TA22 163 E4
Brutasche Terr BA16 207 D7
Bruton BS24 49 A2
Bruton Ave
  Bath BA2 44 F4
  Portishead BS20 2 A5
Bruton Avenue Garages BA2 44 F4
Bruton Cl BS48 18 E8
Bruton La BA4 142 F2
Bruton Mus* BA10 215 E6
Bruton Pl BS8 226 B3
Bruton Prim Sch BA10 215 E6
Bruton Rd BA4 141 F1
Bruton Sch for Girls BA10 215 C3
Bruton Sta BA10 215 F6
Brutton Way TA20 223 B3
Bryant's Hill TA22 148 C2
Bryant Ave BA3 78 D1
Bryant Gdns BS21 6 C1
Bryer Cl
  Bridgwater TA6 208 E1
  Chard TA20 223 D3
Brymore Cl TA6 208 D5
Brymore Sch TA5 135 A2
Brympton Ave BA22 186 D2
Brympton Way BA20 218 C3
Bsns Courtyard The BA11 143 C7
Bubwith Cl TA20 223 D3
Bubwith Ho 4 BA5 203 D4
Bubwith Rd TA20 223 D3
Bubwith Wlk BA5 203 B3
Buces Rd TA1 212 B1
Buck Cl BA6 206 C3
Buckhill TA24 131 B4
Buckhill Cl TA18 224 C4
Buckingham Cl TA6 209 A2
Buckingham Pl BS8 226 A3
Buckingham Rd BS24 49 B2
Buckingham Vale BS8 226 A4
Buckland Cl TA8 104 C8
Buckland Gn BS22 32 A5
Buckland La BA22 175 C3
Buckland Rd
  Shepton Mallet BA4 205 A5
  Taunton TA2 213 B8
Buckland Rd continued
  Yeovil BA21 219 E6
Buckland St Mary CE Prim Sch TA20 193 A8
Bucklands Batch BS48 18 F8
Buckland Sch TA23 202 C6
Bucklands Dr BS48 19 A8
Bucklands End BS48 18 F8
Bucklands Gr BS48 18 F8
Bucklands La BS48 18 F8
Bucklands View BS48 19 A8
Buckle Pl BA22 218 B6
Bucklers Mead Rd BA21 219 D8
Bucklers Mead Sch BA21 219 C8
Bucklers Mead Wlk BA21 219 D8
Bucklers Way BA4 204 F6
Bucklewell Cl BS11 4 F6
Buckshots Cross EX14 192 D4
Buckwell TA21 222 E6
Bude Cl BS48 9 B1
Budge La BA11 144 A8
Budgett's Cross TA21 180 F6
Budgetts TA21 180 F6
Bughole La TA21 179 E8
Bugle Ct 11 BA8 190 A6
Building of Bath Mus* BA1 228 C3
Bulford TA21 222 D5
Bulford La TA21 222 D5
Bull's Hill BA2 62 E1
Bull's La
  Tatworth TA20 198 C8
  Upton Noble BA4 142 F2
Bull's Quarr BA11 143 E8
Bull's Quarries Rd BA11 143 F7
Bull Bridge Mead BA22 197 D3
Bullen Mead BA11 117 F2
Bullens Cl TA19 183 F4
Buller Ave BA22 218 A6
Bull Horn Dro TA7 154 D5
Bull La BS20 4 C4
Bull Mdw TA4 167 F7
Bullmead Cl BA16 207 B5
Bullmead La BA11 143 C7
Bullock Field Hill TA21 166 B2
Bullocks La BS21 16 C4
Bullon Dro TA5 134 B7
Bull Plot Hill BA6 158 C8
Bulls La TA18 224 B6
Bull St TA3 169 D4
Bulwarks La BA6 206 F4
Bumper's Batch BA2 63 A8
Bunce's La TA19 184 E3
Buncombe Hill TA5 152 C3
Bune Villas TA6 208 E7
Bunford Hollow Rdbt BA20 218 D1
Bunford La BA20, BA21 218 C4
Bungalows The
  Axbridge BS26 70 C2
  Chard TA20 223 D5
  Monkton Heathfield TA2 213 F8
  Nether Stowey TA5 134 A2
  Poyntington DT9 188 E7
Bungay's Hill BA2, BS39 59 E1
Bunker Military Mus The* TA9 104 D3
Bunns La
  Horningsham BA11 144 A5
  Witham Friary BA11 143 F5
Bunting Ct BS22 31 E1
Burch's Cl TA1 212 C2
Burchill's Hill TA21 222 B7
Burchill Cl BS39 58 F3
Burchills Cl TA21 222 A6
Burcott La
  Coxley BA5 139 E7
  Wells BA5 203 A3
Burcott Rd BA5 203 B3
Burdenham Dro TA7 155 A6
Burfoote Gdns BS14 23 E4
Burfoot Rd BS14 23 E4
Burford Cl
  Bath BA2 44 B3
  Portishead BS20 2 E4
Burford Cross BA4 204 C2
Burford Gr BS11 4 F5
Burgage TA21 222 D6
Burgage La TA4 167 A4
Burgage Rd TA5 134 C6
Burge's Hill BA3 116 B1
Burge's La BA3 116 B1
Burge Cres TA4 167 E6
Burge Mdw TA4 167 E6
Burges Cl
  Marnhull DT10 190 F6
  Wiveliscombe TA4 210 C5
Burges La TA4 210 C5
Burgess Cl TA1 212 B1
Burgess La BA6 157 F6
Burgis Rd BS14 23 D6
Burgundy Rd TA24 201 A8
Burleigh Gdns BA1 44 A8
Burleigh La BA16 207 C4
Burlescombe CE Prim Sch EX16 179 B3
Burley Gdns BA16 207 D4
Burlingham's La BA22 186 C8
Burlington Ct BS20 2 E6
Burlington Rd
  Midsomer Norton BA3 78 C2
  Portishead BS20 2 E7
Burlington St
  Bath BA1 228 B4
  15 Weston-Super-Mare BS23 48 E8
Burnbush Cl BS14 23 E6
Burnbush Prim Sch BS14 23 D5
Burnell Dr BS2 227 C4
Burnell Ho 8 BA4 205 B6
Burnett's La BA6 158 A6
Burnett Bsns Pk BS31 25 B1
Burnett Cl TA8 104 C7
Burnett Hill BS31 42 B8
Burnett Ind Est BS40 35 E1
Burnham Cl BS24 48 F1
Burnham Dr BS24 48 F1
Burnham Moor La TA9 105 B5
Burnham-on-Sea Inf Sch TA8 104 C8
Burnham Rd
  Bath BA2 44 C6
  Bristol BS11 4 D6
  Highbridge TA9 104 D4
Burn Hill TA4, TA21 166 F3
Burnshill Dr TA2 212 A7
Burns Rd TA1 213 C4
Burnt House Cotts BA2 62 C8
Burnthouse Dro BA5 141 B8
Burnt House La BA3 116 C2
Burnt House Rd BA2 62 D8
Burrell La BA7 158 F1
Burrells BA22 197 B8
Burridge Cl BA5 139 E6
Burridge Cross TA20 193 E1
Burrington Ave BS24 48 F1
Burrington CE Prim Sch BS40 53 F3
Burrington Cl
  Nailsea BS48 8 E1
  Weston-Super-Mare BS24 48 F1
Burrington Combe BS40 72 C8
Burrington Coombe* BS40 54 A1
Burrington La BS40 54 A3
Burrington Wlk BS13 22 A8
Burroughes Ave BA21 218 E6
Burrough St TA12 185 F7
Burrough Way TA21 222 D4
Burrowbridge CE Sch TA7 154 F1
Burrow Dro
  Burrowbridge TA7 154 F1
  Hambridge TA12 184 F8
Burrowfield BA10 215 F7
Burrowfield Cl BA10 215 F7
Burrow Hill Dro TA7 155 A1
Burrow La
  Ashbrittle TA21 178 D8
  High Ham TA10 156 A1
Burrow Rocks TA4 202 B1
Burrows La BA3 97 B1
Burrows The BS22 32 D3
Burrow Wall TA7 155 A1
Burrow Way
  Hambridge TA12 184 F7
  Kingsbury Episcopi TA12 185 A7
Burstock La DT8 199 F7
Burston La EX16 164 A4
Burt's Hill BA4 142 F3
Burtle Rd
  Burtle TA7 137 D6
  East Huntspill TA9 136 E7
  Westhay BA6 138 A5
Burton Barton BA22 197 C8
Burton Cl BS1 227 B1
Burton Ct BS8 226 B3
Burtonhayes DT10 190 F6
Burton La BA22 197 C8
Burton Pl TA1 212 E3
Burton Row TA9 86 A5
Burton St
  5 Bath BA1 228 B2
  Marnhull DT10 190 F6
Burwalls Rd BS8 11 E6
Bury The BS24 50 A3
Bury View BA2 42 C5
Buscott La TA7 138 B1
Bushfield Rd TA18 224 B4
Bushfurlong Rd TA3 184 B8
Bush La TA5 152 E6
Bush Pl TA10 172 A5
Bush Rd TA5 152 D7
Bushs Orch TA19 221 A4
Bushy Combe BA3 77 F3
Bushy Coombe Gdns BA6 206 F5
Bushy Cross La TA3 169 C3
Bushy Thorn Rd BS40 56 E8
Business Pk The BS13 22 E3
Bussell's Moor Cross EX36 162 C4
Bussex Sq TA7 154 F6
Butcher's Hill TA3 170 F2
Butcher's La TA5 134 A2
Butchers La
  Castle Cary BA7 159 C3
  Shapwick TA7 155 F8
Butcombe BS24 49 A2
Butcombe La BS40 55 B7
Butcombe Wlk BS14 23 B5
Butham La
  Chew Magna BS40 39 A4
  Chew Magna BS40 39 B3
Butlass Cl BS39 59 D1
Butleigh CE Prim Sch BA6 157 E4
Butleigh Cl TA6 209 D4
Butleigh Cross BA6 157 E3
Butleigh Dro
  Ashcott TA7, BA16 156 C5
  Walton BA16 156 D6
Butleigh Old Rd BA6 206 E3

Butleigh Rd
Glastonbury BA6 206 E3
Street BA16 207 E5
Butler's Gdns BA11 120 A4
Butt's Batch BS40 35 D1
Butt Cl BA6 206 E5
Buttercliffe Rise BS41 11 C3
Buttercup La BA16 207 D6
Butterfield Pk BS21 6 C1
Buttermere Rd BS23 49 A5
Butterworth Ct BS4 22 D7
Buttice La BA5 111 B1
Butt La TA10 171 D4
Butt Lake Rd TA9 106 B3
Buttle's Cross TA3 191 F7
Buttle's La TA3 191 E6
Buttle Cl TA19 184 E4
Buttle La TA19 184 E3
Button Cl BS14 23 A6
Button St BA11 119 D5
Butts TA19 221 C4
Butts Batch BS26 69 B3
Butts Castle TA19 221 C4
Butts Cl
Marnhull DT10 190 F5
Williton TA4 202 D4
Butts Cnr TA6 153 F4
Butts Hill BA11 119 E3
Butts La
Ilton TA19 183 D3
Kilmington BA12 161 F7
Langford Budville TA21 166 F2
Rodney Stoke BS27 91 A1
Butts Orch BS40 35 D1
Butts Quarry La TA18 224 E6
Butts The BA11 119 E3
Butts Way TA4 166 F4
Buxtons Cl 5 BA5 139 D8
Byfield BA2 45 B1
Byfield Pl BA2 45 B1
Byfields BS21 16 C8
Byron Cl BS24 50 A4
Byron Ct BS23 48 F8
Byron Pl BS8 226 B3
Byron Rd
Bath BA2 44 F4
Locking BS24 50 A4
Taunton TA1 213 C3
Weston-Super-Mare BS23 49 A4
Byways Cvn Pk BS21 6 C1
Byzantine Ct BS1 227 A1

C

Cabbage La BA8 176 C3
Cabell Ct BA11 119 D2
Cabell Rd BA11 119 E2
Cabot Cl BS31 25 D2
Cabot Prim Sch BS2 227 C4
Cabot Rise BS20 2 A5
Cabot Twr* BS8 226 B2
Cabot Way
Bristol BS8 11 F5
Pill BS20 4 D3
Weston-Super-Mare BS22 32 A3
Cabstand BS20 2 D6
Cadbury Bsns Pk BA22 175 B6
Cadbury Camp La BS20 8 D6
Cadbury Camp La W BS21 7 C5
Cadbury Castle* BA22 175 C4
Cadbury Cl TA8 85 C1
Cadbury Farm Rd BS49 34 C7
Cadbury Halt BS20 1 F1
Cadbury Ho BS20 2 E4
Cadbury La BS20 1 F1
Cadbury Rd
Keynsham BS31 25 A2
Portishead BS20 2 E4
Cadbury Sq BS49 34 E3
Cadby Ho BA2 44 A6
Cadeside Cvn Site TA21 222 F7
Cadogan Rd BS14 23 A8
Cad Rd
Ilminster TA19 221 A8
Ilton TA19 183 E3
Cadwell's La TA9 136 A8
Caernarvon Rd BS31 24 C4
Caernarvon Way TA8 85 B1
Caern Well Pl BA1 228 C4
Cairn Cl BS48 9 A1
Cairo Ct 18 BS23 30 C1
Caitlin Ct BS14 23 D6
Cala Trad Est BS3 11 F3
Calder Cl BS31 25 A4
Calder Cres TA1 213 D4
Cale Cl DT10 190 C4
Caledonia Mews BS8 11 F6
Caledonian Rd
Bath BA2 44 D6
Bristol BS1 226 B1
Caledonia Pl BS8 11 F7
Cale Way BA9 216 B4
Caller's La EX15 180 D1
Callins Ct TA24 201 A5
Callins View TA24 201 A5
Callow Hill BA5 139 C7
Callowhill Ct BS1 227 B3
Calluna Cl BS22 32 A5
Calton Gdns BA2 228 C1
Calton Rd BA2 228 C1
Calton Wlk BA2 228 B1
Calvados Rd TA1 213 C3
Calway Rd TA1 213 B2
Camberley Rd BS4 22 D8
Camberley Wlk BS22 49 E8
Camborne Gr BA21 219 E5
Camborne Pl BA21 219 E5
Camborne St BA21 219 E5
Cambridge Cl BA20 218 D5
Cambridge Ct BS40 35 D2
Cambridge Gr BS21 6 D5
Cambridge Pl
Bath BA2 45 B5
Weston-Super-Mare BS23 48 D8
Cambridge Rd BS21 6 D5
Cambridge St TA20 223 C4
Cambridge Terr
Bath BA2 45 B5
11 Taunton TA2 213 A8
Cam Brook Cl BA2 78 D8
Cambrook Ho BS39 76 F8
Camden Cres BA1 228 B4
Camden Ct
Bath BA1 228 B4
Bridgwater TA6 208 E5
Camden Orch TA11 211 C4
Camden Pl TA6 208 E5
Camden Rd
Bath BA1 28 A1
Bridgwater TA6 208 E5
Bristol BS3 226 B1
Somerton TA11 211 C4
Camden Row BA1 228 B4
Camden Terr
Bath BA1 228 C4
Bristol BS8 226 A2
Weston-Super-Mare BS23 48 E7
Camel Cross BA22 174 C3
Cameley CE Prim Sch
BS39 58 E1
Cameley Cl BS39 76 E8
Cameley Gn BA2 43 F6
Cameley La BS39 75 F7
Cameley Rd BS39 76 C8
Camelot Ct TA11 211 B5
Camelot Sh Ctr BA9 216 C4
Camel St BA22 174 F2
Cameroons Cl BS31 24 E4
Camerton CE Prim Sch
BA2 78 E8
Camerton Cl BS31 25 E3
Camerton Hill BA2 78 E8
Camerton Rd BA2 60 E1
Camomile Wlk BS20 2 F5
Campian Wlk BS4 22 D6
Campion Cl 4 BS22 49 D7
Campion Dr
Taunton TA1 213 C1
Yeovil BA22 218 B5
Campion Gdns TA20 223 D5
Campkin Rd BA5 203 B4
Camplins BS21 6 C1
Camp Rd
Bristol BS8 11 F7
Weston-Super-Mare BS23 30 C1
Yeovil BA22 186 D1
Camp Rd N BS23 30 B1
Camp View BS48 8 D2
Camvale BA2 79 B8
Camview BS39 77 D6
Canada Coombe BS24 50 A1
Canada Way BS1 226 B1
Canal Cl TA21 222 B8
Canal Dro BS27, BS28 90 A3
Canal Rd TA1 212 F5
Canal Terr
Bathampton BA2 28 F1
Taunton TA1 212 F5
Canal View TA6 209 A4
Canal Way TA19 221 A3
Canberra Cres BS24 50 B6
Canberra Rd BS23 48 F3
Canford La BS9 5 E8
Canford Rd BS9 5 F8
Cannard's Grave Rd BA4 205 C4
Cannards Grave Rdbt
BA4 205 D3
Cannington CE Prim Sch
TA5 135 C2
Cannington College Gdns*
TA5 135 B2
Cannington Countryside Vst
Ctr* TA5 135 B2
Cannon Cl TA6 209 B5
Cannon Court Mews
DT9 217 D1
Cannons Gate BS21 16 C8
Cannon St BS1 227 A4
Cannus La
9 North Petherton TA6 153 F4
Puriton TA7 136 C4
Cann St TA1 212 E3
Cannwood La BA10 161 B8
Canon's Rd BS1 226 C1
Canons Cl BA2 44 B2
Canons Gate BA22 173 E1
Canons Rd BS1 226 C2
Canon St TA1 213 A4
Canons Way BS1 226 C1
Canons Wlk BS22 31 D2
Cantell Gr BS14 23 F5
Canterbury Cl BS22 32 B3
Canterbury Dr TA3 170 C4
Canterbury Rd BA2 44 D5
Cantock's Cl BS8 226 C3
Canvin Ct TA11 211 B5
Canworth Way TA6 209 C3
Canynge Ho 2 BS1 227 B1
Canynge Rd BS8 11 F8
Canynge Sq BS8 11 F8
Canynge St BS1 227 B2
Capell Cl BS22 49 B8
Capenor Cl BS20 2 C4
Capes Cl TA6 209 A5
Capital Edge BS8 226 B1
Capland Ct TA3 183 A5
Capland La TA3 183 A5
Caple La BS40 56 B5
Cappards Rd BS39 57 D4
Capricorn Pl BS8 226 B2
Capri Villas BS23 30 C2
Capton TA4 132 C2
Capton Cross TA4 132 C2
Caradon Pl TA6 208 F7
Caramia Pk TA9 136 A8
Carantoc Pl 3 TA24 131 A5
Caraway Cl TA20 223 F5
Caray Gr TA3 169 D4
Carberry View BS24 50 A8
Card Cl BS27 90 F3
Cardigan Cres BS22 49 C8
Cardill Cl BS13 22 A8
Cardinal Cl BA2 62 D8
Carditch Dro BS49 52 B8
Carey's Cl BS21 6 F4
Carey's Hollow TA13 220 B4
Carey Cl BA4 141 E6
Carey Developments 1
BS21 6 C1
Careys Mead BA3 116 F7
Careys Way BS24 49 E7
Carhampton Cross TA24 131 B5
Carice Gdns BS21 16 D8
Carisbrooke Gdns BA20 218 F5
Carisbrooke Rd BS4 22 D7
Carlan Stepps TA19 183 C2
Carlingford Terr BA3 79 A2
Carlingford Terrace Rd
BA3 79 A2
Carlow Rd BS4 22 E8
Carlton Cl BS39 58 F3
Carlton Ct
Minehead TA24 200 F7
Wells BA5 203 E4
Carlton Dr TA6 208 F7
Carlton Mans BS23 48 D7
Carlton Mews BA5 203 E4
Carlton St BS23 48 D7
Carmine Cl BA6 206 C4
Carnival Cl TA19 221 A4
Carolina Ho BS2 227 A4
Caroline Bldgs BA2 45 B5
Caroline Cl BS31 24 C4
Caroline Pl BA1 228 B4
Carpenter Cl BS23 49 A7
Carpenters Cl TA3 169 C3
Carpenters Ho TA19 221 B3
Carpenters La BS31 24 E5
Carpenters Terr TA12 185 E7
Carraway La DT10 190 F5
Carre Gdns BS22 31 F4
Carr Ho BA2 44 A6
Carrick Ho 7 BS8 11 F6
Carriels Ho 12 BA4 205 B6
Carrier's La TA21 166 C2
Carrington Way BA9 216 C4
Carrs Cl BA2 44 A6
Carstons Cl BS48 18 F6
Carter Rd BS39 77 D5
Carters La BA22 196 E8
Carters Way
Chilcompton BA3 96 D3
Somerton TA11 211 C4
Cart Gate TA14 185 F5
Cartwright Cl BA5 139 E6
Carvers Rd TA6 209 A5
Cary Ct TA11 211 B5
Caryedge La BA7 160 A2
Cary Hill
Castle Cary BA7 214 D5
Kingsdon TA11 173 E5
Cary Moor Dro BA7 159 C1
Cary Rd BA22 175 D6
Cary Way
Kingsdon TA11 173 D5
Somerton TA11 211 C5
Cashford Gate TA2 213 C7
Casion Ct BS1 227 B1
Casley La BA11 102 D6
Cassino Rd TA23 202 E6
Cassis Cl TA8 104 C5
Castlake La TA4 150 F7
Castle Batch Prim Sch
BS22 32 A5
Castle Bow TA1 212 F4
Castle Cary Com Prim Sch
BA7 214 C4
Castle Cary Mus* BA7 214 C5
Castle Cary Sta BA7 214 B8
Castle Cl BS48 19 F7
Castle Cnr BA11 101 D3
Castle Cotts TA21 180 D8
Castle Cross EX13 198 D4
Castle Ct
Othery TA7 155 C2
Shepton Mallet BA4 205 A4
Castle Farm La BS41 21 B2
Castle Field Ind Est TA6 209 A6
Castlefield La TA4 168 B1
Castle Gdns BA2 44 E3
Castle Gn TA1 212 F4
Castle Hill
Banwell BS29 51 C2
Dunster TA24 201 E2
Nether Stowey TA5 134 A2
Nunney BA11 143 B8
Castle La
Cranmore BA4 142 A6
South Cadbury BA22 175 D4
Wedmore BS28 108 A1
West Pennard BA6 140 C1
Wiveliscombe TA4 210 F6
Yarley BA5 139 D7
Castlemans Rd TA1 212 B1
Castle Mead TA23 131 E4
Castle Moat TA6 208 F5
Castle Neroche Forest Trail*
TA20 182 D2
Castle Prim Sch BS31 24 D4
Castle Rd
Clevedon BS21 6 E6
Sherborne DT9 225 F5
Wellington TA21 180 D8
Weston-Super-Mare BS22 31 E3
Castle Rise BA7 214 C5
Castle Sch The TA1 212 D4
Castle St
Bampton EX16 164 B1
Bridgwater TA6 208 F5
Bristol BS1 227 B3
Frome BA11 119 E5
Keinton Mandeville TA11 158 B1
Nether Stowey TA5 134 B2
Nunney BA11 143 B8
Stogursey TA5 134 C5
Stoke sub Hamdon TA14 185 F4
Taunton TA1 212 E4
Castleton
Haselbury Plucknett
TA18 196 C5
1 Sherborne DT9 225 E4
Castleton Rd DT9 225 F4
Castle Town Way DT9 225 E6
Castle View 2 BS24 49 F8
Castle View Rd BS21 6 D5
Castle Way TA1 212 F4
Castlewood Cl BS21 6 D4
Castle Wood La EX13,
TA20 193 C1
Caswell Hill BS20 3 B1
Caswell La BS20 3 B2
Cat's Ash
Fitzhead TA4 166 F7
Shepton Mallet BA4 205 B6
Catash Cl BA22 175 D6
Catch Gate La TA20 223 A5
Catch Rd BA11 143 B7
Catcott Broad Dro TA7 137 D5
Catcott Prim Sch TA7 137 D2
Catcott Right Dro TA7 155 D6
Catemead BS21 16 C8
Cater Rd BS13 22 B6
Cathanger La
Fivehead TA3 170 D1
Stogursey TA5 134 D5
Catharine Pl BA1 228 B3
Cathay La BS27 90 B7
Cathcart Ho 7 BA1 28 A1
Cathead Cross TA14 185 E1
Cathedral Church of The
Holy & Undivided Trinity*
BS1 226 C2
Cathedral Gn BA5 203 E4
Catherine Hill BA11 119 F5
Catherines Cl BA7 214 C6
Catherine St
Avonmouth BS11 4 C8
East Huntspill TA9 136 D8
Frome BA11 119 E5
Catherine Way BA1 29 A5
Catherson Cl BA11 119 D3
Cathill La DT9 176 A2
Cathole Bridge Rd TA18 224 A4
Cat La
Stalbridge DT10 190 A1
Stourton Caundle DT10 189 F1
Catley Gr BS41 11 B2
Catmoor Cross EX13 198 A5
Catnip Cl 2 EX13 198 A1
Cats' Castle Hill TA4 150 E5
Catsgore Rd TA11 173 C5
Cats La
Minehead TA24 201 A6
Taunton TA2 168 F6
Cat St TA14 185 E1
Catt's La TA21 180 E6
Cattle Hill
Bratton Seymour BA9 176 A8
Welham BA7 160 A1
Cattle Market Rd BS1 227 C1
Catwell TA4 202 E2
Caulfield Rd BS22 32 B4
Caundle La
Stalbridge Weston DT10 190 A3
Stourton Caundle DT10 189 F1
Causeway
Nailsea BS48 8 B3
Woolavington TA7, TA9 136 E6
Causeway Cl TA7 136 E4
Causeway Council Hos
TA9 106 B4
Causeway La DT8 199 D6
Causeway Terr TA23 202 C6
Causeway The
Congresbury BS49 34 D4
Nailsea BS20 8 F8
Street BA16 207 D8
Yatton BS49 34 C7
Causeway View BS48 8 C2
Cautletts Cl BA3 96 F8
Cavalier Cl BA21 219 D8
Cavalier Way
Wincanton BA9 216 C3
Yeovil BA21 219 E8
Cavalier Wlk BA21 219 D8
Cave Ct BS2 227 B4
Cavell Ct BS21 6 C1
Cavendish Cl BS31 25 D2
Cavendish Cres BA1 228 A4
Cavendish Ct BA22 173 E2
Cavendish Dr BA14 83 F6
Cavendish Gdns BS9 5 C4
Cavendish Lodge BA1 228 A4
Cavendish Pl BA1 228 A4
Cavendish Rd BA1 228 A4
Caveners Ct BS22 31 B1
Caversham Dr BS48 9 A2
Cave St BS2 227 B4
Cawley Ave EX13 198 A2
Caxton Ct 4 BA2 228 C3
Caxton Rd BA11 120 A3
Cecil Rd
Bristol, Clifton BS8 11 F8
Weston-Super-Mare BS23 30 E1
Cecil St BA20 219 B5
Cecil Terr TA6 209 B4
Cedar Ave
Butleigh BA6 157 D5
Weston-Super-Mare BS22 31 C1
Cedar Cl
Brent Knoll TA9 86 B2
Bridgwater TA6 209 C3
Chard TA20 223 B5
Long Ashton BS41 10 F1
Taunton TA1 213 D2
Cedar Ct
Bristol, Combe Dingle BS9 5 D7
Bristol, Sneyd Park BS9 5 C4
Bristol, Westbury on T BS9 5 F8
Martock TA12 185 E7
Wellington TA21 222 E5
Cedar Dr BS31 24 D4
Cedar Falls TA4 151 E1
Cedar Fields
Sparkford BA22 175 A5
West Coker BA22 197 A8
Cedar Gr
Bath BA2 44 D3
Bristol BS9 5 D5
Somerton TA11 211 D4
Yeovil BA21 218 E6
Cedarhurst Rd BS20 1 E4
Cedarn Ct BS22 31 B4
Cedar Pk BS9 5 D5
Cedar Row BS11 4 F6
Cedars The
Chew Stoke BS40 56 D8
Evercreech BA4 141 E1
Minehead TA24 200 F7
Cedar Terr BA3 78 D1
Cedar Villas BA2 228 A1
Cedar Way
Bath BA2 228 A1
Nailsea BS48 9 A2
Portishead BS20 2 C4
Cedar Wlk BA6 157 E5
Cedern Ave BS24 50 C3
Cedric Cl BA1 44 C7
Cedric Rd BA1 44 C8
Cefn Ct TA24 201 B4
Celandine Mead TA1 169 A1
Celandine Rd BA22 218 A5
Celtic Way BS24 67 B7
Cemetery La
Street BA16 207 A7
Wincanton BA9 216 B3
Centenary Cotts DT9 176 A1
Centenary Gdns BA8 190 A6
Centenary Way BS27 90 A7
Central Acre BA20 219 B4
Central Ave BA22 173 E2
Central Pk BS14 23 B7
Central Rd BA20 219 B5
Central Way BS21 6 E1
Centre Dr BS29 50 E4
Centre Quay BS20 2 E7
Centre Rd TA7 137 C2
Centre The
Keynsham BS31 24 F5
10 Weston-Super-Mare
BS23 48 E7
Centurion Bsns Ctr BA4 205 D4
Century Pk BA20 218 E5
Cerdic Cl TA20 223 E4
Cerdic Terr TA20 223 D4
Cerney Gdns BS48 9 A2
Cerney La BS11 4 E5
Chackrell La EX16 178 F2
Chad's Hill TA5 135 B2
Chadleigh Gr BS4 22 D7
Chaffcombe La TA20 194 B5
Chaffcombe Rd TA20 223 E6
Chaffeymoor Hill SP8 161 E1
Chaffinch Ave BA11 120 B6
Chaffinch Cl TA1 212 B4
Chaffinch Dr BA3 97 B8
Chaffins The BS21 6 E2
Chain Gate Ct BA6 206 D4
Chains Rd EX16 178 D1
Chalcombe Rocks La
TA4 164 E5
Chalcot La BA13 121 F5
Chalcroft Wlk BS13 21 E4
Chalfield Cl BS31 25 A2
Chalfont Rd BS22 49 C8
Chalice Ct BA6 206 E4
Chalice Hill Cl BA6 206 E4
Chalice Mews 1 TA6 208 F5
Chalice Way BA6 206 F3
Chalice Well* BA6 206 F4
Chalk Farm Cl BS39 40 A7
Chalks The BS40 39 B3
Challenger Way BA22 218 B6
Challick La TA4 166 A6
Challoner Ct BS1 227 A1
Challow Dr BS22 31 B2

Chamberlain Ho TA1 .... 212 D5
Chamberlain St BA5 .... 203 D4
Chamberlain Ave TA6 .... 209 C6
Champford La TA21 .... 222 D5
Champford Mews 2 TA21 .... 222 D5
Champion Cross TA4 .... 165 E3
Champney Rd BA11 .... 120 A7
Chancel Cl
Bristol BS9 .... 5 D3
Nailsea BS48 .... 8 D1
Chancellor's Pound BS40 .36 D3
Chancellor Cl BA16 .... 156 D7
Chancellor Rd BA16 .... 156 D7
Chandag Inf Sch BS31 .... 25 A4
Chandag Jun Sch BS31 ... 25 A4
Chandag Rd BS31 .... 25 A4
Chandler Cl BA1 .... 27 B1
Chandlers DT9 .... 225 E5
Chandlers La TA7 .... 137 C3
Chandos Ct BS23 .... 48 D6
Chandos Rd BS31 .... 24 E7
Chandos St TA6 .... 208 F5
Change La TA4 .... 164 D6
Channel Cl TA5 .... 134 A2
Channel Ct
Burnham-on-S TA8 .... 104 B5
Weston-Super-Mare BS22 ... 31 B3
Channel Dash Pl BA22 ... 173 E2
Channel Hts BS24 .... 48 F1
Channells La TA19 .... 183 C1
Channel Rd BS21 .... 6 E5
Channel View Cres BS20 ... 2 B5
Channel View Rd BS20 .... 2 B5
Channing Cl TA8 .... 104 B5
Chantry Cl
Nailsea BS48 .... 8 C1
Taunton TA2 .... 213 B7
Chantry Ct
Bristol BS1 .... 226 C2
Somerton TA11 .... 211 C3
Chantry Dr BS22 .... 32 A4
Chantry Dro TA7 .... 155 B1
Chantry Gdns BA14 .... 83 F3
Chantry Ho 2 BA4 .... 205 B6
Chantry La BA22 .... 174 D3
Chantry Mead Rd BA2 .... 44 E3
Chantry The BS26 .... 87 B5
Chantry View BA22 .... 197 D8
Chapel Barton
High Littleton BS39 .... 59 D1
Nailsea BS48 .... 8 C2
Chapel Cl
Castle Cary BA7 .... 214 C5
Chew Stoke BS40 .... 56 E8
Chilton Polden TA7 .... 137 B2
Farrington Gurney BS39 .... 76 F4
Keinton Mandeville TA11 .. 158 A1
Nailsea BS48 .... 8 E2
North Curry TA3 .... 170 B4
Winford BS40 .... 38 A6
Chapel Cross
North Cadbury BA22 .... 175 D5
Porlock TA24 .... 129 C7
Chapel Ct
Bath BA1 .... 228 B2
Clandown BA3 .... 78 E4
Clevedon BS21 .... 6 D3
Chapelfield BA3 .... 115 A3
Chapel Field BA2 .... 79 E8
Chapel Forge Cl TA9 .... 136 B8
Chapel Hill
Ashcott TA7 .... 156 B8
Backwell BS48 .... 19 D7
Chewton Mendip BA3 .... 94 E5
Clevedon BS21 .... 6 D3
Kingsdon TA11 .... 173 D5
Kington Magna SP8 .... 177 E1
Odcombe BA22 .... 186 C2
Ubley BS40 .... 55 C5
Wrington BS40 .... 35 D3
Chapel La
Bishops Lydeard TA4 .... 167 E8
Butleigh BA6 .... 157 E4
Chew Stoke BS40 .... 56 D8
Claverham BS49 .... 34 F8
Cleeve BS49 .... 35 B7
Dinnington TA17 .... 195 B7
East Huntspill TA9 .... 136 E8
Gurney Slade BA3 .... 114 E7
Holcombe BA3 .... 116 C8
Milborne Port DT9 .... 217 D2
North Cadbury BA22 .... 175 D6
Oxenpill BA6 .... 138 C4
Penselwood BA9 .... 161 E2
South Cadbury BA22 .... 175 F5
Sparkford BA22 .... 175 A6
Winford BS40 .... 38 A6
Wingfield BA14 .... 83 C6
Yenston BA8 .... 189 F7
Yeovil Marsh BA21 .... 187 A5
Zeals BA12 .... 161 F3
Chapel Lawns BA3 .... 78 E4
Chapel Leigh La TA4 .... 167 A8
Chapel Rd
Bristol, Bishopsworth BS13 .... 22 A6
Clandown BA3 .... 78 E4
Fordgate TA7 .... 154 C3
Isle Abbotts TA3 .... 183 E7
Pawlett TA6 .... 135 F6
Rooks Bridge BS26 .... 87 C5
South Cadbury BA22 .... 175 D4
Chapel Row
Bath BA1 .... 228 B2
Chapel Row *continued*
Bathford BA1 .... 29 C2
Dunster TA24 .... 201 D2
Norton St Philip BA2 .... 81 F4
Pill BS20 .... 4 C4
Chapel St
Bridgwater TA6 .... 209 A5
Burnham-on-S TA8 .... 104 A7
Dulverton TA22 .... 163 D6
Exford TA24 .... 128 D1
Horningsham BA12 .... 144 D4
Upton Noble BA4 .... 142 F2
Chapel Wlk BA2 .... 60 C2
Chapel Yd BA7 .... 214 B4
Chaplains Wood BS20 .... 1 E5
Chapman Ct TA1 .... 212 C1
Chapmans Cl
Frome BA11 .... 119 F6
Wookey BA5 .... 139 D8
Chapmanslade CE Prim Sch BA13 .... 121 D4
Chapter St BS2 .... 227 B4
Charbury Wlk BS11 .... 4 E5
Charcroft Hill BA10 .... 160 F6
Chard Bsns Pk TA20 .... 223 D6
Chard Cl BS48 .... 18 F8
Chard Ct BS14 .... 23 B6
Chard & District Hospl TA20 .... 223 E4
Chard La
Chard TA20 .... 223 B1
Drimpton DT8 .... 199 F8
Ilminster TA19 .... 194 D6
Tatworth EX13, TA20 .... 193 E1
Woolminstone TA18, TA20 .. 195 B2
Chard Mus* TA20 .... 223 B4
Chard Rd
Axminster EX13 .... 198 B4
Clevedon BS21 .... 6 E1
Crewkerne TA18 .... 224 A6
Drimpton DT8 .... 199 F7
Chard Sch TA20 .... 223 C4
Chard St
Chardstock EX13 .... 198 B7
Thorncombe TA20 .... 199 B6
Chardstock Ave BS9 .... 5 D8
Chardstock La TA20 .... 223 C2
Chardyke Dr BS39 .... 58 E1
Charing Cross DT6 .... 199 E1
Charity La BA11 .... 98 C1
Charlcombe La BA1 .... 27 F3
Charlcombe Pk BS20 .... 1 D3
Charlcombe Rise BA1 .... 27 F2
Charlcombe View Rd BA1 .28 A2
Charlcombe Way BA1 .... 27 F2
Charlcome Rise BS20 .... 1 D3
Charlecombe Ct BS9 .... 5 F6
Charlecombe Rd BS9 .... 5 F6
Charlecote BA1 .... 27 F1
Charles Cres TA1 .... 213 D4
Charles Ct 1 BS8 .... 226 A2
Charles Pl BS8 .... 226 A2
Charles Rd
Frome BA11 .... 119 F3
Yeovil BA21 .... 219 D6
Charles St
Bath BA1 .... 228 B2
Bristol BS1 .... 227 A4
Charlestone Rd TA8 .... 104 B8
Charleton Ho 8 BS2 .... 227 C3
Charlock Cl 3 BS22 .... 49 D7
Charlock Rd BS22 .... 49 D7
Charlotte Ct BA20 .... 219 A4
Charlotte St S BS1 .... 226 C2
Charlotte St
Bath BA1 .... 228 B2
Bristol, Brandon Hill BS1 .. 226 C3
Bristol, St Pauls BS2 .... 227 C4
Charlton Ave BS23 .... 48 D4
Charlton Cl
Bridgwater TA6 .... 209 C4
Crewkerne TA18 .... 224 D5
Shepton Mallet BA4 .... 205 D5
Yeovil BA21 .... 219 D5
Charlton Crossroads BA4 .... 205 D5
Charlton Dr BS48 .... 9 C7
Charlton Field La DT9 .... 175 D1
Charlton Hill DT9, BA8 .... 176 B3
Charlton Horethorne CE Prim Sch DT9 .... 176 A1
Charlton La
Creech St Michael TA3 .... 169 E5
Radstock BA3 .... 97 D6
Sparkford DT9 .... 175 F3
Charlton Mackrell CE Prim Sch TA11 .... 173 E7
Charlton Pk
Keynsham BS31 .... 24 D5
Midsomer Norton BA3 .... 97 B7
Charlton Rd
Creech St Michael TA3 .... 169 E6
Holcombe BA3 .... 97 D3
Keynsham BS31, BS14 .... 24 C3
Midsomer Norton BA3 .... 97 B8
Shepton Mallet BA4 .... 205 D5
Weston-Super-Mare BS23 ... 48 D4
Charlton Road Cotts TA3 .... 169 D6
Charlton Trad Est BA4 .... 205 E5
Charlton View BS20 .... 2 C5
Charlynch Hill TA5 .... 152 F8
Charlynch La TA5 .... 153 B8
Charlynch Rd TA5 .... 153 A8
Charmborough Farm Rural Bsns Pk BA3 .... 97 D3
Charmoor Dro TA20 .... 182 F1
Charmoor La TA20 .... 182 F1
Charmouth Rd BA1 .... 44 B7
Charnwood Cl TA6 .... 208 F7
Charnwood Dr BS27 .... 90 B7
Charnwood Rd BS14 .... 23 B4
Charter Cl TA6 .... 209 A4
Charter Ho BS1 .... 226 B2
Charterhouse Cl
Cheddar BS27 .... 90 C6
Nailsea BS48 .... 8 F1
Charterhouse Dr BA11 .. 120 C7
Charter Rd BS22 .... 49 B8
Charter Way BA5 .... 203 B4
Charter Wlk
Bristol BS14 .... 23 A6
Taunton TA1 .... 213 C5
Chartley BS9 .... 5 D2
Chase Cl BA6 .... 206 C3
Chasey's Dro BA6 .... 139 C4
Chatham Ave TA6 .... 208 E6
Chatham Ct TA10 .... 171 C4
Chatham Pk BA2 .... 45 C6
Chatham Pl TA10 .... 171 C4
Chatham Row BA1 .... 228 C3
Chatley Furlong BA2 .... 81 F3
Chatsworth Rd BA21 .... 219 D7
Chattenden Ho BS9 .... 5 F3
Chatterton Gn BS14 .... 22 F3
Chatterton Ho 5 BS1 .... 227 B1
Chatterton Sq BS1 .... 227 C1
Chatterton St BS1 .... 227 C1
Chaucer Cl 4 TA6 .... 153 F4
Chaucer Rd
Bath BA2 .... 44 F4
Midsomer Norton BA3 .... 97 B8
Weston-Super-Mare BS23 ... 49 A4
Chaundey Gr BS13 .... 22 B5
Cheapside
Bristol BS2 .... 227 C4
Langport TA10 .... 171 F5
Taunton TA1 .... 212 F3
Wiveliscombe TA4 .... 210 C4
Cheap St
Bath BA1 .... 228 C2
Frome BA11 .... 119 F5
Sherborne DT9 .... 225 D4
Cheats Rd TA3 .... 169 C3
Checcombe La DT9 .... 188 B4
Checkridge La EX13 .... 198 D2
Cheddar Bsns Pk BS27 .... 90 A6
Cheddar Cl
Burnham-on-S TA8 .... 104 C8
Frome BA11 .... 120 C7
Nailsea BS48 .... 18 F8
Cheddar Ct BS27 .... 90 B7
Cheddar Fields BS27 .... 90 A7
Cheddar Fst Sch BS27 .... 90 B7
Cheddar Gorge* BS27 .... 71 E1
Cheddar Gorge Rural Village* BS27 .... 90 C8
Cheddar Gr BS13 .... 22 A8
Cheddar Grove Prim Sch BS13 .... 22 A8
Cheddar Moor Dro BS27 .. 90 C4
Cheddar Rd
Axbridge BS26 .... 70 E2
Chewton Mendip BA3 .... 94 D6
Clewer BS28 .... 89 D2
Wedmore BS28 .... 108 D6
Cheddar Valley Bldgs 2 BA5 .... 203 C3
Cheddon Fitzpaine CE Prim Sch TA2 .... 168 F6
Cheddon Lawns TA2 .... 169 A6
Cheddon Mews TA2 .... 212 F7
Cheddon Rd TA2 .... 212 F7
Chedworth Cl BA2 .... 45 F3
Chedzoy La TA7 .... 209 E7
Cheeks La BA10 .... 215 E6
Cheer La TA7 .... 154 F5
Cheese Hill BA11 .... 143 D8
Cheese La BS2 .... 227 B2
Chelmer Cl TA1 .... 213 D4
Chelmer Gr BS31 .... 24 F4
Chelscombe BA1 .... 27 B1
Chelsea Cl BS31 .... 25 A5
Chelsea Rd BA1 .... 44 C7
Chelsfield BS48 .... 19 A7
Chelston Ave BA21 .... 219 B7
Chelston Bsn Pk TA21 .... 180 D8
Chelston Rd BS4 .... 22 D7
Chelston Terr TA21 .... 180 D8
Chelswood Ave BS22 .... 49 C8
Chelswood Gdns BS22 .... 49 D8
Cheltenham St BA2 .... 228 A1
Chelvey Batch BS48 .... 18 F3
Chelvey La BS48 .... 18 E4
Chelvey Rd BS48 .... 18 D5
Chelvey Rise BS48 .... 9 A1
Chelvy Cl BS13 .... 22 D3
Chelwood BS23 .... 48 F8
Chelwood Dr
Bath BA2 .... 44 D1
Taunton TA1 .... 212 E1
Chelwood Rd
Bristol BS11 .... 4 D7
Saltford BS31 .... 25 E4
Chelwood Rdbt BS39 .... 58 E8
Chelynch Pk BA4 .... 141 E6
Chelynch Rd BA4 .... 141 F7
Chepstow Ave TA6 .... 209 A2
Chepstow Ct BA21 .... 219 D6
Chepstow Ho BA10 .... 215 D6
Chepstow Rd BS4 .... 22 D8
Chepstow Wlk BS31 .... 24 D5
Cher TA24 .... 200 F6
Cherfield TA24 .... 200 F6
Cherington Rd BS48 .... 9 A2
Cheriton St BA8 .... 176 D3
Cherry Ave BS21 .... 6 E2
Cherry Cl
Bridgwater TA6 .... 209 C3
Yatton BS49 .... 34 B8
Cherry Ct 12 BS1 .... 227 A4
Cherry Garden La BA2 .. 100 D7
Cherry Gr
Frome BA11 .... 119 E3
Taunton TA2 .... 212 F6
Yatton BS49 .... 34 B8
Cherry Hay BS21 .... 6 D1
Cherry La
4 Bristol BS1 .... 227 B4
Odcombe BA22 .... 186 C2
Cherry Orch TA3 .... 168 D1
Cherry Orchard Dr BA5 .. 203 C5
Cherry Pie La BA22 .... 175 A5
Cherry Rd
Long Ashton BS41 .... 10 F1
Nailsea BS48 .... 8 D1
Cherry Tree Cl
Keynsham BS31 .... 24 C4
Radstock BA3 .... 78 E1
Cherry Tree Ct
Crewkerne TA18 .... 224 D8
Kingston Seymour BS21 .... 16 C2
1 Wells BA5 .... 203 C3
Wincanton BA9 .... 216 D4
Cherry Tree Dr BA20 .... 218 D2
Cherry Tree La TA1 .... 212 F1
Cherry Tree Rd EX13 .... 198 A1
Cherry Tree Way TA23 .... 202 D6
Cherrywood Rd BS22 .... 31 F2
Cherrywood Rise BS22 .... 31 F2
Chertsey Cl TA7 .... 136 E4
Cherwell Rd BS31 .... 25 A4
Chescombe Rd BS49 .... 34 B7
Chesham Rd N BS22 .... 49 B8
Chesham Rd S BS22 .... 49 B8
Cheshay's Hill TA19 .... 183 D1
Chesle Cl BS20 .... 1 E3
Cheslefield BS20 .... 1 E3
Chesle Way BS20 .... 1 E3
Chessell La BA4 .... 140 C4
Chessels Cl BA22 .... 197 B8
Chessels La TA11 .... 173 F7
Chessington Ave BS14 .... 23 B5
Chesterblade Rd
Chesterblade BA4 .... 142 A4
Evercreech BA4 .... 141 F3
Chester Cl BS24 .... 50 A8
Chester Cres BS13 .... 22 B8
Chesterfield TA20 .... 223 D4
Chesterfield Cl BS29 .... 50 F3
Chesterfield Ho BA3 .... 78 B1
Chesterfield Hospl BS8 . 226 A2
Chester Terr TA20 .... 223 D4
Chesterton Dr BS48 .... 9 A2
Chesterton Ho 6 BS2 .... 227 B4
Chestertons The BA2 .... 45 F8
Chestnut Ave
Axbridge BS26 .... 70 C2
Chapel Cleeve TA24 .... 131 D5
Crewkerne TA18 .... 224 D7
Weston-Super-Mare BS22 ... 32 A1
Chestnut Barn Ind Est BS24 .... 33 D3
Chestnut Chase BS48 .... 9 A3
Chestnut Cl
Baltonsborough BA6 .... 158 A5
Banwell BS29 .... 51 A3
Bridgwater TA6 .... 209 C4
Bristol BS14 .... 23 F5
1 Carhampton TA24 .... 131 A5
Congresbury BS49 .... 34 D4
Frome BA11 .... 120 C7
Maiden Bradley BA12 .... 144 C2
Paulton BS39 .... 77 E6
Radstock BA3 .... 78 E1
Somerton TA11 .... 211 C3
Wellington TA21 .... 222 E5
Chestnut Ct BS13 .... 22 A7
Chestnut Dr
Claverham BS49 .... 17 F1
Taunton TA1 .... 213 C1
Yeovil BA20 .... 218 F3
Chestnut Gr
Bath BA2 .... 44 C4
Clevedon BS21 .... 6 E4
Westwood BA15 .... 64 F4
Chestnut Ho
Brean TA8 .... 65 F2
Bristol BS13 .... 22 D3
Chestnut La
Ashcott TA7 .... 156 B8
Bleadon BS24 .... 67 B7
Chestnut Par BA4 .... 205 D4
Chestnut Rd
Long Ashton BS41 .... 11 B2
11 Martock TA12 .... 185 E6
Chestnuts The
Cheddar BS27 .... 71 A1
Winscombe BS25 .... 70 A7
Chestnut Way TA24 .... 201 A5
Chestnut Wlk
Bristol BS13 .... 22 A6
Saltford BS31 .... 25 E3
Chever's La BA2 .... 81 E5
Cheverton Ho 1 BA21 .... 219 B5
Chew Cotts BS31 .... 24 F5
Chew Court Farm BS40 ... 39 B3
Chew Hill BS40 .... 39 A4
Chew La BS40 .... 38 F1
Chew Magna Prim Sch BS40 .... 39 B3
Chew Rd BS40 .... 38 C5
Chew St BS40 .... 39 A3
Chew Stoke CE Prim Sch BS40 .... 56 D8
Chewton Cheese Dairy* BA3 .... 94 E6
Chewton Hill BA3 .... 95 A7
Chewton Mendip CE Prim Sch BA3 .... 94 F7
Chewton Rd BS31 .... 24 F2
Chew Valley Lake Nature Trails* BS39 .... 57 B7
Chew Valley Sch BS40 .... 38 F1
Cheyne Rd BS9 .... 5 D6
Chibbet Hill TA24 .... 146 B8
Chibbet Post TA24 .... 146 C8
Chichester Cl TA8 .... 104 B8
Chichester Pl BA3 .... 79 A2
Chichester Rd BA16 .... 207 C4
Chichester Way BS24 .... 50 A8
Chick's La TA4 .... 210 C6
Chicks La BA3 .... 95 D7
Chickwell La BA3 .... 81 A1
Chidgey Cl TA6 .... 208 F5
Chilcombe La TA4 .... 132 F1
Chilcompton Rd BA3 .... 96 E7
Chilcote Dro BA5 .... 113 E2
Chilcote La BA5 .... 113 D1
Chilcott Cross TA22 .... 163 A7
Chilcott La TA22 .... 163 A7
Childhay La DT8 .... 199 F6
Chilkwell St BA6 .... 206 E4
Chillington Down TA19, TA20 .... 194 F4
Chilliswood Cres TA1 .... 212 B2
Chilliswood La
Staplehay TA3 .... 181 B8
Taunton TA3 .... 168 B1
Chill Pits La EX13 .... 198 B8
Chillybridge Rocks TA22 .. 147 E1
Chillyhill La BS40 .... 38 F2
Chilpitts TA7 .... 136 F4
Chiltern Cl BS14 .... 23 B4
Chiltern Cross EX16 .... 164 B2
Chilthorne Domer CE Sch BA22 .... 186 E5
Chilthornehill La BA22 .. 186 D6
Chilton Cantelo House (Sch) BA22 .... 174 C1
Chilton Cl TA6 .... 208 F7
Chilton Ct 7 BA1 .... 28 B1
Chilton Dro TA7 .... 137 C6
Chilton Gr BA21 .... 219 A7
Chilton Pk TA6 .... 208 F7
Chilton Rd
Bath BA1 .... 28 B1
Bridgwater TA5, TA6 .... 208 F8
Bristol BS4 .... 23 A8
Chilton Polden TA7 .... 137 B4
Chilton Right Dro TA7 .... 155 B6
Chilton St TA6 .... 208 F7
Chilton Trinity Tech Coll TA6 .... 208 F7
Chilworthy La TA19, TA20 .. 193 F7
Chimes The BS48 .... 18 C8
Chinehorn Dro TA5 .... 135 F3
Chinnock Hollow BA22 ... 196 E8
Chinnock Rd BA6 .... 206 F5
Chip La TA1 .... 212 E5
Chippel La DT10 .... 190 F5
Chipping Cross BS21 .... 16 C8
Chi-Rio Cl BA4 .... 205 E4
Chisland Dr TA24 .... 129 C8
Chistles La TA11 .... 158 A1
Chitcombe Rocks La TA4 .... 149 C1
Cholwell Cotts BS39 .... 58 D2
Chorwell La TA21 .... 166 E2
Chovel La BA11 .... 142 F6
Chowins Rd TA18 .... 224 C5
Christchurch CE Fst Sch BA11 .... 119 F2
Christ Church CE Prim Sch
Bristol BS8 .... 226 A3
Weston-Super-Mare BS23 ... 48 E8
Christ Church Cl 1 BS48 .... 8 E2
Christ Church Ct 9 TA18 .... 224 C6
Christchurch Hall 2 BA1 .... 228 B3
Christ Church Path S 12 BS23 .... 48 E8
Christchurch Rd BS8 .... 226 A3
Christchurch St E BA11 .. 119 F4
Christchurch St W BA11 .. 119 E4
Christian's Cross BA6 .... 157 E1
Christian Cl BS22 .... 32 A3
Christina Terr BS8 .... 226 A1
Christmas St 6 BS1 .... 227 A3
Christmas Stps 2 BS1 .... 227 A3
Christon Rd
Banwell BS29 .... 51 A1
Loxton BS26 .... 68 C6
Christon Terr BS23 .... 48 F2
Christopher Cl BA20 .... 218 E5
Christopher Way BA4 .... 205 A5
Chritchard Way TA1 .... 213 B4
Chrysanthemum Cl 3 DT9 .... 225 E4
Chrysanthemum Flats 2 DT9 .... 225 E4
Chrysanthemum Row 4 DT9 .... 225 E4
Chubbards Cross Cvn Site TA19 .... 183 E5
Chubbs Lawn TA18 .... 224 C5
Chubworthy Cross TA4 .. 165 D5
Church Ave BS9 .... 5 E4
Church Cl
Bathampton BA2 .... 28 F2

Church Cl *continued*
Bathford BA1 . . . 29 B2
Bourton SP8 . . . 161 E1
7 Carhampton TA24 . . . 131 A5
Clevedon BS21 . . . 6 A2
East Huntspill TA9 . . . 136 E8
Evercreech BA4 . . . 141 E1
Great Elm BA11 . . . 118 F7
Lydeard St Lawrence TA4 . 151 A3
24 Martock TA12 . . . 185 E6
Norton Fitzwarren TA2 . . . 168 B4
Portishead BS20 . . . 2 D5
Shapwick TA7 . . . 137 F1
South Brewham BA10 . . . 160 F6
Stoke St Gregory TA3 . . . 170 E6
Stoke St Mary TA3 . . . 169 C1
West Chinnock TA18 . . . 196 B8
Yatton BS49 . . . 34 C7
Church Cnr BS24 . . . 67 B1
Church Cotts
Chilton Trinity TA5 . . . 135 F2
Monkton Combe BA2 . . . 63 E8
Newton St Loe BA2 . . . 43 B6
Church Ct
Midsomer Norton BA3 . . . 78 A1
Redhill BS40 . . . 36 D3
Churchdown Wlk BS11 . . . 4 E5
Church Dr
Congresbury BS49 . . . 34 D4
West Buckland TA21 . . . 180 F7
Church Farm Bsns Pk
BA2 . . . 43 A7
Church Farm Cl
Marksbury BA2 . . . 42 B1
Stawell TA7 . . . 137 A1
Church Farm Pl 18 BA8 . 190 A6
Churchfield La TA3 . . . 183 F7
Church Field La TA7 . . . 136 C4
Churchfields
Rode BA11 . . . 101 F8
Wellington TA21 . . . 222 D7
Church Fields
Wellington TA21 . . . 222 E6
Wincanton BA9 . . . 216 C3
Churchfields Dr BA7 . . . 214 C6
Church Gdns BA6 . . . 206 D5
Church Hayes Cl BS48 . . . 18 E8
Church Hayes Dr BS48 . . . 18 E8
Church Hill
Beckington BA11 . . . 101 E4
Buckhorn Weston SP8 . . . 177 D3
Charlton Adam TA11 . . . 173 F7
Combwich TA5 . . . 135 B5
Dinnington TA17 . . . 195 B7
Exford TA24 . . . 128 D1
Freshford BA3 . . . 64 B5
Kington Magna SP8 . . . 177 E2
Pitney TA10 . . . 172 C7
Radstock BA3 . . . 79 C3
South Cadbury BA22 . . . 175 C3
Stalbridge DT10 . . . 190 B5
Templecombe BA8 . . . 176 E1
Timsbury BA2 . . . 60 B2
Church Ho BA4 . . . 141 F1
Church House Rd TA8 . . . 84 F5
Churchill Ave
Clevedon BS21 . . . 6 C2
Wells BA5 . . . 112 E1
Churchill Bsns Pk BS23 . . 49 A7
Churchill CE Prim Sch
BS40 . . . 53 A5
Churchill Cl
Burnham-on-S TA8 . . . 104 C5
5 Clevedon BS21 . . . 6 C2
Wells BA5 . . . 112 E1
Churchill Dr BS9 . . . 5 D7
Churchill Gate BS25 . . . 52 F4
Churchill Gn BS25 . . . 52 C5
Churchill La
Axminster EX13 . . . 198 A5
Chipstable TA4 . . . 165 C5
Churchill Rd
Frome BA11 . . . 119 D4
Shepton Mallet BA4 . . . 205 A5
Wells BA5 . . . 112 E1
Weston-Super-Mare BS23 . . 49 A7
Churchill Rd E BA5 . . . 112 E1
Churchill Sch & Sixth Form Ctr BS25 . . . 52 D5
Churchill Way
Taunton TA1 . . . 212 F1
Watchet TA23 . . . 202 C6
Church La
Axbridge BS26 . . . 70 C2
Backwell BS48 . . . 19 C5
Badgworth BS26 . . . 88 A6
Baltonsborough BA6 . . . 158 A5
Bath BA2 . . . 45 C4
Batheaston BA1 . . . 28 F4
Bicknoller TA4 . . . 132 F2
Bishop Sutton BS39 . . . 57 D4
Bitton BS30 . . . 25 E7
Blackford BS28 . . . 107 D5
Brent Knoll TA9 . . . 86 A2
Bristol BS1 . . . 227 B2
Bristol, Clifton Wood BS8 . . 226 B2
Bristol, Dundry Hill BS14 . . . 23 B3
Carhampton TA24 . . . 131 B5
Chew Stoke BS40 . . . 56 D8
Chewton Mendip BA3 . . . 94 F7
Chilcompton BA3 . . . 96 D5
Chilton Polden TA7 . . . 137 B2
Churchill BS25 . . . 52 D5
Clutton BS39 . . . 58 E3
Coleford BA3 . . . 116 F7
Compton Bishop BS26 . . . 69 B3
Compton Dando BS39 . . . 41 D6
Doulting BA4 . . . 141 E6
Church La *continued*
Dulverton TA22 . . . 163 D6
East Coker BA22 . . . 197 E8
East Harptree BS40 . . . 74 E4
East Huntspill TA9 . . . 136 E8
East Lambrook TA13 . . . 220 C8
Evercreech BA4 . . . 141 E1
Farmborough BA2 . . . 60 A6
Farrington Gurney BS39 . . . 77 A4
Flax Bourton BS48 . . . 19 F7
Glastonbury BA6 . . . 206 D5
Haselbury Plucknett TA18 . 196 C5
Hatch Beauchamp TA3 . . . 182 E8
Horningsham BA12 . . . 144 E4
Horton TA19 . . . 183 C2
Hutton BS24 . . . 49 E2
Ilminster TA19 . . . 221 C4
Kingston St Mary TA2 . . . 168 E8
Limpley Stoke BA3 . . . 64 A5
Long Ashton BS41 . . . 11 C2
Long Sutton TA10 . . . 172 D2
Loxton BS26 . . . 68 D4
Lympsham BS24 . . . 67 B1
Lynford-on-F TA11 . . . 158 D2
Meare BA6 . . . 138 D4
Midsomer Norton BA3 . . . 78 A1
Milborne Port DT9 . . . 217 D2
Misterton TA18 . . . 224 E3
Nailsea BS21 . . . 8 C4
Nailsea BS48 . . . 8 C1
North Perrott TA18 . . . 196 C4
Norton Sub Hamdon, Chiselborough TA14 . . . 185 E1
Norton Sub Hamdon TA14 . . 185 F2
Paulton BS39 . . . 77 E6
Portbury BS20 . . . 3 E3
Rimpton BA22 . . . 188 B8
Rode BA11 . . . 101 F8
Ruishton TA3 . . . 169 C4
Ruishton, Thornfalcon TA3 . . 169 E2
Seavington St Mary TA19 . . 184 E1
22 Shepton Mallet BA4 . . . 205 B6
Shepton Mallet, Cannards Grave BA4 . . . 205 D2
Sherborne DT9 . . . 225 D4
Stratton-on-t F BA3 . . . 96 F2
Timsbury BA2 . . . 60 B2
Westonzoyland TA7 . . . 154 F5
West Pennard BA6 . . . 140 B1
Wingfield BA14 . . . 83 C6
Winscombe BS25 . . . 69 E6
Yatton BS49 . . . 34 C7
Churchlands TA9 . . . 106 D4
Churchlands Ct TA8 . . . 104 A7
Churchland Way BS22 . . . 50 B8
Church Lane Cnr TA9 . . . 86 A2
Church Lane End BS48 . . . 19 F8
Church Leaze BS11 . . . 4 D6
Church Mdw TA6 . . . 208 E6
Church Mdws BS14 . . . 23 C4
Church Mead SP8 . . . 161 E1
Churchmoor La BA6 . . . 158 A5
Church Pass 4 TA6 . . . 208 F5
Church Path
Aller TA10 . . . 171 D8
Bridgwater TA6 . . . 208 E5
Crewkerne TA18 . . . 224 B6
Meare BA6 . . . 138 D4
Minehead TA24 . . . 200 F8
Queen Camel BA22 . . . 174 F3
South Petherton TA13 . . . 220 C2
2 Yeovil BA20 . . . 219 B5
Church Path Rd BS20 . . . 4 C4
Church Pl
Milborne Port DT9 . . . 217 D2
Pill BS20 . . . 4 C4
Church Rd
Abbots Leigh BS8 . . . 11 A8
Bath, Combe Down BA2 . . . 45 C1
Bath, Weston Park BA1 . . . 27 C1
Bawdrip TA7 . . . 136 E2
Bitton BS30 . . . 25 E7
Bourton SP8 . . . 177 F8
Bradford Abbas DT9 . . . 187 E1
Brean TA8 . . . 65 F4
Bristol, Bishopsworth BS13 . . 22 A6
Bristol, Sneyd Park BS9 . . . 5 D3
Chapel Leigh TA4 . . . 167 A7
Churchinford TA3 . . . 191 F8
Churchstanton TA3 . . . 181 B1
Coxley BA5 . . . 139 E6
Dundry BS41 . . . 21 D2
East Brent TA9 . . . 86 C4
Easton-in-G BS20 . . . 4 A4
Edington TA7 . . . 137 C2
Fitzhead TA4 . . . 166 F7
Fordgate TA7 . . . 154 D3
Huntspill TA9 . . . 136 A8
Ilton TA19 . . . 183 E4
Keenthorne TA5 . . . 134 D3
Kilmington BA12 . . . 161 F7
Leigh Woods BS8 . . . 11 D6
Lympsham BS24 . . . 67 B1
Middlezoy TA7 . . . 155 B3
Minehead TA24 . . . 200 F8
North Curry TA3 . . . 170 B4
North Newton TA7 . . . 154 A2
Peasedown St John BA2 . . . 79 B8
Pensford BS39 . . . 40 A7
Redhill BS40 . . . 36 D3
Shapwick TA7 . . . 137 F1
South Cadbury BA22 . . . 175 D4
Sparkford BA22 . . . 175 A4
Spaxton TA5 . . . 152 E7
Street BA16 . . . 207 D7
Sutton Mallet TA7 . . . 155 B7
Taunton TA3 . . . 168 D1
Wembdon TA6 . . . 208 D6
Church Rd *continued*
Weston-Super-Mare BS22 . . . 31 E2
Whitchurch BS14 . . . 23 C4
Winford BS40 . . . 38 A7
Winscombe BS25 . . . 69 E7
Yatton BS49 . . . 34 C7
Church Rd N BS20 . . . 2 D5
Church Rd S BS20 . . . 2 D4
Church Rise BS40 . . . 38 A7
Church Row BA3 . . . 96 F2
Church Row Cotts TA3 . . . 181 E6
Church Sq
Clutton BS39 . . . 58 E2
Midsomer Norton BA3 . . . 78 A1
8 Taunton TA1 . . . 212 F4
Church St
Babcary TA11 . . . 174 C7
Banwell BS29 . . . 51 B3
Barton St David BA6 . . . 157 F2
6 Bath BA1 . . . 228 C2
Bathford BA1 . . . 29 B2
Bath, Weston park BA1 . . . 27 B1
Bath, Widcombe BA2 . . . 45 B4
Beckington BA11 . . . 101 E4
Bishops Lydeard TA4 . . . 167 E8
Blackford BS28 . . . 107 D4
Blagdon BS40 . . . 54 F2
Bridgwater TA6 . . . 209 A5
Bristol BS1 . . . 227 B2
5 Cannington TA5 . . . 135 B2
Castle Cary BA7 . . . 214 B4
Chard TA20 . . . 223 C3
Cheddar BS27 . . . 90 B7
Coleford BA3 . . . 116 F7
Crewkerne TA18 . . . 224 C6
Croscombe BA5 . . . 204 C7
Dinder BA5 . . . 140 D7
Donyatt TA19 . . . 183 D1
Drayton TA10 . . . 171 E3
Dunster TA24 . . . 201 E2
2 Frome BA11 . . . 119 F4
Halstock BA22 . . . 197 C3
8 Henstridge BA8 . . . 190 A6
Highbridge TA9 . . . 104 E4
Hinton St George TA17 . . . 195 C7
Horningsham BA12 . . . 144 D4
Ilchester BA22 . . . 173 E1
Isle Abbotts TA3 . . . 183 F7
Keinton Mandeville TA11 . . 158 A1
Kilmersdon BA3 . . . 98 B5
Kingsbury Episcopi TA12 . . . 185 B8
Kington Magna SP8 . . . 177 E2
Lopen TA13 . . . 185 A1
Maiden Bradley BA12 . . . 144 C1
Mark TA9 . . . 106 D4
Martock TA12 . . . 185 E6
Merriott TA16 . . . 195 F7
Milborne Port DT9 . . . 217 D2
Minehead, Alcombe TA24 . . 201 B5
Minehead TA24 . . . 200 F8
Norton St Philip BA2 . . . 81 E4
Nunney BA11 . . . 143 B8
Paulton BS39 . . . 77 D6
Pensford BS39 . . . 40 D4
Podimore BA22 . . . 174 A3
Radstock BA3 . . . 78 F2
Shepton Beauchamp TA19 . . 184 E4
Southwick BA14 . . . 83 F3
Stogursey TA5 . . . 134 C5
Stoke St Michael BA3 . . . 116 A2
Taunton TA1 . . . 213 B3
Timberscombe TA24 . . . 130 B5
Tintinhull BA22 . . . 186 B6
Upton Noble BA4 . . . 142 F2
Wanstrow BA4 . . . 142 F4
Wedmore BS28 . . . 108 D4
West Coker BA22 . . . 197 A8
Wincanton BA9 . . . 216 C4
Winsham TA20 . . . 194 E1
Wiveliscombe TA4 . . . 210 C4
Woolavington TA7 . . . 136 E4
Woolley BA1 . . . 27 F6
Yeovil BA20 . . . 219 B5
Yeovilton BA22 . . . 174 A1
Churchstanton Prim Sch
TA3 . . . 191 E8
Church Stps TA24 . . . 200 F8
Church Terr
7 Bampton EX16 . . . 164 B1
East Coker BA22 . . . 197 C7
Odcombe BA22 . . . 186 C2
4 Yeovil BA20 . . . 219 B5
Church Tk SP8 . . . 161 E1
Church Town BS48 . . . 19 C5
Church View
Bourton SP8 . . . 161 E1
Chilton Trinity TA5 . . . 135 F2
Clatworthy TA4 . . . 149 F1
Evercreech BA4 . . . 141 E1
North Wootton BA4 . . . 140 C4
Porlock TA24 . . . 124 A3
Wraxall BS48 . . . 9 B2
Church View Cl TA10 . . . 171 E8
Churchview Ct BA6 . . . 206 D4
Churchward Dr BA11 . . . 120 C6
Churchward Rd BS22 . . . 32 B3
Churchway
Curry Rivel TA10 . . . 171 D4
Faulkland BA3 . . . 80 D1
Church Way TA7 . . . 137 D2
Churchway Cl TA10 . . . 171 D4
Churchways BS14 . . . 23 C4
Churchwell Cl DT9 . . . 187 E1
Churchwell St DT9 . . . 187 E1
Church Wlk
Baltonsborough BA6 . . . 158 A5
Bawdrip TA7 . . . 136 E2
Bratton Seymour BA9 . . . 176 B8
Church Wlk *continued*
Ilminster TA19 . . . 221 C4
Leigh u M BA3 . . . 117 A3
Long Sutton TA10 . . . 172 F4
Marston Magna BA22 . . . 174 F1
9 North Petherton TA6 . . . 153 E3
Pill BS20 . . . 4 C4
Wrington BS40 . . . 35 D2
Chur La BA22 . . . 197 A8
Churlands Cl BA22 . . . 197 A8
Churston Cl BS14 . . . 23 A3
Cinder Ash La TA18 . . . 195 D4
Cinnamon La BA6 . . . 206 F3
Circle The BA2 . . . 44 B3
Circular Rd BS9 . . . 5 E2
Circus Field Rd BA6 . . . 206 D4
Circus Mews BA1 . . . 228 B3
Circus Pl BA1 . . . 228 B3
Circus The BA1 . . . 228 B3
City Mus & Art Gal★ BS8 226 C3
City of Bath Coll BA1 . . . 228 B2
City of Bristol Coll BS1 . 226 C2
City of Bristol Coll (Hartcliffe Ctr) BS13 . . . 22 D4
City Rd BS2 . . . 227 B4
City The TA9 . . . 106 C4
City View BA1 . . . 228 C4
Clammer Hill La TA18 . . . 224 D6
Clanage Rd BS3 . . . 11 E4
Clanders Batch BS40 . . . 54 D3
Clandown CE Prim Sch
BA3 . . . 78 E4
Clandown Rd BS39 . . . 77 F4
Clanfield DT9 . . . 225 B2
Clan Ho BA2 . . . 45 C7
Clanville TA24 . . . 200 F7
Clanville Rd TA24 . . . 200 F7
Clapton Court Gdns★
TA18 . . . 195 D1
Clapton Dro BS20 . . . 2 D1
Clapton Gate TA18 . . . 195 C2
Clapton La
Holton BA9 . . . 176 B6
Portishead BS20 . . . 2 E2
Clapton Rd
Hewish TA18 . . . 195 D2
Midsomer Norton BA3 . . . 77 D1
Clapton Wlk BS9 . . . 5 C5
Clare Gdns BA2 . . . 44 D1
Clareham La
Buckland Dinham BA11 . . . 99 D2
Buckland Dinham BA11 . . . 99 F3
Claremont Bldgs BA1 . . . 28 A1
Claremont Cres BS23 . . . 30 B1
Claremont Ct TA1 . . . 212 C1
Claremont Cvn Pk TA8 . . . 84 F6
Claremont Dr TA1 . . . 212 C1
Claremont Gdns
Clevedon BS21 . . . 6 E1
Hallatrow BS39 . . . 77 B7
4 Nailsea BS48 . . . 8 D1
Claremont Gr TA6 . . . 209 D6
Claremont Hall BS21 . . . 6 E4
Claremont La TA1 . . . 212 C1
Claremont Pl 13 BA1 . . . 28 A1
Claremont Rd BA1 . . . 28 B1
Claremont Wlk BA1 . . . 28 A1
Clarence Ct 1 BA20 . . . 219 A5
Clarence Dr 1 TA6 . . . 153 F4
Clarence Grove Rd BS23 . . 48 E5
Clarence Pl
Bath BA1 . . . 44 B6
Bristol BS2 . . . 226 C4
Clarence Rd BS1 . . . 227 B1
Clarence Rd E BS23 . . . 48 E5
Clarence Rd N BS23 . . . 48 D5
Clarence Rd S BS23 . . . 48 D5
Clarence St
Bath BA1 . . . 228 C4
Taunton TA1 . . . 212 E4
Yeovil BA20 . . . 219 A5
Clarence Terr
Bath BA2 . . . 45 D5
8 Yeovil BA20 . . . 219 B4
Clarendon Rd
Bath BA2 . . . 45 B5
Weston-Super-Mare BS23 . . . 48 F8
Clarendon Villas BA2 . . . 45 B5
Clare St
Bridgwater TA6 . . . 208 F5
Bristol BS1 . . . 227 A2
2 North Petherton TA6 . . . 153 F4
Clark's La TA18 . . . 224 F3
Clark Cl
Woolavington TA7 . . . 136 E4
Wraxall BS48 . . . 9 B2
Clarke's Cl TA20 . . . 223 D4
Clarke's Row TA20 . . . 223 D4
Clarken Cl BS48 . . . 8 E1
Clarken Coombe BS41 . . . 11 B3
Clarkes Ct BA20 . . . 219 A4
Clarkham Cross BA22 . . . 197 E2
Clarks Cl BA22 . . . 218 A5
Clarkson Ave BS22 . . . 31 C1
Clarkson Ho BA1 . . . 228 A2
Clarks Rd TA6 . . . 209 C4
Clarks Shopping Village
BA16 . . . 207 C6
Classic Bldgs TA6 . . . 208 F4
Clatcombe La DT9 . . . 188 D6
Clatworthy Dr BS14 . . . 23 A7
Clatworthy Resr★ TA4 . . . 149 D2
Claude Ave BA2 . . . 44 C5
Claude Terr BA2 . . . 44 C5
Claverham Cl BS49 . . . 34 D7
Claverham Dro BS49 . . . 17 D5
Claverham Pk BS49 . . . 34 F8
Claverham Rd BS49 . . . 34 E8
Claverton Bldgs BA2 . . . 228 C1
Claverton Ct BA2 . . . 45 E4
Claverton Down Rd BA2 . . 45 F3
Claverton Dr BA2 . . . 45 F3
Claverton Hill BA2 . . . 46 A4
Claverton Lodge BA2 . . . 45 C5
Claverton Pumping Sta★
BA2 . . . 46 C5
Claverton Rd BS31 . . . 25 E2
Claverton Rd W BS31 . . . 25 D3
Claverton St BA2 . . . 228 C1
Clay Castle TA18 . . . 196 C5
Clay Castle La TA18 . . . 196 C6
Claydon Cl TA23 . . . 131 E4
Claydon Gn BS14 . . . 22 F3
Clayford La TA22 . . . 163 C5
Clayford Rd TA22 . . . 163 C5
Clayhanger Cross TA20 . . 193 E6
Clayhanger La
Chard TA20 . . . 223 A8
Combe St Nicholas TA20 . . . 193 E6
Clayhidon Crossway
EX15 . . . 180 E2
Clay La
Barrington TA19 . . . 184 B5
Bitton BS30 . . . 25 D8
Chewton Mendip BA3 . . . 94 C5
Higher Chillington TA19 . . . 194 F5
Millmoor EX15 . . . 179 A1
Rode BA11 . . . 101 F8
Claylands Cnr TA5 . . . 134 E5
Claypiece Rd BS13 . . . 22 A4
Clayton Cl
Portishead BS20 . . . 2 E4
Yeovil BA22 . . . 218 A6
Clearwood BA13 . . . 121 F8
Clearwood View BA13 . . . 121 E4
Cleaveside Cl BA22 . . . 174 F3
Cleeve Abbey★ TA23 . . . 131 E3
Cleevedale Rd BA2 . . . 45 A1
Cleeve Dr BS49 . . . 35 B8
Cleeve Gn BA2 . . . 44 A6
Cleeve Gr BS31 . . . 24 D5
Cleeve Hill
Ubley BS40 . . . 73 E8
Watchet TA23 . . . 202 A7
Cleeve Hill Rd BS40 . . . 35 C7
Cleeve Pk TA24 . . . 131 D5
Cleeve Pl BS48 . . . 9 A1
Cleeve Rd TA2 . . . 213 B7
Cleeveways DT9 . . . 176 A2
Clemence Rd BA16 . . . 207 D4
Clements Cl BA5 . . . 203 C3
Clement St BS2 . . . 227 C4
Cleve Ct 3 BS8 . . . 11 F6
Clevedon Com Sch BS21 . . 6 F5
Clevedon Craft Ctr★ BS21 . . 7 A1
Clevedon Ct★ BS21 . . . 7 A4
Clevedon Hospl BS21 . . . 6 E3
Clevedon La BS21 . . . 8 B7
Clevedon Min Rly★ BS21 . . . 6 B3
Clevedon Pier★ BS21 . . . 6 C4
Clevedon Rd
Flax Bourton BS48 . . . 9 F2
Midsomer Norton BA3 . . . 78 A2
Nailsea BS21 . . . 8 B4
Portishead BS20 . . . 2 D3
Weston-Super-Mare BS23 . . . 48 E6
Wraxall BS48 . . . 9 B4
Wraxall BS48 . . . 9 D6
Clevedon Terr BS6 . . . 227 A4
Clevedon Wlk 2 BS48 . . . 8 E2
Cleveland Cotts BA1 . . . 228 C4
Cleveland Ct BA2 . . . 45 C6
Cleveland Pl BA1 . . . 228 C4
Cleveland Pl E BA1 . . . 228 C4
Cleveland Pl W BA1 . . . 228 C4
Cleveland Reach BA1 . . . 228 C4
Cleveland Row BA1 . . . 45 B8
Clevelands TA24 . . . 200 F8
Cleveland St TA1 . . . 212 E4
Cleveland Terr BA1 . . . 228 C4
Cleveland Wlk BA2 . . . 45 C6
Cleve The BA21 . . . 218 C6
Clewson Rise BS14 . . . 22 F3
Cleyhill Gdns BA13 . . . 121 D4
Cliffe Dr BA3 . . . 64 A6
Clifford Ave TA2 . . . 212 E8
Clifford Cres TA2 . . . 212 E8
Clifford Gdns BS11 . . . 4 E6
Clifford Ho BS23 . . . 48 D6
Clifford Lodge 3 TA5 . . . 135 B2
Clifford Mews TA21 . . . 222 E6
Clifford Pk TA5 . . . 135 B2
Clifford Terr TA21 . . . 222 E6
Cliff Rd
Cheddar BS27 . . . 71 E1
North Petherton TA6 . . . 153 E3
Weston-Super-Mare BS22 . . . 31 A2
Cliff St BS27 . . . 90 C8
Cliffs The BS27 . . . 90 C8
Clift House Rd BS3 . . . 11 F4
Clift House Spur BS3 . . . 11 F4
Clifton Ave BS23 . . . 48 E5
Clifton Cl
1 Bristol BS8 . . . 11 F7
Yeovil BA21 . . . 219 E6
Clifton Coll BS8 . . . 226 A4
Clifton College Prep Sch
BS8 . . . 5 F1
Clifton Ct 10 BS21 . . . 6 C2
Clifton Down BS8 . . . 11 F7
Clifton Down Rd BS8 . . . 226 A3
Clifton High Gr BS9 . . . 5 E5
Clifton High Sch BS8 . . . 226 A4

Clifton Hill
Barwick BA22 . . . . 197 F8
Bristol BS8 . . . . 226 A2
Clifton Park Rd BS8 . . . . 11 F8
Clifton Pk BS8 . . . . 226 A3
Clifton Rd
Bristol BS8 . . . . 226 A2
Weston-Super-Mare BS23 . . . 48 E5
Clifton St BS20 . . . . 2 C2
Clifton Suspension Bridge*
BS8 . . . . 11 E7
Clifton Terr 7 TA2 . . . . 212 F6
Clifton Vale BS8 . . . . 226 A2
Clifton Vale Cl BS8 . . . . 226 A2
Clifton View 9 BA22 . . . . 197 F8
Cliftonwood Cres BS8 . . . . 226 B2
Clifton Wood Ct BS8 . . . . 226 B2
Clifton Wood Rd BS8 . . . . 226 B2
Cliftonwood Terr BS8 . . . 226 A2
Clift Pl BS1 . . . . 227 A1
Clifts Bldgs BA11 . . . . 119 F4
Clink Farm Ct BA11 . . . . 120 C6
Clink Rd BA11 . . . . 120 D6
Clink The TA6 . . . . 209 A5
Clipper Cl TA6 . . . . 209 C4
Clipper Quay TA24 . . . . 201 B7
Clitsome View TA23 . . . . 131 D2
Clive Rd BS14 . . . . 23 C8
Clivey BA13 . . . . 102 E1
Clock Ho TA5 . . . . 134 B2
Clock Ho The BA10 . . . . 160 D4
Clockhouse Mews BS20 . . . . 2 D6
Clockhouse The TA4 . . . . 167 E6
Clockhouse View BA16 . . 207 D6
Cloisters Croft TA8 . . . . 104 B6
Cloisters The BA5 . . . . 203 D3
Cloister The DT9 . . . . 225 D4
Closemead BS21 . . . . 6 D1
Close The
Glastonbury BA6 . . . . 206 E5
9 Merriott TA16 . . . . 195 F7
Minehead TA24 . . . . 201 B5
North Cadbury BA22 . . . . 175 D6
Portishead BS20 . . . . 1 F1
Clotfurlong La DT9 . . . . 188 F1
Clothier Mdw BA7 . . . . 214 B6
Cloudberry Cl TA20 . . . . 223 F5
Cloud Hill Ind Est BS39 . . . 77 A8
Clovelly Rd BS22 . . . . 32 A2
Clover Cl
Clevedon BS21 . . . . 6 F3
Paulton BS39 . . . . 77 E4
Clover Ct 2 BS22 . . . . 49 D7
Clover Gd BA4 . . . . 205 C5
Clover Mead TA1 . . . . 213 C1
Clover Rd BS22 . . . . 32 A6
Cloverton Dr TA6 . . . . 209 D7
Clover Way TA9 . . . . 104 E4
Clumber Dr BA11 . . . . 119 F6
Clumber Ho BA11 . . . . 119 F6
Clutton Hill BS39 . . . . 59 B4
Clutton Prim Sch BS39 . . . . 58 E3
Clyce Rd TA9 . . . . 104 D3
Clyde Ave BS31 . . . . 24 F4
Clyde Gdns BA2 . . . . 44 B6
Clydesdale Cl BS14 . . . . 23 A6
Clynder Gr BS21 . . . . 6 E6
Clyntonville BS22 . . . . 31 A4
Coach House Mews BS23 . 30 D1
Coachmans Yd BA6 . . . . 206 D5
Coach Rd TA24 . . . . 124 A3
Coalash La BA11 . . . . 119 D8
Coal Barton BA3 . . . . 116 E8
Coalbridge Cl BS22 . . . . 31 F2
Coaley Rd BS11 . . . . 4 D5
Coal La BA11 . . . . 119 C8
Coal Orch TA1 . . . . 212 F4
Coalpit La
Chilcompton BA3 . . . . 96 A2
Stoke St Michael BA3 . . . . 116 B3
Coalpit Rd BA1 . . . . 29 A4
Coape Rd BS14 . . . . 23 F5
Coast Cvn Pk BS21 . . . . 1 B1
Coastguard Cotts TA24 . . 201 A8
Coast Rd TA8 . . . . 84 F7
Coates Est BS48 . . . . 8 F3
Coates Gr BS48 . . . . 9 A2
Coates Wlk BS4 . . . . 22 D6
Coate Turn TA4 . . . . 166 A6
Coat Rd TA12 . . . . 185 D7
Cobblestone Mews BS8 . 226 A4
Cob Castle TA21 . . . . 180 D8
Cobhorn Dr BS13 . . . . 21 F4
Cobley Croft BS21 . . . . 16 C8
Cobthorn Way BS49 . . . . 34 E5
Coburg Cl TA21 . . . . 180 F7
Coburg Villas 11 BA1 . . . . 28 A1
Cock-Crowing Stone
TA20 . . . . 193 D4
Cockers Hill BS39 . . . . 41 C5
Cockhill Elm La BA7 . . . . 214 B4
Cockhill La BA22 . . . . 175 D7
Cockland Hill TA21 . . . . 166 C1
Cockmill La BA4 . . . . 140 F1
Cockpit Hill DT6, DT8 . . . . 199 F4
Cockpit La BA4 . . . . 142 C2
Cock Rd
Buckland Dinham BA2,
BA11 . . . . 100 B5
Horningsham BA12 . . . . 144 C4
Cockrod BA16 . . . . 207 B2
Cock & Yew Tree Hill
BS40 . . . . 38 A2
Cod La BA22 . . . . 196 D7
Codrington Pl BS8 . . . . 226 A3
Cogsall Rd BS14 . . . . 23 F6
Coity Pl BS21 . . . . 6 C4
Coker's La BA12 . . . . 161 F8
Coker Hill BA22 . . . . 196 F8
Coker Hill La BA22 . . . . 197 A7
Coker Ho BA22 . . . . 197 C8
Coker Marsh BA22 . . . . 197 D7
Coker Rd BS22 . . . . 32 B2
Colbourn Cl BA3 . . . . 114 E7
Colbourne Rd BA2 . . . . 44 D1
Colchester Cres BS4 . . . . 22 D7
Cold Harbour
Milborne Port DT9 . . . . 217 D2
Sherborne DT9 . . . . 225 E5
Coldharbour Bsns Pk
DT9 . . . . 225 E6
Coldharbour La BS23 . . . . 48 D3
Cold Harbour La BA22 . . . 196 F6
Coldhills La BA8 . . . . 176 D2
Cold Nose BS28 . . . . 138 D8
Coldpark Gdns BS13 . . . . 21 E5
Coldpark Rd BS13 . . . . 21 E5
Cold Rd TA3 . . . . 182 D6
Coldrick Cl BS14 . . . . 22 F3
Cole's La
Chewton Mendip BA3 . . . . 95 A6
South Petherton TA13 . . . . 220 D3
Cole Cl
Cotford St Luke TA4 . . . . 167 E6
Nether Stowey TA5 . . . . 134 A3
Cole Cross BA22 . . . . 186 C6
Colehouse La BS21 . . . . 16 C8
Cole La 5 TA14 . . . . 185 F4
Colemead BS13 . . . . 22 B5
Cole Mead BA10 . . . . 215 D5
Cole Rd BA10 . . . . 215 D5
Coleridge Cottage* TA5 . . 134 B2
Coleridge Cres TA1 . . . . 213 B3
Coleridge Gdns TA8 . . . . 85 B2
Coleridge Gn TA6 . . . . 208 E5
Coleridge Rd
Bridgwater TA6 . . . . 208 E6
Clevedon BS21 . . . . 6 C3
Nether Stowey TA5 . . . . 134 A2
Weston-Super-Mare BS23 . . . 49 A4
Coleridge Sq TA6 . . . . 208 E6
Coleridge Vale Rd E 1
BS21 . . . . 6 D2
Coleridge Vale Rd N BS21 . . 6 C2
Coleridge Vale Rd S BS21 . . 6 D2
Coleridge Vale Rd W 2
BS21 . . . . 6 C2
Coles's La EX13 . . . . 198 B1
Coles Cotts TA5 . . . . 135 F2
Coles Cross Cotts DT8 . . 199 D5
Coles Gdns BA3 . . . . 98 B5
Coleshill Dr BS13 . . . . 22 B5
Colesmore TA4 . . . . 167 A4
Coles Pl TA20 . . . . 223 C3
Coley La TA19 . . . . 194 F5
Coley Rd BS40 . . . . 75 B4
Colham La TA20 . . . . 194 E1
Colin Ave TA2 . . . . 212 F7
Colin Rd TA2 . . . . 213 A7
Collarway La BA22 . . . . 196 F8
College BA22 . . . . 196 E8
College Cl TA10 . . . . 172 E2
College Ct TA8 . . . . 104 A7
College Fields BS8 . . . . 11 F8
College Gn
Bristol BS1 . . . . 226 C2
Yeovil BA21 . . . . 219 B6
College Rd
Bath BA1 . . . . 27 E1
Bristol, Clifton BS8 . . . . 11 F8
Taunton TA2 . . . . 212 D6
Wells BA5 . . . . 203 E5
College Sq BS1 . . . . 226 C2
College St
Bristol BS1 . . . . 226 C2
Burnham-on-S TA8 . . . . 104 A7
College View
18 Bath BA1 . . . . 28 A1
Taunton TA1 . . . . 212 C2
College Way
Bridgwater TA6 . . . . 209 C6
Taunton TA1 . . . . 212 C1
Colles Cl BA5 . . . . 203 F5
Colles Rd BA5 . . . . 203 F5
Collett Ave BA4 . . . . 205 C5
Collett Cl BS22 . . . . 32 C4
Collett Way BA11 . . . . 120 C7
Colley La TA6 . . . . 209 B4
Colleylake Cotts TA3 . . . . 181 C5
Colley Lane Ind Est TA6 . . 209 B3
Collickshire La TA3 . . . . 170 E6
Collie Cnr BA11 . . . . 118 A1
Collier's La BA11 . . . . 99 D2
Collier Cl BA2 . . . . 78 D8
Colliers La BA1 . . . . 27 F4
Colliers Rise BA3 . . . . 79 A3
Colliers Wlk 4 BS48 . . . . 8 E2
Collin's Farm TA19 . . . . 183 E2
Collingwood Cl
Saltford BS31 . . . . 25 E2
Weston-Super-Mare BS22 . . . 31 E4
Collingwood Ct TA6 . . . . 208 F5
Collins' La TA11 . . . . 173 F7
Collinson Rd BS13 . . . . 22 B5
Collins St BS11 . . . . 4 B8
Collum La BS22 . . . . 31 E6
Colman Rd TA1 . . . . 212 B1
Colmer Rd
Bridgwater TA6 . . . . 208 F7
Yeovil BA21 . . . . 219 B6
Colne Gn BS31 . . . . 25 A4
Colombo Cres BS23 . . . . 48 E3
Colston's Almshouses 1
BS1 . . . . 227 A3
Colston Ave BS1 . . . . 227 A2
Colston Cross EX13 . . . . 198 B4
Colston Fort 2 BS2 . . . . 227 A4
Colston Par BS1 . . . . 227 B1
Colston St BS1 . . . . 227 A3
Colston Yd BS1 . . . . 227 A3
Colton La TA4 . . . . 149 F7
Columbus Ho BA2 . . . . 45 D8
Colyton 11 BS22 . . . . 32 A2
Combe Ave BS20 . . . . 2 C6
Combe Batch BS28 . . . . 108 D4
Combe Batch Rise BS28 . 108 D4
Combe Beacon La TA20 . 193 C7
Combe Cl
Bicknoller TA4 . . . . 132 E2
Yeovil BA21 . . . . 219 A8
Combe Cross
Halse TA4 . . . . 167 B7
Monksilver TA4 . . . . 150 C8
Shillingford EX16 . . . . 164 D4
Combecross Hill TA4 . . . . 150 B8
Combecross La
Monksilver TA4 . . . . 150 B8
Stogumber TA4 . . . . 150 C8
Combe Down CE Prim Sch
BA2 . . . . 45 B1
Combe Down La TA4 . . . . 151 C2
Combe Fields BS20 . . . . 2 C6
Combe Gn BA5 . . . . 204 B7
Combe Gr BA1 . . . . 44 B8
Combe Hay La BA2 . . . . 62 B6
Combe Hill
Barton St David TA11 . . . . 158 A2
Combe St Nicholas TA20 . . 193 D5
Hemyock EX15 . . . . 180 C2
Milborne Port DT9 . . . . 217 B3
Templecombe BA8 . . . . 176 E1
Yenston BA8 . . . . 189 F8
Combe Hill Dro TA20 . . . . 193 C5
Combe Hill La TA7 . . . . 156 B7
Combe La
Brompton Ralph TA4 . . . . 150 B3
Charlton Adam TA11 . . . . 173 F8
Chilton Polden TA7 . . . . 137 B3
Churchstanton TA3 . . . . 181 A2
Combe St Nicholas TA20 . . . 193 B5
Dulverton TA22 . . . . 163 D6
East Anstey TA22 . . . . 162 F6
Exford TA24 . . . . 128 D1
Hallatrow BS39 . . . . 77 B6
Langport TA10 . . . . 171 F7
North Curry TA3 . . . . 170 A4
Parbrook BA4 . . . . 158 D8
Rodhuish TA24 . . . . 131 B3
Wedmore BS28 . . . . 108 D4
Wiveliscombe TA4 . . . . 210 C8
Woolavington TA7 . . . . 136 F4
Combeland La TA22 . . . . 164 A5
Combeland Rd TA24 . . . . 201 B4
Combe Pk
Bath BA1 . . . . 44 C8
Yeovil BA21 . . . . 218 F8
Combe Rd
Bath BA2 . . . . 45 B1
Portishead BS20 . . . . 2 D5
Combe Road Cl BA2 . . . . 45 B1
Combeshead Hill TA22 . . 148 A3
Combeshead La
Brompton Regis TA22 . . . . 148 A4
West Anstey EX36 . . . . 162 A7
Combeside BA2 . . . . 45 A3
Combe Side BS48 . . . . 19 A7
Combe St TA20 . . . . 223 C4
Combe Street La BA21 . . 219 A8
Combe Street Lane Rdbt
BA21 . . . . 218 F8
Combe Sydenham Ctry Pk*
TA4 . . . . 150 A7
Combe Terr TA9 . . . . 136 E8
Combe The
Burrington BS40 . . . . 53 F2
Lydeard St Lawrence TA4 . 151 C2
Comer's Cross TA24 . . . . 146 E6
Comer's Gate TA24 . . . . 146 E6
Comer Rd BS27 . . . . 90 A7
Comeytrowe Ctr TA1 . . . . 212 C1
Comeytrowe La TA1, TA4 . 212 A2
Comeytrowe Orch TA1 . . 212 A2
Comeytrowe Rd TA1 . . . . 212 B1
Comeytrowe Rise TA1 . . . . 212 B2
Comfortable Pl BA1 . . . . 228 A3
Commerce Way TA9 . . . . 104 F2
Commercial Rd
Bristol BS1 . . . . 227 A1
Shepton Mallet BA4 . . . . 205 B6
Commercial Row TA20 . . 223 C4
Commercial Way BS22 . . . 32 B2
Common La
Charlton Adam TA11 . . . . 174 A8
Churchill Green BS25 . . . . 52 B5
Easton-in-G BS20 . . . . 4 B2
Halstock BA22 . . . . 197 C2
Hardington Mandeville
BA22 . . . . 197 A5
Holcombe BA3 . . . . 116 D7
Huish Champflower TA4 . . . 165 D7
Kington Magna SP8 . . . . 177 E1
Marnhull DT10 . . . . 190 E4
North Perrott TA18 . . . . 196 D4
Templecombe BA8 . . . . 177 A1
Wincanton BA9 . . . . 216 D3
Yenston BA8 . . . . 189 F8
Common Moor Dro BA6 . . 206 E7
Common Rd BA9 . . . . 216 E3
Como Ct BS20 . . . . 2 C6
Compass Hill TA1 . . . . 212 E3
Compass Rise TA1 . . . . 212 E3
Compton Acres DT9 . . . . 187 E4
Compton Cl
Shepton Mallet BA4 . . . . 205 B5
Taunton TA2 . . . . 213 A6
Yeovil BA21 . . . . 219 E8
Compton Cnr BA4 . . . . 205 B5
Compton Ct Mews DT9 . . . 187 F3
Compton Dr
Bristol BS9 . . . . 5 C7
Weston-Super-Mare BS24 . . 49 E7
Compton Dundon CE Prim
Sch TA11 . . . . 157 A3
Compton Flats BA21 . . . . 219 C6
Compton Gdns BA11 . . . . 120 D7
Compton Gn BS31 . . . . 24 E4
Compton Hill TA13 . . . . 220 A5
Compton La
Axbridge BS26 . . . . 70 B1
Shepton Mallet BA4 . . . . 205 B2
Compton Rd
Shepton Mallet BA4 . . . . 205 B4
South Cadbury BA22 . . . . 175 D4
South Petherton TA13 . . . . 220 B5
Yeovil BA21 . . . . 187 E3
Compton St
Butleigh BA6 . . . . 157 D4
Compton Dundon TA11 . . . . 157 B4
Comrade Ave BS25 . . . . 70 E8
Concorde Dr BS21 . . . . 6 B1
Condell Cl TA6 . . . . 208 F7
Condor Cl BS22 . . . . 49 D8
Conduit Hill BA11 . . . . 99 B1
Conegore BA22 . . . . 174 D4
Conegore Cnr BA22 . . . . 174 D4
Coneygree BS13 . . . . 21 F6
Conference Ave BS20 . . . . 2 F5
Conference Cl BS20 . . . . 2 F4
Conies The TA2 . . . . 168 E8
Conifer Cl TA24 . . . . 128 D1
Conifer Way BS24 . . . . 49 E5
Coniston Ave BS9 . . . . 5 E6
Coniston Cres BS23 . . . . 48 F4
Coniston Gdns BA21 . . . . 219 A7
Connaught Ho TA6 . . . . 209 C5
Connaught Mans BA2 . . . 228 C3
Connaught Pl BS23 . . . . 48 D8
Connaught Rd BS4 . . . . 22 E8
Connection Rd BA2 . . . . 44 A6
Connelly Dr BS28 . . . . 108 C4
Connock Sq BA4 . . . . 205 C4
Conquest Bsns Pk TA19 . 184 A4
Constable Cl
Keynsham BS31 . . . . 24 F6
Yeovil BA21 . . . . 219 E8
Constable Dr BS22 . . . . 31 F3
Constantine Ct BA4 . . . . 205 E4
Constitution Hill BS8 . . . . 226 B2
Convocation Ave BA2 . . . . 45 E5
Conway Cres TA8 . . . . 85 C1
Conway Gn BS31 . . . . 25 A3
Conway Rd TA5 . . . . 135 B2
Conygar Cl BS21 . . . . 6 F5
Conygar View TA24 . . . . 201 E3
Conygre Gn BA2 . . . . 60 B2
Conygre Rise BA2 . . . . 59 F6
Cook's Folly Rd BS9 . . . . 5 D3
Cook's La
Banwell BS29 . . . . 51 A4
Clevedon BS21 . . . . 7 B2
Cranmore BA4 . . . . 142 A6
Milverton TA4 . . . . 167 B5
Stalbridge DT10 . . . . 190 B2
Cook Ave TA20 . . . . 223 D3
Cooke's La TA10 . . . . 156 B2
Cookley La TA4 . . . . 150 F8
Cooks Bridle Path BS48 . . 36 D8
Cooks Cl TA3 . . . . 169 D5
Cooks Gdns BS48 . . . . 9 A2
Cooks La DT9 . . . . 225 D3
Cooksley La TA4 . . . . 149 A2
Cookson Cl TA8 . . . . 104 D5
Cook St BS11 . . . . 4 C8
Cook Way TA2 . . . . 212 C6
Coombe's Cider Farm &
Mus* TA9 . . . . 106 A4
Coombe's Way BS26 . . . . 87 E8
Coombe DT9 . . . . 225 C5
Coombe Bridge Ave BS9 . . 5 D6
Coombe Brook BA5 . . . . 203 A7
Coombe Cl BA7 . . . . 214 C6
Coombe Cotts BA5 . . . . 204 C7
Coombe Dale
Backwell BS48 . . . . 37 A8
Bristol BS9 . . . . 5 C6
Coombe Dell BA4 . . . . 205 A6
Coombe Gdns BS9 . . . . 5 E6
Coombe Hill
Blagdon Hill TA21 . . . . 181 A5
Bruton BA10 . . . . 215 E7
Coombe La
Bristol BS9 . . . . 5 E6
Compton Bishop BS26 . . . . 69 B4
East Harptree BS40 . . . . 74 E4
Easton-in-G BS8 . . . . 4 A2
Kingsbury Episcopi TA12 . . 185 B8
Shepton Mallet BA4 . . . . 205 A6
Coomb End BA3 . . . . 78 F3
Coombend Ho BA3 . . . . 78 F3
Coombe Rd
Dinnington TA17 . . . . 195 B7
Nailsea BS48 . . . . 8 E1
Weston-Super-Mare BS23 . . . 30 E1
Coombe Side TA9 . . . . 86 B2
Coombe St
Bruton BA10 . . . . 215 E7
Penselwood BA9 . . . . 161 E2
Coombe Terr
Glastonbury BA6 . . . . 206 E5
Sherborne DT9 . . . . 225 C5
Coombe The
Blagdon BS40 . . . . 54 C3
Compton Martin BS40 . . . . 74 A6
Coombe View BA4 . . . . 205 A6
Coombe Water La DT8 . . 199 E5
Coomb Rocke BS9 . . . . 5 D6
Cooper's Ash La BA7,
BA22 . . . . 214 A2
Cooperage La BS3 . . . . 226 B1
Cooperage The BA11 . . . . 119 F3
Cooper Rd BS9 . . . . 5 F7
Coopers Barns BA22 . . . . 174 F1
Coopers Hts TA4 . . . . 210 C4
Coopers Mead BA4 . . . . 205 D4
Coopers Mill TA2 . . . . 168 B4
Coot Hide EX16 . . . . 178 D1
Coots The BS14 . . . . 23 E6
Copeland Dr BS14 . . . . 23 B5
Copford La BS41 . . . . 11 B1
Copis La TA11 . . . . 158 B3
Coplestons TA3 . . . . 168 D1
Copley Gdns BS22 . . . . 31 F2
Coppack Ho 6 BS21 . . . . 6 C2
Copper Beeches TA1 . . . . 212 A2
Copper Beech Rd TA11 . . 173 D5
Copper Cl BS27 . . . . 90 A8
Copperfield Dr BS22 . . . . 31 F4
Coppern Way DT10 . . . . 190 B4
Coppice Cl BA20 . . . . 218 D2
Coppice End Cnr BS24 . . . . 67 C2
Coppice Mews BS21 . . . . 6 C4
Coppice The BS13 . . . . 21 E4
Coppin Cl BA6 . . . . 206 F3
Coppin Rd TA2 . . . . 168 B4
Coppits Hill La
Yeovil BA21 . . . . 218 D8
Yeovil Marsh BA21 . . . . 187 A5
Copplesbury La BA4,
BA10 . . . . 160 D8
Copse Cl
Watchet TA23 . . . . 202 C5
Weston-Super-Mare BS24 . . 49 A1
Copse Cnr BS24 . . . . 67 C2
Copse Dro
Baltonsborough BA6 . . . . 158 C5
Barrington TA19 . . . . 184 B5
Copse End BS25 . . . . 51 F2
Copse La
Ashill TA19 . . . . 183 D4
Barrington TA19 . . . . 184 D4
Hambridge TA3 . . . . 184 B7
Ilton TA19 . . . . 183 F4
Pilton BA4 . . . . 140 F3
Copseland BA2 . . . . 45 D5
Copse Rd
Clevedon BS21 . . . . 6 C4
Keynsham BS31 . . . . 25 C4
Yeovil BA22 . . . . 218 B7
Copse Shoot La TA19 . . . . 184 C5
Copse Stile TA20 . . . . 193 F1
Copse The
Bridgwater TA6 . . . . 209 D5
Cossington TA7 . . . . 136 F3
Frome BA11 . . . . 120 B6
Weston-Super-Mare BS22 . . . 32 D2
Copsewood La BS26 . . . . 88 B2
Copthorne Cl BS14 . . . . 23 B5
Coralberry Dr BS22 . . . . 31 F1
Corams La TA21 . . . . 222 B6
Cording's Ball TA4 . . . . 150 A1
Corewell La TA5 . . . . 133 E3
Corfe Cl BS48 . . . . 8 D1
Corfe Cres BS31 . . . . 24 E4
Corfe Rd BS4 . . . . 22 D7
Corinthian Ct 9 BS1 . . . . 227 B1
Cork Pl BA1 . . . . 44 D7
Corkscrew La
North Cadbury BA22 . . . . 175 E7
Staplegrove TA2 . . . . 212 D8
Cork St
Bath BA1 . . . . 44 D7
Frome BA11 . . . . 119 F5
Cork Terr BA1 . . . . 44 D7
Cormorant Cl
Bridgwater TA6 . . . . 209 C3
Weston-Super-Mare BS22 . . . 31 F1
Cornborough Pl TA6 . . . . 209 B5
Corner Cl TA21 . . . . 222 D4
Corner Croft BS21 . . . . 6 D1
Cornfields The BS22 . . . . 31 F5
Cornhill
Bridgwater TA6 . . . . 208 F5
Shepton Mallet BA4 . . . . 205 C6
Sherborne DT9 . . . . 225 C4
5 Wellington TA21 . . . . 222 D6
Cornhill Dr BS14 . . . . 23 A7
Cornish Gr BS14 . . . . 23 E6
Cornish Rd BS14 . . . . 23 E6
Cornishway E TA1 . . . . 212 B3
Cornishway N TA1 . . . . 212 B3
Cornishway S TA1 . . . . 212 B2
Cornishway W TA1 . . . . 212 B3
Cornish Wlk BS14 . . . . 23 E6
Cornlands EX16 . . . . 178 D1
Cornleaze BS13 . . . . 22 A5
Cornmoor Cres TA9 . . . . 136 E7
Cornmoor La TA9 . . . . 136 E7
Corn St
Bath BA1 . . . . 228 B2
Bristol BS1 . . . . 227 A3
Cornwallis Ave
Bristol BS8 . . . . 226 A2
Weston-Super-Mare BS22 . . . 31 F4
Cornwallis Cres BS8 . . . . 11 F6
Cornwallis Gr BS8 . . . . 226 A2

Cornwall Rd BA4 205 A6
Coromandel Hts BA1 228 B4
Coronation Ave
Bath BA2 44 C4
Keynsham BS31 24 D4
Yeovil BA21 218 F7
Coronation Cl
Ruishton TA3 169 C3
Wanstrow BA4 142 F4
Coronation Ct BA3 115 A3
Coronation Est BS23 48 F3
Coronation Ho TA6 209 C6
Coronation Pl BS1 227 A2
Coronation Rd
Banwell BS29 51 A3
Bath BA1 44 D7
Bleadon BS24 67 C6
Bridgwater TA6 208 E5
Bristol BS3 226 B1
Frome BA11 120 B5
Highbridge TA9 104 D4
Wells BA5 203 B4
Weston-Super-Mare BS22 31 E2
Coronation St TA20 223 C3
Coronation Terr
Chilcompton BA3 96 D5
Oakhill BA3 115 A3
Coronation Villas BA8 176 E1
Corondale Rd BS22 49 D8
Corporate Rd BS22 174 A2
Corporation St TA1 212 F3
Corpus Christi RC Prim Sch
BS23 48 D6
Corrick Cl BS27 90 F2
Corridor The 2 BA1 228 C2
Corsham Dr TA8 104 C8
Corsley CE Prim Sch
BA12 121 D2
Corsley Wlk BS4 22 F8
Corston BS24 49 A2
Corston Dr BA2 43 B6
Corston La BA2 43 A8
Corston View BA2 44 C2
Corston Wlk BS11 4 D7
Corton Cl BA21 219 E8
Coryate Cl BA22 186 C2
Cory Rd TA2 213 A8
Cosgates Feet or County
Gate EX35 122 D5
Cossington La TA7 136 E3
Cossington Prim Sch
TA7 136 F3
Cossington Rd BS4 22 F8
Cossins La TA18 224 C6
Costello Hill BA22 173 F2
Costiland Dr BS13 21 F6
Cote Cnr TA9 136 F7
Cote House La BS9 5 F5
Cote La BA12 161 F6
Cote Paddock BS9 5 F4
Cote Pk BS9 5 E6
Cotford St Luke Prim Sch
TA4 167 E5
Cotham Hill BS6 226 C4
Cotham Lawn Ho BS6 226 C4
Cotham Lawn Rd BS6 226 C4
Cotham Pl BS6 226 C4
Cotham Rd BS6 226 C4
Cotham Rd S BS6 227 A4
Cotham Sch BS6 226 C4
Cothay Manor Gdns*
TA21 179 C8
Cothelstone Cl TA6 208 B4
Cothelstone Rd TA4 151 F1
Cotlake Cl TA1 212 F1
Cotlake Rise TA1 168 E1
Cotleigh Crossing EX14 191 F1
Cotley La TA20 193 D2
Cotman Wlk 1 BS22 31 F2
Cotswold Cl BS20 2 E4
Cotswold Rd BA2 44 E4
Cotswold View BA2 44 B5
Cotswold Way SN14 13 A6
Cottage Cnr TA19 183 F4
Cottage La TA22 163 D6
Cottage Pl
3 Bath BA1 28 C2
Bristol BS2 227 A4
Cottage Row TA8 104 A6
Cottages The BS40 35 D2
Cotterell Ct BA1 228 B2
Cottle Gdns BS14 23 F6
Cottle Rd BS14 23 F6
Cottles La
West Pennard BA6 140 B1
Winsley BA15 64 F6
Cotton's La TA11 158 B2
Cotton Cnr 18 BA8 190 A6
Cotton Mead BA2 43 B7
Coulson's Cl BS14 23 A3
Coulson's Rd BS14 23 A3
Coulson Dr BS22 32 B3
Council Hos
Babcary TA11 174 D7
Bleadon BS24 67 B5
Clapton TA18 195 C1
Hewish TA18 195 D3
Kingston Seymour BS21 16 C3
Podimore BA22 174 A4
Wick St Lawrence BS22 32 B8
Council Houses BS24 33 C3
Council Houses The
Butcombe BS40 55 B8
Hinton Blewett BS39 75 E6
Counterslip BS1 227 B2
Counterslip Gdns BS14 23 C6
Countess Ave TA6 208 E7
Countess Gytha Prim Sch
BA22 174 F3
County Wlk TA1 213 A3
Couple Cross TA24 130 B1
Coursing Batch BA6 206 F3
Court's Barton BA11 119 D2
Court Acres 6 BA22 197 F8
Court Ash BA20 219 B5
Court Ave BS49 34 C7
Court Barton
Crewkerne TA18 224 B6
Ilminster TA19 221 C4
Court Cl
Backwell BS48 19 C5
Portishead BS20 2 D4
Court Cotts SP8 177 D3
Court-de-Wyck CE Prim Sch
BS49 17 F1
Court Dr
Sandford BS25 52 B4
Wellington TA21 222 D5
Courtenay Cres BS4 22 D7
Courtenay Rd BS31 25 B2
Courtenay Wlk BS22 32 A3
Court Farm BA11 100 A3
Court Farm Cl TA20 194 E1
Court Farm Pk* BS29 50 F5
Court Farm Rd BS14 22 F3
Courtfield
Langport TA10 172 A5
Milverton TA4 166 F4
Court Field La TA20 193 B5
Court Fields Com Sch
TA21 222 C5
Court Gdns
Batheaston BA1 29 A4
Marston Magna BA22 174 F1
Yeovil BA21 218 E8
Court Gr TA7 136 C4
Court Hay BS20 4 A4
Court Hill
Compton Dando BS39 41 D5
Taunton TA1 212 D2
Court Ho BS26 70 B2
Court La
7 Barwick BA22 197 F8
Bathford BA1 29 B2
Clevedon BS21 7 A3
Lye's Green BA12 121 B1
Milborne Port DT9 217 C3
Morebath EX16 164 D4
Shipham BS25 70 F8
Courtland Rd TA21 222 D6
Courtlands
Keynsham BS31 24 E5
Norton Fitzwarren TA2 168 B5
Courtlands Cl TA23 202 C6
Courtlands La BS3 11 E4
Courtlands Unit BS4 22 D8
Courtmead BA2 62 F7
Courtmead La TA24 123 F4
Court Mill La TA20 223 A8
Court Moors La TA21 179 E5
Court Orch TA5 135 B2
Court Pl BS22 31 F2
Court Place La TA24 131 B4
Court Rd
Norton Fitzwarren TA2 168 B4
Weston-Super-Mare BS22 31 A5
Court St
5 Bridgwater TA6 208 F5
Winsham TA20 194 E1
Court Terr TA21 222 C5
Court The TA24 131 A5
Court Way EX16 178 D1
Courtway Ave TA6 209 C4
Courtyard The
Dunster TA24 201 E2
Evercreech BA4 141 F2
Minehead TA24 200 F7
Shapwick TA7 137 F1
3 Taunton TA1 212 F4
West Harptree BS40 74 E6
Coverdale Ct BA21 218 F6
Coveyhill La BA4 142 E5
Cowan Cl TA8 104 C7
Cowbridge Cross TA24 200 D1
Cow Bridge Rd BA6 157 C7
Cow Down Rd TA20 194 C1
Cowdray Cl TA24 200 E6
Cowdray Rd
Bristol BS4 22 D7
Minehead TA24 200 E6
Cowen Cl TA18 224 C4
Cowleaze Dro TA3 169 D3
Cowleaze La BS40 74 C6
Cowler Wlk BS13 21 F4
Cowling Dr BS14 23 C5
Cowling Rd BS14 23 D5
Cowl St BA4 205 B7
Cowpath La DT9 176 A1
Cowslip La BS26 68 D3
Cox's Cl
Bruton BA10 215 E5
Glastonbury BA6 206 E6
Cox's Dr BA6 158 A5
Cox's Gn BS40 35 E1
Cox's La TA4 167 C5
Coxbridge Dro BA6 158 A6
Cox Hill DT10 190 E4
Coxland's Rock TA4 167 B7
Coxley Dr BA1 28 B2
Coxley Prim Sch BA5 139 E6
Coxley Vineyard* BA5 139 E6
Cox Rd TA21 222 C4
Coxs Cl BA22 175 D6
Coxton End La BA5 92 B3
Coxway BS21 6 F2
Coxwithy La BA6 139 D1
Coxwynne Cl BA3 97 C8
Crabtree Cl BS41 21 D1
Crab Tree Dro BA6 206 F8
Crabtree La
Curry Rivel TA10 171 C1
Dundry BS41 21 D2
Wyke Champflower BA10 215 B7
Crackmore DT9 217 C1
Craig Lea TA2 212 E7
Cranberry Wlk BS9 5 C8
Cranbourne Chase BS23 31 A1
Cranbourne Cl TA6 208 F6
Crancombe La TA7 136 D3
Crandale Rd 3 BA2 44 D5
Crane Cotts BA4 142 B6
Crane Hill TA10, TA11 173 C4
Cranes Cl TA2 213 D7
Cranford Cl BS22 31 D1
Crangs La BA22 175 D4
Cranhill Rd
Bath BA1 44 D8
Street BA16 207 B6
Cranleigh BA2 62 F8
Cranleigh Ct TA13 220 B4
Cranleigh Gdns
Bridgwater TA6 209 A4
Bristol BS9 5 E4
Cranleigh Rd BS14 23 B5
Cranmer Rd TA1 213 A4
Cranmore BS24 49 A2
Cranmore Ave BS31 24 E6
Cranmore Ct 3 BA11 119 E3
Cranmore Pl BA2 62 E8
Cranmore Sta* BA4 142 A5
Cranmore View BA11 119 D2
Cranmore West Sta*
BA4 142 A5
Cransey La
Washford TA4, TA23 131 F2
Williton TA4 132 A2
Crantock Ave BS13 22 B8
Cranway La TA20 223 F2
Cranwell Cl TA7 154 F5
Cranwell Gr BS14 23 A5
Cranwell Rd BS24 50 C5
Cranwells Pk BA1 44 D8
Crapnell La BA5 140 F8
Crawford Cl 1 BS21 6 B1
Crawford La BA22 175 D7
Crawlic La TA4 151 E1
Crawl La BA3 78 C4
Crawter Dr TA24 124 A3
Craydon Gr BS14 23 D4
Craydon Rd BS14 23 D5
Craydon Wlk BS14 23 D5
Crease Cl BA5 203 B4
Create Ctr* BS1 11 F5
Crediton 5 BS22 32 A2
Creechbarrow Rd TA1 213 C5
Creechberry Orch TA1 213 D5
Creeches La BA16 156 D7
Creech Hill La BA10 215 B7
Creech Mill Est TA3 169 C4
Creech Paper Mill TA3 169 C4
Creech St Michael CE Prim
Sch TA3 169 D4
Creechwood Terr TA3 169 D5
Creedwell Cl TA4 167 A4
Creedwell Orch TA4 167 A4
Creighton Cl BA5 140 C8
Crescent Gdns BA1 228 A3
Crescent La BA1 228 B4
Crescent The
Backwell BS48 19 A6
Bristol, Sea Mills BS9 5 C6
4 Carhampton TA24 131 A5
Coleford BA3 117 A7
Farrington Gurney BS39 77 B3
Golsoncott TA23 131 D1
Ilminster TA19 221 B2
Lympsham BS24 67 C5
South Cadbury BA22 175 E4
Stanton Drew BS39 39 F1
Taunton TA1 212 F3
Weston-Super-Mare BS22 31 B1
Yeovil BA20 219 A4
Crescent View BA2 228 B1
Crescent View Ct BS22 31 B1
Crescent Way TA1 212 F3
Creslands Ind Units BS24 49 A3
Cressey The TA19 184 E4
Cresswell Ave TA2 212 D7
Cresswell Cl BS22 32 A2
Crestfield Ave TA6 208 F7
Creswicke Rd BS4 22 E7
Creswick Way TA8 104 C8
Crewkerne Bsns Pk
TA18 224 D6
Crewkerne Cl BS48 9 B1
Crewkerne Hospl TA18 224 B5
Crewkerne Rd TA20 223 E4
Crewkerne Sta TA18 224 E4
Crewkerne Turning
EX13 198 C6
Cribb's La BS40 36 D1
Crib Cl TA20 223 D6
Crib House La BS28 89 C1
Crickback La BS40 39 A3
Cricket Cotts TA3 170 B3
Cricket Cross TA19 194 C6
Cricket Field Gn BS48 8 D2
Cricket La TA19, TA20 194 C6
Cricket St Thomas Miniature
Rly* TA20 194 E3
Cricket St Thomas Wildlife
Pk* TA20 194 E3
Cricket View DT9 225 D3
Crickham La BS28 108 D8
Cricklade Ct BS48 9 A1
Cridlake 7 EX13 198 A1
Cridlands Mdw TA6 208 E6
Crimchard TA20 223 B5
Crimthorne Cotts TA3 183 A7
Cripple St TA12 185 D7
Crispin Ctr BA16 207 C6
Crispin Sch BA16 207 D7
Critch Hill BA11 119 C3
Critchill Cl BA11 119 D3
Critchill Gr BA11 119 D3
Critchill Rd BA11 119 D3
Critchill Sch BA11 119 C4
Crocker's Hill BA9 175 F8
Crockerne CE Prim Sch
BS20 4 C4
Crockerne Dr BS20 4 C3
Crockerne Ho BS20 4 D4
Crockers Hill TA7 136 E4
Crocombe BA2 60 C3
Crocombe La BA2 60 C3
Croford Hill TA4 166 E6
Croft Cl BS30 25 D8
Croft Cotts
Moorlinch TA7 155 E7
Wrantage TA3 170 B1
Croft La
Brushford TA22 163 C4
Skilgate TA4 164 E6
Westbury-sub-Mendip BA5 110 C6
Croftland La TA10 171 E2
Croft Mdw TA4 202 F1
Crofton Ave BA21 219 B6
Crofton Ct BA21 219 B5
Crofton Pk BA21 219 B5
Crofton Rd BA21 219 B6
Croft Rd
Bath BA1 28 B1
Holcombe BA3 116 C8
Crofts Mead BA9 216 C2
Croft The
Backwell BS48 19 A7
Cheddar BS27 90 C8
Clevedon BS21 6 F4
Hutton BS24 49 E3
Mark TA9 106 A4
Monkton Combe BA2 45 E1
Watchet TA23 202 C7
Westwood BA15 64 F3
Williton TA4 202 D3
Wookey Hole BA5 203 A8
Yeovil BA20 218 C2
Croft Way TA4 210 C4
Croftways TA4 202 D4
Cromer Ct BS21 6 D5
Cromer Rd BS23 48 E5
Cromwell Dr BS22 32 A4
Cromwell Rd
Bridgwater TA6 209 A2
Taunton TA1 213 B5
Yeovil BA21 219 D6
Crooked La
Brent Knoll TA9 85 E3
Burnham-on-S TA8 85 D1
Cucklington SP8 177 E6
Rode BA11 101 E7
Crookes La BS22 31 A4
Crookhorn Hill TA24 129 C7
Cropmead Trad Est
TA18 224 D6
Crosby Row BS8 226 A2
Croscombe CE Prim Sch
BA5 204 C7
Croscombe Gdns BA11 120 D6
Crossacre TA6 208 D6
Crosscombe Dr BS13 22 C3
Cross Combe Wlk BS13 22 B3
Crosscroft Cotts TA4 151 A3
Crosselm Rd BA4 143 A2
Cross Elms Hill TA5 133 F7
Cross Elms La BS9 5 E5
Cross Farm Cl TA24 201 A5
Cross Farm Rd BS27 90 F3
Crossfield Cl TA6 208 D6
Crossfields DT9 187 F4
Crossing Dro BS28 109 D3
Cross Keys Cl TA2 212 A7
Cross La
Axbridge BS26 70 A2
Brendon EX35 122 A4
Long Sutton TA10 172 F4
Crossland La EX14 191 F2
Crosslands TA21 222 B8
Cross Lanes BS20 4 C4
Crossman Wlk BS21 6 F2
Crossmead TA7 136 E4
Cross Moor Dr BS26 70 B1
Cross Moor Dro BS26 69 E1
Cross Moor Rd BS26 70 B1
Crosspost La BA2 42 B4
Cross Rd DT9 187 E1
Crossroads The BA9 216 C3
Cross St
Burnham-on-S TA8 104 A7
Keynsham BS31 24 F7
3 Weston-Super-Mare
BS23 48 E7
Cross The
Baltonsborough BA6 158 A5
Bradford Abbas DT9 187 E1
Buckland Dinham BA11 100 A3
East Harptree BS40 74 F4
9 Henstridge BA8 190 A6
Ilminster TA19 221 C3
Milverton TA4 167 A4
Minehead TA24 200 F8
Nether Stowey TA5 134 B2
Cross The *continued*
Street BA16 207 D7
Cross View Rise TA6 208 D6
Crossway TA1 213 C5
Cross Way DT9 187 E1
Crossway La BA3 96 B7
Crossways
Coleford BA3 116 F7
Tatworth TA20 198 D8
Crossways Cvn Pk BA2 61 F5
Crossways Rd TA6 209 B1
Crosswell Cl 7 TA6 153 E3
Cross Wlk BS14 23 A6
Crouds La TA10 172 E4
Crow's Hill BA4 142 C1
Crow Castle La TA18 224 B7
Crowcombe CE Fst Sch
TA4 151 C7
Crowcombe Heathfield Sta*
TA4 151 B5
Crowcombe Rd TA2 212 F8
Crowcombe Wlk TA6 208 C4
Crowe Hill BA3 64 B5
Crowe La BA3 64 B5
Crow La
Ashill TA19 183 C4
Bridgwater TA7 209 E7
Bristol BS1 227 A2
Broadway TA19 194 A8
Slape Cross TA7 209 E6
Westbury-sub-Mendip BA5 110 E6
Crown Cl TA2 213 C6
Crowne Trad Est BA4 205 D5
Crown Gdns BA11 119 F3
Crown Glass Pl 5 BS48 8 E2
Crown Hill
Bath BA1 27 C1
West Buckland TA21 180 F7
Winford BS40 38 A5
Crown Ho BS48 8 C1
Crown Ind Est TA2 213 C6
Crown La
Creech St Michael TA3 169 D6
South Petherton TA13 220 C4
Crown Mews TA21 180 F7
Crown Rd BA1 27 B1
Crown Wlk TA1 212 F3
Crowpill Cotts TA6 208 F6
Crowpill La TA6 208 F6
Crowshute Flats TA20 223 C3
Crowshute Link TA20 223 C3
Crufts Mdw TA3 169 D4
Crusader Cl TA6 208 E6
Crusty La BS20 4 C5
Cruwy's Cross TA4 210 B7
Crypton Tech Bsns Pk
TA6 209 B8
Cuck Hill BS25 70 E7
Cuckold's Row TA5 152 E8
Cuckoo Cnr TA1 213 B2
Cuckoo Hill
Bruton BA10 160 D6
Frome BA11 119 E8
Cuckoo La
Frome BA11 119 F8
High Littleton BS39 59 B3
Thorncombe TA20 199 C7
Wraxall BS48 9 A6
Cuffs Mead TA20 223 F1
Cufic La BS27 90 C8
Culliford Cl BA16 207 D7
Culliver's Grave BA22 197 C8
Culmhead Cl TA1 212 D1
Culmstock Prim Sch
EX15 179 E1
Culvecliffe Ct TA24 125 C4
Culvercliffe Rd TA23 202 D7
Culverhay BS39 41 D6
Culverhay Cl TA7 136 C4
Culverhayes TA20 223 C2
Culverhay La TA4 210 B4
Culverhay Sch BA2 44 B2
Culverhays La TA4 132 F1
Culverhill BA11 119 F3
Culver Hill TA10 172 B7
Culver La
Carhampton TA24 131 B4
East Harptree BS40 74 F3
Culverlake La EX13 199 A3
Culvers Cl
Keynsham BS31 24 E6
Sherborne DT9 225 C4
Culvers Rd BS31 24 E6
Culver St BS1 226 C2
Culver Street La TA5 134 A7
Culvert Dro BS27 109 B6
Culverwell Cotts BA4 140 F3
Culverwell Rd BS13 22 A4
Cumberland Basin Rd
BS8 11 F5
Cumberland Cl BS1 226 A1
Cumberland Ho BA1 228 A2
Cumberland Pl 6 BS8 11 F6
Cumberland Rd BS1 226 B1
Cumberland Row BA1 228 B2
Cumberland St BS2 227 B4
Cumhill Hill BA4 140 E3
Cumnock Cres BA7 214 C6
Cumnock Rd BA7 214 C6
Cumnock Terr BA7 214 C6
Cunningham Ave EX13 198 A2
Cunningham Rd TA8 104 C7
Curdleigh La TA3 181 D5
Curland Gr BS14 23 B5
Curlew Cl TA24 201 C4

Curlew Gdns BS22 ... 31 F1
Currells La BS40 ... 20 B1
Curriott Hill TA18 ... 224 B4
Curriott Hill Rd TA18 ... 224 B5
Curry Hole La BA22 ... 197 C2
Curry La TA3 ... 169 E6
Curry Mallet CE Prim Sch TA3 ... 183 D8
Currymead La TA10 ... 171 C2
Currypool La TA5 ... 134 E1
Curry Rivel CE Prim Sch TA10 ... 171 D4
Currywoods Way TA10 ... 171 D4
Curtis Units BA11 ... 119 E2
Curvalion House Gdns TA3 ... 169 D4
Curvalion Rd TA3 ... 169 D4
Cushuish La TA2, TA5 ... 152 C2
Cushuish Lane Cotts TA2 ... 152 B1
Cussacombe Gate EX36 ... 145 J1
Custom Cl BS14 ... 23 A7
Custom Ho
Bristol BS1 ... 227 A1
Minehead TA24 ... 201 B7
Cutcombe CE Fst Sch TA24 ... 129 E1
Cutcombe Cross TA24 ... 129 E1
Cutcombe Hill TA24 ... 129 F2
Cuthays La EX13 ... 198 B1
Cuthbert St TA9 ... 104 D3
Cutler Rd BS13 ... 21 F6
Cutliff Cl TA1 ... 212 E1
Cuts Rd TA3, TA7 ... 170 E8
Cutter's Wharf TA24 ... 201 B7
Cutt Mill La DT10 ... 190 F3
Cut Tongue La TA20 ... 193 C7
Cutty Cotts BA22 ... 175 D6
Cutty La BA22 ... 175 D6
Cygnet Cres BS22 ... 31 F1
Cynthia Rd BA2 ... 44 D5
Cypress Ct
Bristol BS9 ... 5 D3
Somerton TA11 ... 211 E4
Cypress Dr
Puriton TA7 ... 136 C4
Yeovil BA20 ... 218 F2
Cypress Gdns BS8 ... 11 E6
Cypress Terr BA3 ... 78 D1
Cypress Way BA11 ... 120 C7
Cyril St W TA2 ... 212 E6
Cyril St TA2 ... 212 E6

D

Dabinett Cl TA2 ... 168 B5
Dafford's Bldgs BA1 ... 28 C2
Dafford St BA1 ... 28 C2
Dagg's La BS28 ... 138 E8
Dagg's Lane Dro BA5, BS28 ... 138 D7
Daghole BS27 ... 90 C8
Daglands The BA2 ... 78 E8
Dahlia Gdns BA2 ... 45 B7
Dairs Orch TA20 ... 198 C8
Dairy Cl BA5 ... 203 B5
Dairycroft BS2 ... 227 B4
Dairy Ct 3 TA18 ... 224 C5
Dairy Flats DT9 ... 225 E5
Dairy Hill BA2 ... 80 B5
Dairy House La TA3 ... 182 E5
Dairylands TA24 ... 131 D4
Daisey Bank BA2 ... 45 B4
Daisyfield BA22 ... 188 A8
Dakota Dr BS14 ... 23 A4
Dale La BA5 ... 92 C3
Dale St BS2 ... 227 C4
Daley Cl BS22 ... 32 B3
Dalimores La BA11 ... 143 B8
Dalleston BA3 ... 114 C8
Dallimore Mead BA11 ... 143 B8
Dalton Sq BS2 ... 227 B4
Dalwood 12 BS22 ... 32 A2
Dalwoods DT9 ... 225 D3
Dame Court Cl BS22 ... 31 F4
Dame Withycombe Villas TA5 ... 135 B5
Dampier Pl BA21 ... 219 C5
Dampier St BA21 ... 219 C5
Dampiet St TA6 ... 208 F4
Damson Rd BS22 ... 49 E7
Dancey Mead BS13 ... 21 F6
Dancing Cross BA9 ... 176 B5
Dancing Hill TA6 ... 153 E4
Dancing La BA9 ... 216 A4
DandO's La BS28 ... 108 C4
Dandy's Mdw BS20 ... 2 E4
Dane's Lea BS28 ... 108 C4
Daneacre Rd BA3 ... 79 A3
Dane Cl BA15 ... 64 E7
Dane Rise BA15 ... 64 E7
Danesboro Rd TA6 ... 208 C4
Danesborough View TA4 ... 202 D3
Danesborough View E TA4 ... 202 D3
Danesborough View W TA4 ... 202 D3
Danes Cl EX14 ... 191 F2
Danesfield CE Com Mid Sch TA4 ... 202 D4
Dangerfield Ave BS13 ... 21 F6
Daniel Cl BS21 ... 6 F3
Daniel Mews BA2 ... 45 B7
Danielsfield Rd BA20 ... 218 F2
Daniels La BA5 ... 111 A4
Daniel St BA2 ... 45 B7
Dapps Hill BS31 ... 24 F5
Dapwell La BS14, BS31 ... 24 A1
Darby's Knap TA24 ... 147 C5
Darby Cl SP8 ... 161 F1
Darby Way TA4 ... 151 F1
Darcis Row TA20 ... 223 B4
Dare Cl TA2 ... 213 A8
Darkey La BA10 ... 215 F7
Darkfield Way TA7 ... 136 E3
Dark La
Backwell BS48 ... 19 B5
Banwell BS29 ... 51 C2
Berkley BA11 ... 120 E8
Blagdon BS40 ... 54 E3
Chew Magna BS40 ... 38 F3
Freshford BA3 ... 64 B5
Hockworthy EX16 ... 178 B8
Holcombe BA3 ... 97 C1
Kilmersdon BA11 ... 98 A1
North Wootton BA4 ... 140 C5
Sandford Orcas DT9 ... 188 C7
Seavington St Mary TA19 ... 184 E1
Stoke St Gregory TA3 ... 170 F6
Stoke St Michael BA3 ... 116 C2
Upton Noble BA4 ... 142 F2
Wellington TA21 ... 222 D5
Witham Friary BA11 ... 143 D2
Darlick Cnr EX36 ... 145 G4
Darlington Mews BA2 ... 45 B7
Darlington Pl BA2 ... 45 B6
Darlington Rd BA2 ... 45 B8
Darlington St BA2 ... 45 B7
Darmead BS24 ... 32 B1
Dartmouth Ave BA2 ... 44 C5
Dartmouth Cl BS22 ... 32 A2
Dartmouth Wlk BS31 ... 24 D4
Dart Rd BS21 ... 6 D1
Darwin Cl TA2 ... 212 B6
Dashwoods La TA4 ... 132 E2
Daubeny Ct BS1 ... 227 A1
Daunton Cl TA9 ... 104 D4
David's La TA19 ... 184 F2
David's Rd BS14 ... 23 C6
David St BS2 ... 227 C3
Davies Cl
Bridgwater TA6 ... 208 F2
Winsham TA20 ... 194 E1
Davies Ct BA5 ... 203 B4
Davin Cres BS20 ... 4 C3
Davis La BS21 ... 16 F8
Davis St BS11 ... 4 B8
Davis Terr 5 BA5 ... 203 C4
Daw's La DT9 ... 176 A3
Dawbins Dr TA7 ... 136 E4
Dawes Cl BS21 ... 6 D1
Dawes Ct 2 BS8 ... 11 F6
Daws Cl TA6 ... 208 E2
Daws La TA6 ... 153 E3
Daws Mead TA1 ... 212 A3
Day Cres BA2 ... 43 F6
Deacon Rd TA6 ... 209 C6
Deacons Cl BS22 ... 31 E2
Deacons Ct BS22 ... 31 C1
Deacons La BA21 ... 187 D6
Deacon Way TA8 ... 104 B6
Deadlands La TA12, TA13 ... 185 A6
Dead Maids Cross Rd BA13 ... 121 E5
Deadman's Hill DT9 ... 176 A1
Deadmill La BA1 ... 28 C3
Dead Woman's Cnr BA12 ... 161 F8
Deal Cl TA6 ... 209 D5
Dean's Cross
Allerford TA24 ... 124 E3
Lydeard St Lawrence TA4 ... 151 A4
Dean's La
Allerford TA24 ... 124 E3
Brompton Ralph TA4 ... 150 F4
Dean Cl
Frome BA11 ... 120 C6
Weston-Super-Mare BS22 ... 32 B3
Deane Cl TA4 ... 150 D8
Deane Dr TA1 ... 212 B2
Deane Gate Ave TA1 ... 213 E5
Deanery Rd BS1 ... 226 C2
Deanery Wlk BA3 ... 64 C6
Deanesly Way BA9 ... 216 D3
Deane Way TA20 ... 198 D8
Deanhill La BA1 ... 27 A2
Dean La
Dunster TA24 ... 201 D3
Milverton TA4 ... 167 A6
Oakhill BA3 ... 115 A3
Deansley Way BA9 ... 216 E3
Deans Mead BS11 ... 5 A8
Deans Pl 8 BA5 ... 203 D4
Dean St BS2 ... 227 B4
Deans The BS20 ... 2 B4
Dean Vale Pk TA4 ... 167 C4
Debecca's La BS20 ... 4 B4
De Combe Ho TA18 ... 224 D6
De Corcis Cl TA5 ... 134 A3
Decoy La TA11 ... 157 A2
Deep La BA12 ... 121 E1
Deepleigh La TA4 ... 210 C7
Deerleap
Easton BA5 ... 111 B6
Shipham BS25 ... 70 F8
Deer Mead BS21 ... 6 B1
Deerswood Gdns BA16 ... 207 A6
Deer View TA24 ... 201 C4
Delapre Rd BS23 ... 48 D3
Delhorn La BS24 ... 86 C7
Delius Gr BS4 ... 22 D7
Deller's Wharf TA1 ... 212 F5
Dellers Ct TA1 ... 212 F5
Dellshore Cl TA20 ... 223 D4
Dell The
Bristol, Westbury on T BS9 ... 5 F5
Minehead TA24 ... 200 E6
Nailsea BS48 ... 8 D2
Weston-Super-Mare BS22 ... 31 E4
Delmore Rd BA11 ... 119 E3
Delta Cl BA11 ... 119 F5
Delta Ct 1 BA11 ... 119 F5
Delta Rise TA4 ... 151 E1
Demelza Ct BA22 ... 174 D3
De Montalt Pl BA2 ... 45 B1
Dempier Mews BA22 ... 218 B6
Dene Cl BS31 ... 24 F3
Dene Cross TA4 ... 167 F7
Dene Gdns TA24 ... 201 B4
Dene Rd
Cotford St Luke TA4 ... 167 F6
Whitchurch BS14 ... 23 C4
Dening Cl TA20 ... 223 C6
Denleigh Cl BS14 ... 23 A4
Denman's La
Barrington TA19 ... 184 D5
Cannington TA5 ... 135 B2
Denmark Ave BS1 ... 226 C2
Denmark Rd BA2 ... 44 D6
Denmark St BS1 ... 226 C2
Denmark Terr TA2 ... 212 F7
Dennett Cl BA4 ... 205 E4
Denning Cl TA1 ... 212 B1
Denning Ct BS22 ... 32 B4
Dennington La
Churchinford EX14 ... 192 C6
Dulverton TA22 ... 163 B4
Dennor Pk BS14 ... 23 B7
Denny Cl BS20 ... 2 A5
Denny La BS40 ... 39 B1
Denny View BS20 ... 2 A5
Dennyview Rd BS8 ... 10 F8
Denston Dr BS20 ... 2 E4
Denston Wlk BS13 ... 22 A7
Dentwood Gr BS9 ... 5 B8
Denzil Cl BA22 ... 197 A8
Derham Cl BS49 ... 34 B8
Derham Ct BS49 ... 34 B8
Derham Pk BS49 ... 34 B8
Derham Rd BS13 ... 22 A5
Derricke Rd BS14 ... 23 F6
Dertfords BA12 ... 144 D8
Derwent Gdns BA21 ... 219 D6
Derwent Gr
Keynsham BS31 ... 25 A5
Taunton TA1 ... 213 E4
Derwent Rd BS23 ... 49 A5
Derwent Way BA21 ... 218 C6
Devenish La BA9 ... 216 F4
Deveron Gr BS31 ... 25 A4
Devonia Pk TA4 ... 168 A1
Devonshire Bldgs BA2 ... 44 F4
Devonshire Ct BS23 ... 48 E4
Devonshire Dr BS20 ... 1 F5
Devonshire Mews BA2 ... 44 F3
Devonshire Pl BA2 ... 44 F4
Devonshire Rd
Bathampton BA2 ... 28 E1
Weston-Super-Mare BS23 ... 48 E4
Devonshire St TA6 ... 209 B5
Devonshire Villas BA2 ... 44 F3
Dewar Cl TA8 ... 104 C7
Dew Water La TA11 ... 211 D5
Dial's Gate La BA6, TA11 ... 158 D4
Dial Hill Rd BS21 ... 6 D4
Dial La BS40 ... 20 D1
Diamond Batch BS24 ... 32 B1
Dibbens Row BA9 ... 161 A2
Dibbles La BA22 ... 197 A8
Dickenson's Gr BS49 ... 34 E3
Dickenson Rd BS23 ... 48 E6
Digby Ct DT9 ... 225 D3
Digby Rd DT9 ... 225 D3
Dighton Ct 3 BS2 ... 227 A4
Dighton St BS2 ... 227 A4
Digland La TA24 ... 129 F5
Dilkes La TA11 ... 174 C7
Dillington Farm Cotts TA19 ... 221 E5
Dillington Ho TA19 ... 221 D6
Dillons Rd TA3 ... 169 D4
Dimmer La BA7 ... 159 B2
Dinder Cl BS48 ... 18 E8
Dinghurst Rd BS25 ... 52 E4
Dingle Cl BS9 ... 5 C6
Dingle Ct BS13 ... 21 F7
Dingle Rd BS9 ... 5 D7
Dingle The BS9 ... 5 D7
Dingle View BS9 ... 5 C7
Dinglewood Cl BS9 ... 5 D7
Dinhams TA3 ... 169 C4
Dinhay DT10 ... 190 F6
Dipford Rd TA3 ... 168 D1
Dipland Gr BS40 ... 54 F2
Disraeli Pl TA1 ... 212 D5
Ditcheat Prim Sch BA4 ... 159 C7
Ditch Furlong Rd TA7 ... 137 A2
Ditton St TA19 ... 221 C3
Dixon Gdns BA1 ... 27 F1
Dobree Pk TA21 ... 222 A4
Dock Gate La BS8 ... 226 A1
Doctor's Hill BA5 ... 111 B1
Dodd's Cnr BA9 ... 215 E1
Dodd Ave BA5 ... 203 F5
Dodge Cross DT9 ... 225 F5
Dodham Cres BA20 ... 218 F4
Dod La BA6 ... 206 E4
Dog Down Cross EX16 ... 178 A8
Doleberrow BS25 ... 52 F3
Dolebury Warren Nature Reserve* BS40 ... 53 A3
Dolemead La BS27 ... 90 E2
Dolemoor La
Congresbury BS49 ... 34 A4
Congresbury BS49 ... 34 C3
Dolling's Rd TA3 ... 181 B4
Dolling Cl TA20 ... 223 D6
Dolphin Sq BS23 ... 48 D7
Dominion Rd BA2 ... 44 A6
Dominy Cl TA20 ... 223 D3
Dommett's La BA11 ... 119 D4
Dommett Cl EX13 ... 198 A2
Domus Dr BA4 ... 205 E4
Donald Rd BS13 ... 21 F7
Doniford Beach Halt TA23 ... 202 E6
Doniford Dr TA4 ... 202 D3
Doniford Mdw TA23 ... 202 F6
Doniford Orch TA23 ... 202 F6
Doniford Rd
Watchet TA23 ... 202 E6
Williton TA4 ... 202 D4
Donne La BA22 ... 186 C2
Donnes Terr BA7 ... 214 B5
Donnington Wlk BS31 ... 24 D4
Donstan Rd TA9 ... 104 E5
Donyatt Hill TA19 ... 183 D1
Donyatt Hill Est TA19 ... 183 D1
Doone Way TA24 ... 201 B4
Dorchester Cl 6 BS48 ... 8 D1
Dorchester Rd
Barwick BA22 ... 197 F7
East Coker BA22 ... 197 F5
Taunton TA2 ... 213 A8
Yeovil BA22 ... 219 A1
Dorchester St BA1 ... 228 C1
Dore Cl BA21 ... 218 C7
Dormeads View 6 BS24 ... 49 F7
Dorset Cl
Bath BA2 ... 44 D6
Frome BA11 ... 119 E5
Highbridge TA9 ... 104 E2
Dorset Ho BA2 ... 44 D3
Dorset Rd TA6 ... 209 C3
Dorset St BA2 ... 44 D6
Doster's La TA2 ... 169 C6
Double Gates Dro TA11 ... 158 A3
Double Hill BA2 ... 79 F7
Douglas Ct 3 BS23 ... 48 F5
Douglas Dr BA4 ... 205 B5
Douglas Rd BS23 ... 48 F5
Douglas Yates Ct BA3 ... 116 F7
Doulting Ct BA11 ... 120 D7
Doulting Hill BA4 ... 205 F4
Doulton Way BS14 ... 23 B5
Dovai Dr TA6 ... 208 E7
Dove Cots Cl BA16 ... 207 C7
Dove La BS2 ... 227 C4
Dover Ho BA1 ... 228 C4
Dover Pl
6 Bath BA1 ... 28 A1
Bristol BS8 ... 226 B3
Dover Rd TA2 ... 213 A8
Dovers La BA1 ... 29 C2
Dovers Pk BA1 ... 29 C2
Dovery Manor Mus* TA24 ... 124 A3
Dove St S BS2 ... 227 A4
Dove St BS2 ... 227 A4
Doveswell Gr BS13 ... 22 A4
Dovetail Ct 1 TA1 ... 212 E3
Dovetail Dr BS23 ... 49 A7
Dovetons Cl TA4 ... 202 E3
Dovetons Dr TA4 ... 202 E3
Dowding Rd BA1 ... 28 B1
Dowell Cl TA2 ... 212 C6
Dowland 13 BS22 ... 32 A2
Dowland Gr BS4 ... 22 D6
Dowling La BA6 ... 158 A5
Dowling Rd BS13 ... 22 D3
Dowlish La TA19 ... 194 F5
Down's Orch BA6 ... 138 C4
Downash La EX13 ... 198 E3
Down Ave BA2 ... 45 A1
Down Cl BS20 ... 1 F4
Downclose La TA18 ... 196 C3
Downend Cres TA6 ... 136 B4
Downend Rd TA6 ... 136 B4
Downend Terr TA6 ... 136 B4
Downey Field La TA18 ... 196 D6
Downfield
Bristol BS9 ... 5 C7
Keynsham BS31 ... 24 D5
Downhall Dr TA6 ... 208 D6
Downhead La BA22 ... 174 C5
Down La
Bathampton BA2 ... 28 F1
Buckland Dinham BA11 ... 99 C3
Shepton Montague BA9 ... 160 B2
Sherborne DT9 ... 188 A5
Trent DT9 ... 187 F5
West Pennard BA4, BA6 ... 140 C1
Downland Cl 5 BS48 ... 8 D1
Downlands La EX15, TA3 ... 181 A2
Downleaze
Bristol, Stoke Bishop BS9 ... 5 F3
Portishead BS20 ... 2 A5
Yeovil BA20 ... 218 D2
Downleaze Rd BS9 ... 5 F3
Down Rd BS20 ... 1 F4
Downs Cl BS22 ... 31 F1
Downs Cote Ave BS9 ... 5 F6
Downs Cote Dr BS9 ... 5 F6
Downside
Portishead BS20 ... 2 C5
Street BA16 ... 207 D6
Downside Abbey* BA3 ... 96 E2
Downside Cl
Bathampton BA2 ... 28 F1
Chilcompton BA3 ... 96 D3
Downside Rd
Backwell BS48 ... 36 E8
Weston-Super-Mare BS23 ... 48 F4
Downside Sch BA3 ... 96 E2
Downslade La TA10 ... 172 D5
Downs Rd BS41 ... 21 D2
Downs Sch The BS48 ... 9 C8
Downs The BS20 ... 2 B4
Downsway BS39 ... 77 D6
Downton Rd BS13 ... 22 D8
Down View BA3 ... 97 F8
Dowry Pl 3 BS8 ... 11 F5
Dowry Rd BS8 ... 226 A2
Dowry Sq BS8 ... 226 A2
Dowsland Way TA1 ... 213 C1
Dozen's Cnr TA17 ... 195 A7
Dragon Cross TA24 ... 131 D3
Dragonfly Chase BA22 ... 173 E2
Dragons Hill Cl BS31 ... 24 F5
Dragons Hill Ct BS31 ... 24 F5
Dragons Hill Gdns BS31 ... 24 F5
Drake's Cl TA3 ... 169 C4
Drake Ave BA2 ... 44 F2
Drake Cl
Saltford BS31 ... 25 D2
Staplegrove TA2 ... 212 B7
Weston-Super-Mare BS22 ... 31 F4
Drake Rd BA5 ... 203 F6
Drakes Cl TA6 ... 208 F5
Drakes Cres TA20 ... 198 D8
Drakes Mdw
East Coker BA22 ... 197 C7
Yarcombe EX14 ... 192 D3
Drakes Pk TA21 ... 222 D7
Drakes Pk N TA21 ... 222 D7
Drakes Way BS20 ... 2 B5
Drang The
Coxley BA5 ... 139 E6
Evercreech BA4 ... 141 E1
Porlock TA24 ... 124 A3
Dransfield Way BA2 ... 44 C4
Drapers Way TA24 ... 129 D2
Drappel La BA5 ... 110 E7
Draycot Pl BS1 ... 227 A1
Draycott Ave TA2 ... 213 A6
Draycott Ct 1 BA2 ... 228 C3
Draycott Moor Dro BS27 ... 90 D1
Draycott Rd
Cheddar BS27 ... 90 D5
Shepton Mallet BA4 ... 205 B6
Draycott & Rodney Stoke CE Fst Sch BS27 ... 90 F3
Draydon Rd BS4 ... 22 D8
Dray Rd BA22 ... 186 C2
Drayton BS24 ... 49 A2
Drayton Cl BS14 ... 23 B8
Drayton La TA10 ... 171 D3
Drayton Rd BS9 ... 5 C8
Drew's La DT10 ... 190 B5
Drials La BA3 ... 94 F6
Drift Rd TA24 ... 201 D4
Drift The
Chard Junction TA20 ... 198 E8
Chard TA20 ... 194 B3
Drill Hall La BA4 ... 205 C5
Drimpton Cross DT8 ... 199 F7
Dring The BA3 ... 78 E2
Drive The
Bristol BS14 ... 23 C6
Burnham-on-S TA8 ... 85 A2
Churchill BS25 ... 52 E4
Shipham BS25 ... 70 E8
Stanton Drew BS39 ... 39 F1
Taunton TA1 ... 212 D1
Weston-Super-Mare BS23 ... 48 F8
Woolavington TA7 ... 136 E4
Dropping La BA10 ... 160 D5
Drove Cl DT10 ... 189 F2
Drove Ct BS48 ... 8 E3
Drove La
East Pennard BA4 ... 158 E8
Shepton Beauchamp TA19 ... 184 E4
Drove Rd
Congresbury BS49 ... 34 D3
Stourton Caundle DT10 ... 189 F2
Weston-Super-Mare BS23 ... 48 F5
Drove The
Bridgwater TA6 ... 209 A6
Portbury BS20 ... 3 D6
Droveway TA13 ... 220 B5
Drove Way
Churchinford TA3 ... 191 F8
Sandford BS24, BS25 ... 51 E7
Droveway Cl TA13 ... 220 C5
Droveway La BA21 ... 187 C7
Druid Cl BS9 ... 5 E5
Druid Hill BS9 ... 5 E5
Druid Rd BS9 ... 5 D4
Druids Garth BA2 ... 28 D1
Druid Stoke Ave BS9 ... 5 D5
Druids Wlk TA20 ... 223 C5
Druid Woods BS9 ... 5 C5
Druley Hill BA10 ... 161 D8
Drum Ave BA6 ... 206 C5
Drumhead Way The BS25 ... 70 E8
Dr White's Cl BS1 ... 227 B1
Dryleaze BS31 ... 24 E7
Drysdale Cl BS22 ... 31 D1
Duchess Cl TA6 ... 208 E7
Duchy Cl BA3 ... 78 E5
Duchy Rd
Clandown BA3 ... 78 E5
Shepton Mallet BA4 ... 205 A5
Duck La
Chard TA20 ... 223 C3

Duck La *continued*
Churchill BS40 53 A8
Horsington BA8 176 E2
Ilchester BA22 173 F1
Kenn BS21 17 A6
Stalbridge DT10 190 B5
Westbury-sub-Mendip BA5 110 E6
Duck Pool Dro BA6 206 B7
Duckpool La TA18 196 B8
Duck Pool La BA11 102 B6
Ducks' Field Crossing
TA18 224 C1
Ducks Hill TA10 172 B5
Ducks La BS22 32 A8
Duck St BS25 52 C5
Dudley Cl BS31 24 E4
Dudmoor TA12 185 B7
Dudwell La BA3 95 A5
Dugdale St TA24 200 F6
Duke's Cl BA9 216 E3
Duke's La
Horningsham BA12 144 A1
Kilmington BA12 161 F8
Duke Ave 7 TA5 135 B2
Duke Ho TA19 221 B3
Dukes Field BA4 205 C5
Dukes Mead TA6 209 A2
Duke St
Bath BA2 228 C2
Bridgwater TA6 208 E7
Frome BA11 119 E5
Taunton TA1 213 A4
Dull Cross TA4 151 D3
Dulverton La TA4 165 D7
Dulverton Mid & Com Sch
TA22 163 D6
Dumfries Pl BS23 48 E5
Dummis La BA5 111 A1
Dumper's La BA3 94 F7
Dumpers La BS40 39 B2
Dunball Ind Est TA6 136 B4
Dunbar Cl TA9 104 C4
Duncan Gdns BA1 27 A3
Duncart La BA5 204 C7
Duncliffe Cl DT10 190 B4
Duncombe Cl TA6 209 D5
Dundas Row TA4 167 E8
Dundry CE Prim Sch
BS41 21 D2
Dundry La
Dundry BS41 21 C3
Winford BS40 38 A7
Dunedin Way BS22 32 C4
Dunford Terr BA6 158 A5
Dungarvon Rd BS24 49 F7
Dungeon BS28 108 D7
Dungeon La BA5 204 C6
Dunkerry Rd BS26 88 C4
Dunkerton Cl BA6 206 F3
Dunkerton Hill BA2 61 E2
Dunkerton Rise TA2 168 B5
Dunkery Cl BS48 8 E1
Dunkery Rd
Bridgwater TA6 208 D4
Weston-Super-Mare BS23 30 F1
Dunkery Vineyard*
TA24 200 A1
Dunkirk Bsns Pk BA14 83 D2
Dunkleys Way TA1 213 C2
Dunn's Hill TA21 179 A6
Dunningham La BS28 107 E7
Dunns Cl BS28 108 C4
Dunsford Pl BA2 45 B6
Dunsgreen La EX15 191 A8
Dunsham La TA18 195 C2
Dunsley Hill EX16, EX36 162 D5
Dunstan Dr DT9 225 E5
Dunstan Rd
Burnham-on-S TA8 104 B7
Glastonbury BA6 206 F5
Dunstan Way BS27 90 B6
Dunster Beach Chalets
TA24 201 F4
Dunster Castle* TA24 201 E1
Dunster Cl
Minehead TA24 201 B4
Taunton TA2 213 B7
Dunster Cres BS24 49 A2
Dunster Ct BS25 70 A8
Dunster Fst Sch TA24 201 D2
Dunster Gdns 5 BS48 8 E1
Dunster Ho BA2 45 A2
Dunster Rd
Bristol BS4 22 F8
Keynsham BS31 24 E4
Dunsters Rd BS49 17 F1
Dunster Sta* TA24 201 F4
Dunster Steep
Dunster TA24 201 E2
Porlock, Doverhay TA24 124 A3
Porlock, West Porlock
TA24 123 F4
Dunster Visitor Ctr*
TA24 201 E2
Dunster Wood Forest Trails*
TA24 130 D5
Dunster Working Water
Mill* TA24 201 E1
Dunwear Ho 8 TA6 209 C4
Dunwear La TA6 209 D3
Durban Way BS49 17 B1
Durbin Park Rd BS21 6 D5
Durcott Rd BA2 78 D8
Durham Gr BS31 24 D4
Durham Pl 9 TA2 213 A8
Durhams Cotts TA4 210 C5
Durkheim Dr 2 BA5 203 C4
Durleigh Cl
Bridgwater TA6 208 D3
Bristol BS13 22 A7
Durleigh Hill TA5 208 A2
Durleigh Rd TA6 208 C3
Durley Hill BS31 24 C7
Durley La BS31 24 D7
Durleymoor Cross EX16 178 F4
Durley Pk BA2 44 E4
Durnhill BS40 73 F7
Durrant Cl DT9 225 D3
Dursdon Dro
Priddy BA5 111 C8
Wells BA5 112 B6
Dursley Rd BS11 4 E5
Durston BS24 49 A2
Durston Cl BA16 207 C5
Durston Ho 3 BA16 207 C5
Durston Way TA1 212 E1
Durville Rd BS13 22 B6
Durweston Wlk BS14 23 C8
Dutch Rd TA9 105 E5
Dutton Cl BS14 23 D6
Dutton Rd BS14 23 D6
Dutton Wlk BS14 23 D6
Dwelly Cl TA20 223 C3
Dyehouse Cnr TA22 164 A6
Dyehouse Cross TA22 163 F5
Dyehouse La
Bury TA22 164 A5
Glastonbury BA6 206 C5
Dye La BA3 115 A3
Dyer's La TA2 213 E7
Dyers' Close La BA11 119 E5
Dyers Cl
Bristol BS13 22 D4
Curry Rivel TA10 171 D4
West Buckland TA21 180 F7
Dyers Gn TA6 153 F3
Dyers Rd TA10 171 D4
Dyke's Way BA9 216 B3
Dyke Hill Terr TA20 198 D8
Dymboro Ave BA3 77 F1
Dymboro Cl BA3 77 F1
Dymboro Gdns BA3 77 F1
Dymboro The BA3 77 F1
Dyrham Cl TA8 104 D7
Dyson Cl BS49 34 B8

E

Eagle Cl
Ilchester BA22 173 E2
Weston-Super-Mare BS22 49 D8
Eagle Gdns BA22 173 E2
Eagle La 1 BA11 119 F4
Eagle Pk BA1 28 F5
Eagle Rd BA1 28 F5
Eagles The BS49 34 B8
Eames Orch TA19 221 C2
Earlesfield BS48 8 C1
Earle St BA20 219 C5
Earlham Gr BS23 49 A7
Earls Cl
Bridgwater TA6 208 E7
Sherborne DT9 225 F5
Earl St BS1 227 A4
East Anstey Prim Sch
EX16 162 E5
East Approach Rd TA7 136 D4
East Ave TA9 104 C4
Eastbourne Ave 15 BA1 28 B1
Eastbourne Ct 13 TA1 213 A4
Eastbourne Gate TA1 213 A4
Eastbourne Rd TA1 213 A4
Eastbourne Terr 12 TA1 213 A4
East Brent CE Fst Sch
TA9 86 C4
East Bridgwater Com Sch
TA6 209 C5
Eastbrook Terr TA3 168 D1
Eastbury Hill TA24 131 B5
Eastbury Rd TA24 131 B5
East Cl
Bath BA2 44 A5
Haselbury Plucknett TA18 196 B5
East Clevedon Triangle
BS21 6 F3
Eastcliff BS20 2 E7
East Coker Com Prim Sch
BA22 197 C7
East Coker Rd BA20 218 F2
East Coker Sawmills
BA22 197 C7
Eastcombe Gdns BS23 30 F1
Eastcombe La BA4 142 E2
Eastcombe Rd BS23 30 F1
East Compton Rd
Pilton BA4 204 E1
Shepton Mallet BA4 205 B1
East Coombe La TA4 165 D8
Eastcote Pk BS14 23 B5
Eastcourt Rd BS39 76 F8
Eastcroft BS40 54 E2
Eastcroft Cl BS40 54 E2
East Ct
Bristol BS3 11 F3
Horrington BA5 113 A1
Eastdown Rd BA3 78 D5
East Dr TA9 86 E4
East Dundry La BS41 22 A1
East Dundry Rd BS13,
BS14 22 F2
East End BS26 88 D7
East End La BA3 94 E4
Easterdown Hill
Dinnington TA17 195 B8
Easterdown Hill *continued*
Seavington St Mary TA19 184 E1
Easter La EX35 122 B4
Eastermead La BS29 51 C3
Eastern Ave TA6 209 D4
Eastern Ho BS23 30 E1
Eastertown BS24 67 D1
Eastfield
Bruton BA10 215 F7
29 Martock TA12 185 E6
Shepton Mallet BA4 205 B6
Yarlington BA9 175 F8
Eastfield Ave BA1 27 B2
Eastfield Cl 30 TA12 185 E6
Eastfield Gdn 12 DT9 225 E4
Eastfield Gdns BS23 30 F1
Eastfield La
Barrington TA19 184 D5
Blackford BS28 107 F6
Ditcheat BA4 159 C7
East Chinnock BA22 196 D8
Hambridge TA3 184 B8
Lydford Fair Place TA11 158 D3
North Perrott TA18 196 C4
Norton Sub Hamdon BA22 185 F1
Eastfield Pk BS23 30 F1
Eastfield Rd
Hutton BS24 49 E2
Wincanton BA9 216 D4
East Gate 11 TA1 213 A4
Eastgate Gdns 10 TA1 213 A4
Easthams Rd TA18 224 D6
East Harptree CE Prim Sch
BS40 74 F4
Easthay La TA20 199 A4
Easthill BA11 120 B4
Easthill La BA7 159 D5
East Huntspill Prim Sch
TA9 136 E8
East La TA18 196 B7
East Lambrook Manor Gdns*
TA13 220 C8
East Lambrook Rd TA13 220 D7
Eastland Rd BA21 219 C5
East Lanes BA21 187 D6
Eastlea BS21 6 B1
East Lea Rd BA1 44 A8
Eastleigh Cl
Burnham-on-S TA8 104 C8
Frome BA11 120 A7
Wiveliscombe TA4 210 C5
Eastleigh Rd TA1 213 B3
Eastlyn Rd BS13 22 B8
East Mead BA3 78 B2
Eastmead Ct BS9 5 E4
Eastmead La BS9 5 E4
East Mead La
Street BA16 207 F5
Walton BA16 156 E6
East Mere Cross EX16 178 B2
East Mill Ct 11 DT9 225 E4
East Mill La DT9 225 E4
Eastmoor La TA4 164 E8
Eastnor Rd BS14 23 A3
Easton Ct BA3 76 E1
Easton Ho 9 BA1 28 C1
Easton La
Pylle BA4 141 C1
Sampford Peverell EX16 178 D1
Easton Rd BS20 4 C4
Easton Town La BA4 158 F4
Easton Trow La BA4 159 B5
Eastop La DT10 190 A3
Eastover
Bridgwater TA6 209 A5
Langport TA10 172 A6
Eastover Cl TA10 172 A5
Eastover Com Prim Sch
TA6 209 B5
Eastover Gr BA2 44 C1
Eastover Rd BS39 59 D1
East Par BS9 5 C6
East Quay TA6 209 A6
East Quay Mews TA6 209 A6
East Rd BA16 207 E6
East Reach TA1 213 A4
East Ride TA9 86 B1
East Ridge Dr BS13 21 F5
East Side La TA7 136 F2
East Somerset Rly* BA4 205 F3
East Somerset Way BA5 203 D3
East St
Banwell BS29 51 C3
Bourton SP8 161 F1
Bristol BS2 227 C4
Cannington TA5 135 C2
Chard TA20 223 D4
Crewkerne TA18 224 C6
Drayton TA10 171 E3
East Coker BA22 197 B8
Ilminster TA19 221 C4
Martock TA12 185 E6
Milborne Port DT9 217 D2
North Perrott TA18 196 C4
Norton Sub Hamdon TA14 185 F1
Shepton Montague BA9 160 B2
Taunton TA1 212 F3
Templecombe BA8 176 F1
East Stoke TA14 185 F4
East Street Dro TA12 185 E6
East Street La BA6 140 A1
East Tapps La EX16 163 B2
East Town La TA4 150 E3
East Town La (Platterwell
La) BA4 141 B3
Eastville
Bath BA1 28 B1
Yeovil BA21 219 C5
Eastville La BS27 90 F1
East Water La BA5 92 F2
Eastway BS48 8 E3
East Way BA2 44 A5
Eastway Cl BS48 8 D2
Eastway Sq BS48 8 E3
Eastwell La BS25 69 E6
Eastwick Ave TA2 212 F7
Eastwick Rd TA2 213 B7
Eastwood BA2 45 F6
Eastwood Cl
Bridgwater TA6 209 C4
Frome BA11 119 C4
High Littleton BS39 59 C1
East Woodlands Rd
BA11 144 A7
East Wood Pl BS20 2 E7
Eastwoods BA1 29 B3
Eaton Cl BS14 23 E5
Eaton Cres
Bristol BS8 226 A4
Taunton TA2 213 A6
Ebben La TA20 194 F1
Ebbor Gorge Nature
Reserve* BA5 111 D6
Ebbor Gorge Nature Trail*
BA5 111 C5
Ebbor La BA5 111 B5
Ebden Lo 15 BS22 32 A2
Ebdon La BS22 32 C5
Ebdon Rd BS22 31 F4
Ebenezer La BS9 5 E5
Eckweek Gdns BA2 79 D8
Eckweek La BA2 79 E8
Eckweek Rd BA2 79 D8
Ecos Ct BA11 119 D4
Edbrooke Rd TA24 147 C5
Edbrook La TA5 134 F3
Eddington Ct BS23 48 D7
Eden Croft BS22 49 E8
Eden Park Cl BA1 29 A4
Eden Park Dr BA1 29 A4
Eden Terr BA1 28 B2
Eden Villas 4 BA1 28 C2
Edford Hill BA3 116 C6
Edgar Bldgs BA1 228 B3
Edgarley Ct BS21 6 C5
Edgarley Field La BA6 157 E8
Edgarley Rd
Glastonbury BA6 139 D1
West Pennard BA6 139 F1
Edgcott Rd TA24 128 C1
Edgebury TA7 136 E4
Edgecombe Ave BS22 31 D2
Edgecombe Mews BA1 27 B1
Edgefield Cl BS14 22 F3
Edgefield Rd BS14 22 F3
Edgehill Rd BS21 6 D6
Edgemoor Rd TA24 201 B4
Edgewood Cl BS14 23 B8
Edgeworth Rd BA2 44 C2
Edinburgh Pl 1 BS23 48 E8
Edinburgh Rd
Bridgwater TA6 208 E2
Keynsham BS31 24 E4
Edington Rd TA7 137 D4
Edington Right Dro TA7 155 B7
Edington & Shapwick Sch
Burtle TA7 137 D6
Shapwick TA7 137 F1
Edingworth Rd BS24 86 F7
Edith Cl TA8 85 A2
Edithmead La TA9 105 A6
Edmond's Hill TA11 173 D4
Edmund Hill La BA6 206 F6
Edmunds Way BS27 90 C7
Edward Cl BA22 218 B6
Edward Ct BS31 24 F4
Edward Park Dr BS21 6 E5
Edward Rd BS21 6 E5
Edward Rd S BS21 6 E5
Edward Rd W BS21 6 E6
Edward St
Bath, Bathwick BA2 45 B7
Bath, Lower Weston BA1 44 C7
Bridgwater TA6 209 B5
Edwin Short Cl BS30 25 E8
Egerton Rd BA2 44 E4
Egford Hill BA11 119 C5
Egford La BA11 119 C5
Egg Moor La EX13 198 A7
Eggwood La TA13, TA16 195 E8
Eglin Croft BS13 22 B4
Eglinton Rd BA16 207 B4
Egremont Ct TA4 202 D2
Egrove Way TA4 202 E4
Eight Acre Dro TA7, TA9 137 A5
Eight Acre La
Wellington TA21 222 E5
Wootton Courtenay TA24 129 F8
Eighteen Arce La BA21 218 C6
Eighth Ave BS14 23 A7
Eileen Cl BA16 207 E5
Eirene Terr BS20 4 D4
Elberton Rd BS9 5 B7
Elborough Ave BS49 34 B8
Elborough Gdns BS24 50 C3
Elbridge Ho 3 BS2 227 C3
Elderberry Wlk BS22 31 F1
Elder Cl
Chard TA20 223 C5
Highbridge TA9 104 D5
Eldergrove Cl TA6 209 D7
Elder Ho TA8 65 E2
Elderwood Rd BS14 23 B7
Eldon Pl BA1 28 B2
Eldred Cl BS9 5 D5
Eleanor Cl BA2 44 A5
Eleanor Cotts BA2 44 A6
Electric Ho TA14 185 E3
Eleven Ct TA6 208 E4
Elfrida Terr BA5 203 A5
Elgar Cl
Bristol BS4 22 D6
Clevedon BS21 6 E1
Eliot Cl BS23 49 A3
Eliotts Dr BA21 218 E7
Elizabeth Cl BS24 49 D3
Elizabeth Ct
Burnham-on-S TA8 104 B6
4 Martock TA12 185 E6
Elizabeth Flats BA21 219 C6
Elizabeth Gdns 16 BA8 190 A6
Elizabeth Way
Bridgwater TA6 209 C5
Chard TA20 223 C5
Ellbridge Cl BS9 5 D5
Ellenborough Cres BS23 48 E6
Ellenborough Ct BS23 48 E6
Ellenborough Ho BS8 226 A2
Ellenborough Park Rd
BS23 48 E6
Ellenborough Pk N BS23 48 D6
Ellenborough Pk S BS23 48 D6
Ellen Cl 8 TA6 153 F4
Ellen Ho BA2 44 A5
Ellersdown La TA22 163 E4
Ellesmere Rd
Bristol BS4 23 D8
Weston-Super-Mare BS23 48 D2
Ellfield Cl BS13 21 F6
Ellick Rd BS40 54 D1
Ellicombe La TA24 201 C4
Ellicombe Mdw TA24 201 C4
Elliot Cl BA11 119 F6
Elliots La BA11 119 B8
Elliott's Hill BA22 196 D7
Ellis's La TA5 152 C6
Ellis Ave BS13 22 A8
Elliscombe Pk BA9 176 B6
Ellis Gr TA2 168 B5
Ellis Pk BS22 32 C4
Elliston Dr BA2 44 B4
Ellsbridge Cl BS31 25 B5
Ellsbridge Ho Norton
Radstock Coll BS31 25 B5
Ellworthy Ct BA11 120 B4
Elm Ave TA8 104 B6
Elmbrook BA1 44 D8
Elm Cl
Banwell BS29 50 E4
Broadway TA19 183 C2
Nailsea BS48 8 C1
Star BS25 52 D1
Wells BA5 203 A4
Yatton BS49 34 B7
Elm Ct
Bristol BS14 23 A6
Keynsham BS31 24 C4
Elmdale Rd BS8 226 B3
Elm Dr BA9 216 C3
Elm Farm BS48 9 A2
Elm Gr
Bath, Larkhill BA1 28 C2
Bath, The Oval BA2 44 C4
Locking BS24 49 F4
Minehead TA24 201 A5
Taunton TA1 212 E5
Elmgrove Cl TA6 209 D7
Elmham Way BS24 32 B1
Elm Hayes BS13 21 F6
Elmhurst Ave BA21 219 B7
Elmhurst Est BA1 29 A4
Elmhurst Gdns BS41 20 F8
Elmhurst Jun Sch BA16 207 D6
Elmhurst La BA16 207 D6
Elmhurst Rd BS24 49 E2
Elmhyrst Rd BS23 48 F8
Elm La
Great Elm BA11 119 A6
Shalford BA9 216 B7
Woolavington TA7 136 F4
Elmlea Ave BS9 5 F5
Elm Lea Cl TA7 136 C4
Elmlea Jun & Inf Schs BS9 5 F5
Elmleigh BA21 218 C7
Elm Leigh BA11 120 C6
Elmleigh Rd 21 TA12 185 E6
Elm Lodge Rd BS48 9 B2
Elm Pk TA1 212 E5
Elm Pl BA2 44 F4
Elm Rd BS39 77 E5
Elms Cl TA1 212 E5
Elms Est TA2 213 F8
Elmside Cl BA16 207 D5
Elmside Ho TA6 208 F2
Elmside Rd TA6 208 E2
Elms La BA7 214 B7
Elmsleigh Rd BS23 48 E4
Elmsley La BS22 31 C5
Elms Rd TA21 222 F5
Elm St TA20 223 C5
Elms The
Banwell BS29 51 A4
Bath, Lambridge BA1 28 C2
Bath, Weston Park BA1 27 C1
Elmswood BS23 48 F8
Elm Terr BA3 97 C8
Elm Tree Ave
Nailsea BS21 8 A4
Radstock BA3 78 D1
Elm Tree Cl TA7 155 C2
Elmtree Dr BS13 21 F5
Elm Tree Pk BS20 3 D3

Elm Tree Rd
Clevedon BS21 6 D2
Locking BS24 50 A4
Elmvale Dr BS24 49 F3
Elm View
Midsomer Norton BA3 78 B1
Temple Cloud BS39 58 E1
Elm Way BA4 205 A6
Elm Wlk
Portishead BS20 2 C4
Yatton BS49 34 B7
Elmwood Ave TA6 208 F3
Elmwood Sch TA6 208 F3
Elsbert Dr BS13 21 E6
Elscombe La
Timberscombe TA24 130 A4
Wootton Courtenay TA24 129 F4
Elton Ho 2 BS2 227 C3
Elton Rd
Bristol BS8 226 C3
Clevedon BS21 6 C3
Weston-Super-Mare BS22 32 A4
Elton St BS2 227 C4
Elvard Cl BS13 22 A4
Elvard Rd BS13 22 A4
Elwell La BS40, BS41 21 A1
Elworthy Cross TA4 150 C5
Elworthy Dr TA21 222 D4
Elworthy La TA4 150 C5
Ely Gr BS9 5 B7
Embankment The TA10 172 A5
Embercourt Dr BS48 19 A6
Emery Gate BS29 51 B3
Emlet DT9 187 E1
Emley La BS40 54 B6
Emlyn Cl 6 BS22 32 B4
Emmanuel Ct BS8 226 A4
Emmett Wood BS14 23 B3
Empress Menen Gdns BA1 44 A8
Enderleigh Gdns BS25 52 F4
Enfield Dr BA4 141 E2
Enfield Rd BA4 141 E2
Engine La BS48 18 B8
Englands La BA22 174 F3
Englands Mead BA22 174 F3
Englands Rd TA24 124 A3
Englands Way TA20 223 D6
Englishcombe La BA2 44 D3
Englishcombe Rd BS13 22 C3
Englishcombe Rise BA2 44 A3
Englishcombe Tithe Barn* BA2 43 F2
Englishcombe Way BA2 44 E3
Enmore BS24 49 A2
Enmore CE Prim Sch TA5 152 F5
Enmore Cl TA8 104 C8
Enmore Rd
Bridgwater TA5 153 B6
Taunton TA2 212 F7
Ennerdale Cl BS23 49 A5
Enterprise Ctr The BS24 49 A3
Enterprise Mews BA20 218 D3
Enterprise Trade Ctr BS4 22 E7
Entry Hill BA2 44 F2
Entry Hill Dr BA2 44 F3
Entry Hill Gdns BA2 44 F3
Entry Hill Pk BA2 44 F2
Entry Rise BA2 44 F1
Erin Wlk BS4 22 D8
Erlon La BA5 110 F4
Ermine St BA21 218 D7
Ermine Way BS11 4 C7
Ernest Ashman Pl TA20 223 D5
Ervine Terr BS2 227 C4
Escott Ct TA6 208 F6
Escott La TA4 132 D1
Esgar Rise BS22 31 E3
Eskdale Cl BS22 49 D8
Esmonde Dr BA22 173 E2
Esmond Gr BS21 6 D4
Esplanade
Burnham-on-S TA8 104 A7
Minehead TA24 201 A7
Esplanade La TA23 202 C7
Esplanade Rd BS20 2 C7
Esplanade The TA23 202 C7
Essex Cl TA20 223 C4
Essex Ct TA1 212 C2
Essex Dr TA1 212 C2
Estuary Ho BS20 2 E7
Estuary Pk TA5 135 B5
Estune Wlk BS41 11 A2
Esworthy Cross EX16 162 F1
Ethel St BA5 203 C3
Ethpark Gr 1 TA2 212 F6
Etonhurst BS23 48 D6
Eton La BS29 50 E7
Eton Rd TA8 104 B6
Etsome Cl TA11 211 C4
Etsome Hill TA11 211 C7
Etsome Rd TA11 211 C5
Etsome Terr TA11 211 C4
Ettlingen Way BS21 6 F2
Eugene Flats 7 BS2 227 A4
Eugene St
Bristol, Kingsdown BS2 227 A4
Bristol, St Pauls BS2, BS5 227 C4
Evelyn Rd BA1 44 B8
Evelyn Terr 14 BA1 28 A1
Evenlode Gdns BS11 4 F5
Evenlode Way BS31 25 A3
Evercreech CE Prim Sch BA4 141 E2
Evercreech Rd BS14 23 B4
Evercreech Way TA9 104 F2
Everett Cl BA5 112 E1
Evergreen Cl BS25 51 F1
Evergreen Path TA16 195 F7
Everton Rd BA20 219 A4
Evesham Ave BA21 218 C6
Evesham Dr TA6 209 A1
Ewart Rd BS22 49 C8
Ewell Cl TA19 183 C1
Exbourne 10 BS22 32 A2
Exbury Cl TA8 104 C7
Excelsior St BA2 45 B5
Excelsior Terr BA3 78 B1
Exchange Ave BS1 227 A2
Exebridge Ind Est TA22 163 F3
Exeter Cl
Burnham-on-S TA8 104 C7
Nether Stowey TA5 134 B2
Exeter Rd
Portishead BS20 2 E4
Rockwell Green TA21 222 B5
Weston-Super-Mare BS23 48 E5
Exeter Road Cvn Pk TA21 222 A4
Exford CE Fst sch TA24 128 D1
Exford Cl BS23 48 F2
Exford Rd TA24 147 C6
Exmoor Falconry & Animal Farm* TA24 124 B4
Exmoor Gdns TA22 163 D6
Exmoor Rd BA2 44 F2
Exmoor Way TA24 200 E6
Exmouth Rd BS4 22 F8
Express Pk TA6 136 A2
Exton BS24 49 A2
Exton Cl BS14 23 B5
Exton La TA22 147 E4
Eyer's La BS2 227 C3
Eyers Rd BS24 49 F7

F

Faber Gr BS13 22 C4
Factory Hill SP8 161 F2
Factory La
East Huntspill TA9 136 E8
Tatworth TA20 198 D8
Failand Cres BS9 5 C5
Failand La
Easton-in-G BS8 4 A1
Portbury BS20 3 F2
Failand Wlk BS9 5 C6
Fairacre Cl BS24 50 B4
Fairacres Cl BS31 24 F5
Fair Cl BA2 81 E4
Fairclose TA20 193 D6
Fair Cross TA23 131 F2
Fairdean Rd TA9 104 E4
Fairfax Cl TA6 209 C6
Fairfax Rd TA6 209 C5
Fairfax St BS1 227 B3
Fairfield
Coleford BA3 116 E8
Crewkerne TA18 224 B5
Ilminster TA19 221 A4
7 Martock TA12 185 E6
Rode BA11 82 F1
Sampford Peverell EX16 178 D1
Sherborne DT9 225 D5
Somerton TA11 211 E4
Tunley BA2 61 A3
Yarlington BA9 175 F7
Fairfield Ave BA1 28 A2
Fairfield Cl
Backwell BS48 19 D7
Frome BA11 120 A7
Marshfield SN14 13 F8
Weston-Super-Mare BS22 31 B1
Fairfield Dr TA4 202 E3
Fairfield Gdns BA6 206 D4
Fairfield Gn TA3 192 A7
Fairfield Hts DT9 225 D5
Fairfield Mdws BA14 83 F3
Fairfield Mead BS48 19 D7
Fairfield Park Rd BA1 28 A2
Fairfield Pneu Sch BS48 19 C6
Fairfield Rd
Bath BA1 28 B1
Taunton TA2 213 B7
Fairfield Terr
Bath BA1 28 A1
Fitzhead TA4 166 F5
Peasedown St John BA2 79 C7
Fairfield View BA1 28 A2
Fairfield Way BS48 19 C6
Fairford Cl TA9 104 E4
Fairford Rd
Bristol BS11 4 D7
Highbridge TA9 104 E4
Fair Furlong BS13 22 A4
Fair Furlong Prim Sch BS13 22 B4
Fair Hill BS25 70 F8
Fairhouse Rd BA22 197 F8
Fairlands Mid Sch BS27 90 C7
Fairlands Way BS27 90 C7
Fairmead Rd BA21 219 C8
Fairmead Sch BA21 219 C8
Fairmont Terr 7 DT9 225 E4
Fair Pl TA11 158 D3
Fairseat Workshops BS40 56 E7
Fairview
Mells BA11 118 B7
Weston-Super-Mare BS22 31 F4
Fair View BA10 161 A7
Fairview Ho BS9 5 F8
Fairview Terr
Taunton TA3 168 D1
Yeovilton BA22 187 A8
Fairwater Cl TA2 212 D6
Fairway BS4 23 D8
Fairway Cl
Berrow TA8 84 F4
Weston-Super-Mare BS22 31 E2
Fairway Rise TA20 223 E5
Fairways
Saltford BS31 25 E2
Wells BA5 203 C4
Fairways Cvn Pk TA7 136 E3
Fairways The TA1 212 F1
Fairway View BA21 219 D6
Fairwood Rd BA13 102 F5
Fairy Hill BS39 41 D6
Falcon Cl
Bristol, Westbury on T BS9 5 F8
Portishead BS20 2 D4
Falcon Cres BS22 49 D8
Falcon Ct TA1 212 C4
Falcondale Rd BS9 5 F7
Falconer Rd BA1 27 A3
Falconsmead Wlk BA21 219 D8
Falkland Ho 7 TA18 224 C6
Falkland Sq 6 TA18 224 C6
Falklands Rise TA24 200 D7
Fallowfield
Blagdon BS40 54 E2
Weston-Super-Mare BS22 31 F3
Falmouth Cl BS48 9 A1
Fanshawe Rd BS14 23 A7
Faraday Rd 2 BS8 11 F5
Farleigh Ct BS48 20 B8
Farleigh Hungerford Castle* BA2 82 E8
Farleigh Rd
Backwell BS48 19 C6
Clevedon BS21 6 B1
Keynsham BS31 24 D4
Norton St Philip BA2 81 F5
Farleigh Rise BA15 29 E1
Farleigh View BA15 64 F3
Farleigh Wlk BS13 22 A8
Farler's End BS48 18 F8
Farley Cl BA11 120 C6
Farley Dell BA3 116 E8
Farmborough CE Prim Sch BA2 59 F6
Farm Cl
Somerton TA11 211 B3
Westbury-sub-Mendip BA5 110 D6
Weston-Super-Mare BS22 32 C4
Farm Ct TA13 220 C5
Farm Dr TA11 211 B3
Farmer Rd BS13 21 E4
Farm Hill TA7 156 B8
Farmhouse Cl 7 BS48 8 E2
Farmhouse Ct 1 BS48 8 E1
Farmhouse Dr BA11 119 F7
Farm La
Buckland St Mary TA20 182 A2
Coultings TA5 134 E4
Stogursey TA5 134 D4
Street BA16 207 C7
Wellow BA2 62 E1
Farm Orch DT9 188 C7
Farm Rd
Bradford Abbas DT9 187 E1
Doulting BA4 141 E5
Hutton BS24 49 E2
Street BA16 207 C6
Weston-Super-Mare BS22 31 B1
Farm St BA22 186 C6
Farm View TA2 168 F6
Farmwell Cl BS13 22 B5
Farnaby Cl BS4 22 C7
Farnborough Rd BS24 50 C4
Farncombe La BA9 160 B1
Farndale Rd BS22 49 D8
Farr's La BS1 227 A2
Farr's Orch 6 TA16 195 F7
Farrant Cl
Baltonsborough BA6 158 A5
Bristol BS4 22 D6
Taunton TA1 212 A4
Farrant Rd BA11 119 D5
Farriers Gn TA2 213 F7
Farringdon Hill La TA5 134 D6
Farrington Fields BS39 77 C3
Farrington Fields Trad Est BS39 77 C3
Farrington Gurney CE Prim Sch BS39 77 A4
Farrington La BA4 141 F6
Farrington Rd BS39 77 C5
Farrington Way BS39 77 A3
Farrow Cl TA20 223 D3
Farrs La BA2 45 B2
Farr St BS11 4 B8
Farthing's Pitts TA21 222 C4
Farthing Combe BS26 70 D2
Farthing Down TA21 179 E7
Farthing La EX13 193 D1
Farthing Rd TA6 208 E1
Farthing Row BA11 82 E1
Farthings Cl TA21 167 C2
Farthings Paddock BA7 159 A3
Faulkland La BA2, BA3 80 C4
Faulkland Rd BA2 44 D5
Faulkland View BA2 79 E7
Faversham Dr BS24 49 A1
Fawcus Pl TA20 223 C4
Fawn Cl BA6 206 C3
Fayre Way BA5 204 B7
Fearnville Est BS21 6 C2
Featherbed La
Chew Stoke BS40 38 A3
Clayhanger EX16 165 C1
Clutton BS39 58 C6
Fedden Village BS21 1 F5
Feeder Rd BS2 227 C1
Fellowsmead DT10 190 F5
Felon's Oak La TA24 131 B2
Felsberg Way BS27 90 C7
Feltham Dr BA11 120 A3
Feltham La BA11 144 B8
Felton Gr BS13 22 A8
Felton La BS40 37 E7
Felton St BS40 37 C7
Fender Cl TA5 135 B5
Feniton 6 BS22 32 A2
Fennel La BS26 70 B2
Fennel Way BA22 218 A5
Fenners BS22 32 B4
Fennington La TA2 168 B8
Fenns La BS41 10 E1
Fenshurst Gdns BS41 20 F8
Fenswood Cl BS41 10 F1
Fenswood Ct BS41 10 E1
Fenswood Mead BS41 10 E1
Fenswood Rd BS41 10 E1
Fental La BA3 116 C1
Fenton Cl BS31 25 D3
Ferenberge Cl BA2 60 A6
Ferguson Cl TA5 134 A3
Fermoy BA11 120 B6
Fern Cl BA3 78 B1
Ferndale Dr TA1 168 D1
Ferndale Gdns BA21 218 E6
Ferndale Rd
Bath BA1 28 C3
Portishead BS20 2 D6
Ferndown Cl
Bristol BS11 5 A7
Taunton TA1 212 D1
Ferne Animal Sanctuary* TA20 193 A2
Fern Gr BS48 18 C8
Fern Lea BS24 67 B6
Fernlea Gdns BS20 4 B4
Fernlea Rd BS22 49 C7
Fernleigh Ave TA6 209 A3
Fernleigh Cl BA4 141 E1
Fern Lodge BS23 48 D6
Fernside BS48 19 A7
Fernsteed Rd BS13 21 F6
Ferry Ct BA2 45 B6
Ferry La
Bath BA2 45 B6
Lympsham BS24 67 C3
Ferryman's Ct BS2 227 B2
Ferryman Rd BA6 206 E7
Ferry St BS1 227 B2
Fersfield BA2 45 B3
Festival Units TA6 209 B1
Feversham Ave TA6 208 E6
Feversham Ct BA22 173 E2
Feversham La BA6 206 D5
Feversham Way TA2 213 A8
Fiddle La BA22 174 F1
Field Cl BA3 116 A3
Field End
Axminster EX13 198 A1
Minehead TA24 201 A5
Fielders The BS22 32 B4
Fieldgardens Rd BS39 58 F1
Field Gate TA3 183 C8
Fieldgate La TA3 183 B8
Fielding's Rd BA2 44 C6
Fielding Ct BA21 219 C6
Fielding Ho BA2 44 A6
Fielding Path BA6 206 E6
Fielding Rd
Street BA16 207 B7
Yeovil BA21 219 C6
Fieldins BA15 64 E7
Field La
Chewton Mendip BA3 94 F8
Kington Magna SP8 177 E1
Penselwood BA9 161 D2
Field Marshal Slim Ct 24 BS2 227 C3
Field Rd TA10 156 A1
Fields End TA1 213 C2
Fields The BS22 32 D2
Field View BA4 205 C5
Field View Ct BA4 141 E1
Fieldway BS25 52 B4
Field Way TA9 104 D5
Fifehead Bsns Ctr (Manor Farm Trad Est) BA8 190 F8
Fifehead Hill BA8 190 F8
Fifth Ave BS14 23 B7
Filer Cl BA2 79 D8
Fillymead DT10 190 F5
Filwood Broadway BS4 22 E8
Finch Cl
Shepton Mallet BA4 204 F6
Weston-Super-Mare BS22 49 E8
Finches The BS20 2 F6
Finches Way TA8 85 B1
Finger Cnr DT10 190 F5
Finger La DT9 225 D3
Finmere Gdns BS22 32 A4
Fircliff Pk BS20 2 D7
Fire House Mews BA9 216 C3
Firgrove La BA2 61 B1
Fir La BS40 72 B5
Fir Leaze BS48 8 B1
Firs Ct BS31 24 C4
First Ave
Axminster EX13 198 A2
Bath BA2 44 E4
First Ave *continued*
Bristol BS14 23 A7
Portbury BS20 3 E5
Radstock BA3 97 C8
First Dro TA7 155 D3
Firs The
Bath BA2 45 B1
Langport TA10 172 A5
Limpley Stoke BA3 64 A5
Wheddon Cross TA24 129 E1
First Ho BA16 207 B6
First Sedgemoor Dro TA10 155 E4
Fir Tor Ave BA5 203 C5
Fir Tree Ave
Paulton BS39 77 F4
Weston-Super-Mare BS24 49 E4
Firtree Cl TA5 134 A2
Fir Tree Cl TA6 209 D4
Firway Cross EX16 164 C3
Firwood Rd BA11 119 E4
Fisher's Hill
Glastonbury BA6 206 D4
Holywell Lake TA21 179 D7
Fisher's La
Dinnington TA17 195 A7
Mark TA9 106 D5
Fishers Brook BA11 120 A5
Fishers Cl DT9 187 F5
Fishers Mead TA22 163 D6
Fisherway La TA19 195 A5
Fishpond Bottom Rd DT6 199 A1
Fishwell La BA6 157 D4
Fitzharding Ho 8 BS1 227 A3
Fitzharding Rd BS20 4 E3
Fitzroy Circ BS20 2 F6
Fitzroy Ho 3 BA2 228 C3
Fivash Cl TA1 168 D1
Five Acres 3 BA22 197 F8
Five Arches Cl BA3 78 D2
Five Ashes BA22 186 C2
Five Barrows Cross EX36 145 B7
Five Bells TA23 202 B5
Five C Bsns Ctr BS21 6 B1
Five Cross Way TA21 180 F6
Five Cross Ways TA22 162 F7
Five Dials TA19 183 C1
Five Hos TA21 222 B8
Five Lords TA5 134 B2
Fiveways Cl BS27 90 A7
Fiveways Rdbt BA21 219 A6
Fiveways Specl Sch BA21 219 D6
Five Yards 3 TA4 167 F8
Flagstaff Rd BS26 68 D7
Flamingo Cres BS22 49 E8
Flat The BS39 58 D5
Flatwoods Cres BA2 45 F3
Flatwoods Rd BA2 45 F3
Flax Bourton CE Prim Sch BS48 19 F8
Flax Bourton Rd BS8 10 B3
Flaxfield Dr TA18 224 C5
Flax La DT9 187 F4
Flaxpool Hill TA4 151 C6
Flax Row TA18 224 C7
Flax Way BA21 218 C6
Fleed Cross TA4 166 A6
Fleet Air Arm Mus* BA22 174 B3
Fletcher's La BS26 87 D6
Fletcher Cl TA2 213 B8
Fleur De Lys Dr BA14 83 F4
Flingers La BA9 216 D4
Flint Cross TA4 149 C1
Flints Cl BA11 119 D4
Florence Brown Specl Sch BS4 22 D8
Florence Gr BS22 49 B8
Florida Fields BA7 214 B6
Florida St BA7 214 C5
Florida Terr BA3 78 C2
Flowerdale Rd TA23 202 C6
Flowerdown Bridge BS22 49 D7
Flowerdown Rd BS24 50 D4
Flowerfield BA11 143 B8
Flowers Hill BS4 23 E8
Flowers Ho 1 BA20 219 B4
Flowerstone BA3 114 D7
Flowerwell Rd BS13 22 B5
Flushing Mdw BA21 219 E5
Foghamshire La BA11 143 D6
Foldhill Cl 25 TA12 185 E6
Foldhill La
Ash BA22 186 A6
Martock TA12 185 F6
Folke La DT9 189 A1
Folleigh Cl BS41 11 B2
Folleigh Dr BS41 11 B2
Folleigh La BS41 11 B2
Folliott Rd BA6 206 E6
Folly Cl
Cannington TA5 135 B2
Midsomer Norton BA3 96 E7
Folly Dr BA4 159 C7
Folly Dro TA19 183 A5
Folly Farm Nature Reserve* BS39 58 B5
Folly Fields BA21 219 B7
Folly La
Buckland St Mary TA20 182 E1
Kington Magna SP8 177 F2
Nether Compton DT9 187 F4
North Wootton BA4 140 C4
Shipham BS25 70 E7
South Cadbury BA22 175 D4

Folly La *continued*
Weston-Super-Mare BS23 . . . 48 E1
Folly Rd TA12 . . . 185 B7
Folly The
Cold Ashton SN14 . . . 12 F6
Ditcheat BA4 . . . 159 C7
Paulton BS39 . . . 77 F6
Saltford BS31 . . . 25 F2
Fons George TA1 . . . 212 F2
Fons George Cl TA1 . . . 212 E2
Fons George Rd TA1 . . . 212 F2
Fonthill Rd BA1 . . . 27 E2
Font La BA22 . . . 197 B7
Fontmell Ct BS14 . . . 23 D7
Font Villas BA22 . . . 197 B8
Football La BA9 . . . 216 B4
Footlands Cl TA1 . . . 212 F1
Forbes Fraser Hospl BA1 . . . 44 B8
Forche's La TA24 . . . 131 D3
Forches Cnr EX15 . . . 181 A4
Forde Abbey & Gdns★
TA20 . . . 198 F8
Forde Pk BA21 . . . 218 C7
Fordhay BA22 . . . 196 E7
Fordhay Terr BA22 . . . 196 E7
Ford La
Chewton Mendip BA3 . . . 94 D8
Pilton BA4 . . . 140 F3
Stawell TA7 . . . 137 A1
Yarley BA5 . . . 139 B8
Fordmill Cross EX16 . . . 164 D1
Ford Orch EX16 . . . 178 D1
Ford Rd
Bampton EX16 . . . 164 C1
Peasedown St John BA2 . . . 79 D8
Wellow BA2 . . . 62 F1
Wiveliscombe TA4 . . . 210 C4
Ford St TA21 . . . 222 F4
Forefield Pl BA2 . . . 228 C1
Forefield Rise BA2 . . . 45 B4
Forefield Terr BA2 . . . 45 A4
Forelands BS23 . . . 30 B1
Fore Leaze Dro TA12 . . . 184 E7
Fore St
9 Bampton EX16 . . . 164 B1
Bridgwater TA6 . . . 208 F5
Cannington TA5 . . . 135 B2
Castle Cary BA7 . . . 214 C5
Chard TA20 . . . 223 C4
Dulverton TA22 . . . 163 D6
Holcombe Rogus TA21 . . . 178 F5
Milverton TA4 . . . 167 A4
North Petherton TA6 . . . 153 E3
Othery TA7 . . . 155 C2
Tatworth TA20 . . . 198 D8
Taunton TA1 . . . 212 F3
Thorncombe TA20 . . . 199 B6
Wellington TA21 . . . 222 D6
West Camel BA22 . . . 174 D3
Westonzoyland TA7 . . . 154 E5
Williton TA4 . . . 202 D3
Winsham TA20 . . . 194 E1
Forest Dr BS23 . . . 31 A1
Forest Dro TA3 . . . 182 F5
Forester Ave BA2 . . . 45 B8
Forester Ct BA2 . . . 228 C4
Forester La BA2 . . . 45 B8
Forester Rd
Bath BA2 . . . 45 B8
Portishead BS20 . . . 2 D4
Foresters Cl TA4 . . . 202 E3
Forest Hill BA20 . . . 218 E2
Forest La TA20 . . . 193 E8
Forest Mill La TA19 . . . 183 B1
Forest Rd
Frome BA11 . . . 120 B7
Horningsham BA11, BA12 . . . 144 B4
Forest Wlk BA13 . . . 121 C4
Forge Cnr
Somerton TA11 . . . 211 C4
Stogursey TA5 . . . 134 B6
Forge End BS20 . . . 3 E3
Forge La
East Chinnock BA22 . . . 196 E8
Zeals SP8, BA12 . . . 161 F2
Forgotten World Mus★
BS26 . . . 68 D4
Fortescue Rd BA3 . . . 78 F2
Fortfield Rd BS14 . . . 23 B5
Forth Cl BA16 . . . 207 A4
Fortnum Pl TA19 . . . 221 D3
Forton La
Chard TA20 . . . 223 F1
Tatworth TA20 . . . 194 A1
Forton Rd TA20 . . . 223 D2
Forts Orch BA22 . . . 186 E6
Forum Bldgs BA1 . . . 228 C1
Forum La BA4 . . . 205 A7
Forum The BA21 . . . 218 C6
Forward's La TA3 . . . 181 C5
Fosgrove La TA3 . . . 181 E7
Fosse Barton BS48 . . . 8 D2
Fosse Cl
Nailsea BS48 . . . 8 C2
Yeovil BA21 . . . 218 D7
Fossedale Ave BS14 . . . 23 C6
Fossefield Rd BA3 . . . 97 B6
Fosse Gdns BA2 . . . 62 D8
Fosse Gn BA3 . . . 78 E4
Fosse La
Batheaston BA1 . . . 29 A4
Blackford BS28 . . . 107 C3
Clandown BA3 . . . 78 D3
Nailsea BS48 . . . 8 D2
Shepton Mallet BA4 . . . 205 D4
Fosse Lane Junc BA4 . . . 205 E5
Fosse Lane Trad Est
BA4 . . . 205 D5
Fosse Rd BA3 . . . 115 C3
Fosse The TA3 . . . 170 C4
Fosseway
Clandown BA3 . . . 78 E4
Clevedon BS21 . . . 6 C2
Midsomer Norton BA3 . . . 97 A5
Radstock BA3 . . . 97 C8
Fosse Way
Nailsea BS48 . . . 8 C2
Yeovil BA21 . . . 218 D7
Fosseway Cl BA2 . . . 79 C7
Fosse Way Cotts BA3 . . . 78 D2
Fosseway Ct
Bristol BS8 . . . 226 A2
Ilchester BA22 . . . 173 E2
Fosse Way Est BA2 . . . 44 D1
Fosseway Gdns BA3 . . . 78 D1
Fosseway S BA3 . . . 97 B7
Fosse Way Sch BA3 . . . 97 C8
Fosseway The BS8 . . . 226 A3
Foster's Almshouses 3
BS1 . . . 227 A3
Foster's La BA22 . . . 175 A7
Foster Cl BA5 . . . 112 E1
Foster Rd BA11 . . . 120 A3
Fosters 10 DT9 . . . 225 E4
Foundry Barton 2 BA11 . . . 119 F5
Foundry Cotts BA2 . . . 60 B4
Foundry Mews
Chard TA20 . . . 223 C4
2 Crewkerne TA18 . . . 224 C5
Foundry Rd TA1 . . . 212 F4
Foundry Sq 1 TA18 . . . 224 C5
Foundry The BA1 . . . 228 C3
Fountain Bldgs 7 BA1 . . . 228 B3
Fountain Ho 8 BA1 . . . 228 B3
Fountain La BS25 . . . 70 B7
Fountains Cl BA21 . . . 218 C7
Four Acre Mdw TA6 . . . 208 E6
Four Acre Mead 1 TA4 . . . 167 F8
Four Acres
Bristol BS13 . . . 21 E4
Shepton Mallet BA4 . . . 205 C5
Fouracres Cl TA1 . . . 213 B1
Four Acres Cl
Bristol BS13 . . . 21 F4
Nailsea BS48 . . . 18 E8
Four Acres Prim Sch
BS13 . . . 21 E4
Four Elms TA21 . . . 179 A6
Four Forks La TA5 . . . 152 F7
Four Lanes TA20 . . . 193 F6
Fourth Ave
Bristol BS14 . . . 23 B7
Radstock BA3 . . . 97 D8
Fourways Cl BA7 . . . 214 D6
Fouts Cross TA19 . . . 184 F2
Fowey Cl BS48 . . . 19 A8
Fowey Rd BS22 . . . 32 A4
Fowler St TA2 . . . 212 E6
Fownes Rd TA24 . . . 201 B5
Fox's Dro BA11 . . . 102 C1
Foxbury Cl BA11 . . . 119 F6
Fox Cl TA21 . . . 222 A6
Foxcombe La DT9 . . . 176 C1
Foxcombe Rd
Bath BA1 . . . 44 B7
Bristol BS14 . . . 23 B4
Foxcote BA20 . . . 218 C2
Foxcote Ave BA2 . . . 79 E7
Foxcote Gdns BA11 . . . 120 C7
Foxdon Hill TA20 . . . 223 A7
Foxdown Hill TA21 . . . 222 C4
Foxdown Ho TA21 . . . 222 C4
Foxdown Terr TA21 . . . 222 D4
Foxglove Cl BS22 . . . 32 A5
Foxglove Way
Chard TA20 . . . 223 F5
Yeovil BA22 . . . 218 A5
Foxhanger La TA22 . . . 148 A2
Fox Hill BA2 . . . 45 A2
Foxhill Ho BA2 . . . 45 A1
Foxhole La TA3 . . . 169 E5
Foxholes La BA2, BA11 . . . 100 D5
Fox & Hounds La BS31 . . . 24 F5
Fox Mdws TA18 . . . 224 D7
Fox Rd BA16 . . . 207 A5
Fox Way TA5 . . . 134 B2
Foxwell La BA22 . . . 196 C7
Foye Ho BS8 . . . 11 E6
Frampton Rd TA6 . . . 208 F2
Francis Cl TA3 . . . 169 D5
Francis Fox Rd 7 BS23 . . . 48 E7
Francis Ho BS2 . . . 227 A4
Francis Reed Cl TA7 . . . 154 F5
Francis Wlk DT9 . . . 225 E5
Francombe Ho BS1 . . . 227 A1
Frankcom Ho BA2 . . . 45 B7
Frankford Mans 7 BS23 . . . 30 C1
Frankland Cl BA1 . . . 27 B1
Frankley Bldgs BA1 . . . 28 B1
Frankley Terr 6 BA1 . . . 28 B1
Franklin's Way BS49 . . . 17 F1
Franklin Cl TA2 . . . 212 B7
Franklin Ct BS1 . . . 227 B1
Franklyn Terr BS39 . . . 77 A4
Frank Webber Rd TA21 . . . 222 A5
Fraser Cl
Burnham-on-S TA8 . . . 104 C7
Weston-Super-Mare BS22 . . . 31 F4
Frederick Ave BA2 . . . 79 C7
Frederick Ct BA5 . . . 203 C4
Frederick Pl BS8 . . . 226 B3
Frederick Rd TA6 . . . 209 C6
Fredrick Pl 5 BA20 . . . 219 B4
Freedom Ave BA21 . . . 218 E6
Free Hill BA5 . . . 110 E6
Freeland Pl BS8 . . . 11 F6
Freelands BS21 . . . 16 C8
Freeling Ho BS1 . . . 227 B1
Freemans La BS48 . . . 20 B2
Freemantle Ho BS2 . . . 227 A4
Free St BA22 . . . 173 E1
Freeview Rd BA2 . . . 44 A5
Freezinghill La BS30 . . . 12 B4
Fremantle Rd TA1 . . . 213 B1
Frenchay Rd BS23 . . . 48 E4
French Cl
Nailsea BS48 . . . 8 F3
Peasedown St John BA2 . . . 79 D7
Frenchfield Rd BA2 . . . 79 D7
French Weir Ave TA1 . . . 212 E5
French Weir Cl TA1 . . . 212 E4
Freshford CE Prim Sch
BA3 . . . 64 B5
Freshford La BA3 . . . 64 A4
Freshford Sta BA3 . . . 64 C5
Freshmoor 6 BS21 . . . 6 F3
Frethey Rd TA1, TA4 . . . 168 B3
Friar Ave BS22 . . . 31 E3
Friarn Ave TA6 . . . 208 F4
Friarn Lawn TA6 . . . 208 F4
Friarn St TA6 . . . 208 F4
Friars Ave BA21 . . . 218 D6
Friars Cl BA22 . . . 173 D1
Friars Way TA8 . . . 104 B6
Friary BS1 . . . 227 C1
Friary Cl
Clevedon BS21 . . . 6 C5
Westwood BA15 . . . 64 E4
Witham Friary BA11 . . . 143 C3
Friary Rd BS20 . . . 2 B5
Friday St TA24 . . . 200 F7
Friendly Row BS20 . . . 4 C5
Friendship Gr 2 BS48 . . . 8 F2
Friendship Rd BS48 . . . 8 F3
Friggle St BA11 . . . 120 D1
Frithfield La BA4 . . . 205 C6
Frobisher Ave BS20 . . . 2 B5
Frobisher Cl
Burnham-on-S TA8 . . . 104 D8
Portishead BS20 . . . 2 A5
Weston-Super-Mare BS22 . . . 31 E4
Frobisher Way TA2 . . . 212 B6
Frog La
Bristol BS1 . . . 226 C2
Combe St Nicholas TA20 . . . 193 D6
Creech St Michael TA3 . . . 169 F6
Dinnington TA17 . . . 195 B8
Enmore TA5 . . . 153 A6
Felton BS40 . . . 37 C8
Galhampton BA22 . . . 175 E8
Haselbury Plucknett TA18 . . . 196 C6
Holcombe Rogus TA21 . . . 178 F5
Ilminster TA19 . . . 221 C4
Kingsdon TA11 . . . 173 D5
Langport TA10 . . . 171 F5
North Curry TA3 . . . 170 D5
Shepton Mallet BA4 . . . 205 E4
Stoke St Michael BA3 . . . 116 A4
Ubley BS40 . . . 55 D1
Wanstrow BA4 . . . 142 F4
West Camel BA22 . . . 174 D3
Winford BS40 . . . 37 F5
Froglands La BS27 . . . 90 C7
Froglands Way BS27 . . . 90 C7
Frogmore St BS1 . . . 226 C2
Frogs La TA21 . . . 180 F7
Frog St
Bampton EX16 . . . 164 B1
East Quantoxhead TA5 . . . 133 B6
Lopen TA13 . . . 185 A1
Frogwell Cross TA4 . . . 164 D6
Frome Com Coll BA11 . . . 120 A7
Fromefield BA11 . . . 120 A6
Fromefield Ho BA11 . . . 120 A6
Frome Mus★ BA11 . . . 119 F5
Frome Old Rd BA3 . . . 79 A2
Frome Rd
Bath BA2 . . . 44 D1
Beckington BA11 . . . 101 D3
Bruton BA10 . . . 215 F7
Maiden Bradley BA12 . . . 144 B3
Norton St Philip BA2 . . . 81 F3
Nunney BA11 . . . 143 B8
Radstock BA3 . . . 79 B2
Rode BA11 . . . 101 F7
Southwick BA14 . . . 83 F3
Wingfield BA14 . . . 83 C5
Frome St BS2 . . . 227 C4
Frome Sta BA11 . . . 120 A4
Frome View BA12 . . . 144 C2
Front St
Chapel Allerton BS26 . . . 88 D1
Chedzoy TA7 . . . 154 D8
Churchill BS25 . . . 52 E4
Monksilver TA4 . . . 150 B8
Frost Hill BS49 . . . 34 D7
Frost La TA19 . . . 183 F4
Fry's La BS40 . . . 53 F3
Fry's Well BA3 . . . 96 D3
Fry's Wlk BA4 . . . 205 A5
Frys House of Mercy 11
BS1 . . . 227 B1
Frys La TA7 . . . 154 E8
Frys Leaze BA1 . . . 28 B2
Frys Mews TA1 . . . 213 C2
Fryth Ho BS48 . . . 9 D3
Fryth Way BS48 . . . 8 C2
Fulford Ct TA24 . . . 200 F7
Fulford Rd BS13 . . . 22 C5
Fulford Wlk BS13 . . . 22 B5
Fullands Ave TA1 . . . 168 F1
Fullands Ct TA1 . . . 168 F1
Fullands Rd TA1 . . . 213 B1
Fullens Cl BS22 . . . 49 D7
Fuller Cl BA4 . . . 205 D5
Fuller Rd BA1 . . . 28 C2
Fullers La BS25 . . . 70 A6
Fullers Way BA2 . . . 62 D8
Fullwell Cl BA3 . . . 80 D1
Fulmar Rd BS22 . . . 31 F1
Fulwell La BA3 . . . 80 D1
Fulwood Cl TA1 . . . 212 D1
Furge Gr BA8 . . . 190 A6
Furge La BA8 . . . 190 A6
Furland Rd
Crewkerne TA18 . . . 224 C5
Weston-Super-Mare BS22 . . . 31 C2
Furland Way TA18 . . . 224 C5
Furlong Cl BA3 . . . 96 F7
Furlong Cotts EX16 . . . 179 A4
Furlong Gn TA3 . . . 168 D1
Furlong La
Curry Rivel TA10 . . . 171 C3
Milborne Port DT9 . . . 217 B3
Furlong Pl BS26 . . . 70 C1
Furlongs Ave TA6 . . . 208 E2
Furlongs The DT9 . . . 225 D5
Furnham Cl TA20 . . . 223 D5
Furnham Cres TA20 . . . 223 D6
Furnham Rd TA20 . . . 223 D5
Furnleaze BS39 . . . 58 E3
Furpits La TA10 . . . 172 B6
Furringdons Cross TA18 . . . 195 F6
Furze Cl
Bridgwater TA6 . . . 208 D4
Weston-Super-Mare BS22 . . . 31 B2
Furzeclose La BA4 . . . 142 C7
Furzehill TA20 . . . 223 D5
Furzehill La TA24 . . . 147 C6
Furzeland Rd TA24 . . . 124 A4
Furze Rd BS22 . . . 31 A3
Furze The BA20 . . . 218 C2
Fylton Croft BS14 . . . 23 B3
Fyne Court Nat Res & Visitor
Ctr★ TA5 . . . 152 E3

G

Gables Cl BS29 . . . 51 B3
Gables The TA21 . . . 222 C6
Gabriel Cl BA11 . . . 120 C6
Gadd's La BS27 . . . 90 B8
Gagley La BA5 . . . 111 B2
Gainesmarsh La TA10 . . . 172 C5
Gainsborough DT9 . . . 217 C2
Gainsborough Ct BA1 . . . 27 B1
Gainsborough Dr
Sherborne DT9 . . . 225 B3
Weston-Super-Mare BS22 . . . 31 F3
Gainsborough Gdns BA1 . . . 44 C8
Gainsborough Hill DT9 . . . 225 E2
Gainsborough Rd BS31 . . . 24 F5
Gainsborough Way BA21 . . . 219 E8
Gale's Dro BA6 . . . 139 D3
Galhampton Hill BA7,
BA22 . . . 214 C2
Galingale Way BS20 . . . 2 F5
Gallagher Ret Pk BS23 . . . 49 A5
Galleries The BS1 . . . 227 B3
Galley Batch BA3 . . . 114 F4
Galley Batch La BA3 . . . 114 F4
Galloping Bottom La
TA23 . . . 149 E5
Galmington Cl TA1 . . . 212 C3
Galmington Dr TA1 . . . 212 C2
Galmington La TA1 . . . 212 C2
Galmington Rd TA1 . . . 212 C2
Gamblyn Cross TA4 . . . 164 F5
Gammins Cotts TA24 . . . 129 E2
Gander Cl BS13 . . . 22 B5
Gandstone Cross TA4 . . . 150 D2
Ganesfield BA4 . . . 141 E6
Gange's Hill TA3 . . . 170 F2
Ganges Cl TA3 . . . 170 F2
Gannet Rd BS22 . . . 31 F1
Gants Mill La BA10 . . . 215 D5
Gaol La BA4 . . . 205 C6
Garamond Ct BS1 . . . 227 B1
Garden City TA10 . . . 172 A6
Garden Cl
Bristol BS9 . . . 5 C5
Norton Fitzwarren TA2 . . . 168 B4
Weston-Super-Mare BS22 . . . 31 E2
Garden Ct BS8 . . . 226 A4
Gardeners Cl
Bradford On Tone TA4 . . . 167 F1
Cheddar BS27 . . . 90 B8
Gardeners Wlk BS41 . . . 11 B1
Garden Ground BA4 . . . 205 C4
Gardenhurst TA8 . . . 85 B1
Garden Hurst Cl TA8 . . . 104 B8
Garden Plot Hill TA3 . . . 183 E7
Gardens Rd BS21 . . . 6 C4
Gardens The
Dulverton TA22 . . . 163 D7
East Pennard BA4 . . . 158 F8
Sherborne DT9 . . . 225 C3
1 Wellington TA21 . . . 222 D5
2 Wells BA5 . . . 203 D4
Garden Terr TA21 . . . 222 B7
Garden Way TA24 . . . 200 D7
Garden Wlk TA6 . . . 208 E2
Gardiners Bsns Pk TA7 . . . 136 F3
Gardiners Orch BS28 . . . 108 C4
Gardner Ave BS13 . . . 21 F7
Gardner Rd BS20 . . . 2 D6
Garfield Terr 1 BA1 . . . 28 C2
Garlandhayes La EX15 . . . 180 E2
Garland Ho 7 BS21 . . . 6 C2
Garner Ct 4 BS22 . . . 32 B4
Garonor Way BS20 . . . 3 F5
Garre Ho BA2 . . . 43 F5
Garrett Rd BA20 . . . 218 D3
Garrick Rd BA2 . . . 43 F5
Garsdale BA11 . . . 120 A4
Garsdale Rd BS22 . . . 49 D8
Garston Cotts BS40 . . . 54 E3
Garstone La TA16 . . . 195 F8
Garston La
Blagdon BS40 . . . 54 E3
Frome BA11 . . . 120 A4
Marston Magna BA22 . . . 174 F1
Garston Lodge 11 BA11 . . . 119 F4
Garston Rd BA11 . . . 120 A4
Garstons
Bathford BA1 . . . 29 D2
7 Clevedon BS21 . . . 6 B1
Wrington BS40 . . . 35 E1
Garstons Cl
Backwell BS48 . . . 18 F6
Wrington BS40 . . . 35 E2
Garstons Orch BS40 . . . 35 D1
Garston St BA4 . . . 205 C6
Garstons The BS20 . . . 2 D4
Garth Rd BS13 . . . 22 A8
Gartons Mead BA4 . . . 141 E1
Gartons Mead Rd BA4 . . . 141 E1
Garvins Rd BA6 . . . 206 C4
Gasferry Rd BS1 . . . 226 B1
Gashay La EX13 . . . 199 B3
Gas La TA17 . . . 195 D7
Gason La BA22 . . . 174 F4
Gasper St BA12 . . . 161 E3
Gass Cl TA9 . . . 104 F4
Gasson's La TA11 . . . 211 C3
Gaston's La TA12 . . . 185 D5
Gaston Ave BS31 . . . 24 F6
Gaston Cl BA16 . . . 207 C4
Gastons The BS11 . . . 5 A8
Gaswell La TA7 . . . 155 E8
Gatchell's La TA3 . . . 181 B5
Gatchell Gn TA3 . . . 168 D1
Gatchell Mdw TA3 . . . 168 D1
Gatchells La TA4 . . . 132 F2
Gatcombe Farm Ind Est
BS40 . . . 35 D3
Gatcombe Rd BS13 . . . 22 B5
Gate Cl EX13 . . . 198 E3
Gatehouse Ave BS13 . . . 22 A5
Gatehouse Cl BS13 . . . 22 A5
Gatehouse Ct BS13 . . . 22 B5
Gatehouse Ctr The BS13 . . . 22 B5
Gatehouse Way BS13 . . . 22 A5
Gate La BA5 . . . 203 D2
Gaulden Manor★ TA4 . . . 150 F2
Gaunt's La BS1 . . . 226 C2
Gaunton Cl TA1 . . . 212 D2
Gaunts Cl BS20 . . . 1 F4
Gaunts Rd TA6 . . . 135 E6
Gay's Hill BA1 . . . 228 C4
Gay Cl TA21 . . . 222 E6
Gay Ct BA1 . . . 28 E3
Gay Elms Prim Sch BS13 . . . 22 A4
Gay Elms Rd BS13 . . . 22 A4
Gaylard's La TA20 . . . 194 B5
Gay St
Bath BA1 . . . 228 B3
Mells BA11 . . . 118 B7
Wellington TA21 . . . 222 E6
Gazelle Rd
Weston-Super-Mare BS24 . . . 49 B3
Yeovil BA20 . . . 218 D3
Gefle Cl BS1 . . . 226 B1
Geldof Dr BA3 . . . 78 A2
Gelosia Cl TA7 . . . 154 F6
General Higgins Ho TA9 . . . 104 E3
Gennes Gr BA9 . . . 216 C4
Gentle St
Frome BA11 . . . 119 F4
Horningsham BA12 . . . 144 E4
Geoffrey Cl BS13 . . . 21 E6
George's Pl BA2 . . . 45 B6
George's Rd BA1 . . . 28 A1
George Cl BS48 . . . 19 D7
George & Crown Cotts
TA17 . . . 195 C7
George La
Marshfield SN14 . . . 13 E8
South Petherton TA13 . . . 220 C4
George Maher Ct TA19 . . . 221 C3
Georges Bldgs BA1 . . . 28 C3
Georges Ground BA11 . . . 119 E2
George Sh Ctr The TA18 . . . 224 C6
Georges Ho BA2 . . . 45 B6
Georges Mews TA1 . . . 213 C2
George Smith Way BA22 . . . 218 A6
Georges Sq BS1 . . . 227 B2
George St
Bath BA1 . . . 228 B3
Bath, Bathwick BA2 . . . 45 B6
Bridgwater TA6 . . . 208 F5
Burnham-on-S TA8 . . . 104 A7
Charlton Adam TA11 . . . 173 F7
Glastonbury BA6 . . . 206 D5
Portishead BS20 . . . 2 C2
Sherborne DT9 . . . 225 D4
Taunton TA2 . . . 212 F6
Wellington TA21 . . . 222 D6
Weston-Super-Mare BS23 . . . 48 E7
George Sweetman Cl
BA9 . . . 216 D4
George Whitefield Ct
BS1 . . . 227 B3
George William Ct TA6 . . . 208 F4
Georgian Ct BA11 . . . 119 D3
Georgian Ho BA2 . . . 228 C2

Georgian House (Mus)★ BS1 226 C2
Georgian View BA2 44 C2
Gerard Rd BS23 48 F8
Gerbestone La TA21 180 E6
Gerrard Bldgs BA2 45 B7
Gerrard Cl BS4 22 D7
Geys Hill BA12 144 D8
Giant's Grave TA20 193 A7
Giant's Grave Rd TA20 193 A7
Gibbet La BS14 23 D1
Gibbet Rd BA9 176 B6
Gibbs' La TA19 184 D5
Gibbsfold Rd BS13 22 C4
Gibbs Marsh Trad Est DT10 190 D6
Gibraltar Cotts TA24 123 E4
Giddy La BA3 116 A4
Gielgud Cl TA8 104 D6
Gifford Cl TA20 223 D5
Giffords La TA18 196 C5
Giffords Orch TA12 185 A7
Giffords Pl BS13 22 A7
Gigg La SP8 177 C2
Gilbeck Rd BS48 8 C2
Gilberts Cnr BA6 158 A6
Gilbert Scott Ho BA5 113 A1
Gilbert Scott Mews BA5 113 A2
Gilbert Scott Rd BA5 113 A1
Gilberyn Dr BS22 32 A3
Gilda Cl BS14 23 C5
Gilda Cres BS14 23 B6
Gilda Par BS14 23 C5
Gilda Sq W BS14 23 B5
Giles Cl TA10 171 D4
Giles Farm BA5 113 A1
Gillards TA1 212 B4
Gillards Cl TA21 222 B4
Gillards Mead TA3 192 A7
Gill Cres TA1 212 B1
Gillebank Cl BS14 23 D5
Gillingham Ct TA20 223 D5
Gillingham Terr 3 BA1 28 B1
Gill Mews BS22 32 B4
Gillmore Cl BS22 31 D1
Gillmore Rd BS22 31 D1
Gills La BS26 87 B5
Gillson Cl BS24 49 D2
Gimblett Rd BS22 32 B4
Gipsy Cross TA4 166 A2
Gipsy Dro TA20 193 C4
Gipsy La
Burcott BA5 139 E8
Frome BA11 120 B7
Glastonbury BA6 139 D1
Halse TA4 167 B6
Sampford Arundel TA21 179 D5
Staplegrove TA2 212 D7
Street BA16 207 E4
Taunton TA1 212 C3
Wells BA5 203 A4
Gladstone Ct BA2 45 C2
Gladstone Pl BA2 45 C2
Gladstone Rd
Bath BA2 45 C2
Bristol BS14 23 B6
Gladstone St
Midsomer Norton BA3 78 B3
Taunton TA2 212 E6
Gladstone Terr
Minehead TA24 201 A5
Wellington TA21 222 E6
Gladstone Villas BA3 115 C5
Glanfield Cl TA4 167 E8
Glanfield Terr BA22 173 F1
Glanvill Ave TA20 223 C5
Glanville Dr BS39 75 E6
Glanville Rd BS28 108 C4
Glanvill Rd BA16 207 C3
Glass's Cross TA4 149 E1
Glass's Rocks La TA4 149 D1
Glasses Mead TA1 212 B2
Glass House Hill DT9 225 E3
Glastonbury Abbey★ BA6 206 E4
Glastonbury Cl BS48 9 B1
Glastonbury Ct BA21 218 D6
Glastonbury Rd
Meare BA6 138 E4
Wells BA5 203 B2
Glastonbury Tor★ BA6 139 D1
Glastonbury Way BS22 32 A2
Glaston Ho BA16 207 D7
Glaston Rd BA16 207 D7
Glebe Ave BS20 2 E4
Glebe Cl BS41 11 C2
Glebe Cotts TA3 169 E2
Glebe Cres TA24 200 E8
Glebe Ho
Bath BA2 45 B5
Portishead BS20 2 E4
Weston-Super-Mare BS22 31 F3
Glebe Inf Sch The BS49 34 C4
Glebeland Cl TA7 156 B8
Glebelands
7 Merriott TA16 195 F7
Minehead TA24 200 E8
Norton Sub Hamdon TA14 185 F3
Nunney BA11 143 B7
Radstock BA3 78 D1
Glebelands Cl BS27 90 B6
Glebe Paddock BA5 139 E8
Glebe Rd
Bath BA2 44 B4
Clevedon BS21 6 C2
Glebe Rd *continued*
Long Ashton BS41 11 C2
Portishead BS20 2 E4
Weston-Super-Mare BS23 48 E8
Glebe The
Fivehead TA3 170 F1
Freshford BA3 64 B4
Hinton Charterhouse BA2 63 D2
Queen Camel BA22 174 F3
Timberscombe TA24 130 B4
Timsbury BA2 60 B3
Wrington BS40 35 D2
Glebe Way BS27 90 C6
Glebe Wlk BS31 24 C4
Glebe Yd TA10 172 E4
Glen Ave BS8 10 F8
Glenavon Pk BS9 5 C4
Glen Brook BS9 5 D4
Glencairn Ct BA2 45 B6
Glen Cl TA2 168 B5
Glencoe Bsns Pk BS23 49 A7
Glencoe Terr TA3 168 D1
Glencot La BA5 203 A7
Glencot Rd BA5 203 A6
Glencroft Way BS22 31 E3
Glendale 16 BS8 11 F6
Glendevon Rd BS14 23 A3
Glen Dr
Bristol BS9 5 D5
Taunton TA2 168 F6
Gleneagles Cl
Nailsea BS48 9 A1
Weston-Super-Mare BS22 31 F3
Glenmore Rd TA24 201 A7
Glen The
Saltford BS31 25 F1
Weston-Super-Mare BS22 31 B2
Glenthorne Ave BA21 219 B7
Glenthorne Nature Trail Gate★ EX35 122 D5
Glenthorne Rd 9 TA2 212 F6
Glentworth Ct 19 BS23 30 C1
Glentworth Rd BS8 226 B2
Glen View BA3 115 E7
Glenview Ho BA2 79 D8
Glenville Rd BA21 219 D6
Glenwood Gdns TA2 212 F8
Glenwood Mans BS23 30 D1
Glenwood Rise BS20 1 F5
Glen Yeo Terr BS49 34 C4
Globe Orch TA18 196 C6
Gloucester Ho 11 BS2 227 C3
Gloucester La 18 BS2 227 C3
Gloucester Rd
Bath BA1 28 C3
Bridgwater TA6 208 F2
Burnham-on-S TA8 104 C7
Upper Swainswick BA1 28 A7
Gloucester Row 6 BS8 11 F7
Gloucester St
4 Bath BA1 228 B3
5 Bristol BS2 227 B4
8 Bristol, Clifton BS8 11 F7
Taunton TA1 213 A4
Weston-Super-Mare BS23 48 D7
Glovers DT9 225 D5
Glovers Cl
Milborne Port DT9 217 D2
4 Stoke sub Hamdon TA14 185 F4
Glovers Ct BA20 218 F4
Glovers Field BS25 70 F7
Glovers Wlk 18 BA20 219 B4
Glynsmead TA20 198 C8
Glynswood TA20 223 C5
Goathill La BA8 176 C3
Goathill Rd DT9 189 B4
Godhams La TA4 165 A7
Godminster Ct BA10 215 E6
Godminster La BA10 215 E4
Godney Dro BA5 139 B6
Godney Rd BA5, BA6 139 A4
Godwin Dr BS48 8 C3
Goeffrey Farrant Wlk TA1 213 A5
Goes La BA7 158 F2
Gogs Orch BS28 108 C3
Gold Corner Dro TA9 137 A6
Goldcrest Way BS20 2 F6
Goldcroft BA21 219 B6
Goldcroft Ct BA21 219 B6
Goldenhaye La TA20 194 D3
Golden Hill
Stourton Caundle DT10 189 F1
Wiveliscombe TA4 210 C5
Golden Lion Ct BS1 227 B2
Golden Valley La BS30 25 E8
Golden Valley Prim Sch BS48 8 F2
Goldfinches La BA6 139 D3
Gold Hill
Batcombe BA4 142 D2
Shepton Mallet BA4 205 B7
Golding's La DT9 217 C1
Golding Cl BA5 203 C4
Goldney Ave BS8 226 A2
Goldney Cl BS39 58 F1
Goldney Rd BS8 226 A2
Goldney Way BS39 58 F1
Goldsmiths La EX13 198 A4
Goldsmoor Cross EX16 178 E3
Gold St DT10 190 B4
Golf Club La BS31 25 E2
Golf Course Rd BA2 45 D6
Golf Links La BA3 114 E3
Golf Links Rd TA8 85 A2
Golledge Cl BA3 96 C4
Gooch Cl
Bridgwater TA6 209 B4
Frome BA11 120 D6
Gooch Way BS22 32 B3
Good's La TA5 152 C5
Goodard Dr BS22 32 B4
Goodeaves Cl BA3 117 A7
Goodeaves Cotts BA3 117 A7
Goodeve Pk BS9 5 D3
Goodeve Rd BS9 5 D3
Good Hill BA4 142 E2
Goodlands La TA1 212 F4
Goodwin Dr BS14 22 F4
Goodymoor Ave BA5 203 B5
Goodymoor La BA5 203 B5
Goold Cl BA2 43 A8
Goosander Cl TA24 201 C4
Goosard La BS39 77 E8
Gooseacre Ct BA22 197 B8
Gooseacre La
East Coker BA22 197 B8
Yeovil BA22 218 A1
Gooseham La BS28 108 F4
Gooseham Mead BS49 34 D4
Goose La
Chilton Polden TA7 137 B3
Horton TA19 183 C2
Gooselade BA16 207 C3
Gooseland Cl BS14 22 F3
Goose St BA11 101 E5
Goosey La BS22 32 C2
Gordano Bsns Pk BS20 2 E5
Gordano Gdns BS20 4 B4
Gordano Rd BS20 3 D7
Gordano Sch BS20 2 D3
Gordano View BS20 2 C5
Gordano Way BS20 3 F5
Gordon's Cl TA1 213 B1
Gordon Bldgs BA3 79 A3
Gordon Rd
Bath BA2 45 B5
Bristol BS8 226 B3
Peasedown St John BA2 79 D8
Taunton TA1 213 A3
Weston-Super-Mare BS23 48 F7
Yeovil BA21 219 C6
Gordon Terr TA6 209 A5
Gorefield TA13 220 D2
Gorehedge 14 BA11 119 F4
Gore La
Chapmanslade BA13 121 B4
Pitney TA10 172 C7
Gore Rd TA8 85 A1
Gores Pk BS39 59 B2
Gore Sq TA4 167 E8
Gorlangton Cl BS14 23 A7
Gorlegg TA21 179 E5
Gorpit La TA5 134 F8
Gorse La
Bristol BS8 226 B2
Cold Ashton BS30, SN14 12 D7
Gort Rd TA2 168 B6
Gosford Mans 6 BS23 30 C1
Goslet Rd BS14 23 E5
Goss Barton BS48 8 D1
Goss Cl BS48 8 C1
Goss Dr BA16 207 B3
Goss La BS48 8 C1
Goss View BS48 8 C1
Goswell Cl BA16 207 C5
Goswell Rd BA16 207 C5
Gough's Cave★ BS27 90 D8
Gough Cl 11 TA16 195 F7
Gough Pl BS27 90 A8
Gould's Ground 2 BA11 119 E5
Gould's La 1 BA11 119 E5
Gould Cl BA16 207 E6
Gouldsbrook Terr TA18 224 B6
Gouldsbrook View TA18 224 C7
Goulston Rd BS13 22 A5
Goulston Wlk BS13 22 A5
Gournay Ct BS39 77 A3
Governors Ho BA2 44 D6
Govier's La TA23 202 C7
Grace Cl BS49 34 B8
Grace Dr BA3 78 A2
Grace Martin's La BA22 174 F3
Grace Rd BS22 32 B4
Gradwell Cl BS22 32 B3
Grafton Cl TA2 213 A8
Graham Rd BS23 48 E7
Graham Way TA4 167 E6
Grainger Ct BS11 4 E7
Grain Store The 9 BS1 227 A2
Graitney Cl BS49 35 A8
Granary Orch DT9 187 F5
Granary The 8 BS1 227 A2
Granary Way TA3 181 D8
Granby Hill BS8 11 F6
Granby Rd BA22 174 A2
Grand Par BA2 228 C2
Grand Pier★ BS23 48 D7
Grand Western Canal (Country Pk)★ EX16 178 F2
Granfield Gdns BS40 53 A5
Grange Ave
Highbridge TA9 104 E3
Street BA16 207 B6
Grange Bsns Pk The BS24 33 A5
Grange Cl
Cannington TA5 135 C2
Wellington TA21 222 E5
Weston-Super-Mare BS23 48 E1
Grange Cnr DT8 199 E7
Grange Dr
Bridgwater TA6 208 D4
Taunton TA2 213 A6
Grange End BA3 97 B7
Grange Farm Rd BS49 17 A1
Grangefields BA16 207 D5
Grange Gdns TA2 213 A7
Grange Paddock TA9 106 E4
Grange Rd
Bristol, Bishopsworth BS13 22 A5
Bristol BS8 226 A3
Frome BA11 120 A7
Huntspill TA9 136 A8
Saltford BS31 25 C3
Street BA16 207 D7
Weston-Super-Mare BS23 48 E1
Grange The
Bath BA1 27 C1
Bristol BS9 5 D7
Chilton Polden TA7 137 B2
Flax Bourton BS48 19 F7
Kingston St Mary TA2 168 E8
Langport TA10 171 E5
Grange Way TA6 135 F5
Grange Wlk TA2 213 A6
Grant's Hill EX16, TA22 163 F2
Grant's La
Wedmore BS28 108 D4
Wiveliscombe TA4 210 D6
Grants Cl BA9 216 B4
Grants La BA9 216 D4
Granville Chapel 5 BS8 11 F5
Granville Rd BA1 27 E4
Granville Way DT9 225 E6
Grasmere TA6 208 C5
Grasmere Dr BS23 48 F4
Grass Meers Dr BS14 23 A4
Grassmere Rd BS49 34 B8
Grass Rd TA8 65 F4
Grass Royal BA21 219 C6
Grass Royal Jun Sch BA21 219 C6
Gratton La EX35 122 A4
Gravelands La TA3 169 D3
Gravel Hill BS40 56 B7
Gravel La TA3, TA19 183 F6
Gravel Pit Cross EX36 145 E6
Gravel Pits DT9 225 D3
Gravel Wlk BA1 228 B3
Gravenchon Way BA16 207 A6
Graves Cl 7 TA6 209 B4
Gray's Almshouses 17 TA1 213 A4
Gray's Hill EX15 180 D1
Gray's La EX15 180 D1
Gray Hollow BS40 74 F4
Grayling Ho BS9 5 F7
Grays Ave TA7 154 E6
Grays Hill BA2 80 B5
Grays Rd TA1 213 B4
Grays Terr TA1 213 B4
Great Ann St BS2 227 C3
Great Barton BA4 205 D6
Great Bedford St BA1 228 B4
Great Bow Yd TA10 171 F5
Great Britain S.S.★ BS1 226 B1
Great Brockeridge BS9 5 F6
Great Cl EX15 179 E1
Great Cnr 5 BA21 218 C6
Great Field La TA14 185 F4
Great Gdns BA4 205 C6
Great George St
Bristol, Brandon Hill BS1 226 C2
Bristol, St Pauls BS2 227 C3
Great Hayles Rd BS14 23 A6
Great Hill BA9 161 D2
Great House Ct BA6 138 D4
Great House St TA24 130 B5
Great La
Knole TA10 173 A4
Shepton Beauchamp TA19 184 E4
Great Mdw TA22 163 D6
Great Mead TA1 212 B3
Great Orch BA22 173 E2
Great Ostry BA4 205 B6
Great Pit La BA22, DT9 188 B7
Great Pulteney St BA2 228 C3
Great Ringaton La EX36 162 B6
Great St TA14 185 E2
Great Stanhope St BA1 228 A2
Greatstone La BS40 37 F5
Great Western La TA11 211 D3
Great Western Rd
Chard TA20 223 D5
Clevedon BS21 6 D2
Martock TA12 185 E7
Great Western Terr BA21 219 D5
Great Withy Dro BA5 206 C8
Greatwood Cl TA6 209 A2
Great Wood Cl BS13 22 C4
Grebe Cl TA6 209 B4
Grebe Ct TA6 209 B4
Grebe Rd
Bridgwater TA6 209 B4
Taunton TA2 213 B6
Green's Dro BA6 206 C7
Green's Hill TA4 151 C5
Greenacre
Wembdon TA6 208 D6
Weston-Super-Mare BS22 31 B2
Green Acre Rd BS14 23 A3
Greenacres
Bath BA1 27 B3
Bristol BS9 5 E7
Midsomer Norton BA3 77 E1
Greenacres Pk BA21 187 A5
Greenaleigh Lower Rd TA24 125 C4
Greenaleigh Upper Rd TA24 125 C4
Greenbank Gdns BA1 27 B1
Greenbrook Terr TA1 212 E4
Green Cl
Holford TA5 133 D4
Paulton BS39 77 E6
Sparkford BA22 175 A4
Green Cotts BA2 45 C2
Greendale TA19 221 B3
Greenditch Ave BS13 22 C5
Greenditch Cl BA3 96 C3
Green Ditch La BA3 96 B6
Greendown Pl BA2 45 A1
Green Dragon Ct 4 TA6 208 F4
Green Dro TA11 158 A4
Green Farm Ind Est BA13 121 C4
Greenfield Cres BS48 8 E3
Greenfield La TA7 136 D2
Greenfield Pk BS20 2 C3
Greenfield Pl BS23 48 C8
Greenfield Prim Sch BS4 22 C7
Greenfields
Bridgwater TA6 208 F3
Crewkerne TA18 224 C7
Greenfields Ave BS29 51 A3
Greenfield Terr TA20 198 D8
Greenfield Wlk BA3 78 A3
Greenfylde CE First Sch TA19 221 C3
Greengage Cl 6 BS22 49 E8
Green Gate EX16 178 B2
Greenham's Cross TA14 185 F2
Greenham Bsns Pk TA21 179 C5
Greenham La TA18 199 E7
Greenham Yd TA18 199 E7
Greenhayes BS27 90 B8
Greenhays Foot EX13 198 B6
Greenhill DT9 225 D4
Greenhill Cl
Nailsea BS48 8 D2
Weston-Super-Mare BS22 32 A3
Greenhill Croft BS25 52 B4
Greenhill Cross EX36 162 B2
Greenhill La
Alston Sutton BS26 88 E5
Sandford BS25 52 B4
Greenhill Pl BA3 78 A3
Greenhill Rd
Midsomer Norton BA3 78 A3
Sandford BS25 52 B4
Yeovil BA21 219 D7
Green Knap La TA20 193 C2
Green La
Bristol BS11 4 B8
Brompton Regis TA22 148 B1
Butcombe BS40 55 A7
Castle Cary BA7 214 F4
Chard Junction TA20 198 D7
Chardstock EX13 198 B7
Chard TA20 193 F1
Charlton Horethorne DT9 176 A2
Charlton Horethorne, Sigwells DT9 175 F2
Corfe TA3 181 E7
Corsley Heath BA12 144 E7
Cricket St Thomas TA20 194 F3
East Chinnock BA22 196 E8
East Coker BA22 197 B8
Failand BS8 10 C4
Farrington Gurney BS39 76 F6
Felton BS40 37 C3
Fivehead TA3 170 E2
Freshford BA3 64 B2
Frome BA11 119 D4
Hinton Charterhouse BA2 63 E1
Ilminster TA19 183 E2
Kington Magna SP8 177 E2
Leigh u M BA3, BA11 117 B2
Marshfield SN14 13 E8
Oakhill BA3 114 E4
Pitcombe BA7 215 A1
Priddy BS40 73 B7
Queen Camel BA22 174 F3
Sampford Arundel TA21 179 F4
Shepton Beauchamp TA19 184 E3
Sherborne DT9 188 E1
Southwick BA14 83 D2
Stoke St Michael BA3 116 B5
Stratton-on-t F BA3 96 E1
Street BA16 207 C4
Tatworth TA20 193 D1
Winsley BA15 64 F6
Greenland La TA24 131 B1
Greenland Rd BS22 31 D1
Greenlands TA1 213 B2
Greenlands Rd BA2 79 C8
Green Lane Ave BA16 207 C4
Green Lane End TA19 184 E3
Green Lane Gate BA9 176 A8
Green Mead BA21 218 C5
Greenmoor La BA21 187 A5
Green Ore Est BA5 94 B1
Green Park La BA11 101 F6
Green Park Mews BA1 228 A2
Green Park Rd BA1 228 B2
Green Parlor Rd BA3 79 D1
Green Pastures Rd BS48 9 B2
Green Pits La BA11 143 B7
Green Pk
Bath BA1 228 B2
Rode BA11 101 E8
Green Quarry BA21 219 A6
Green Ride BA12 161 F7
Greenridge BS39 58 F3
Greenridge Cl BS13 21 E4
Greenslade Gdns BS48 8 D3
Greens Pl BA5 203 D3

Green St
Bath BA1 228 C2
Hinton St George TA17 195 D7
Shoscombe BA2 79 E5
Ston Easton BA3 95 E8
Greenstalls Pk BA22 173 F2
Green The
Backwell BS48 19 A5
8 Barwick BA22 197 F8
Bath BA2 44 D1
Bridgwater TA6 208 E2
Brushford TA22 163 E4
Coleford BA3 116 F6
Easton BA5 111 A4
Faulkland BA3 80 D2
Hinton Charterhouse BA2 63 F1
Ilchester BA22 173 E2
Locking BS24 50 A4
33 Martock TA12 185 E6
Pill BS20 4 D4
Pitminster TA3 181 E6
1 Sherborne DT9 225 D4
Williton TA4 202 D3
Winscombe BS25 70 A7
Green Tree Rd BA3 78 B3
Greenvale Cl BA2 60 B1
Greenvale Dr BA2 60 B1
Greenvale Rd BS39 77 D5
Greenway
Bishops Lydeard TA4 167 E8
Faulkland BA3 80 C1
Ilminster TA19 221 B1
Minehead TA24 200 D6
Monkton Heathfield TA2 169 B6
North Curry TA3 170 B3
Watchet TA23 202 B7
Greenway Ave TA2 212 E6
Greenway Cl BA9 216 D4
Greenway Cotts TA4 167 E8
Greenway Cres TA2 212 E7
Greenway Ct BA2 44 F4
Greenway La
Barrington TA13 184 E5
Bath BA2 45 A4
Blagdon Hill TA3 181 B5
Cold Ashton SN14 12 D5
Combe St Nicholas TA20 193 E6
Stoke St Mary TA3 169 D2
Wiveliscombe TA4 210 A5
Greenway Pk 3 BS21 6 F3
Greenway Rd
Castle Cary BA7 214 B6
Rockwell Green TA21 222 A5
Taunton TA2 212 E6
Greenways BA3 96 C2
Greenway Terr TA2 168 D8
Greenwell La BS40 53 C7
Greenwood Cl TA9 136 B8
Greenwood Rd
Weston-Super-Mare BS22 31 E2
Yeovil BA21 218 D7
Gregory Mead BS49 17 A1
Gregorys Gr BA2 62 D8
Gregorys Tyning BS39 77 F6
Greinton BS24 49 A2
Grenville Ave BS24 50 A4
Grenville Cl BA6 157 E4
Grenville Ho TA6 208 F2
Grenville Pl 7 BS1 11 F5
Grenville Rd TA8 104 C7
Grenville View TA4 167 E6
Grey's Cnr BA9 161 A3
Greyfield Comm BS39 59 C2
Greyfield Rd BS39 59 C2
Greyfield View BS39 58 F1
Greyhound Cl BA9 216 C4
Greylands Rd BS13 21 F7
Greys Rd TA16 195 F7
Greystoke Bsns Ctr BS20 2 D4
Gribb View TA20 199 B6
Grib La BS40 54 F2
Griffen Cl TA6 208 E6
Griffen Rd BS24 49 E7
Griffin Cl
Wells BA5 203 B6
Weston-Super-Mare BS22 32 B2
Griffin Ct BA1 228 B2
Griffin La TA3 182 F7
Griffin Rd
Clevedon BS21 6 E3
Hatch Beauchamp TA3 182 F7
Griggfield Wlk BS14 23 A7
Grimsey La SP8 177 F8
Grinfield Ave BS13 22 C4
Grinfield Ct BS13 22 C4
Groats 9 TA4 167 F8
Grooms Orch TA21 222 C5
Grosvenor Bridge Rd BA1 28 C1
Grosvenor Ct BA22 173 E2
Grosvenor Pk BA1 28 C1
Grosvenor Pl BA1 28 C1
Grosvenor Rd
Bristol BS2 227 C4
Stalbridge DT10 190 B4
Grosvenor Terr BA1 28 C2
Grosvenor Villas 9 BA1 28 B1
Grove Alley BA10 215 E6
Grove Ave
Bristol BS1 227 A1
Bristol, Coombe Dingle BS9 5 C7
Yeovil BA20 218 F5
Grove Cl
Penselwood BA9 161 E2
Watchet TA23 202 C6
Grove Ct BS9 5 E5
Grove Dr
Taunton TA2 212 F8
Weston-Super-Mare BS22 31 C1
Grove Hill TA7 155 B1
Grove Ho
Bath BA2 45 B6
Burnham-on-S TA8 104 A8
Grove Jun Sch BS48 18 D8
Grove La
Faulkland BA3 80 D2
Frome BA11 119 E3
Knole TA10 173 A4
North Cheriton BA8 176 E5
Stalbridge DT10 190 B4
West Anstey EX36 162 D6
Weston-Super-Mare BS23 48 D8
Grove Lane Cl DT10 190 B4
Grove Leaze BS11 4 D6
Grove Mead BA11 119 E2
Grove Orch BS40 54 E2
Grove Park Ct BS23 30 D1
Grove Park Rd BS23 30 D1
Grove Pl TA24 201 B4
Grove Rd
Banwell BS29 50 E4
Blue Anchor TA24 131 B6
Bristol, Coombe Dingle BS9 5 D8
Burnham-on-S TA8 104 A8
Huntspill TA9 136 A8
Weston-Super-Mare BS23 48 D8
Weston-Super-Mare, Milton BS22 31 C1
Groves La TA24 131 B6
Grove St BA2 228 C3
Groves The BS13 22 D4
Grove Terr 8 TA2 212 F6
Grove The
Bath BA1 27 C1
Bristol BS1 227 A1
Burnham-on-S TA8 85 B1
Frome BA11 119 E2
Hallatrow BS39 77 B7
Ruishton TA3 169 C3
Sherborne DT9 225 D3
Winscombe BS25 51 F1
Wraxall BS48 9 C3
Grove Wood Rd BA3 78 F1
Grughay La TA3 182 E5
Grunter's La BA3 114 F7
Gryphon Sch The DT9 225 E6
Guard Ave BA22 218 B6
Guard House La 9 BA5 203 D4
Gug The BS39 59 C2
Guild Ct BS1 227 B2
Guildford Pl TA1 212 F3
Guildhall La BS28 108 C4
Guineagore La DT9 188 B4
Guinea La BA1 228 C3
Guinea St BS1 227 A1
Guinevere Cl BA21 218 D7
Gullen BA2 80 A6
Gulliford's Bank BS21 6 F2
Gulliford Cl TA9 104 D4
Gullimores Gdns BS13 22 B4
Gullock Tyning BA3 78 B1
Gullons Cl BS13 22 A6
Gullon Wlk BS13 21 F5
Gulway Mead TA20 198 D8
Gumbrells Ct TA6 209 A4
Gunners La BA22 218 A5
Gunning's La BA4 142 F2
Gunville La
Charlton Horethorne DT9 176 A2
East Coker BA22 197 D8
Gunwyn Cl BA6 206 E6
Gurney St TA5 135 C2
Gurnville Cotts BA11 119 F2
Guthrie Rd BS8 226 A4
Gwynne La TA1 213 A3
Gyffarde Ct 4 TA1 213 A4
Gyffarde St TA1 213 A4
Gypsy La
Cheddar BS28 89 D6
Keynsham BS31 42 B8
Marshfield SN14 13 F7

H

Haberfield Hill BS8 4 E2
Haberfield Ho 1 BS8 11 F6
Hacketty Way TA24 124 B3
Hack La
Holford TA5 133 F2
Nether Stowey TA5 134 A2
Hack Mead La TA9 105 E1
Hackness Rd TA9 136 E8
Haddon Cl TA22 148 B2
Haddon La
Hartford TA4 164 C7
North Petherton TA6 153 C2
Stalbridge DT10 190 C5
Haddon View TA22 148 B2
Hadley Rd BA2 45 B2
Hadrian Cl BS9 5 C4
Hadspen Gdn* BA7 160 A2
Hadworthy La TA6 153 F4
Hagget Cl TA6 208 F1
Hagleys Gn TA4 151 B7
Haig Cl BS9 5 B7
Haig Rd TA2 168 B6
Haines Hill TA1 212 E2
Haines La DT8 199 D5
Haines Pk TA1 212 E1
Hains La DT10 190 F7
Halcombe TA20 223 C2
Halcon Cnr TA1 213 D4
Halcon Com Prim Sch TA1 213 D4
Hale La BA9 177 C6
Halesleigh Rd TA6 208 E5
Hales Mdw BA21 187 D6
Hale Way TA2 213 D7
Half Acre TA4 202 D2
Half Acre Cl
Bristol BS14 23 A3
Williton TA4 202 D2
Halfacre La BS14 23 B4
Half Acres DT9 225 C3
Half Moon St 6 DT9 225 D3
Halfpenny Row BA11 82 E1
Halfway BA22 186 F6
Half Yd BS40 53 D8
Hallam Ct BS21 6 C4
Hallam Rd BS21 6 C4
Hallards Cl BS11 4 F8
Hallatrow Rd BS39 77 C6
Hallen Dr BS9 5 C7
Hallet Gdns BA20 219 A4
Hallets Orch BA22 186 B6
Hallett Rd BA7 214 B7
Halletts Way
Axminster EX13 198 A1
Portishead BS20 2 D5
Hall Hill EX35 122 B5
Halliwell Rd BS20 1 D4
Hall La BA1 12 B3
Hall Sch The BS25 70 B8
Hall Terr TA8 104 A8
Halse Cnr TA4 167 D5
Halse La TA24 147 B5
Halse Manor TA4 167 B6
Halston Dr BS2 227 C4
Halsway TA6 209 C5
Halsway Hill TA4 132 F1
Halsway La
Bicknoller TA4 133 A1
Crowcombe TA4 151 A8
Halswell Cl TA6 208 E4
Halswell Gdns BS13 22 B4
Halswell Rd BS21 6 D1
Halt End BS14 23 C3
Halter Path Dro TA7 137 C7
Halves La BA22 197 C7
Halwyn Cl BS9 5 D5
Halyard Dr TA6 208 E7
Halyard Pl TA24 201 B7
Ham's La TA11 174 D7
Hamber Lea TA4 167 F8
Hambledon Rd BS22 32 C4
Hambridge Com Prim Sch TA10 184 D8
Ham Cl BS39 58 F1
Hamdon Cl 12 TA14 185 F4
Hamdon Hill Country Pk* TA14 185 F3
Hamdon View TA14 185 E3
Hamdown Ct TA10 172 B6
Ham Gn
Hambridge TA10 184 D8
Pill BS20 4 D3
Ham Gr BS39 77 E5
Ham Hill
Coleford BA3 116 D6
Combe St Nicholas TA20 193 D8
High Ham TA10 156 A2
Langford Budville TA21 166 A1
Radstock BA3 78 F3
Ham Hill Ctry Pk* TA14 186 A3
Ham Hill Rd
Odcombe BA22 186 C2
Stoke sub Hamdon TA14 185 F4
Hamilton Ct
11 Bristol BS1 227 A4
Taunton TA1 213 C4
Wells BA5 203 B4
Hamilton Ho BA1 27 E3
Hamilton Rd
Bath BA1 27 E2
Taunton TA1 213 C4
8 Weston-Super-Mare BS23 30 C1
Hamilton Terr BA2 79 F5
Ham La
Bishop Sutton BS39 57 C5
Burnham-on-S TA8 104 B6
Compton Dundon TA11 157 A3
Croscombe BA4, BA5 204 E7
Dundry BS41 21 D3
Farrington Gurney BS39 76 F5
Kingston Seymour BS21 16 B2
Marnhull DT10 190 F6
North End BS49 17 A3
Paulton BS39 77 E5
Pawlett TA6 135 E6
Rodhuish TA23 149 C8
Shepton Mallet BA4 205 A7
Sherborne DT9 188 A5
Trent DT9 187 F5
Wraxall BS48 9 B4
Yatton BS49 17 A3
Ham La E BA4 204 F7
Hamlands La TA21 167 D1
Hamlet The
Nailsea BS48 9 A3
Templecombe BA8 176 E1
Hamley La
Buckland St Mary TA20 193 B8
Combe St Nicholas TA20 182 F1
Ham Link BS40 53 F3
Hamlyn Cl TA1 212 C1
Hamlyn Rd BA6 206 E6
Ham Mdw DT10 190 E6
Hammer La BA2, BA3 100 C8
Hammer St BA10 161 B8
Hammet St
8 North Petherton TA6 153 E3
Taunton TA1 212 F4
Hammets Wharf 1 TA1 212 F4
Hammond Gdns BS9 5 E7
Hamp Ave TA6 208 F3
Hamp Brook Way TA6 208 E2
Hamp Com Jun Sch TA6 208 F3
Hampden Rd BS22 31 E2
Hamp Green Rise TA6 209 A3
Hamp Ind Est TA6 209 A3
Hamp Inf Sch TA6 208 F3
Hamp St TA6 208 F3
Hampton Cl
5 Barwick BA22 197 F8
Bridgwater TA6 209 D7
Hampton Cnr BS11 4 E6
Hampton H BA2 45 D8
Hampton Ho 10 BA1 28 C1
Hampton La BS8 226 B4
Hampton Rd BS6 226 C4
Hampton Row BA2 45 B8
Hampton View BA1 28 B1
Ham Rd
Brean BS24, TA8 66 B3
Burnham-on-S TA9 85 E4
Creech St Michael TA3 169 D4
Wellington TA21 180 D8
Hamrod La TA7 154 E5
Hams La BS26 68 C3
Hams Rd BS31 24 F7
Ham St BA6 158 B5
Hamway La TA20 193 C8
Hamwood TA1 212 B4
Ham Wood Cl BS24 49 B2
Hamwood Cotts TA1 212 B4
Hamwood La TA3 181 B8
Hamwood Terr TA1 212 B4
Hanbury Ct BS8 226 A4
Hanbury Rd BS8 226 A4
Handel Rd BS31 24 E5
Handlemaker Rd BA11 119 E2
Handy Cross TA4 151 A2
Hanford Ct BS14 23 D7
Hanger's Way TA24 201 D2
Hangerland La TA4 150 E6
Hang Hill BA2 80 A6
Hanging Hill La TA13 184 F4
Hanglands La BA8 176 C2
Hanham La BS39 77 F7
Hanham Way BS48 8 B2
Hankridge Way TA1 213 E5
Hanna Cl BA2 44 B6
Hannah More Cl
Cheddar BS27 90 B7
Wrington BS40 35 E2
Hannah More Inf Sch BS48 18 D8
Hannah More Prim Sch BS1 227 C2
Hannah More Rd BS48 18 C8
Hannahs La BA5 110 E6
Hannay Rd BS27 71 B1
Hann Cl BA5 203 B2
Hanning Cl TA19 221 F6
Hanning Pk TA19 183 C1
Hanning Rd TA19 183 C1
Hanny's La BS40 39 C3
Hanover Cl
Shepton Mallet BA4 205 A6
Weston-Super-Mare BS22 32 A4
Hanover Ct
Bath BA1 28 B2
Bristol BS1 227 B3
Castle Cary BA7 214 C5
Dulverton TA22 163 D7
Radstock BA3 79 C2
Hanover Gdns BA11 119 D3
Hanover Ho BS20 2 B5
Hanover Pl
Bath BA1 45 B8
Bristol BS1 226 B1
Hanover St
2 Bath BA1 28 B1
2 Bristol BS1 227 A2
Hanover Terr 5 BA1 28 B1
Hansetown Rd TA4 148 F1
Hansford Cl BA2 44 E1
Hansford Mews BA2 44 F1
Hansford Sq BA2 44 E1
Hanson's Way 4 BS21 6 C2
Hans Price Cl 18 BS23 48 E8
Hans Price Ho 13 BS23 48 E8
Hantone Hill BA2 45 F8
Happerton La BS20 4 D2
Hapsburg Cl BS22 32 A4
Hapsford Hill BA11 119 C8
Harbour BA21 218 C5
Harbour Cres BS20 2 E5
Harbour Ct TA5 135 B5
Harbourne Cl TA8 104 C8
Harbour Rd
Portishead BS20 2 D6
Sherborne DT9 225 E5
Watchet TA23 202 C7
Harbour Road Trad Est BS20 2 F6
Harbour Terr DT9 225 E5
Harbour View TA5 135 B5
Harbour Wall BS9 5 B4
Harbour Way
Bristol BS1 226 C1
Sherborne DT9 225 E5
Harbour Wlk BS1 226 C1
Harbutts BA2 28 F1
Harcourt Cl BS31 25 E2
Harcourt Gdns BA1 27 B2
Harcourt Mews BA11 120 A4
Harcourt St TA2 212 E6
Harden Rd BS14 23 E5
Harding's Hill TA10, TA11 172 F5
Harding's House La DT9 225 A6
Harding's La BA8 176 D4
Harding Ct TA11 211 D3
Harding Pl BS31 25 B5
Hardings Cl 8 TA6 153 F3
Hardings Ct TA13 220 C5
Hardington Dr BS31 25 A2
Hardmead La BS27 90 E2
Hardwarden Terr BA22 175 A5
Hardwick Rd BS20 4 C5
Hardy Cres DT10 190 B4
Hardy Ct TA18 224 C5
Hardy Mead Dro TA9 136 B7
Hareclive Prim Sch BS13 22 C4
Hareclive Rd BS13 22 C4
Hare La TA20 182 E2
Harepark Terr TA24 201 A5
Hare Path TA24 147 F8
Hare Path Cross TA24 129 D1
Harepits La BA6 157 E3
Hare Pk TA24 124 C4
Harestone Cross EX13 198 B7
Harewell Wlk BA5 203 B3
Harfield Terr 10 BA20 219 B4
Harford Cl BS9 5 C7
Harford Sq BS40 39 B3
Hargrove La DT10 190 C2
Harington Pl 2 BA1 228 B2
Harley Ct 3 BS8 11 F7
Harley La BS21 7 C6
Harley Mews 2 BS8 11 F7
Harley Pl 4 BS8 11 F7
Harley St BA1 228 B4
Harmony Dr BS20 1 F4
Harnell Cl TA1 213 C3
Harnhill Cl BS13 22 B4
Harp Chase TA1 213 B1
Harper's La TA23 131 D1
Harper Rd TA18 224 C5
Harpitts La SP8 177 F2
Harp Rd
Brent Knoll TA9 105 E6
South Petherton TA13 220 C3
Harptree BS24 49 A2
Harptree Cl BS48 18 D8
Harptree Hill BS40 74 B5
Harrier Path 3 BS22 49 E8
Harriets Yd BS31 24 F5
Harrington Ave BS14 23 E6
Harrington Cl BS30 25 E8
Harrington Gr BS14 23 E6
Harrington Rd BS14 23 E6
Harrington Wlk BS14 23 E6
Harris Cl EX16 179 A4
Harris Gr BS13 22 B3
Harris La
Abbots Leigh BS8 10 F8
Curry Mallet TA3 183 C8
Harrison's La TA19 184 E1
Harris Vale BA3 116 F7
Hart's La
Hallatrow BS39 77 B7
Huish Champflower TA4 165 D7
Sherborne DT9 188 A3
Hart Cl BS20 4 E4
Hartcliffe Engineering Com Coll BS13 22 E4
Hartcliffe Rd BS4 22 E8
Hartcliffe Way BS3, BS4, BS13 22 C7
Hartcliffe Wlk BS4 22 F8
Harter's Hill La BA5 139 E6
Harters Cl BA5 139 E6
Hartfield Ave BS6 226 C4
Hartgill Cl BS13 22 B3
Hartland 14 BS22 32 A2
Hartley Cotts BA4 204 B1
Hartley Ho BA1 228 B3
Hartley Way TA1 213 D2
Hartmoor Hill SP8 177 E3
Hartrow Cl TA1 212 E1
Harts Cl TA19 221 A4
Hartsfield TA20 223 D2
Harts Paddock BA3 77 F3
Hartswell TA4 210 C3
Harvesters Dr BA16 207 B4
Harvest La
Charlton Horethorne DT9 176 A2
Weston-Super-Mare BS22 50 B8
Harvest Way BS22 32 A5
Harvey's Rd TA13 220 C4
Harvey Cl BS22 32 A4
Harvey Way TA19 183 B4
Harwood Cross TA24 130 A4
Harwood Gn BS22 31 E4
Harwood La
Timberscombe TA24 130 A4
Wootton Courtenay TA24 129 F4
Haselbury Gr BS31 25 E2
Haselbury Plucknett CE Fst Sch TA18 196 C5
Haseley Ct TA1 212 D2
Haslands BS48 18 D8
Hassage Hill BA2 80 E7
Hassock's La BA10 160 E8
Hastings Cross TA19 183 B3
Hatch Beauchamp CE Prim Sch TA3 183 A7
Hatch Ct* TA3 183 A8
Hatcher Cl TA8 104 D5
Hatchers Ct TA2 212 F7
Hatchet Hill BA3, BA11 98 E4
Hatch Green La TA3 182 F6

Hatch Mews Bsns Pk TA3 183 A7
Hatfield Bldgs BA2 45 B5
Hatfield Rd
Bath BA2 44 F3
Weston-Super-Mare BS23 49 A8
Hathaway Ho 13 BS2 227 A4
Hathermead Gdns BA21 219 D7
Haunts TA18 196 C8
Havage Cl TA9 104 E5
Havage Dro BS24 51 D8
Haven Cl TA24 201 F3
Haversham Cl BS22 31 D1
Haviland Gr BA1 27 B3
Haviland Ho 7 BS2 227 C3
Haviland Pk BA1 27 B2
Havory BA1 28 C1
Havyat Rd BS40 53 E8
Havyat Road Trad Est BS40 35 E1
Hawarden Terr BA1 28 B1
Hawcombe View TA24 124 A3
Hawk's Worth Cl BA11 120 C7
Hawkchurch CE Prim Sch EX13 198 E3
Hawkchurch Cross EX13 198 E2
Hawkchurch Rd EX13 198 E3
Hawker's La BA5 112 E1
Hawke Rd BS22 31 E4
Hawkers Cl 9 TA5 135 B2
Hawkfield Bsns Pk BS14 22 D5
Hawkfield Cl BS14 22 D5
Hawkfield Rd BS13 22 D5
Hawkfield Way BS14 22 D5
Hawkin's La TA4 165 E7
Hawkins Cl
Burnham-on-S TA8 104 C7
Street BA16 207 E6
Hawkins St BS2 227 C3
Hawkins Way 2 BA21 218 C6
Hawkmoor Hill DT6, EX13 199 B2
Hawkridge Cross TA22 146 D1
Hawkridge Rd TA6 208 B4
Hawksmoor Cl BS14 23 A6
Hawks Rise BA22 218 B5
Hawksworth Dr BS22 32 C4
Hawksworth Rd TA24 201 B6
Hawkwell Cross EX16 162 F4
Hawley Way TA8 104 C7
Hawthorn Cl
Bridgwater TA6 209 D4
High Ham TA10 156 A2
Portishead BS20 1 F5
Hawthorn Coombe BS22 31 E3
Hawthorn Cres
Shepton Mallet BA4 205 A6
Yatton BS49 17 A2
Hawthorne Cl TA18 224 D7
Hawthorne Rd TA21 222 F5
Hawthorn Gdns BS22 31 D2
Hawthorn Gr BA2 45 A1
Hawthorn Hill
Kingsbury Episcopi TA13 185 B6
Weston-Super-Mare BS22 31 E2
Hawthorn Hts BS22 31 D3
Hawthorn Pk BS22 31 E3
Hawthorn Rd
Frome BA11 120 A6
Minehead TA24 200 D7
Radstock BA3 79 B2
Street BA16 207 E6
Taunton TA1 213 C1
Yeovil BA21 219 D7
Hawthorns La BS31 24 E5
Hawthorns The
Clevedon BS21 6 C3
Stalbridge DT10 190 C4
Hawthorn Way BS48 9 A2
Haxen La TA17 195 A8
Hayboro Way BS39 77 E4
Haybridge Villas BA5 203 A5
Haycombe BS14 22 F6
Haycombe Dr BA2 44 A4
Haycombe La BA2 44 A3
Hayden Cl BA2 228 A1
Haydon Cl TA1 212 B4
Haydon Dro BA5 113 C6
Haydon Gate BA3 97 F8
Haydon Hill BA3 98 A8
Haydon Hollow DT9 189 B3
Haydon Ind Est BA3 97 F8
Haydon La TA1, TA3 213 E2
Haydon Rd TA1 213 A4
Hayesdown Fst Sch BA11 120 B5
Hayes End TA13 220 D4
Hayes End Manor TA13 220 D4
Hayesfield Pk BA2 228 B1
Hayesfield School Tech Coll BA2 228 A1
Hayesfield Sch Tech Coll BA2 44 D6
Hayes La TA11 156 F2
Hayes Park Rd BA3 77 F2
Hayes Pl BA2 228 B1
Hayes Rd
Compton Dundon TA11 156 F3
Midsomer Norton BA3 77 F1
Hayes The BS27 90 B8
Hayeswood Farm BA15 46 F5
Hayeswood Rd BA2 59 E3
Hayfield Rd TA24 201 B6
Haygarth Ct BA1 228 B4
Haygrove La TA6 208 C3
Haygrove Pk TA3 168 D1
Haygrove Rd TA6 208 C3
Haygrove Sch TA6 208 C4
Hay Hill
Bath BA1 228 B3
Croscombe BA5 204 B8
Hay La BS40 37 D6
Hayleigh Ho BS13 22 C4
Hayman Rd TA24 200 F7
Haymarket The BS1 227 A3
Haymarket Wlk 9 BS1 227 A4
Haymoor Dro BA5 139 D7
Haymoor La
Coxley BA5 139 E6
Long Sutton TA10 172 D4
Hayne Cross EX16 164 B4
Hayne La TA5 153 B7
Haynes Motor Mus* BA22 175 A6
Hayne Wlk TA7 137 B2
Hay St BA3 96 A8
Haytor Pk BS9 5 D6
Hayward Cl BS21 6 C1
Hayward Dr BA6 158 A6
Haywood Cl BS24 49 A1
Haywood Gdns BS24 49 B1
Haywood Rd TA1 213 D2
Hazel Barrow BS40 74 A7
Hazelbury Rd
Bristol BS14 23 C7
Nailsea BS48 8 D1
Hazel Cl TA1 213 C1
Hazel Cote Rd BS14 23 B4
Hazel Ct BA11 120 A3
Hazeldene Rd BS23 49 A8
Hazel Gr
Bath BA2 44 D4
Midsomer Norton BA3 97 B8
Hazelgrove House (Sch) BA22 174 F5
Hazell Cl BS21 6 E1
Hazel Terr BA3 97 C8
Hazel View TA18 224 D7
Hazel Way BA2 62 D8
Hazelwell La TA19 221 A4
Hazelwood Ct BS9 5 D3
Hazelwood Dr TA6 209 E5
Hazelwood Rd BS9 5 D3
Hazleton Gdns BA2 45 F3
Head Croft BS48 20 B8
Head Dro
Catcott TA7 137 D3
Othery TA7 155 D3
Headley Ct BS13 22 B6
Headley La BS13 22 B7
Headley Park Ave BS13 22 B7
Headley Park Prim Sch BS13 22 B6
Headley Park Rd BS13 22 A7
Headley Rd BS13 22 A6
Headley Wlk BS13 22 B7
Headon Cross TA24 129 F8
Head St BA22 186 B6
Headstock Cross TA20 198 E6
Headstock Rd TA20 198 E7
Headwell TA3 183 C8
Headwell Cl TA3 183 C8
Headwell Hill TA3 183 C8
Heal's Field EX13 198 A2
Heal Cl TA8 104 D5
Heale La TA10 171 C4
Healeys TA24 124 A4
Healys Mdw TA4 167 E6
Hearn La BA22 175 D8
Heart Meers BS14 23 B5
Heath Cl BA12 144 D8
Heathcombe Rd TA6 208 B4
Heathcote Rd BA22 174 A2
Heath Dr BA11 119 F6
Heather Cl
Bridgwater TA6 209 B3
Minehead TA24 201 C4
Taunton TA1 169 A1
Heatherdene BS14 22 F7
Heather Dr BA2 62 D8
Heather Rd BA21 219 D7
Heatherton Park Ho TA4 180 E8
Heather Way BA22 218 A5
Heathfield TA4 151 E4
Heathfield Cl
Bath BA1 27 A3
Creech St Michael TA3 169 D6
Keynsham BS31 24 C5
5 North Petherton TA6 153 F4
West Bagborough TA4 151 E4
Heathfield Com Sch TA2 213 F8
Heathfield Cres BS14 23 B4
Heathfield Dr TA2 213 F8
Heathfield Rd BS48 8 E3
Heathfield Way BS48 8 E2
Heathgate BS49 34 B8
Heathgates BS23 48 D4
Heath Rd BS48 8 F3
Heath Ridge BS41 11 A2
Heathstock Hill TA4 210 D5
Heathway BA12 144 D8
Heathway La BA6 138 B4
Heavitree Way TA2 213 A6
Hebden Rd BA15 64 F3
Heber's La TA19 195 A5
Heckley La BA3 115 B5
Hector Rd TA7 137 D2
Hectors La TA3 170 D8
Hectors Stones TA7 136 E4
Heddon Oak TA4 151 A8
Hedge La BA4 141 B2
Hedgemead Ct BA1 228 C4
Hedges Cl 3 BS21 6 B1
Hedges The BS22 32 C3
Hedgestocks BA4 160 C8
Hedging La TA7 170 A8
Heggard Cl BS13 22 A5
Heights The TA19 221 B4
Hele La
Langport TA10 172 C4
South Petherton TA13 220 C4
Helena Rd BA20 218 D1
Helens Rd BS25 52 B4
Helland Hill TA3 170 C3
Helland La TA3 170 D4
Helliar's La
Curry Mallet TA3 183 D8
Fivehead TA3 170 D1
Hellier's Cl TA20 223 B4
Hellier's La BS27 89 E6
Helliers Rd TA20 223 B4
Hellier Wlk BS13 22 C3
Helling's Cross TA4 166 A4
Helmstedt Way TA20 223 D6
Helston Rd BS48 9 A1
Helvier's La TA4 167 A7
Helwell Gn TA23 202 D6
Helyar Cl BA6 206 D5
Hembridge La BA4 158 E7
Hembury La BA5 139 C7
Hemington Prim Sch BA3 99 B7
Hemming Way BS24 49 E3
Hemp Gdn TA24 200 F8
Hempitts Rd BA16 156 E7
Hemplow Cl BS14 23 D7
Hemstich Hill TA7 138 C1
Henacre Rd BS11 4 F8
Henbury Hill BS9 5 F8
Henbury Ho BA2 45 E4
Henbury Rd BS9 5 F8
Hencliffe Rd BS14 23 D7
Henderson Cl TA1 212 C2
Henderson Dr TA20 223 D2
Henderson Ho 1 BS2 227 B4
Henderson Pl 5 BA5 203 D4
Hendford BA20 219 A4
Hendford Ct BA20 219 A3
Hendford Gr BA20 219 A4
Hendford Hill BA20 219 A3
Hendon Cl TA9 104 E5
Hendon Cross EX16 178 B8
Hengrove Ave BS14 23 B8
Hengrove Com Arts Coll BS14 23 B7
Hengrove La BS14 23 B8
Hengrove Way BS14 22 E6
Henhayes La TA18 224 C6
Hen La BS40 37 E3
Henley Cl EX13 198 B7
Henley Gr TA1 212 D4
Henley La
Butleigh BA6 157 E4
Wookey BA5 139 E8
Yatton BS49 34 D7
Henley Lodge BS49 34 D7
Henley Pk BS49 34 C7
Henley Rd
High Ham TA10 156 B3
Kingsdon TA11 173 E5
Taunton TA1 212 D3
Henley Rise BA4 205 D4
Henley View
Crewkerne TA18 224 C4
Wellow BA2 62 D1
Henley Way BA11 119 F5
Henmore La BS26 88 E6
Hennessy Cl BS14 22 F3
Henning Way DT9 217 D3
Henrietta Ct BA2 228 C4
Henrietta Gdns BA2 228 C3
Henrietta Mews BA2 228 C3
Henrietta Pl BA2 228 C3
Henrietta Rd BA2 228 C3
Henrietta St
Bath BA2 228 C3
Bristol BS2 227 A4
Henry Butt Ho 11 BS23 48 E8
Henry Rogers Ho 2 TA5 135 B2
Henry St BA1 228 C2
Hensley Gdns BA2 44 E4
Hensley Rd BA2 44 E3
Hensman's Hill BS8 226 A2
Henson Pk TA20 223 E5
Hensons Dr EX16 179 A3
Henstridge Trad Est BA8 190 C7
Hepburn Rd BS2 227 B4
Herald Cl BS9 5 D5
Herbert Ho TA22 163 D6
Herbert Rd
Bath BA2 44 D5
Burnham-on-S TA8 104 A8
Clevedon BS21 6 D4
Herbert St TA2 212 E6
Herblay Cl BA21 219 E6
Hereford Dr TA2 213 A8
Heritage Cl BA2 79 D8
Heritage Ct BA6 206 D4
Heritage Ctyd BA5 203 D4
Heritage The BA2 78 E8
Herluin Way BS22, BS23 49 B6
Hermes Cl BS31 25 D2
Hermes Pl BA22 173 E2
Hermitage Cl BS11 4 E7
Hermitage Hill TA10 172 D6
Hermitage Rd
Bath BA1 27 E1
Langport TA10 172 D6
Hermitage St TA18 224 C5
Herne Rise TA19 221 B2
Hern La BS48 20 E5
Heron Cl
Minehead TA24 201 C4
Heron Cl *continued*
Weston-Super-Mare BS22 49 E8
Heron Ct BS21 6 C2
Heron Dr TA1 212 B4
Heron Gate TA1 213 E6
Heron Gate Office Pk TA1 213 E5
Heron Gdns BS20 2 E4
Heron Ho 2 TA6 209 C4
Heron Pk TA8 84 E8
Herons La TA4 167 A4
Heronsmead Wlk BA21 219 D8
Herons Moor Prim Sch BS24 50 A8
Heron Way TA19 221 C2
Herridge Cl BS13 22 B4
Herridge Rd BS13 22 B4
Hersey Gdns BS13 21 E3
Hertford Rd BA21 219 E8
Hervey Cl BS28 108 C4
Hervey Rd
Chard TA20 223 D3
Wells BA5 112 E1
Hestercombe Cl TA6 208 B4
Hestercombe House Gdns* TA2 169 A7
Hestercombe Rd
Bristol BS13 22 B6
Taunton TA2 169 A7
Hetling Ct 7 BA1 228 B2
Hewett Cl TA3 168 D1
Hewish Ct BS23 48 E8
Hewish La
Crewkerne TA18 224 A5
Hewish TA18 195 D3
Hext Ct TA11 211 D3
Hexton Rd BA6 206 E5
Heyron Wlk BS13 22 B4
Heywood Rd BS20 4 C4
Heywood Terr BS20 4 C4
Hibbs Cl SN14 13 F8
Hicks's La BA22 214 D1
Hidcote Mews BS24 49 E7
Hide Mkt BS2 227 C3
Hidewood La EX15 180 F1
Higgin's Grave La TA13 220 B1
High Acre BS39 77 F4
Highaton Head Cross EX36 162 C4
High Bank
Porlock TA24 124 A3
Watchet TA23 202 C7
High Bannerdown BA1 29 B4
High Bolham EX16 163 C1
Highbridge TA4 202 F4
Highbridge & Burnham Sta TA9 104 E3
Highbridge Rd TA8 104 B5
Highbrooks Rd TA11 173 B5
Highburn Cl TA8 104 C4
Highbury Cotts
8 Bath BA1 28 A1
Coleford BA3 116 F7
Highbury Ct 15 BS23 30 C1
Highbury Farm Bsns Pk BS39 77 A8
Highbury Par BS23 30 C1
Highbury Pl BA1 28 A1
Highbury Rd
Hallatrow BS39 77 B7
Weston-Super-Mare BS23 30 C1
Highbury St BA3 117 A7
Highbury Terr 10 BA1 28 A1
Highbury Villas
9 Bath BA1 28 A1
Bristol BS2 226 C4
Highcroft
Weston-Super-Mare BS23 30 F1
Woolavington TA7 136 E4
High Cross EX16 164 A1
Highdale Ave BS21 6 E3
Highdale Cl BS14 23 B4
Highdale Rd BS21 6 E3
High Down Jun & Inf Schs BS20 2 A4
Higher Actis BA6 206 E3
Higher Backway BA10 215 E6
Higher Barton
Martock TA12 185 D4
Trent DT9 187 F5
Higher Beacon TA19 221 B4
Higher Beadon TA16 195 E7
Higher Brooks BA16 207 C2
Higher Bullen BA22 197 F8
Higher Burton BA22 197 C8
Higher Cheap St 3 DT9 225 D4
Higher Coombses TA20 198 D8
Higher Cross EX15 179 C1
Higher Easthams La TA18 224 F7
Higher Farm La
Podimore BA22 174 A4
Sparkford BA22 175 B3
Higher Farm Trad Est BA20 218 C5
Higher Gunville DT9 217 D2
Higher Heathfield TA4 151 E4
Higher Kingsbury DT9 217 D3
Higher Kingsbury Cl DT9 217 C3
Higher Kingston BA21 219 B5
Higher Mead TA19 221 B3
Higher Millhayes EX15 180 B1
Higher North Town La BA22 175 D7
Higher Orch
Martock TA12 185 D4
Minehead TA24 200 C8
Higher Palmerston Rd TA2 212 D6
Higher Park La TA24 129 E2
Higher Pk TA24 200 D6
Higher Rd
Chedzoy TA7 154 D8
Horsington BA8 176 D3
Shepton Beauchamp TA19 184 E3
Woolavington TA7 136 E4
Higher Ream BA21 218 C6
Higher Rodhuish Rd TA24 131 B3
Higher St
Curry Mallet TA3 183 C8
East Quantoxhead TA5 133 B5
Martock TA12 185 D4
Merriott TA16 195 F8
Norton Sub Hamdon TA14 185 E2
West Chinnock TA18 196 B8
Higher Tolbury BA10 215 E6
Higher Town EX16 178 C1
Higher Westbury DT9 187 E1
Higher West Hatch La TA3 182 D7
Higher Westholme Rd
North Wootton BA4 140 D4
Pilton BA4 204 A1
Highfield
Coleford BA3 116 E8
Ilminster TA19 221 B4
Taunton TA1 212 A2
Taunton TA1 212 C3
Wells BA5 140 C7
West Chinnock TA18 196 B8
Highfield Cl
Bath BA2 44 B5
Somerton TA11 211 C4
Taunton TA1 212 A2
Highfield Cres
Chilcompton BA3 96 C4
Taunton TA1 212 A2
Highfield Dr BS20 1 E3
Highfield La
Compton Martin BS40 74 B6
East Harptree BS40 75 A3
Highfield Rd
Keynsham BS31 24 F2
Peasedown St John BA2 79 C8
Street BA16 207 B5
Weston-Super-Mare BS24 49 A1
Yeovil BA21 219 C6
Highfields
Barrington TA19 184 C5
Clandown BA3 78 E4
Midsomer Norton BA3 78 D2
Stanton Drew BS39 39 F1
Highfield Terr TA12 185 D5
Highfield Trad Est BA21 219 C6
Highfield View BA3 116 E8
Highfield Way TA11 211 C4
High Gn BA5 111 A4
High Gr BS9 5 B7
Highgrove TA1 212 E1
Highgrove Cl TA6 209 A2
Highgrove Wlk BS24 50 A8
High Ham CE Prim Sch TA10 156 A1
High Kingsdown BS2 226 C4
High La
Barton St David TA11 158 A2
Shapwick TA7 155 F8
Highland Cl BS22 31 B2
Highland Ct BA21 219 C6
Highland Rd BA2 44 B5
Highlands TA1 212 E1
Highlands La BS24 50 A8
Highlands Rd
Long Ashton BS41 11 A2
Portishead BS20 2 B5
Highland Terr BA2 44 D6
High Lea BA21 219 B8
High Littleton CE Prim Sch BS39 59 C1
High Mdws BA3 77 F1
Highmead Gdns BS13 21 E4
High Mead Gdns BS39 57 D3
Highmore Rd DT9 225 C5
High Path TA21 222 C7
High Pk BS39 77 D6
High Rd BA22 175 D8
Highridge Cres BS13 21 F5
Highridge Gn BS13 21 E6
Highridge Inf Sch BS13 21 F6
Highridge Pk BS13 21 F6
Highridge Rd BS13, BS41 21 E4
Highridge Wlk BS13 21 E7
High St
Aller TA10 171 E8
Ashcott TA7 156 B8
Axbridge BS26 70 B2
Bampton EX16 164 B1
Banwell BS29 51 A2
Bathampton BA2 28 F1
Bath BA1 228 C2
Batheaston BA1 28 F3
Bathford BA1 29 D2
Bath, Twerton BA2 44 B6
Bath, Weston BA1 27 B1
Bishops Lydeard TA4 167 E8
Bitton BS30 25 E8
Blackford BS28 107 E4
Blagdon BS40 54 E3
Bourton SP8 161 F2
Bridgwater TA6 208 F5
Bristol BS1 227 A2
Bristol, Shirehampton BS11 4 E6
Bruton BA10 215 E6
Buckland Dinham BA11 100 A3

High St *continued*
Burnham-on-S TA8 104 A6
Butleigh BA6 157 E4
Cannington TA5 135 B2
Carhampton TA24 131 A5
Castle Cary BA7 214 C5
Chapmanslade BA13 121 C4
Chard TA20 223 B4
Charlton Adam TA11 173 F7
Chew Magna BS40 39 A3
Chewton Mendip BA3 94 F7
Claverham BS49 17 F1
Coleford BA3 116 F6
Congresbury BS49 34 D4
Dulverton TA22 163 D6
Dunster TA24 201 E2
East Chinnock BA22 196 E8
East Harptree BS40 74 F5
Evercreech BA4 141 E1
Faulkland BA3 80 D1
Freshford BA3 64 B5
Frome BA11 119 E5
Glastonbury BA6 206 E4
Hardington Mandeville BA22 197 A6
Henstridge BA8 190 A6
High Littleton BS39 59 D1
Hinton Charterhouse BA2 63 E1
Hinton St George TA17 195 D7
Ilchester BA22 173 E1
Ilminster TA19 221 B4
Keinton Mandeville TA11 158 A1
Keynsham BS31 24 E6
Kingweston BA6 157 E1
Lynford-on-F TA11 158 C2
Maiden Bradley BA12 144 C2
Marshfield SN14 13 F8
Midsomer Norton BA3 78 B1
Milborne Port DT9 217 D2
Milton Clevedon BA4 160 A8
Milverton TA4 166 F5
Monksilver TA4 150 B8
Nailsea BS48 8 F3
North Cadbury BA22 175 D6
North Petherton TA6 153 E4
North Wootton BA4 140 C4
Norton St Philip BA2 81 E4
Nunney BA11 143 B8
Oakhill BA3 115 A3
Othery TA7 155 C2
Paulton BS39 77 E5
Paulton, Plummer's Hill BS39 77 E6
Pensford BS39 40 E4
Porlock TA24 124 A3
Portbury BS20 3 E3
Portishead BS20 2 D5
Queen Camel BA22 174 F3
Rimpton BA22 188 A8
Rode BA11 101 E8
Saltford BS31 25 F3
Shepton Mallet BA4 205 B5
Sparkford BA22 175 A5
Spaxton TA5 152 E7
Stalbridge DT10 190 B5
Stogumber TA4 150 D8
Stogursey TA5 134 C5
Stoke sub Hamdon TA14 185 F4
Ston Easton BA3 95 E8
Stoney Stratton BA4 141 F2
Stourton BA12 161 F5
Stourton Caundle DT10 189 F2
Street BA16 207 C6
Taunton TA1 212 F3
Templecombe BA8 176 E1
Thorncombe TA20 199 B6
Timsbury BA2 60 B2
Wellington TA21 222 E6
Wellow BA2 62 D1
Wells BA5 203 D4
West Coker BA22 197 A8
Weston-Super-Mare BS23 48 D8
Weston-Super-Mare, Worle BS22 31 E2
Williton TA4 202 D2
Wincanton BA9 216 C4
Winford BS40 38 A7
Winsham TA20 194 E1
Wiveliscombe TA4 210 C4
Wookey BA5 139 D8
Wookey Hole BA5 203 A8
Woolley BA1 27 F6
Wrington BS40 35 D2
Yatton BS49 34 C8
Yenston BA8 189 F8
Yeovil BA20 219 B4
High View BS20 2 A4
High View Dr TA7 156 B8
Highwall La BS14, BS31 23 F1
Highwoods Cl TA14 185 F2
Higson Cl BA22 186 D3
Hilary Rd TA1 212 D3
Hildesheim Bridge BS23 48 F7
Hildesheim Cl BS23 48 F6
Hildesheim Ct 9 BS23 48 E7
Hilhouse BS9 5 C6
Hill's La 10 TA12 185 E6
Hill Ave BA2 44 F1
Hillborne Gdns BA21 218 C5
Hillbrook Ct DT9 225 D4
Hill Brow DT9 225 B2
Hill Cl BA9 216 D4
Hillclose La TA19 221 F2
Hillcote Est BS24 67 B8
Hillcrest
Crowcombe TA4 151 B7
Peasedown St John BA2 79 C7
Pensford BS39 40 E3
Hillcrest Cl
Nailsea BS48 8 E1
Yeovil BA21 219 C7
Hillcrest Dr BA2 44 C4
Hillcrest Rd
Nailsea BS48 8 E1
Portishead BS20 1 E4
Templecombe BA8 176 E1
Hill Crest Rd BA21 219 C6
Hillcroft Cl BS22 31 A2
Hill Cross BA22 196 F6
Hill Ct BS39 77 E6
Hilldale Rd BS48 19 B5
Hill Dr BS8 10 C3
Hillend BS22 31 E3
Hillfield BS27 90 B7
Hill Gay Cl BS20 1 F4
Hill Ground BA11 119 E5
Hillgrove Ave BA20 218 F2
Hillgrove Cl TA6 208 E5
Hillgrove Rd BA5 93 C1
Hillgrove St N BS2 227 A4
Hillgrove St BS2 227 B4
Hillgrove Terr BS23 48 D1
Hill Head BA6 206 D3
Hill Head Cl
Glastonbury BA6 206 D3
Taunton TA1 213 A3
Hillhead Cotts TA2 212 C8
Hillhead Cross TA24 128 D3
Hillhouse EX14 192 D3
Hill House Cl DT9 225 E5
Hillier's La
Churchill BS25 52 D4
Yarley BA5 139 C8
Hillingdon Ct BA21 218 C6
Hill La
Bicknoller, Culverhays TA4 133 A1
Bicknoller TA4 132 F2
Brent Knoll TA9 86 B3
Carhampton TA24 131 A4
Chipstable TA4 165 C6
Clevedon BS21 7 C4
Draycott BS27 90 C2
Portishead BS20 1 F1
Rodney Stoke BS27 91 B2
Rowberrow BS25 53 A1
Shepton Mallet BA4 205 B6
Waterrow TA4 165 E5
West Quantoxhead TA4 132 F4
Hill Lea Gdns BS27 90 B8
Hillmead
Churchill BS40 53 A5
Shepton Mallet BA4 205 B6
Hillmer Rise BS29 50 F3
Hill Moor BS21 6 E2
Hillpath BS29 51 B2
Hill Pk BS49 34 E5
Hill Rd
Allerford TA24 124 E4
Clevedon BS21 6 D4
Dundry BS41 21 D2
Minehead TA24 125 B4
Sandford BS25 52 A3
Weston-Super-Mare BS23 48 F8
Weston-Super-Mare, Worle BS22 31 E2
Hill Rd E BS22 31 E2
Hillsboro TA7 136 E4
Hillsborough BS8 226 A2
Hillsborough Gdns TA8 85 B1
Hillsborough Ho BS23 49 A4
Hills Cl BS31 25 A5
Hills Cotts TA4 167 A7
Hillsdon Rd BS9 5 F8
Hillside
Bristol BS6 226 C4
Chard TA20 223 B4
Horrington BA5 113 A2
Portbury BS20 3 D3
Puriton TA7 136 C4
West Pennard BA6 140 B1
Hillside Ave
Frome BA11 119 F2
Midsomer Norton BA3 96 F8
Hillside Cl
Curry Rivel TA10 171 D4
Paulton BS39 77 F6
Hill Side Cl BA5 203 C5
Hillside Cres
Midsomer Norton BA3 96 E8
Puriton TA7 136 C4
Hillside Dr TA7 136 C4
Hillside Fst Sch BS22 31 E2
Hillside Gdns
Bishop Sutton BS39 57 C3
Weston-Super-Mare BS22 31 B1
Hillside Gr TA1 212 C1
Hillside Ho BA11 119 F3
Hillside Rd
Backwell BS48 19 A4
Bath BA2 44 D4
Bleadon BS24 67 B8
Clevedon BS21 6 D3
Long Ashton BS41 11 B2
Midsomer Norton BA3 96 F8
Portishead BS20 1 D4
Hillside Terr BA21 219 C5
Hillside View
1 Barwick BA22 197 F8
Midsomer Norton BA3 78 A3
Peasedown St John BA2 79 C8
Yeovil BA22 219 D1
Hillside W BS24 49 F2
Hills Orch 9 TA12 185 E6
Hill St
Bristol BS1 226 C2
Hill St *continued*
Stogumber TA4 150 D8
Hill Terr TA1 212 A4
Hill The
Freshford BA3 64 C5
Langport TA10 172 A5
Hill Top BS20 2 A4
Hilltop La TA5 133 D6
Hilltops TA8 65 F6
Hillview
Midsomer Norton BA3 96 E7
Timsbury BA2 60 B1
Hill View
Brean TA8 65 E2
Bristol BS8 226 B2
Brompton Ralph TA4 150 C3
Farrington Gurney BS39 77 B3
Marksbury BA2 42 B1
Mudford BA21 187 D6
Priston BA2 61 A5
Queen Camel BA22 174 F4
Yeovil BA21 219 C5
Hillview Ave BS21 6 D2
Hillview Cl TA24 200 D7
Hill View Cl
Ilton TA19 183 F4
7 Stoke sub Hamdon TA14 185 F4
West Chinnock TA18 196 B8
Hill View Ct
Evercreech BA4 141 E1
Weston-Super-Mare BS22 49 D8
Hill View Cvn Pk BS40 20 B1
Hillview Gdns BS40 37 C8
Hill View Park Homes BS22 49 D8
Hillview Rd
Loxton BS26 68 C4
Minehead TA24 200 D7
Hill View Rd
Bath BA1 28 B2
Bristol BS13 22 A8
Carhampton TA24 131 A5
Weston-Super-Mare BS23 49 A7
Hillview Terr TA12 185 D5
Hill View Terr
Ilminster TA19 221 B4
Lyng TA3 170 C7
Hill View Trad Est TA4 151 E4
Hillway TA11 173 E7
Hillworth Ho 26 BA4 205 B6
Hillyfield Rd BS13 22 A6
Hillyfields
Taunton TA1 213 C2
Winscombe BS25 70 B8
Hillyfields Way BS25 70 A8
Hilly Head TA21 222 B5
Hilly Pk TA2 168 B5
Hinam Cross TA22 163 B7
Hinckley Cl BS22 32 C4
Hincombe Hill BA4 142 E2
Hindhayes Inf Sch BA16 207 D5
Hindhayes La BA16 207 D6
Hind Pitts BS25 70 F7
Hine Rd TA1 212 B1
Hinkley Point Nature Trail* TA5 134 C8
Hinkley Point Visitor Ctr* TA5 134 C8
Hinton BS24 49 A2
Hinton Cl
Bath BA2 43 F6
Hinton St George TA17 195 D7
Saltford BS31 25 E3
Hinton Cross BA22 187 D7
Hinton Dr TA1 212 E1
Hinton Hill BA2, BA3 63 A1
Hinton La 12 BS8 11 F6
Hinton Rd TA18 224 B8
Hinton St George CE Sch TA17 195 C7
Hinton Villas BA2 63 E1
Hippisley Dr BS26 70 D2
Hippisley Ho BA5 113 A1
Hiscocks Dr BA2 44 E4
Hiscocks La BA8 176 E2
Hitchen TA16 195 F7
Hitchen Cl SN14 13 F8
Hitchen Hill BA4 140 F3
Hitchings La TA3 170 B7
Hitchin La BA4 205 A5
Hither Acre TA19 221 A4
Hither Bath Bridge BS4 23 C8
Hither Gn BS21 6 F2
Hither Green Ind Est BS21 6 F2
Hither Mead TA4 167 F8
Hittsford La EX36 162 A1
Hoare's La BA11 98 B3
Hobart Rd BS23 48 F3
Hobb's La BS1 226 C2
Hobbiton Rd BS22 32 A4
Hobbs Ct 1 BS48 8 F2
Hobbs La BS48 20 E3
Hobbs Mead 7 TA4 167 F8
Hob La TA2 168 E8
Hobwell La BS41 11 C2
Hoccombe Ford TA4 150 F1
Hocken Cl TA20 223 D6
Hockley Ct BA1 27 D1
Hockley La BA22 175 E5
Hockpitt La TA5 134 A2
Hodder's Cl BA11 119 E5
Hodges Barton TA11 211 C4
Hodshill BA2 62 F6
Hoecroft BA3 96 D2
Hoecroft Gdns BA3 96 D3
Hogarth Mews BS22 32 A3
Hogarth Wlk BS22 32 A3
Hoggington La BA14 83 E3
Hogues Wlk BS13 22 B4
Holbeach Way BS14 23 A2
Holbear TA20 223 D2
Holbrook Cres BS13 22 D4
Holbrook Pk TA13 220 C5
Holburne Mus & Crafts Study Ctr* BA2 45 B7
Holcombe BS14 23 A5
Holcombe Cl BA2 28 F1
Holcombe Gn BA1 27 B2
Holcombe Gr BS31 24 D5
Holcombe Hill BA3 116 C7
Holcombe La
Bathampton BA2 28 F1
Doulting BA4 141 E4
Holcombe Vale BA2 28 F1
Holden's Way
Curry Rivel TA10 171 C3
Curry Rivel TA10 171 D3
Holders Wlk BS41 20 F8
Holdfast La TA14 185 D1
Holditch Court La TA20 198 E5
Holditch La EX13, TA20 198 E5
Holdscroft La DT6 199 B1
Holeground Villas BA5 203 A8
Holemore Cross EX14 191 F5
Holes La BA11 118 B6
Holes Sq TA24 130 B5
Holford Cl BS48 8 E1
Holford Ct BS14 23 B5
Holford La TA4 151 C5
Holford Rd
Bridgwater TA6 208 B4
Taunton TA2 212 E8
Hollam Cross TA22 163 E7
Hollam Dr TA22 163 D6
Hollam La TA22 163 D7
Holland's La TA4 149 E1
Holland's Wash Dro TA20 193 C5
Holland Ct BA16 207 D7
Holland Rd
Bath BA1 28 B1
Clevedon BS21 6 B1
Holland St BS23 49 A8
Holleys Cl TA20 198 D8
Hollies Cl
Martock TA12 185 D5
Middlezoy TA7 155 B3
Shepton Mallet BA4 205 C6
Hollies La BA1 29 A6
Hollies The
Crewkerne TA18 224 C4
Midsomer Norton BA3 78 A1
Yeovil BA21 219 C7
Hollis Ave BS20 2 C3
Hollis Cl
Halstock BA22 197 D3
Long Ashton BS41 21 A8
Hollis Cres BS20 2 C3
Hollister's Dr BS13 22 D4
Hollis Way
Halstock BA22 197 D3
Southwick BA14 83 F3
Holloway
Bath BA2 228 B1
Lopen TA13 185 A1
Minehead TA24 200 F7
Holloway Rd TA7 155 B2
Holloway St TA24 200 F7
Holloway The TA21 179 E7
Hollowbrook La BS39, BS40 57 D6
Hollowell Hill
Norton Sub Hamdon TA14, TA18 185 E1
West Chinnock TA18 196 B8
Hollow La
Baltonsborough BA6 158 B8
Dinnington TA17 195 B7
Lopen TA13 185 A1
Montacute TA15 186 B3
Wembdon TA5, TA6 208 C7
Weston-Super-Mare BS22 31 F3
Hollow Marsh La BA3, BS39 76 B4
Hollowmead BS49 34 E8
Hollowmead Cl BS49 34 F8
Hollow Rd
Shepton Beauchamp TA19 184 D3
Shipham BS25 70 F8
Hollow The
Bath BA2 44 B4
Corsley Heath BA12 144 E8
Dunkerton BA2 61 D4
Westbury-sub-Mendip BA5 110 D7
Hollway Cl BS14 23 E5
Hollway Rd BS14 23 E5
Hollybush Cl BA15 64 E7
Hollybush La
Bristol BS9 5 E5
Bristol BS9 5 F4
Leigh u M BA3 117 A2
Holly Cl
Bridgwater TA6 209 E5
Nailsea BS48 9 A3
7 North Petherton TA6 153 F3
Taunton TA1 213 C1
Weston-Super-Mare BS22 32 A1
Holly Ct
Bristol BS2 226 C4
Frome BA11 120 B7
Holly Dr BA2 62 D8
Holly Gr TA18 224 D7
Holly Hill BA4 142 C1
Holly La
Clevedon BS21 6 F6
Drimpton DT8 199 F8
Shepton Mallet BA4 205 C4
Hollyman Wlk 5 BS21 6 F3
Hollymead La BS9 5 E4
Hollyridge BS14 23 C6
Holly Ridge BS20 2 A5
Holly Terr
Chard TA20 223 C4
Odcombe BA22 186 C2
Holly Tree Wlk BA20 218 E3
Holly Wlk
Keynsham BS31 24 D4
Radstock BA3 78 E1
Holman's BA6 157 E4
Holman Cl BA6 206 E6
Holmbury Cl BA11 120 D6
Holmbush TA24 128 E8
Holm Cl TA8 104 B5
Holmlea
Portishead BS20 2 F5
1 Wookey BA5 139 D8
Holmoak Rd BS31 24 C4
Holm Oaks BA6 157 E4
Holm Rd BS24 49 E2
Holms Rd BS23 49 A5
Holsom Cl BS14 23 F6
Holsom Rd BS14 23 F6
Holst Gdns BS4 22 D7
Holt Ball Steep TA24 129 D7
Holten's La BA22 196 E6
Holt Hill DT9 189 C1
Holt La
Halstock BA22 197 F3
South Perrott DT8 196 D1
Stourton Caundle DT9, DT10 189 E1
West Pennard BA6 140 D2
Holton Cross BA9 176 C6
Holton St BA9 176 C5
Holt Rd
North Brewham BA11 161 E8
Witham Friary BA11 143 D1
Holtsdown La BA1 28 F7
Holvert La TA20 194 F1
Holway
North Petherton TA6 153 F4
Tatworth TA20 198 D8
Holway Ave TA1 213 B3
Holway Deane TA1 213 D2
Holway Gn TA1 213 C2
Holway Hill TA1 213 B2
Holway House Pk TA19 183 E2
Holway Park Com Prim Sch TA1 213 C3
Holway Rd TA1 213 B3
Holwell Cl BS39 77 E4
Holwell Hill BA11 143 B7
Holwell La BS27 89 F8
Holworthy La TA22 148 E2
Holy Moor Cross EX36 162 C1
Holy Moor La EX36 162 C1
Holyoake St TA21 222 C7
Holyrood Com Sch (Lower) TA20 223 C4
Holyrood Com Sch (Upper) TA20 223 C5
Holyrood St TA20 223 C3
Holy Tree Cross TA14 185 E3
Holy Trinity CE Prim Sch
Taunton TA1 213 A3
Yeovil BA20 218 E2
Holy Well Rd TA7 137 C2
Homberg Way TA6 208 E6
Homeavon Ho BS31 24 F5
Homecanton Ho BA9 216 C4
Homecastle Ho 2 TA6 208 F5
Homechime Ho BA5 203 D3
Home Cl
Westbury-sub-Mendip BA5 110 E6
West Camel BA22 174 D3
Wrington BS40 35 E3
Homeclose La EX13, TA20 198 A8
Home Cotts TA1 212 D5
Home Dr
Wincanton BA9 216 C3
Yeovil BA21 218 E5
Home Farm* TA24 131 D6
Home Farm Cl BA2 79 B7
Home Farm La BA22 188 A8
Home Farm Pk TA19 183 E2
Home Farm Rd BS8 11 B8
Home Farm Way TA19 183 E2
Homefield
Bishops Lydeard TA4 167 E8
Congresbury BS49 34 E3
Locking BS24 50 A5
Timsbury BA2 60 C2
Wellington TA21 222 E4
Homefield Cl
Beckington BA11 101 E4
Creech St Michael TA3 169 D4
Locking BS24 50 A5
Saltford BS31 25 E3
Winscombe BS25 51 F1
Home Field Cl TA11 157 B4
Homefield Ct BA22 174 F1
Homefield Ind Est BS24 50 A5
Homefield Rd BS31 25 F3
Homefields BA5 110 E6
Home Fields BA4 205 C4
Homeground BS21 6 F2

Home Ground BS11 .... 4 D7
Homelea Pk E BA1 .... 44 A7
Homelea Pk W BA1 .... 44 A7
Home Mdw TA24 .... 200 D7
Homemead BA2 .... 43 A8
Home Mead BS4 .... 22 E7
Home Orch
Chew Stoke BS40 .... 56 D8
Hatch Beauchamp TA3 .... 183 A7
Homestead BS20 .... 1 E3
Homestead Pk BA5 .... 203 A7
Homestead The
Clevedon BS21 .... 6 C3
Keynsham BS31 .... 24 F2
Homestead Way BS25 .... 70 A8
Homeville Ho BA20 .... 219 A4
Home Way Cnr BA6 .... 138 B4
Hone Cross EX16 .... 164 F5
Hone La TA22 .... 147 F4
Honeycombe Rise DT9 .... 225 B2
Honey Crock La TA7 .... 155 E8
Honeygar La BA6 .... 138 B5
Honey Garston Cl BS13 .... 22 B4
Honey Garston Rd BS13 .... 22 B4
Honeyhall La BS49 .... 52 D7
Honeyhurst La BS27 .... 109 F8
Honeylands
Curry Rivel TA10 .... 171 D4
Portishead BS20 .... 2 C3
Honeymead
Bristol BS14 .... 23 C6
Croscombe BA5 .... 204 B8
Honey Mead La BA6, TA11 .... 158 B4
Honeypot La TA11 .... 158 C1
Honey Pot La BA11 .... 144 A4
Honey Row La TA4 .... 132 E2
Honeysuckle Pl BS24 .... 50 A8
Honeywell La BA3 .... 94 F4
Honiton 9 BS22 .... 32 A2
Honiton Rd
Clevedon BS21 .... 6 E1
Taunton TA3 .... 168 D1
Hood Cl BA6 .... 206 E3
Hookedmead La BS26 .... 88 A1
Hook Hill BA2 .... 60 D2
Hook La
Hinton Blewett BA3, BS39 .... 75 E4
North Cheriton BA9 .... 176 C5
Hooks Batch BS40 .... 54 C4
Hookway Hill TA24 .... 123 A3
Hooper's Cl TA1 .... 212 B2
Hooper's La
East Coker BA22 .... 197 F7
Fordgate TA7 .... 154 E3
Hooper Ave BA5 .... 112 E1
Hooper Cl
Burnham-on-S TA8 .... 104 D5
Highbridge TA9 .... 104 F4
Hooper Rd
Bristol BS14 .... 23 D5
Street BA16 .... 207 B5
Hoopers Barton 9 BA11 .... 119 E5
Hoopers Cross EX16 .... 164 D3
Hopcott Cl TA24 .... 200 E6
Hopcott Rd TA24 .... 200 F5
Hopcott Terr TA24 .... 201 A5
Hopechapel Hill 10 BS8 .... 11 F6
Hope Cl BA5 .... 203 C4
Hope Corner Cl TA2 .... 212 E8
Hope Corner La TA2 .... 212 F8
Hope Cote Lodge BA2 .... 45 C1
Hope Cotts
Highbridge TA9 .... 104 D3
Kingston Seymour BS21 .... 16 B2
Hope Cross SP8 .... 177 D3
Hope Ct BS1 .... 226 B1
Hope Sq BS8 .... 11 F6
Hope Terr BA3 .... 78 B1
Hopewell Gdns BS11 .... 4 F7
Hopkins Ct BA9 .... 216 C2
Hopkins Ho BA22 .... 218 A5
Hopkins St BS23 .... 48 E8
Hopton Ct BA4 .... 141 E1
Horesham Gr BS13 .... 22 C5
Horfield Rd BS2 .... 227 A4
Horn's La BS26 .... 70 B2
Hornbeam Cl
Bridgwater TA6 .... 209 D5
Frome BA11 .... 120 C6
Taunton TA1 .... 213 D2
Hornbeam Wlk BS31 .... 24 C3
Horne Cl BA3 .... 96 F1
Horner Nature Trails★ TA24 .... 129 B8
Horner Rd TA2 .... 213 B7
Horningsham Prim Sch BA12 .... 144 D4
Horn La TA20 .... 194 B2
Hornsbury Hill TA20 .... 223 E8
Hornsbury Mill Mus★ TA20 .... 223 E8
Hornsey La TA20 .... 182 B1
Horns La BA9 .... 160 B2
Horn St BA11 .... 143 B8
Hornswell DT9 .... 189 D4
Horrington Prim Sch BA5 .... 113 B3
Horsecastle Cl BS49 .... 17 A1
Horsecastle Farm Rd BS49 .... 17 A1
Horsecastle La DT9 .... 225 C3
Horsecastles DT9 .... 225 D3
Horse Cl BA11 .... 101 D5
Horsecombe Brow BA2 .... 45 A1
Horsecombe Gr BA2 .... 45 A1
Horsecombe Vale BA2 .... 45 A1
Horsecroft La TA3 .... 170 B4
Horsefair The BS1 .... 227 B3
Horseham La TA5 .... 134 E8
Horsehill La BA4 .... 142 D2
Horse La DT9 .... 176 A2
Horseland La TA24 .... 131 A5
Horseleaze La BS25 .... 52 D1
Horsemans Mews BA6 .... 206 D5
Horse Mill Cross DT6 .... 199 D3
Horse Mill La TA11 .... 211 E4
Horsepark La TA24 .... 130 A4
Horse Pond La TA6 .... 208 F4
Horsepool Rd BS13 .... 21 E3
Horse Race La BS8 .... 10 A6
Horse Rd TA24 .... 130 F5
Horseshoe Cotts TA12 .... 185 E7
Horseshoe Dr BS9 .... 5 C4
Horseshoe Rd TA20 .... 199 A6
Horseshoe Wlk BA2 .... 45 B5
Horsey La
Horsey TA7 .... 136 C2
Langport TA10 .... 172 B4
Yeovil BA20 .... 219 A4
Horsey Rdbt BA20 .... 219 A3
Horsington CE Prim Sch BA8 .... 176 D3
Horsington Ho BA8 .... 176 E2
Horstmann Cl 2 BA1 .... 44 B7
Hortmead La TA19 .... 183 E3
Horton Cl BA21 .... 218 D6
Horton Ho BA2 .... 228 C4
Horton St
Bristol BS2 .... 227 C3
Frome BA11 .... 119 D5
Horton Way TA7 .... 136 E4
Horts Rd TA1 .... 212 C1
Horwood Rd BS48 .... 8 F1
Hosey Wlk BS13 .... 22 A5
Hoskins Cl TA10 .... 171 C4
Hospital La
Sherborne DT9 .... 225 D4
South Petherton TA13 .... 220 D5
Hospital Rdbt BA20 .... 219 A5
Host St BS1 .... 227 A3
Hot Bath St 6 BA1 .... 228 B2
Hotwell Rd BS8 .... 226 B1
Hotwells Prim Sch BS8 .... 11 F6
Houlgate Way BS26 .... 70 B1
Houlton St BS2 .... 227 C4
Houndsmill BA8 .... 176 E2
Houndsmoor La TA4 .... 167 A4
Hound St DT9 .... 225 D4
Houndstone Bsns Pk BA22 .... 218 B6
Houndstone Cl BA21 .... 218 C5
Houndstone Cnr BA22 .... 218 A5
Houndstone Ct BA22 .... 218 A5
Houndstone Pk BA22 .... 218 A5
Houndstone Ret Pk BA22 .... 218 B5
Houndwood Cl BA16 .... 207 A6
Houndwood Dro BA16 .... 207 A6
House's La TA20 .... 193 F1
House Gate Rd BA11 .... 143 F2
Housman Rd BA16 .... 207 D5
Houston Way BA11 .... 119 D5
Hoveland Cres TA1 .... 212 D2
Hoveland Ct TA1 .... 212 E2
Hoveland Dr TA1 .... 212 D1
Hoveland La TA1 .... 212 C2
Howard Cl
Burnham-on-S TA8 .... 104 C7
Saltford BS31 .... 25 D3
Howard Rd
Wellington TA21 .... 222 D7
Yeovil BA21 .... 219 E6
Howards Row TA20 .... 223 C4
Howecroft Ct BS9 .... 5 E4
Howecroft Gdns BS9 .... 5 E4
Howell's La TA2, TA6 .... 153 D1
Howell Hill BA22 .... 174 D4
Howgrove Hill La BS40 .... 37 C2
How Hill BA2 .... 44 A6
Howitt Way 1 BS24 .... 49 F7
Howleigh La TA3 .... 181 C5
Hownel La TA22 .... 147 F2
Hoyles Cl TA21 .... 222 E4
Hoyles Rd TA21 .... 222 E4
Hozzard La BS28 .... 107 E2
Huckeymead La BA4 .... 158 F7
Huddleston Ct 10 BA5 .... 203 D4
Hudson St TA8 .... 104 B6
Hudson Way TA2 .... 212 C6
Huett Cl TA8 .... 65 F3
Hugdole La TA7 .... 137 D2
Hughenden Rd BS23 .... 49 A8
Hughes Cl 6 TA6 .... 209 B4
Hughes Ct BA11 .... 101 E8
Hugh Sexey CE Mid Sch BS28 .... 107 E3
Hugo St TA1 .... 213 A4
Huish BA20 .... 219 A5
Huish Ball Steep TA24 .... 129 D7
Huish Cl
Highbridge TA9 .... 104 D4
Taunton TA1 .... 213 D4
Huish Cleeve TA4 .... 165 E7
Huish Ct BA3 .... 79 B2
Huish Episcopi Prim Sch TA10 .... 172 A5
Huish Episcopi Sch TA10 .... 172 A5
Huish Gdns 2 BA20 .... 219 A5
Huish La
Alweston DT9 .... 189 B2
Washford TA23 .... 131 E4
Huish La *continued*
Wyke Champflower BA10 .... 215 C7
Huish Mdw TA23 .... 131 E4
Huish Park (Yeovil Town FC) BA22 .... 218 B7
Huish Prim Sch BA20 .... 219 A5
Huish Rd TA11 .... 173 C7
Huish Row TA24 .... 129 A8
Hukeley Head Cross EX16 .... 164 D3
Hulk Moor Dro BA16, BA16 .... 207 C8
Hulkshay La TA6 .... 153 E3
Hull La DT9, BA8 .... 176 B3
Humber Gr TA1 .... 213 D3
Humberstan Wlk BS11 .... 4 E8
Humphreys Rd TA21 .... 222 E7
Humphry Davy Way 6 BS8 .... 11 F5
Humpy La DT9 .... 189 A1
Hundredstone Cl BA21 .... 219 B8
Hundry La TA10 .... 184 C8
Hungerford Cl BS4 .... 23 E8
Hungerford Gdns BS4 .... 23 E8
Hungerford Rd
Bath BA1 .... 44 C7
Bristol BS4 .... 23 E8
Hungerford Terr BA2 .... 62 D1
Hung Rd BS11 .... 4 E5
Hunstrete Rd BA2 .... 59 F7
Hunt's La BS49 .... 34 E8
Huntash La TA4 .... 167 A4
Huntenhull Gn BA13 .... 121 C3
Huntenhull La BA13 .... 121 D4
Hunter's Hill EX15 .... 179 E1
Hunter's Way EX15 .... 179 E1
Hunters Moon Touring Pk EX13 .... 198 E1
Hunters Rest Miniature Rlwy★ BS39 .... 59 A5
Huntham Cl TA3 .... 170 E6
Huntham La TA3 .... 170 E5
Huntham Rd TA3 .... 170 D4
Huntingham Rd BS13 .... 21 F4
Huntley Cl EX13 .... 198 A2
Huntley Gr BS48 .... 9 A1
Huntley La
Chardstock EX13 .... 198 A8
Tatworth EX13, TA20 .... 193 D1
Hunts La TA5 .... 133 D5
Huntsmans Ridge BS27 .... 90 C7
Hunts Mead DT9 .... 225 B2
Huntspill Rd TA9 .... 104 D2
Huntworth Bsns Pk TA6 .... 154 A5
Huntworth La
Fordgate TA7 .... 154 C5
North Petherton TA6 .... 153 F4
Hurcott Cross TA19 .... 184 D3
Hurcott La TA19 .... 184 D4
Hurd's Bldgs BA11 .... 119 F4
Hurdle Way TA1 .... 213 A3
Hurley La TA4 .... 151 B8
Hurlstone Pk TA24 .... 124 B3
Hurmans Cl TA7 .... 156 B8
Hurn Dro BA5 .... 139 B6
Hurn La
Berrow TA8 .... 84 F7
Keynsham BS31 .... 25 A3
Pitcombe BA7 .... 215 A1
Shepton Montague BA7 .... 160 A2
Hurn Rd BS21 .... 6 F2
Hursley Hill
Bristol BS14 .... 40 D8
Whitchurch BS14 .... 23 D1
Hursley La BS14 .... 23 E1
Hurst TA12 .... 185 D5
Hurst Dro
Compton Dundon TA11 .... 157 A3
Hambridge TA10, TA12 .... 184 E8
Hurst Mews TA12 .... 185 D5
Hurston Rd BS4 .... 22 D7
Hurst Pk TA12 .... 185 D5
Hurst Rd
Bristol BS4 .... 22 F8
Weston-Super-Mare BS23 .... 49 A6
Hurst Wlk BS4 .... 22 F8
Hussey's DT10 .... 190 F5
Hutchin's La BA10 .... 160 F8
Hutchings's La TA4 .... 167 D4
Hutton CE Prim Sch BS24 .... 49 E2
Hutton Cl
Bristol BS9 .... 5 E7
Keynsham BS31 .... 25 A2
Hutton Hill BS24 .... 49 F2
Hutton Moor La BS22, BS24 .... 49 C6
Hutton Moor Pk BS24 .... 49 C6
Hutton Moor Rd BS22 .... 49 C7
Hutton Moor Rdbt BS22 .... 49 C7
Huxham La BA4 .... 158 F7
Hyacinth Terr TA21 .... 222 C5
Hyatt Pl BA4 .... 204 F5
Hyatts Wood Rd BS48 .... 19 E1
Hyde's La SN14 .... 13 A6
Hyde Ct BA21 .... 218 C6
Hyde La
Monkton Heathfield TA2 .... 169 C5
Taunton TA2 .... 213 F6
Hyde Lane Cotts TA2 .... 169 C5
Hyde Park Ave 4 TA6 .... 153 E3
Hyde Pk 5 TA6 .... 153 E3
Hyde Rd
Minehead TA24 .... 200 E6
Montacute TA15 .... 186 B4
Hyde The
Clevedon BS21 .... 16 C8
Keynsham BS31 .... 24 F6
Hyland Gr BS9 .... 5 F8
Hylton Cl TA2 .... 212 F8
Hynicombe La TA4 .... 165 D6
Hythe La BS27 .... 89 E5

I

Iberry La TA3 .... 183 E8
Idwal Cl BA2 .... 79 C8
Iford Cl BS31 .... 25 E3
Iford Fields BA15 .... 64 E2
Iford Hill BA15 .... 64 E2
Iford La BA3, BA15 .... 64 C3
Ilchester Com Prim Sch (Inf) BA22 .... 173 E2
Ilchester Com Prim Sch (Jun) BA22 .... 173 E2
Ilchester Cres BS13 .... 22 B8
Ilchester La TA10 .... 172 F4
Ilchester Mead BA22 .... 173 D1
Ilchester Mus★ BA22 .... 173 E1
Ilchester Rd
Bristol BS13 .... 22 B8
Charlton Mackrell TA11 .... 173 F6
Chilthorne Domer BA21, BA22 .... 186 F6
Yeovil BA21 .... 218 F8
Ile Ct TA19 .... 221 C4
Ilex Ave BS21 .... 6 E2
Ilex Cl
Bristol BS13 .... 21 F6
Huntspill TA9 .... 136 B8
Ilex La BS25 .... 51 F1
Ilford Ct TA1 .... 212 C2
Illustrious Cres BA22 .... 173 E2
Ilminster BS24 .... 49 A2
Ilminster Ave BS4 .... 22 F8
Ilminster Avenue Prim Sch BS4 .... 23 A8
Ilminster Cl
Clevedon BS21 .... 6 E2
Nailsea BS48 .... 18 D8
Ilminster Rd TA1 .... 213 D4
Ilsyn Gr BS14 .... 23 D7
Ilton Bsns Pk TA19 .... 183 F5
Imbercourt Cl BS14 .... 23 B8
Immenstadt Dr TA21 .... 222 D4
Imperial Pk BS13 .... 22 C6
Imperial Rd BS14 .... 23 C8
Improvement Pl 5 TA21 .... 222 D5
Inchalloch 19 BA1 .... 28 A1
Incline The TA19 .... 221 B3
Inclosures The 5 BS22 .... 49 F8
Ingleton Dr BS22 .... 32 A4
Ingrams Mdw TA23 .... 202 C6
Inkerman Ct TA1 .... 213 A3
Inman Ho BA1 .... 228 C4
Inn Cotts BS11 .... 5 A7
Inner Circ TA1 .... 213 D5
Inner Elm Terr BA3 .... 78 C1
Inner Gullands TA1 .... 212 D3
Innicks Cl BS40 .... 55 D1
Innox Gdns BS13 .... 22 A5
Innox Gr BA2 .... 43 F2
Innox Hill BA11 .... 119 E6
Innox La BA1 .... 28 B5
Innox Rd BA2 .... 44 B5
Inns Court Ave BS4 .... 22 D7
Inns Court Dr BS4 .... 22 D6
Inns Court Gn BS4 .... 22 D7
Innsmead La TA7 .... 137 B1
Instow 7 BS22 .... 32 A2
Instow Rd BS4 .... 22 E8
Instow Wlk BS4 .... 22 E8
International Coll Sherborne Sch DT9 .... 225 D5
International Helicopter Mus★ BS24 .... 49 E5
Inverness Rd BA2 .... 44 C6
Inwood Rd TA6 .... 208 C5
Irene Cl TA6 .... 209 D7
Ireson Cl BA9 .... 216 D4
Ireson La BA9 .... 216 D4
Irnham Rd TA24 .... 201 A7
Iron Dish La TA13 .... 184 E6
Iron Mill La BA11 .... 101 A1
Ironmould La BS31 .... 24 A8
Iron Post TA22 .... 163 B5
Irvine Cl TA2 .... 212 C6
Irving Cl BS21 .... 6 F3
Irving Ho BS1 .... 226 C3
Irving Rd TA11 .... 158 A1
Irwell Gn TA1 .... 213 D4
Isaacs Cl BA16 .... 207 B4
Island The BA3 .... 78 A1
Islemoor Dro TA3 .... 184 A8
Islemoor La TA13 .... 220 B6
Islemoor Rd TA3 .... 183 F8
Isleport Bsns Pk TA9 .... 104 F4
Isleport Rd TA9 .... 104 F3
Isles La
East Coker, Lyatts BA22 .... 197 C6
East Coker, Sutton Bingham BA22 .... 197 D6
Ivel Ct BA21 .... 219 C5
Ivel Gdns BA22 .... 173 E1
Ivel Sq BA20 .... 219 B5
Ivelway TA18 .... 224 C5
Ivo Peters Rd BA2 .... 228 A2
Ivors Way TA6 .... 153 E4
Ivy Ave BA2 .... 44 C4
Ivy Bank Pk BA2 .... 44 F2
Ivybridge 8 BS22 .... 32 A2
Ivy Cl BS48 .... 8 D1
Ivy Cotts TA3 .... 181 E3
Ivy Cross TA21 .... 179 D7
Ivy Ct BS20 .... 1 F5
Ivy Gn TA20 .... 223 C3
Ivy Gr BA2 .... 44 C4
Ivy Grove Cl TA6 .... 209 D7
Ivy Ho
Chard TA20 .... 223 B4
Wellington TA21 .... 222 C6
Ivy House Cotts BS29 .... 50 D7
Ivy House Pk TA3 .... 169 C2
Ivy La BS24 .... 50 A8
Ivyleaf Rd TA11 .... 211 C4
Ivy Pl BA2 .... 44 C4
Ivythorn Cl BA16 .... 207 C4
Ivy Thorn La BA16 .... 207 A1
Ivythorn Rd BA16 .... 207 C4
Ivywell Rd BS9 .... 5 E3
Ivy Wlk
Banwell BS29 .... 50 E4
Midsomer Norton BA3 .... 97 B8
Yeovil BA20 .... 218 E3
Iwood La BS40 .... 35 A2

J

Jack's Dro BS28 .... 137 F8
Jack's La
Croscombe BA5 .... 204 C7
Frome BA11 .... 119 D7
Jack Price Cl BS13 .... 22 C3
Jackson's La TA5 .... 134 A2
Jack White's Gibbet BA9 .... 176 B8
Jacob's Ct BS1 .... 226 C2
Jacob's Wells Rd BS8 .... 226 B2
Jacobs Cl BA6 .... 206 E5
Jacobs Mdw BS20 .... 2 F4
Jacob St
Bristol BS2 .... 227 B3
Bristol BS2 .... 227 C3
Jagaar Ct TA7 .... 137 D5
Jaguar Ho 3 BA1 .... 228 B3
Jamaica St BS2 .... 227 B4
James's Hill BA10 .... 161 A8
James Cl
Holcombe BA3 .... 116 C8
Shepton Mallet BA4 .... 205 C4
James La EX14 .... 192 F2
James Lane Cross EX13 .... 193 A1
James St W BA1 .... 228 B2
James St BS5 .... 227 C4
Janson Cl TA6 .... 209 D6
Japonica Cl TA6 .... 209 D5
Jarman Way TA20 .... 223 D6
Jarmany Hill BA6 .... 157 F3
Jarmyns TA1 .... 212 A3
Jarvis Cl DT10 .... 190 B4
Jarvis La TA9 .... 86 D4
Jarvis Way DT10 .... 190 B4
Jasmine Cl
Crewkerne TA18 .... 224 D7
Highbridge TA9 .... 104 D4
Weston-Super-Mare BS22 .... 32 A1
Yeovil BA22 .... 218 B5
Jasmine Ct 8 BS23 .... 48 E8
Jasmine La BS49 .... 17 F2
Jasmine Way BS24 .... 32 A1
Jay Cl BA11 .... 120 B6
Jaycroft Rd TA8 .... 104 B6
Jay View BS23 .... 49 A5
Jeffreys' Way TA1 .... 212 A2
Jeffries Cl TA19 .... 183 C4
Jeffs Way 3 EX13 .... 198 A1
Jellalabad Ct TA1 .... 212 F3
Jellicoe Ct BS22 .... 31 E4
Jena Ct BS31 .... 25 D3
Jesmond Rd
Clevedon BS21 .... 6 C3
Weston-Super-Mare BS22 .... 32 C4
Jesse Hughes Ct BA1 .... 28 C2
Jessop Ct BS1 .... 227 B2
Jessop Underpass BS3 .... 11 F4
Jews La
Bath BA2 .... 44 C6
Churchill BS25 .... 52 F4
Wiveliscombe TA4 .... 210 B5
Jill's Cl BA4 .... 142 A6
Jim O'Neil Ho BS11 .... 4 D7
Jocelin Dr BS22 .... 31 F4
Jocelin Rd BA6 .... 206 F5
Jocelyn Dr BA5 .... 203 B3
John Beales Hill BA4 .... 140 F3
John Cabot Ct BS1 .... 226 A1
John Carr's Terr BS8 .... 226 B2
John Cozens Ho 6 BS2 .... 227 C3
John Grinter Way TA21 .... 222 D4
John Gunn Cl TA20 .... 223 C5
John St S TA8 .... 104 A7
John Slessor Ct BA1 .... 228 B4
Johnson's Ctyd DT9 .... 225 D3
Johnson Cl
East Brent TA9 .... 86 D5
Wells BA5 .... 203 F5
Johnson Flats BA21 .... 219 C7
John St
Bath BA1 .... 228 B3
Bristol BS1 .... 227 A3
Burnham-on-S TA8 .... 104 A7
Highbridge TA9 .... 104 D3
Johnstone Ct BA16 .... 207 B3
Johnstone St BA2 .... 228 C2
John Wesleys Chapel★ BS1 .... 227 B3
Joles La BA11 .... 120 F1
Jones Cl BS49 .... 17 A1
Joselin Ct DT9 .... 225 D5
Joyden Ct TA20 .... 223 D2
Joy Hill BS8 .... 11 F6
Juan's La SP8 .... 177 E1
Jubilee Cl
Bridgwater TA6 .... 209 C4

Jubilee Cl *continued*
Castle Cary BA7 214 C6
Chard TA20 223 C3
Jubilee Cotts 10 BA11 119 F4
Jubilee Ct
8 Wellington TA21 222 D5
Weston-Super-Mare BS23 48 F8
Jubilee Dr BS8 10 B4
Jubilee Gdns
Milverton TA4 167 A4
South Petherton TA13 220 C4
Jubilee La BS40 53 A6
Jubilee Path BS22 31 C1
Jubilee Pl
Bristol BS1 227 A1
Clevedon BS21 6 D1
Yeovil BA21 218 D5
Jubilee Rd
Axbridge BS26 70 C2
Radstock BA3 78 D1
Street BA16 207 C4
Weston-Super-Mare BS23 48 E7
Jubilee St
Bristol BS2 227 C2
Burnham-on-S TA8 104 B6
Taunton TA2 212 E6
Jubilee Terr
Frome BA11 119 E5
Hemington BA3 99 C7
Paulton BS39 77 E6
Jubilee Way BS22 32 C3
Judy's Orch TA7 154 F5
Julian's Acres TA8 84 F4
Julian Cl
Bristol BS9 5 E3
Shepton Mallet BA4 205 C4
Julian Ct BS9 5 E3
Julian Rd
Bath BA1 228 B3
Bristol BS9 5 E3
Julier Ho BA1 228 C4
Jumpers Combe TA23 148 E8
Junction Ave BA2 228 A1
Junction Dro TA3 170 C2
Junction Rd BA2 228 A1
Juniper Cl
Bridgwater TA6 209 E4
Yeovil BA20 218 F3
Juniper Pl BS22 31 F4
Juniper Rd TA1 213 C2
Jurston La
Wellington TA21 222 E6
Wellington TA21 222 F5
Jury Hill TA22 163 E6
Jury Rd TA22 163 E6
Justice Ave BS31 25 E3
Justice La BA11 119 F5

K

Kale St BA4 142 D2
Kale Street Cotts BA4 142 D2
Karen Cl BS48 19 A4
Karen Dr BS48 19 A5
Kaynton Mead BA1 44 B7
Keats Ho 4 BS23 48 F4
Keats Rd
Radstock BA3 97 C8
Taunton TA1 213 C3
Kebby's Farm Cl TA4 202 E3
Keble Ave BS13 21 F5
Keeds La BS41 10 F1
Keedwell Hill BS41 10 F1
Keel's Hill BA2 79 C8
Keen's Elm La BA16 207 E4
Keene's Way BS21 6 C2
Keens Cl BA16 207 D5
Keens La TA7 155 C2
Keep St BA22 174 D3
Keep The BS22 32 A3
Keg Store The BS1 227 B2
Keinton Mandeville Prim Sch TA11 158 A1
Kellways BS48 19 A4
Kelson's La BS28 108 B3
Kelso Pl BA1 44 D7
Kelso Villas BA1 44 D7
Kelston Cl BS31 25 D4
Kelston Gdns BS22 32 B5
Kelston Rd
Bath BA1 26 E1
Keynsham BS31 24 D5
Weston-Super-Mare BS22 32 B5
Kelston View BA2 44 A5
Kelting Gr BS21 6 F2
Keltings TA6 208 C6
Kelway Rd TA21 222 E7
Kember's Hill BA22, DT9 175 C3
Kemble Cl BS48 9 A1
Kemble Gdns BS11 4 F5
Kemm Cl BS27 90 B6
Kemp's La BA11 120 F7
Kempe's Cl BS41 11 A2
Kempe Way BS24 49 E7
Kemps La TA24 147 B7
Kemps Way TA22 163 D6
Ken Cl
Chard TA20 223 D3
Wells BA5 140 C8
Kencot Wlk BS13 22 B3
Kendale Rd TA6 208 E6
Kendall Cl TA3 169 D6
Kendrick Ct 1 BA5 203 D4
Kenilworth Cl BS31 24 D4
Kenilworth Ct BA1 45 B8
Kenmare Rd BS4 22 E8
Kenmeade Cl BS25 70 E8
Kenmore Dr BA21 219 B6
Kennard Cl BA6 206 F3
Kennard Moor Dro
Butleigh BA6 157 E7
Glastonbury BA6 206 F1
Kennaway Rd BS21 6 E2
Kenn Bsns Pk BS21 16 E8
Kenn Cl BS23 49 A5
Kenn Ct BS4 22 E7
Kennedy Cl TA9 104 E4
Kennel Batch BA5 111 D4
Kennel La
Compton Bishop BS26 68 E3
East Pennard BA4 158 F8
Langport TA10 172 A6
West Bagborough TA4 151 D4
Kennel Lodge Rd BS3 11 E4
Kenn Est BS21 16 E5
Kennet Gr TA1 213 D4
Kennet Ho 10 BA1 228 B2
Kennet Pk BA2 28 E1
Kennet Rd BS31 25 A4
Kennford 6 BS22 31 F2
Kennington Rd BA1 44 B7
Kennion Cl TA20 223 D3
Kennion Rd BA5 203 C5
Kenn Moor Dr BS21 6 E1
Kennmoor Rd BS21 17 A6
Kenn Moor Rd BS49 17 B1
Kenn Rd BS21 16 F6
Kenn St BS21 16 F7
Kensington Ct
Bath BA1 28 B2
Bristol BS8 226 A3
Kensington Fields BA14 83 F7
Kensington Gdns
Bath BA1 28 B1
Bridgwater TA6 209 D6
Kensington Gr TA24 200 E6
Kensington Pl
Bath BA1 28 B1
Bristol BS8 226 A3
Kensington Rd BS23 48 F5
Kent's Bglws TA20 198 D8
Kent's Cotts TA20 198 D8
Kent's Orch TA20 198 D8
Kent Ave TA6 209 A2
Kentisworth Rd DT10 190 F5
Kent La
Shapwick TA7 137 F1
Shepton Mallet BA4 205 A5
Kent Rd
Congresbury BS49 34 D5
Tatworth TA20 198 D8
Kents Cl TA20 198 C8
Kentshare La BS40 38 B6
Kents La TA20 198 D8
Kent St BS27 71 B1
Kent Way BS22 32 B4
Kenwyn Cl TA1 213 D3
Keppel Cl BS31 25 D2
Kerry Croft BA11 143 C3
Kersey Ct BA11 119 C5
Kersham La TA24 130 A1
Kestrel Cl TA6 209 C3
Kestrel Dr BS22 31 E1
Keward Ave BA5 203 B3
Keward Cl BA5 203 B3
Keward Mill Trad Est BA5 203 B2
Keward Wlk BA5 203 C3
Kew Rd BS23 30 E1
Kewside BS22 31 B4
Kewstoke Prim Sch BS22 31 B3
Kewstoke Rd
Bath BA2 45 A2
Bristol BS9 5 E4
Weston-Super-Mare BS22 31 C3
Kew Wlk BS4 23 C8
Keyes Path BS22 31 F4
Keyford BA11 119 F3
Keyford Cotts 15 BA11 119 F4
Keyford Ct BA11 119 F2
Keyford Field Cotts BA11 119 F2
Keyford Gdns BA11 119 F3
Keyford Pl BA11 119 F4
Keyford Rdbt BA22 197 E8
Keyford Terr BA11 119 F4
Keyhaven Bglws BS22 31 B4
Key Hill BA22 197 E8
Keynsham By-Pass BS31 24 E7
Keynsham Hospl BS31 24 F4
Keynsham Prim Sch BS31 24 D5
Keynsham Rd BS30, BS31 25 A8
Keynsham Sta BS31 24 F6
Keyton Hill BS28 107 E2
Kicks Hill TA7 155 B4
Kicks Hill La TA7 155 B4
Kidd's La BA4 205 D6
Kidder Bank BA5 203 F5
Kiddles BA21 219 C5
Kid Gate Dro TA9, BS28 137 D8
Kidner Cl TA7 136 E4
Kidsbury Rd TA6 208 E5
Kielder Dr BS22 31 F3
Kilbirnie Rd BS14 23 A3
Kilburn Dr TA6 209 D6
Kildare BA2 45 B7
Kildare Gdns TA24 200 F6
Kildare Rd BS13 22 D8
Kilkenny Ave 5 TA2 212 F6
Kilkenny Ct TA2 212 F6
Kilkenny La
Bath BA2 62 B8
Wraxall BA4 159 A6
Kilkenny Pl BS20 2 C6
Killams Ave
Staplehay TA3 181 F8
Taunton TA1 168 F1
Killams Cl TA1 168 F1
Killams Cres TA1 168 F1
Killams Dr TA1 168 F1
Killams Gn TA1 168 F1
Killams La TA1 168 F1
Killarney Ave TA8 104 C6
Killick Way TA4 202 D3
Kilmersdon CE Prim Sch BA3 98 A6
Kilmersdon Hill BA3 98 A5
Kilmersdon Rd
Bristol BS13 22 B4
Radstock BA3 97 E8
Kilminster Rd BS11 4 D7
Kilmorie Cl TA1 212 C2
Kiln Cl TA5 135 B5
Kiln Dr
Evercreech BA4 141 E1
Highbridge TA9 104 D3
Kiln Pk BS23 49 A6
Kilton Cross TA5 133 E5
Kilve BS24 49 A2
Kilve Cl TA2 212 F7
Kilve Cres TA2 212 F7
Kilve Ct TA5 133 C5
Kilver St BA4 205 D6
Kilver Street Hill BA4 205 D7
Kimber Cl TA9 104 D3
Kimberley Rd BS21 6 C2
Kimberley Terr TA6 209 B7
Kinber Cl BA1 27 A3
Kinforde TA20 223 C5
King's Castle Rd BA5 112 E1
King's Cnr TA22 163 D6
King's Coll TA1 213 B2
King's Hall Sch TA2 168 E6
King's Head La BS13 21 F7
King's Hill BA3 94 F7
King's La
Binegar BA3 95 E1
Clevedon BS21 6 D5
6 Weston-Super-Mare BS23 48 E8
King's Mill Rd DT10 190 D3
King's Pl TA6 208 F5
King's Rd
Bristol BS8 226 A3
Clevedon BS21 6 D5
Doulting BA4 141 E7
Portishead BS20 1 F4
King's Sch BA10 215 E6
King Alfred Cl 3 TA6 153 F4
King Alfred Dr TA20 223 C2
King Alfred Sch The TA9 104 C5
King Alfreds Ctyd 7 BA5 203 D4
King Alfreds Way BS28 108 B4
King Alfred Way BA15 64 D7
King Arthur Dr BA21 218 D7
King Arthurs Com Sch BA9 216 A4
King Athelstan Dr TA20 223 D2
King Ceol Cl TA20 223 D2
King Cerdic Cl TA20 223 D2
Kingcott Mill Farm Cvns BS48 20 B8
King Cuthred Cl TA20 223 C2
King Cuthred Dr TA20 223 C2
Kingdom BA5 113 A4
Kingdom La TA2 168 B4
Kingdon Mead TA3 169 D4
Kingdown Rd BS40 37 C5
King Edward's Jun Sch BA2 45 C7
King Edward's Pre-Prep Sch BA1 44 C8
King Edward's Sch BA2 45 C7
King Edward Cl BS14 23 A6
King Edward Rd
Bath BA2 44 D5
Minehead TA24 201 A6
Kingfisher Cl
Bridgwater TA6 209 C3
Yeovil BA20 218 D3
Kingfisher Ct BA3 64 C6
Kingfisher Dr BA3 97 B8
Kingfisher Rd BS22 49 F8
King George's Rd
Bath BA2 44 C6
Bristol BS13 21 F5
King George Ave TA6 208 F2
King George Cl TA6 209 A2
King George Rd TA24 201 A6
King George St 2 BA20 219 B4
King George V Pl 7 BS1 227 A2
King Ina Rd TA11 211 D4
King Ine Cl N TA20 223 C2
King Ine Cl S TA20 223 C2
King La BS39 58 F4
Kinglake Villas TA6 209 A2
King Rd BS49 52 E6
Kingsacre BA7 214 B5
Kings Acre TA4 151 B5
Kingsbury Episcopi Prim Sch TA12 185 A6
Kings Castle Bsns Est TA6 209 A6
Kings Cl
Shepton Mallet BA4 205 B5
Taunton TA1 213 A2
Kingscliffe Terr TA6 209 A2
Kingscombe BA3 114 E6
Kingscourt Cl BS14 23 A4
Kings Cres DT9 225 D5
Kings Croft BS41 10 E1
Kings Ct
Bath BA1 228 B2
Bristol BS1 227 A2
Bristol, St Pauls BS1 227 B4
2 Bristol, Withywood BS13 21 F4
Sherborne DT9 225 D6
Yeovil BA21 219 C6
Kingsdon CE Prim Sch TA11 173 D5
Kingsdon Hill TA11 173 D5
Kingsdon Manor Sch TA11 173 D4
Kingsdown Cl TA6 209 D6
Kingsdown Gr SN13 29 F3
Kingsdown Par BS6 227 A4
Kingsdown View 16 BA1 28 A1
Kings Dr TA7 154 E6
Kingsettle Hill BA10 161 B5
Kingsfield BA2 44 C3
Kingsford Gate Cross TA24 145 B7
Kingsford Hill TA24 145 C7
Kingshams BA22 173 E1
Kingshill BS48 8 C2
Kings Hill BA22 186 E6
Kingshill CE Prim Sch BS48 8 D3
Kingshill Gdns BS48 8 C1
Kingshill La BS40 56 C4
Kingsholme Ct BS23 30 E1
Kings La TA7 156 B8
Kingsland TA23 202 D7
Kingsland Grange 1 BA21 218 C6
Kingsland La TA24 148 D5
Kingsland Rd BA4 205 B5
Kingsland Trad Est BS2 227 C3
Kings Lear TA19 183 F4
Kingsley Cl TA1 212 C1
Kingsley Ho BS2 227 C2
Kingsley Rd
Clevedon BS21 6 D2
Radstock BA3 78 C1
Weston-Super-Mare BS23 48 F3
Kingsmead BS48 8 C2
Kingsmead Cl
Holcombe BA3 116 C8
Wiveliscombe TA4 210 C3
Kingsmead Com Sch TA4 210 C3
Kingsmead Ct 8 BA1 228 B2
Kingsmead N BA1 228 B2
Kingsmead Sq BA1 228 B2
Kingsmead St BA1 228 B2
Kingsmead W BA1 228 B2
Kingsmill BS9 5 D5
Kingsmoor Prim Sch TA7 136 E2
Kings Oak Mdw BS39 58 E2
Kings of Wessex Com Sch The BS27 90 B7
King Sq
Bridgwater TA6 208 F5
Bristol BS2 227 A4
King Square Ave BS2 227 A4
Kings Rd
Sherborne DT9 225 D5
Stoke sub Hamdon TA14 185 F5
Wells BA5 140 C8
Wrington BS40 35 D1
Kings Ride TA20 223 B6
Kings Sq BS30 25 D8
King St
Bridgwater TA6 209 A5
Bristol BS1 227 A2
Frome BA11 119 F5
Glastonbury BA6 206 D5
Highbridge TA9 104 D3
Yeovil BA21 219 B6
Kingston BA20 219 A5
Kingston Ave
Clevedon BS21 6 E3
Saltford BS31 25 C3
Kingston Bldgs 5 BA1 228 C2
Kingston Cl
Street BA16 207 D6
Taunton TA2 212 E7
Kingston Dr BS48 18 C8
Kingstone Cross TA19 221 F2
Kingstone Hill TA19 221 F2
Kingston La
Felton BS40 37 F8
Maiden Bradley BA12 144 C1
Kingston Mead BS40 37 F7
Kingston Mews 3 TA2 212 F6
Kingston Rd
Bath BA1 228 C2
Nailsea BS48 18 C8
Taunton TA2 212 E7
Kingston St Mary CE Prim Sch TA2 168 D8
Kingston View BA21 219 B6
Kingston Way BS48 18 C8
Kingston Well La TA20 194 C2
Kingsway
Bath BA2 44 C3
Holcombe BA3 116 C8
Mark BS26, TA9 87 D3
Portishead BS20 1 F4
Taunton TA1 168 F1
Kingsway Ctr BA11 119 F4
Kingsway Rd TA8 104 B7
Kingswear 3 BS22 32 A2
Kings Weston Ave BS11 4 E8
Kings Weston La BS11 5 A8
Kings Weston Rd BS9 5 B8
Kingsweston Sch BS11 5 A8
Kings Wlk BS13 21 E7
Kingswood Chase BA14 83 F6
Kingswood Prep Sch BA1 27 E1
Kingswood Rd TA18 224 C4
Kingswood Sch BA1 27 E2
Kington View BA8 176 E1
Kingwell View BS39 59 D2
Kingweston Rd
Butleigh BA6 157 E3
Charlton Mackrell TA11 173 E8
King William Ave BS1 227 A2
King William Rd TA7 137 D2
Kinsale Rd BS14 23 C7
Kinvara Rd BS4 22 E8
Kinver Terr TA8 104 A7
Kipling Ave BA2 44 F4
Kipling Rd
Radstock BA3 78 C1
Weston-Super-Mare BS23 49 A3
Kippax Ave BA5 203 F5
Kipscombe Cross EX35 122 A6
Kirk Dr TA7 154 E6
Kirke Gr TA2 213 B8
Kirkham St TA11 211 E4
Kirlegate BA6 138 C4
Kissing Batch BA11 119 C6
Kit's La TA4 166 A6
Kitchener Rd TA2 168 A6
Kitchens La TA13 185 A1
Kite's Nest La SP8 161 F1
Kite La BA4 159 C6
Kites Croft BA5 110 E7
Kite Wlk 2 BS22 49 E8
Kithill TA18 224 D4
Kitley Hill BA3 78 C4
Kitridge La TA24 146 B7
Kitrow La TA24 131 A6
Kitswall La TA24 130 D5
Kitt Hill DT9 225 C4
Kitton La DT9 188 A4
Kitts TA21 222 D4
Knacker's Hole La
Churchinford TA3 192 A6
Thorncombe DT6, TA20 199 C4
Knap Hill BA3 117 B2
Knapp TA16 195 F7
Knapp Cotts TA4 151 E1
Knapp Hill Cl BA5 113 A2
Knapp La
Bishops Lydeard TA4 151 E1
North Curry TA3 170 B4
Knapp Rd
Creech St Michael TA3 169 F4
North Curry TA3 170 A4
Knapps Cl BS25 69 F8
Knapps Dr BS25 69 F8
Knapps La
Chard TA20 194 C4
Langport TA10 172 B5
Knapp The TA24 130 B4
Knap The BA8 176 E1
Knaptons Hill BA11 118 C6
Kneller Cl BS11 5 A8
Knight's Cross TA21 181 A5
Knight's Ct BA11 119 F4
Knight's La
Axminster EX13 198 A4
Higher Chillington TA19 194 E5
Knight Cl BS22 32 A5
Knightcott BS29 50 F3
Knightcott Gdns BS29 50 F3
Knightcott Ind Est BS29 50 E3
Knightcott Pk BS29 51 A3
Knightcott Rd
Abbots Leigh BS8 10 F8
Banwell BS29 50 F3
Knightlands La TA10 172 F4
Knighton TA5 134 B7
Knighton Dro TA10 184 D7
Knightsbridge Pk BS13 22 E4
Knightsbridge Way TA6 209 D6
Knight Shute La TA20 193 D6
Knights Rd TA21 180 D8
Knights Templar CE Meth Com Sch TA23 202 D6
Knightstone TA3 169 D3
Knightstone Cl
Axbridge BS26 70 C1
Kingsbury Episcopi TA12 185 B8
Peasedown St John BA2 79 B8
Knightstone Cswy BS23 48 C8
Knightstone Ct
Burnham-on-S TA8 104 B6
Clevedon BS21 6 D1
Stalbridge DT10 190 B4
Taunton TA2 213 A6
Weston-Super-Mare BS23 30 D1
Knightstone Gn BS23 48 E6
Knightstone Ho
1 Bristol BS2 227 A4
Weston-Super-Mare BS23 48 D8
Knightstone Hts BA11 119 F3
Knightstone Mead TA22 148 A2
Knightstone Pk 4 BS23 48 E5
Knightstone Pl
Bath BA1 27 B1
7 Weston-Super-Mare BS22 31 F2
Knightstone Rd BS23 48 C8
Knightstone Sq BS14 23 C5
Knightstone Wlk BS2 226 C4
Knights Yd BA7 214 C5
Knobsbury Hill BA3 98 D6
Knobsbury La BA3 98 C7

Knole Cswy
Knole TA10 173 A4
Long Sutton TA10 172 F4
Knole Pit La TA10 173 A4
Knoll Ct BS9 5 D3
Knoll Green La TA5 134 F2
Knoll Hill BS9 5 D3
Knoll Hill View BA11 143 C6
Knoll Ho [5] BA11 119 F4
Knoll La BA4 142 E3
Knoll Pk TA8 65 F2
Knoll The BS20 2 D7
Knoll View
Burnham-on-S TA8 104 C8
[4] Frome BA11 119 F4
Knotcroft La TA2 153 D1
Knotts Paddock DT9 225 E4
Knowle Cross DT8 199 F6
Knowle Dro
Middlezoy TA7 155 A4
Westonzoyland TA7 154 F5
Knowle End TA7 136 E3
Knowle La
Chard TA20 194 B6
Dunster TA24 201 B1
Misterton DT8, TA18 224 E2
Shepton Mallet BA4 204 E5
Wookey BA5 110 E1
Knowle Moor Dro BA5 110 C2
Knowle Rd TA6 209 C6
Knowles Rd BS21 6 C2
Knowleyards Rd TA7 155 B4
Kuching Rd BA22 174 A2
Kylross Ave BS14 23 B5
Kyrle Gdns BA1 28 F3
Kyte Rd BA4 205 C5

L

Labbott The BS31 24 E5
Labourham Dro BS27 90 B5
Labourham Way BS27 90 B6
Laburnum Cl
Bridgwater TA6 209 D4
Frome BA11 120 B7
Midsomer Norton BA3 96 F8
Somerton TA11 211 D4
Laburnum Cotts [7] TA21 222 D5
Laburnum Cres TA18 224 D7
Laburnum Ct
[7] Taunton TA1 213 A4
Weston-Super-Mare BS23 49 B7
Laburnum Dr TA11 211 D4
Laburnum Gr BA3 96 F8
Laburnum Lodges TA9 136 A8
Laburnum Rd
Wellington TA21 222 E5
Weston-Super-Mare BS23 49 B7
Laburnum St TA1 213 A4
Laburnum Terr
Batheaston BA1 28 F3
Creech St Michael TA3 169 D4
Laburnum Way BA20 218 D2
Laburnum Wlk BS31 24 C3
Lacey Rd BS14 23 B6
La Ciotat Ho TA6 209 A4
Ladd Cl TA9 104 D3
Ladies Mile BS8 5 F1
Ladman Gr BS14 23 E6
Ladman Rd BS14 23 E5
Ladycroft [5] BS21 6 B1
Ladye Bay BS21 6 D7
Ladye Wake BS22 31 F4
Lady Harriet Acland's Dr
TA22 164 A8
Lady Lawn TA3 168 D1
Ladymead BS20 2 F5
Ladymead Cl TA6 208 B4
Ladymead Com Sch TA2 168 E6
Ladymeade
Backwell BS48 19 A7
Ilminster TA19 221 B3
Ladymead Ho BA1 228 C3
Ladymead La BS40 52 F5
Ladymead Rd TA2 168 F6
Lady St TA22 163 D7
Lady Victoria's Dr TA22 163 E6
Ladywell BS40 35 D2
Laggan Gdns BA1 27 E1
Laggan Ho BA1 27 E1
Lagger Hill TA5 133 C5
Lahs Pl BA11 101 E4
Lakefields BA22 197 B8
Lakemead Gdns [3] BS13 21 F4
Lakemead Gr BS13 21 F6
Lake Mews BA22 219 B1
Lake Rd BS20 2 D7
Lakeside TA9 104 E4
Lakeside Cl BS40 55 D5
Lakeside Ct BS24 32 B1
Lakeside Pk
Bridgwater TA6 209 A3
Vobster BA11 117 E8
Lakeview Cres TA9 104 E3
Lake Wall TA7 154 E4
Lambert's Hill BA4 204 F3
Lambert Cl DT9 217 C2
Lambert Ct DT9 217 D2
Lambert La TA19 194 F5
Lambert Pl BS4 22 D6
Lamberts Marsh BA14 83 E2
Lamb La TA6 208 F4
Lambourne Ct TA18 224 D7
Lambourne Way BS20 2 F5
Lambourn Rd BS31 25 A4
Lambpark Ct TA3 191 F6
Lambridge [6] BA1 28 C1
Lambridge Bldgs [1] BA1 28 C1
Lambridge Grange [6]
BA1 28 C2
Lambridge Mews [5] BA1 28 C1
Lambridge Pl BA1 28 C1
Lambridge St BA1 28 C1
Lambrok Cl BA14 83 F6
Lambrok Rd BA14 83 F6
Lambrook Cl TA1 213 B4
Lambrook Gate TA13 184 F5
Lambrook Ho BA9 216 C4
Lambrook Rd
Shepton Beauchamp
TA19 184 E4
Taunton TA1 213 B4
Lambrook St BA6 206 E4
Lambrook Way TA1 213 C4
Lambs Field DT9 225 E5
Lamb St BS2 227 C3
Lamington Cl BS13 21 F6
Lamont Ho [7] BA1 28 C1
Lampard's Bldgs BA1 228 B4
Lamparts Way TA19 183 C2
Lampeter Rd BS9 5 F7
Lampley Rd BS21 16 D2
Lampreys La TA13 220 C3
Lampton Ave BS13 22 E3
Lampton Gr BS13 22 E3
Lampton Rd BS41 10 F1
Lancaster House Sch
BS23 48 F8
Lancer Ct TA21 222 D6
Lanch La SP8 177 F5
Lancock St TA21 222 A5
Lancombe La BA10 215 C3
Landacre La TA24 146 A7
Landemann Cir BS23 30 E1
Landemann Path [2] BS23 48 E8
Landlord's Hill TA21 179 E7
Landmark Ct BS1 226 C1
Landmead BA6 206 D5
Landmoor La TA10 172 D4
Landsdown Mews BA11 119 D5
Landseer BA8 176 D4
Landseer Cl BS22 31 F3
Landseer Rd BA2 44 B6
Landshire La
Charlton Horethorne
DT9 176 A1
Chilton Polden TA7 137 A3
Henstridge BA8 190 C6
Odcombe BA22 186 C1
Lane End BA12 144 D8
Lane Foot TA24 129 D7
Lane Head TA24 123 E4
Lanesborough Rise BS14 23 D7
Lanes End Hill BA11,
BA12 144 D8
Laneys Dro BS24 49 E5
Lang's Cnr TA19 183 B1
Langaller Hill TA22 163 D4
Langdon Cl TA20 223 D6
Langdon Rd BA2 44 B4
Langdons DT9 225 E5
Langdons Way TA20 198 C8
Langdown Ct BS14 23 E5
Langer's La TA19 194 E5
Langford's La BS39 59 D1
Langford Budville CE Prim
Sch TA21 166 F1
Langford Cl TA3 170 F1
Langford Ct [14] TA1 213 A4
Langford Ct Cotts BS40 53 E5
Langford Gate TA4 166 F2
Langford La
Fivehead TA3 170 F2
Lower Langford BS40 53 E5
Norton Fitzwarren TA2 168 C6
Langford Rd
Bristol BS13 21 F8
Lower Langford BS40 53 C6
Weston-Super-Mare BS23 49 A6
Langfords La BS39 77 C8
Langham Dr TA1 212 C1
Langham Gdns TA1 212 C1
Langham La SP8 177 F5
Langham Pl BA11 82 F1
Langhill Ave BS4 22 D7
Langland's La TA9 104 B1
Langland La TA7 137 D2
Langlands [8] TA14 185 F4
Langlands La TA3 169 F2
Langley's La BA3, BS39 77 C1
Langley Cres BS3 11 E1
Langley Cross TA4 210 B6
Langleys Cotts BA3 96 B8
Langmead Dro
Middlezoy TA7 155 A4
Westonzoyland TA7 154 F5
Langmead La TA7 155 A4
Langmead Pl TA18 224 C4
Langmead Rd TA18 224 C4
Langmead Sq TA18 224 C4
Langmoor La EX13 198 D2
Langport Gdns BS48 18 E8
Langport Rd
Long Sutton TA10 172 E5
Middlezoy TA7 155 B4
Somerton TA11 211 B4
Weston-Super-Mare BS23 48 E5
Lang Rd TA18 224 C4
Langridge La BA1 27 D8
Langton Ho [9] BS2 227 C3
Langworthy Orch TA19 183 C1
Lansdown Cres
[2] Bath BA1 27 F1
Timsbury BA2 60 C2
Lansdown Ct BS23 48 F8
Lansdowne Pl BA9 216 C4
Lansdowne Rd TA2 213 A6
Lansdown Gdns BS22 32 B5
Lansdown Gr BA1 228 B4
Lansdown Grove Ct BA1 228 B4
Lansdown Grove Lodge
BA1 228 B4
Lansdown Ho BA1 27 F1
Lansdown Hts BA1 27 F1
Lansdown La
Bath BA1 27 B4
Upton Cheyney BS30 26 D8
Lansdown Mans BA1 228 B4
Lansdown Pk BA1 27 E3
Lansdown Pl
Bristol BS8 226 A3
Frome BA11 119 D5
High Littleton BS39 59 D1
Lansdown Pl E BA1 228 B4
Lansdown Pl W [1] BA1 27 F1
Lansdown Rd
Bath BA1 27 E2
Bristol BS8 226 A3
Saltford BS31 25 E3
Lansdown View
Bath BA2 44 C5
Faulkland BA3 80 D1
Timsbury BA2 60 C2
Tunley BA2 61 B4
Lanthony Cl BS24 50 A8
Lapwing Cl TA24 201 C5
Lapwing Gdns BS22 31 F1
Larch Ave TA20 223 B5
Larch Cl
Bridgwater TA6 209 D6
Churchill BS40 53 A5
Nailsea BS48 9 A2
Taunton TA1 213 D2
Larch Ct BA3 97 D8
Larches The BS22 32 A3
Larchfield Cl BA11 120 B7
Larchfield Trad Est TA19 221 B1
Larchgrove Cres BS22 31 F1
Larchgrove Wlk BS22 31 F1
Larchwood Ct BA3 79 A3
Lark Cl BA3 97 B8
Larkhall Pl BA1 28 C2
Larkhall Terr BA1 28 C2
Larkhill Rd
Locking BS24 50 B6
Yeovil BA21 218 D7
Lark Pl BA1 44 D7
Lark Rd BS22 31 F1
Larks Mdw DT10 190 C4
Larkspur Cl TA1 213 C1
Larkspur Cres BA21 218 D7
Larkspur Ct TA2 212 D7
Larviscombe Cl TA4 202 D4
Larviscombe Rd TA4 202 D4
Lasbury Gr BS13 22 C5
Lascot Hill BS28 108 C5
Latcham Dro BS27, BS28 109 A4
Latches La BS27 90 D3
Latchmoor Ho BS13 22 A8
Late Broads BA15 64 D7
Lauder Ct DT9 217 D2
Launcherley Cross BA5 140 A6
Launcherley Rd BA4, BA5 140 B5
Launder Cl BA6 206 E4
Laura Pl BA2 228 C3
Laurel Ave TA9 86 A2
Laurel Cl
East Coker BA22 197 B8
Frome BA11 120 B7
Taunton TA1 213 C1
Laurel Dr
Nailsea BS48 8 F2
Paulton BS39 77 E5
Weston-Super-Mare BS23 48 E2
Laurel Gdns
Chard TA20 223 B5
Timsbury BA2 60 B1
Yatton BS49 17 B1
Laurel La BA22 174 F3
Laurel St BA6 140 A1
Laurels The
Churchill BS25 52 F4
Crewkerne TA18 224 D7
Wembdon TA6 208 C6
Weston-Super-Mare BS23 48 E2
Westwood BA15 64 F3
Laurel Terr BS49 17 B1
Lavender Cl BS22 32 A5
Lavender Ct
Frome BA11 120 B7
Street BA16 207 B4
Lavender Gr TA1 212 C3
Laver's La TA20 198 F5
Laverley Cotts BA6 140 C2
Laverock Ct TA1 212 E5
Lavers Ct TA12 186 A7
Lavers Oak TA12 185 E7
Lavington Cl BS21 6 B1
Lawfords Gate BS2 227 C3
Lawfords Gate Ho [17]
BS2 227 C3
Lawford St BS2 227 C3
Law La
Drayton TA10 171 F3
Langport TA10 172 A3
Lawn La
Galhampton BA22 175 D8
Shapwick TA7 137 F1
Lawn Mdw TA3 169 C3
Lawnmoor La TA10 184 C6
Lawn Rd TA2 212 C8
Lawnside BS48 19 B5
Lawns The
Bristol BS11 4 E7
Combe St Nicholas TA20 193 D6
Weston-Super-Mare BS22 32 B3
Yatton BS49 17 A1
Lawn The [1] TA21 222 D6
Lawpool Ct [12] BA5 203 D4
Lawrence Cl
Burnham-on-S TA8 104 D5
Highbridge TA9 104 F4
Somerton TA11 211 D3
Weston-Super-Mare BS22 31 E2
Lawrence Hayes BA9 216 D3
Lawrence Hill BA9 216 A2
Lawrence Hill Bsns Ctr
BA9 216 B3
Lawrence Mews BS22 31 E2
Lawrence Rd
Coleford BA3 116 F7
Weston-Super-Mare BS22 31 E2
Wrington BS40 35 E2
Laws Dr BS24 49 F7
Lawson Cl
[5] Martock TA12 185 E6
Saltford BS31 25 C2
Lawyer's Hill TA5 152 C7
Lax Ct BA5 203 B4
Laxton Cl TA1 213 D5
Laxton Rd TA1 213 E5
Laxton Way BA2 79 D7
Laycock Hill DT9 217 D7
Layfield La TA3 170 C3
Layne Terr TA18 196 B8
Lays Bsns Ctr BS31 24 C4
Lays Dr BS31 24 C5
Lays La BS40 54 D4
Lays The BA11 101 E5
Leach's Field TA2 168 D8
Leach Cl BS21 6 D1
Leaches Cl BA22 186 B6
Leach Rd TA20 223 D7
Lea Cl BA21 219 B8
Lea Croft BS13 22 A4
Leading Edge The BS8 226 B2
Leadon Gr TA1 213 D4
Leafield Cl TA2 168 B5
Leafy Way BS24 50 B4
Lea Grove Rd BS21 6 C4
Leaholme Gdns BS14 23 A3
Lear's La BA9 177 C6
Leat The [8] TA4 167 F8
Leawood Ct [3] BS23 30 C1
Leaze Cl BA11 119 D5
Leaze Dro BA5 139 A7
Leaze Ho BA11 119 D5
Leaze House Mews
BA11 119 D5
Leaze La
Blagdon BS40 72 E8
West Chinnock TA18 196 B8
Yeovil BA21 219 F4
Leazemoor La TA10 172 B8
Leaze Rd BA11 119 D5
Leaze The
Radstock BA3 97 D8
Rode BA2 82 C1
Leazeway Dro TA7 155 C1
Lecher La DT8, TA18 196 B1
Leda Ave BS14 23 A7
Leedham Rd BS24 50 C5
Leeford La EX35 122 B5
Leeming Way BS11 4 C8
Lee Pk TA21 180 F7
Leeside BS20 2 C5
Leet Ct DT9 225 B2
Leeward Cl TA6 209 C4
Leewood Rd BS23 30 F1
Leffman Ct TA11 211 C4
Leggar The TA6 209 A6
Legion Rd BA21 218 F6
Leg La BS40 54 B3
Leg Of Mutton Rd BA6 206 E6
Leg Sq BA4 205 C6
Leg Square Ct BA4 205 C6
Leigh Cl BA1 28 A2
Leigh Court Bsns Ctr BS8 5 A2
Leigh Furlong Rd BA16 207 B4
Leigh La
Cold Ashton BA1 13 B3
Crowcombe TA4 151 A7
Halstock BA22 197 C3
Winsford TA22 147 C2
Winsham TA20 199 A8
Leigh Rd
Bristol BS8 226 B4
Leigh u M BA11 117 C2
Street BA16 207 C5
Taunton TA2 213 B8
Leigh St BA3 116 F3
Leighton Cl BA4 141 E1
Leighton Cres BS24 67 A8
Leighton La BA4 141 E1
Leighton Lane Ind Est
BA4 141 E1
Leighton Rd BA1 27 A3
Leigh upon Mendip Fst Sch
BA3 117 A3
Leigh View Rd BS20 2 E7
Leighwood Dr BS48 8 B1
Leigh Woods Forest Walks*
BS8 5 C1
Leinster Ave BS4 22 D8
Lemon La BS2 227 C4
Lenover Gdns BS13 22 B4
Lenthay Cl DT9 225 C2
Lenthay Ct DT9 225 C3
Lenthay Rd DT9 225 B2
Leonard's Barton BA11 119 E6
Leonard Houlden Ct [7]
TA2 213 A8
Leonard La BS1 227 A3
Leopold Bldgs BA1 228 C4
Lerburne The BS28 108 D4
Leslie Ave TA2 212 E6
Leslie Rise BA15 64 F3
Les Rosiers Gdns BA9 216 C4
Lester Dr BS22 32 A3
Lester La DT9 176 A2
Letham Ct TA19 221 B4
Lethbridge Pk TA4 151 D1
Lethbridge Rd BA5 203 C4
Level La DT9 176 A2
Level View TA10 172 C5
Leversedge Rd BA11 120 A7
Lewins Mead BS1 227 A3
Lewis's Dro BA5 138 E7
Lewis Cres BA11 119 F6
Lewisham Gr BS23 49 A8
Lewis Rd
Bristol BS13 22 A8
Taunton TA2 212 E7
Lewmond Ave BA5 203 F5
Leycroft Cl TA1 213 B4
Leycroft Gr TA1 213 B4
Leycroft Rd TA1 213 B4
Leyland Wlk BS13 21 F4
Leys Hill BA11 120 A6
Leys La BA11 119 F7
Leys The BS21 6 B1
Leystone Cl BA11 120 A6
Leyton Dr TA6 209 D6
Lias Rd BA16 207 B4
Liberty Gdns BS1 226 C1
Liberty La BS40 54 E2
Liberty Pl TA6 209 B4
Liberty The BA5 203 E5
Liddon Hill TA18 195 C5
Liddymore La
Watchet TA23 202 D5
Williton TA4, TA23 202 E4
Liddymore Rd TA23 202 C6
Lightermans Cl TA24 201 B7
Lightgate TA13 220 D5
Lightgate La TA13 220 D4
Lightgate Rd TA13 220 D4
Lilac Cl TA1 213 C2
Lilac Ct BS31 24 C4
Lilac Terr BA3 78 C2
Lilac Way BS22 32 A5
Lilian Terr BS39 77 E5
Lillebonne Cl TA21 222 F6
Lillesdon Terr TA3 170 A2
Lillington Cl BA3 79 B2
Lillington Rd BA3 79 B2
Lillington Way TA20 223 C5
Lilly Batch BA11 119 F7
Lillycombe La TA3, EX15 191 B8
Lillypool Cheese & Cider
Farm* BS25 70 F6
Lily La BA8 176 E1
Limber Rd BA22 218 A6
Limbers La BA5 139 B8
Limbury [2] TA12 185 E6
Limbury Cotts [3] TA12 185 E6
Limebreach Wood BS48 8 D3
Limeburn Hill BS40 38 E5
Lime Cl
Frome BA11 120 B7
Locking BS24 50 B4
Minehead TA24 200 D7
Street BA16 207 C5
Weston-Super-Mare BS22 32 A1
Lime Cres TA1 213 C2
Lime Ct BS31 24 C4
Lime Gr
Bath BA2 45 B6
Shepton Mallet BA4 205 A6
Lime Grove Gdns BA2 45 B6
Lime Kiln BA21 218 C5
Limekiln La
Bath BA2 45 F4
Chard, Forton TA20 223 D1
Chard, Lydmarsh TA20 194 C3
Cricket St Thomas TA20 194 E2
Leigh u M BA11 117 C3
Oakhill BA3 114 E5
Stoke St Michael BA3 115 F4
Tatworth TA20 193 F1
Lime Kiln La
Castle Cary BA7 214 E4
Clevedon BS21 6 D3
Henstridge BA8 190 A6
Wookey Hole BA5 203 B7
Lime Kiln Rd BS1 226 B2
Limekilns Cl BS31 24 F5
Limepits La TA10 172 D5
Limerick Cl DT9 217 D2
Limerick La BA11 101 F2
Limes Cl TA4 202 E3
Lime St
Nether Stowey TA5 134 B2
Stogursey TA5 134 C6
Limestone Hill TA5 135 C1
Lime Terr BA3 78 D1
Lime Tree Ave BA20 218 E2
Lime Tree Cl TA6 209 D4
Lime Tree Gr BS20 4 D3
Limington Rd BA22 173 E1
Limpetshell La TA4 202 E3
Limpley Stoke Rd BA15 64 D6
Linch La BA4 142 D2
Lincoln Hill TA19 184 E4
Lincoln Cl BS31 24 C4

Lincombe Rd BA3 97 D8
Lincott View BA2 79 C8
Linden Ave BS23 49 B8
Linden Cl
Bridgwater TA6 209 C4
Bristol BS14 23 E6
Frome BA11 119 D5
Radstock BA3 97 E8
Linden Ct BS21 6 D4
Linden Gdns BA1 44 D8
Linden Gr TA1 212 E5
Linden Hill TA21 222 A6
Linden Rd
Clevedon BS21 6 D4
Yeovil BA20 218 F5
Lindens The BS22 31 E4
Lindisfarne Cl BA15 64 E6
Lindsey Cl BS20 1 F4
Lindsey Cres 1 TA6 153 F3
Linemere Cl BS48 19 D6
Lines Way BS14 23 C3
Liney Rd TA7 154 F6
Lingfield Ave BA21 219 D7
Linham Rd TA6 208 F6
Linhay Cl EX15 179 E1
Linkhay TA20 198 D8
Linkhay Cl TA20 198 D8
Link La
Burrington BS40 53 F3
Monkton Farleigh BA15 46 F8
Linkmead BA3 96 F2
Link Rd
Nailsea BS48 8 F2
Portishead BS20 2 C5
Links Ct BS23 48 D4
Links Gdns TA8 84 F3
Linkside BS21 6 E6
Links Rd BS23 48 C2
Link The BS27 90 B8
Linley Cl
Bath BA2 44 A5
Bridgwater TA6 209 D7
Linleys The BA1 44 C7
Linne Ho BA2 44 A5
Linnet Cl
Taunton TA1 212 B4
Weston-Super-Mare BS22 31 E1
Linnet Gdns BS20 2 F6
Linnet Way
Frome BA11 120 B6
Midsomer Norton BA3 97 B8
Linsvale Cl BA11 120 C5
Linsvale Dr BA11 120 C5
Lintern Cl BA4 159 C7
Linton's Wlk BS14 23 A7
Lion Cl BS48 8 D2
Lion D'angers TA4 210 D4
Lion Ho 20 BA4 205 B6
Lion Mews TA11 211 E4
Lipe Hill La TA3, TA4 168 B1
Lipe La TA3 169 C3
Lipgate Pl BS20 2 D3
Lippetts Way TA7 137 D1
Lippiat Hill BA3 80 C3
Lippiatt La
Cheddar BS27 90 C7
Shipham BS25 70 F8
Timsbury BA2 60 B3
Lippiatt The BS27 90 C8
Lisieux Ct TA1 213 D2
Lisieux Way TA1 213 C3
Lisle Rd BS22 32 B4
Lister's Hill TA19 221 C2
Listercombe Cl TA19 221 C2
Lister Gr BA15 64 F3
Litfield Pl BS8 11 F7
Litfield Rd BS8 11 F8
Litt Hill BA3 75 F2
Little Ann St BS2, BS5 227 C4
Little Birch Croft BS14 23 A3
Little Bishop St BS2 227 B4
Littlebrook BS39 77 E6
Little Brooks La BA4 205 C4
Little Burrow Dro TA7 155 A1
Little Caroline Pl 4 BS8 11 F5
Little Cl TA2 212 C8
Little Elm Rd TA7 155 C4
Little England TA7 155 C2
Little Entry BA5 203 F5
Littlefield DT9 225 B3
Littlefield Cl BA16 156 E7
Littlefield La TA10 172 E4
Little Field La BA5 110 F7
Littlefields Ave BS29 51 B3
Littlefields La TA19 184 F3
Littlefields Rd BS29 51 B3
Littlefields Rise BS29 51 B3
Little George St
Bristol BS2 227 C4
Weston-Super-Mare BS23 48 E7
Little Gn BA5 111 A4
Little Halt BS20 1 E4
Little Ham BS21 16 C8
Littleham Cotts TA3 181 E6
Little Headley Cl BS13 22 B7
Little Keyford La BA11 119 E1
Little King St BS1 227 A2
Little La
Farmborough BA2 60 A6
Kingsbury Episcopi TA12 185 A7
Little Leaze La TA7 137 D2
Little Lester TA19 221 C2
Little Marston Rd BA22 174 F1
Little Mdw
6 Bishops Lydeard TA4 167 F8
Ilchester BA22 173 E2
Little Mead TA14 185 F2
Little Mead Cl BS24 49 E3
Little Meadow End BS48 18 E8
Little Moor Rd TA9 106 F3
Littlemore Dro TA7 154 C3
Little Orch
Cheddar BS27 90 C8
34 Martock TA12 185 E6
Street BA16 207 D7
Weston-Super-Mare BS23 48 D1
Little Paul St BS2 226 C4
Little Pen TA8 84 F5
Little Plover Cl TA24 201 C5
Little Sammons BA22 186 E5
Little Silver Ct TA23 202 C7
Little Silver La TA21 222 D2
Little St TA14 185 E2
Little Stanhope St BA1 228 A4
Little Stoke Rd BS9 5 E4
Littleton Hill TA11 211 E6
Littleton La
Wellow BA2 80 C7
Winford BS40 38 D5
Little Trumps BA22 186 B7
Little Withey Mead BS9 5 F5
Little Wiveliscombe La
TA4 165 D6
Littlewood BA11 143 C4
Littlewood Cl BS14 23 B3
Littlewood La BS49 18 C2
Litton BS24 49 A2
Liver Moor Dro TA11 156 E2
Livingstone Rd BA2 44 D5
Livingstone Terr BA2 228 A1
Livingstone Way TA2 212 B6
Llewellyns Almshouses 6
BA5 203 D4
Llewellyn Way BS22 32 B3
Lloyd Cl TA1 212 B1
Load La TA7 154 E5
Load Pool TA7 155 C2
Lobelia Cl TA9 104 D5
Lock's Hill BA11 119 F3
Lock's La BA9 216 C4
Lockemor Rd BS13 22 F4
Locketts Barton TA3 170 D7
Lockey Rd BA4 205 B4
Lock Gdns BS13 21 E7
Locking Farm Ind Est
BS24 50 A5
Locking Head Dro
Locking BS24 49 F5
Weston-Super-Mare BS24 50 A6
Locking Moor Rd
Locking BS24 50 B5
Weston-Super-Mare BS22 49 D8
Locking Prim Sch BS24 50 B4
Locking Rd BS22, BS23 49 B7
Lockingwell Rd BS31 24 D5
Locksbrook Ct 8 BA1 44 B6
Locksbrook Rd
Bath BA1 44 C6
Weston-Super-Mare BS22 32 B5
Locksbrook Trad Est 7
BA1 44 B6
Lockside BS20 2 E7
Lockside Sq BS20 2 E7
Locks Way TA7 136 F3
Lockswell TA7 136 E4
Lockswell Cotts BA4 141 B1
Lockwood Ct 4 BA21 218 F7
Lockyer Dro TA7 156 A5
Lodes La TA2 168 E8
Lodge Cl
Taunton TA1 212 A2
Wellington TA21 222 D6
Yatton BS49 34 B8
Lodge Cotts TA3 181 D6
Lodge Ct
Bristol BS9 5 E4
Castle Cary BA7 214 B4
Lodge Dr
Long Ashton BS41 11 B2
Weston-Super-Mare BS23 31 A1
Lodge Gdns BA2 44 D1
Lodge Hill
Berkley BA11, BA13 120 F5
Bratton Seymour BA9 176 A7
Somerton TA11 211 F4
Westbury-sub-Mendip
BA5 110 D5
Yarlington BA9 175 F7
Lodge Hill Ind Pk BA5 110 D5
Lodge La
Axminster EX13 198 B2
Wraxall BS48 9 B2
Lodge Pl BS1 226 C3
Lodge Rd
Horningsham BA12 144 D4
Kingsdon TA11 173 D4
Lodge Rocks TA24 131 D3
Lodge St BS1 226 C3
Lodges The BA3 96 D1
Lodway BS20 4 C4
Lodway Cl BS20 4 C5
Lodway Gdns BS20 4 C4
Lodwells Orch TA3 170 B4
Lombardy Cl 5 BS22 49 E8
London Cross TA4 151 E4
London Dro BA6, BS28 138 D7
London Ho TA4 210 C4
London Rd
Bath BA1 228 C4
Milborne Port DT9 217 E1
London Rd E BA1 29 A3
London Rd W BA1 28 E2
London Sq
28 Martock TA12 185 E6
Portishead BS20 2 E7
London St BA1 228 C4
Longacre BS21 16 B8
Long Acre BA4 205 C4
Longacre Cl TA2 212 E7
Longacre Dro TA7 154 D7
Long Acre Ho BA1 228 C4
Longacre La TA19 194 F6
Long Acre Rd BS14 23 A3
Long Acres Cl BS9 5 D7
Long Ashton Bsns Pk
BS41 11 B1
Long Ashton Rd BS41 11 B2
Long Ave BS21 6 B2
Long Barnaby BA3 78 A2
Longbottom BS25 71 A6
Longbridge 16 BA4 205 B6
Longbrook Trad Est BS3 11 E3
Long Cl
Ilminster TA19 221 C2
Yeovil BA21 218 C5
Longcombe Dr BA12 144 F6
Longcroft Rd BA21 219 C6
Long Cross
Bristol BS11 4 F8
Doulting BA4 141 F8
Felton BS40 37 D7
Nether Stowey TA5 134 A3
Long Cross Bottom
Doulting BA3 142 A8
Stoke St Michael BA3 116 A1
Longdown Dr BS22 32 B4
Long Dro
Broadway TA19, TA20 183 A2
Buckland St Mary TA20 182 F2
Glastonbury BA5 139 E4
Westbury-sub-Mendip
BS27 110 A4
Long Eaton Dr BS14 23 B7
Longfellow Ave BA2 44 F4
Longfellow Rd BA3 97 C8
Longfield BA11 118 A7
Longfield Cl TA4 202 E2
Longforth Rd TA21 222 D6
Longforward Hill
Dinnington TA17 195 A8
Seavington St Mary TA19 184 D1
Longforward La
Dinnington TA17 195 B8
Seavington St Mary TA19 184 D1
Long Furlong La
East Coker BA22 197 C8
Long Sutton TA10 172 E5
Long Ground BA11 119 F3
Long Hay Cl BA2 44 B5
Long Hill
Clewer BS28 89 D2
Shepton Mallet BA4 141 C8
Long Holcombe Cross
EX36 145 E6
Long La
Backwell BS48 19 C2
Bourton SP8 161 D1
Cucklington BA9 177 D5
Dinder BA5 140 D7
Felton BS40 37 B5
Fishpond Bottom DT6 199 B1
Walton BA16 156 D7
Wanstrow BA4 142 F5
West Chinnock TA18 196 B7
Wheddon Cross TA24 129 C2
Wootton Courtenay TA24 129 E8
Wrington BS40 36 B2
Long Lakes TA4 202 E4
Longlands La
East Coker BA22 197 C8
Westbury-sub-Mendip BA5 110 E7
Longleat Cl BA11 119 F3
Longleat Ct BA11 119 E4
Longleat Forest Holiday
Village★ BA12 144 F5
Longleat Ho★ BA12 144 D6
Longleat La BA3 116 C8
Longleat Rd BA3 116 B8
Longleat Rly★ BA12 144 C6
Longleat Saf Pk★ BA12 144 D6
Longleaze Gdns BS24 49 F3
Long Load Rd TA12 185 E8
Longman's Lea BA4 159 C7
Longmarsh La TA10 172 E6
Longmead TA4 165 E8
Long Mead BA21 218 C5
Longmead Cl
Norton St Philip BA2 81 F4
Taunton TA1 212 D2
Wellington TA21 222 B8
Longmead Cotts TA21 222 B8
Longmead Croft BS13 21 F4
Longmeadow Rd BS31 24 C4
Longmead Way TA1 212 D2
Long Moor Dro TA7, TA9 137 A7
Long Orchard Hill TA19 221 E3
Longreach Gr BS14 23 D6
Long Ride Dro BA6 157 F3
Longridge Way BS24 49 F7
Long Row BS1 227 B2
Long Run BA22 186 C2
Longrun La TA1 212 D4
Longs Field TA3 170 C4
Long St
Croscombe BA5 204 B7
Galhampton BA22 175 E8
High Ham TA10 156 A1
Sherborne DT9 225 E4
Williton TA4 202 E3
Longstone Ave TA6 209 C5
Longstone Cl TA5 134 B2
Longstrings La TA18 224 C8
Long Sutton CE Prim Sch
TA10 172 E4
Long-Thorn BS48 18 F6
Longthorne Pl BA2 44 F2
Long Thorn La BS40 55 E7
Longton Grove Rd 3
BS23 48 E8
Longton Ind Est BS23 48 F6
Long Valley Rd BA2 43 F5
Longvernal BA3 77 F1
Longvernal Prim Sch BA3 77 F1
Longway Ave BS13, BS14 22 F4
Longwood Ho BS8 10 D4
Longwood La
Burlescombe TA21 179 C4
Long Ashton BS8, BS41 10 F4
Lonsdale Ave BS23 48 F4
Lonsdale Rd TA5 135 C2
Look's La BA6 157 C6
Looseall La TA22 163 D8
Lopen Head TA13 220 A1
Lopen La TA13 220 C1
Lopen Rd TA13, TA17 195 D8
Lordsleaze La TA20 223 D3
Lords Meadow La 5
EX16 164 B1
Lords Way TA6 208 E6
Loretto Gdns 5 EX13 198 A1
Loretto Rd EX13 198 A1
Lorne Pl BA5 203 E5
Lorne Rd BA2 44 D6
Lotment Hill TA11 173 D5
Lottisham La BA4, BA6 158 D6
Lottisham Rd BA6 158 C6
Lotts' Ave BS48 19 B5
Lotus Ct BS22 31 C1
Louisa Gate TA22 163 F7
Louisa St BS2 227 C2
Loundshay La TA4 167 A4
Louvigne Cl TA8 104 C7
Love's La BA2 59 F6
Love La
Burnham-on-S TA8 104 C7
Ilminster TA19 221 C3
Marnhull DT10 190 F6
Shepton Beauchamp TA19 184 E4
Wincanton BA9 216 F5
Lovelands DT2 197 A1
Lovelinch Gdns BS41 10 F1
Lovell Dr BS39 57 C4
Lovells Mead DT10 190 F6
Lovells Mill BS39 57 D4
Lovells The BS20 4 B4
Loveridge La TA20 198 D8
Lovers' Wlk
4 Cannington TA5 135 B2
Weston-Super-Mare BS23 48 D8
Lovers La BA3, BS39 78 A5
Lovers Wlk BA5 203 D5
Loves Hill BA2 60 A1
Loves La BA14 83 C7
Lovington CE Prim Sch
BA7 158 F2
Low's Hill La DT9 188 B3
Lowbourne BS14 22 F6
Lower Acreman St 3
DT9 225 D3
Lower Actis BA6 206 E3
Lower Ansford BA7 214 B7
Lower Backway BA10 215 E6
Lower Batch BS40 39 B3
Lower Bath Rd TA6 209 B6
Lower Beadon TA16 195 F7
Lower Borough Walls
BA1 228 C2
Lowerbourne Terr TA24 124 A3
Lower Boyston La DT9 188 F5
Lower Bristol Rd
Bath BA2 44 B6
Clutton BS39 58 F4
Lower Burlington Rd BS20 2 E7
Lower Camden Pl BA1 228 C4
Lower Castle St BS1 227 B3
Lower Chapel Ct BA5 113 A1
Lower Cheriton La BA8 176 D4
Lower Church La BS2 227 A3
Lower Church Rd BS23 48 D8
Lower Claverham BS49 17 F3
Lower Clifton Hill BS8 226 B2
Lower College St BS1 226 C2
Lower Coombses TA20 198 D8
Lower Cross EX15 179 C1
Lower Down Rd BS20 2 B5
Lower East Coker Rd
BA20 218 F1
Lower East Hayes BA1 45 B8
Lower Fairfield TA4 166 F5
Lower Fairmead Rd
BA21 219 D8
Lower Fallow Cl BS14 22 F3
Lower Farm DT9 187 E4
Lower Farm La BA2 43 B7
Lowerfield La TA19 184 E1
Lower Foxmoor Rd TA21 222 B5
Lower Gay St BS2 227 A4
Lower Guinea St BS1 227 A1
Lower Gully Dro BS28 89 F3
Lower Gunville DT9 217 D2
Lower Hedgemead Rd
BA1 228 C4
Lower High St BS11 4 D7
Lower Holway Cl TA1 213 D2
Lower Hyde Rd TA15 186 B4
Lower Innox BA11 119 E6
Lower Keyford BA11 119 F3
Lower Kingsbury DT9 217 D3
Lower Kingsdown Rd
SN13 29 F3
Lower Knowles Rd BS21 6 C2
Lower La
Shepton Mallet BA4 205 C6
Weston Town BA4 142 E5
Lower Lamb St BS1 226 C2
Lower Linden Rd BS21 6 D3
Lower Lodfin EX16 164 B2
Lower Marshfield Rd
TA24 201 B6
Lower Maudlin St BS1 227 A3
Lower Mdw TA19 221 A4
Lower Meadow Rd TA24 201 B5
Lower Middle St TA1 212 F4
Lower New Rd BS27 90 A7
Lower Northend BA1 28 F5
Lower North St BS27 90 B8
Lower North Town La
BA22 175 D7
Lower Norton La
Weston-Super-Mare BS22 31 E4
Weston-Super-Mare, Norton
BS22 31 C4
Lower Notlake Dro BS28 89 E4
Lower Odcombe BA22 186 C2
Lower Oldfield Pk BA2 228 A1
Lower Orch TA19 184 C5
Lower Parade Ground Rd
BS24 50 C5
Lower Park La TA24 129 E1
Lower Park Row BS1 227 A3
Lower Pk TA24 200 E7
Lower Queen's BS21 6 D3
Lower Rd
Hinton Blewett BS39 75 E6
Horsington BA8 176 D3
Kingsdon TA11 173 D5
Stalbridge DT10 190 C4
Woolavington TA7 136 E4
Lower Ream BA21 218 C5
Lower Rocke's Cotts
BA6 157 D4
Lower Severalls Gdn★
TA18 196 A6
Lowerside La BA6 206 D7
Lowerside Rd BA6 206 E6
Lower Silk Mill BA4 204 F6
Lower Somerton TA11 211 F3
Lower St
Buckland Dinham BA11 100 A2
Carhampton TA24 131 B4
Chewton Mendip BA3 94 F7
Curry Mallet TA3 183 C8
Merriott TA16 195 F7
Pilton BA4 140 F3
Rode BA11 101 E8
Upton Noble BA4 142 F2
West Chinnock TA18 196 B8
Lower Stoke BA2, BA3 64 A8
Lower Strode BS40 56 A7
Lower Strode Rd BS21 16 A7
Lower Touches TA20 223 E5
Lower Town
Montacute TA15 186 B4
Sampford Peverell EX16 178 D1
Lower Turners Barn La
BA20 218 F2
Lower Vellow TA4 132 D2
Lower Westholme Rd
BA4 140 D3
Lower Whitelands BA3 79 B3
Lower Woodcock St
BA7 214 C5
Lower Wraxhill Rd BA20 218 F1
Low Ham Rd TA10 172 B8
Lowlands Terr TA1 212 B4
Lowman Cross EX16 178 B2
Lowmoor Ind Est TA21 222 B8
Lowsome La DT9 188 A5
Lowther Rd BA21 219 E7
Lowtrow Cross TA4 165 A8
Loxhams TA10 156 B2
Loxleigh Ave TA6 209 B4
Loxleigh Gdns TA6 209 B4
Loxley Batch TA7 156 A8
Loxley Gdns BA2 44 C4
Loxley Terr TA6 208 F7
Loxton Dr BA2 44 B6
Loxton Rd BS23 48 F2
Loxton Sq BS14 23 A6
Lubborn La BA6 158 B5
Luckes La TA4 132 E3
Luckington Cross BA11 98 B2
Lucklands Rd BA1 27 C1
Luckley Ave BS13 22 C5
Luckwells La TA24 129 E2
Lucott Cross TA24 128 C6
Ludbourne Rd DT9 225 E3
Ludlow Ave TA2 213 A8
Ludlow Cl
Bridgwater TA6 209 A2
Frome BA11 120 C6
Keynsham BS31 24 D5
Ludney Cross TA19 194 F7
Ludney La
Dinnington TA17 195 A8
Ilminster TA19 194 F7
Ludwells Orch BS39 77 E5
Lufton Coll of FE BA22 186 D4
Lufton Heights Commerce Pk
BA22 218 A7
Lufton Trad Est BA22 218 A7
Lufton Way BA22 218 A6
Luggard's Cross BS21 8 C4
Lugshorn La TA11 211 C8
Luke's Cl BA3 78 F3
Lukes Gdn TA24 131 B4

Luke St EX16 164 B1
Lullington La BA11 101 B3
Lulsgate Rd BS13 22 A8
Lulworth Rd BS31 24 E4
Lundy Dr TA8 104 B5
Luns Hill BA6 157 F1
Lunty Mead BS48 18 F6
Lupin Way BA22 218 B5
Lush Path DT9 225 E4
Lusty Gdns BA10 215 E5
Luttrell Cl TA2 213 B8
Luttrell Gdns TA24 200 F6
Luvers La BS40 54 D1
Luxborough Rd TA6 208 B4
Lux Furlong BS9 5 B7
Luxhay Cl TA2 213 B8
Luxton's La BA3, BA4 116 F1
Lyatt La BA5 140 E8
Lyatts Hill BA22 197 B6
Lychgate Pk BS24 50 A4
Lyddieth Ct BA15 64 E7
Lyddon's Hill TA22 148 A1
Lyddon Cl TA21 222 D4
Lyddon Rd BS22 32 B3
Lyddons Mead TA20 223 E4
Lydeard Cross TA5 152 E3
Lydeard Down Hill TA4 151 B4
Lydeard Mead TA4 167 E8
Lydeard St Lawrence Com Prim Sch TA4 151 A3
Lyde Ct BA21 219 E6
Lyde Gn BA2 81 E5
Lyde La BA21 219 F6
Lyde Rd BA21 219 E7
Lydon La TA4 165 D5
Lye Cross Rd BS40 36 C1
Lyefield Rd BS22 31 E4
Lye Hole La BS40 36 D2
Lye La BA4 158 F6
Lye Mead BS40 38 A6
Lyes The BS49 34 D3
Lyewater TA18 224 B6
Lyme Gdns BA1 44 B7
Lyme Rd
Axminster EX13 198 A1
Bath BA1 44 B7
Crewkerne TA18 224 B4
Lymore Ave BA2 44 C5
Lymore Gdns BA2 44 C5
Lymore Terr BA2 44 C4
Lympsham CE Fst Sch BS24 67 B1
Lympsham Gn BA2 62 D8
Lympsham Rd BS24 67 B1
Lynbrook BS41 10 F1
Lynbrook La BA2 44 F3
Lynch Cl BS22 31 F3
Lynchcombe La BA5 110 F6
Lynch Cres BS25 69 F7
Lynch Hill BA3 96 A3
Lynch La
Cheddar BS27 90 C8
Hardington Mandeville BA22 197 A6
Westbury-sub-Mendip BA5 110 D8
Lynchmead BS25 70 A7
Lynch The BS25 69 F7
Lyncombe Hall BA2 45 A4
Lyncombe Hill BA2 228 C1
Lyncombe Vale BA2 45 B4
Lyncombe Vale Rd BA2 45 A4
Lyndale Ave
Bridgwater TA6 208 E5
Bristol BS9 5 D5
Lynde Cl BS13 22 B4
Lyndhurst Cres TA6 208 C5
Lyndhurst Gr TA12 185 D7
Lyndhurst Rd
Bath BA2 44 C6
Bristol BS9 5 F7
Keynsham BS31 24 F3
Midsomer Norton BA3 97 B8
Weston-Super-Mare BS23 48 E4
Lyndhurst Terr BA1 228 C4
Lynfield Pk BA1 27 C1
Lynfield Rd BA11 119 D5
Lynford La TA11 158 C1
Lyngford Cres TA2 213 A7
Lyngford La TA2 168 F6
Lyngford Park Prim Sch TA2 213 B8
Lyngford Pl TA2 213 A7
Lyngford Rd TA2 213 A7
Lyngford Sq TA2 213 A7
Lynmouth Cl BS22 32 A2
Lynor Cl TA1 213 D3
Lynton Cl BS20 2 E4
Lynton Rd
Burnham-on-S TA8 104 B6
Midsomer Norton BA3 97 B8
Lynwood Cl
Frome BA11 119 D4
Midsomer Norton BA3 97 A8
Lynx Cres BS24 49 B2
Lynx Trad Est BA20 218 D3
Lynx West Trad Est BA20 218 C3
Lyons Court Rd BS14 23 D7
Lyons Ct BS23 48 F7
Lype La TA22 147 E4
Lypstone Cl BS24 50 A8
Lypyatt La BA6 206 F4
Lysander Rd BA20 218 E3
Lysander Ret Pk BA20 219 A3
Lysander Road Rdbt BA20 218 C3
Lyster Cl BA22 173 E1
Lyster Gdns BA22 173 E1
Lyte's Cary* TA11 173 F5
Lytes Cary Rd BS31 25 A3
Lytton Gdns BA2 44 B4
Lytton Gr BS31 25 A5
Lyveden Gdns BS13 22 B5
Lyvedon Way BS41 11 B1

M

McAdam Way BS1 11 F5
MacAulay Bldgs BA2 45 C4
McCrae Rd BS24 50 B5
McCreath Cl [3] TA6 153 F3
Mc Creery Rd DT9 225 D6
Macey's Rd BS13 22 D3
Macfarlane Chase BS23 49 A5
Machine Cross TA22 163 F6
Macies The BA1 27 B3
McKinley Terr TA23 131 E4
Mackley La BA2 81 E3
MacLeod Cl BS21 6 A2
Macquarie Farm Cl BS49 17 A1
Macrae Rd BS20 4 E4
Madam's Paddock BS40 39 B3
Madam La
Weston-Super-Mare BS22 31 F2
Weston-Super-Mare BS22 32 A3
Weston-Super-Mare BS22 32 A4
Madden Cl TA8 104 C7
Maddocks Pk BA9 216 C3
Maddocks Slade TA8 104 A8
Madeira Ct BS23 48 C8
Madeira Rd
Clevedon BS21 6 D3
Weston-Super-Mare BS23 30 C1
Madgeon La TA20 192 E8
Madison Ct [5] TA18 224 C6
Madwoman's La BS28 108 B2
Maesbury Rd BS31 25 A2
Maesdown Cl BA4 141 E2
Maesdown Cotts BA4 141 E2
Maesdown Hill BA4 141 E3
Maes Down Ho [10] BA4 205 B6
Maesdown Rd
Doulting BA4 141 E4
Evercreech BA4 141 E2
Maesknoll La BS14, BS39 40 B8
Magdalana Ct BS1 227 B1
Magdalen Ave BA2 228 B1
Magdalene Cl BA6 206 D4
Magdalene Ct [9] TA1 212 F4
Magdalene La [10] TA1 212 F4
Magdalene Rd BA3 79 C2
Magdalene St
Glastonbury BA6 206 D4
Taunton TA1 212 F4
Magdalen La BA14 83 B7
Magdalen Rd BA2 228 B1
Magdalen Way BS22 32 A3
Magellan Cl BS22 31 F4
Maggs Folly BS39 59 D2
Maggs Hill BA2 60 B2
Maggs La
Castle Cary BA7 214 C7
Whitchurch BS14 23 C4
Maglands Rd TA23 202 D6
Magna Cl BA21 219 D8
Magnolia Ave BS22 32 A1
Magnolia Cl
Frome BA11 120 C7
Weston-Super-Mare BS22 49 E7
Magnolia Rd BA3 78 E1
Magnolia Tree Rd TA6 209 E5
Magpie Cl
Burnham-on-S TA8 85 B1
Weston-Super-Mare BS22 49 E8
Maiden Beech Mid Sch TA18 224 B4
Maidenbrook La TA2 169 A6
Maiden Croft La BA6 139 D2
Maidenhead Cross EX16 179 C2
Maidenhead Rd BS13 22 D3
Maiden Way BS11 4 C8
Maidstone Gr BS24 49 A1
Maincombe Cl TA18 224 C4
Main Rd
Brockley BS49 18 D2
Burrowbridge TA7 154 F1
Cannington TA5 135 C1
Coxley BA5 139 E6
Flax Bourton BS48 19 F7
Huntspill TA9 136 B8
Hutton BS24 49 E2
Kilve TA5 133 C5
Lyng TA3, TA7 170 C7
Middlezoy TA7 155 B3
Othery TA7 155 B2
Shapwick TA7 155 F8
Westhay BA6 138 B5
Westonzoyland TA7 154 F5
Main St
Babcary TA11 174 C7
Barton St David TA11 158 A3
Chilthorne Domer BA22 186 E6
Farrington Gurney BS39 77 A4
Martock TA12 185 F7
Walton BA16 156 D7
Mal's Mead La TA20 194 C3
Malago Wlk BS13 21 E4
Malden Mead BS14 23 A5
Malherbie Ct TA20 194 B6
Malin Par BS20 2 F6
Mallard Pl TA9 104 C4
Mallard Rd TA24 201 C5
Mallard Way TA6 209 B4
Mallard Wlk [7] BS22 49 E8
Mallory Cl TA2 212 C6
Mallow Cl BS21 6 E2
Mall The
Bath BA1 228 C2
Bristol, Clifton BS8 11 F7
Malmesbury Ct [6] BA21 218 C6
Malmesbury Way BA21 218 C6
Malta Way BA22 174 A2
Malt Ho The TA4 210 C4
Malthouse Cl BA9 216 C4
Malthouse Ct
Frome BA11 119 E3
Taunton TA1 212 A4
Malthouse La DT9 187 F5
Malthouses TA21 167 A1
Maltings Ind Est The BA1 44 B6
Maltings The
Chard TA20 223 C3
Frome BA11 119 F4
Midford BA2 63 C5
Sherborne DT9 225 E4
Weston-Super-Mare BS22 31 F2
Maltlands BS22 49 D8
Malvern Bldgs BA1 28 A2
Malvern Cl TA6 209 D6
Malvern Ct BA21 218 D6
Malvern Rd BS23 48 E5
Malvern Terr
[4] Bath BA1 28 A1
Taunton TA2 212 F6
Malvern Villas [3] BA1 28 A1
Mamsey La TA4 202 C3
Manchester Cotts BS22 31 E3
Mancroft Ave BS11 4 F7
Mandarin Cl TA6 209 B4
Mandy Mdws BA3 77 F1
Mangle Cave Hill TA18 195 C5
Manilla Cres BS23 30 C1
Manilla Pl BS23 30 C1
Manilla Rd BS8 226 A3
Manleaze Cvn Pk BA4 205 D3
Manleys Cotts TA2 168 C6
Manmoor La BS21 7 A1
Manning's La BA3 94 F3
Manning Cl BA5 203 F5
Manning Rd TA4 167 E6
Manor Barton TA14 185 E2
Manor Bldgs TA18 196 C4
Manor Cl
Berrow TA8 84 F6
Bradford Abbas DT9 187 E1
Chard TA20 223 C2
Charlton Horethorne DT9 176 A2
Cossington TA7 136 F3
Ditcheat BA4 159 C7
East Brent TA9 86 D5
Easton-in-G BS20 4 A4
Farrington Gurney BS39 77 A3
Glastonbury BA6 206 D5
Kingsdon TA11 173 D5
Portishead BS20 2 A5
South Perrott DT8 196 C1
Sparkford BA22 175 A4
Taunton TA1 212 E3
Templecombe BA8 189 E8
Wellow BA2 62 D1
Manor Cl The BS8 11 A8
Manor Copse Rd BA3 79 C2
Manor Court Prim Sch TA20 223 C3
Manor Ct
Backwell BS48 19 A5
Burnham-on-S TA8 104 B7
Cossington TA7 136 F3
Easton BA5 111 A4
Horsington BA8 176 D2
Locking BS24 50 B4
Sherborne DT9 225 D5
Stawell TA7 137 A1
Weston-Super-Mare BS23 49 A8
Manor Dr
Bathford BA1 29 C2
Berrow TA8 84 F6
Chedzoy TA7 154 D8
East Coker BA22 197 B8
[10] Merriott TA16 195 F7
Staplegrove TA2 212 C7
Taunton TA1 212 E3
Manor Farm
Chard TA20 223 C3
East Coker BA22 197 B8
Manor Farm Barns TA7 169 E8
Manor Farm Cl
Tatworth TA20 198 C8
Weston-Super-Mare BS24 49 B2
Manor Farm Cres BS24 49 B2
Manor Furlong BA11 119 E2
Manor Gdns
Farmborough BA2 59 F6
Farrington Gurney BS39 77 A3
Ilchester BA22 173 E1
Locking BS24 50 A4
Weston-Super-Mare BS22 31 B4
Manor Gn EX14 191 F2
Manor Grange BS24 67 B7
Manor Ho BS2 226 C3
Manor House Gdns BA6 206 D5
Manor House Rd BA6 206 D5
Manor La
Abbots Leigh BS8 10 F8
Wedmore BS28 108 D5
Manor Mews TA2 212 D8
Manor Orch TA1 212 D2
Manor Park Cl BA3 79 C2
Manor Pk
Bath BA1 44 B8
Keinton Mandeville TA11 158 B1
Norton Fitzwarren TA2 168 B4
Pawlett TA6 135 F6
Radstock BA3 79 C2
Weston-Super-Mare BS23 48 E1
Manor Pl TA11 158 B1
Manor Rd
Abbots Leigh BS8 10 F7
Bath BA1 27 C1
Bridgwater TA6 209 C6
Bristol, Bishopsworth BS13 22 A6
Burnham-on-S TA8 104 B7
Chedzoy TA7 154 D8
Cossington TA7 136 F3
Edington TA7 137 D2
Frome BA11 119 E2
Isle Abbotts TA3 183 F7
Kingsdon TA11 173 D5
Milborne Port DT9 217 C3
Minehead TA24 201 B4
Pawlett TA6 135 F6
Radstock BA3 79 C2
Saltford BS31 25 C2
Staplegrove TA2 212 C8
Taunton TA1 212 D3
Weston-Super-Mare BS23 49 A8
Yeovil BA20 219 A4
Manor Ride TA9 86 B2
Manor St BA22 197 A8
Manor Terr BA3 79 C2
Manor Valley BS23 31 A1
Manor View
Crewkerne TA18 224 C4
Golsoncott TA23 131 D1
Manor Villas BA1 27 C1
Manor Way
Berrow TA8 84 F6
Failand BS8 10 C4
Frome BA11 119 E2
Manse La TA7 136 C4
Mansel Cl BS31 25 C3
Mansfield Ave BS23 49 B8
Mansfield Rd TA1 213 A3
Manshay La DT6 199 D1
Manship Gn BA4 205 B4
Manston Cl BS14 23 C7
Mantle St TA21 222 C5
Mantle VC Rd BA22 174 A2
Manvers St BA1 228 C1
Manworthy Cross TA4 166 C4
Maperton Rd DT9 176 A2
Maple Cl
Bristol BS14 23 D5
Evercreech BA4 141 F1
North Petherton TA6 153 F3
Puriton TA7 136 C4
Street BA16 207 C5
Taunton TA2 213 A7
Weston-Super-Mare BS23 49 A8
Wincanton BA9 216 C2
Maple Ct
Bridgwater TA6 209 D6
Bristol BS9 5 F8
Frome BA11 120 A7
[9] Weston-Super-Mare BS23 30 C1
Maple Dr
Burnham-on-S TA8 104 B5
Crewkerne TA18 224 D7
Radstock BA3 78 E1
Yeovil BA20 218 F3
Maple Gdns BA2 44 E4
Maple Gr BA2 44 E4
Maple Ho BS2 227 A4
Maple Leaf Ct BS8 226 A3
Maple Rd
Curry Rivel TA10 171 D4
Langport TA10 172 A6
Maple Rise BA3 79 B2
Maples The
Nailsea BS48 8 C1
Shepton Mallet BA4 205 C6
Maplestone Rd BS14 23 A3
Maple Tree Ct TA7 136 F3
Maple Wlk BS31 24 D4
Mapstone Cl BA6 206 E3
Marchant's Hill BA3 95 F2
Marchant-Holliday Sch BA8 176 C5
Marchants Pass BA1 228 C1
Marchfields Way BS23 49 A5
March La BA22 175 D8
Marconi Cl BS23 49 B7
Marconi Rd BS20 1 F5
Marden Gr TA1 213 D3
Marden Rd BS31 25 A4
Mardi's La TA11 158 C2
Mardyke Ferry Rd BS1 226 B1
Mare La TA13 220 C5
Mares La BA5 110 E7
Margaret's Bldgs BA1 228 B3
Margaret's Hill BA1 228 C4
Margaret Cres TA8 104 A5
Margaret Rd [4] BS13 21 F4
Margery Fish Gdns* TA13 220 C8
Marguerite Rd BS13 21 F7
Marina Row TA6 209 B4
Marindin Dr BS22 32 B4
Marine Ct BA21 219 D5
Marine Dr TA8 104 B5
Marine Hill BS21 6 C5
Marine Par
Clevedon BS21 6 C4
Pill BS20 4 C5
Weston-Super-Mare BS23 30 B1
Marine Par *continued*
Weston-Super-Mare BS23 48 D6
Mariner's Cl BS22 31 D1
Mariner's Way BS20 4 C5
Mariners' Path BS9 5 E3
Mariners Cl
Backwell BS48 19 A6
Bridgwater TA6 209 A5
Minehead TA24 201 B7
Mariners Ct TA6 209 A5
Mariners Dr
Backwell BS48 19 A6
Bristol BS9 5 D4
Mariners Way TA23 202 D6
Maritime Heritage Ctr* BS1 226 B1
Marjoram Way BS20 2 F5
Mark CE Fst Sch TA9 106 A4
Mark Coll TA9 106 E4
Mark Cswy TA9 106 B4
Market Ave BS22 32 C3
Market Cl
[4] Bampton EX16 164 B1
Brushford TA22 163 E4
Market Ct
[8] Bridgwater TA6 208 F5
[2] Crewkerne TA18 224 C6
Market Gate BS2 227 A3
Market House La TA24 200 F7
Market House Mus The* TA23 202 C7
Market Ind Est BS49 17 B1
Market La BS23 48 D8
Market Pl
Burlescombe EX16 179 B4
Castle Cary BA7 214 C5
Frome BA11 119 F5
Glastonbury BA6 206 D4
Ilchester BA22 173 E1
Radstock BA3 78 F2
[23] Shepton Mallet BA4 205 B6
Somerton TA11 211 E4
Wells BA5 203 E4
Wincanton BA9 216 C4
Winford BS40 37 F7
Wiveliscombe TA4 210 C4
Market Pl The BA11 143 B8
Market Sq
Crewkerne TA18 224 C6
South Petherton TA13 220 C4
Market St
Bridgwater TA6 208 F5
Crewkerne TA18 224 C6
Highbridge TA9 104 E3
Watchet TA23 202 C7
Wells BA5 203 D4
Yeovil BA20 219 B5
Market Terr TA9 104 E3
Mark La BS1 226 C2
Marklands BS9 5 E3
Mark Rd
Burtle TA7 137 D6
Highbridge TA9 105 A2
Marksbury CE Prim Sch BA2 42 B2
Marks Cl TA3 169 C4
Marksmead DT8 199 F8
Marksview Bsns Ctr BA21 219 F7
Marlborough Ave TA6 209 A2
Marlborough Bldgs
Bath BA1 228 A3
Langport TA10 171 F5
Marlborough Cl TA6 209 A2
Marlborough Ct TA8 85 B1
Marlborough Dr BS22 32 B2
Marlborough Flats [8] BS2 227 A4
Marlborough Hill BS2 227 A4
Marlborough Hill Pl BS2 227 A4
Marlborough La BA1 228 A3
Marlborough Rd BA21 219 E6
Marlborough St
Bath BA1 228 A4
Bristol BS2 227 A4
Marl Cl BA21 218 E7
Marle Ground TA19 184 E2
Marlepit Gr BS13 21 F6
Marley's Row TA24 124 A3
Marley Cl TA24 201 A5
Marleys Way BA11 119 C5
Marlfield Wlk BS13 21 E7
Marling Ho TA24 201 B7
Marl La DT9 187 E3
Marlowe Ho [3] BS23 48 F4
Marl Pits [1] BS48 19 A6
Marl Pits La BA11 143 C7
Marne Cl BS14 23 D5
Marnhull Cl DT10 190 F6
Marriage La DT10 190 F3
Marron Cl BS26 70 C2
Marsden Rd BA2 44 B3
Marshall Wlk BS4 22 D7
Marshalsea Est DT6 199 C3
Marshbridge Cross TA22 163 C7
Marshclose Hill TA22 146 E2
Marsh Cross TA24 200 D1
Marshfield Rd TA24 201 B5
Marshfield Way BA1 28 A1
Marsh Hill TA22 163 C8
Marsh La
Barrington TA19 184 E5
Barton St David TA11 158 A3
Bridgwater TA6 209 B1
Buckhorn Weston BA9 177 C4
Cannington TA5 135 C2
Dunster TA24 201 E3
Easton-in-G BS20 4 A4

Marsh La *continued*
Farrington Gurney BS39 77 A3
Henstridge BA8 190 B7
Holcombe BA3 116 C5
Penselwood BA9 161 D2
Pitney TA10 172 D7
Portbury BS20 3 F6
South Cheriton BA8 176 E4
Temple Cloud BS39 59 A1
Tintinhull BA22 186 A5
Yeovil BA21 218 F8
Yeovil Marsh BA21 187 A5
Marsh Lane Ind Est BS20 3 F7
Marsh Pottinson Ho 16 BA20 219 B4
Marsh Rd
Bristol BS3 11 F3
Rode BA11 82 F1
Standerwick BA11 102 D1
Yatton BS49 34 B8
Marsh St
Avonmouth BS11 4 C8
4 Bristol BS1 227 A2
Dunster TA24 201 E3
Marshway TA3 170 D1
Marshwood CE Prim Sch DT6 199 C2
Marshwood Cross DT6 199 E1
Marson Rd BS21 6 D3
Marston Cl
Frome BA11 119 D2
Taunton TA1 212 E1
Marston La BA11 119 D2
Marston Mead BA11 119 D2
Marston Rd
Frome BA11 119 D1
Nunney BA11 143 D8
Sherborne DT9 225 B5
Marston Trad Est BA11 119 E2
Martcombe Rd BS20 4 C2
Martha's Orch BS13 21 E7
Martin's Cl TA8 85 A3
Martindale Ct BS22 49 D8
Martindale Rd BS22 49 D8
Martins TA3 169 C4
Martins Bldgs 4 TA21 222 D5
Martins Cl
Evercreech BA4 141 E1
Wellington TA21 222 D5
Wells BA5 203 B3
Martins Gr BS22 31 E2
Martins La BA4 205 E5
Martins Paddock BA4 142 A6
Martin St BA6 158 A5
Martins The BS20 3 A6
Martland Cl TA7 136 E3
Martlet Rd TA24 200 F7
Martock BS24 48 F2
Martock Bsns Pk TA12 185 D7
Martock CE Prim Sch TA12 185 D6
Martock La TA12 185 F7
Martock Rd
Keynsham BS31 25 A3
Long Sutton TA10 172 E4
Mart Rd TA24 201 B7
Mart The 6 BS23 48 E7
Martyn Cl TA5 135 B5
Marwin Cl TA12 185 E7
Marwood Cl TA8 104 C8
Marwood Rd BS4 22 E8
Mary Brown Davis La 6 BA5 139 D8
Marybush La BS2 227 B3
Mary Elton Prim Sch BS21 6 B1
Mary Hart Cl BA16 207 B7
Mary La 10 EX16 164 B1
Mary Rd BA5 203 C5
Mary St
Taunton TA1 212 F3
Yeovil BA21 219 B5
Masefield Ho BS23 49 A4
Mason's Way BS27 90 C7
Mason La TA15 186 B4
Masons Way BA11 119 D1
Mason Way BA4 205 A4
Massingham Pk TA2 213 B6
Materman Rd BS14 23 E5
Matfurlong Cl TA12 185 D5
Matt's La TA14 185 F4
Matthews Cl BS14 23 F6
Matthews Rd
Taunton TA1 212 B1
Yeovil BA21 219 C5
Mattock's Tree Hill TA3 169 E1
Mattys Cross EX14 191 D3
Maudlin Cross TA20 199 C8
Maudlin La TA20 199 C8
Maudslay Field BA22 197 C8
Maunsell Rd BS24 49 E7
Maunsel Rd TA7 153 F1
Max Mill La BS25 69 C8
Maxwell Rd BA4 205 B4
Maxwell St TA2 212 E6
May's La BS24 33 C3
Maybrick Rd BA2 44 D5
Mayfair Ave BS48 8 F1
Mayfield Ave BS22 31 E1
Mayfield Cl BA22 175 D8
Mayfield Dr TA6 208 B4
Mayfield Rd
Bath BA2 44 D5
Yeovil BA21 219 D6
Mayfields BS31 24 E5
Mayfield Terr TA4 210 C4
Mayflower Cl TA6 209 D5
Mayflower Gdns BS48 9 A2
Maynard Cl
Bristol BS13 22 C5
4 Clevedon BS21 6 F3
Maynard Rd BS13 22 C5
Maynard Terr BS39 58 F3
Maypole Cl BS39 58 E3
May Pole Knap TA11 211 C4
Maysfield Cl BS20 2 D3
Maysgreen La BS24 33 B3
Maysmead La BS40 53 C6
May Terr TA23 131 E3
Maytree Ave BS13 22 B7
Maytree Cl
Bristol BS13 22 B7
Frome BA11 120 B7
May Tree Cl BS48 8 C1
May Tree Rd BA3 78 E1
May Tree Wlk BS31 24 C3
Mead Ave BA22 218 B6
Mead Cl
Bath BA2 44 E3
Bristol BS11 4 E6
Cheddar BS27 90 B6
East Huntspill TA9 136 E8
Stoke St Michael BA3 116 B2
Meade Cl TA6 153 F3
Meade Ho BA2 44 A5
Meade La TA19 184 E1
Mead La
Blagdon BS40 54 E3
Lydford Fair Place TA11 158 C3
Saltford BS31 25 F4
Sandford BS25 51 E4
Stocklinch TA19 184 C4
Wanstrow BA4 142 F4
West Pennard BA6 140 C2
Meadlands BA2 43 B7
Meadowbank BS22 31 F3
Meadow Cl
Backwell BS48 19 B6
Chilton Trinity TA5 135 F2
Farrington Gurney BS39 77 A3
Henstridge BA8 190 A7
Highbridge TA9 104 D4
Kingston St Mary TA2 168 E8
Langport TA10 172 A6
Nailsea BS48 8 E3
Nether Stowey TA5 134 A2
Stalbridge DT10 190 B4
Street BA16 207 B4
Wincanton BA9 216 D3
Meadow Cotts TA24 131 B4
Meadow Croft BS24 49 B2
Meadowcroft Dr TA8 104 C8
Meadow Ct BA1 44 A7
Meadow Dr
Bath BA2 62 D8
Locking BS24 50 B4
Portishead BS20 1 F1
Meadow Gdns
Bath BA1 27 A1
Stogursey TA5 134 C6
Meadow Gr BS11 4 D7
Meadow La
Bathampton BA2 28 D1
Walton BA16 156 E7
Meadowland BS49 17 A1
Meadowlands BS22 32 C2
Meadowlands Ave TA6 208 E6
Meadow Pk
Bathford BA1 29 B3
Wembdon TA6 208 C5
Meadow Pl BS22 32 D3
Meadow Rd
Clevedon BS21 6 E3
Frome BA11 119 F7
Paulton BS39 77 F4
Yeovil BA21 219 E7
Meadow Rise BA4 205 B7
Meadow Sch The BA10 215 E6
Meadows Cl BS20 1 F5
Meadows End BS25 52 D4
Meadowside
Carhampton TA24 131 A5
Rockwell Green TA21 222 B5
Meadowside Cl TA1 212 B4
Meadowside Dr BS14 23 A3
Meadows Prim Sch The BS30 25 D8
Meadow St
Axbridge BS26 70 C2
Bristol BS2 227 C4
Weston-Super-Mare BS23 48 E7
Meadows The
2 Bourton SP8 161 F1
Drayton TA10 171 E3
Porlock TA24 124 A3
Meadow Terr TA24 201 A5
Meadow View
2 Bampton EX16 164 B1
4 Barwick BA22 197 F8
East Coker BA22 197 C8
Glastonbury BA6 206 E3
Long Sutton TA10 172 E1
Radstock BA3 79 A1
Timberscombe TA24 130 B5
Meadow View Cl BA1 44 A8
Meadow Villas 14 BS23 48 E8
Mead Rd BS20 2 C2
Meads Ct TA6 208 E3
Meads Droveway TA3 169 D5
Mead St BS3 227 C1
Meads The DT9 217 D2
Mead Terr BS40 54 E2
Mead The
Clutton BS39 58 E3
Dundry BS41 21 D2
East Brent TA9 86 E5
Mead The *continued*
Farmborough BA2 60 A6
Henstridge BA8 190 A6
Holcombe BA3 116 C8
Ilchester BA22 173 D1
Ilminster TA19 221 B3
Paulton BS39 77 D5
Rode BA11 101 E8
14 Shepton Mallet BA4 205 B6
Shipham BS25 70 E8
Stoke St Michael BA3 116 B2
Stratton-on-t F BA3 96 F2
Street BA16 207 D7
Timsbury BA2 60 C3
Winsley BA15 64 E7
Mead Vale BS22 49 E8
Mead Vale Com Prim Sch BS22 31 E1
Meadway
Bristol BS9 5 C6
Farmborough BA2 60 A6
Temple Cloud BS39 58 E1
Woolavington TA7 136 E4
Mead Way TA2 169 B6
Meadway Ave BS48 8 D2
Mearcombe La BS24 67 F6
Meardon Rd BS14 23 E6
Meare BS24 48 F2
Meare Rd
Bath BA2 45 A2
Glastonbury BA6 206 B6
Meare Village Prim Sch BA6 138 D4
Meareway BA6 138 C5
Mearn's Cross BA3 94 B6
Mede Cl BS1 227 B1
Medical Ave BS2, BS8 226 C3
Medway Cl
Keynsham BS31 25 A3
Taunton TA1 213 D4
Medway Dr BS31 25 A3
Meetinghouse La BS49 18 A1
Melbourne House Mews BA5 203 D4
Melbourne Pl TA6 209 B6
Melbourne Terr 2 BS21 6 D2
Melcombe Ct BA2 44 D4
Melcombe La TA6 153 E3
Melcombe Rd BA2 44 D4
Mellanby Cl BA16 207 D5
Mellent Ave BS13 22 C3
Mells CE Fst Sch BA11 118 A6
Mells Cl BS31 25 A2
Mells La BA3 79 B1
Melrose Ave
Bristol BS8 226 B4
Wells BA5 203 C4
Melrose Ct 3 BA5 203 C4
Melrose Gr BA2 44 B3
Melrose Pl BS8 226 B4
Melrose Rd BA21 219 B6
Melrose Terr BA1 28 A2
Melsbury La BA5 139 E6
Memorial Ave TA18 224 C5
Memorial Rd
Wrington BS40 35 E2
Yeovil BA22 218 B6
Mendip Ave
Shepton Mallet BA4 205 E4
Weston-Super-Mare BS22 31 F2
Mendip Cl
Axbridge BS26 70 D2
Frome BA11 120 A7
Keynsham BS31 24 D5
3 Nailsea BS48 8 E1
Paulton BS39 77 E4
Yatton BS49 34 B7
Mendip Dr BA11 120 A7
Mendip Edge BS24 66 F8
Mendip Fields BA3 96 C2
Mendip Gdns
Bath BA2 62 D8
Frome BA11 120 B7
Yatton BS49 34 B7
Mendip Green Fst Sch BS22 31 E1
Mendip Ho TA1 212 F3
Mendip Lea Cl BS27 90 F2
Mendip Lodge BS25 70 A8
Mendip Rd
Bridgwater TA6 209 C4
Locking BS24 50 D4
Portishead BS20 2 B5
Rooks Bridge BS26 87 A6
Stoke St Michael BA3 116 A2
Weston-Super-Mare BS23 49 A7
Yatton BS49 34 B7
Mendip Rise BS24 50 B4
Mendip Vale BA3 116 E7
Mendip Vale Sta* BA4 205 F3
Mendip Vale Trad Est BS27 90 A7
Mendip View
Coleford BA3 116 F7
Street BA16 207 B7
Mendip Villas
Cheddar BS27 71 A1
Compton Martin BS40 73 F7
Emborough BA3 95 E3
Mendip Way
Burnham-on-S TA8 104 B7
Radstock BA3 78 F3
Menlea BS40 54 D3
Mercer Ct BS14 23 B8
Merchants' Barton 3 BA11 119 F4
Merchants Almshouses 6 BS1 227 A2
Merchants Barton Ind Est BA11 119 F4
Merchants Ct BS8 226 A1
Merchants Quay BS1 227 A1
Merchants Rd
Bristol BS8 226 A3
Bristol, Hotwells BS8 226 A1
Merchants Row BS1 226 C1
Merchant St BS1 227 B3
Meredith Cl BA22 197 C3
Meredith Ct BS1 226 A1
Merevale Way BA21 218 C7
Meriden BA1 44 D8
Meridian Pl BS8 226 B3
Meridian Vale BS8 226 B3
Meriet Ave BS13 22 B4
Merle Cl TA6 209 B4
Merlin Cl
Bristol BS9 5 F8
1 Weston-Super-Mare BS22 49 E8
Merlin Dr BA5 203 B5
Merlin Ind Pk TA2 213 B6
Merlin Pk BS20 2 A4
Merrick Ct BS1 227 A1
Merrick Rd BA6 206 E7
Merridge Cl TA6 208 A4
Merridge Hill TA5 152 D6
Merrifields TA4 167 E6
Merriman Gdns BA16 207 C5
Merriman Rd BA16 207 C5
Merrimans Rd BS11 4 D8
Merriott Fst Sch TA16 195 F7
Merriott Rd
Hinton St George TA17 195 D7
Merriott TA16 195 F6
Merry-field BA3 116 E8
Merryfield La
Doulting BA4 141 F5
Ilton TA19 183 E4
Merryfield Lane Halt* BA4 141 F5
Merryfield Rd BS24 50 B6
Merryfields TA9 106 D5
Merry La TA9 136 F8
Merthyr Guest Cl BA8 176 E1
Merton Dr BS24 50 A8
Mervyn Ball Cl TA20 223 C5
Methwyn Cl BS22 49 C7
Metropole Ct TA24 201 A7
Metropolitan The BS1 227 B1
Mews The
Bath BA1 44 A8
5 Bridgwater TA6 209 B4
East Coker BA22 197 C7
Minehead TA24 201 A7
Wiveliscombe TA4 210 C4
Mewswell Dr BS27 71 B1
Mezellion Pl 14 BA1 28 B1
Mianda Terr TA19 221 C3
Michaels Mead BA1 27 B2
Midas Ct TA11 211 D3
Middle's La BA4 140 C4
Middle Ave BS1 227 A2
Middle Brooks BA16 207 C3
Middlecombe Cross TA24 200 C6
Middle Dro
Baltonsborough BA6 158 B4
Compton Dundon TA11 156 F3
Glastonbury BA6 206 B5
Hambridge TA10, TA12 184 F8
Lydford Fair Place TA11 158 C3
Rodney Stoke BS27 109 C6
Street BA6 157 C7
Middlefield La
Barrington TA10 184 D6
Norton Sub Hamdon TA13, TA16 185 D1
West Chinnock TA16 196 A8
Middle Field La DT9 188 B7
Middlefield Rd TA10 172 C7
Middleford Ho BS13 22 C4
Middle Gate TA10 172 D8
Middlegate Rd TA10 172 C7
Middle Green Rd TA21 222 E3
Middle La
Bath BA1 28 B1
Kingston Seymour BS21 15 F4
Middle Leaze Dro TA12 185 F7
Middle Leigh BA16 207 C5
Middlemead BA3 96 F3
Middle Moor Dro TA5 134 D7
Middle Moor La BS27 89 E7
Middlemoor Water Pk* TA7 136 F5
Middle Path TA18 224 B5
Middlepiece La BA2, BS31 42 B7
Middle Rd TA7 137 A3
Middle Ridge La DT9 175 D1
Middleroom Dro TA3 182 E4
Middle St
Ashcott TA7 156 B7
Burnham-on-S TA9 85 E5
East Harptree BS40 74 F4
East Lambrook TA13 220 C8
Galhampton BA22 175 D8
Kingsdon TA11 173 D5
Martock TA12 185 D4
Minehead TA24 200 F8
Misterton TA18 224 F3
Montacute TA15 186 B3
North Perrott TA18 196 C4
Puriton TA7 136 C4
Rimpton BA22 188 A8
Shepton Beauchamp TA19 184 E3
Taunton TA1 212 F4
Yeovil BA20 219 B4
Middle Stoke BA3 64 A6
Middle Stream Cl TA6 208 D2
Middleton La
Clatworthy TA4 149 C2
Shepton Mallet BA4 205 B4
Middleton Rd BS11 4 F8
Middle Touches TA20 223 E5
Middleway TA1 212 E2
Middle Way TA11 157 B4
Middleway Ct TA1 212 E2
Middleway Rd BA4 158 E8
Middle Yeo Gn BS48 8 D3
Middlezoy Prim Sch TA7 155 B3
Midelney Rd TA10 171 E2
Midford BS24 48 F2
Midford Hill BA2, BA3 63 C5
Midford La BA2, BA3 63 E7
Midford Rd
Southstoke BA2 63 B7
Taunton TA1 213 B4
Midhaven Rise BS22 31 E4
Midland Bridge Rd BA1, BA2 228 A2
Midland Mews BS2 227 C3
Midland Rd
Bath BA1 44 D7
Bristol BS2 227 C3
Midland St BS2 227 C2
Midleaze DT9 225 A3
Midney La BA9 177 D8
Midsomer Ent Pk BA3 78 C2
Midsomer Norton Prim Sch BA3 78 B1
Midsomer Norton S* BA3 97 A8
Midsummer Bldgs BA1 28 B2
Milborne Port Bsns Ctr DT9 217 D2
Milborne Port Prim Sch DT9 217 D2
Milburn Rd BS23 48 F7
Milbury Gdns BS22 31 C2
Mildmay's Rd TA10 155 F1
Mildmay Dr BA22 174 F3
Mildred Rd BA16 156 E7
Miles's Bldgs BA1 228 B3
Miles Cl BS20 4 E3
Miles St BA2 228 C1
Milestone Cl TA6 153 F4
Milestone Ct BS22 32 D2
Mile Wlk BS14 23 A6
Milford Inf Sch BA21 219 B7
Milford Jun Sch BA21 219 B7
Milford Pk BA21 219 C7
Milford Pl 3 TA1 213 A4
Milford Rd BA21 219 C7
Milking La BS27 90 E2
Milk St
Bath BA1 228 B2
Frome BA11 119 E5
Millands La TA5 133 C6
Millands The TA11 211 E4
Millard's Hill
Batcombe BA4 142 D2
Midsomer Norton BA3 78 C3
Millards Ct BA3 78 B3
Millards Hill BA3 78 B3
Mill Ave BS1 227 A2
Millbatch BA6 138 C4
Mill Batch Farm Ind Est TA9 86 F4
Mill Bay TA6 153 E4
Millbourn Cl BA15 64 D7
Millbourne Rd BS27 90 C7
Millbridge Gdns TA24 200 F7
Millbridge Rd TA24 200 E7
Millbrook BA20 219 A4
Millbrook Cross 1 EX13 198 A1
Millbrook Ct BA2 228 C1
Millbrook Dale EX13 198 A1
Millbrook Gdns BA7 214 B5
Millbrook Pl BA2 228 C1
Mill Cl
Cannington TA5 135 B2
East Coker BA22 197 C8
Frome BA11 119 F6
Nether Stowey TA5 134 A2
Portbury BS20 3 D2
Mill Cotts
Creech St Michael TA3 169 D4
Saltford BS31 25 F2
Millcross BS21 16 C8
Mill Cross
Halstock BA22 197 C3
Kingston St Mary TA2 168 E7
Mill Ct
Midsomer Norton BA3 78 A1
Watchet TA23 202 B7
Millennium Cl BA3 116 A3
Millennium Sq BS1 226 C2
Miller's Hill DT9 217 A5
Miller Cl BS23 48 F8
Miller Ho BS8 226 A2
Millers Cl
Bourton SP8 161 F1
Pill BS20 4 C4
Millers Ct BS21 16 E8
Millers Gdns BA5 203 E5
Millers Orch TA3 170 F1
Millers Rise BS22 32 A4
Millers Way 11 TA4 167 F8
Miller Way DT9 225 E5
Miller Wlk BA2 28 F1
Milletts Cl 2 TA24 131 A5
Mill Farm Hill TA5 134 F1

Millfield
Chard TA20 223 D3
Ilchester BA22 173 E2
Midsomer Norton BA3 96 F8
Millfield Cl TA20 223 D3
Millfield Ind Est TA20 223 E3
Millfield Prep Sch BA6 139 D1
Millfield Sch BA16 207 E5
Millford La BA4 159 C6
Mill Gdns TA24 201 D1
Millgreen Cl TA9 136 B8
Millground Rd BS13 21 F5
Millham La TA22 163 D6
Mill Hill BA2 62 E1
Mill Ho BS1 227 A2
Mill House Ct BA11 119 F5
Millier Rd BS49 35 B8
Milliman Cl BS13 22 C5
Milliner Ct BA4 205 B5
Mill La
Alhampton BA4 159 C5
Axminster EX13 198 F3
Batcombe BA4 142 C1
Bathampton BA2 28 F2
3 Bath BA2 44 B6
Beckington BA11 101 D5
Bishops Lydeard TA4 167 F8
Bitton BS30 25 E8
Bourton SP8 161 F1
Bradford Abbas DT9 187 E1
Bruton BA10 215 E6
Butcombe BS40 55 A8
Cannington TA5 135 B2
Chard TA20 223 C3
Chard, Wambrook TA20 193 C2
Charlton Mackrell TA11 173 E7
Chew Stoke BS40 56 D8
Clatworthy TA4 149 E2
Compton Martin BS40 74 A7
Congresbury BS49 34 D4
Corfe TA3 181 F6
Corsley Heath BA11, BA12 144 C8
Creech St Michael TA3 169 D4
Crewkerne, Misterton TA18 196 B3
Crewkerne TA18 224 D5
Dinnington TA17 195 B8
Dowlish Wake TA19 194 E7
Dunster TA24 201 D1
East Coker BA22 197 C7
East Coker, Holywell BA22 197 B8
East Huntspill TA9 136 D8
Exford TA24 128 C2
Halstock BA22 197 C3
Higher Chillington TA19 194 E5
Ilchester BA22 173 F1
Ilminster TA19 221 B7
Kingstone TA19 221 F1
Lopen TA13 185 A1
Lynford-on-F TA11 158 C2
Maiden Bradley BA12 144 B3
Marnhull DT10 190 F6
Milverton TA4 167 A5
Monkton Combe BA2 63 E8
Nether Stowey TA5 134 A2
North Wootton BA4 140 D5
Othery TA7 155 C2
Pitcombe BA10 215 C3
Porlock TA24 124 A3
Portbury BS20 3 E3
Priston BA2 61 A7
Shapwick TA7 155 F8
Shepton Mallet BA4 204 E4
Somerton TA11 211 D2
South Petherton TA13 220 E6
Stoke St Michael BA3 116 B3
Stone Allerton BS26 88 D4
Taunton TA3 168 D1
Thurloxton TA2 153 D1
Timsbury BA2 60 B1
Trent DT9 187 F5
Watchet TA23 202 C7
Wedmore BS28 108 E3
Wells BA5 203 A1
West Monkton TA2 169 D8
Wiveliscombe TA4 210 C4
Wrington BS40 53 F8
Yeovil BA20 219 B4
Mill Lane Cl TA3 168 D1
Mill La Trad Est BA20 219 C4
Mill Leat BA6 157 F5
Mill Leg BS49 34 D4
Millmead Ho BS13 22 C4
Millmead Rd BA2 44 C5
Millmoot La TA7 136 F3
Millpill Cl BS9 5 D5
Mill Rd
Barton St David TA11 158 A3
Radstock BA3 79 B2
Mill Rise
Bourton SP8 161 F1
Staplegrove TA2 212 B7
Mill Road Ind Est BA3 79 B3
Mill St
Carhampton TA24 131 B4
North Petherton TA6 153 F3
Rimpton BA22 188 A8
Watchet TA23 202 C7
Wells BA5 203 D4
Wincanton BA9 216 C4
Millstream Cl TA24 200 F6
Mill Stream Cl BS26 70 C1
Mill Stream Gdns TA21 222 B7
Mill Street Cl BA9 216 C4
Millthorn Ho 2 BA16 207 C5

Millward Terr BS39 77 E6
Millway
Chard TA20 193 C2
Rodney Stoke BS27 110 B8
Millway Rise Ind Est EX13 198 A2
Millwey Ave EX13 198 A2
Mill Wlk TA7 136 E3
Millwood Cl TA6 208 E2
Milne Cl TA6 208 F2
Milsom Pl TA4 167 F6
Milsom St BA1 228 B3
Milton Ave
Bath BA2 44 F4
Weston-Super-Mare BS23 49 A8
Milton Brow BS22 31 B2
Milton Cl
Nailsea BS48 8 E3
Taunton TA1 213 C3
Yeovil BA21 218 C6
Milton Ct BA4 205 B7
Milton Gn BS22 31 C1
Milton Hill
Monkton Heathfield TA2 213 E7
Weston-Super-Mare BS22 31 B2
Milton Ho BA21 187 D6
Milton Jun & Inf Schs BS22 31 C1
Milton La
Martock TA12 185 E8
Wells BA5 203 D5
Wookey Hole BA5 203 B8
Milton Leaze TA10 172 E2
Milton Lodge Gdn* BA5 203 D7
Milton Park Rd BS22 31 C1
Milton Pl TA6 208 E4
Milton Rd
Radstock BA3 78 C1
Taunton TA1 213 C3
Weston-Super-Mare BS22, BS23 49 B8
Milton Rise BS22 31 C1
Miltons Cl BS13 22 D4
Milton Terr BA5 203 A8
Milverton BS24 48 F2
Milverton Com Prim Sch TA4 166 F4
Milverton Rd TA21 222 B8
Milward Rd BS31 24 E6
Minchington's Cl TA14 185 F2
Minehead First Sch TA24 200 F6
Minehead Hospl TA24 200 F7
Minehead La TA22 164 A7
Minehead Mid Sch TA24 201 A6
Minehead Rd
Bishops Lydeard TA4 167 E8
Bristol BS4 23 A8
Minehead Sta* TA24 201 B7
Miners Cl BS41 10 F2
Minerva Ct BA2 228 C3
Minerva Gdns BA2 44 C4
Minnows The TA20 223 C3
Minsmere Rd BS31 25 A4
Minster Cl TA1 212 C1
Minster Ct TA1 212 C1
Minster Way BA2 45 C8
Minton Cl BS14 23 B5
Mintons TA20 223 B3
Mintons Orch TA20 223 B3
Mint The BA11 119 E5
Misburg Cl BA4 204 F6
Misterton CE Fst Sch TA18 224 F3
Mitchell's Pool TA21 222 E6
Mitchell's Row BA22 175 D6
Mitchell Gdns TA20 223 B3
Mitchell La BS1 227 B2
Mitchell St TA21 222 C7
Mitchell Terr BA5 112 E1
Mitchelmore Rd BA21 219 B5
Mitford-Slade Ct BS49 34 C7
Mitre Ct TA1 213 B4
Mizzymead Cl 1 BS48 8 D1
Mizzymead Rd BS48 8 E1
Mizzymead Rise BS48 8 E1
Moffats Dr BA5 113 A2
Molesworth Cl BS13 22 A4
Molesworth Dr BS13 22 A4
Molly Cl BS39 76 E8
Monarch Ctr TA2 213 C6
Monday's Court La TA10 172 E5
Money Pit La EX13 193 A1
Monger Cotts BS39 77 F4
Monger La
Midsomer Norton BA3 78 A3
Paulton BS39 78 A4
Monington Rd BA6 206 E6
Monk Barton Cl BA21 218 C7
Monk Cross TA24 128 D1
Monkley La BA11 83 C1
Monks' Path TA23, TA24 131 E4
Monks Cl
Rooks Bridge BS26 87 B5
Taunton TA1 213 B5
Monks Dale BA21 218 D6
Monksdale Rd BA2 44 D4
Monks Dr TA7 137 F1
Monks Ford BA5 139 D8
Monksford La BA5 139 C8
Monks Hill BS22 31 B3
Monkstone Dr TA8 84 F5
Monkstone Gdns 6 EX13 198 A1
Monksway TA23 131 E4
Monks Way TA8 104 B6
Monkton Ave BS24 49 A2

Monkton Combe Jun Sch BA2 45 C1
Monkton Combe Jun Sch (Pre-Prep) BA2 45 C1
Monkton Combe Sch BA2 45 E1
Monkton La TA5 134 D5
Monmouth Cl
Chard TA20 223 E4
Glastonbury BA6 206 D5
Portishead BS20 1 F4
Westonzoyland TA7 154 F6
Monmouth Ct
Bath BA1 228 A2
Chard TA20 223 E4
Pill BS20 4 C5
Monmouth Dr BA11 120 B6
Monmouth Farm Cl TA6 135 F5
Monmouth Paddock BA2 81 E5
Monmouth Pl BA1 228 B2
Monmouth Rd
Keynsham BS31 24 D5
Pill BS20 4 C5
Shepton Mallet BA4 205 A5
Taunton TA1 213 B5
Westonzoyland TA7 154 F6
Yeovil BA21 219 D7
Monmouth St
Bath BA1 228 B2
Bridgwater TA6 209 A5
Montacute Cir 4 BS22 49 F8
Montacute Ho* TA15 186 B4
Montacute Rd
Montacute TA14, TA15 186 B4
Tintinhull BA22 186 B6
Montague Ct 4 BS2 227 A4
Montague Flats 6 BS2 227 A4
Montague Gdns BA7 214 B5
Montague Hill BS2 227 A4
Montague Hill S 5 BS2 227 A4
Montague Ho 8 BA1 28 C1
Montague Pl BS6 227 A4
Montague Rd
Saltford BS31 25 D2
Shoscombe BA2 79 E5
Montague St BS1 227 A4
Montague Way TA20 223 C3
Monteclefe CE Jun Sch TA11 211 E3
Montepelier BS23 48 F8
Montgomery Ct BA11 120 A4
Montpelier E BS23 30 F1
Montrose Cotts BA1 27 C1
Montrose Rd BA21 219 E7
Montrose Villas BS27 90 C7
Montsurs Cl BA3 96 D3
Montys La TA2 168 A6
Monument Cl TA21 222 E4
Monument Rd TA21 222 E3
Moolham La
Ilminster TA19 194 D7
Kingstone TA19 221 D1
Moon's Dro TA7 155 A1
Moondown La TA13 220 B2
Moonhayes Cross EX14 191 F4
Moon La TA7 153 E1
Moonraker Cl 8 TA6 209 B4
Moons Hill BA3 116 B4
Moonshill Cl BA3 116 A3
Moonshill Cotts BA3 116 A3
Moonshill Rd BA3 116 A3
Moon St BS2 227 B4
Moor Cl
Compton Dundon TA11 156 F2
Langport TA10 172 A6
Wincanton BA9 216 C3
Moorclose Dro TA7 137 C3
Moorclose La BA4 158 E6
Moor Croft Rd BS24 49 E3
Moor Dro TA7 155 F6
Moore's La TA5, TA6 208 C7
Moorend Gdns BS11 4 F7
Moor End Spout BS48 8 D2
Moores Yd BA14 83 C6
Moorfield Gdn TA24 146 C6
Moorfield Rd BS48 19 A6
Moorfields Cl BA2 44 D3
Moorfields Ct BS48 8 D2
Moorfields Dr BA2 44 D4
Moorfields Ho BS48 8 D2
Moorfields Rd
Bath BA2 44 D4
Nailsea BS48 8 D2
Moor Gn BS26 70 C1
Moor Gr BS11 5 A8
Moorgrove Ho BS9 5 C7
Moorham Rd BS25 52 A1
Moorhouse La TA4 165 A8
Moor House La TA5 133 E4
Moorings The
Bath BA2 45 B6
Pill BS20 4 C4
Moor La
Alhampton BA4 159 C5
Backwell BS48 18 F6
Batcombe BA4 142 D1
Brushford TA22 163 F4
Churchinford TA3 192 A7
Clapton in G BS20 2 E1
Clevedon BS21 6 E2
Clevedon BS21 7 A2
Cucklington SP8 177 E5
Draycott BS27 90 F1
East Coker BA22 197 D7
Hardington Mandeville BA22 197 A7
Higher Chillington TA20 194 F5
Hutton BS24 49 D3
North Curry TA3 170 B4

Moor La *continued*
South Petherton TA13 220 B3
Tickenham BS21 7 F4
Walton in G BS21 7 C6
Westbury-sub-Mendip BA5 110 C5
Weston-Super-Mare BS24 49 F7
Wincanton BA9 216 C2
Moorland Cl TA1 213 C5
Moorland Cotts BS26 69 F2
Moorland Pk BS24 33 E5
Moorland Pl TA1 213 C5
Moorland Rd
Bath BA2 44 D5
Bridgwater TA6 209 D4
Street BA16 207 B7
Taunton TA1 213 C5
Weston-Super-Mare BS23 48 E4
Moorlands TA4 167 F8
Moorlands Cl
16 Martock TA12 185 E6
Nailsea BS48 8 D2
Moorlands Ct TA16 195 F7
Moorlands Inf Sch BA2 44 D4
Moorlands Jun Sch BA2 44 D3
Moorlands Pk 18 TA12 185 E6
Moorlands Pk Sh Ctr 19 TA12 185 E6
Moorlands Rd TA16 195 E6
Moorland St BS26 70 C1
Moorlands The BA2 44 D3
Moorland Way TA6 209 D5
Moor Lane Cl TA3 170 B4
Moorlay Cres BS40 37 F8
Moorledge La BS39, BS40 57 F7
Moorledge Rd BS40 39 B1
Moorlinch Right Dro TA7 155 D6
Moorlinch Vineyard* TA7 155 E7
Moor Park Rd TA10 171 F5
Moor Pk
Clevedon BS21 6 E2
Langport TA10 171 F5
Moor Rd
Banwell BS29 51 B5
Middlezoy TA7 155 B4
Minehead TA24 200 E8
Moorlinch TA7 155 D7
Sutton Mallet TA7 155 B8
Yatton BS49 17 B2
Moorsfield BS39 58 F3
Moor Sherd BS28 110 C1
Moorside BS49 17 B1
Moorside Ct BS21 6 E2
Moorside Villas BS21 6 E2
Moortown La TA10 171 B2
Moorview Cl BA6 138 C4
Moor Villas TA13 220 B3
Moorway La DT9 188 C6
Moots La TA6 209 D4
Morangis Way TA20 223 B6
Moravia Cl TA6 208 E6
Morden Wlk BS14 23 D7
Moreton Cl BS14 23 A4
Moreton La BS40 56 E2
Moreton Mans 5 BS23 30 C1
Morford St BA1 228 B4
Morgan's La
East Harptree BS40 74 F2
8 Frome BA11 119 E5
Morgan Cl
Saltford BS31 25 D2
Weston-Super-Mare BS22 50 B8
Morgan Pl BS48 20 B8
Morgans Bldgs BS20 8 F8
Morgans Hill Cl BS48 18 D8
Morgans Rise TA1 212 A3
Morgan Way BA2 79 E7
Morland Rd TA9 104 D4
Morlands Ind Pk TA9 104 D4
Morley Terr
Bath BA2 44 D6
Radstock BA3 79 A3
Mornington Pk TA21 222 E5
Morpeth Rd BS4 22 D8
Morrell's Cross EX16 164 B4
Morrell's La EX16 178 B6
Morris Cl
Barrington TA19 184 C5
Bathford BA1 29 B3
Morris La BA1 29 B3
Morston Ct BS22 49 C7
Mortimer Cl
Bath BA1 27 B2
Woolavington TA7 136 E4
Mortimer Rd BS8 226 A3
Morton's La TA10 156 C1
Moseley Gr BS23 48 E2
Moss Cl TA6 209 C6
Moss La TA3 169 C3
Mosterton Down La DT8 196 A1
Moulton Cl BA4 205 A4
Mound The BA6 206 C4
Mounsdon Cl BA6 157 E4
Mountain's La BA2 59 E6
Mountain Ash BA1 27 D1
Mountain Wood BA1 29 C2
Mountbatten Cl
Burnham-on-S TA8 85 A1
Weston-Super-Mare BS22 31 E4
Mountbatten Ho TA6 209 C5
Mount Beacon BA1 28 A1
Mount Beacon Pl 3 BA1 27 F1
Mount Beacon Row 1 BA1 28 A1
Mounter's Hill EX13, TA20 193 B2
Mounters Cl DT10 190 F5

Mountery Cl BA5 203 D5
Mountery Rd BA5 203 D5
Mountfields Ave TA1 213 B1
Mountfields Pk TA1 213 B1
Mountfields Rd TA1 213 B1
Mount Gr BA2 44 B3
Mount Hey TA11 211 E3
Mount Hindrance Cl TA20 223 D6
Mount Hindrance La TA20 223 D6
Mount Ho TA1 212 F3
Mount La
Charlton Horethorne DT9 176 A1
Golsoncott TA23, TA24 131 C1
Mount Nebo TA1 212 E2
Mount Pleasant
Bath BA2 45 D1
Castle Cary BA7 214 C5
Crewkerne TA18 224 D6
Frome BA11 119 F2
Kilmington BA12 161 F6
Pill BS20 4 D4
Pilton BA4 140 F3
Radstock BA3 79 B2
Yeovil BA21 219 C5
Mount Pleasant Ave BA5 203 B5
Mount Rd
Bath BA1 228 B4
Bath, Southdown BA2 44 B3
Nether Stowey TA5 134 A2
Mountsfield BA11 120 A2
Mount St
Bishops Lydeard TA4 167 E8
Bridgwater TA6 208 F5
Taunton TA1 212 F3
Mount Terr TA1 213 A3
Mount The
Frome BA11 119 F2
Taunton TA1 212 F3
Yatton BS49 34 C8
Mount View
Bath, Beacon Hill BA1 28 A1
Bath, Southdown BA2 44 B3
Woolavington TA7 136 E4
Mount View Terr TA6 135 F6
Mountway TA1 213 A3
Mountway Cl TA1 212 C4
Mountway La TA1 212 C4
Mountway Rd TA1 212 C4
Movey La BA22 173 F1
Mow Barton
Bristol BS13 21 F6
8 Martock TA12 185 E6
Mow Barton Rd TA11 173 D5
Mowbray Rd BS14 23 C7
Mowcroft Rd BS13 22 D4
Mowes La DT10 190 F4
Mowground La TA7 137 A3
Mowleaze 11 BA22 197 F8
Mowries Ct TA11 211 D4
Moxham Dr BS13 22 C4
Muchelney Abbey* TA10 172 A3
Muchelney Hill BA6 158 B5
Muchelney Ho TA19 221 B3
Muchelney Way BA21 218 C7
Muckleditch La TA19 184 D3
Muddicombe Cross TA24 128 B2
Muddicombe La TA24 128 B2
Muddyford La TA4 151 A3
Muddy La BS22 32 A8
Mudford Hill BA21 187 C5
Mudford Rd BA21 219 B8
Mudgley Cross Roads BS28 108 F1
Mudgley Hill BS28 108 E1
Mudgley Rd
Rooks Bridge BS26 87 A4
Wedmore BS28 108 E3
Mud La BS49 17 D2
Mulberry Ave BS20 2 E5
Mulberry Cl
Backwell BS48 19 A6
Portishead BS20 2 F5
Taunton TA1 213 C2
Weston-Super-Mare BS22 32 A1
Mulberry Ct BA11 120 B7
Mulberry Farm BA6 140 B1
Mulberry Gdns
4 Crewkerne TA18 224 C5
Sherborne DT9 225 C5
Mulberry La
Bleadon BS24 67 C6
Stoke Sub Hamdon TA14 186 A4
Mulberry Rd BS49 34 E3
Mulberry Tree Cl TA6 209 D5
Mulberry Wlk BS9 5 C8
Mullins Cl BA5 203 B3
Mullins Way BA7 214 B6
Mundays Mead BA9 216 D3
Munden's La DT9 189 A1
Murford Ave BS13 22 B4
Murford Wlk BS13 22 B4
Murhill BA3 64 C6
Muriel Terr BA5 203 D3
Murray-Smith Dr BA22 218 A6
Murray Way BA9 216 B3
Murtry Hill La BA11 100 C2
Musbury Cl DT10 190 F6
Musbury La DT10 190 F6
Museum of South Somerset* BA20 219 B4
Musgraves TA22 163 E6
Musgrove Rd TA1 212 C3
Musmoor La BA22 174 F7

Mus of Bath at Work★ BA1 228 B4
Mus of Costume★ BA1 228 B3
Mus of East Asian Art★ BA1 228 B3
Mutton La BS28 108 D4
Mutton St DT6 199 D1
Mux's La TA4 151 B3
Myrtleberry Mead BS22 32 A5
Myrtle Cl TA6 209 D5
Myrtle Dr
Bristol BS11 4 E5
Burnham-on-S TA8 104 A7
Myrtle Gdns BS49 34 C8
Myrtle Hill BS20 4 C5
Myrtle La TA21 179 E7
Myrtle Rd
Bristol BS2 226 C4
22 Martock TA12 185 E6
Myrtles The BS24 49 D2
Myrtle Tree Cres BS22 31 A6
Myrtlle Cotts TA3 182 D7

N

Nag's La TA18 195 B1
Nailsea & Backwell Sta BS48 18 F7
Nailsea Cl BS13 22 A7
Nailsea Com Sch BS48 8 E1
Nailsea Moor La BS48 17 F7
Nailsea Park Cl BS48 8 F2
Nailsea Pk BS48 8 F2
Nailsea Wall BS21 17 C8
Nailsea Wall La BS48 17 E7
Naish's Cross BA3 96 D3
Naish's St BA11 119 E5
Naishes Ave BA2 79 D8
Naish Farm BA3 96 D3
Naish Hill BS20 2 F1
Naish Ho BA2 44 A6
Naish La BS48 20 D3
Naisholt Rd BA4 204 F6
Naish Rd TA8 85 A3
Nanga-gat Rd BA22 174 A2
Nanny Hurn's La BS39 58 A1
Napier Ct
Bristol BS1 226 B1
Sherborne DT9 225 B2
Napier Miles Rd BS11 5 A8
Napier Rd BA1 27 A3
Naples View TA6 208 E7
Narfords La TA20 193 C1
Narrow Plain BS2 227 B2
Narrow Quay BS1 227 A2
Nash Barton BA22 197 C8
Nash Cl BS31 25 A5
Nash Gn TA2 212 B7
Nash La
Dinnington TA17, TA19 195 A6
East Coker BA22 197 C8
Marshwood DT6 199 B2
Yeovil BA20 218 D1
Nates La BS40 35 F1
Nathan Cl BA20 218 D2
Naunton Way BS22 31 B2
Neale's Way BA4 141 E2
Neathem Rd BA21 219 C7
Neat La BA4 204 D1
Nedge Cnr BA3 94 D4
Nedge Hill BA3 94 D3
Nedge La BA3 94 C4
Needhams Patch TA4 167 E6
Nelson Bldgs BA1 228 C4
Nelson Ct
Bridgwater TA6 208 F5
Weston-Super-Mare BS22 31 E4
Nelson Ho
Bath BA1 228 A3
5 Bristol BS1 227 A3
Nelson Pl BA1 228 C4
Nelson Pl E BA1 228 C4
Nelson Pl W BA1 228 A2
Nelson St BS1 227 A3
Nelson Terr BA1 228 C4
Nelson Villas BA1 228 A2
Nempnett St BS40 55 D5
Neroche Prim Sch TA19 183 C2
Neroche View TA3 183 A7
Nerrols Dr TA2 213 C7
Neston Wlk BS4 22 F8
Netherclay TA1 212 A4
Netherclay La TA3 182 B7
Nethercoombe La DT9 225 C5
Nethercott La TA4 151 C3
Nethercott Way TA4 151 A3
Netherhay La DT8 199 F8
Nethermoor Rd TA7 155 B3
Netherstoke La BA22 197 C3
Nether Stowey CE Prim Sch TA5 134 A2
Netherton Cross BA22 197 E6
Netherton La
East Coker BA22 197 F6
Marston Magna BA22 175 A1
Netherton Rd BA21 219 D7
Netherton Wood La BS48 18 A6
Netherways BS21 6 B1
Netley BA21 218 D6
Nettlebridge Hill BA3 115 D5
Nettlecombe Hill
Castle Cary BA7 214 F6
Pitcombe BA7 215 A2
Nettlecombe Ho BA5 113 A1
Nettlecombe Park Rd
Monksilver TA4 132 A1
Sticklepath TA4 149 F7
Nettle Combe View BA5 113 A2
Neva Rd BS23 48 E6
Neville Cl 1 TA11 173 F7
Neville Pk BA6 158 A5
Nevys La TA4 150 E8
Newark St BA1 228 C1
Newbarn Park Rd TA1 212 B1
Newberrys Patch TA3 192 A7
Newbery Cl 4 EX13 198 A1
Newbery La TA18 224 F3
New Bglws TA20 223 C3
New Bldgs
3 Bampton EX16 164 C1
Dunwear TA7 209 D1
Frome BA11 119 F3
Ilminster TA19 221 B1
North Perrott TA18 196 C4
Oake TA4 167 C4
Peasedown St John BA2 79 B8
New Bond St BA1 228 C2
New Bond Street Pl BA1 228 C2
Newbourne Rd BS22 49 C8
Newbridge Ct BA1 44 B7
Newbridge Dro TA9 105 A1
Newbridge Gdns BA1 44 A8
Newbridge Hill BA1 44 B7
Newbridge Ho BS9 5 C4
Newbridge La TA9 104 F1
New Bridge Prim Sch BA1 44 B7
Newbridge Rd BA1, BA2 44 B7
New Bristol Rd BS22 31 E1
New Buildings La BA11 119 F3
Newbury BA12 144 E4
Newbury Cotts BA3 117 A8
Newbury Terr 3 BA21 218 F7
Newchester Cross TA16 195 E7
New Church Rd BS23 48 D2
New Cl
Bourton SP8 161 F1
Haselbury Plucknett TA18 196 B5
Horrington BA5 113 A4
Street BA16 207 B4
Newclose La BS40 56 D1
Newclose Terr TA14 185 E4
Newcombe Cvn Pk TA8 104 B8
Newcombe Dr BS9 5 C4
Newcombe La BS25 70 B7
Newcombe Rd BS9 5 F7
Newcot Cross EX15 191 A5
New Cotts
Milton Clevedon BA4 160 A8
West Chinnock TA18 196 B8
New Cross TA11 211 C3
New Cross Hill
Barrington TA12, TA13 184 F6
Kingsbury Episcopi TA12 185 A6
New Cut BA5 203 D7
New Cut Bow BS21 16 A6
Newditch La BS40 20 C1
Newell DT9 225 C4
Newfield TA4 166 F4
Newfields BS40 72 C8
New Fosseway Rd BS14 23 B6
New Fosseway Sch BS14 23 B6
Newfoundland Rd BS2 227 C4
Newfoundland St BS2 227 C4
Newfoundland Way
Bristol BS2 227 C4
Portishead BS20 2 E6
New Friary Cotts BA11 143 C3
Newgate BS1 227 B3
Newgate Cross TA22 163 D7
Newgate La TA4 210 C5
Newhaven Pl BS20 1 E4
Newhaven Rd BS20 1 D4
New Hill TA11 211 E4
Newhouse La TA4 165 E6
Newington Cl BA11 119 E3
Newington Terr BA11 119 E4
New Kingsley Rd BS2 227 C2
New King St BA1 228 B2
New La
Bampton EX16 163 F2
Charlton Horethorne DT9 176 A1
Creech St Michael TA3 169 D5
Cricket St Thomas TA20 194 E4
Haselbury Plucknett TA18 196 C6
Tatworth TA20 198 C8
Witham Friary BA11 143 C4
Newland DT9 225 E4
Newland Cross TA24 128 B1
Newland Dr BS13 22 A4
Newland Flats 5 DT9 225 E4
Newland Gdn 8 DT9 225 E4
Newland Ho BA1 27 F1
Newland Rd
Bristol BS13 22 A3
Weston-Super-Mare BS23 48 F6
Newlands Cl BS20 2 C5
Newlands Cres TA3 169 C3
Newlands Gn BS21 6 E1
Newlands Gr TA3 169 C3
Newlands Hill BS20 2 C4
Newlands Rd
Keynsham BS31 24 D4
Ruishton TA3 169 C3
Newland Wlk BS13 22 A3
Newlyn Ave BS9 5 D5
Newlyn Cres TA7 136 B4
Newman Cl BA6 206 E6
Newmans La
East Huntspill TA9 105 C1
Timsbury BA2 60 B2
Newmarket Ave 9 BS1 227 A3
New Mdws BS14 23 A6
Newnham Cl BS14 23 D7
New Oak Prim Sch BS14 23 B7
New Orchard St BA1 228 C2
New Park Ho BS21 6 D5
New Pit Cotts BA2 60 F1
New Pk EX16 162 E4
Newport Cl
Clevedon BS21 6 C2
Portishead BS20 1 F4
Newport Hill TA3 170 B2
Newport Rd BS20 4 C5
Newquay Rd BS4 22 F8
New Rd
Banwell BS29 50 E4
Barwick BA22 197 F8
Bathford BA1 29 D2
Bawdrip TA7 136 D2
Bridgwater TA6 209 A5
Burrowbridge TA3, TA7 170 E8
Cannington TA5 135 C1
Carhampton TA24 131 A5
Chapel Allerton BS26 88 C2
Chard Junction TA20 198 F8
Churchill BS25 52 F4
Clevedon BS21 6 D2
Combe St Nicholas TA20 193 D6
Crewkerne TA18 195 B4
Crickham BS28 108 D8
Draycott BS27 91 C3
East Huntspill TA9 136 D8
Freshford BA3 64 B5
Frome BA11 120 B4
Hambridge TA12 184 E7
Haselbury Plucknett TA18 196 E6
High Littleton BS39 59 C3
Hinton St George TA17 195 C7
Ilminster TA19 221 B4
Kilmersdon BA3 98 E4
Kilmington BA12 161 E7
Lyng TA3 170 B6
North Wootton BA4 140 A4
Norton Sub Hamdon, Chiselborough TA14 185 F1
Norton Sub Hamdon TA14 185 E3
Oare EX35 122 D4
Odcombe BA22 186 D3
Othery TA7 155 C2
Pensford BS39 40 D3
Pill BS20 4 C4
Porlock TA24 123 E3
Rawridge EX14 191 E1
Redhill BS40 37 A4
Seavington St Mary TA19 184 E1
Sherborne DT9 225 E3
Shipham BS25 52 E1
South Cadbury BA22 175 E4
Stalbridge DT10 190 B4
Staple Fitzpaine TA3 182 D5
Taunton TA3 168 D1
West Bagborough TA4 151 E4
Weston Town BA4 142 D5
Wiveliscombe TA4 166 A6
Yeovil BA22 218 A5
New Road Gate EX35 122 D5
New Rock Ind Est BA3 96 D2
Newsome Ave BS20 4 C4
New Sq BA5 113 A2
New St
Bath BA1 228 B2
Bristol BS2 227 C3
Long Sutton TA10 172 E4
Marnhull DT10 190 F5
Mells BA11 118 B7
North Perrott TA18 196 C4
Somerton TA11 211 E4
Wells BA5 203 D5
New Street Flats 4 BS2 227 C3
New Thomas St BS2 227 C2
Newton's Rd
Weston-Super-Mare BS22 31 E3
Weston-Super-Mare BS22 31 E4
Newton Cl
Burnham-on-S TA8 85 A2
West Harptree BS40 74 E6
Newton Ct 14 EX16 164 B1
Newton Gn BS48 18 C8
Newton La
Bicknoller TA4 132 E1
Corfe TA3 181 F6
Newton Rd
Barwick BA22 197 F8
Bath BA2 43 F6
North Petherton TA6 153 F3
Taunton TA1 213 E4
Weston-Super-Mare BS23 48 E6
Yeovil BA20 219 D3
Newton Sq 8 EX16 164 B1
Newtown TA12 185 E7
Newtown La BA6 140 A1
Newtown Pk TA10 172 A6
Newtown Rd
Highbridge TA9 104 D3
Langport TA10 172 A6
New Way TA10 172 B7
Nibley Rd BS11 4 E5
Nichol's Rd BS20 1 F5
Nicholas Cl TA22 163 E4
Nicholls Cl TA6 208 D4
Nichol Pl TA4 167 F6
Nick Reed's La EX15 180 D1
Nidon La TA7 137 D3
Nigel Pk BS11 4 E7
Nightingale Acre TA3 183 A7
Nightingale Ave BA11 120 B6
Nightingale Cl
1 Bridgwater TA6 209 C4
Burnham-on-S TA8 85 B1
Wells BA5 203 B3
Weston-Super-Mare BS22 31 E1
Nightingale Ct
16 Taunton TA1 213 A4
Weston-Super-Mare BS22 31 E1
Nightingale Gdns BS48 8 D2
Nightingale Gr BA4 205 C5
Nightingale La BA22 174 F6
Nightingale Rise BS20 1 F3
Nightingales TA4 167 E6
Nightingale Way BA3 97 B8
Nile St BA1 228 A2
Nine Acre Dro TA7 138 B2
Nine Acre La TA3 170 C4
Nine Barrows La BA5 92 E4
Nippors Way BS25 69 F8
Nithsdale Rd BS23 48 E4
Nixon Trad Units BS24 49 A3
No 1 Royal Cres Mus★ BA1 228 B3
Noah's Hill TA2 169 B7
Noake Rd DT9 225 B3
Noble St TA1 213 B4
Noel Coward Cl TA8 104 C6
Nomis Pk BS49 34 E2
No Place La TA5 152 E5
Norbins Rd BA6 206 D5
Nordens Mdw TA4 210 D4
Nordrach La BS40 73 D5
Nore Gdns BS20 2 C6
Nore Park Dr BS20 1 F5
Nore Rd BS20 2 A6
Norfolk Ave BS2 227 B4
Norfolk Bldgs BA1 228 A2
Norfolk Cl TA6 209 C3
Norfolk Cres BA1 228 A2
Norfolk Gr BS31 24 C4
Norfolk Hts 10 BS2 227 B4
Norfolk Rd
Portishead BS20 2 E4
Weston-Super-Mare BS23 48 F5
Norland Rd BS8 11 F8
Norlet Ct BA6 206 D5
Normandy Ave TA23 202 E6
Normandy Dr TA1 213 C3
Normandy Ho BA16 207 B6
Norman La TA7 156 B7
Norman Rd BS31 25 E3
Normans The BA2 28 F1
Normans Way BS20 3 E7
Norrington Way TA20 223 D2
Northam Farm Cvn Pk & Camp Site TA8 65 F4
Northampton Bldgs BA1 228 B4
Northampton Ho BS48 9 D3
Northampton St BA1 228 B4
Northanger Ct 5 BA2 228 C3
North Ave TA9 104 C4
Northay Cross EX13 199 B3
Northay La
Axminster EX13 199 A3
Combe St Nicholas TA20 193 B6
North Bank BA5 203 A8
Northbrook Dr TA7 137 F1
Northbrook Rd
Cannington TA5 135 C2
Shapwick TA7 138 A1
Yeovil BA21 219 D7
North Cadbury CE Prim Sch BA22 175 D6
North Chew Terr BS40 39 B3
North Chine Dro BA5 138 D8
North Cl BS27 90 F3
Northcombe La TA22 163 E7
Northcote Cres BA11 120 A7
Northcote Rd BS8 5 F1
North Cres DT9 217 D3
North Croft TA4 202 D3
North Curry CE Prim Sch TA3 170 B3
North Down Cl BS25 70 F8
North Down La BS25 70 F8
Northdown Rd BA3 78 E5
North Dro BS48 8 A2
North End
Charlton Horethorne DT9 176 A2
Creech St Michael TA3 169 D5
Midsomer Norton BA3 78 B2
North End Rd BS49 16 F3
Northern Path BS21 6 F3
Northern Way BS21 6 F3
Northfield
Bridgwater TA6 208 E4
Radstock BA3 79 A3
Somerton TA11 211 C4
Timsbury BA2 60 C3
Winsley BA15 64 F7
Northfield Ave TA1 212 E4
Northfield Cl TA5 134 C6
Northfield Gdns TA1 212 E5
Northfield Ho
Bath BA1 27 F1
Glastonbury BA6 206 E4
Northfield La
Dinnington TA17 195 B8
South Petherton TA13 220 C2
Northfield Rd
Minehead TA24 201 A8
Portishead BS20 1 E3
Taunton TA1 212 E4
Northfields
Bath BA1 27 F1
Taunton TA1 212 B3
Northfields Cl BA1 27 F1
Northfield Way TA11 211 C5
Northgate
Bridgwater TA6 208 F5
Wiveliscombe TA4 210 C5
Northgate St BA1 228 C2
North Gr
Pill BS20 4 C4
Wells BA5 203 E5
North Green St 11 BS8 11 F6
North Hill Ho BA11 120 A6
North Hill Mews BA11 119 F5
North Hill Rd TA24 200 F8
North Hills Cl BS24 49 B2
North Hill Woodland Trail★ TA24 125 B4
North La
Bath BA2 45 D5
Berrow TA8 65 F1
Challacombe EX31, TA24 126 B4
East Coker BA22 197 A7
Nailsea BS48 8 B1
Othery TA7 155 C2
Stogursey TA5 134 C7
2 Weston-Super-Mare BS23 48 E7
Yeovil BA20 219 B5
Northleach Wlk BS11 4 F5
North Leaze BS41 11 B2
Northleaze CE Prim Sch BS41 11 B2
Northleaze Ho BA16 207 C6
North Leaze La BA22 175 C7
Northleigh Ave BS22 31 C1
Northleigh Rd TA1 213 B3
Northload Bridge BA6 206 C5
Northload Bridge Rdbt BA6 206 D5
Northload Dro BS28 109 E2
Northload La BS28 109 D1
Northload St BA6 206 D5
Northload Terr BA6 206 D5
North Mdws BA2 79 E8
Northmead Ave BA3 77 F2
Northmead Cl BA3 77 F2
Northmead Dro TA3 170 A1
Northmead Rd BA3 77 F2
North Mills La TA13 220 C5
Northmoor La TA3 170 C7
Northmoor Rd
Dulverton TA22 163 D7
Othery TA10 155 D1
Northover Bldgs BA6 206 B3
Northover Dr TA20 223 B5
Northover Farmhouse BA6 207 D8
North Par
Bath BA2 228 C2
Frome BA11 119 F5
North Parade Bldgs 8 BA1 228 C2
North Parade Pas 7 BA1 228 C2
North Parade Rd BA2 45 B6
North Perrott Rd TA18 196 C5
North Petherton Com Jun Sch TA6 153 F3
North Petherton Inf Sch TA6 153 F3
North Rd
Banwell BS29 51 A3
Bath, Bathwick BA2 45 C6
Bath, Combe Down BA2 45 B2
Charlton Horethorne DT9 176 A2
Eastertown BS24 67 D2
Leigh Woods BS8 11 D7
Midsomer Norton BA3 78 A1
Minehead TA24 201 A7
Sherborne DT9 225 E5
Timsbury BA2 60 C2
Wells BA5 203 E5
Williton TA4 202 D4
Northside
Castle Cary BA7 214 C6
Rockwell Green TA21 222 B5
North Side Rd BS48 36 F8
North St
Babcary TA11 174 C7
Bradford Abbas DT9 187 E1
Bridgwater TA6 208 E4
Bristol BS1 227 B4
Castle Cary BA7 214 C5
Crewkerne TA18 224 C7
Drayton TA10 171 E3
Haselbury Plucknett TA18 196 C6
Ilminster TA19 221 C4
Langport TA10 172 A5
Martock TA12 185 E6
Milborne Port DT9 217 D2
Milverton TA4 167 A4
Nailsea BS48 8 B1
North Petherton TA6 153 E4
Norton St Philip BA2 81 E4
Norton Sub Hamdon TA14 185 E1
Shepton Beauchamp TA19 184 E4
Somerton TA11 211 E4
South Petherton TA13 220 C5
Stoke sub Hamdon TA14 185 F4
Taunton TA1 212 F4
Wellington TA21 222 D6
Weston-Super-Mare BS23 48 E8
Williton TA4 202 D3
Wincanton BA9 216 C4
Wiveliscombe TA4 210 B4
North Stoke La BS30 26 B8
North Terr BA21 219 C6
North Town TA11 173 D5
North Town Com Prim Sch TA1 212 E4
Northtown La
North Wootton BA4 140 C4

Northtown La *continued*
Taunton TA1 . . . . .212 E4
North Town Mews TA1 . .212 E5
Northumberland Bldgs �１
BA1 .228 B2
Northumberland Pl �１
BA1 . . . . 228 C2
North View BA3 . . . . .79 B2
North View Ct BA2 . . . . .44 B5
North View Dr BS29 . . . . . .51 A2
North Villas TA4 . . . . .167 F6
North Way
Bath BA2 . . . . .44 A5
Midsomer Norton BA3 . . . . .78 A1
Northwick Gdns BS39 . . . .57 D4
Northwick Rd
Chew Magna BS39, BS41 . .39 D7
Mark TA9 . . . . .106 B5
Northwood Cl TA2 . . . . . . .168 B4
Northwood Dro BA6 . . . . .158 A6
Norton Cl
Chew Magna BS40 . . . . .39 B3
Shepton Mallet BA4 . . . . . .205 A5
Norton Dro TA12 . . . . .185 B8
Norton Fitzwarren CE Prim
Sch TA2 . . . . .168 B5
Norton Grange BA2 . . . . . . .81 E5
Norton Hill Sch BA3 . . . . . .97 B8
Norton Ho �７ BS1 . . . . . . .227 B1
Norton La
Chew Magna BS39, BS40 . .39 C5
Wellow BA2 . . . . .81 B7
Weston-Super-Mare BS22 . .31 C4
Whitchurch BS14 . . . . .23 C2
Norton Radstock Coll BA3 78 F2
Norton Rd TA14 . . . . .185 E3
Norton St Philip CE Fst Sch
BA2 .81 E4
Norton sub Hamdon CE Prim
Sch TA14 . . . . .185 F3
Nortons Wood La BS21 . . . . .7 A5
Norville Cl BS27 . . . . .90 B8
Norville La BS27 . . . . .90 B8
Norwich Cl TA1 . . . . .212 C1
Norwich Ct TA1 . . . . .212 D2
Norwood Ave BA2 . . . . .45 E5
Norwood Farm* BA2 . . . . . .81 F7
Norwood Gr BS21 . . . . .1 F5
Notgrove Cl BS22 . . . . .31 B2
Notlake Dro BS27 . . . . .89 E4
Notting Hill Way BS6 . . . . . .88 D6
Nova Scotia Pl BS1 . . . . . .226 A1
Novers Cres BS4 . . . . .22 C8
Novers Hill BS4 . . . . .22 C8
Novers La BS4 . . . . .22 D7
Novers Park Dr BS4 . . . . . . .22 C8
Novers Park Rd BS4 . . . . . .22 D8
Novers Rd BS4 . . . . .22 C8
Nowers La TA21 . . . . .222 C3
Nowhere La BA8 . . . . .217 F7
Nunney Barton BA11 . .119 D4
Nunney Castle* BA11 . . . .143 B8
Nunney Catch Rbt BA11 .143 B7
Nunney Cl
Burnham-on-S TA8 . . . . .85 C1
Keynsham BS31 . . . . .25 A2
Nunney Fst Sch BA11 . . . .143 B8
Nunney Rd BA11 . . . . .119 D4
Nurcott La TA24 . . . . .147 C7
Nursery Cl TA5 . . . . .135 B5
Nursery Gdns TA20 . . . . . .223 E4
Nursery La BA9 . . . . .216 C4
Nursery Rd BA20 . . . . .219 A3
Nursery Rise BA3 . . . . .96 E4
Nursery Terr TA6 . . . . .208 E5
Nursery Villas TA20 . . . . . .223 E4
Nutgrove La BS40 . . . . .39 A4
Nutshole La TA20 . . . . .194 B2
Nut Tree Cl TA9 . . . . .136 E8
Nut Tree La TA18 . . . . .224 D7
Nutts La BA11 . . . . .101 F8
Nutwell Rd BS22 . . . . .31 E2
Nutwell Sq BS22 . . . . .31 E2
Nydon The TA7 . . . . .137 D3
Nye Cl BS27 . . . . .90 C7
Nye Dro BS24 . . . . .51 A5
Nye Rd BS25 . . . . .51 F5
Nyland Dro BS27 . . . . .90 B1
Nyland La BA8 . . . . .190 C8
Nyland View BS27 . . . . .90 F3
Nynehead Hollow BA11 . .167 C1
Nynehead Prim Sch
TA21 . . . . .167 B1
Nynehead Rd
Nynehead TA21 . . . . .167 C1
Wellington TA21 . . . . .222 F8
Nythe Rd TA7 . . . . .156 A5

O

Oak's Dro BA5 . . . . .138 E8
Oak Apple Dr TA6 . . . . . . .208 D6
Oak Ave BA2 . . . . .44 C3
Oak Cl TA24 . . . . .200 D7
Oak Ct
Bristol BS16 . . . . .23 A5
Weston-Super-Mare BS22 . .32 C3
Oakdale Gdns BS22 . . . . . .31 F2
Oakdale Rd BS14 . . . . .23 A8
Oak Dr
Crewkerne TA18 . . . . .224 D7
Portishead BS20 . . . . .2 B4
Oake Acres TA4 . . . . .167 D4

Oake & Bradford Com Prim
Sch TA4 . . . . .167 D4
Oake Cl TA4 . . . . .167 D4
Oake Gn TA4 . . . . .167 D4
Oak End Way TA20 . . . . . .223 C5
Oaken Ground TA21 . . . . .222 B5
Oakfield Cl
Bath BA1 . . . . .44 D8
Frome BA11 . . . . .119 D5
Oakfield Gr BS8 . . . . .226 B4
Oakfield Pk TA1 . . . . .222 E4
Oakfield Pl BS8 . . . . .226 B4
Oakfield Rd
Bridgwater TA6 . . . . .208 C4
Bristol BS8 . . . . .226 B4
Frome BA11 . . . . .119 D4
Keynsham BS31 . . . . .24 F2
Street BA16 . . . . .207 B4
Oakfield Sch BA11 . . . . . .119 D4
Oakford La BA1 . . . . .28 B3
Oak Gr BS20 . . . . .4 C5
Oakgrove Way TA6 . . . . . .209 D6
Oakhill BS24 . . . . .49 A2
Oakhill CE Prim Sch
BA3 . . . . .115 B3
Oakhill Cl BS48 . . . . .9 B1
Oakhill Ct BA3 . . . . .116 E3
Oakhill Rd BA2 . . . . .44 F2
Oak Ho
Brean TA8 . . . . .65 E2
Bristol BS13 . . . . .22 D4
Oakhurst Rd BS9 . . . . .5 F5
Oak La
East Anstey TA22 . . . . .162 E6
Rodhuish TA24 . . . . .131 A3
Taunton TA2 . . . . .212 F6
Oakland Ct TA12 . . . . .185 E7
Oakland Dr
Hutton BS24 . . . . .49 E3
Martock TA12 . . . . .185 E7
Oakland Rd TA12 . . . . .185 E7
Oaklands
Cheddar BS27 . . . . .90 A8
Clevedon BS21 . . . . .6 E3
Paulton BS39 . . . . .77 F4
Temple Cloud BS39 . . . . . . .58 E1
Oaklands Ave TA20 . . . . . .223 F4
Oaklands Rd BA21 . . . . . . .219 D7
Oakleigh BA20 . . . . .218 D2
Oakleigh Cl BS48 . . . . .19 B5
Oakley
Bath BA2 . . . . .45 E5
Clevedon BS21 . . . . .16 B8
Oakley Cl TA7 . . . . .154 F5
Oakley La BA22 . . . . .186 F6
Oak Lodge Cres TA24 . . . .200 F7
Oak Rd
Nether Stowey TA5 . . . . . . .134 B2
Winscombe BS25 . . . . .70 A8
Oakridge Cl BS25 . . . . .70 B7
Oakridge La BS25 . . . . .70 C6
Oakridge Pk BA21 . . . . . . .219 A6
Oaksey Gr BS48 . . . . .9 A1
Oak St BA2 . . . . .228 B1
Oaks The
Nailsea BS48 . . . . .9 A2
Taunton TA1 . . . . .213 C1
Wembdon TA6 . . . . .208 C6
Winford BS40 . . . . .37 F7
Oak Terr BA3 . . . . .78 D1
Oak Tree Cl EX14 . . . . .191 F2
Oaktree Ct BS11 . . . . .4 E7
Oaktree Gdns BS13 . . . . . . .21 E5
Oaktree Pk BA21 . . . . .219 A6
Oaktree Pl BS22 . . . . .32 C3
Oak Tree Way TA5 . . . . . . .135 B2
Oak Trek BS31 . . . . .24 D3
Oak Vale La BA8 . . . . .190 A6
Oak Way BA22 . . . . .218 A7
Oare Post TA24 . . . . .123 B3
Oatfield BS48 . . . . .19 F1
Oathill Cotts BA4 . . . . .140 F3
Oathill La
Clapton TA18 . . . . .195 C1
Winsham TA18 . . . . .199 E8
Oatlands Ave BS14 . . . . .23 A6
Oatley La TA5 . . . . .134 F2
Oborne Rd DT9 . . . . .225 F5
Obridge Cl TA2 . . . . .213 A6
Obridge Cres TA2 . . . . . . .213 A6
Obridge La TA2 . . . . .213 A6
Obridge Rd TA2 . . . . .213 A6
Obridge Viaduct TA2 . . . .213 B6
Observatory Field BS25 . . .70 B8
Observatory The BS22 . . . .31 D3
Ocean Way BA22 . . . . .174 B3
Octagon The �6 TA1 . . . . . .212 F4
Odcombe Hollow BA22 . .196 E8
Odeon Bldgs BS23 . . . . . . .48 E7
Odins Rd BA2 . . . . .44 D1
Old Acre Rd BS14 . . . . .23 A3
Old Airfield Cvn Pk The
TA7 .155 A4
Old Ansford Inn BA7 . . . . .214 C6
Old App BA7 . . . . .159 E2
Old Banwell Rd BS24 . . . . . .50 B4
Oldbarn La
Bampton EX16 . . . . .163 E1
Compton Martin BS40 . . . . .56 D1
Old Barn La
Halse TA4 . . . . .37 A5
Hatch Beauchamp TA3 . . . .182 F6
Old Barn Way BS20 . . . . . .218 E3
Old Barrow Hill BS11 . . . . . .4 D7

Old Basin TA6 . . . . .209 B2
Oldberry La TA22 . . . . .163 D6
Old Bond St �4 BA1 . . . . . .228 B2
Old Bowden Way DT9 . . . .217 D4
Old Bread St BS2 . . . . .227 C2
Old Brewery Ind Est The
TA4 .210 C4
Old Brewery Rd TA4 . . . . .210 C4
Old Brewery The
�6 Frome BA11 . . . . .119 F4
Rode BA11 . . . . .101 E8
Old Brewhouse The BA1 . .27 B2
Old Bridge Cl BA6 . . . . . . .206 D5
Oldbridge Rd BS14 . . . . . . .23 C3
Old Bristol Rd
East Brent TA9 . . . . .86 E4
Oakhill BA3, BA4 . . . . .114 E1
Priddy BA5, BS40 . . . . .93 A6
Shepton Mallet BA4 . . . . . . .141 C8
Weston-Super-Mare BS23 . .48 D2
Weston-Super-Mare BS22 . .32 A2
Old Bull La BA4 . . . . .141 F7
Old Burnham Rd TA9 . . . .104 D4
Old Chapel BA1 . . . . .228 C4
Old Chapel Ct TA10 . . . . . .172 A6
Old Chapel Rd TA7 . . . . . .155 B3
Old Chelsea La BS8 . . . . . . .10 C4
Old Church Rd
Axbridge BS26 . . . . .70 C1
Clevedon BS21 . . . . .6 C3
Nailsea BS48 . . . . .8 D2
Weston-Super-Mare BS23 . .48 D2
Old Cleeve CE Sch TA23 . .131 E4
Old Coach Rd BS26 . . . . . . .69 E2
Old Combe Hill TA4 . . . . . .181 F5
Old Co-op Cotts BA3 . . . . .117 A7
Old Dairy Ct BS21 . . . . .6 F3
Old Dairy The BA2 . . . . .44 D4
Old Ditch BA5 . . . . .110 E7
Old Ditch La TA7 . . . . .155 E7
Old Down La BA4 . . . . .142 A6
Old Drill Hall The BS2 . . . .227 C3
Old England Way BA2 . . . . .79 E8
Old Farm DT9 . . . . .225 C4
Old Farm Cl TA24 . . . . .200 E6
Old Farm Ct
Blackford BS28 . . . . .107 E4
Queen Camel BA22 . . . . . . .174 F3
Old Farm Pl TA17 . . . . .195 C7
Old Farm Rd
Minehead TA24 . . . . .200 E6
Nether Stowey TA5 . . . . . . .134 B2
Old Ferry Rd BA2 . . . . .44 C6
Oldfield BS21 . . . . .6 E3
Oldfield La BA2 . . . . .44 D4
Oldfield Girls Sch BA1 . . . .26 F1
Oldfield Park Inf Sch BA2 44 D6
Oldfield Park Jun Sch
BA2 .44 C4
Oldfield Park Sta BA2 . . . .44 D6
Oldfield Pl BS8 . . . . .11 F5
Oldfield Rd
Bath BA2 . . . . .228 A1
Bristol BS8 . . . . .226 A1
Oldfield BA11 . . . . .101 B1
Oldfield Residential Pk
BA11 . . . . .101 B1
Old Forge The BA2 . . . . .61 B4
Old Forge Way BA2 . . . . . . .79 E8
Old Fosse Rd BA2 . . . . .44 C1
Old Frome Rd
Bath BA2 . . . . .62 E8
Doulting BA4 . . . . .141 E8
Horrington BA5 . . . . .113 D3
Oakhill BA3, BA4 . . . . .115 B1
Old Glove Factory The
BA22 . . . . .186 B6
Old Gore La BA3 . . . . .95 E3
Old Green The 🚂 DT9 . . . .225 D4
Old Ham TA5 . . . . .133 D6
Old Hill
Wincanton BA9 . . . . .216 C5
Winford BS40 . . . . .37 D6
Wrington BS40 . . . . .35 F3
Old Hitchen 🚂 TA16 . . . . .195 F7
Old Ho The BA3 . . . . .64 C5
Old Junction Rd BS23 . . . . .49 B5
Old King St BA1 . . . . .228 B3
Old King Street Ct BS1 . . .227 B3
Old La
Farmborough BA2 . . . . .60 A6
Nailsea BS21 . . . . .8 C4
Porlock TA24 . . . . .124 B3
Old Main Rd TA6 . . . . .135 F5
Old Malt Ho BS2 . . . . .227 C4
Old Maltings The BA3 . . . .115 A3
Old Manor Est BA3 . . . . . . .116 F4
Old Market 🚂 TA12 . . . . . .185 E6
Old Market Cl BA4 . . . . . . .206 D5
Old Market Ctr TA1 . . . . . .212 F3
Old Market Mews DT10 . .190 B4
Old Market Rd BA4 . . . . . . .205 B6
Old Market St BS2 . . . . . . .227 C3
Old Market Rdbt BS2 . . . .227 C3
Old Mdws La BS26 . . . . . . .87 C5
Oldmead Wlk BS13 . . . . . . .21 E7
Old Midford Rd BA2 . . . . . .63 B7
Old Millard's Hill BA3 . . . . .78 B3
Old Mill Rd
Portishead BS20 . . . . .2 D5
Woolavington TA7 . . . . .136 E4
Old Mills Ind Est BS39 . . . .77 E2
Old Mills La BS39 . . . . .77 D3
Old Mill Way
Wells BA5 . . . . .203 B2
Weston-Super-Mare BS24 . .50 A8
Oldmixon Cres BS24 . . . . . .49 A3

Oldmixon Prim Sch BS24. .49 A2
Oldmixon Rd BS24 . . . . .49 B1
Old Mixon Rd BS24 . . . . . . .49 C2
Old Newbridge Hill BA1 . .44 A8
Old Oaks Cl TA6 . . . . .208 D5
Old Orch
Bath BA1 . . . . .228 C3
Chard TA20 . . . . .223 F1
Old Orchard Cl TA19 . . . . .183 F4
Old Orchards TA20 . . . . . . .223 B4
Old Orchard St BA1 . . . . . .228 C2
Old Orchard The TA11 . . . .221 A5
Old Orch The TA13 . . . . . . .220 D4
Old Park Hill BS2 . . . . .226 C3
Old Park Rd
Bristol BS11 . . . . .4 D7
Clevedon BS21 . . . . .6 E4
Old Pawlett Rd TA9 . . . . . .136 A7
Old Pit Rd BA3 . . . . .97 C8
Old Pit Terr BA3 . . . . .78 E4
Old Pk BS2 . . . . .226 C3
Old Police Station The
BA9 . . . . .216 C4
Old Post Office Cotts
TA7 .153 F2
Old Post Office La BS23 . .48 D8
Old Pound Ct SP8 . . . . . . .161 E1
Old Print Works 🚂 BA11 .119 E5
Old Priory Rd BS20 . . . . .4 B4
Old Quarry BA2 . . . . .44 D2
Old Quarry Rd BS11 . . . . . . .4 E7
Old Quarry Rise BS11 . . . . . .4 E7
Old Rd
North Petherton TA6 . . . . . .153 F4
Odcombe BA22 . . . . .186 C2
Pensford BS39 . . . . .40 E3
Radstock BA3 . . . . .79 C1
South Cadbury BA22 . . . . . .175 E4
Taunton TA3 . . . . .168 D1
Old Rd The BA8 . . . . .189 D6
Old Rectory The TA9 . . . . . .86 C4
Oldrey La TA24 . . . . .147 C8
Old Saw Mills The BA3 . . .117 A3
Old Sawmill The BA12 . . .161 F6
Old School Cl
Alweston DT9 . . . . .189 A1
Ashcott TA7 . . . . .156 B8
Churchill BS25 . . . . .52 F4
Yeovil BA21 . . . . .218 C5
Old School Hill BA2 . . . . . . .62 F7
Old School Ho BA21 . . . . . .219 C5
Old School Ho The
Bath BA1 . . . . .228 B4
Whatley BA11 . . . . .118 A3
Old School La
Bleadon BS24 . . . . .67 C6
Catcott TA7 . . . . .137 D2
Lynford-on-f TA11 . . . . .158 C2
Old School Pl
Sherborne DT9 . . . . .225 D3
Wells BA5 . . . . .203 E5
Old School The BA11 . . . . .119 E4
Oldshute La TA22 . . . . .163 C7
Old Sneed Ave BS9 . . . . .5 D4
Old Sneed Cotts BS9 . . . . . .5 E4
Old Sneed Pk BS9 . . . . .5 D4
Old Sneed Rd BS9 . . . . .5 D4
Old St BS21 . . . . .6 E3
Old Station Cl
Cheddar BS27 . . . . .90 A7
Wrington BS40 . . . . .35 D1
Old Station Ct TA20 . . . . . .223 D5
Old Station Gdns BA8 . . . .190 A7
Old Station La BA10 . . . . . .215 C4
Old Station Rd BA20 . . . . .219 C4
Old Station Way BS24 . . . . .219 C4
Old Stream Farm TA10 . . .171 E3
Old Street La BA5 . . . . .204 B7
Old Tannery The 🚂 BS2 . .227 C3
Old Tarnwell BS39 . . . . .40 B2
Old Taunton Rd TA6 . . . . . .209 A4
Old Threshing Mill The
BA4 . . . . .141 B2
Old Tiverton Rd EX16 . . . .164 C1
Old Tk BA2 . . . . .63 F7
Old Town TA20 . . . . .223 C3
Old Vicarage Cl TA7 . . . . . .137 B2
Old Vicarage Ct BS14 . . . . .23 C4
Old Vicarage Gdns TA13 . .220 C4
Old Vicarage Gn BS31 . . . .24 E6
Old Vicarage La TA4 . . . . . .167 E8
Old Vicarage The TA21 . . .222 E6
Oldville Ave BS21 . . . . .6 D2
Old Walcot Sch The BA1 .228 B3
Old Wall BS24 . . . . .66 D5
Old Water Gdns The BS40 .54 E2
Old Way
Chipstable TA4 . . . . .165 D6
Stogumber TA4 . . . . .150 D8
Oldway Ho TA21 . . . . .222 F4
Oldway La TA3 . . . . .183 A8
Oldway Pk TA21 . . . . .222 F4
Oldway Pl TA9 . . . . .104 D4
Oldway Rd
East Anstey TA22 . . . . .162 F5
Wellington TA21 . . . . .222 E4
Old Wells Rd
Bath BA2 . . . . .44 F3
Croscombe BA5 . . . . .204 D6
Doulting BA4 . . . . .142 A8
Glastonbury BA6 . . . . .206 F6
Leigh u M BA3, BA4, BA11 .117 B2
Shepton Mallet BA4, BA5 . .205 A5
Old Weston Rd
Congresbury BS49 . . . . .34 B5
Flax Bourton BS48 . . . . .20 B8
Old Yarn Mills The DT9 . . .225 D2
Oliver's La TA19 . . . . .183 B2
Oliver Brooks Rd BA3 . . . . .96 E7

Olivier Cl TA8 . . . . .104 C6
One Elm TA10 . . . . .172 B7
Onega Ctr BA1 . . . . .228 A3
Onega Terr BA1 . . . . .228 A3
Oolite Gr BA2 . . . . .44 D1
Oolite Rd BA2 . . . . .44 D1
Orange Gr BA1 . . . . .228 C2
Orange St BS2 . . . . .227 C4
Orchard Ave
Bristol BS1 . . . . .226 C2
Midsomer Norton BA3 . . . . .77 F1
Portishead BS21 . . . . .7 E4
Orchard Cl
Banwell BS29 . . . . .51 B3
Bishop Sutton BS39 . . . . . . .57 C3
Bradford On Tone TA4 . . . .167 F1
Bristol, Westbury on T BS9 . .5 F5
Carhampton TA24 . . . . .131 B5
Castle Cary BA7 . . . . .214 B7
Cheddar BS27 . . . . .90 B8
Coleford BA3 . . . . .117 A7
Congresbury BS49 . . . . .34 D4
Cossington TA7 . . . . .137 A3
Coxley BA5 . . . . .139 E6
Drimpton DT8 . . . . .199 F8
East Brent TA9 . . . . .86 E4
East Chinnock BA22 . . . . . .196 E8
East Huntspill TA9 . . . . . . .136 B5
Felton BS40 . . . . .37 C8
Flax Bourton BS48 . . . . .20 A8
Frome BA11 . . . . .119 D4
Highbridge TA9 . . . . .104 E4
Keynsham BS31 . . . . .24 D6
Long Sutton TA10 . . . . .172 E4
🔒 North Petherton TA6 . . .153 E3
Odcombe BA22 . . . . .186 C2
Portishead BS20 . . . . .2 D5
Queen Camel BA22 . . . . . . .174 F3
Rockwell Green TA21 . . . . .222 A5
South Petherton TA13 . . . . .220 C5
Sparkford BA22 . . . . .175 A5
Taunton TA3 . . . . .168 D1
Wedmore BS28 . . . . .108 C4
West Coker BA22 . . . . .197 A8
Weston-Super-Mare, Kewstoke
BS22 . . . . .31 B3
Weston-Super-Mare, Worle
BS22 . . . . .31 F2
Westwood BA15 . . . . .64 F3
Wincanton BA9 . . . . .216 D3
Wrington BS40 . . . . .35 E2
Yeovil Marsh BA21 . . . . . . .187 A5
Orchard Cl The BS24 . . . . . .49 F4
Orchard Cotts
Croscombe BA5 . . . . .204 B7
Timsbury BA2 . . . . .60 F1
Orchard Cres BS11 . . . . .4 D7
Orchard Ct
Claverham BS49 . . . . .17 F1
Highbridge TA9 . . . . .104 E3
Minehead TA24 . . . . .201 B4
Street BA16 . . . . .207 C6
Wellington TA21 . . . . .222 E6
Orchard Dr
Bristol BS13 . . . . .22 A6
Sandford BS25 . . . . .52 A4
Southwick BA14 . . . . .83 E3
Taunton TA1 . . . . .212 A3
Orchard End BS40 . . . . .74 F4
Orchard Gdns
Paulton BS39 . . . . .77 E6
West Buckland TA21 . . . . . .180 F7
Orchard Gn TA2 . . . . .212 F8
Orchard Ho
Weston-Super-Mare BS22 . .31 F2
Yeovil BA21 . . . . .219 A6
Orchard La
Allerford TA24 . . . . .124 B4
Bristol BS1 . . . . .226 C2
Chewton Mendip BA3 . . . . . .94 F6
Crewkerne TA18 . . . . .224 C6
Evercreech BA4 . . . . .141 E1
Kingsbury Episcopi TA12 . .185 B8
Thorncombe TA20 . . . . .199 B6
Wembdon TA6 . . . . .208 D5
Orchard Lea
Coxley BA5 . . . . .139 E7
Pill BS20 . . . . .4 D4
Wells BA5 . . . . .203 C5
Orchardleigh BA22 . . . . . . .196 E8
Orchardleigh View BA11 . .119 D6
Orchard Lodge BA2 . . . . . . .45 F8
Orchard Mead TA19 . . . . . .183 C1
Orchard Paddock BA5 . . . .203 A7
Orchard Pk
Bristol BS16 . . . . .23 D4
West Camel BA22 . . . . .174 D3
Orchard Pl
Aller TA10 . . . . .171 D8
🔒 Weston-Super-Mare
BS23 . . . . .48 E7
Orchard Rd
Axbridge BS26 . . . . .70 C1
Backwell BS48 . . . . .19 A6
Carhampton TA24 . . . . .131 B5
Clevedon BS21 . . . . .6 D2
Hutton BS24 . . . . .49 E2
Long Ashton BS41 . . . . .10 F1
Milborne Port DT9 . . . . . . .217 C2
Minehead TA24 . . . . .200 F8
Nailsea BS48 . . . . .8 D1
Paulton BS39 . . . . .77 E6
Somerton TA11 . . . . .211 B4
Street BA16 . . . . .207 C6
Orchard Rise
Crewkerne TA18 . . . . .224 C5
Fivehead TA3 . . . . .170 F2
Porlock TA24 . . . . .124 A3

Orchard Rise *continued*
Ruishton TA3 . . . . . 169 C4
Orchard St
Bristol BS1 . . . . . 226 C2
Frome BA11 . . . . . 119 E5
Weston-Super-Mare BS23 . . . 48 E8
Yeovil BA20 . . . . . 219 A4
Orchards The
Bristol, Shirehampton BS11 . . 4 E6
Horrington BA5 . . . . . 113 A2
Stocklinch TA19 . . . . . 184 C4
Orchard Terr
5 Bath BA2 . . . . . 44 B6
Glastonbury BA6 . . . . . 206 D5
Orchard The
Banwell BS29 . . . . . 51 A3
Bath, Combe Down BA2 . . . . 45 B1
Bath, Newbridge BA1 . . . . . 44 A7
Corston BA2 . . . . . 43 B8
Freshford BA3 . . . . . 64 C5
Holywell Lake TA21 . . . . . 179 E7
Locking BS24 . . . . . 50 A5
Meare BA6 . . . . . 138 D4
Pensford BS39 . . . . . 40 E4
Pill BS20 . . . . . 4 C4
Ruishton TA3 . . . . . 169 C2
Upper Stanton Drew BS39 . . 40 A2
Orchard Vale
Ilminster TA19 . . . . . 221 B3
Langport TA10 . . . . . 172 A5
Midsomer Norton BA3 . . . . . 77 F1
Orchard View
Baltonsborough BA6 . . . . . 158 B6
Haselbury Plucknett TA18 . 196 C6
Orchard Way
Charlton Horethorne
DT9 . . . . . 176 A2
Cheddar BS27 . . . . . 90 B8
Keinton Mandeville TA11 . . 158 A1
Misterton TA18 . . . . . 224 F3
Peasedown St John BA2 . . . 79 D7
Shapwick TA7 . . . . . 137 F1
Taunton TA1 . . . . . 213 D5
Timberscombe TA24 . . . . . 130 B5
Williton TA4 . . . . . 202 E4
Woolavington TA7 . . . . . 136 E3
Orchard Wlk
Churchill BS25 . . . . . 52 E4
Milborne Port DT9 . . . . . 217 C2
Orchard Wyndham* TA4 . 132 B2
Orchid Cl TA1 . . . . . 169 A1
Orchids The TA8 . . . . . 85 A2
Oriel Dr BA6 . . . . . 206 D4
Oriel Gdns BA1 . . . . . 28 C2
Oriel Gr BA2 . . . . . 44 B4
Oriel Rd BA16 . . . . . 207 C5
Orme Dr BS21 . . . . . 6 D5
Ormerod Rd BS9 . . . . . 5 E5
Orneage Cl BA11 . . . . . 101 E8
Orwell Dr BS31 . . . . . 25 A4
Osborne Ave BS23 . . . . . 48 F7
Osborne Gr TA1 . . . . . 212 E3
Osborne Pl TA16 . . . . . 195 F7
Osborne Rd
Bath BA1 . . . . . 44 B7
Bridgwater TA6 . . . . . 208 F6
Bristol BS3 . . . . . 226 C1
Weston-Super-Mare BS23 . . . 48 F7
Yeovil BA20 . . . . . 219 A5
Osborne Villas BS2 . . . . . 226 C4
Osborne Wallis Ho BS8 . 226 A1
Osborne Way TA1 . . . . . 212 E3
Osborne Wlk TA8 . . . . . 104 C6
Osmond Dr BA5 . . . . . 203 B3
Osmond Rd 2 BS24 . . . . . 49 F7
Osprey Ct BS14 . . . . . 22 D5
Osprey Gdns BS22 . . . . . 31 F1
Ostlings La BA1 . . . . . 29 B2
Ostrey Mead BS27 . . . . . 90 B7
Otago Terr 5 BA1 . . . . . 28 C2
Othery Village Prim Sch
TA7 . . . . . 155 C2
Ottawa Rd BS23 . . . . . 48 F3
Otterford Cl BS14 . . . . . 23 B5
Otterford Gypsy Pk TA3 . 181 D2
Otterford Lakes Nature
Trail* TA3 . . . . . 181 E1
Otterham La TA3 . . . . . 183 F8
Otterhampton Prim Sch
TA5 . . . . . 135 B5
Otter Rd 1 BS21 . . . . . 6 E1
Otter Vale Cl EX14 . . . . . 191 F1
Ottery La DT9 . . . . . 225 C3
Our Lady of Mount Carmel
RC Prim Sch BA9 . . . . . 216 C3
Our Lady of the Rosary RC
Prim Sch BS11 . . . . . 5 A8
Outer Circ TA1 . . . . . 213 D5
Outer Gullands TA1 . . . . . 212 D2
Oval The BA2 . . . . . 44 C4
Overbrook Bsns Ctr
BS28 . . . . . 107 D4
Overcombe BA8 . . . . . 189 E8
Overdale
Clandown BA3 . . . . . 78 E5
Peasedown St John BA2 . . . . 60 F3
Overhill BS20 . . . . . 4 D4
Over Innox BA11 . . . . . 119 F6
Overland La TA3 . . . . . 170 C3
Overlands
North Curry TA3 . . . . . 170 C4
Ruishton TA3 . . . . . 169 C4
Overleigh
Street BA16 . . . . . 207 C3
Street BA16 . . . . . 207 C4
Overstables La BS21 . . . . . 6 D3
Overton BA9 . . . . . 216 D4
Owen Dr BS8 . . . . . 10 B4
Owen St TA21 . . . . . 222 C6
Owlaborough La EX36 . . . 162 B2
Owl St
South Petherton TA13 . . . . . 220 B8
Stocklinch TA19 . . . . . 184 C3
Owsley Cotts TA19 . . . . . 184 E4
Oxendale BA16 . . . . . 207 B5
Oxen La TA3 . . . . . 170 B3
Oxenpill BA6 . . . . . 138 C4
Oxen Rd TA18 . . . . . 224 C6
Oxford Pl
Bath BA2 . . . . . 45 C2
19 Bristol, Clifton BS8 . . . . . 11 F6
10 Taunton TA2 . . . . . 213 A8
Weston-Super-Mare BS23 . . . 48 D7
Oxford Rd BA21 . . . . . 219 E7
Oxford Row BA1 . . . . . 228 B3
Oxford Sq BS24 . . . . . 50 B6
Oxford St
Bristol BS2 . . . . . 227 C2
Bristol, Tyndall's Park BS2 . 226 C4
Burnham-on-S TA8 . . . . . 104 B6
Evercreech BA4 . . . . . 141 E1
Weston-Super-Mare BS23 . . . 48 D7
Oxford Terr 4 TA6 . . . . . 209 B4
Oxhayes DT8 . . . . . 199 F8
Oxhouse La
Failand BS8 . . . . . 10 B6
Winford BS40 . . . . . 37 D6
Oxleaze
5 Bishops Lydeard TA4 . . . 167 F8
Bristol BS13 . . . . . 22 D4
Oxleaze La BS41 . . . . . 21 E3
Oxley Cotts DT9 . . . . . 225 C4
Ozenhay BS39 . . . . . 75 E6

P

Packers' Way TA18 . . . . . 196 B3
Pack Horse La BA2 . . . . . 62 F7
Packsaddle Way BA11 . . . . 119 F7
Pacquet Ho BS20 . . . . . 4 D5
Paddles La BA11 . . . . . 119 D1
Paddock Cl TA3 . . . . . 169 D5
Paddock Dr TA9 . . . . . 104 D4
Paddock Gdn BS14 . . . . . 22 F4
Paddock Pk BS22 . . . . . 32 B2
Paddocks Cvn Pk The
BS26 . . . . . 87 A7
Paddocks The
Bath BA2 . . . . . 45 B1
Ilchester BA22 . . . . . 173 E1
Sandford BS25 . . . . . 52 C4
Wellington TA21 . . . . . 222 E5
Weston-Super-Mare BS23 . . . 48 D2
Paddock The
Banwell BS29 . . . . . 51 A3
Clevedon BS21 . . . . . 6 D2
Corston BA2 . . . . . 43 B7
Dulverton TA22 . . . . . 163 D6
Galhampton BA22 . . . . . 175 D8
Portishead BS20 . . . . . 2 D4
Taunton, Dowsland TA1 . . . 168 F1
Taunton, Trull TA3 . . . . . 168 D1
Paddock Wlk DT9 . . . . . 217 C2
Paddock Woods BA2 . . . . . 45 D2
Padfield Cl BA2 . . . . . 44 B5
Padfield Gn BA4 . . . . . 141 E6
Padleigh Hill BA2 . . . . . 44 B2
Padstow Rd BS4 . . . . . 22 F8
Paganel Cl TA24 . . . . . 200 F6
Paganel Rd TA24 . . . . . 200 F6
Paganel Rise TA24 . . . . . 200 E6
Paganel Way TA24 . . . . . 200 E6
Pagans Hill BS40 . . . . . 38 D2
Page's Ct BS49 . . . . . 34 C8
Page's Hill BA16 . . . . . 207 C1
Pageant Dr DT9 . . . . . 225 D3
Page La BA6 . . . . . 140 A2
Pages Mead BS11 . . . . . 4 C8
Paintmoor La TA20 . . . . . 194 B4
Palace Ct BA5 . . . . . 203 D3
Palace Gdns TA4 . . . . . 210 C4
Palace Yard Mews BA1 . . . 228 B2
Palfrey's La TA20 . . . . . 193 D3
Palmer's Elm BS24 . . . . . 33 B4
Palmer's End La TA12 . . . . 184 F7
Palmer's Way BS24 . . . . . 49 D2
Palmer Cl TA6 . . . . . 208 F2
Palmer Row 7 BS23 . . . . . 48 E8
Palmers Cl TA8 . . . . . 104 D8
Palmers La BA2 . . . . . 61 B3
Palmers Rd BA6 . . . . . 206 D4
Palmer St
Frome BA11 . . . . . 119 F4
South Petherton TA13 . . . . 220 C4
Weston-Super-Mare BS23 . . . 48 E8
Palmerston Rd TA1 . . . . . 212 D5
Palm Tree Cl TA6 . . . . . 209 E5
Panborough Dro BA5 . . . . 138 F8
Panoramic The BS1 . . . . . 226 C3
Parade Nurseries TA24 . . . 200 F7
Parade The
1 Bath BA2 . . . . . 44 B6
Bristol, Bishopsworth BS13 . . 22 A6
Bristol, Shirehampton BS11 . . 4 E6
Chardstock EX13 . . . . . 198 A7
Minehead TA24 . . . . . 200 F7
Paradise Cres BA4 . . . . . 141 E2
Paradise La
Croscombe BA5 . . . . . 204 B7
Glastonbury BA6 . . . . . 139 D2
Langport TA10 . . . . . 172 A7
Tatworth TA20 . . . . . 193 F1
Paradise Rd BA6 . . . . . 206 D5
Paradise Row BS39 . . . . . 41 A6
Paragon Ct 13 BS23 . . . . . 30 C1
Paragon Rd BS23 . . . . . 30 C1
Paragon Sch The BA2 . . . . . 45 A3
Paragon The
Bath BA1 . . . . . 228 C3
Bristol BS8 . . . . . 11 F6
Paray Dr BA5 . . . . . 203 F5
Parbrook Ct BS14 . . . . . 23 B5
Parbrook La BA6 . . . . . 158 D7
Parcroft Com Jun Sch
BA20 . . . . . 218 F5
Parcroft Gdns BA20 . . . . . 218 F5
Pardlestone La TA5 . . . . . 133 C5
Parfields BA20 . . . . . 218 F5
Parish Brook Rd BS48 . . . . . 8 B2
Parish Hill BA22 . . . . . 175 D5
Parish Land La TA5 . . . . . 152 D5
Parish Mews BA20 . . . . . 218 C5
Park Ave
Bath BA2 . . . . . 228 B1
Bridgwater TA6 . . . . . 208 D4
Castle Cary BA7 . . . . . 214 B4
Yatton BS49 . . . . . 17 B1
Park Barn La TA19 . . . . . 183 C4
Park Batch BS40 . . . . . 54 F3
Park Bglws EX16 . . . . . 179 B3
Park Cl
Barton St David TA11 . . . . 158 A3
Cossington TA7 . . . . . 136 F3
Keynsham BS31 . . . . . 24 D5
Paulton BS39 . . . . . 77 D5
Staplehay TA3 . . . . . 181 D8
Street BA16 . . . . . 207 C5
Park Cnr
Hambridge TA3 . . . . . 184 B7
Leigh u M BA11 . . . . . 117 D3
Park Cotts TA20 . . . . . 223 B5
Park Cres
Chard TA20 . . . . . 223 B5
Cossington TA7 . . . . . 136 F3
Park Ct 5 BS23 . . . . . 48 E5
Park End BS29 . . . . . 50 E4
Parker Cl TA21 . . . . . 222 E6
Parkes Rd BS24 . . . . . 50 C5
Park Farm BA6 . . . . . 206 C4
Park Farm Rd BA6 . . . . . 206 C4
Parkfield Cl TA6 . . . . . 153 F4
Parkfield Cres TA1 . . . . . 212 D2
Parkfield Dr TA1 . . . . . 212 D3
Parkfield Gdns BS39 . . . . . 57 D3
Parkfield Prim Sch TA1 . 212 D3
Parkfield Rd
Axbridge BS26 . . . . . 70 D1
Taunton TA1 . . . . . 212 D3
Parkfields Orch BA6 . . . . 157 E4
Parkfields Residential Home
BA6 . . . . . 157 E4
Park Gate TA2 . . . . . 168 F7
Parkgate La BA11 . . . . . 101 E7
Park Gdns
Bath BA1 . . . . . 44 D8
Yeovil BA20 . . . . . 219 A5
Park Gr DT10 . . . . . 190 B4
Park Hayes BA3 . . . . . 116 F3
Park Hill
Bristol BS11 . . . . . 4 F6
Mells BA11 . . . . . 118 C7
Pilton BA4 . . . . . 140 E3
Park Hill Dr BA11 . . . . . 119 F6
Park Ho BA2 . . . . . 44 E4
Parkhouse La BS31 . . . . . 24 C2
Parkhouse Rd TA24 . . . . . 200 E7
Parkhurst Rd BS23 . . . . . 49 A7
Park La
Barton St David TA11 . . . . 158 A3
Bath BA1 . . . . . 44 D7
Blagdon BS40 . . . . . 54 F3
Bristol BS2 . . . . . 226 C3
Cannington TA5 . . . . . 135 B3
Carhampton TA24 . . . . . 131 A5
Castle Cary BA7 . . . . . 214 D7
Clapton TA18 . . . . . 195 B1
Combe St Nicholas TA20 . . 193 C6
Downhead BA4 . . . . . 117 A1
Faulkland BA3 . . . . . 80 B1
Goathurst TA5 . . . . . 153 C4
Henstridge BA8 . . . . . 190 A8
High Ham TA10 . . . . . 156 D1
Ilminster TA19 . . . . . 183 E1
Kingsdon TA11 . . . . . 173 E5
Kingston St Mary TA2 . . . . 168 C8
Langport TA10 . . . . . 171 E4
Montacute BA22, TA15 . . . 186 B3
North Newton TA7 . . . . . 154 A3
North Petherton TA6 . . . . . 153 F4
Seavington St Mary TA19 . . 184 C1
Thorncombe TA20 . . . . . 199 A7
Wellington TA21 . . . . . 222 C1
West Buckland TA21 . . . . . 180 E7
Yenston BA8 . . . . . 189 F8
Parklands BS39 . . . . . 59 D2
Parklands Ave BS22 . . . . . 32 A4
Parklands Rd
Bristol BS3 . . . . . 11 E4
Wellington TA21 . . . . . 222 D7
Parklands Rise TA24 . . . . . 200 D7
Parklands Way TA11 . . . . . 211 B4
Parkland Wlk TA18 . . . . . 224 C4
Park Lane Cl TA24 . . . . . 131 A5
Park Lodge BA20 . . . . . 219 A5
Parkmead TA2 . . . . . 213 E8
Park Pl
Bath BA1 . . . . . 228 A4
Bristol BS2 . . . . . 226 C3
Bristol BS8 . . . . . 226 B3
Castle Cary BA7 . . . . . 214 C5
Weston-Super-Mare BS23 . . . 48 D8
Park Rd
Bath BA1 . . . . . 44 B7
Park Rd *continued*
Bridgwater TA6 . . . . . 208 D4
Bristol BS3 . . . . . 226 B1
Bristol, Shirehampton BS11 . . 4 F6
Bruton BA10 . . . . . 215 E5
Chard TA20 . . . . . 223 C4
Clevedon BS21 . . . . . 6 D4
Congresbury BS49 . . . . . 34 E3
Frome BA11 . . . . . 119 E4
Henstridge BA8 . . . . . 190 A6
Keynsham BS31 . . . . . 24 E4
Paulton BS39 . . . . . 77 D5
Shepton Mallet BA4 . . . . . 205 B5
Stalbridge DT10 . . . . . 190 B4
Street BA16 . . . . . 207 C5
Yeovil BA20 . . . . . 219 B5
Park Row BS1 . . . . . 226 C3
Park Sch The BA20 . . . . . 219 A5
Parks Cotts TA2 . . . . . 168 D8
Parkside Ct 1 TA6 . . . . . 209 B4
Parkside Inf Sch BA1 . . . . 228 B3
Parks La
Brompton Ralph TA4 . . . . . 150 C3
Minehead TA24 . . . . . 200 F7
Park St
Bath BA1 . . . . . 228 A4
Bristol BS1 . . . . . 226 C3
Castle Cary BA7 . . . . . 214 C5
Dunster TA24 . . . . . 201 D1
Exford TA24 . . . . . 128 D1
Minehead TA24 . . . . . 200 F7
Taunton TA1 . . . . . 212 E3
Yeovil BA20 . . . . . 219 B4
Parks The
Bridgwater TA6 . . . . . 208 D4
Minehead TA24 . . . . . 200 E7
Parkstone Ave TA6 . . . . . 209 A2
Park Street Ave BS1 . . . . . 226 C3
Park Street Mews BA1 . . 228 A4
Parks View TA24 . . . . . 124 A4
Parksway Ct TA24 . . . . . 200 E7
Park Terr
Chard TA20 . . . . . 223 B6
Glastonbury BA6 . . . . . 206 D4
Minehead TA24 . . . . . 200 F7
Park The
Castle Cary BA7 . . . . . 214 B4
Keynsham BS31 . . . . . 24 E6
Portishead BS20 . . . . . 2 F5
Yatton BS49 . . . . . 17 B1
Yeovil BA20 . . . . . 219 A5
Park View
Axminster EX13 . . . . . 198 A3
Bath BA2 . . . . . 44 D6
Cotford St Luke TA4 . . . . . 167 F6
Crewkerne, Misterton
TA18 . . . . . 196 B3
Crewkerne TA18 . . . . . 224 C4
Montacute TA15 . . . . . 186 B3
Stogursey TA5 . . . . . 134 C5
Park Villas BS23 . . . . . 48 D8
Park Wall BA10 . . . . . 215 F5
Park Wall Dro TA7 . . . . . 209 F4
Park Water La DT8 . . . . . 199 F5
Parkway
Bridgwater TA6 . . . . . 209 C5
Timsbury BA2 . . . . . 60 E2
Park Way
Bruton BA10 . . . . . 215 E5
Midsomer Norton BA3 . . . . . 97 A8
Ruishton TA3 . . . . . 169 C3
Weston-Super-Mare BS22 . . . 32 B1
Parkway La BA2 . . . . . 60 D3
Park Wlk BS20 . . . . . 4 D4
Park Wood Cl BS14 . . . . . 22 F4
Parlour Ho TA1 . . . . . 213 B5
Parmin Cl TA1 . . . . . 213 C3
Parmin Way TA1 . . . . . 213 C3
Parnell Rd BS21 . . . . . 6 D3
Parnell Way TA8 . . . . . 104 B8
Parrett Cl TA10 . . . . . 171 F5
Parrett Mead
South Perrott DT8 . . . . . 196 C1
Taunton TA1 . . . . . 213 D3
Parrett Way TA6 . . . . . 209 B3
Parrett Works Cotts
TA12 . . . . . 220 F8
Parricks La EX13 . . . . . 198 D3
Parrocks La TA20 . . . . . 198 C8
Parry's Cl BS9 . . . . . 5 E5
Parry's La BS9 . . . . . 5 F5
Parry Cl BA2 . . . . . 44 B4
Parrys Gr BS9 . . . . . 5 E5
Parson's Batch BA4 . . . . . 140 E3
Parson's Dro BS28 . . . . . 138 C7
Parson's La TA11 . . . . . 173 D5
Parson's St TA24 . . . . . 124 A3
Parsonage Cl
Langport TA10 . . . . . 172 A5
Somerton TA11 . . . . . 211 E3
Winford BS40 . . . . . 37 F6
Parsonage Cotts
Kingston St Mary TA2 . . . . 168 D8
West Camel BA22 . . . . . 174 D3
Parsonage Cres BA7 . . . . . 214 B6
Parsonage Ct
Puriton TA7 . . . . . 136 B4
Taunton TA1 . . . . . 212 A4
Parsonage Hill TA11 . . . . . 211 E3
Parsonage La
Ashill TA19 . . . . . 183 C4
Axbridge BS26 . . . . . 70 E2
Bath BA1 . . . . . 228 B2
Charlton Musgrove BA9 . . . 161 B1
Chilcompton BA3 . . . . . 96 C4
Kingston St Mary TA2 . . . . 168 D8
Milverton TA4 . . . . . 167 A4
Pensford BS39 . . . . . 40 D6
Parsonage La *continued*
Staple Fitzpaine TA3 . . . . . 182 C4
Winford BS40 . . . . . 37 F6
Parsonage Pl TA10 . . . . . 171 D4
Parsonage Rd
Berrow TA8 . . . . . 84 F5
Long Ashton BS41 . . . . . 11 C2
West Camel BA22 . . . . . 174 D3
Parsons' La TA5 . . . . . 152 A7
Parsons Cl
Bicknoller TA4 . . . . . 132 F2
Long Sutton TA10 . . . . . 172 F4
Nether Stowey TA5 . . . . . 134 A3
Parsons Gate BA7 . . . . . 214 B7
Parsons Gn
Clevedon BS21 . . . . . 16 C8
Weston-Super-Mare BS22 . . . 32 A3
Parsons Mead BS48 . . . . . 19 F7
Parsons Paddock BS14 . . . 23 A7
Parsons Pen BS27 . . . . . 90 B7
Parsons Rd TA9 . . . . . 104 C4
Parsons Way
Wells BA5 . . . . . 203 B4
Winscombe BS25 . . . . . 69 E6
Partis Coll BA1 . . . . . 44 A8
Partis Way BA1 . . . . . 44 A8
Partition St BS1 . . . . . 226 C2
Partman's Hill BA3 . . . . . 116 B3
Partridge Cl
Moorlinch TA7 . . . . . 155 F7
Weston-Super-Mare BS22 . . . 31 F1
Partway La
Chard Junction TA20 . . . . . 198 F6
East Chinnock BA22 . . . . . 196 F7
Passage Leaze BS11 . . . . . 4 D6
Passage St BS2 . . . . . 227 B2
Pastures Ave BS22 . . . . . 32 C3
Pastures The BA15 . . . . . 64 E3
Patch Croft BS21 . . . . . 16 C8
Pathe Rd TA7 . . . . . 155 B1
Pathfinder Terr 3 TA6 . . . 209 B4
Patrick's Way TA3 . . . . . 181 D8
Patrum Cl TA1 . . . . . 212 B1
Patson Hill La DT9 . . . . . 188 B5
Patterson Ho 8 BS1 . . . . . 227 B1
Pattinson Cl BA21 . . . . . 219 D6
Pattons TA3 . . . . . 169 C1
Patwell La BA10 . . . . . 215 E6
Patwell St BA10 . . . . . 215 E6
Paul's Cswy BS49 . . . . . 34 D4
Paull's La TA19 . . . . . 183 B2
Paullet EX16 . . . . . 178 C1
Paulls Cl TA10 . . . . . 172 A6
Paulman Gdns BS41 . . . . . 20 F8
Paulmont Rise BS39 . . . . . 58 E1
Pauls Rd TA11 . . . . . 211 C3
Paul St
Bristol BS2 . . . . . 226 C4
Frome BA11 . . . . . 119 F5
Shepton Mallet BA4 . . . . . 205 B6
Taunton TA1 . . . . . 212 F3
Paulto' Hill BA3, BS39 . . . . 78 B6
Paulton Inf Sch BS39 . . . . 77 E5
Paulton Jun Sch BS39 . . . . 77 E5
Paulton La BA2, BA3 . . . . . 78 D7
Paulton Meml Hospl BS39 77 F4
Paulton Rd
Farrington Gurney BS39 . . . . 77 B4
Hallatrow BS39 . . . . . 77 B7
Midsomer Norton BA3 . . . . . 77 F1
Paulwood Rd BS39 . . . . . 58 E1
Pavement The TA3 . . . . . 170 B4
Pavey Cl BS13 . . . . . 22 C4
Pavey Rd BS13 . . . . . 22 C4
Pavyotts La BA22 . . . . . 197 E8
Pawelski Cl BA4 . . . . . 142 B7
Pawlett BS24 . . . . . 49 A2
Pawlett Mead Dro TA6 . . 136 A5
Pawlett Prim Sch TA6 . . . . 135 F5
Pawlett Rd
Bristol BS13 . . . . . 22 C3
Walpole TA6 . . . . . 136 B4
West Huntspill TA6, TA9 . . . 136 A7
Pawletts Almshouses
TA5 . . . . . 134 C5
Pawlett Wlk BS13 . . . . . 22 C3
Paybridge Rd BS13 . . . . . 21 F4
Payne's La TA12 . . . . . 185 E8
Payne Rd BS24 . . . . . 49 D2
Paynes Ho 17 BS23 . . . . . 48 E8
Paynes La TA7 . . . . . 155 C2
Payton Rd
Holywell Lake TA21 . . . . . 179 F7
Rockwell Green TA21 . . . . . 222 A5
Peace Cl TA6 . . . . . 209 D6
Peacehay La TA21 . . . . . 179 E4
Peach Tree Cl TA6 . . . . . 209 E5
Peacocks Cl TA21 . . . . . 180 F7
Peacocks Hill TA11 . . . . . 158 A2
Peadon La TA5 . . . . . 134 C4
Peak La
Compton Dundon TA11 . . . . 157 A2
Shepton Beauchamp TA19 . 184 D3
Pear Ash La BA9 . . . . . 161 E2
Pearce Dr TA9 . . . . . 104 D4
Pearmain Rd BA16 . . . . . 207 B4
Pearse Cl BS22 . . . . . 32 B5
Pearson Ho BA21 . . . . . 219 A6
Peart Cl BS13 . . . . . 21 E5
Peart Dr BS13 . . . . . 21 E4
Peartree Cl BS13 . . . . . 22 B4
Pear Tree Cl
Bridgwater TA6 . . . . . 209 D4
Westleigh EX16 . . . . . 179 A4
Peartree Field BS20 . . . . . 2 F5

Peartree Gdns BS24 ......67 C6
Pear Tree Ind Est BS40 ....53 C4
Peartwater Hill TA5 ...... 152 D8
Peartwater Rd TA5 ...... 152 D7
Peasedown St John Prim Sch BA2 ....79 C7
Peat Moors Visitor Ctr* BA6 .... 138 A4
Pebbles Orch TA19 ....184 E4
Pecking Mill Rd BA4 .....141 E1
Pedder Rd BS21 ....6 D1
Peddles Cl TA10 .... 171 D8
Peddles La TA11 ....173 E8
Pedlars Gr
Chapmanslade BA13 ..... 121 C4
Frome BA11 ....119 E7
Pedwell Cvn Pk TA7 ..... 156 A7
Pedwell Hill TA7 .... 156 A7
Pedwell La TA7 .... 156 A7
Peel Ct TA23 .... 202 C7
Peel St BS5 .... 227 C4
Peerage Ct TA24 .... 201 A6
Pegasus Ct 17 BA20 ......219 B4
Peggy's La TA18 .... 196 C5
Peile Dr TA2 ....212 E7
Peir Cl BS20 ....2 E7
Pelham Ct TA6 .... 209 D7
Pelican Cl BS22 ....49 F8
Pelting Dro BA5 ....92 D1
Pembroke Ave BS11 ....4 E6
Pembroke Cl
Burnham-on-S TA8 ....85 B1
Taunton TA1 .... 212 C1
Yeovil BA21 ....219 E7
Pembroke Ct BS21 ....6 C4
Pembroke Gr BS8 .... 226 A3
Pembroke Ho 1 BS23 ....30 C1
Pembroke Mans BS8 .... 226 A4
Pembroke Pl BS8 .... 226 A1
Pembroke Rd
Bridgwater TA6 .... 209 C3
Bristol BS8 .... 226 A4
Bristol, Shirehampton BS11 ..4 E6
Portishead BS20 ....1 E4
Weston-Super-Mare BS23 ...48 F4
Pembroke St BS2 ....227 B4
Pembroke Vale BS8 ..... 226 A4
Pemswell Rd TA24 ....200 F8
Penarth Dr BS24 ....49 A1
Penarth Rd TA6 .... 208 D4
Pen Cross BA22 ....197 B6
Pendle Cl BS25 ....70 A7
Pendlesham Gdns BS23 ...31 A1
Pendomer Rd BA22 ......197 B5
Pendragon Pk BA6 .... 206 D5
Pen Elm Cotts TA2 ....168 B5
Pen Elm Hill TA2 ....168 B6
Penel Orlieu TA6 ....208 F4
Penfield BA21 .... 219 C5
Pen Hill BA9 .... 161 C4
Penlea Ave TA6 ....208 E2
Penlea Cl TA6 ....208 E2
Penlea Ct BS11 ....4 D7
Pen Mill Hill SP8, BA12 ...161 F2
Pen Mill Inf Sch BA21 ... 219 D6
Pen Mill Sta BA21 ....219 E5
Pen Mill Trad Est BA21 ...219 F6
Penmoor Pl TA8 ....84 F5
Penmoor Rd TA8 ....84 F5
Penmore Rd BA22, DT9 ...188 B7
Pennard BS24 ....49 A2
Pennard Ct
Bath BA2 ....44 A6
Bristol BS14 ....23 B5
Pennard Gn BA2 ....44 A6
Pennard La BA6 .... 140 A2
Penn Cl
Cheddar BS27 ....90 C7
Wells BA5 ....112 E2
Penn Ct BS26 ....70 C1
Penneys Piece BA11 .... 120 C6
Penn Gdns BA1 ....44 A8
Penn Hill BA20 ....219 B4
Penn Hill Pk BA20 ....219 B4
Penn Hill Rd BA1 ....27 A1
Pennine Gdns BS23 ....31 A1
Penn La BA22 .... 197 A6
Pennlea BS13 ....22 C7
Penn Lea Ct BA1 ....44 B8
Penn Lea Rd BA1 ....44 B8
Pennon Rise BS1 .... 226 C1
Penn Rd BS27 ....90 C7
Penn St BS1 ....227 B3
Penns The BS21 ....6 E2
Penn View BA9 .... 216 D4
Penn Way BS26 ....70 C1
Penny's Meade TA19 .....183 F4
Penny Batch La BA5 .....139 E8
Penny Cl TA21 .... 222 D7
Pennycress BS22 ....49 D7
Penny Lea TA23 .... 202 C6
Pennyquick BA2 ....43 D6
Pennyquick View BA2 .....43 F6
Pennywell Est 3 BS21 .....6 D2
Pennywell Rd BS2 ...... 227 C4
Penpole Ave BS11 ....4 E6
Penpole Cl BS11 ....4 D7
Penpole La BS11 ....4 E7
Penpole Pk BS11 ....4 E7
Penpole Pl BS11 ....4 E6
Penrice Cl BS22 ....31 C2
Penrose BS14 ....22 F7
Penrose Sch TA6 ....208 E4
Pensford Ct BS14 ....23 D5
Pensford Hill BS39 ....40 D5
Pensford La BS39 ....40 A3
Pensford Old Rd BS39 .....40 E3
Pensford Prim Sch BS39 ..40 D4
Pensford Way BA11 ..... 120 D7
Pentagon The BS9 ....5 B5
Penthouse Hill BA1 ....28 F3
Pentire Ave BS13 ....22 A6
Pentridge La DT10 ....190 E2
Penzoy Ave TA6 ....209 B4
Pepperall Rd TA9 .... 104 D4
Peppershells La BS39 .....41 C6
Pepys Cl BS31 ....25 D2
Pera Pl BA1 .... 228 C4
Pera Rd BA1 .... 228 C4
Perch Hill BA5 ....110 E6
Percival Rd BS8 ....11 F8
Percy Pl 13 BA1 ....28 B1
Percy Rd BA21 .... 219 D6
Peregrine Cl BS22 ....31 F1
Perfect View BA1 ....28 A1
Periton Cross TA24 ...... 200 D6
Periton Ct TA24 .... 200 D6
Periton La TA24 .... 200 D7
Periton Mead Sch TA24 . 200 D6
Periton Rd TA24 .... 200 D6
Periton Rise TA24 .... 200 D6
Periton Way TA24 .... 200 D6
Perkins Ct BA5 ....203 B4
Perley La TA23 .... 148 D8
Perrett Ho 22 BS2 ...... 227 C3
Perretts Ct BS1 .... 226 C1
Perrett Way BS20 ....4 E4
Perridge Hill BA4 .... 140 D4
Perrin Cl BS39 ....76 E8
Perrings The BS48 ....18 E8
Perrott Hill Sch TA18 .....196 B4
Perrow La BS28 ....89 C2
Perry's Cider Mills* TA19 ....194 E7
Perry's Cl BS27 ....90 A7
Perry Court Inf Sch BS14 ..23 A6
Perry Court Jun Sch BS14 ....23 A6
Perrycroft Ave BS13 ......22 A6
Perrycroft Rd BS13 ....22 A6
Perry Hill TA11 .... 174 D8
Perry Hill Rd TA11 ...... 211 D2
Perry La TA9 ....106 F5
Perry Lake La BA5 ....139 B7
Perrymans Cl BS30 ....12 A8
Perrymead
Bath BA2 ....45 B3
Weston-Super-Mare BS22 ...32 B5
Perrymead Ct BA2 ....45 B4
Perrymead Pl BA2 ....45 B4
Perry New Rd TA22 ......163 F4
Perry Pl BA21 .... 219 C5
Perry Rd
Blackford TA9 .... 107 A6
Bristol BS1 .... 227 A3
Perry St TA20 .... 198 D8
Pesley Cl BS13 ....22 A4
Pesters La TA11 ....211 E3
Pestlefield La TA3 ...... 170 C1
Peter's Gore DT6 ....199 B1
Petercole Dr BS13 ....22 A6
Peterside BS39 ....76 E8
Peterson Sq BS13 ....22 C3
Peter St
Shepton Mallet BA4 ....205 B6
Taunton TA2 ....212 F6
Yeovil BA20 ....219 B4
Petherton Gdns BS14 .....23 B7
Petherton Rd
Bristol BS14 ....23 B7
North Newton TA7 ....153 F2
Pethick Ho BS4 ....22 F8
Peto Garden at Iford Manor The* BA15 ....64 E3
Peto Gr BA15 ....64 F3
Petrel Cl TA6 .... 209 D7
Petter's Way BA20 ....219 B4
Petticoat La BA4 ....205 B6
Pettitts Cl DT9 ....187 E1
Petton Cross EX16 ...... 165 A3
Petvin Cl BA16 .... 207 D4
Petvins Ct TA18 .... 196 C5
Pevensey Wlk BS4 ....22 D7
Pharmacy Flats The DT10 ....190 F6
Pheasant The TA19 ....184 E1
Phelps Cl TA20 .... 223 D6
Philadelphia Ct BS1 .....227 B3
Philippa Cl BS14 ....23 A7
Philips Ho 2 BS2 ....227 B4
Phillip's Dro TA3 .... 170 D7
Phillip Ho TA6 ....208 F2
Phillips Cl TA6 ....208 D4
Phillips Rd BS23 ....49 A6
Phillis Hill BS39 ....77 F4
Phippen St 1 BS1 ....227 B1
Phoenix Ct
Frome BA11 .... 119 D4
Taunton TA1 ....212 F3
Phoenix Ho
Bath BA1 ....228 B4
Frome BA11 .... 119 D4
Phoenix Rd TA6 ....209 B3
Phoenix Terr TA8 ....104 B6
Phoenix Way BS20 ....2 F6
Piccadilly Pl BA1 ....45 B8
Piccadilly Ho 13 BA4 .....205 B6
Pickeridge Cl TA2 ....213 B7
Picket La DT8 .... 196 C1
Pickett La BA21 .... 219 A7
Pickney La TA2 ....168 B7
Pickpurse La TA4 ....150 E8
Pickwick Rd BA1 ....28 A2
Piece TA19 ....184 E4
Piece La TA19 ....184 E4
Piece Rd DT9 .... 217 C3
Piece The 2 TA16 ....195 F7
Pier Rd BS20 ....2 E7
Pierrepont Pl 9 BA1 .... 228 C2
Pierrepont St BA1 ...... 228 C2
Piers Rd BA4 .... 142 A6
Pier St TA8 .... 104 A6
Piffin La TA4 ....167 E8
Pigeon House Dr BS13 ....22 D4
Pigeon La BS40 ....36 E1
Pig Hill BA22 .... 197 A7
Pightley La TA5 ....152 F6
Pightley Rd TA5 ....152 E7
Pig La TA7 .... 154 D8
Pig Market La TA1 ....212 F3
Pigott Ave BS13 ....22 A4
Pigs Hill La TA5 .... 134 D1
Pike Cl BA6 .... 206 C5
Pike Hill BA4 .... 205 A7
Pike La BA4 ....205 B6
Pikes Cres
Dunster TA24 .... 201 D2
Taunton TA1 ....212 E1
Pilcorn St BS28 .... 108 C4
Pile La
Curry Mallet TA3 .... 183 C8
Stourton Caundle DT10 ....189 F3
Piley La TA21 .... 179 D8
Pilgrim's Way TA6 ....135 F5
Pilgrims Way
Bristol BS11 ....4 C7
Chew Stoke BS40 ....56 D8
Lovington BA7 ....158 E2
Weston-Super-Mare BS22 ...31 E3
Pillar La BA11 ....99 D4
Pill Bridge La BA22 ...... 173 D1
Pill Head La TA18 .... 196 C4
Pill Mdw SP8 ....177 E2
Pillmead La BS28 .... 108 D5
Pillmoor Dro BA5 ....139 F6
Pillmoor La BA5 ....139 F6
Pillmore La
Highbridge TA9 .... 105 A4
Watchfield TA9 .... 105 C4
Pill Rd
Abbots Leigh BS8 ....4 F1
Pill BS20 ....4 E2
Rooks Bridge BS26, TA9 ....87 C2
Pill St BS20 ....4 D4
Pill Way BS21 ....6 B2
Pilots Helm TA6 ....153 E4
Pilsdon La DT6 ....199 F3
Pilton Hill BA4 .... 140 C4
Pilton Manor Vineyard* BA4 ....140 E3
Pimm's La BS22 ....31 B2
Pimms La BS22 ....31 B3
Pimpernel Cl BA16 ....207 B7
Pince's Knap TA20 ....198 F5
Pinchay La BS40 ....38 A4
Pinckney Gn BA15 ....46 E5
Pincushion Cnr BA22 .... 197 E6
Pine Ave TA20 .... 223 C5
Pine Cl
Street BA16 ....207 B3
Taunton TA1 .... 213 D2
Weston-Super-Mare BS22 ...31 D2
Pinecroft
Bristol BS14 ....22 F7
Portishead BS20 ....1 F6
Pine Ct
Chew Magna BS40 ....39 B3
Frome BA11 ....120 B7
Keynsham BS31 ....24 C4
Radstock BA3 ....79 A2
Pine Hill BS22 ....31 D2
Pine Lea BS24 ....67 B6
Pine Ridge Cl BS9 ....5 C4
Pines Cl
Chilcompton BA3 ....96 D3
Wincanton BA9 .... 216 C3
Pines Residential Site The BA11 .... 120 D8
Pines Way
Bath BA2 .... 228 A2
Radstock BA3 ....79 A2
Pines Way Ind Est BA2 .. 228 A2
Pine Tree Ave BA20 ......218 F3
Pine Tree Cl TA6 .... 209 D4
Pinetree Rd BS24 ....50 D4
Pine Wlk BA3 ....78 E1
Pinewood TA11 .... 211 D4
Pinewood Ave BA3 ....77 F1
Pinewood Dr TA11 ...... 211 D4
Pinewood Gr BA3 ....77 F1
Pinewood Rd BA3 ....77 F1
Pinewood Way TA8 ....65 F3
Pinford La DT9 ....188 F3
Pinhay Rd BS13 ....22 B6
Pinkham Hill TA20 ....194 B6
Pinkhams Twist BS14 .....23 A5
Pink Knoll Hollow DT9 .. 188 C8
Pinksmoor La TA21 ......179 E7
Pinkwood La BA10 ....160 E7
Pinmore BA11 ....119 E2
Pinney Cl TA1 ....212 B1
Pinnockscroft TA8 ....84 F5
Pintail Rd TA24 .... 201 C5
Pinter Cl TA8 .... 104 C6
Pioneer Ave BA2 ....44 F1
Pipehouse BA2 ....63 E4
Pipehouse La BA2 ....63 F4
Pipe La BS1 .... 226 C2
Piper's Alley TA19 ....221 B4
Pipers Cl BS26 ....88 E6
Pipers Pl EX14 ....191 F2
Pippard Cl BA16 ....207 E5
Pippin Cl BA2 ....79 D7
Pippins The
Portishead BS20 ....2 F5
Wembdon TA6 .... 208 D6
Pipplepen La DT8, TA18 ...196 B2
Pitchcombe Gdns BS9 .....5 D7
Pitcher's Hill TA2 ....168 F7
Pitching The
Castle Cary BA7 .... 214 C5
Chilcompton BA3 ....96 D5
Pitch & Pay La BS9 ....5 E3
Pitch & Pay Pk BS9 ....5 E3
Pitcombe Hill BA10 ....215 B2
Pitcombe La TA4 ....165 B5
Pitcombe Rock BA10 .... 215 C3
Pitcot La BA3 ....115 F7
Pitfield Cnr BA22 .... 188 A7
Pitfour Terr BA2 ....60 B2
Pithay Ct BS1 .... 227 A3
Pithay The
Bristol BS1 .... 227 A3
Paulton BS39 ....77 E6
Pit Hill TA17 ....195 B7
Pit Hill La TA7 .... 155 C7
Pit La
Sticklepath TA23 .... 149 D7
Sutton Mallet TA7 ...... 155 C7
Ubley BS40 ....55 F5
Pitman Ct BA1 ....28 C2
Pitman Ho BA2 ....44 D4
Pitman Rd BS23 ....48 E6
Pitney Hill TA10 .... 172 C6
Pit Rd
Dinnington TA17 .... 195 C7
Midsomer Norton BA3 ......78 B1
Pitsham La TA4 ....164 E6
Pitt's La BS40 ....39 B1
Pitt Ct TA10 ....171 B3
Pitten St BA3 ....116 E3
Pitt La
Huish Champflower TA4 ....165 E8
Porlock Weir TA24 ...... 123 C3
Waterrow TA4 ....165 F5
Pitts Cl TA1 .... 212 C1
Pitts La TA3 ....183 F7
Pitway TA13 .... 220 D5
Pitway Cl BS39 ....76 F4
Pitway Hill TA13 .... 220 D6
Pitway La BS39 ....76 E4
Pixash Bsns Ctr BS31 .....25 B5
Pixash La BS31 ....25 C5
Pix La TA4 ....167 B4
Pixton Way TA22 ....163 E6
Pizey Ave
Burnham-on-S TA8 ....85 A1
Clevedon BS21 ....6 B2
Pizey Ave Ind Est BS21 ....6 C2
Pizey Cl BS21 ....6 B2
Place Dro TA7 ....154 F4
Placket La BA20 .... 218 D1
Plain Pond TA4 .... 210 C5
Plain The BA2 ....81 E4
Plais St TA2 ....212 F6
Plantaganet Chase BA20 218 D2
Plantagenet Pk BA20 ....218 E3
Platterwell La (East Town La) BA4 ....141 B3
Players La TA8 ....85 A1
Playfield Cl 2 BA8 ..... 190 A6
Playford Gdns BS11 ....4 E8
Playses Gn TA10 .... 184 D8
Pleasant Pl BA1 ....29 D2
Pleshey Cl BS22 ....31 D2
Plimsoll Ho 3 BS1 ....227 B1
Plot La DT9 ....187 F5
Plott La BA8 ....190 B7
Plough Cl BA16 .... 207 A4
Ploughed Paddock BS48 ...8 D1
Plover Cl
Milborne Port DT9 .... 217 C2
Minehead TA24 .... 201 C5
Weston-Super-Mare BS22 ...31 F1
Plover Ct BA21 .... 218 D6
Plover Rd DT9 .... 217 C2
Plovers Rise BA3 ....79 A3
Plowage La BA22 .... 174 D3
Plox BA10 ....215 E6
Plox Gn BA10 ....215 E6
Plucknett Row BA20 .... 218 D5
Plud St BS28 ....108 B3
Plumber's Barton 9 BA11 ....119 F4
Plumers Cl 4 BS21 ....6 E1
Plum La TA6 .... 209 C2
Plumley Cres BS24 ....50 A4
Plumley Ct BS23 ....48 D4
Plummer's La BA5 ....92 D5
Plum Orch DT9 ....187 F4
Plumptre Ave BA5 ....203 F5
Plumptre Cl BS39 ....77 E5
Plumptre Rd BS39 ....77 E5
Plumtree Cl BS25 ....52 A1
Plum Tree Cl TA6 ....209 E5
Plum Tree Rd BS22 ....49 E8
Plunder St BS49 ....35 B7
Plunging Dr BA6 ....206 F1
Plymor Rd TA9 .... 136 A8
Poachers End TA24 ..... 201 C4
Pococks Yd TA10 ....171 F5
Podger's La TA19 ....183 F4
Podgers Dr BA1 ....27 B2
Podium The BA1 .... 228 C2
Poets Cnr BA3 ....97 C8
Polden Bsns Ctr The TA6 ....136 B2
Polden Cl BS48 ....8 E1
Polden Ct TA6 ....209 B5
Polden Rd
Portishead BS20 ....2 B5
Weston-Super-Mare BS23 ...48 F8
Polden St TA6 ....209 B5
Polden View BA6 ....206 E3
Polden Wlk TA7 ....136 E3
Pole Rue La TA20 .... 193 C6
Polestar Way BS24 ....50 A8
Polham La TA11 .... 211 D3
Polkes Field TA3 ....170 F6
Pollard's La TA21 ....180 F7
Pollard Rd
Bridgwater TA6 .... 209 D6
Weston-Super-Mare BS22 ...49 F8
Pollards Ct TA24 .... 124 A3
Pollards Way TA1 ....212 E4
Polygon Rd BS8 .... 226 A2
Polygon The 15 BS8 ....11 F6
Pomeroy La BA14 ....83 B6
Pomfrett Gdns BS14 ......23 E5
Pond Cl 5 BA8 .... 190 A6
Pond Cotts BA3 ....80 D2
Pond Head BS20 ....4 D4
Pondhead Cross TA4 .....202 E3
Pond La TA21 .... 179 D3
Pond Orch TA4 ....150 B8
Pondpool La TA3 .... 170 C3
Pond Wlk DT10 ....190 B4
Ponsford Rd
Bristol BS14 ....23 B8
Minehead TA24 .... 201 A6
Pookfield Cl BA11 ....143 B7
Poolbridge Rd BS28 .... 107 C4
Pool Cl TA7 .... 136 C4
Poole Hill TA22 ....163 B5
Poole Ho BA2 ....43 F5
Poolemead Rd BA2 ....43 F5
Pooles Cl TA5 .... 134 A2
Pooles La TA20 ....194 E1
Poole St BS11 ....4 B8
Pooles Wharf BS8 ...... 226 A1
Pooles Wharf Ct BS8 .... 226 A1
Pool Hill TA21 ....165 E1
Pool La BS40 ....38 A2
Poop Hill TA18 .... 196 C8
Poop Hill La TA18 ...... 196 C8
Poor Hill BA2 ....59 F6
Poorhouse La DT6 ....199 E1
Pope's La
Milborne Port DT9 .... 217 D2
Rockwell Green TA21 ....222 B4
Pope's Wlk BA2 ....45 B3
Pope Cl TA1 .... 168 D1
Popery La TA24 ....129 E1
Popham Cl
Bridgwater TA6 .... 209 D5
East Brent TA9 ....86 D5
Popham Flats TA21 ..... 222 D6
Pop La EX13, TA20 ....198 B8
Poplar Ave BS9 ....5 D6
Poplar Cl
Bath BA2 ....44 D4
Frome BA11 ....120 B7
Poplar Dr BA21 .... 218 C7
Poplar Est TA9 .... 104 D3
Poplar Farm BA5 .... 111 A4
Poplar La
Catcott TA7 .... 137 D1
Mark TA9 ....105 E3
Poplar Pl 16 BS23 ....48 E8
Poplar Rd
Bath BA2 ....62 D8
Bridgwater TA6 .... 209 D7
Bristol, Highridge BS13 ....21 F7
Burnham-on-S TA8 ...... 104 A8
Street BA16 .... 207 C3
Taunton TA1 .... 213 D2
Poplars Cl BA21 .... 187 A5
Poplars The
Easton-in-G BS20 ....4 B4
Porlock TA24 .... 124 A3
Weston-Super-Mare BS22 ...32 A1
Poplar Tree La BA14 ......83 C2
Poplar Wlk BS24 ....49 E5
Pople's La BA11 ....117 F8
Pople's Well TA18 ....224 B6
Poples Bow TA9 ....104 E5
Poppy Cl
Weston-Super-Mare BS22 ...32 A5
Yeovil BA22 ....218 B5
Porch EX13 .... 198 A3
Porch Cl BA6 ....206 E3
Porchestall Dro BA6 .....206 B4
Porlock Cl
3 Clevedon BS21 ....6 E1
Weston-Super-Mare BS23 ...48 F2
Porlock Dr TA1 ....212 E1
Porlock Gdns BS48 ....8 E1
Porlock Hill TA24 ....123 F3
Porlock Rd
Bath BA2 ....45 A1
Minehead TA24 .... 200 C7
Porlock Visitor Ctr* TA24 .... 124 A3
Portal Rd BS24 ....50 D4
Portbury Comm BS20 ......2 E4
Portbury Gr BS11 ....4 D6
Portbury Hundred The BS20 ....3 C4
Portbury La BS20 ....9 E7
Portbury Way BS20 ....3 E5
Portbury Wlk BS11 ....4 D6
Portcullis Rd TA10 ..... 172 A6
Porter's Hatch BA6 ..... 138 D4
Portfield La TA10 ....171 F5
Portishead Bsns Pk BS20 ...2 E5
Portishead Lodge BS20 ....2 D6

Portishead Prim Sch
Portishead BS20 2 C5
Portishead BS20 2 E6
Portishead Rd BS22 32 B4
Portishead Way BS3 11 E3
Port La TA22 164 A5
Portland Cl
Cannington TA5 135 B2
Nailsea BS48 8 D1
Portland Ct BS1 226 B1
Portland Dr BS20 2 E4
Portland Grange 6 TA1 212 E3
Portland Lofts 8 BS2 227 B4
Portland Mans 9 BS2 227 B4
Portland Pl
Bath BA1 228 B4
Brent Knoll TA9 86 B1
Bridgwater TA6 208 D5
Frome BA11 119 D5
Portland Rd
Bath BA1 228 B4
Frome BA11 119 D5
Langport TA10 172 B5
Street BA16 207 A6
Portland Sq BS2 227 B4
Portland St
Bristol, Clifton BS8 11 F7
Taunton TA1 212 E4
Portland Terr
Bath BA1 228 B4
Watchet TA23 202 C7
Portman Cres 9 TA6 153 F3
Portman Ct BA22 196 E8
Portman Dr TA6 153 E3
Portman Rd TA6 153 E3
Portmans TA3 170 B3
Portman St TA2 212 F6
Portmeade Dro BS26 70 C1
Portmeirion Cl BS14 23 B5
Portnell's La BA12 161 F2
Portobello Bldgs TA20 223 B4
Portreeve Dr BA21 219 B6
Port View BS20 4 C5
Portview Rd BS11 4 B8
Portwall Dro TA7 209 F5
Portwall La BS1 227 B1
Portwall La E 10 BS1 227 B1
Portway
Bristol, Shirehampton BS11 4 C6
Bristol, Sneyd Park BS8 5 C3
Frome BA11 120 A4
Holford TA5 133 D4
Street BA16 207 D4
Wells BA5 203 C4
Port Way BA2 100 D7
Portway Ave BA5 203 D4
Portway Com Sch BS11 4 E7
Portway Hill
Batcombe BA4 142 C1
Bruton BA4 159 F6
Portway La
Binegar BA3 95 E1
Holford TA5 133 E4
Portway Lodge 1 BA5 203 C4
Portway Rdbt BS11 4 C8
Portway Villas BA11 120 A4
Positano Ct TA6 208 E7
Poskitt Ho TA6 208 F6
Post Cl TA21 222 E4
Post La
Malmsmead EX35 122 C4
Skilgate TA4 164 E7
Post Office La
Blagdon BS40 54 D3
Flax Bourton BS48 19 F7
Minehead TA24 200 F7
Tatworth TA20 198 C8
Post Office Rd BS24 50 C5
Post Office Yd DT8 199 F7
Poston Way BA15 64 E7
Pot La BA11 120 F8
Potter's Cross TA4 165 C7
Potters Ho 1 BA4 205 B6
Potterton Cl TA6 208 F1
Pottery Cl BS23 49 A6
Pottery Rd TA19 183 C1
Pottery View TA19 183 C1
Pottle St BA12 144 D3
Potts Cl BA1 28 F3
Poulett Cotts TA17 195 D7
Pound Cl
Glastonbury BA6 206 D5
Stalbridge DT10 190 B4
Yeovil BA21 218 C5
Pound Farm Cl TA6 208 D3
Poundfield Rd TA24 200 E6
Pound Fold BA5 204 C7
Pound Hill TA21 179 A5
Poundisford Cl TA1 212 D1
Pound La
Bishops Lydeard TA4 151 F1
Buckland St Mary TA20 193 A8
Downhead BA4 117 A1
Easton BA5 111 A4
Lydford Fair Place TA11 158 C3
Martock TA12 185 D6
Nailsea BS48 8 D3
Oakhill BA3 115 B5
Rawridge EX14 191 F1
Yarcombe EX14 192 E2
Yarlington BA9 175 F8
Yeovil BA22 218 A2
Pound Mead BS40 37 C8
Pound Orch TA4 151 C7
Pound Pool TA11 211 C4
Pound Rd
Axminster EX13 198 F2
Broadway TA19 183 B2
Pound Rd *continued*
Pawlett TA6 135 F5
Poundsclose TA22 163 E4
Pound Terr 3 TA21 222 D5
Pound The BS40 36 D3
Pound Way TA10 172 B3
Pounsell La TA10 172 B5
Pow's Hill BA3 78 D5
Pow's Orch BA3 78 A1
Powell Cl TA3 169 D4
Powell Ct BA5 203 B4
Powells Acres BS21 6 E3
Powis Cl BS22 31 C2
Powlett Ct BA2 45 B7
Powlett Rd BA2 45 B8
Powy's Gn DT9 225 C4
Powy's La DT9 225 C4
Poyntz Rd BS4 22 F8
Prankerds Rd DT9 217 C2
Preachers Vale BA3 116 F7
Preanes Gn BS22 32 A2
Precinct The BS20 2 D5
Prescot Cl BS22 31 B2
Prescott Rd EX15 179 D1
Prestleigh La BA4 141 E4
Prestleigh Rd BA4 141 E2
Preston CE Prim Sch
BA21 218 C7
Preston Cross TA4 150 E6
Preston Gr BA20 218 F5
Preston La TA4 150 E6
Preston Rd
Yeovil BA20 218 E5
Yeovil, Houndstone BA22 218 B5
Preston Road Rdbt BA21 218 C5
Preston Sch BA21 218 D5
Prestor 9 EX13 198 A1
Pretwood Cl TA19 221 C3
Prewett St BS1 227 B1
Prey La TA3 182 D7
Preywater Rd BA5 139 D8
Prices Bldgs TA6 209 A4
Priddles La TA20 193 C8
Priddy Cl
Bath BA2 44 B5
Frome BA11 120 C7
Priddy Ct BS14 23 B5
Priddy Dr BS14 23 B5
Priddy Prim Sch BA5 92 D3
Priddy Rd BA5 112 E8
Priddy Veal La BA5 111 A5
Priest's Ho* TA10 172 A3
Priestlands DT9 225 D5
Priestlands La DT9 225 D5
Priestley Way TA8 104 C5
Priest Row BA5 203 D4
Priest St TA4 202 C2
Priests Way BS22 31 D2
Prigg La TA13 220 C4
Primmerfield La BA3 94 C8
Primrose Hill
Bath BA1 27 D1
Charlton Mackrell TA11 173 F7
East Coker BA22 197 B7
Nunney BA11 143 B8
Primrose Hill Pk Homes
TA11 173 F7
Primrose La
Midsomer Norton BA3 78 B1
Yeovil BA21 187 D5
Prince's Bldgs 17 BS8 11 F6
Prince's Cl 11 TA14 185 F4
Prince's Rd
Clevedon BS21 6 D3
Shepton Mallet BA4 205 C6
Street BA16 207 B5
Prince's St
Bristol BS2 227 C4
Clandown BA3 78 E5
Prince Philip Cl TA20 223 B3
Princes' La BS8 11 F6
Princes Bldgs BA1 228 B3
Princes Rd BA5 203 D4
Princess Anne Rd BA11 120 A7
Princess Cl
Keynsham BS31 24 E4
12 North Petherton TA6 153 F4
Princess Rd TA1 212 D2
Princess Row BS2 227 A4
Princess St TA8 104 B7
Princes St
Bath BA1 228 B2
Taunton TA1 213 B4
Yeovil BA20 219 B5
Princess Victoria St BS8 11 F6
Prince St BS1 227 A1
Prince Street Rdbt BS1 227 A2
Printers Ct 32 TA12 185 E6
Prior's Wlk TA1 212 F4
Prior Park Bldgs BA2 45 B5
Prior Park Coll BA2 45 C2
Prior Park Cotts BA2 228 C1
Prior Park Gdns BA2 45 B5
Prior Park Landscape Gdn*
BA2 45 C3
Prior Park Rd BA2 45 B4
Priors Hill BA2 60 A2
Priorswood Ind Est TA2 213 B6
Priorswood Pl 8 TA2 213 A8
Priorswood Prim Sch
TA2 212 F6
Priorswood Rd TA2 213 A6
Priory TA21 222 E6
Priory Ave TA1 213 A4
Priory Bridge Rd TA1 213 A5
Priory Cl
Bath BA2 45 B2
Cannington TA5 135 C2
Priory Cl *continued*
Castle Cary BA7 214 B5
Chilton Polden TA7 137 B2
Ilchester BA22 173 E1
Midsomer Norton BA3 78 A1
Yeovil BA20 218 D1
Priory Com Sch BS22 32 B3
Priory Ct
Bridgwater TA6 208 F4
9 Stoke sub Hamdon
TA14 185 F4
5 Taunton TA1 213 A4
Wellington TA21 222 E7
Priory Farm Trad Est BS20 3 D3
Priory Fields TA1 213 A5
Priorygate Ct BA7 214 B6
Priory Gdns
Bristol, Shirehampton BS11 4 D7
Burnham-on-S TA8 104 B6
Easton-in-G BS20 4 B4
Wellington TA21 222 E6
Priory Glade BA21 218 C6
Priory Gn TA24 201 E2
Priory Hill TA5 134 C5
Priory Hospl BA5 203 C3
Priory Mead BA10 215 F8
Priory Mews BS23 49 B7
Priory Path BA7 214 C5
Priory Pl BA5 203 D3
Priory Rd
Bristol BS8 226 C4
Bristol, Shirehampton BS11 4 D6
Chilton Polden TA7 137 B2
Easton-in-G BS20 4 B4
Ilchester BA22 173 E1
Keynsham BS31 24 E7
Portbury BS20 3 D3
Wells BA5 203 D3
Weston-Super-Mare BS23 49 A7
Priory Sch The TA2 213 B7
Priory View BA7 214 B6
Priory Villas BA9 216 C3
Priory Way TA1 213 B5
Priory Way Ind Est TA1 213 B5
Priory Wlk
Portbury BS20 3 D3
Taunton TA1 213 A5
Priston Cl BS22 32 B5
Priston La BA2, BA3 61 A5
Priston Rd BA2 61 D6
Pritchard St BS2 227 B4
Private Rd
North Brewham BA11 161 E8
Staplegrove TA2 212 D7
Privet Dr BS13 22 C5
Proctor Ho BS1 227 B1
Prophet's La TA14 185 E3
Prospect Cl
East Brent TA9 86 E5
Shepton Mallet BA4 205 A6
Prospect Gdns BA1 28 F5
Prospect Ho BS22 31 E3
Prospect Pl
Bath, Beacon Hill BA1 28 A1
Bathford BA1 29 D2
Bath, Weston BA1 27 C2
9 Weston-Super-Mare
BS23 48 E8
Prospect Rd BA2 45 C4
Prospect Row TA18 224 F3
Prospect Terr TA1 212 F5
Prospect Villas BA4 159 C7
Protheroes Ho BS1 226 C2
Proud Cross BS40 74 E4
Providence La BS41 10 F2
Providence Pl
Bristol BS2 227 C2
Bruton BA10 215 D6
Providence Rise BS41 10 F2
Providence View BS41 11 A1
Provident Pl TA6 208 E5
Prowle's Cross BA22 197 F5
Prowse's La BS26 70 A1
Prowse La TA9 106 C7
Prowses Mdw TA2 168 B4
Publow La BS39 40 E5
Pud Brook DT9 217 D1
Pudding Pie Cl BS40 53 A5
Pudding Pie La BS40 53 A6
Puddle Town TA18 196 B5
Puddy's La TA9 105 D4
Pudleigh La TA20 223 B8
Puffin Cl
Minehead TA24 201 C5
Weston-Super-Mare BS22 49 F8
Pullen Ct BA4 205 B4
Pulmans La TA18 224 C5
Pulpitsway Dro TA12 185 A8
Pulteney Ave BA2 45 B6
Pulteney Bridge BA2 228 C2
Pulteney Gdns BA2 45 B6
Pulteney Gr BA2 45 B6
Pulteney Mews BA2 45 B7
Pulteney Rd BA2 45 B6
Pulteney Terr BA2 45 B6
Pump La
Bathford BA1 29 B2
Bristol BS1 227 B1
Redhill BS40 36 D2
Pump Sq BS20 4 D5
Punnet Cl BS27 90 B7
Puppy Cross Ways BA3 94 F5
Puppy La BA3 94 F5
Purcell Wlk BS4 22 D7
Purdue Cl BS22 32 B3
Purewell TA7 136 C4
Puriton Hill TA7 136 C3
Puriton Manor TA7 136 C4
Puriton Pk TA7 136 C4
Puriton Prim Sch TA7 136 C4
Puriton Rd
Pawlett TA6 136 A5
West Huntspill TA9 136 B7
Purlewent Dr BA1 27 C1
Purley Dr TA6 209 D6
Purn La BS24 67 A8
Purn Rd BS24 66 F8
Purn Way BS24 67 B7
Purse Caundle Manor Ho*
DT9 189 D4
Pursey Ave BA16 207 E5
Purving Row BS24 67 C1
Purving Row La BS24 67 C1
Putham La TA24 129 F1
Putsham Hill TA5 133 D5
Putsham Mead TA5 133 D5
Putt's La DT9 188 D8
Puttingthorpe Dr BS22 49 C7
Putts La DT9 175 D1
Puxley Cl BS14 23 E6
Puxton La BS24 33 D3
Puxton Moor La BS24 33 E2
Puxton Rd BS24 33 C2
Pyde La TA10 184 D6
Pye Cnr
Churchill BS25 52 D4
Merriott TA16 195 F6
Somerton TA11 211 D4
Pye La TA20 198 E8
Pyleigh La TA4 151 A1
Pyle La BA22 174 A2
Pyles Thorne TA21 222 F4
Pyles Thorne Cl TA21 222 E5
Pyles Thorne Rd TA21 222 E4
Pylewell La BS25 52 D1
Pyle Well La TA11 174 E8
Pylle Hill BA4 141 A1
Pylle La BA4 141 B1
Pylle Rd BA4 141 A2
Pyncombe La TA4 210 B3
Pyne Point BS21 6 C3
Pynne Cl BS14 23 F5
Pynne Rd BS14 23 F5
Pyracantha Wlk BS14 23 A6
Pyrland Ave TA2 212 F8
Pyrland Pl TA2 213 A8
Pyrland Wlk TA6 208 B4

Q

Quab La
Alston Sutton BS26 88 F3
Wedmore BS28 108 B5
Quab Lane Cl BS28 108 B4
Quaish La BA4 140 C4
Quaker's La TA4 210 C3
Quakers' Friars BS1 227 B3
Quakinghouse La TA4 166 E5
Quantick Gdns TA24 201 B5
Quantock Ave TA6 208 D4
Quantock Cl
Burnham-on-S TA8 104 B7
North Petherton TA6 153 E4
Quantock Ct
Burnham-on-S TA8 104 A5
Ilminster TA19 221 C4
Street BA16 207 B5
Williton TA4 202 D2
Quantock Gr TA4 202 E2
Quantock Ho TA6 153 E4
Quantock Mdw TA6 208 C5
Quantock Par TA6 153 E4
Quantock Rd
Bridgwater TA5, TA6 208 B5
Cannington TA5 135 C1
Portishead BS20 2 B5
Taunton TA2 212 E8
Watchet TA23 202 C6
Wellington TA21 222 D7
Weston-Super-Mare BS23 48 E4
Quantock Rise
Kingston St Mary TA2 168 E8
Pawlett TA6 135 F5
Quantocks BA2 45 A1
Quantock Terr TA6 209 A6
Quantock View
Bishops Lydeard TA4 167 F8
Highbridge TA9 104 D3
Kilve TA5 133 C6
Quantock Way
Bridgwater TA6 208 C5
Kingston St Mary TA2 168 D8
Quaperlake St BA10 215 F7
Quarme La TA24 147 E7
Quarr BA4 205 C6
Quarr Cross SP8 177 E4
Quarr Dr DT9 225 D6
Quarr La DT9 225 D6
Quarr Lane Pk DT9 225 D6
Quarry Batch
Street BA16 207 A5
Walton BA16 156 E7
Quarry Cl
Bath BA2 44 F1
Limpley Stoke BA3 64 D6
Minehead TA24 201 B5
Quarry Cotts BA22 197 F8
Quarry Hay BS40 56 D8
Quarry Hill BA22 175 F4
Quarry La
Blagdon Hill TA3 181 D4
Bradford Abbas DT9 187 E1
Butleigh BA6 157 D3
Combe St Nicholas TA20 193 D6
Kingston St Mary TA2 168 F7
Quarrylands La BS26 88 B4
Quarrymans Ct BA2 45 B1
Quarry Rd
Bath BA2 45 D6
Kingsdon TA11 173 D5
Portishead BS20 2 C4
Sandford BS25 52 A2
Street BA16 207 B4
Washford TA23 131 F4
Quarry Rise BS24 66 F8
Quarry Rock Gdns BA2 45 D4
Quarry Vale Cotts BA2 45 B1
Quarry Way BS48 8 D2
Quartley Hill EX16 164 E4
Quay La TA24 201 A8
Quays Ave BS20 2 E5
Quayside TA6 208 F5
Quay St
Bristol BS1 227 A3
Minehead TA24 201 A8
Quays The BS1 226 C1
Quay W TA24 125 D4
Quebec BA2 44 A6
Queen's Ave
Bristol BS8 226 B3
Portishead BS20 2 C5
Queen's Coll TA1 212 D1
Queen's Coll Jun Sch
TA1 212 D1
Queen's Ct BS8 226 B3
Queen's Down TA3 169 C4
Queen's Dr BA2 45 A2
Queen's Par BA1 228 B3
Queen's Parade Pl BA1 228 B3
Queen's Rd
Bridgwater TA6 208 F2
Bristol, Bishopsworth BS13,
BS41 21 F4
Bristol BS8 226 B3
Clevedon BS21 6 D3
Evercreech BA4 141 E2
Radstock BA3 79 B2
Shepton Mallet BA4 205 A5
Weston-Super-Mare BS23 30 D1
Queen's Terr
Sherborne DT9 225 D6
Wiveliscombe TA4 210 C4
Queen's Way BS22 31 F4
Queen Anne Ct TA24 200 F7
Queen Charlotte St BS1 227 A2
Queen Charlton La BS14 23 E2
Queen Elizabeth's Hospital
Sch BS8 226 B3
Queen Elizabeth Ct
Bridgwater TA6 209 A5
Street BA16 207 C6
Queen Quay BS1 227 A2
Queens Cl TA20 223 B2
Queenscote BS20 2 F5
Queens Cres TA14 185 F5
Queens Dr TA1 168 D1
Queens Gate BS9 5 D5
Queens Gate Terr TA1 213 A3
Queens Gr BA9 161 E2
Queens Par BS1 226 C2
Queens Pl BA2 45 B5
Queen Sq
Bath BA1 228 B2
Bristol BS1 227 A2
North Curry TA3 170 B4
Saltford BS31 25 F3
Queen Square Ave 10
BS1 227 A2
Queen Square Pl BA1 228 B3
Queens Rd
Banwell BS29 51 A3
Bradford Abbas DT9 187 E1
Frome BA11 119 D4
Keynsham BS31 24 D4
Minehead TA24 201 A6
Nailsea BS48 8 D1
Portishead BS20 1 E4
Somerton TA11 211 D4
Street BA16 207 B5
Wellington TA21 222 E4
Queens Row BS27 90 C8
Queens Sq TA9 104 C4
Queen St
Bath BA1 228 B2
Bridgwater TA6 208 F5
Bristol BS2 227 B3
Keinton Mandeville TA11 158 A1
North Petherton TA6 153 F4
Taunton TA1 213 B4
Tintinhull BA22 186 B7
11 Wells BA5 203 D4
Yarlington BA9 175 F8
Queens Terr TA1 213 A3
Queensway
Taunton TA1 212 B1
Yeovil BA20 219 A4
Queens Way BS20 1 E4
Queensway Cl TA9 106 E5
Queensway Ctr BS22 32 B2
Queensway Pl BA20 219 A4
Queenswood Rd TA6 208 C4
Queenwood Ave BA1 28 A1
Quicksilver Rdbt BA20 218 F2
Quickthorn Cl BS14 23 A6
Quiet St BA1 228 B2
Quilter Gr BS4 22 D7
Quirke St TA24 200 F7

R

Raby Mews BA2 45 B7
Raby Pl BA2 45 B7
Rackclose Gdns TA20 223 A4
Rackclose Ho TA20 223 A4
Rackclose Pk TA20 223 B4
Rackfield TA21 222 A5
Rackfield Pl BA2 44 B6
Rackhay BS1 227 A2
Rackley La
Buckland St Mary TA20 182 B1
Compton Bishop BS26 69 B2
Rackstile TA20 223 A7
Rackvernal Ct BA3 78 B1
Rackvernal Rd BA3 78 B1
Raddon Cl BA4 205 B6
Radford Hill
Camerton BA2, BA3 78 C7
Timsbury BA2 60 C1
Radigan La TA3, TA19 183 C5
Radlet Cl TA2 213 B7
Radnidge La EX16 162 D4
Radstock & District Mus* BA3 78 F2
Radstock Rd BA3 78 C2
Ragged Dro BA6 158 A7
Rag Hill BA3 79 D5
Rag La
Babcary BA22 174 B6
Yarcombe EX14 192 D2
Raglan's Cross TA4 202 F2
Raglan Cl
Bridgwater TA6 209 D7
Chilcompton BA3 96 C4
Raglan Ct 4 TA2 212 F6
Ragland La BA1 28 A2
Ragland St BA1 28 A2
Raglan La BS40 37 E7
Raglan Pl 20 BS23 30 C1
Raglan Terr
Bath BA1 28 A2
Yeovil BA21 218 F7
Raglan Wlk BS31 24 D4
Railford Hill BA11 118 B3
Railway Arches BS2 227 C2
Railway Cotts BA11 143 C3
Railway La BA2 62 D1
Railway Pl BA1 228 C1
Railway St
Bath BA1 228 C1
Taunton TA2 212 F6
Railway Terr BA2 79 E4
Railway View Pl BA3 78 B2
Rainbow La TA3 191 C7
Rainham Ct 2 BS23 30 C1
Rains Batch BS40 72 E6
Raisey La TA20 193 C7
Raleigh Cl
Bridgwater TA6 209 C5
Saltford BS31 25 D2
Raleigh Ct
Sherborne DT9 225 E4
3 Weston-Super-Mare BS23 48 E5
Raleigh Ho TA6 209 C5
Raleigh Rd DT10 190 B4
Raleigh Rise BS20 2 B5
Raliegh Pl DT9 225 D2
Ralph Allen Dr BA2 45 B3
Ralph Allen Sch BA2 45 E2
Ralston Ct BA9 216 C4
Rambler Way TA6 208 E6
Ramon Ave TA23 202 D7
Ramsay Cl BS22 31 E4
Ramsay Way TA8 104 C8
Ramscombe Forest Wlks* TA5 151 E8
Ramscombe La BA1 28 F6
Ramsey La TA21 179 F8
Ramshorn Cl TA1 212 C2
Ramshorn Gn TA1 212 D2
Ramshorn Pl TA1 212 D3
Ranchways BS20 1 F4
Randall Rd BS8 226 B2
Randolph Ave BS13 22 B5
Randolph Cl BS13 22 B5
Randolph Rd BA11 119 F4
Ranger Rd BA6 206 C3
Rangoon Rd TA23 202 E6
Rankers La BS39 41 C5
Rank The
Coxley BA5 139 F6
Maiden Bradley BA12 144 C2
Vobster BA3 117 D6
Ranscombe Ave BS22 31 D2
Ransford BS21 6 B1
Raphael Ct BS1 227 B1
Raps Cl TA1 213 E5
Raps Gn TA1 213 E5
Rashwood La BA11 118 B6
Ratleigh La DT9 188 A3
Rattigan Cl TA8 104 C6
Rattle Row TA24 131 B4
Raven Cl BS22 31 E1
Raven Ct BS9 5 F8
Ravenhead Dr BS14 23 B8
Ravensmead TA20 223 C5
Ravenswood Special Sch BS48 8 D3
Ravensworth Terr TA8 104 B7
Rawle's Bldgs TA24 124 A3
Rawlings La BS26 88 E2
Rawlins Ave BS22 32 A5
Rayens Cl BS41 10 F1
Rayens Cross Rd BS41 10 F1
Rayleigh Rd BS9 5 E7
Raymar Flats TA19 221 A4
Raymond St TA2 212 E6
Raymore Rise BS41 10 F1
Rayneswood BS23 48 F8
Read Mead BA6 206 E3
Reakes Cl BA5 203 C4
Rebels Way BA6 206 D5
Reckleford BA20, BA21 219 B5
Reckleford Inf Sch BA21 219 C5
Rector's Cl TA8 65 F3
Rector's Way BS23 48 F6
Rectory Cl
Farmborough BA2 60 A6
6 North Petherton TA6 153 E3
Staplegrove TA2 212 C8
Wraxall BS48 9 A2
Rectory Ct TA20 193 D6
Rectory Dr
Burnham-on-S TA8 104 B8
Staplegrove TA2 212 C7
Yatton BS49 34 C7
Rectory Farm Cl BA22 174 F3
Rectory Gdns TA20 193 D6
Rectory Hill
Chapel Allerton BS26 88 D2
Pitney TA10 172 C7
South Cadbury BA22 175 C3
Rectory La
Bleadon BS24 67 C6
Compton Martin BS40 74 B6
Hardington Mandeville BA22 197 A6
Horsington BA8 176 E2
Norton Sub Hamdon TA14 185 F2
Shalford BA9 216 E6
Sparkford BA22 175 A3
Timsbury BA2 60 B2
Rectory Lawn TA8 104 B8
Rectory Pl TA8 104 C8
Rectory Rd
Ashbrittle TA21 178 F8
Burnham-on-S TA8 104 B8
Easton-in-G BS20 4 B3
Norton Fitzwarren TA2 168 B5
Shepton Mallet BA4 205 B6
Staplegrove TA2 212 C8
Rectory Way
Lympsham BS24 66 F2
Yatton BS49 34 C7
Recurium Lodge BS26 70 B2
Redacre BS40 36 D3
Red Barn La TA20 193 D4
Redcliff Backs BS1 227 B2
Redcliffe Cl BS20 1 E3
Redcliffe Par E BS1 227 A1
Redcliffe Par W BS1 227 A1
Redcliffe St BS27 90 C7
Redcliffe Way BS1 227 B1
Redcliff Hill BS1 227 B1
Redcliff Mead La BS1 227 B1
Redcliff St BS1 227 B2
Red Cotts
Blagdon BS40 54 D6
Corsley Heath BA12 144 E8
Redcroft BS40 36 D3
Redcross Mews 14 BS2 227 C3
Redcross St BS2 227 C3
Redding Pit La BS40 37 E4
Reddings The BS40 74 B7
Redfield Gr BA3 97 A8
Redfield Rd BA3 97 A8
Redford Cres BS13 21 F3
Redford Wlk BS13 21 F3
Redgate Pk TA18 224 C8
Redgates Rd TA24 200 E7
Redgate St TA6 209 B4
Red Hill
Peasedown St John BA2 60 E1
Redhill BS40 36 D2
West Monkton TA2 169 B7
Redhill La BA3 95 A2
Red Hill La TA7 155 E7
Redhole La DT9 225 D8
Red House La BS9 5 E6
Red House Rd TA9 86 D5
Red La
Churchinford TA3 191 F7
Hemyock EX15 180 E3
Seaborough DT8 195 E1
Staplehay TA3 181 E8
Redlake Dr TA1 213 D3
Redland Ave BS20 3 F6
Redland La TA3 183 C8
Redland Pk BA2 43 F6
Redlands La TA7 137 C2
Redlands Terr BA3 96 F8
Redland Terr BA11 119 F3
Red Lion Ct
3 Crewkerne TA18 224 C6
Somerton TA11 211 E4
Red Lodge Bsns Pk BS24 32 D1
Redlynch Cross BA10 160 E4
Redlynch La BS31 24 D2
Redmans Hill BS28 107 E4
Redpoll Dr BS20 3 A6
Red Post
Chard TA20 193 D3
Isle Abbotts TA3 183 E7
Porlock TA24 124 B3
Red Post Cross TA11 173 D4
Red Post Ct BA2 79 B7
Red Rd
Berrow TA8 85 A7
Brean TA8 66 A2
Redshard La BS40 53 B7
Redstart Prim Sch The TA20 223 C5
Redstart Rd TA20 223 C6
Redway TA24 124 A3
Red Way The BA12 144 F6
Redwing Dr BS22 31 F1
Red Wing Rd DT9 217 C2
Redwood Cl
Nailsea BS48 9 A2
Radstock BA3 97 E8
Redwood Ho BS13 22 D3
Redwood La BS48 20 C7
Redwood Rd BA21 219 E8
Reed Cl
Bridgwater TA6 208 F2
Chard TA20 223 D6
Watchet TA23 202 D6
Reedley Rd BS9 5 F5
Reedmoor Gdns TA6 208 E7
Reeds Dr TA7 136 F4
Reed Way BS22 32 C3
Rees Way BS26 87 E7
Reeves Cl BS27 90 F2
Regal Rd BA4 205 B6
Regal Way 24 BA4 205 B6
Regency Cl TA8 85 A2
Regency Ct BA5 203 C4
Regency Wlk BA11 119 E4
Regent Ct BA22 173 E2
Regent Gn TA4 167 F1
Regent Mews TA20 223 C3
Regent St
Bradford On Tone TA4 167 F1
Bristol BS8 226 A2
Burnham-on-S TA8 104 A7
Weston-Super-Mare BS23 48 E7
Regents The
Cotford St Luke TA4 167 E6
Keynsham BS31 24 F6
4 Yeovil BA21 218 C6
Regents Way TA24 200 E6
Regent Way TA6 209 A2
Regil La BS40 38 A6
Regil Rd BS40 37 F3
Regina The BA1 228 B3
Reid Ct BA5 203 B4
Remalard Ct BA7 214 B5
Rendcomb Cl BS22 31 B2
Rennison Ct BS23 48 E4
Reservoir La BA5 203 C6
Retford Ho BA2 45 E5
Retreat Cvn Pk The TA8 85 A2
Retreat The
Foxcote BA3 79 E3
Frome BA11 120 B4
Taunton TA2 168 F6
Weston-Super-Mare BS23 30 C1
Reubens Ct BS22 31 F3
Rex's La
Barwick BA22 197 F8
Yeovil BA22 219 C1
Rex Rd BA22 186 C2
Rexton La TA4 150 F5
Reynald's Way
Butleigh BA6 157 C4
Street BA16 207 D1
Reynolds TA21 166 F2
Reynolds Cl BS31 25 A5
Rhode Cl BS31 25 A3
Rhode La TA6 208 E2
Rhodes Cl TA2 212 C7
Rhodyate BS40 54 D2
Rhodyate Hill BS49 34 F6
Rhodyate La BS49 35 A7
Rhodyate The BS29 51 C1
Rhydderch Way TA18 224 C5
Rhyll Gate Cross TA22 162 E7
Rhyne Terr BS23 48 D2
Rhyne View BS48 8 B1
Rich's Farmhouse Cider Farm* TA9 105 D3
Richard Beadon Cl TA4 210 B4
Richard Huish Coll TA1 213 A2
Richards Cl
Wellington TA21 222 C8
Weston-Super-Mare BS22 32 B4
Richards Cres TA2 169 B6
Richmond Cl
Bath BA1 27 F1
Bridgwater TA6 208 F7
Keynsham BS31 24 D4
Minehead TA24 200 E6
Portishead BS20 2 E5
Sampford Peverell EX16 178 D1
Sherborne DT9 225 C3
Richmond Ct BA22 173 E2
Richmond Gn
Nailsea BS48 8 F1
Sherborne DT9 225 C4
Taunton TA1 212 D5
Richmond Hill
Bath BA1 27 F1
Bristol BS8 226 B3
Richmond Hill Ave BS8 226 B3
Richmond Ho
Crewkerne TA18 224 C6
9 Shepton Mallet BA4 205 B6
Yeovil BA20 219 A4
Richmond Hts
Bath BA1 27 F2
Bristol BS8 226 B3
Richmond La
Bath BA1 27 F1
Bristol BS8 226 B3
Richmond Mews BS8 226 A3
Richmond Park Rd BS8 226 A3
Richmond Pk TA1 212 C4
Richmond Pl BA1 27 F1
Richmond Rd
Bath BA1 27 F1
2 Frome BA11 119 E3
Sherborne DT9 225 C3
Taunton TA1 212 D5
Yeovil BA20 219 A4
Richmond St BS23 48 D7
Richmond Terr BS8 226 A3
Richmond Villas BA6 206 E4
Richmond Way BA21 218 C6
Ricketts La BS22 32 A2
Rickford La BS40 54 A3
Rickford Rd BS48 8 F1
Rickford Rise BS40 54 A3
Rickhayes BA9 216 B4
Rickhay Rise TA18 196 B8
Ricklands The BS40 38 A6
Ricksey Cl TA11 211 B3
Ricksey La TA11 211 B3
Ricksmead Dro TA7 155 B2
Rickyard Rd BS40 35 E2
Ridge Cl BS20 2 A4
Ridge Cres BS40 74 E6
Ridge Green Cl BA2 62 D8
Ridge Highway TA4 166 A3
Ridge Hill TA4 210 D5
Ridge La
Corton Denham DT9 175 D1
East Chinnock BA22 196 F8
East Coker BA22 197 A7
Pitcombe BA7, BA10 215 A2
Ridge BS40 74 D5
Shepton Mallet BA4 205 B3
Ridgemead BA20 218 D2
Ridgemeade BS14 23 B4
Ridgemount Gdns BS14 23 B5
Ridge Rd
Croscombe BA4, BA5 204 D5
West Anstey TA22 162 D7
Ridge The
Bristol BS11 4 E7
Porlock TA24 124 B3
Poyntington DT9 188 F7
Yatton BS49 34 B8
Ridgeview BS41 11 B2
Ridgeview Ho BS20 2 E3
Ridgeway
Ashcott TA7 156 B8
Nailsea BS48 8 C1
Nunney BA11 143 C8
Sherborne DT9 225 B3
Ridgeway Ave BS23 48 E6
Ridgeway Cl BS40 74 E6
Ridgeway Ct BS14 23 C5
Ridgeway Gdns
Bristol BS14 23 C5
Glastonbury BA6 206 F5
Ridgeway La
Bristol BS14 23 B5
Moorlinch TA7 155 F7
North Cadbury BA22 175 D6
Nunney BA11 143 C8
Shillingford EX16 164 D2
Stolford TA5 134 E8
Ridgeway Rd BS41 11 A2
Ridgeway The BS22 31 B2
Ridgewood BS9 5 D3
Ridgewood Cross EX15 191 B8
Ridgewood La EX15 191 A8
Ridgway TA18 196 B8
Ridgway Cross EX36 145 K1
Ridings The BS13 21 E4
Ridley Cnr TA10 171 C5
Ridley Hill TA10 171 E8
Riec-Sur-Belon Way TA19 221 A4
Rigg La DT9 187 F5
Rigg Lane Cotts DT9 187 F5
Riggles Cross EX14 191 D3
Rimpton Hill BA22 188 A7
Rimpton Rd BA22 174 F1
Ringdown La EX15 180 F2
Ringolds Way BA16 207 B4
Ringspit La BS14, BS39 40 E8
Ring St DT10 190 B4
Ringstone TA9 136 B8
Ringswell Gdns BA1 28 B1
Ringwell BA2 81 E4
Ringwell Hill TA12 185 D4
Ringwell La BA2 81 E4
Ringwood Gr BS23 31 A1
Ringwood Rd
Bath BA2 44 C5
Bridgwater TA6 209 A2
Riphay Cross TA22 163 E3
Rippleside BS20 2 C5
Rippleside Rd BS21 6 E5
Ripple The BS21 8 D4
Risdale Rd BS3 11 F1
Risdon Rd TA23 202 C6
Risedale Cl TA6 208 C5
Risedale Rd BS25 70 A8
Risemoor Rd TA6 208 E2
Ritchie Rd BA22 218 A5
Rivendell BS22 32 A4
Riverbed Ho TA9 104 D3
River Dro TA7 155 E4
River La TA7 209 E1
Riverland Dr BS13 21 F5
Riverleaze
Bristol BS9 5 C5
Portishead BS20 1 F6
River Mead BS21 16 D8
River Pl BA2 44 B6
River Rd
East Huntspill TA7 137 B8
Mark TA9 106 D1
River Rd *continued*
Pawlett TA6 135 F5
Portbury BS20 3 F8
Riversgate BS1 227 C2
Riverside
Banwell BS24, BS29 51 B5
Bridgwater TA6 208 F6
Burrowbridge TA7 154 F1
Combwich TA5 135 C5
Dinder BA5 140 D7
Horton TA19 183 C2
Meare BA5 138 F5
Taunton TA1 212 E4
Wellington TA21 222 B7
Riverside Cl
Bristol BS11 4 F5
Clevedon BS21 6 B1
Midsomer Norton BA3 96 F7
Weston-Super-Mare BS22 32 C3
Riverside Cotts BA3 79 A2
Riverside Ct BA2 228 B1
Riverside Gdns
Bath BA1 228 B2
Dunster TA24 201 E3
Midsomer Norton BA3 96 F7
Riverside Pl 2 TA1 212 F4
Riverside Rd
Bath BA2 228 B2
Midsomer Norton BA3 96 F7
Riverside Row TA24 124 A3
Riverside Terr BA11 119 F5
Riverside Wlk BA3 96 F7
Rivers Rd
Bath BA1 228 C4
Yeovil BA21 219 D8
Rivers Reach BA11 120 A5
Rivers St BA1 228 B3
Rivers Street Mews BA1 228 B3
River St BS2 227 C3
River Street Pl 5 BA1 228 B3
River Terr BS31 24 F5
Riverton Rd TA7 136 B4
River View
Bridgwater TA6 208 F6
Combwich TA5 135 B5
Exebridge TA22 163 F3
Riverway BS48 8 F3
River Wlk BS22 32 D2
Roachill Cross EX36 162 C1
Road Hill
Alcombe SN13 29 E8
Langford Budville TA4 166 B3
Roath Rd BS20 2 D5
Robbins Cl SN14 13 F8
Robert Blake Science Coll TA6 208 F3
Robert Ct BS8 11 D7
Roberts Dr TA6 209 A2
Roberts Rd TA2 168 A6
Robert St TA4 202 D2
Robin Cl
Bristol BS14 23 D6
Midsomer Norton BA3 97 B8
Taunton TA1 212 B4
Weston-Super-Mare BS22 49 E8
Robin Dr BS24 49 E2
Robinia Wlk BS14 23 A7
Robin La BS21 6 D5
Robins Ct
Chard TA20 223 C5
Frome BA11 119 D5
Robins Dr
Bridgwater TA6 209 A6
Burtle TA7 137 D6
Robins La
Burtle TA7 137 C6
Frome BA11 119 D5
Shepton Beauchamp TA19 184 E4
Robinson Cl BS48 19 A5
Robinson Hts DT10 190 B4
Robinson Way BS48 19 A5
Rob-Lynne Ct BS25 69 F8
Roche Cl BA21 218 C7
Rochester Cl BS24 49 A1
Rochester Rd TA2 213 A8
Rochfort Ct BA1 45 B8
Rock's Dro BA16 138 F3
Rock Ave BS48 8 C2
Rock Cotts BS20 4 E4
Rockeries Dr BS25 69 F8
Rockeries The BS25 69 F8
Rocketts Cl TA3 169 D4
Rocketts Cotts TA3 169 C4
Rockfield Cotts TA21 179 F7
Rock Hall Cotts BA2 45 B1
Rockhall Ho 10 BS23 30 C1
Rock Hall Ho BA2 45 B1
Rock Hall La BA2 45 B1
Rock Hill TA3 170 C1
Rockhill Est BS31 24 F4
Rockingham Gdns BS11 5 A8
Rockingham Gr BS23 31 A1
Rock La
Bath BA2 45 B1
Exford TA24 128 D1
West Bagborough TA4 151 E5
Rockleaze
Bristol BS9 5 E2
Evercreech BA4 141 E2
Rockleaze Ave BS9 5 E3
Rockleaze Ct BS9 5 E3
Rockleaze Mans 12 BS23 30 C1
Rockleaze Rd BS9 5 E3
Rockliffe Ave BA2 45 B8
Rockliffe Rd BA2 45 B8
Rock Rd
Chilcompton BA3 96 D2
Keynsham BS31 24 E5

Roc–St G 265

Rock Rd *continued*
Midsomer Norton BA3 78 B2
Yatton BS49 34 C7
Rocks La BS40 20 E1
Rocks St BA5 204 C7
Rocks The BA4 142 B7
Rock Terr BA3 116 F6
Rockway TA3 170 C1
Rockwell Gate TA21 222 B5
Rockwell Green CE Prim Sch TA21 222 B5
Rocky Hill TA11 173 D5
Rocky La TA23 131 E2
Rodber Cl BA9 216 B4
Rodber Gdns BA9 216 B4
Roddenbury Cl BA11 120 B5
Roddenbury View BA12 144 D8
Rodden Rd BA11 120 A5
Rode Hill
Rode BA11 82 E1
Southwick BA11 83 A1
Rode Methodist Fst Sch BA11 101 E8
Rodfords Mead BS14 23 A7
Rodhuish Cross TA24 131 B3
Rodhuish Hill La TA24 131 A3
Rod La TA19 183 F4
Rodmead La BA5 110 E4
Rodmead Wlk BS13 22 A4
Rodmoor Rd BS20 2 D6
Rodmore Cres BA4 141 E1
Rodmore Rd BA4 141 E1
Rodney BS24 49 A2
Rodney Ct BA22 218 A5
Rodney Ho BA2 44 A6
Rodney Pl BS8 226 A3
Rodney Rd
Backwell BS48 19 A6
Saltford BS31 25 E2
Rodney Stoke National Nature Reserve* BS27 91 B2
Rodway TA5 135 B3
Rodwell La TA13 184 E5
Roe Ave BA22 218 A5
Roebuck Cl BS22 32 B4
Roebuck Gate La TA4 151 B6
Roe Cl TA6 209 D4
Roe La BA22 188 B8
Roemead La BA3 114 C5
Roemead Rd BA3 114 C4
Rogers Cl
Buckland Dinham BA11 100 A3
Clutton BS39 58 E3
North Petherton TA6 153 F3
Rogers Wlk TA4 167 E6
Roland Cl TA1 212 C2
Roman Baths The* BA1 228 C2
Roman Ct BA21 219 D6
Roman Farm Rd BS4 22 E7
Roman Ho BA1 228 C4
Roman La TA6 208 C3
Roman Rd
Bath BA1 228 C3
Bleadon BS24 67 C8
Sandford BS25 51 F4
Taunton TA1 213 C5
Roman Villas BA4 205 E4
Roman Way
Bristol BS9 5 C4
Coleford BA3 116 F7
Paulton BS39 77 C6
Peasedown St John BA2 79 E7
Watchet TA23 202 C7
Roman Way The BA6 206 C3
Romney Mead TA1 213 D4
Romsey Rd BA21 219 E8
Ron Jones Ho 3 BS1 227 B4
Rook's Meade La TA19 184 E1
Rookery Cl
Puriton TA7 136 C4
Rooks Bridge BS26 87 A6
Weston-Super-Mare BS22 31 E3
Rookery La
Croscombe BA5 204 B7
Drimpton DT8 199 F6
Rookery Terr TA21 222 C5
Rookery The BA5 140 D7
Rookery Way BS14 22 F4
Rook La BA11 119 F4
Rooksbridge Rd BS24, BS26 87 B6
Rooksbridge Wlk BA2 44 B5
Rooks La BA11 120 E7
Room Hill Rd TA24 146 D7
Roper's La BS40 35 E3
Rope Walk Ho 23 BS2 227 C3
Ropewalk The TA20 223 B5
Rope Wk TA24 201 B7
Rope Wlk
Backwell BS48 19 A5
Bridgwater TA6 209 A5
Coleford BA3 116 E8
Evercreech BA4 141 E1
14 Martock TA12 185 E6
Wellington TA21 222 C4
Rope Wlk The TA23 202 C7
Roping Rd BA21 219 B6
Rosary Dr TA6 208 B4
Rosebank Rd TA4 167 A4
Roseberry Cotts BA3 117 A7
Roseberry Pl BA2 44 C6
Roseberry Rd BA2 44 C6
Roseberry Terr TA1 212 D5
Rosebery Ave
Bridgwater TA6 209 B5
Yeovil BA21 219 D6
Rosebery St TA2 212 E7
Rosebery Terr BS8 226 B2
Rose Cotts
Taunton TA1 213 B3
Weston-Super-Mare BS22 32 C2
Rose & Crown Cotts BA3 116 F6
Rose Ct
Keinton Mandeville TA11 158 A1
Shepton Mallet BA4 205 B6
Rosedale Ave BS23 49 A7
Rose Dale Wlk BA11 119 F6
Rose Gdns BS22 32 B4
Rose Hill
Bath BA1 28 C3
Spaxton TA5 152 F2
Rose La
Crewkerne, Misterton TA18 196 B3
Crewkerne TA18 224 B6
Purtington TA20 195 A3
Roseland Cl BA1 28 C3
Roselyn Cres DT9 189 A1
Rosemary Cres BS20 2 F5
Rosemary La
Dulverton TA22 163 D6
Freshford BA3 64 B4
Rosemarylane Cross EX15 180 D1
Rosemary St DT9 217 C2
Rose Meare Gdns BS13 21 E7
Rose Mills Ind Est TA19 183 E2
Rosemont Terr BS8 226 A2
Rosemount La BA2 45 B4
Rosemount Rd BS48 20 B8
Roseneath Ave TA8 84 F4
Rose Terr
Bath BA2 45 C2
Bristol BS8 226 B3
Rose Tree Paddock TA8 84 F4
Rosette Cotts TA12 185 B7
Rosevean Cl TA6 209 D7
Rose Villas TA5 135 B2
Rosewarn Cl BA2 44 A4
Rosewell Ct BA1 228 B2
Rosewood Ave TA8 104 C6
Rosewood Cl TA8 104 C7
Rosewood Dr TA8 104 C6
Roslyn Ave BS22 31 C1
Rossendale Cl BS22 31 F3
Rosshayne La EX14 192 C2
Rossiter's Hill BA11 119 F3
Rossiter's Rd BA11 119 E3
Rossiter Grange 5 BS13 21 F4
Rossiter Rd BA2 228 C1
Rosslyn Cl 1 BA1 44 B7
Rosslyn Rd BA1 44 B7
Rotcombe La BS39 59 D2
Rotcombe Vale BS39 59 D2
Rotton Row TA4 210 C4
Roughmoor TA4 202 E4
Roughmoor Cl TA1 212 D5
Roughmoor Cotts TA1 212 D5
Roughmoor Cres TA1 212 D5
Roughmoor La BA5 110 C7
Roundhill Gr BA2 44 B3
Roundhill Pk BA2 44 A4
Roundmoor Cl BS31 25 D3
Roundmoor Gdns BS14 23 D7
Roundoak Gdns TA21 167 C2
Round Oak Gr BS27 90 A8
Round Oak Rd BS27 90 A8
Round Pool La TA4 151 B7
Roundwell Cl BA4 204 F6
Roundwell St TA13 220 C4
Rowacres
Bath BA2 44 B3
Bristol BS14 22 F6
Rowan Cl
Nailsea BS48 9 A2
Puriton TA7 136 C4
Wincanton BA9 216 D2
Rowan Ct
Frome BA11 120 B7
Radstock BA3 78 E1
Rowan Dr
Berrow TA8 84 F5
Taunton TA1 213 D1
Rowan Ho BS13 22 D4
Rowan Pl BS24 32 B1
Rowans Cl TA6 209 C6
Rowans The BS20 2 B4
Rowan Way
Churchill BS40 53 A5
Yeovil BA20 218 F3
Rowan Wlk BS31 24 C4
Rowbarrow Hill
Rimpton DT9 188 A7
Trent DT9 187 F6
Rowbarton Cl TA2 212 F7
Rowberrow BS14 22 F7
Rowberrow La BS25 70 F8
Rowberrow Way BS48 8 E1
Rowcliffe Cotts TA21 178 F8
Rowdells Orch TA19 184 D1
Rowden Mill La DT10 189 F1
Rowdens Rd BA5 203 D3
Rowditch La TA5 133 D5
Rowe's Hill BA12 144 E4
Rowe Cl TA21 222 A4
Row La
Keinton Mandeville TA11 158 A1
Laverton BA2 100 D8
Rowlands Cl BA1 29 B2
Rowlands Rise TA7 136 C4
Rowley Rd BA6 206 E5
Rowls La BA9 177 E6
Rowmarsh La TA10 172 D5
Rownham Cl BS3 11 E4
Rownham Ct BS8 226 A1
Rownham Hill BS8 11 E6
Rownham Mead BS8 226 A1
Row Of Ashes La BS40 36 F4
Rows La EX16 164 A1
Rows The BS22 31 E2
Row The
Hambridge TA10 184 D8
Langport TA10 172 B3
Royal Ave BA1 228 B3
Royal Cl BA21 219 C6
Royal Cres
Bath BA1 228 A3
Weston-Super-Mare BS23 48 D8
Royal Ct BS23 48 D4
Royal Fort Rd BS2, BS8 226 C3
Royal High Sch The BA1 228 B4
Royal Ho 4 BA4 205 B6
Royal Hospl for Sick Children BS2 226 C3
Royal National Hospl for Rheumatic Diseases BA1 228 B2
Royal Par
Bristol BS8 226 B3
Weston-Super-Mare BS23 48 D8
Royal Park Mews BS8 226 A3
Royal Photographic Society* BA1 228 B3
Royal Pk BS8 226 A3
Royal Portbury Dock Rd BS20 3 E5
Royal Prom BS8 226 B3
Royal Sands BS23 48 D4
Royal Sch The BA1 27 F2
Royal United Hospl BA1 44 B8
Royal West of England Acad BS8 226 B3
Royal York Cres BS8 11 F6
Royal York Ho 7 BS8 226 A2
Royal York Mews 6 BS8 226 A2
Royal York Villas BS8 226 A2
Royces La TA19 184 C5
Roynon Way BS27 90 B7
Royston Lodge BS23 48 D6
Royston Rd TA3 192 A7
Rozel Ho 14 BS23 30 C1
Rubbery La TA11 158 D1
Rubens Cl BS31 25 A5
Ruborough Rd TA6 209 C4
Ruckley Ford BA3 80 A2
Ruddock Cl BA22 197 B8
Ruddock Way BA22 197 B8
Ruddymead BS21 6 D2
Rudge Hill BA11 102 D5
Rudge La
Beckington BA11 102 B6
Standerwick BA11 102 D3
Rudge Rd BA11 102 B2
Rudgeway Rd BS39 77 E4
Rudgewood Cl BS13 22 D4
Rudgleigh Ave BS20 4 C4
Rudgleigh Rd BS20 4 C4
Rudhall Gn BS22 32 B3
Rudmore Pk BA1 44 A7
Rue La
Alweston DT9 189 C2
Hambridge TA3 184 B7
Ruett La BS39 77 B4
Rugg's Dro
Chedzoy TA7 154 D7
West Huntspill TA9 136 B7
Rugg's Hill TA22 148 E2
Rughill BS28 108 D8
Rugosa Dr TA8 84 F4
Ruishton CE Prim Sch TA3 169 C3
Ruishton La TA3 169 C3
Ruishton Lane Cotts TA3 169 C3
Runnymede Rd BA21 219 D8
Rupert St
Bristol BS1 227 A3
Taunton TA2 212 E6
Rusham BS13 21 F4
Rush Ash La BA3 116 E8
Rushgrove Gdns BS39 57 C4
Rush Hill
Bath BA2 44 C2
Farrington Gurney BS39 76 F3
Rush Hill La BS28 107 F3
Rushmoor BS21 6 A1
Rushmoor Gr BS48 19 A5
Rushmoor La BS48 19 A5
Rushway BS40 53 F4
Ruskin Cl TA1 213 C4
Ruskin Rd BA3 78 C1
Ruskway La TA10 184 C6
Russell's TA4 210 C4
Russell's Barton BA11 143 B8
Russell Cl BS40 38 A6
Russell Pl
Bridgwater TA6 208 F6
Milborne Port DT9 217 C3
Russell Pope Ave TA20 223 D2
Russell Rd
Clevedon BS21 6 C3
Locking BS24 50 C6
Russell St BA1 228 B3
Russets The BS20 2 F4
Russett Cl BS48 19 B6
Russett Gr BS48 18 C8
Russett Rd
Street BA16 207 C4
Taunton TA1 213 E5
Russet Way
Peasedown St John BA2 79 D7
Yeovil BA20 218 D2
Russ La BS21 16 E4
Russ St BS2 227 C2
Rusty Well BA20 218 F3
Rusty Well Pk BA20 218 F3
Ruthven Rd BS4 22 E8
Rutland Cl BS22 49 C8
Rutter's La TA19 221 B4
Ryalls Ct BA21 219 C5
Ryburn Cl TA1 213 D3
Rydal Ave BS24 50 A4
Rydal Rd BS23 48 F4
Rydon Cres TA5 135 C2
Rydon La
Lopen TA13 185 A1
South Petherton TA13 220 A5
Taunton TA2 212 F8
Rye TA7 136 C4
Rye Cl BS13 21 E6
Ryecroft Ave BS22 31 E2
Ryecroft Rise BS41 11 B1
Ryefields Cl BA22 197 B8
Rye Gdns BA20 218 D2
Rye La TA7 155 C2
Rylands Farm Ind Est TA21 222 B3
Ryepool TA4 167 F8
Ryesland Way TA3 169 D4
Rye Water La DT2 197 A1
Rylands BA11 101 E4
Rylands Cl TA4 202 D2
Rylestone Gr BS9 5 F5
Rysdale Rd BS9 5 F6

S

Sabrina Way BS9 5 C4
Sackmore Gn DT10 190 F6
Sackmore La DT10 190 F5
Saco Ho BS1 227 B2
Sacred Heart Prep Sch BS40 39 A3
Sadborow La TA20 199 B4
Sadborow Pound TA20 199 B5
Sadbury Cl BS22 32 B4
Sadler St BA5 203 D4
Sadlier Cl BS11 5 A8
Saffron Cl TA1 168 F1
Saffron Ct
Bath BA1 228 C4
Sherborne DT9 225 E4
Saffron Ho 10 BS23 48 E8
Saffrons The 7 BS22 32 B4
Sage's La BA3 94 D6
Sage Cl BS20 1 E4
Sainsbury Cl TA24 200 D7
Sainsbury Rd TA24 200 D7
St Agnes Cl BS48 9 A1
St Albans Pl TA2 212 F8
St Aldhelm's CE Prim Sch BA4 141 E6
St Aldhelm's Cl BA11 119 D4
St Aldhelm's Rd DT9 225 D6
St Aldhelms Ct BA11 119 D4
St Algars Yd BA11 144 A4
St Andrew's CE Jun Sch
Burnham-on-S TA8 104 B7
Congresbury BS49 34 C4
St Andrew's CE Prim Sch
Bath BA1 228 B4
Taunton TA2 212 F6
St Andrew's CE Sch EX13 198 A7
St Andrew's Cl
Congresbury BS49 34 C4
Curry Rivel TA10 171 D4
High Ham TA10 156 A2
St Andrew's Ct BA5 203 F5
St Andrew's Dr BS21 6 A2
St Andrew's Par 1 BS23 48 F4
St Andrew's Rd
Burnham-on-S TA8 104 B7
Stogursey TA5 134 C5
6 Taunton TA2 212 F6
St Andrew's Terr BA1 228 B3
St Andrews Cl
Castle Cary BA7 214 B7
Nailsea BS48 9 A1
Weston-Super-Mare BS22 31 F3
St Andrews Ct TA24 200 F7
St Andrews Dr EX13 198 A2
St Andrews La TA24 200 F7
St Andrews Mews 4 BA5 203 C3
St Andrews Pk BA5 203 D3
St Andrews Rd
Backwell BS48 19 B5
Cheddar BS27 90 C7
Yeovil BA20 218 F5
St Andrew St BA5 203 E4
St Andrews View TA2 212 F6
St Andrews Wlk 5 BA5 203 C3
St Ann's Cl TA2 212 E7
St Ann's Dr TA8 85 A1
St Ann's Pl BA1 228 B2
St Ann's Way BA2 45 C6
St Anne's Ave BS31 24 D6
St Anne's CE Prim Sch BS24 33 B5
St Anne's Cl BA6 158 A5
St Anne's Ct BS31 24 D6
St Anne's Gdns BA21 218 E6
St Anthony's Cl BA3 78 A2
St Antonys Sq 1 DT9 225 D3
St Aubyn's Ave BS23 48 D2
St Audries Cl TA5 134 C6
St Audries Ct TA23 202 B7
St Augustine's Par BS1 227 A2
St Augustine's Pl 1 BS1 227 A2
St Augustine of Canterbury Sch The TA2 213 A7
St Augustines Ct 1 TA1 213 A4
St Augustine St TA1 213 A4
St Austell Cl BS48 19 A8
St Austell Rd BS22 49 B8
St Barnabas CE Prim Sch BS20 2 B5
St Barnabas Cl BA3 78 B3
St Bartholomew's CE Fst Sch TA18 224 D5
St Benedict's CE Jun Sch BA6 206 D4
St Benedict's Cl BA6 206 D4
St Benedict's RC Prim Sch BA3 97 C7
St Bernadette RC Prim Sch BS14 23 B6
St Bernadette RC Sch BS14 23 B6
St Bernard's RC Prim Sch BS11 4 E6
St Bernard's Rd BS11 4 E6
St Brandon's Sch BS21 6 B3
St Brides Cl BA6 206 D5
St Bridges Cl BS22 31 A6
St Bridges Ct BS22 31 A6
St Bridget's Cl TA8 65 F5
St Cadoc Ho BS31 24 F5
St Catherine's Cl BA2 45 C6
St Catherine's Cres DT9 225 B3
St Catherine's Ct 10 BA11 119 E5
St Catherine's Mead BS20 4 D3
St Catherine's Way DT9 225 B3
St Catherines Hill BA10 215 E6
St Chad's Ave BA3 78 A1
St Chad's Gn BA3 97 A8
St Charles Cl BA3 78 A2
St Christopher's Ct BS21 6 C5
St Christopher's Way TA8 85 A2
St Christophers Cl BA2 45 C8
St Cleer's Orch TA11 211 C3
St Cleers TA11 211 C3
St Cleers Way TA11 211 C3
St Clements Ct
Bath BA1 27 C1
Bristol BS2 227 C4
Clevedon BS21 6 C4
Keynsham BS31 24 E4
2 Weston-Super-Mare BS22 32 A2
St Clements Rd BS31 24 F4
St Cuthbert's CE Inf Sch BA5 203 C3
St Cuthbert's Lodge 3 BA5 203 D4
St Cuthbert's Villas BA5 203 A5
St Cuthbert Ave BA5 203 B5
St Cuthbert St BA5 203 D4
St Cuthbert Way BA5 203 B5
St David's Cl
Glastonbury BA6 206 E4
Taunton TA2 213 A8
Weston-Super-Mare BS22 31 B2
St David's Cres BA21 219 B7
St David's Ct BS21 16 E8
St David's Dr EX13 198 A2
St David's Gdns TA2 212 F8
St Davids Cl EX13 198 A2
St Davids Ct TA6 209 D3
St Davids Mews BS1 226 C2
St Davids Pl BA10 215 E7
St Decuman's Rd TA23 202 C7
St Dubricius CE Sch TA24 124 A3
St Dunstan's Com Sch BA6 206 D5
St Dunstan's Pk BA6 158 A5
St Dunstans Cl
Glastonbury BA6 206 D5
Keynsham BS31 24 E6
St Edmund's Rd BA6 206 D5
St Edmund's Terr BA3 117 C7
St Edmunds Rd BA6 206 E5
St Edward's Cl TA7 137 B2
St Edward's Rd BS8 226 B2
St Edyth's Rd BS9 5 C6
St Elizabeth's Way TA13 220 C4
SS Peter & Paul RC Cath* BS8 226 A4
SS Peter & Paul RC Prim Sch BS8 226 C4
St Francis Prim Sch BS48 8 F1
St Francis Rd BS31 24 D6
St George's Ave
Taunton TA2 212 F8
Yeovil BA21 219 B7
St George's CE Sch, Bourton SP8 161 E1
St George's Cl TA24 201 D2
St George's Cross BA11 101 E1
St George's Hill
Bath BA2 45 D8
Easton-in-G BS20 4 A3
St George's Ho BS8 226 B2
St George's Pl TA1 212 F3
St George's RC Prim Sch TA1 213 A3
St George's Rd
Keynsham BS31 24 D6
Portbury BS20 3 E7
St George's St TA24 201 D2
St George CE Prim Sch BS1 226 B2

St Georges Ave EX13 198 A2
St Georges Bldgs BA1 228 A3
St Georges Ct BA6 206 E5
St Georges Mews TA1 212 F3
St Georges Pl BA1 228 A3
St Georges Prim Sch BS22 32 C3
St Georges Rd BS1 226 C2
St Georges Sq TA1 212 F3
St Georges Way TA1 212 E2
St Gilda's Cl TA10 172 A5
St Gilda's Way BA6 206 D4
St Gildas TA20 223 D4
St Gildas Ct TA10 172 A5
St Gildas RC Prim Sch BA21 219 B5
St Gregory's CE Prim Sch DT10 190 F5
St Gregory's RC Sch BA2 62 D8
St Helens BA22 175 D8
St Hilary Cl BS9 5 D5
St Ives Cl BS48 9 A1
St Ives Rd BS23 49 A5
St James' Barton BS1 227 B4
St James's Cl BA21 218 D5
St James's Par BA1 228 B2
St James's Pk
Bath BA1 228 B4
Yeovil BA20 218 C5
St James' Sq BA6 157 D4
St James's Sq BA1 228 A4
St James's St
Bath BA1 228 B4
South Petherton TA13 220 C4
St James Cl TA1 212 F4
St James Ct
Bridgwater TA6 209 D3
4 Taunton TA1 212 F4
St James Mews TA13 220 C4
St James St
Taunton TA1 212 F4
Weston-Super-Mare BS23 48 D7
St James Terr BA22 197 A7
St John's BA1 44 B8
St John's Ave BS21 6 D3
St John's Bridge 4 BS1 227 A3
St John's CE Fst Sch BA11 119 F4
St John's CE Inf Sch BA6 206 E5
St John's CE Jun Sch TA9 104 D4
St John's CE Prim Sch
Keynsham BS31 24 E5
Midsomer Norton BA3 78 A1
Wellington TA21 222 E6
St John's Cl
Peasedown St John BA2 79 B7
Skilgate TA4 164 E6
Weston-Super-Mare BS23 30 D1
St John's Cres
Midsomer Norton BA3 78 A2
Trowbridge BA14 83 F6
St John's Pl BA1 228 B2
St John's RC Prim Sch BA2 45 B6
St John's RC Prim Sch (Annexe) BA2 44 D4
St John's Rd
Backwell BS48 19 B5
Bath BA2 228 C3
Bath, Lower Weston BA1 44 C7
Burnham-on-S TA8 104 B7
Clevedon BS21 6 D3
Frome BA11 120 B5
Taunton TA1 212 E3
Yeovil BA21 219 D7
St John's Sq BA6 206 D5
St John's Terr BA11 119 E3
St John & St Francis CE Prim Sch TA6 209 D4
St Johns Cl TA21 222 E6
St Johns Ct
Axbridge BS26 70 B2
Bath BA2 228 C3
Keynsham BS31 24 E6
Wells BA5 203 D3
St Johns Ho 3 BA20 219 B5
St Johns Rd BA2 60 B1
St Johns Ret Pk TA1 213 B5
St John St
Bridgwater TA6 209 B4
Wells BA5 203 D4
St Johns Wlk BA6 206 D5
St John the Evangelist CE Prim Sch BS21 6 C1
St Joseph's RC Prim Sch
Bridgwater TA6 208 D4
Burnham-on-S TA8 104 B6
Portishead BS20 2 D3
St Joseph's Rd BS23 30 E1
St Joseph & St Teresa RC Prim Sch BA5 203 D4
St Josephs Field TA1 213 A3
St Jude's Terr BS22 31 C1
St Judes Ho 21 BS2 227 C3
St Julian's CE Prim Sch BA2 62 E1
St Julian's Cl BS39 77 E4
St Julian's Rd BA2 79 F5
St Juthware Cl BA22 197 C3
St Katherine's CE Prim Sch BS40 37 A7
St Katherine's Sch BS20 4 E3
St Kenya Ct BS31 24 F5
St Keyna Rd BS31 24 E5
St Kilda's Rd BA2 44 D5
St Ladoc Rd BS31 24 D6
St Laud Cl BS9 5 D5
St Lawrence's CE Prim Sch BA5 110 E6
St Leonards Ct BA20 219 A4
St Loe Cl BS14 22 F3
St Louis RC Prim Sch BA11 119 E5
St Luke's Cl TA8 104 B7
St Luke's Rd
Bath BA2 44 F3
Midsomer Norton BA3 77 F2
St Lukes Mews TA4 167 E6
St Lukes Rd BA11 101 E5
St Margaret's Cl BS31 24 D6
St Margaret's La BS48 19 A5
St Margaret's Rd BA22 186 B6
St Margaret's Sch BA22 186 C6
St Margaret's Terr BS23 48 D8
St Margarets Cl BS48 19 A5
St Margarets Ct TA1 213 B4
St Margarets La TA20 198 C8
St Mark's CE Sch BA1 28 B2
St Mark's Ecumenical CE/ Methodist Prim Sch BS22 31 F4
St Mark's Rd
Bath BA2 228 C1
Burnham-on-S TA8 104 B8
Midsomer Norton BA3 78 A2
Weston-Super-Mare BS22 32 A3
St Marks Cl
Chedzoy TA7 154 E8
Keynsham BS31 24 E6
St Marks Ct TA6 209 D3
St Marks Gdns BA2 228 C1
St Martin's CE Jun Sch BS22 31 D2
St Martin's Cl
Fivehead TA3 170 F1
Zeals BA12 161 F3
St Martin's Ct BA2 44 E1
St Martin's Garden Prim Sch BA2 44 D1
St Martin's La SN14 13 F8
St Martin's Pk SN14 13 F8
St Martin's Sch TA18 224 B6
St Martins BS21 6 C5
St Martins Ct BS22 31 E3
St Martins Hospl BA2 44 E1
St Martins Way BA20 218 D2
St Mary's Bldgs BA2 228 B1
St Mary's CE Prim Sch
Bradford Abbas DT9 187 E1
Bridgwater TA6 208 C4
Radstock BA3 79 C1
Thorncombe TA20 199 B6
Timsbury BA2 60 C3
St Mary's Cl
10 Axminster EX13 198 A1
Bath BA2 45 B6
Chard TA20 223 C2
Cossington TA7 136 F3
Timsbury BA2 60 B2
St Mary's Cres
Chard TA20 223 C3
13 North Petherton TA6 153 F4
Yeovil BA21 219 C8
St Mary's Ct
1 Bridgwater TA6 208 F4
Weston-Super-Mare BS24 49 A1
St Mary's Gdns BS40 53 B5
St Mary's Gr BS48 18 C8
St Mary's Hospl BS8 226 B3
St Mary's La BA4 140 E3
St Mary's Park Rd BS20 2 C4
St Mary's Pk
Langport TA10 172 A5
Nailsea BS48 18 C8
St Mary's Prim Sch BS20 3 E3
St Mary's RC Prim Sch
Axminster EX13 198 A1
Bath BA1 27 B1
St Mary's Rd
Bristol BS11 4 D7
Burnham-on-S TA8 104 B7
Frome BA11 120 B5
Hutton BS24 49 D2
Leigh Woods BS8 11 D6
Meare BA6 138 D4
Oxenpill BA6 138 C4
Portishead BS20 2 C4
Sherborne DT9 225 B3
Westonzoyland TA7 154 F5
St Mary's St BS26 70 C2
St Mary's View BA22 196 F7
St Mary's Wlk BS11 4 D6
St Mary CE Prim Sch BA2 45 C8
St Mary Redcliffe & Temple CE Sch BS1 227 B1
St Mary & St Peter's CE Fst Sch
Barrington TA19 184 D5
Ilton TA19 183 E4
St Marys Cl
Hutton BS24 49 D2
Seavington St Mary TA19 184 D1
Wedmore BS28 108 C4
St Marys Ct TA6 153 E4
St Marys Pl BA4 142 F4
St Marys Rise BA3 79 C2
St Mary St
Bridgwater TA6 208 F4
Nether Stowey TA5 134 B2
St Mathew's Pl BA2 45 B5
St Mathias Ho BS2 227 C3
St Matthew's Cl BS23 30 D1
St Matthew's Field TA6 208 E4
St Matthew's Rd BS6 227 A4
St Matthews Gn TA6 208 E4
St Matthias Pk BS2 227 C3
St Medard Rd BS28 108 C4
St Michael's Ave
Clevedon BS21 6 D1
Weston-Super-Mare BS22 32 A3
Yeovil BA21 219 C7
St Michael's CE First Sch TA24 200 F7
St Michael's CE Jun Sch BA2 44 A6
St Michael's Cl
Buckland Dinham BA11 100 A3
Glastonbury BA6 206 E3
Nether Stowey TA5 134 A2
St Michael's Cres TA2 213 A8
St Michael's Ct BA2 63 E8
St Michael's Gdns TA13 220 D5
St Michael's Hill
Bristol BS2 226 C4
Milverton TA4 167 A4
St Michael's Hospl BS2 226 C4
St Michael's Pk BS2 226 C4
St Michael's Pl BA1 228 B2
St Michael's Rd
Bath BA1 44 D7
Burnham-on-S TA8 104 B7
Minehead TA24 200 F8
Yeovil BA21 219 D6
St Michael's View TA15 186 B4
St Michael Cl TA3 169 D4
St Michael on the Mount CE Prim Sch BS2 226 C3
St Michael Rd TA3 169 D4
St Michaels Cl
Nether Compton DT9 187 F3
Stoke St Michael BA3 116 B3
St Michaels Ct
Bawdrip TA7 136 E2
Walton BA16 156 D7
Yeovil BA21 219 C8
St Michaels Rd BA2 44 A5
St Nicholas' CE Prim Sch BA3 79 A2
St Nicholas Almshouses 5 BS1 227 A2
St Nicholas CE Prim Sch
Combe St Nicholas TA20 193 D6
Henstridge BA8 190 A7
St Nicholas Chantry CE Prim Sch BS21 6 E3
St Nicholas Cl
4 Henstridge BA8 190 A6
Winsley BA15 64 D7
Yeovil BA20 219 B4
St Nicholas Ct BA2 28 F1
St Nicholas Pk BA20 219 B4
St Nicholas Rd
Bristol BS2 227 C4
Weston-Super-Mare BS23 48 D2
Whitchurch BS14 23 C4
St Nicholas St BS1 227 A2
St Nicholas Way BS48 18 D2
St Oswald's Ct BS13 22 A8
St Patrick's Ct BA2 45 B6
St Patrick's Rd
Taunton TA2 213 A8
Yeovil BA21 218 D7
St Patricks Cl 3 TA2 213 A8
St Patricks Ct BS31 24 E5
St Paul's CE Jun Sch BA4 205 B5
St Paul's Cl DT9 225 E6
St Paul's Flats DT9 225 E6
St Paul's Gn DT9 225 E6
St Paul's Rd
Bristol BS8 226 B4
Burnham-on-S TA8 104 B7
Weston-Super-Mare BS23 48 E5
St Paul's Terr BA5 111 A4
St Pauls Cl TA13 220 D4
St Pauls Ct TA6 209 D3
St Pauls Pl
Bath BA1 228 B2
Midsomer Norton BA3 78 A2
St Paul St BS2 227 B4
St Peter's Ave BS23 30 D1
St Peter's Cl
Horton TA19 183 C1
Taunton TA2 213 B7
St Peter's Ho BS8 226 B2
St Peter's Rd
Burnham-on-S TA8 104 B7
Radstock BA3 97 C8
St Peter's Rise
Bristol BS13 22 B7
South Petherton TA13 220 D4
St Peter's Terr BA2 44 D6
St Peters CE Fst Sch TA4 202 D4
St Peters CE Prim Sch BS20 2 D4
St Peters Cl
Ilton TA19 183 F4
Staple Fitzpaine TA3 182 C5
Williton TA4 202 D2
St Peters Ct TA6 209 D3
St Peters Lodge BS20 2 D4
St Peters Rd
Portishead BS20 2 D4
Shepton Mallet BA4 205 A6
St Peters Terr 21 BA4 205 B6
St Philip's CE Prim Sch BA2 44 D2
St Philips Rd BS2 227 C3
St Pias X RC Prim Sch BS13 22 A5
St Quintin Pk TA2 213 E6
St Rayn Hill TA17 195 B4
St Saviour's Ave TA6 209 A4
St Saviour's CE Inf Sch BA1 28 B2
St Saviour's CE Jun Sch BA1 28 B2
St Saviour's Rd BA1 28 C2
St Saviour's Terr 10 BA1 28 B1
St Saviours Way 4 BA1 28 C1
St Stephen's Ave 3 BS1 227 A2
St Stephen's CE Prim Sch BA1 27 F1
St Stephen's Cl BA1 27 F1
St Stephen's Ct BA1 228 B4
St Stephen's Pl BA1 228 B4
St Stephen's Rd BA1 228 B4
St Stephen's St BS1 227 A2
St Swithin's Pl BA1 228 C4
St Swithin's Rd DT9 225 E4
St Swithin's Yd BA2 228 C3
St Swithins Cl DT9 225 E4
St Thomas' Ct BA5 203 F5
St Thomas Cross BA21 219 C5
St Thomas Ct TA6 209 D3
St Thomas Mews BA5 203 F5
St Thomas Pl BS1 227 B2
St Thomas Rd BA3 78 B2
St Thomas St E BS1 227 B2
St Thomas St
Bristol BS1 227 B2
Dunster TA24 201 E2
Wells BA5 203 E5
St Thomas Terr BA5 203 F5
St Vigor & St John CE Prim Sch BA3 96 E3
St Vincent's Rd BS8 226 A2
St Whytes Rd BS4 22 D8
St Winifreds Dr BA2 45 D2
Salcombe Gdns BS22 32 A2
Salcombe Rd BS4 23 A8
Salerno Cl BA22 173 E2
Sales Ho 15 BA4 205 B6
Salisbury Rd
Bath BA1 28 B2
Burnham-on-S TA8 104 C7
Paulton BS39 77 F4
Weston-Super-Mare BS22 31 C1
Salisbury St TA2 212 E6
Salisbury Terr
Castle Cary BA7 214 B5
4 Frome BA11 119 E3
Gurney Slade BA3 114 E8
Weston-Super-Mare BS23 48 D7
Sally Hill BS20 2 E7
Sally In The Wood BA1, BA15 46 D6
Sally Lovell's La BA8 189 F8
Sally Lunn's Kitchen Mus* BA1 228 C2
Sallysmead Cl BS13 22 B4
Salmon Par TA6 209 A4
Saltford CE Prim Sch BS31 25 E2
Saltford Ct BS31 25 E3
Salthouse Ct BS21 6 B2
Salthouse La BA20 219 A4
Salthouse Rd BS21 6 B2
Saltings Cl BS21 6 B2
Saltlands TA6 208 F7
Saltlands Ave TA6 208 F7
Saltlands Ho TA6 208 F7
Saltry La TA24 131 A6
Saltwell Ave BS14 23 C5
Salway Cl BS40 38 E1
Salway Gdns 11 EX13 198 A1
Samarate Way BA20 218 D4
Sambourne La BS20 4 C4
Sampford Arundel Com Prim Sch TA21 179 E5
Sampford Peverell CE Prim Sch EX16 178 C1
Sampford Rocks TA4 202 F1
Sampsons Rd BS13 22 D4
Samuel Ct BA8 176 F1
Samuels Ct TA2 212 E6
Samways Cl BA22 218 B5
Sanctuary Gdns BS9 5 D3
Sanctuary La TA22 148 A2
Sandbrook La BA22 175 D7
Sandburrows Rd BS13 21 F6
Sandburrows Wlk BS13 21 F6
Sandcroft BS14 22 F6
Sandcroft Ave BS23 48 D2
Sandene Cl TA2 212 C8
Sand Farm La BS22 31 A6
Sandford Cl 2 BS21 6 B1
Sandford Hill TA5, TA6 208 A6
Sandford Orcas Manor Ho* DT9 188 C8
Sandford Orcas Rd DT9 225 B7
Sandford Pk BA14 83 F7
Sandford Prim Sch BS25 52 B4
Sandford Rd
Bristol BS8 226 A1
Weston-Super-Mare BS23 49 A7
Winscombe BS25 51 F1
Sandhill La TA24 131 C4
Sandhills Dr TA8 84 F4
Sandhurst Rd BA20 218 F1
Sanding's La
Chapel Leigh TA4 167 A8
Fitzhead TA4 166 F8
Lydeard St Lawrence TA4 151 A1
Sandlewood Cl BA21 219 E8
Sandmead Rd BS25 52 A4
Sandown Cl
Bridgwater TA6 209 A2
3 Yeovil BA20 219 A5
Sandpiper Cl
Bridgwater TA6 209 A4
Minehead TA24 201 C5
Sandpiper Dr BS22 31 F1
Sandpiper Rd TA6 209 A4
Sandpits Rd BA6 206 F5
Sand Rd
Wedmore BS28 108 C3
Weston-Super-Mare BS22 31 B5
Sandringham Cl TA6 209 C7
Sandringham Ct 2 BS23 48 F5
Sandringham Rd
1 Weston-Super-Mare BS23 48 F5
Yeovil BA21 219 E6
Sandrocks La TA24 131 B3
Sandscross La BA11 100 A3
Sand St TA4 166 F4
Sandy's Hill La BA11 119 E1
Sandy's La EX14 191 F2
Sandy Cl TA9 104 D4
Sandy Hole TA16 195 F7
Sandy La
Beckington BA11 101 E4
Cannington TA5 135 A3
Easton-in-G BS8 10 A8
Failand BS8 10 C7
Stanton Drew BS39, BS40 39 E3
Wiveliscombe TA4 210 C7
Sandyleaze BS9 5 E7
Sandys Moor TA4 210 D4
Sandy View BA11 101 E4
Sandyway Cross EX36 145 H4
Sansom's Cross DT6 199 F1
Sansome's Hill DT9 217 D2
Sarabeth Dr BA2 61 A4
Saracen St BA1 228 C3
Saunder's Piece La TA18 224 A7
Saunters Cl BA9 216 B4
Saunton Wlk BS4 22 E8
Savernake Rd BS22 31 F3
Savery or Cottage Row TA1 213 B3
Saviano Way TA6 208 E7
Saville Cres BS22 49 C8
Saville Gate Cl BS9 5 F4
Saville Mews BS6 227 A4
Saville Pl BS8 226 A2
Saville Rd
Bristol BS9 5 F3
Weston-Super-Mare BS22 49 C8
Saville Row BA1 228 B3
Savoy The BS11 4 E6
Saw Cl BA1 228 B2
Sawmill Cotts BA11 143 B8
Sawmill Gdns BA3 96 D3
Sawpit La BA6 140 C2
Sawpits Cl TA4 150 D8
Sawyers Cl
Chilcompton BA3 96 D3
Wraxall BS48 9 A2
Sawyers Ct BS21 6 E3
Sawyers Leigh TA2 168 D8
Sawyers Mill EX16 164 E2
Saxby Cl
Clevedon BS21 6 B1
Weston-Super-Mare BS22 32 B4
Saxon Cl
Oake TA4 167 D4
Watchet TA23 202 B7
Saxon Ct
Ilminster TA19 221 B4
Weston-Super-Mare BS22 32 D3
Saxondale Ave TA8 85 A3
Saxon Gn TA6 209 C4
Saxon Pl BS27 90 B7
Saxon Rd
Bridgwater TA6 209 C4
Weston-Super-Mare BS22 49 C8
Saxon Ridge TA23 202 B7
Saxon St BS40 53 D6
Saxonvale BA11 119 F4
Saxon Way
Cheddar BS27 90 B6
Peasedown St John BA2 79 E8
Wedmore BS28 108 C4
Wincanton BA9 216 B3
Winsley BA15 64 F7
Says La BS40 53 B4
Scadden's La BS27 91 B1
Scafell Cl
Taunton TA1 212 C1
Weston-Super-Mare BS23 31 A1
Scamel Ho 11 BA4 205 B6
Scaurs The BS22 31 F2
School Cl
Bampton EX16 164 B1
Banwell BS29 51 B3
Bristol, Whitchurch BS14 22 F4
Tintinhull BA22 186 C6
Watchet TA23 202 C7
School Cotts
13 East Coker BA22 197 F8
Enmore TA5 153 A5
Taunton TA2 168 F6
School Dr DT9 225 E5
School Fields
Cannington TA5 135 C2
2 North Petherton TA6 153 F3
School Hill
Ashcott TA7 156 B8
Cucklington BA9 177 D6
Misterton TA18 224 F3
South Perrott DT8 196 C1
Westbury-sub-Mendip BA5 110 E6

School Hill *continued*
Wookey Hole BA5 203 A8
School La
Barrow Gurney BS48 20 D5
Batheaston BA1 28 F4
Blackford BS28 107 D4
Burrowbridge TA7 154 F1
Chew Stoke BS40 56 D8
Combwich TA5 135 B5
Compton Dundon TA11 157 A3
Doulting BA4 141 E6
Draycott BS27 90 F3
Drimpton DT8 199 E6
Farrington Gurney BS39 77 A4
Horrington BA5 113 A1
Kilmersdon BA3 98 A6
Lopen TA13 185 A1
7 North Petherton TA6 153 F4
Rowberrow BS25 53 A1
Seavington St Michael TA19 184 E2
Shapwick TA7 137 F1
Sherborne DT9 225 D3
Somerton TA11 211 E3
Tatworth TA20 198 C8
Templecombe BA8 176 E1
Wick St Lawrence BS22 32 B7
Woolavington TA7 136 E4
School of Christ the King RC Prim BS4 22 E8
School Rd
Kingsdon TA11 173 D5
Monkton Heathfield TA2 213 F8
Parbrook BA6 158 C7
Westonzoyland TA7 154 E5
Wrington BS40 35 E2
School St
Curry Rivel TA10 171 D4
Drayton TA10 171 E3
School View BS48 9 B1
Schooner Pl TA24 201 B7
Scimitar Rd BA22 218 B6
Scobell Rise BS39 59 C2
Score La BS40 54 E2
Score The BS40 54 E2
Scornfield La BS40 56 D7
Scotch Horn Cl BS48 8 F2
Scotch Horn Way 5 BS48 8 F2
Scot Cl TA6 135 F5
Scot Elm Dr BS24 32 D1
Scot La BS40 38 D1
Scotland La
Axbridge BS26 107 D8
Chapel Allerton BS26 107 D8
Rudge BA11 102 C4
Scots Pine Ave 3 BS48 8 F2
Scott's Hill
Huish Champflower TA4 165 E8
Seavington St Mary TA19 184 D1
Scott's La
Baltonsborough BA6 158 A8
Wellington TA21 222 E6
Scott Cl TA2 212 C6
Scott Rd
Frome BA11 119 F5
Highbridge TA9 104 D3
Weston-Super-Mare BS23 49 A4
Scotts Cl BA3 116 C8
Scotts La TA7 137 D1
Scotts Way TA18 196 B8
Scouse Cross EX13 198 E2
Scouse La EX13 198 E2
Scrapton La TA20 193 D5
Scruibbitts La TA7 137 B2
Scumbrum La BS39 59 C2
Seaborough View TA18 224 C4
Seabrook Rd BS22 31 D1
Sea King Rd BA20 218 D3
Sea La
Carhampton TA24 131 A7
Dunster TA24 201 F4
Kilve TA5 133 C6
Watchet TA23 132 D5
Sealey Cl BS27 90 F3
Sealey Cres BA5 112 E1
Sealeys Cl TA9 136 A8
Sea Mills Inf Sch BS9 5 C7
Sea Mills Jun Sch BS9 5 B5
Sea Mills La BS9 5 C5
Sea Mills Sta BS9 5 B4
SeaQuarium★ BS23 48 D6
Searle Cres BS23 49 A6
Searle Ct
Clevedon BS21 6 E2
Somerton TA11 211 D3
Seat La BA4 142 D1
Seaton Ct BA20 219 A4
Seaton Rd BA20 218 F4
Seavale Mews BS21 6 C4
Seavale Rd BS21 6 C4
Seaview Rd
Portishead, Redcliffe Bay BS20 1 F4
Portishead, West Hill BS20 1 F6
Sea View Rd TA8 104 A8
Seawalls BS9 5 D2
Seawalls Rd BS9 5 D2
Seaward Dr TA6 208 F6
Seaward Way TA24 201 C6
Second Ave
Axminster EX13 198 A2
Bath BA2 44 D5
Bristol BS14 23 B7
Radstock BA3 97 C7
Second Dro TA7 155 D3
Secret World★ TA9 136 C8
Sector Hill EX13 198 B1
Sector La EX13 198 A1
Sedge Cl TA6 208 F2
Sedge Dro TA7 137 C3
Sedge Mead BA11 119 F7
Sedgemoor Cl
Nailsea BS48 18 E8
Yeovil BA21 219 D7
Sedgemoor Coll TA3 170 A2
Sedgemoor Dro
Sutton Mallet TA7 155 A6
Wrantage TA3 170 B2
Sedgemoor Hill Dr TA7 155 B7
Sedgemoor Manor Com Jun Sch TA6 209 C6
Sedgemoor Manor Inf Sch TA6 209 D5
Sedgemoor Rd
Bath BA2 44 F2
Bridgwater TA6 209 C3
Weston-Super-Mare BS23 30 F1
Woolavington TA7 136 E3
Sedgemoor Way
Glastonbury BA6 206 D5
Woolavington TA7 136 E3
Sedgemount Ind Pk TA6 136 A2
Sedgewick Ho BS11 4 E7
Seeley Cres BA16 207 B3
Sefton Sq BS24 50 A8
Selbourne Cl BA1 44 A8
Selbourne Pl TA24 200 F6
Selbourne Rd BS23 48 E4
Selden Rd BS14 23 E5
Sellbed Cross TA24 146 A8
Selley Wlk BS13 22 A5
Selway Ct BA2 45 B2
Selwood TA20 223 C5
Selwood Cl BS22 49 C7
Selwood Cres BA11 120 A7
Selwood Mid Sch BA11 120 B6
Selwood Rd
Frome BA11 119 E5
Glastonbury BA6 206 F6
Selwood St BA11 118 B7
Selworthy Cl
Bridgwater TA6 208 F1
Keynsham BS31 24 D5
Selworthy Gdns 4 BS48 8 E1
Selworthy Ho BA2 44 F2
Selworthy Rd
Taunton TA2 213 B8
Weston-Super-Mare BS23 49 A4
Selworthy Specl Sch TA2 213 A8
Selworthy Terr BA2 44 F2
Semington Cl TA1 213 D4
Septimus Bldgs BS14 22 D5
Serbert Cl BS20 2 E5
Serbert Rd BS20 2 E5
Serbert Way BS20 2 E5
Sercombe Pk BS21 6 E1
Serel Dr BA5 203 B3
Serlo Ct BS22 32 A4
Serotines The TA10 171 D8
Sevenacres TA11 211 C3
Seven Acres La BA1 28 F5
Seven Acres The 3 BS24 49 F7
Seven Dials BA1 228 B2
Seventh Ave BS14 23 A7
Seven Thorns EX35 122 D5
Severalls Park Ave TA18 224 C5
Severn Ave BS23 48 E5
Severn Cl TA6 209 D7
Severn Dr TA1 213 C4
Severn Gr TA8 104 B5
Severnleigh Gdns BS9 5 F3
Severnmeade BS20 1 F5
Severn Rd
Bristol BS11 4 D6
Pill BS20 4 C5
Portishead BS20 2 C5
Weston-Super-Mare BS23 48 E5
Severn Terr TA23 202 C7
Severn Way BS31 25 A5
Sevier Rd BS26 68 C3
Seville Ct
Portishead BS20 2 E7
Taunton TA1 212 D2
Seville Rd BS20 2 E7
Seward Terr BA3 79 C2
Sewell Ho BS25 70 A8
Sexey's Hospl BA10 215 E6
Sexey's Hospl (Almshouses) BA10 215 E6
Sexey's Rd BS28 107 E4
Sexey's Sch BA10 215 D5
Seymour Cl
Clevedon BS21 6 E3
Wells BA5 203 C5
Weston-Super-Mare BS22 31 F4
Seymour Rd
5 Bath BA1 28 A1
Bridgwater TA6 209 D5
Street BA16 207 D4
Seymour St TA21 222 C6
Shackel Cross EX15 191 B8
Shadow Wlk BS24 50 C3
Shadwell Ct BA9 216 C4
Shadwell La BA9 216 C4
Shaftesbury Ave 2 BA1 44 C7
Shaftesbury Cl BS48 18 D8
Shaftesbury La BA9 177 B6
Shaftesbury Mews 7 BA2 44 D5
Shaftesbury Rd
Bath BA2 44 D5
Henstridge BA8 190 C8
Weston-Super-Mare BS23 49 B8
Shaftesbury Terr BA3 79 A3
Shaftgate Ave BA4 205 A6
Shaft Rd BA2 45 E1
Shakespeare Ave
Bath BA2 44 F4
Taunton TA1 213 C3
Shakespeare Ct BS23 48 F2
Shakespeare Rd BA3 78 C1
Shaking Dro TA9 137 B6
Shalford La
Charlton Musgrove BA9 161 A2
Shalford BA9 216 D8
Shallows The BS31 25 F3
Shambles The TA3 170 B4
Sham Castle La BA2 45 C7
Shannon Wlk BS20 2 F6
Shapcott La EX36 162 C2
Shapcott Wood Hill EX36 162 A2
Shaplands BS9 5 F4
Shapway TA19 184 F3
Shapway Cross TA19 184 F3
Shapway La BA4 141 F2
Shapway Rd BA4 141 E2
Shapwick Heath National Nature Reserve★ BA6 138 A3
Shapwick Hill TA7 155 F8
Shapwick Rd BA6 138 A4
Shapwick Right Dro TA7 155 C6
Sharland Cl BS9 5 E3
Sharland Gr BS13 22 C4
Sharlands TA19 184 C5
Sharpenton La TA7 155 D6
Sharpham Dro BA16 138 E1
Sharpham La
Glastonbury BA16 138 D1
Stoke St Gregory TA3 170 E5
Sharpham Rd BS27 89 F7
Shatterwell Cotts BA9 216 C4
Shatt La TA5 152 F3
Shatwell La
Castle Cary BA9 214 F1
Yarlington BA9 175 F8
Shaulders The TA2 213 C7
Shave Cross DT6 199 F1
Shave Hill SP8 177 D4
Shave La
Crewkerne TA18 224 A3
Donyatt TA19 183 D1
Horton TA19 183 C1
South Brewham BA10 161 A6
Shawford La BA11 101 D7
Shaw Gdns BS14 23 A8
Shaw Path TA8 104 C6
Shaws Way BA2 43 F5
Sheafhayne Cross EX14 192 E4
Shearing Cross TA20 199 A5
Shearn La TA8 104 B7
Shearwater Cl TA6 209 D3
Shedrick Hill TA20 199 B8
Sheepfair La SN14 13 F8
Sheephouse Cvn Pk BS20 3 E7
Sheeplands La DT9 225 B5
Sheeplands The DT9 225 B5
Sheeps Croft BS13 22 A5
Sheepstealing La TA4 150 E5
Sheepway BS20 3 B5
Sheep Way TA19 184 E3
Sheepway La BS20 3 C5
Sheldon's La TA22 163 A7
Sheldon Cl BS21 6 F2
Sheldon Ct TA1 212 E4
Sheldon Dr BA5 203 C3
Sheldon Mill 3 BA5 203 C3
Shelduck Cl TA24 201 C5
Shell's La
Chard TA20 193 A3
Shepton Beauchamp TA19 184 E4
Shelley Ave BS21 6 D2
Shelley Cl
Burnham-on-S TA8 85 A2
Yeovil BA21 218 D6
Shelley Dr TA8 85 B2
Shelley Gr TA1 213 B3
Shelley Rd
Bath BA2 44 F4
Radstock BA3 78 C1
Weston-Super-Mare BS23 49 A4
Shellthorn Gr TA6 208 F2
Shelthorn Hill TA5 152 F3
Shelway La TA19 184 C4
Shepherd's Cl TA11 157 A4
Shepherd's Cnr TA23 131 E4
Shepherd's Dro TA7 155 A3
Shepherd's Hay TA1 212 C2
Shepherd's Hill SP8 177 E4
Shepherd's La
Chard TA20 223 B4
Frome BA11 144 B7
Hemyock EX15 180 F1
Shepherds Cl TA6 208 D6
Shepherds Cross BA8 176 C5
Shepherds Way BS22 32 C2
Sheppard's Barton 11 BA11 119 E5
Sheppard's Cnr TA5 153 B5
Sheppards Gdns BA1 27 B1
Sheppards Wlk BA3 96 D3
Sheppy's Cider Farm Ctr★ TA4 167 F1
Sheppy's Mill BS49 34 D5
Shepton BS24 49 A2
Shepton Beauchamp CE Fst Sch TA19 184 E4
Shepton Mallet Com Hospl BA4 204 F6
Shepton Mallet Inf Sch BA4 205 C6
Shepton Mallet Mus★ BA4 205 B5
Shepton Old Rd
Croscombe BA5 204 A6
Dinder BA5 140 D7
Shepton Rd BA4, BA5 204 D7
Sherborne Abbey★ DT9 225 D3
Sherborne Abbey CE Prim Sch DT9 225 B2
Sherborne Castle★ DT9 225 F3
Sherborne Hill DT9 225 E1
Sherborne Mus★ DT9 225 D4
Sherborne Old Castle★ DT9 225 F4
Sherborne Prep Sch DT9 225 D3
Sherborne Prim Sch DT9 225 E5
Sherborne Rd
Milborne Port DT9 217 C2
Yenston BA8 189 E6
Yeovil BA21 219 D5
Sherborne Sch DT9 225 D4
Sherborne Sch for Girls DT9 225 C4
Sherford Rd TA1 212 E1
Sherford Terr TA1 212 E1
Sheridan Cl TA6 209 D3
Sheridan Gdns BA14 83 F6
Sheridan Rd
Bath BA2 43 F5
Burnham-on-S TA8 104 C6
Sherlands 4 TA16 195 F7
Sherlands Gdns 3 TA16 195 F7
Sherring Rd BA4 205 D4
Sherrin Way BS13 21 E3
Sherston Cl BS48 9 A1
Shervage Ct TA6 209 C5
Sherwood Cl BS31 24 E5
Sherwood Cres BS22 31 F3
Sherwood Rd BS31 24 E5
Shetland Way BS48 9 A1
Shickle Gr BA2 44 D1
Shiller's La DT9 188 C7
Shiners Elms BS49 34 B8
Shipham CE Fst Sch BS25 70 E8
Shipham Cl
Bristol BS14 23 B5
Nailsea BS48 18 F8
Shipham La BS25 52 B1
Shipham Rd BS27 71 A3
Ship La
Bristol BS1 227 B1
Combwich TA5 135 B5
Shiplate Rd BS24 67 E6
Shipney La DT10 190 C5
Shircombe La TA22 147 F2
Shire Gdns BS11 4 D8
Shirehampton Prim Sch BS11 4 D6
Shirehampton Rd BS9 5 C6
Shirehampton Sta BS11 4 D5
Shiremoor Hill TA16 195 F7
Shires The TA24 201 C5
Shires Yd BA1 228 B3
Shockerwick La BA1 29 D4
Shoe La TA7 209 E7
Shoot Hill TA17 195 C8
Shophouse Rd BA2 44 B5
Shop La
Pilton BA4 140 E3
Wingfield BA14 83 C6
Shopland Ho 8 BS21 6 C2
Shoreditch BS40 56 C7
Shoreditch Rd
Stoke St Mary TA3 169 A1
Taunton TA1 213 B1
Shoredown La DT9, BA8 217 E6
Short Dro
Mudgley BS28 138 C7
Westbury-sub-Mendip BA5, BS27 110 B4
Short La
Draycott BS27 90 E3
Litton BA3 75 F2
Long Ashton BS41 11 A2
Stone Allerton BS26 88 C2
Shortland La BS28 108 C3
Shortmarsh La BA22 196 F4
Short Way BS8 10 B4
Shortwood Rd BS13 22 E3
Shortwood Wlk BS13 22 E3
Shoscombe CE Prim Sch BA2 79 F5
Shoscombe Gdns BA11 120 C7
Shovel La TA6 153 E3
Showell Pk TA2 212 B7
Showering Cl BS14 23 D5
Showering Rd BS14 23 D5
Showground Rd TA6 209 B1
Shrewsbury Bow BS24 50 A8
Shrewsbury Rd BA22 218 B7
Shrubbery Ave BS23 30 D1
Shrubbery Cl TA8 84 E8
Shrubbery Rd BS23 30 D1
Shrubbery Terr 11 BS23 30 C1
Shrubbery Wlk BS23 30 D1
Shrubbery Wlk W BS23 30 D1
Shudrick La TA19 221 C3
Shums Ct 3 BA1 228 C2
Shurtland La TA4 150 C3
Shurton La TA5 134 C6
Shute's La SP8 177 E4
Shute La
Bruton BA10 215 D6
Huish Champflower TA4 165 C8
Long Sutton TA10 172 E4
Shute Lake La TA18 224 D5
Shuteleigh TA21 222 E5
Shutemead TA1 212 A4
Shute Row TA21 222 E5
Shuter Rd BS13 21 E5
Shutewater Cl TA1 212 A4
Shutewater Hill TA1 212 A4
Shutgate Mdw TA4 202 D3
Shuttern 2 TA1 212 E3
Shuttern Bridge 3 TA1 212 E3
Shutwell La BA4 140 E3
Shyners Terr 8 TA16 195 F7
Sidcot Dr BS25 70 A7
Sidcot La BS25 70 A7
Sidcot Sch BS25 70 B7
Sideland Cl BS14 23 E6
Sidelings The BS40 73 D8
Side Wood La EX36 162 A1
Sidings The DT10 190 C4
Sidmouth Cl TA8 104 C8
Sidney Hill Cottage Homes BS25 52 E4
Silbury Rd BS3 11 E2
Silbury Rise BS31 25 A2
Silcox Rd BS13 22 C4
Silk Cl BA4 205 B7
Silk House Barton DT10 190 B4
Silklands Gr BS9 5 C6
Silk Mills La TA2 212 B6
Silk Mills Rd TA1 212 B4
Silton Rd 1 SP8 161 F1
Silverberry Rd BS22 32 A1
Silvercombe 1 BS23 48 E5
Silver Ct BS48 8 C2
Silverdale Cl
Brushford TA22 163 E4
Wembdon TA6 208 C5
Silverdown Hill TA4 150 C7
Silver La BA11 144 B7
Silverlake Cotts DT9 188 B2
Silverlow Rd BS48 8 D2
Silvermead TA24 201 B5
Silver Mead BS49 34 D2
Silvermead Ct TA24 201 B5
Silver Moor La BS29 50 F7
Silver Rd BA16 207 C5
Silver Springs TA19 184 E3
Silver St
11 Bampton EX16 164 B1
Barrington TA19 184 D5
Barton St David TA11 158 A3
Barwick BA22 197 F8
Bridgwater TA6 208 F4
Bristol BS1 227 A3
Bruton BA10 215 E6
Chard TA20 223 C3
Cheddar BS27 90 B8
Chew Magna BS40 39 B3
Congresbury BS49 34 D2
Crewkerne TA18 196 B3
Curry Mallet TA3 183 C8
Ditcheat BA4 159 C7
East Lambrook TA13 220 C8
Fivehead TA3 170 F1
Glastonbury BA6 206 E4
Holcombe BA3 97 C1
Huntspill TA9 136 A8
Ilminster TA19 221 B4
Kilmersdon BA3 98 B5
Kingsbury Episcopi TA12 185 B8
Kingsdon TA11 173 D5
Langport TA10 172 A3
Midsomer Norton BA3 97 A7
Milverton TA4 167 A4
Nailsea BS48 8 D2
Portishead BS20 1 F1
Shepton Beauchamp TA19 184 E3
South Petherton TA13 220 D5
Taunton TA1 213 A3
Wells BA5 203 E3
West Buckland TA21 180 F7
Wincanton BA9 216 C4
Wiveliscombe TA4 210 C4
Wrington BS40 35 E2
Yeovil BA20 219 B5
Silverstone Way BS49 34 D3
Simbriss Rd BA5 114 F5
Simmons Cl BA16 207 D5
Simon's Cl BS39 77 F5
Simons Cl BS22 32 A2
Simons Mews
Chard TA20 223 E4
3 Weston-Super-Mare BS23 48 F7
Simons Rd DT9 225 D5
Sinclair Ho BS8 226 A2
Singapore Rd BS23 48 E3
Singer's Knoll BA11 119 F4
Singer Ct BA11 119 F5
Single Hill BA2 79 F5
Singleton Ct BA5 203 C5
Sion Hill
Bath BA1 27 E1
Bristol BS8 11 F7
Sion Hill Pl BA1 27 E1
Sion La BS8 11 F7
Sion Pl
Bath BA2 45 B6
Bristol BS8 11 F7
Sion Rd BA1 27 E1
Sir Bevil Grenville's Mon★ BA1 12 A1
Sir Gilbert Scott Ct TA4 202 E3
Siskin Wlk BS22 49 F8
Sisters The BA4 205 A6
Six Acres Cl TA1 213 C5
Sixpence BS39 59 D2
Six Streams BA1 27 B2

Sixteen Acre La TA20 193 D8
Sixth Ave BS14 23 A7
Sixty Acres Cl BS8 10 B4
Six Ways BS21 6 C4
Skillgate La TA14 185 E1
Skimmerton La TA5, TA6 208 A5
Skinner's Hill BA2 78 F7
Skinner's La TA14 185 F2
Skinners La BS25 52 F4
Skitmoor Dro BS28 109 C2
Skylark Ave BS21 1 B1
Slab Dro TA7 155 A1
Sladacre La BS40 54 E2
Slade's Cross TA20 193 D7
Sladebrook Ave BA2 44 C3
Sladebrook Ct BA2 44 C3
Sladebrook Rd BA2 44 B4
Slade Cl TA4 150 E8
Slade La
Barrow Gurney BS48 20 C4
Golsoncott TA23 131 E1
Hawkridge TA22 146 D1
Lympsham BS24 67 B1
Rimpton BA22 188 A7
Rooks Bridge BS26 87 E4
West Anstey EX36 162 B6
Slade Rd BS20 2 D5
Slades Ct 2 BS48 19 A6
Slades Hill BA8 176 E1
Slades Orch TA19 183 C1
Slade Way TA4 202 E4
Slait Hill BA4 142 C7
Slait La BA9 216 C7
Slapes Cl TA2 168 F6
Slate La BS14, BS31 41 B7
Sleep La BS14 23 D3
Sleight Cl BA21 218 C6
Sleight La BA5 140 E8
Slippery Batch TA11 211 A6
Sloe Cl BS22 49 D8
Slopers La BA9 176 D5
Slough Green Cvn Pk
TA3 182 D8
Slough Hill TA3 182 D6
Slough La
Cold Ashton SN14 12 F5
Crowcombe TA4 151 A8
North Wootton BA4 140 B3
Stoke St Gregory TA3 170 F6
Upottery EX14 191 F5
Sloway La TA6, TA9 136 A8
Slow Court La BA22 174 D3
Slowland La BA5 110 D8
Slugg Hill BA16 207 C3
Smallacombe Hill EX16,
EX36 162 D4
Smallbrook La BS39 41 B6
Smallcombe Cl BA3 78 E5
Smallcombe Rd BA3 78 E4
Small Down End BS25 51 F2
Small Down La BA4 142 B2
Small La EX16 179 B2
Small Mead Dro BA6 157 F4
Smallmoor Chase BA16 156 E7
Smallmoor Dro TA7 155 C3
Small Moor La BA16 156 E7
Smallridge Rd EX13 198 A4
Smalls Mead 2 TA11 173 F7
Small St BS1 227 A3
Smallway BS49 34 D5
Small Way La BA22 214 C1
Smallways La TA7 137 B3
Smallwood View BA3 96 E7
Smeathy La EX15 180 F3
Smeaton Rd BS1 11 F5
Sminhays Cnr TA23 149 B5
Smith's Forge Ind Est
BS49 16 F3
Smith's Hill TA18 196 C8
Smith's La BA4 159 C6
Smith's Row TA15 186 B4
Smith's Terr BA21 219 C6
Smithfield Rd BA16 207 B4
Smithick's La BA11 143 E6
Smithmead BS13 22 B5
Smiths Cl BS27 91 A1
Smith Way TA9 104 D3
Smithy TA1 212 B3
Smithyard La TA4, TA23 202 A3
Smithy La BA11 119 E4
Smokeham La TA4 151 D5
Smoky Hole La TA18 185 F1
Smurl La TA9 104 C1
Smythe Croft BS14 23 A3
Smythes Cross EX15 191 C7
Snagg La BA4 159 D5
Snag La BA9 216 E3
Snake La BS28 109 C1
Snakelake Hill BA10 160 C7
Snap Hill TA11 173 D8
Snathe Lea 4 TA4 167 F8
Snedden Gr TA1 213 B5
Snipefield La BS28 108 A6
Snowberry Cl BS22 32 A1
Snowberry Ct TA1 213 C2
Snowdon Cottage La
TA20 223 B4
Snowdon Hts TA20 223 B4
Snowdon Vale BS23 31 A1
Snowdrop Cl BS22 32 A5
Snow Hill BA1 28 A1
Snow Hill Ho BA1 228 C4
Society Rd BA4 205 A6
Sock's La BA10 160 F8
Sock Hill BA21 187 C6
Sock La BA21 187 C6
Soho BA2 81 E5
Solomon's Hollow TA3 169 F2
Solon Ct BS13 21 F5
Solsbury Ct BA1 28 F3
Solsbury La BA1 28 F4
Solsbury View 17 BA1 28 A1
Solsbury Way BA1 28 A2
Somer's Hill BA11 117 D3
Somer Ave BA3 77 F2
Somer Ct BA3 78 B1
Somerdale Ave
Bath BA2 44 D2
Bristol BS4 22 F8
Weston-Super-Mare BS22 49 C8
Somerdale Cl BS22 49 C8
Somerdale Rd BS31 24 F7
Somerdale Rd N BS30,
BS31 24 F8
Somerdale View BA2 44 C2
Somer Ho BA3 78 A1
Somerhouse Orch BA6 206 E5
Somer Lea BA3 96 D5
Somerleaze Cl BA5 203 B3
Somer Rd BA3 77 F2
Somerset Ave
Taunton TA1 212 B2
Weston-Super-Mare BS22,
BS24 50 A8
Somerset Brick & Tile Mus*
TA6 209 A6
Somerset Bridge Prim Sch
TA6 209 B2
Somerset Cl
Martock TA12 185 E7
Shepton Mallet BA4 205 C5
Somerset Coll of Arts & Tech
TA1 212 D4
Somerset Coll of Arts & Tech
(Annexe) TA1 212 E5
Somerset Coll of Arts & Tech
(Bishops Hull Annexe)
TA1 212 C3
Somerset County Mus*
TA1 212 F4
Somerset Ct BA21 219 A6
Somerset Cty Cricket Gd*
TA1 212 F4
Somerset & Dorset Joint
Rly* BA3 97 A8
Somerset & Dorset Rlwy
Trust Mus* TA23 131 E4
Somerset Fire HQ TA2 169 A7
Somerset Folly BA2 60 B2
Somerset Gdns TA6 209 C3
Somerset Ho
Bath BA2 44 D3
12 Bristol BS2 227 C3
Somerset La BA1 27 E1
Somerset Mews BS23 48 F6
Somerset Nuffield Hospl
TA2 212 B7
Somerset Pl
Bath BA1 27 E1
Taunton TA1 213 B4
Yeovil BA20 219 A3
Somerset Rd
Bridgwater TA6 209 C3
Clevedon BS21 6 E3
Frome BA11 119 E4
Portishead BS20 1 F5
Somerset Rural Life Mus*
BA6 206 E4
Somerset Sq
Bristol BS1 227 B1
3 Nailsea BS48 8 E2
Somerset St
Bath BA1 228 C1
Bristol BS1 227 B1
Bristol, Kingsdown BS2 227 A4
Somerset Way
Highbridge TA9 104 E3
Paulton BS39 77 E6
Somerton BS24 49 A2
Somerton Bsns Pk TA11 211 B5
Somerton Cl TA6 209 D4
Somerton Door Dro
Compton Dundon TA11 156 E1
Somerton TA11 211 A7
Somerton Dro TA11 156 E1
Somertonfield Rd TA11 172 E7
Somerton Gdns BA11 120 C7
Somerton Hill
Langport TA10 172 E7
Somerton TA11 211 A3
Somerton Inf Sch TA11 211 C4
Somerton Rd
Clevedon BS21 6 E1
Langport TA10 172 A6
Street BA16 207 D4
Somervale Rd BA3 78 E2
Somervale Sch BA3 78 A1
Somerville Cl
Saltford BS31 25 E2
Shepton Mallet BA4 205 D4
Somerville Cotts BA5 204 B8
Somerville Rd
Sandford BS25 52 A4
Wells BA5 203 C5
Somerville Way TA6 209 D3
Soper Gdns BS4 22 D7
Sopers Field TA20 223 D2
Sophia Gdns BS22 32 B4
Southampton Row 5
TA2 213 A8
South Ave
Bath BA2 44 D5
Highbridge TA9 104 C4
South Ave *continued*
Portishead BS20 2 D6
Sherborne DT9 225 B2
Southay Cross TA20 193 A4
Southay La TA20 192 F4
South Bank
Castle Cary BA7 214 B3
Wookey Hole BA5 203 A8
Southbourne Gdns BA1 28 B1
Southbourne Ho TA6 208 E4
Southbourne Mans BA2 228 C2
South Brent Cl TA9 85 F3
South Bristol Bsns Pk
BS4 22 E7
South Bristol Trad Pk BS3 11 F3
Southbrook TA5 135 C2
Southbrook Cl TA5 135 C2
Southbrook Cotts BA9 216 F4
South Cary La BA7 214 A5
South Cl
Draycott BS27 90 E2
Lympsham BS24 86 B8
Walton BA16 156 E7
South Combe BS24 67 B6
Southcombe House (Queens
Coll) TA3 168 D1
Southcombe Way BA22 186 B6
South Common La EX13 198 A5
Southcot Pl BA2 228 C1
South Croft BS25 51 F2
Southcroft Dr BA13 121 D4
South Ct DT9 225 B3
South Dene BS9 5 E6
Southdown
Charlton Horethorne
DT9 176 A1
Weston-Super-Mare BS22 31 F4
Southdown Ave BA2 44 B3
Southdown Com Inf Sch
BA2 44 B3
Southdown Cross EX16 179 B2
Southdown Jun Sch BA2 44 B3
Southdown Rd
Bath BA2 44 B4
Bristol BS9 5 F8
South Dro
Curry Rivel TA10 171 B4
North Curry TA3 170 D2
Southend Gdns TA9 104 E5
Southend Rd BS23 48 E4
Southernhay BS8 226 B2
Southernhay Ave BS8 226 B2
Southernhay Cres BS8 226 B2
Southern Lea Rd TA8 104 C8
Southern Ring Path 4
BS21 6 B1
Southern Way BS21 6 C1
South Espl TA8 104 A5
Southey Rd BS21 6 D2
Southfield
Cheddar BS27 90 B8
Norton St Philip BA2 81 F4
Radstock BA3 79 A2
Southwick BA14 83 F2
Wiveliscombe TA4 210 C3
Southfield Cl
Nailsea BS48 8 E3
Taunton TA2 168 F6
Weston-Super-Mare BS23 48 D2
Woolavington TA7 136 E3
Southfield Farm Cvn Pk &
Camp Site TA8 65 F4
Southfield Hill BA3 99 A6
Southfield Rd
Nailsea BS48 8 F3
Shepton Mallet BA4 205 A5
Southfield Rd Trad Est
BS48 8 F3
Southfields
Frome BA11 120 A2
Ilminster TA19 183 E2
South Fields BA6 206 E3
Southgate
Bath BA1 228 C2
Wiveliscombe TA4 210 C3
Southgate Ave TA6 209 A3
Southgate Dr BA9 216 C3
Southgate Rd BA9 216 C3
Southgate Sh Ctr BA1 228 C2
South Gr BS20 4 C4
South Green St 8 BS8 11 F6
South Harp TA13 220 E1
South Hele Cross EX16 165 C1
South Hill BS25 51 F2
South La
Challacombe EX31 126 A3
Nether Stowey TA5 134 B2
Southlands
Bath BA1 27 B1
Carhampton TA24 131 B5
Southlands Dr BA2 60 B2
Southlands Way BS49 34 E5
South Lawn BS24 49 F4
South Lawn Cl BS24 49 F4
South Lea Rd BA1 44 A8
Southleaze BS25 70 A6
Southleaze Orch BA16 207 C6
Southleaze Rd BA16 207 B6
Southleigh BS25 69 F8
Southleigh Rd
Bristol BS8 226 B4
Taunton TA1 213 B3
South Mdw BA5 113 A1
South Mdws BS40 35 E2
Southmead
West Camel BA22 174 D3
Winscombe BS25 70 A8
Southmead Cres TA18 224 C5
Southmead La BA8 190 A6
Southmead Rd BS22 49 B7
Southmead Terr TA18 224 C5
South Molton Rd EX16 164 B1
South Moors La TA7 137 B2
Southover BA5 203 D3
Southover Rd BS39 59 D1
South Par
Bath BA2 228 C2
Chew Magna BS40 39 B3
Frome BA11 119 E4
Weston-Super-Mare BS23 48 D8
South Parade Cotts BA2 45 C1
South Petherton Hospl
TA13 220 D5
South Petherton Inf Sch
TA13 220 C4
South Petherton Jun Sch
TA13 220 D3
South Pk TA24 200 D6
South Rd
Brean TA8 65 F3
Lympsham BS24 67 B1
Midsomer Norton BA3 78 B1
Portishead BS20 2 D7
Taunton TA1 213 A2
Timsbury BA2 60 B2
Watchet TA23 202 C6
Weston-Super-Mare BS23 30 C1
Southridge Hts BS24 67 A8
South Road Villas BA9 216 C3
South Rock Ind Est BA3 96 D1
Southside BS23 48 E8
South Side BS49 34 E5
Southside Cl BS9 5 B8
Southside Cres BS22 31 A4
South St
Burnham-on-S TA8 104 A6
Castle Cary BA7 214 B4
Crewkerne TA18 224 D5
Hinton St George TA17 195 D7
Holcombe Rogus TA21 178 F5
Kington Magna SP8 177 E1
Milborne Port DT9 217 D2
Montacute TA15 186 B3
Sherborne DT9 225 E3
South Petherton TA13 220 D4
Stratton-on-t F BA3 96 F2
Taunton TA1 213 A3
Walton BA16 156 E7
Wellington TA21 222 E5
Wells BA5 203 D4
West Camel BA22 174 D3
Wincanton BA9 216 C3
Wiveliscombe TA4 210 C4
Yeovil BA20 219 B4
Southstoke La BA2 62 F8
Southstoke Rd BA2 44 F1
South Terr
Burnham-on-S TA8 104 B6
Weston-Super-Mare BS23 48 D8
Southtown La BA6 158 B8
Southview TA3 168 D1
South View
12 Barwick BA22 197 F8
Bawdrip TA7 136 E2
Bradford Abbas DT9 187 E1
Broadway TA19 183 C2
Clandown BA3 78 E5
Ditcheat BA4 159 C6
Horrington BA5 113 A1
Lynford-on-F TA11 158 C1
Monkton Combe BA2 45 E1
Paulton BS39 77 E6
Portishead BS20 2 D7
Queen Camel BA22 174 F3
Timsbury BA2 60 B2
Westleigh EX16 179 A3
Southview Cl
Hutton BS24 49 E2
Westonzoyland TA7 154 F5
South View Pl BA3 78 B2
Southview Rd TA7 154 F5
South View Rd
Bath BA2 44 D6
Milborne Port DT9 217 C3
South View Terr
Taunton TA3 168 D1
Yatton BS49 17 B1
South Villas TA4 167 F6
Southville BA21 219 C5
Southville Rd BS23 48 E4
Southville Terr BA2 45 B4
Southway Cl BA21 218 F6
Southway Cres BA21 218 F6
Southway Ct BS21 6 D1
Southway Dr BA21 218 F6
Southwell TA3 168 D1
Southwell Cl TA3 168 D1
Southwell Cres TA9 104 E3
Southwell Ct TA9 104 E3
Southwell St BS2 226 C4
South Western Bsns Pk
DT9 225 D3
South Western Terr
BA20 219 C4
Southwick CE Prim Sch
BA14 83 F3
Southwick Ctry Pk* BA14 83 F5
Southwick Rd TA9 106 C1
Southwood BA4 159 D8
Southwood Ave BS9 5 C8
Southwood Dr BS9 5 B8
Southwood Dr E BS9 5 C8
Southwood Gr TA1 212 C2
Southwoods BA20 219 A3
Southwood Way TA3 181 C5
Sovereign Rd TA6 209 D7
Sovereign Sh Ctr BS23 48 D8
Sowden Hill TA5 134 D4
Spanish Hill TA6 153 F2
Spargrove La BA4 142 B1
Sparkford Hill La BA22 175 A4
Sparkford Rd BA22 175 A6
Sparkhayes La TA24 124 A3
Sparks Way TA9 104 D3
Sparrow Hill Way BS26 88 E6
Sparrow La TA24 146 C7
Sparrow Rd BA21 219 B6
Spartley Dr BS13 21 F6
Spartley Wlk BS13 21 F6
Spaxton CE Prim Sch
TA5 152 E7
Spaxton Cl TA8 104 C8
Spaxton Rd TA5 153 C7
Spearcey Cl TA3 181 D8
Spearcey La TA3 181 D8
Spearhay La TA20 198 F5
Spear Mead DT8 199 F7
Spears La TA4 166 A4
Specket La DT8 199 E5
Speckington La BA22 174 B2
Specklemead BS39 77 D5
Speedwell Ind Est 1 BS21 6 C2
Speke Cl
Ilminster TA19 221 B4
Merriott TA16 195 F7
Staplegrove TA2 212 B6
Speke Ct TA19 221 B4
Spencer Ave TA2 212 E6
Spencer Cl TA6 209 D3
Spencer Dr
Midsomer Norton BA3 78 A2
Weston-Super-Mare BS22 32 B3
Spencer Ho 6 BS1 227 B1
Spencers Belle Vue BA1 228 B4
Sperring Ct BA3 96 F8
Sperry Cross TA4 149 B1
Spicer Way TA20 223 D2
Spillers Cl TA6 208 E2
Spindleberry Gr BS48 9 A2
Spiningmill Cotts 3
BA11 119 E5
Spinners End BS22 32 B4
Spinners Ho 5 BA4 205 B6
Spinney Croft BS13 21 F5
Spinneyfield TA4 167 F7
Spinney Rd BS24 50 D4
Spinney The
Ashcott TA7 156 A8
Portishead BS20 2 C4
Taunton TA1 212 D2
Weston-Super-Mare BS24 48 F1
Yeovil BA20 218 D2
Spire Cross TA24 147 A4
Splatt La TA5 152 E8
Splott BS26 88 F6
Spoonbill Rd TA6 209 B4
Spratts Bridge BS40 39 A3
Sprigg Dr BS20 1 F1
Springbok Cl BA16 207 D7
Spring Cres BA2 228 C2
Springer's Hill BA3 116 E6
Springfield
Ilminster TA19 221 B2
Norton St Philip BA2 81 E4
Peasedown St John BA2 79 C7
Street BA16 207 B5
Springfield Ave
Bridgwater TA6 208 C3
Bristol, Shirehampton BS11 4 D6
Weston-Super-Mare BS22 31 D1
Springfield Bldgs
Midsomer Norton BS39 77 D2
Radstock BA3 79 A3
Springfield Cl
Bath BA2 44 B5
Cheddar BS27 90 A8
Cross BS26 69 F2
Springfield Cotts
Upton Cheyney BS30 26 A8
Winsford TA24 147 A6
Springfield Cres BA3 79 A3
Spring Field Cres DT9 225 C3
Springfield Ct BA4 205 A5
Springfield Dr BS28 108 C3
Springfield Flats TA20 223 C4
Springfield Gdns BS29 51 A3
Springfield Ho
Bristol BS6 226 C4
Portishead BS20 2 C4
Springfield Hts BA3 78 E4
Springfield Lawn BS11 4 D6
Springfield Pl
Bath BA1 27 F1
Clandown BA3 78 E4
Yeovil BA21 218 E7
Springfield Rd
Cheddar BS27 90 A8
Highbridge TA9 104 E4
Milborne Port DT9 217 D3
Pill BS20 4 C4
Portishead BS20 2 B5
Wellington TA21 222 C7
Wincanton BA9 216 B4
Yeovil BA21 218 E7
Springfields
East Chinnock BA22 196 E8
Stalbridge DT10 190 C4
Springfield Terr
Street BA16 207 B5
Tatworth TA20 198 D8
Spring Gardens Rd BA2 228 C2
Spring Gdns
Minehead TA24 201 B5
Wiveliscombe TA4 210 C5

Spr–Str 269

Spring Ground Rd BS39 . . . 77 E5
Spring Hill
Bristol BS2 . . . 227 A4
Weston-Super-Mare BS22 . . . 31 D2
Springhill Cl BS39 . . . 77 C6
Spring Hill Dr BS22 . . . 31 E1
Spring La
Bath BA1 . . . 28 B2
Dundry BS41 . . . 22 A1
Sandford Orcas DT9 . . . 188 C7
Springley Rd TA6 . . . 209 D6
Springmead TA20 . . . 223 B3
Springmead Sch BA11 . . . 101 E4
Spring Rd BA11 . . . 119 F6
Spring Rise
Portishead BS20 . . . 2 C3
Puriton TA7 . . . 136 C4
Wells BA5 . . . 203 C3
Spring Terr
Frome BA11 . . . 119 D2
Weston-Super-Mare BS22 . . . 31 C2
Spring Vale BA1 . . . 28 B2
Spring Valley BS22 . . . 31 C2
Springway Ind Est TA7 . . 155 A5
Spring Wood Gdns BS24 . . 49 E3
Spruce Way
Bath BA2 . . . 62 E8
Weston-Super-Mare BS22 . . . 49 E8
Spurwells TA19 . . . 183 F4
Squares Rd TA5 . . . 135 F2
Square The
Axbridge BS26 . . . 70 C2
Banwell BS29 . . . 51 B3
Bath BA2 . . . 228 B1
Edington TA7 . . . 137 C2
Maiden Bradley BA12 . . . 144 C2
Shipham BS25 . . . 70 E7
Taunton TA1 . . . 213 C2
Temple Cloud BS39 . . . 58 E1
Wellow BA2 . . . 62 D1
Westbury-sub-Mendip BA5 . 110 E6
Winscombe BS25 . . . 69 E6
Wiveliscombe TA4 . . . 210 C4
Woolavington TA7 . . . 136 E4
Squibbs Cl TA6 . . . 209 D5
Squibbs Ho TA6 . . . 208 F5
Squire La BS40 . . . 55 C1
Squirrel Ct TA21 . . . 222 D5
Stabbins Cl BS22 . . . 32 B5
Stables The BA3 . . . 98 B5
Stable Yd BA2 . . . 44 D6
Stacey's Ct TA10 . . . 171 F5
Staddlestones BA3 . . . 96 F7
Staddonhill Rd TA24 . . . 146 F8
Stafford Pl BS23 . . . 48 E8
Stafford Rd
Bridgwater TA6 . . . 209 C3
Portishead BS20 . . . 2 E4
Weston-Super-Mare BS23 . . . 48 F7
Stagman La TA7, BA16 . . . 156 C8
Stag Mill Cross EX16 . . . 178 B3
Stag Way BA6 . . . 206 C4
Stainer Cl BS4 . . . 22 D7
Staker's Cross TA20 . . . 195 B2
Staker's Cross La TA18, TA20 . . . 195 B2
Stalbridge Cl DT10 . . . 190 B4
Stalbridge La
Marnhull DT10 . . . 190 F2
Sturminster Newton DT10 . . 190 F1
Stalbridge Pk DT10 . . . 190 A4
Stalbridge Prim Sch DT10 . . . 190 B5
Stalbridge Rd
Henstridge BA8 . . . 190 A6
Stalbridge Weston DT10 . . 190 A3
Stourton Caundle DT10 . . . 189 F2
Stalcombe La BA2 . . . 42 B4
Staling Way BA4 . . . 205 C4
Stallards TA21 . . . 222 C3
Stallgrove La BA16 . . . 207 D3
Stall St BA1 . . . 228 C2
Stalls The BA12 . . . 144 D7
Stambrook Pk BA1 . . . 29 A5
Stammery Hill EX13 . . . 198 C1
Stanchester Com Sch TA14 . . . 186 A4
Stanchester Way TA10 . . . 171 D4
Stancombe La
Flax Bourton BS48 . . . 19 E7
Westbury-sub-Mendip BA5 . 110 F8
Standards Rd TA7 . . . 154 E5
Standards The TA7 . . . 137 D2
Standerwick Cross BA11 . 102 B2
Standerwick Orch TA19 . 183 C2
Standfast Pl TA2 . . . 213 C8
Standhill Rd TA10 . . . 155 F2
Standish Ct TA1 . . . 212 F4
Standish St TA6 . . . 208 F7
Stane Way BS11 . . . 4 C7
Stanford Pl BS4 . . . 22 D7
Stanhope Pl BA1 . . . 228 A2
Stanhope Rd BS23 . . . 48 E3
Stanier Cl BA11 . . . 120 D6
Stanier Rd BA2 . . . 228 A2
Stankley View TA19 . . . 184 F4
Stanley Cl
Bridgwater TA6 . . . 208 F2
Staplegrove TA2 . . . 212 C6
Stanley Ct BA3 . . . 78 B2
Stanley Gr BS23 . . . 48 F7
Stanley Rd 2 BS23 . . . 48 F7
Stanley Rd W BA2 . . . 44 D5
Stanley Terr BA3 . . . 79 A3
Stanley Villas 12 BA1 . . . 28 A1
Stanmoor Rd TA7 . . . 170 F8
Stanshalls Cl BS40 . . . 37 C8
Stanshalls Dr BS40 . . . 37 C8
Stanshalls La BS40 . . . 37 C8
Stanton Drew Prim Sch BS39 . . . 40 A2
Stanton Drew Stone Circles* BS39 . . . 40 A3
Stanton La BS39 . . . 40 D4
Stanton Rd BS40 . . . 39 B3
Stanton Wick La BS39 . . . 40 B1
Stant Way TA20 . . . 193 C6
Stanway Cl
Bath BA2 . . . 44 D1
Taunton TA2 . . . 212 D7
Staple Cl TA4 . . . 132 E4
Staplecombe Vineyard* TA2 . . . 168 C6
Staplegate EX16 . . . 178 A3
Staple Gr BS31 . . . 24 D5
Staplegrove CE Prim Sch TA2 . . . 212 C7
Staplegrove Manor TA2 . 212 D8
Staplegrove Rd
Staplegrove TA2 . . . 212 C7
Taunton TA1, TA2 . . . 212 E5
Staple Hill TA3 . . . 182 C5
Staple La TA4 . . . 132 E4
Staples Cl BS21 . . . 6 E1
Staples Gn BS22 . . . 32 B3
Staples Hill BA3 . . . 64 C4
Staples Mdw TA20 . . . 198 D8
Stapleton Cl TA12 . . . 185 E7
Stapleton Cross TA12 . . . 185 E7
Stapleton Rd TA12 . . . 185 E7
Stapley Cross TA3 . . . 181 B1
Stapling La TA24 . . . 130 F3
Starcross Rd BS22 . . . 32 A2
Star La BS20 . . . 4 D4
Starling Cl BS22 . . . 49 E8
Starrs Cl BS26 . . . 70 B2
Stars La BA20 . . . 219 C4
Statham Cl
Cheddar BS27 . . . 90 B7
Taunton TA1 . . . 212 C2
Statham Gr TA1 . . . 212 C2
Stathe Cotts TA7 . . . 171 B7
Stathe Rd TA7 . . . 171 A8
Station App
Bristol BS1 . . . 227 C1
Frome BA11 . . . 120 A4
Ilminster TA19 . . . 183 E1
Pensford BS39 . . . 40 D5
Weston-Super-Mare BS23 . . . 48 E7
Station Cl
Backwell BS48 . . . 18 F7
Congresbury BS49 . . . 34 C4
Station Lodge 8 BS23 . . . 48 E7
Station Mead BA3 . . . 96 D3
Station Path TA11 . . . 211 D3
Station Rd
Ashcott TA7 . . . 156 B8
Axbridge BS26 . . . 70 C2
Backwell BS48 . . . 19 A6
Bampton EX16 . . . 164 B1
Bath BA1 . . . 44 C7
Binegar BA3 . . . 114 D7
Bishops Lydeard TA4 . . . 167 E8
Blagdon BS40 . . . 54 E3
Bristol, Shirehampton BS11 . . 4 D5
Bristol, Shirehampton BS11 . . 4 E6
Bruton BA10 . . . 215 F6
Burlescombe EX16 . . . 179 B3
Burnham-on-S TA9 . . . 85 F3
Burtle TA7 . . . 137 D6
Castle Cary BA7 . . . 214 B6
Chard Junction TA20 . . . 198 D8
Cheddar BS27 . . . 90 B7
Clevedon BS21 . . . 6 D3
Clutton BS39 . . . 58 E3
Congresbury BS49 . . . 34 C4
Cossington TA7 . . . 136 F3
Draycott BS27 . . . 90 E2
Dunster TA24 . . . 201 E4
Flax Bourton BS48 . . . 20 A8
Freshford BA3 . . . 64 C5
Hatch Beauchamp TA3 . . . 183 A7
Ilminster TA19 . . . 221 A4
Keynsham BS31 . . . 24 E6
Meare TA7 . . . 138 C1
Midsomer Norton BA3 . . . 78 B2
Milborne Port DT9 . . . 217 D4
Milverton TA4 . . . 167 A5
Misterton TA18 . . . 224 E4
Nailsea BS48 . . . 8 F2
Norton Fitzwarren TA2 . . . 168 B4
Pill BS20 . . . 4 C4
Portbury BS20 . . . 3 D3
Portishead BS20 . . . 2 D6
Sandford BS25 . . . 51 F4
Shapwick TA7 . . . 137 F2
Shepton Mallet BA4 . . . 205 B5
Sherborne DT9 . . . 225 E3
Stalbridge DT10 . . . 190 B4
Stogumber TA4 . . . 150 D8
Taunton TA1 . . . 212 F5
Templecombe BA8 . . . 176 E1
Walpole TA6 . . . 136 B3
Wanstrow BA4 . . . 142 F4
Washford TA23 . . . 131 E4
Wellington TA21 . . . 222 C7
Wellow BA2 . . . 62 D1
Westbury-sub-Mendip BA5 . 110 E5
Weston-Super-Mare BS23 . . . 48 E7
Weston-Super-Mare, St Georges BS22 . . . 32 D2
Weston-Super-Mare, Worle BS22 . . . 31 F2
Williton TA4 . . . 202 E3
Wincanton BA9 . . . 216 C3
Wiveliscombe TA4 . . . 210 C4
Station Rd *continued*
Wrington BS40 . . . 35 D2
Yatton BS49 . . . 17 B1
Station Rd (Blackmoor La) BA8 . . . 190 A7
Station Rd Ind Est BA10 . . 215 F6
Station Road Bsns Pk DT10 . . . 190 B5
Station Terr TA24 . . . 201 A7
Station Way BA4 . . . 141 E1
Station Wlk TA9 . . . 104 E3
Staundle La TA3 . . . 183 B8
Staunton Fields BS14 . . . 23 C4
Staunton La
Minehead TA24 . . . 201 A4
Whitchurch BS14 . . . 23 D3
Staunton Rd TA24 . . . 201 A5
Staunton Rise TA24 . . . 201 A5
Staunton Way BS14 . . . 23 D4
Stavordale Gr BS14 . . . 23 B6
Stawell Rd TA7 . . . 137 B1
Stawley Prim Sch TA21 . . . 179 B8
Steamalong TA3 . . . 183 E7
Steam Mills BA3 . . . 96 F8
Steam Packet Terr 2 TA6 . . . 209 B4
Steanbow Cotts BA4 . . . 140 D3
Steart Ave TA8 . . . 104 B6
Steart Cl TA8 . . . 104 B6
Steart Cotts TA3 . . . 169 C3
Steart Ct TA8 . . . 104 A7
Steart Dr TA8 . . . 104 A6
Steart Dro TA10 . . . 156 D1
Steart Gdns TA8 . . . 104 B6
Steart Hill BA22 . . . 174 D5
Steart La
Babcary TA11 . . . 174 B6
Wheddon Cross TA24 . . . 129 F3
Stedhams Cl TA21 . . . 222 D7
Steeds Terr BA3 . . . 115 D6
Steel's La BA9 . . . 161 D2
Steel La TA7 . . . 137 D2
Steel Mills BS31 . . . 24 F4
Steel Well La BA8 . . . 190 A6
Steep La TA22 . . . 164 C8
Steeple View BA3 . . . 116 A3
Steep The TA24 . . . 147 C5
Steevens Ho (Almshouses) 13 BS2 . . . 227 C3
Stembridge Rd TA10 . . . 156 B1
Stembridge Tower Mill* TA10 . . . 156 B1
Stembridge Way TA2 . . . 168 B4
Stephen's Hill TA10 . . . 172 E4
Stephenson Dr BA11 . . . 120 D6
Stephenson Rd TA24 . . . 201 B6
Stephen St TA1 . . . 213 A4
Stephen Way 6 TA1 . . . 213 A4
Steppes Cres 18 TA12 . . . 185 E6
Steppes Mdw TA12 . . . 185 E6
Steps La BA2 . . . 100 E7
Stert Dro TA5 . . . 135 B7
Steven's Cl BA4 . . . 205 A5
Stevens La
Frome BA11 . . . 119 F3
Lympsham BS24 . . . 67 C3
Stewart Ct EX13 . . . 198 A2
Steway La BA1 . . . 29 B6
Stibbear La TA19 . . . 194 A8
Stiby Ct BA21 . . . 218 F7
Stiby Rd BA21 . . . 218 E7
Stickland BS21 . . . 6 C1
Stickleball La BA4, BA6 . . 140 D1
Stickle Hill TA4 . . . 151 B7
Stickle Path EX16 . . . 165 C1
Sticklinch Rd BA6 . . . 140 C2
Stilemead La BS40 . . . 55 D1
Stiles Ct BA5 . . . 203 B4
Stileway BA6 . . . 138 E4
Stileway Bsns Pk BS21 . . . 16 B8
Stiling Cl TA9 . . . 104 D4
Stillingfleet Rd BS13 . . . 22 C5
Stillington Cl BA5 . . . 203 B3
Stillman Cl BS13 . . . 21 E4
Stirling Way
Frome BA11 . . . 120 C6
Keynsham BS31 . . . 24 E4
Stirtingale Ave BA2 . . . 44 C3
Stirtingale Rd BA2 . . . 44 C3
Stitching La BS28 . . . 138 C8
Stitchings La BA2 . . . 61 D7
Stitchings Shord La BS39 . 57 C4
Stoate Cl TA23 . . . 202 C5
Stoberry Ave BA5 . . . 203 E5
Stoberry Cres BA5 . . . 203 E5
Stoberry Park Sch BA5 . . 203 E5
Stock's La
Hatch Beauchamp TA3, TA19 . . . 183 B6
Leigh u M BA3 . . . 116 E3
North Wootton BA4 . . . 140 C4
Stockbridge TA17 . . . 195 D7
Stockbridge La BA6 . . . 140 B2
Stockditch Rd TA12 . . . 185 B7
Stockers Cl TA4 . . . 210 B4
Stockham Cross TA4 . . . 151 D5
Stockham Hill TA22 . . . 163 E8
Stock Hill BA3 . . . 115 B8
Stockhill Cl BA3 . . . 96 C3
Stock Hill Ct BA3 . . . 117 B7
Stockhill Rd BA3 . . . 96 C2
Stock La
Buckhorn Weston SP8 . . . 177 F5
Lower Langford BS40 . . . 53 A7
Stockland Hill EX14 . . . 192 A1
Stockland Manor TA5 . . . 134 F6
Stockman La TA20 . . . 198 C7
Stockmead BS40 . . . 53 B5
Stockmoor Cl TA6 . . . 209 A2
Stock Moor Dro TA6 . . . 209 A1
Stockstyle La EX13 . . . 198 A8
Stockton Cl BS14 . . . 22 F4
Stock Way N BS48 . . . 8 F2
Stock Way S BS48 . . . 8 E2
Stockwitch Cross BA22 . . 174 B3
Stockwood Green Prim Sch BS14 . . . 23 E4
Stockwood Hill BS31 . . . 24 C7
Stockwood La BS14 . . . 23 E5
Stockwood Rd BS4, BS14 . . 24 A7
Stockwood Vale BS31 . . . 24 C6
Stodden's La TA8 . . . 104 E8
Stodden's Rd TA8 . . . 85 C1
Stodden's Wlk TA8 . . . 104 B8
Stodelegh Cl BS22 . . . 32 B3
Stoford La
Broadway TA19 . . . 183 C2
West Buckland TA21 . . . 181 A7
Stoford Pl TA19 . . . 183 C2
Stogumber CE Fst Sch TA4 . . . 150 D8
Stogumber Sta* TA4 . . . 150 E8
Stogursey CE Prim Sch TA5 . . . 134 B5
Stogursey La TA5 . . . 134 A3
Stoke Bishop CE Prim Sch BS9 . . . 5 D5
Stoke Cotts BS9 . . . 5 E4
Stoke Cres BA3 . . . 116 A2
Stoke Cross 10 TA14 . . . 185 F4
Stoke Gr BS9 . . . 5 E6
Stoke Hamlet BS9 . . . 5 F6
Stoke Hill
Bristol BS9 . . . 5 E3
Chew Stoke BS40 . . . 56 D7
Stoke St Mary TA3 . . . 169 D1
Stoke St Michael BA3 . . . 116 A2
Stoney Stoke BA9 . . . 160 E3
Stoke La
Bristol, Westbury on T BS9 . . . 5 F6
Stoke St Mary TA3 . . . 169 A1
Wincanton BA9 . . . 216 F5
Yarlington BA9 . . . 175 E7
Stokeleigh Wlk BS9 . . . 5 C5
Stoke Mead BA2 . . . 63 F7
Stoke Moor Dro BS27 . . . 109 D6
Stoke Paddock Rd BS9 . . . 5 D6
Stoke Park Rd BS9 . . . 5 F4
Stoke Park Rd S BS9 . . . 5 E3
Stoke Rd
Bristol BS9 . . . 5 F3
Martock TA12 . . . 185 E5
North Curry TA3 . . . 170 C4
Portishead BS20 . . . 2 D5
Ruishton TA3 . . . 169 C2
Stoke St Mary TA3 . . . 169 B1
Street BA16 . . . 207 E6
Taunton TA1 . . . 213 B1
Westbury-sub-Mendip BA5 . . . 110 D6
Stoke St Gregory CE Prim Sch TA3 . . . 170 E6
Stoke St Michael Prim Sch BA3 . . . 116 A3
Stokes Croft BS1 . . . 227 B4
Stokes La DT10 . . . 189 F2
Stoke St BS27 . . . 110 B8
Stoke sub Hamdon Castle Prim Sch TA14 . . . 185 F4
Stoke sub Hamdon Priory* TA14 . . . 185 F4
Stolford Hill TA22 . . . 148 A4
Stonage La TA18 . . . 196 C5
Stoneable Rd BA3 . . . 79 A3
Stoneage La BA2 . . . 61 B1
Stone Allerton Dro BS26 . 88 B2
Stonebarrow La EX13 . . . 198 F2
Stoneberry Rd BS14 . . . 23 B3
Stonebridge BS21 . . . 6 D1
Stonebridge Dr BA11 . . . 120 B7
Stonebridge Rd BS23 . . . 48 F4
Stone Cl TA1 . . . 168 D1
Stone Cross TA24 . . . 128 E1
Stonedene DT9 . . . 225 D6
Stone Down La BA6 . . . 139 D1
Stonegallows TA1 . . . 212 A3
Stonehenge La BS48 . . . 8 E4
Stonehill
South Cadbury BA22 . . . 175 C3
Stoke Sub Hamdon TA14 . . 186 A4
Street BA16 . . . 207 B5
Stone Hill Ct TA24 . . . 200 F7
Stone Hill La TA4 . . . 166 D3
Stonehouse Cl BA2 . . . 45 B2
Stonehouse La BA2 . . . 45 B2
Stone La
East Pennard BA4 . . . 158 E6
Exford TA24 . . . 128 E1
Winsford TA24 . . . 147 E6
Yeovil BA21 . . . 187 B5
Stoneleigh
Chew Magna BS40 . . . 39 B3
Wellington TA21 . . . 222 B8
Stoneleigh Cl
Burnham-on-S TA8 . . . 104 C8
Staplegrove TA2 . . . 212 C8
Stoneleigh Ct
Bath BA1 . . . 27 E3
Taunton TA1 . . . 212 C1
Stoneleigh Mews BA21 . . 218 C7
Stoneleigh Rise BA11 . . . 120 A6
Stone Mead La TA10 . . . 173 A4
Stone Rd TA8 . . . 104 D5
Stoneridge La TA4 . . . 165 D5
Stones Cross BA3 . . . 78 B2
Stonesfield TA18 . . . 196 B5
Stones Paddock BA3 . . . 116 C7
Stonewall Terr BA11 . . . 119 F2
Stonewell Dr BS49 . . . 34 D3
Stonewell Gr BS49 . . . 34 D3
Stonewell La BS49 . . . 34 D3
Stonewell Park Rd BS49 . 34 D3
Stoneyard La BA3 . . . 75 D2
Stoney Cl TA24 . . . 129 F6
Stoneyfield Cl BS20 . . . 4 B5
Stoneyfields BS20 . . . 4 B4
Stoney Furlong TA2 . . . 213 B8
Stoney Head Cvn Pk TA3 . 169 F1
Stoneyhurst Dr TA10 . . . 171 C3
Stoney La
Bishops Lydeard TA4 . . . 167 E8
Curry Rivel TA10 . . . 171 C3
East Coker BA22 . . . 197 D6
Stocklinch TA19 . . . 184 C4
Stoney Lane Cross EX16 . . 178 B3
Stoney Littleton Long Barrow* BA2 . . . 80 C7
Stoney St TA24 . . . 129 C7
Stoney Steep BS48 . . . 9 A5
Stonyhead Hill TA3 . . . 169 F1
Stony La
Axminster EX13 . . . 198 A1
Hawkridge TA22 . . . 146 E3
Whatley BA11 . . . 118 A2
Stony St BA11 . . . 119 F5
Stoodham TA13 . . . 220 D5
Stoodly La
North Wootton BA4 . . . 140 D4
Pilton BA4 . . . 204 A2
Stooper's Hill TA20 . . . 193 C6
Stopgate Cross EX14 . . . 192 C4
Stoppard Rd TA8 . . . 104 C6
Stopper's La BA5 . . . 139 F6
Stormont Cl BS23 . . . 48 F3
Stormore BA13 . . . 121 F8
Storridge La
Axminster EX13 . . . 198 B6
Brompton Regis TA22 . . . 148 A1
Storridge View TA22 . . . 148 A2
Stourhead Gdns* BA12 . . 161 F5
Stourhead Ho* BA12 . . . 161 F5
Stour Hill SP8 . . . 177 E1
Stour Hill Pk SP8 . . . 177 F1
Stourton Cl BA11 . . . 119 E3
Stourton Gdns 1 BA11 . . 119 E3
Stourton La BA12 . . . 161 F6
Stourton View BA11 . . . 119 E3
Stourton Way BA21 . . . 218 D6
Stout's Way La
Luxborough TA23 . . . 148 F8
Rodhuish TA24 . . . 131 A1
Stout Cross EX14 . . . 192 C5
Stowborough Cotts BA2 . . 79 C7
Stowell Hill DT9 . . . 176 C1
Stowell La TA20 . . . 198 D8
Stowers Row 31 TA12 . . . 185 E6
Stowey Bottom BS39 . . . 57 E5
Stowey Cross Rds BS39 . . . 57 F5
Stowey La
Curry Mallet TA3 . . . 183 E8
Fivehead TA3 . . . 170 E1
Stowey Pk BS49 . . . 34 D7
Stowey Rd
Pitney TA10 . . . 172 D7
Taunton TA2 . . . 212 E8
Yatton BS49 . . . 34 C8
Stow Ho BS11 . . . 4 E5
Stradling's Hill TA5 . . . 135 B3
Stradling Ave BS23 . . . 48 F5
Stradling Cl TA7 . . . 137 B2
Stradlings Yd BS2 . . . 226 C4
Straight Dro
Burrowbridge TA7 . . . 155 B1
Chilton Trinity TA5 . . . 135 F2
West Huntspill TA9 . . . 136 B7
Woolavington TA9 . . . 137 A6
Straight La BA11 . . . 101 D7
Straightmead BA3 . . . 75 F1
Straight St BS2 . . . 227 C2
Strap La
Ston Easton BA3 . . . 95 F7
Upton Noble BA4, BA10 . . 143 A1
Stratford Cl BS14 . . . 22 F3
Stratford Ct BS9 . . . 5 F8
Stratford La BS40 . . . 56 E1
Stratford Rd BA21 . . . 218 D5
Stratheden BS8 . . . 226 A4
Stratton Cl TA6 . . . 209 D3
Stratton Rd
Holcombe BA3 . . . 116 B8
Saltford BS31 . . . 25 E3
Stratton St BS2 . . . 227 B3
Strawberry Bank TA19 . . . 221 C4
Strawberry Cl BS48 . . . 8 D1
Strawberry Field BS26 . . . 70 D2
Strawberry Gdns BS48 . . . 18 D8
Strawberry Hill
Clevedon BS21 . . . 6 F4
Street BA16 . . . 207 B7
Strawberry La BS13, BS41 . . 21 E3
Strawberry Way BA5 . . . 203 C4
Strawberry Way Rdbt BA5 . . . 203 D3
Streaked La TA3 . . . 170 C6
Streamcombe La TA22 . . . 163 B5
Streamcross BS49 . . . 17 D1
Streamleaze BS40 . . . 39 B3
Streamside
Chew Magna BS40 . . . 39 B3
1 Clevedon BS21 . . . 6 F3
Taunton TA1 . . . 213 C2

Street Ash La TA20 193 C8
Street Dro
Street BA16 207 E7
Street, Marshall's Elm BA16 207 B1
Street End BS40 54 D2
Street End La BS40 54 D2
Street Ho TA19 221 B3
Street La
Odcombe BA22 186 C2
South Brewham BA10 161 A7
Street Rd
Compton Dundon TA11 157 A4
Glastonbury BA6 206 D3
Street BA6 207 D8
Street Rdbt BA16 207 D7
Street Shoe Mus* BA16 207 C6
Street The
Bishop Sutton BS39 57 D4
Chew Stoke BS40 56 D8
Chilcompton BA3 96 D5
Compton Martin BS40 74 B7
Draycott BS27 90 F2
Farmborough BA2 59 F6
Kilmington BA12 161 F6
Radstock BA3 78 F2
Stowey BS39 57 F4
Ubley BS40 55 D1
Wanstrow BA4 142 F4
West Monkton TA2 169 C7
Winford BS40 37 F1
Stretcholt La TA6 135 F6
Stretford La TA19 194 F7
Stringfellow Cres TA20 223 D5
Stringfellow Mews TA20 223 C3
Stringland's La TA24 131 B2
Strode Coll BA16 207 D6
Strode Ho 7 BA4 205 B6
Strode Rd
Clevedon BS21 6 C2
Street BA16 207 D6
Strode Way
Clevedon BS21 6 B1
Shepton Mallet BA4 205 A5
Stroud Rd BS11 4 E5
Stroud Way BS24 49 E7
Strowland La BS24 86 F6
Strowlands BS24, TA9 86 E6
Struthers Cl BA16 207 B7
Strutter's Hill BA10 215 D2
Stuart Ho BS23 30 D1
Stuart Pl BA2 44 D6
Stuart Rd BS23 49 A5
Stuarts Cl BA5 203 D3
Stubb's La BA11 101 D4
Studley La BA4 142 F4
Studley Mdws BA4 142 F4
Stump Cross
Pitcombe BA7 215 A1
Shepton Mallet BA4 204 D5
Sturford La BA12 144 E7
Sturmey Way BS20 4 E3
Sturminster Cl BS14 23 D6
Sturminster Lodge BS14 23 D5
Sturminster Rd BS14 23 D7
Stutts End TA4 167 E6
Style Flats TA4 210 C5
Style Rd TA4 210 C5
Styles Ave BA11 120 C4
Styles Cl BA11 120 B4
Styles Hill BA11 120 B4
Styles Mdw BA11 120 C5
Styles Pk BA11 120 B4
Sub Rd BA6 157 D4
Suffolk Cl TA6 209 C3
Suffolk Cres TA1 212 C1
Suffolk Ct TA1 212 C1
Suffolk Ho BA1 44 C8
Sugg's La TA19 183 C2
Sulis Manor Rd BA2 62 D8
Sullivan Cl BS4 22 D6
Sully Cl TA6 209 D6
Sumerleaze Cres TA2 213 C8
Sumerlin Dr BS21 6 F3
Summer Ct BS8 226 B3
Summerfield BS22 32 A3
Summerfield Ave TA21 180 D8
Summerfield Cl TA7 154 F5
Summerfield Ct TA1 212 E4
Summerfield Rd BA1 28 A1
Summerfields BA8 190 A7
Summerfields Rd TA20 223 C3
Summerfield Terr BA1 28 A1
Summerfield Way TA21 180 D8
Summerhedge Cres TA7 155 C2
Summerhedge Rd TA7 155 C1
Summer Hill
Frome BA11 119 F3
Hinton St George TA17 195 D7
Summerhill Rd BA1 27 D1
Summerhouse BS21 8 D4
Summer House Terr BA20 219 B4
Summerhouse View BA21 219 C6
Summer La
Banwell BS29 50 E5
Chard TA20 194 C4
Hinton St George TA13, TA17 195 C8
Monkton Combe BA2 63 D8
Weston-Super-Mare BS22, BS24 32 B1
Weston-Super-Mare BS29 50 C8
Weston-Super-Mare BS29 50 D7
Summer La N BS22 32 A2
Summerland Ave TA24 201 A7
Summerland Pl TA24 200 F7
Summerland Rd TA24 200 F7
Summerlands
Backwell BS48 19 B5
Yeovil BA21 218 E6
Summerlands Hospl BA21 218 F6
Summerlands Park Ave TA19 221 B4
Summerlands Park Cl TA19 221 B4
Summerlands Park Dr TA19 221 B4
Summerlands Rd BS23 49 B8
Summer Lane Cvn Pk BS29 50 E3
Summer Lane Park Homes BS29 50 E4
Summerlays Ct BA2 45 B6
Summerlays Pl BA2 45 B6
Summerlea BA2 61 A5
Summerleaze BS31 24 E7
Summerleaze Cres TA2 213 C7
Summerleaze Pk BA20 218 F5
Summer Shard TA13 220 C4
Summers Hill La BA4 204 C2
Summerville Terr TA8 104 B6
Summerway TA24 129 E1
Summerway Dro TA7 209 E4
Summerwood Rd BA16 207 B4
Sun Batch BS27 91 A3
Sunderland Pl BS8 226 B3
Sunderland St 2 BA2 228 C3
Sundew Cl TA1 213 C1
Sunfield Rd BS24 49 E3
Sunningdale BS8 226 B4
Sunningdale Cl BS48 9 A1
Sunningdale Rd
Weston-Super-Mare BS22 31 F3
Yeovil BA21 219 C6
Sunnybank BA2 45 B4
Sunny Bank TA4 150 B8
Sunnybank Ct BS24 32 B1
Sunnybank Rd TA6 208 E2
Sunnybank Way BS24 32 B1
Sunnybrow Cl 10 TA6 153 F4
Sunny Cl TA9 136 B8
Sunny Hill
Bristol BS9 5 C7
Pitcombe BA10 215 C4
Sunnyhill Dr BS11 4 E6
Sunnyhill Ho E BS11 4 E6
Sunnyhill Ho W BS11 4 E6
Sunny La BA10 215 C4
Sunnymead
Bridgwater TA6 208 E2
Keynsham BS31 24 F3
Midsomer Norton BA3 77 F2
Oakhill BA3 114 F3
Stratton-on-t F BA3 96 F2
Sunnymeade BA6 138 C4
Sunnymede Rd BS48 8 D3
Sunnyside
Barrington TA19 184 C5
Bristol BS9 5 E5
Burlescombe EX16 179 C2
Clatworthy TA4 149 F1
Clutton BS39 59 B4
Farrington Gurney BS39 77 B3
Frome BA11 119 F3
Sunnyside Cotts TA24 129 A8
Sunnyside Cres BS21 6 D3
Sunnyside Farm Trad Est BS20 4 C2
Sunnyside Gdns BA2 60 B2
Sunnyside Pl BA11 119 F3
Sunnyside Rd
Clevedon BS21 6 D3
Weston-Super-Mare BS23 48 E5
Sunnyside Rd N BS23 48 E6
Sunnyside Terr 6 DT9 225 E4
Sunnyside View BA2 79 C7
Sunnyvale
Camerton BA2 78 E8
Clevedon BS21 6 B1
Sunridge Cl BA3 96 F8
Sunridge Pk BA3 96 F8
Sunset Cl BA2 79 C7
Sun St BA11 119 E5
Suprema Ave TA7 137 C2
Suprema Est TA7 137 D2
Surrey St BS2 227 B4
Susanna's Cross BA3 116 B2
Susanna's La BA3 116 C2
Sussex Ave TA6 209 B3
Sussex Cl TA6 209 B3
Sussex Lodge TA1 212 F5
Sussex Pl BA2 228 C1
Sutherland Ave TA8 104 B6
Sutherland Cl TA1 212 C1
Sutherland Ct TA1 212 C1
Sutherland Dr BS24 49 D2
Sutton Cl
Frome BA11 120 B7
Weston-Super-Mare BS22 49 E8
Sutton Cross TA10 172 F4
Sutton Grange BA21 218 C6
Sutton Hill
East Coker BA22 197 D6
Long Sutton TA10 172 E3
Sutton Hill Rd BS39 57 D4
Sutton La
Redhill BS40 36 F1
Walton BA16 156 D6
Sutton Pk BS39 57 D4
Sutton Rd TA11 211 C2
Sutton St BA2 45 B7
Sutton View TA10 172 E2
Swains TA21 222 D4
Swains La TA21 222 D4
Swain St TA23 202 C7
Swainswick BS14 22 F6
Swainswick CE Prim Sch BA1 28 B5
Swainswick Gdns BA1 28 C2
Swainswick La BA1 28 D4
Swallow Cl BA3 97 B8
Swallowcliffe Ct 5 BA20 219 A5
Swallowcliffe Gdns BA20 219 A5
Swallow Ct
Bristol BS14 23 F6
Sampford Peverell EX16 178 F1
Swallow Dr BA11 120 B6
Swallow Gdns BS22 49 E8
Swallow Hill TA10 172 A6
Swallow St BA1 228 C2
Swallows The BS22 49 D7
Swan Cl BS22 49 E8
Swancombe
Blagdon BS40 54 E2
Clapton in G BS20 8 E8
Swan Down TA20 194 E4
Swane Rd BS14 23 F6
Swan Hill TA18 196 C5
Swan Ho 3 BA4 205 B6
Swanmead Com Sch TA19 221 C3
Swan Prec TA19 221 C3
Swanshard La BA5 139 D6
Swans La BS27 90 F2
Swan Yd DT9 225 D4
Swedish Hos TA13 220 D1
Sweetgrass Rd BS24 50 A8
Sweethay Cl TA3 181 D8
Sweethay Cross TA3 181 C8
Sweethay La TA3 181 C8
Sweetleaze BA3 116 A2
Swell Cl TA9 136 B8
Swell La TA3 171 A2
Swiddacombe La EX36 162 C7
Swift Cl BS22 31 F1
Swift Lodge BA20 219 A4
Swifts TA21 166 F1
Swillbridge Cvn Pk TA23 202 F6
Swingbridge TA2 213 E7
Swiss Dr BS3 11 F2
Swiss Rd
Bristol BS3 11 F1
Weston-Super-Mare BS23 48 F7
Sycamore Cl
Bridgwater TA6 209 D5
Burnham-on-S TA8 104 A5
Nailsea BS48 8 E2
Shipham BS25 70 E8
Taunton TA1 213 C2
Weston-Super-Mare BS23 49 A8
Weston-Super-Mare, Locking BS24 49 E5
Westonzoyland TA7 154 E5
Sycamore Ct TA20 223 C5
Sycamore Dr
Crewkerne TA18 224 D7
Frome BA11 120 B7
Langport TA10 172 A6
Yeovil BA20 218 F2
Sycamore Rd
Minehead TA24 200 D7
Radstock BA3 79 B2
Sycamores BS23 30 E1
Sycamore Sq TA20 223 C5
Sycamore Wlk TA3 169 D4
Sydenham Bldgs BA2 228 A2
Sydenham Cl
Bridgwater TA6 209 C6
Porlock TA24 124 B4
Sydenham Rd
Bath BA2 228 A2
Bridgwater TA6 209 C6
Sydenham Terr BA2 45 C1
Sydling Rd BA21 219 D6
Sydnalls La BA12 144 E8
Sydney Bldgs BA2 45 B6
Sydney Ho BA2 45 B7
Sydney Mews BA2 45 B7
Sydney Pl BA2 45 B7
Sydney Rd BA2 45 B7
Sydney Row BS1 226 B1
Sydney Wharf BA2 45 B7
Sylvan Rd TA21 222 E5
Sylvan Way
Bristol BS9 5 B7
Monkton Heathfield TA2 213 E8
Symes Ave BS13 22 C4
Symes Cl
Chard TA20 223 C4
North Perrott TA18 196 C4
Symes Pk BA1 27 A2
Symons Way
Bridgwater TA6 209 A6
Cheddar BS27 90 C7
Syndercombe La TA4, TA23 149 D2

T

Tabernacle La 4 BA20 219 B4
Tadhill La BA3 116 D2
Tadwick La BA1 28 A6
Tail Mill TA16 195 F7
Tailor's Ct 7 BS1 227 A3
Talbot Cl TA9 104 D3
Tallis Gr BS4 22 D6
Tallowood BA4 205 D5
Tamar Ave TA1 213 B1
Tamar Dr BS31 25 A4
Tamar Rd BS22 32 A2
Tamblyn Cl BA3 79 A3
Tamsin Ct BS31 24 F5
Tamworth Rd BS31 24 E4
Tancred St TA1 213 A4
Tangier TA1 212 E4
Tankard's Cl BS8 226 C3
Tankey's Cl BA11 120 A7
Tan La SP8 161 F1
Tanner's Hill TA4 165 E7
Tanners La SN14 13 F8
Tanners Wlk
Bath BA2 43 F5
Marshfield SN14 13 F8
Tannery Cl BA16 207 C5
Tannery Ct TA18 224 C7
Tanorth Cl BS14 23 A3
Tanorth Rd BS14 22 F3
Tansee Hill TA20 199 B6
Tansey BA4 142 A6
Tansy La BS20 2 F5
Tanyard
Broadway TA19 183 C2
Nether Stowey TA5 134 B2
Tanyard Cotts TA24 131 A5
Tanyard La
Langport TA10 172 A5
North Wootton BA4 140 C4
North Wootton, Lower Westholme BA4 140 D3
Tan Yard La TA13 184 F5
Tanyards BA10 215 F7
Tanyard The BA16 207 C5
Tape La BA3 114 F7
Taphouse La DT6 199 E1
Tapmoor Rd TA7 155 C8
Tappers La 2 TA6 153 E3
Tapps La TA7 136 E4
Tapstone Rd TA20 223 D4
Taranto Hill BA22 173 E2
Taranto Way BA22 174 A2
Target La TA12 185 D4
Tarnock Ave BS14 23 A7
Tarnwell BS39 40 A2
Tarrant La BA20 218 F1
Tarratt La
East Coker BA22 197 E8
Yeovil BA20, BA22 219 A1
Tarratt Rd BA20 218 F1
Tarr Post TA22 146 C1
Tarr Stps* TA22 146 E3
Tarr Water Cotts TA23 148 E8
Tatham Ct TA1 212 D4
Tatworth Prim Sch TA20 198 C8
Tatworth Rd TA20 223 C2
Tatworth St TA20 198 C8
Tauntfield Cl TA1 213 A3
Taunton Rd
Ashcott TA7 156 B7
Bishops Lydeard TA4 167 F7
Bridgwater TA6 209 A3
North Petherton TA6 153 F4
Thurloxton TA6 153 E2
Wellington TA21 222 E7
Weston-Super-Mare BS22 32 B4
Wiveliscombe TA4 210 D4
Taunton Sch TA2 212 D6
Taunton & Somerset Hospl
Musgrove Pk TA1 212 C3
Taunton Sta TA1 212 F5
Taunton Trad Est TA2 212 A7
Taunton Vale Pk TA2 213 F8
Taunusstein Way 12 BA20 219 B4
Taveners Wlk BS48 8 F3
Taverner Cl BS4 22 D7
Taverners Cl 6 BS23 48 F4
Tavistock Rd BS22 32 A2
Tawny Way BS22 49 F8
Taylor's Meade TA20 193 D6
Taylor's Orch TA14 185 E1
Taylor Cl TA2 168 B5
Taylor Ct
Bridgwater TA6 209 A5
Weston-Super-Mare BS22 32 B4
Taylor Gdns BS13 21 F4
Taylor Ho TA19 221 B3
Tayman Ridge BS30 25 D8
Teagle Cl BA5 203 F5
Teak Cl TA6 209 D6
Teal Cl
Bridgwater TA6 209 A4
Weston-Super-Mare BS22 31 F1
Tealham Moor Dro BS28 137 E8
Teal Rd TA24 201 C5
Teals Acre 8 TA5 135 B2
Teapot Lane (Worms Lane) BA6 158 B6
Teasel Wlk BS22 49 D7
Technical St TA8 104 B6
Teck Hill TA6 153 E2
Teckhill La TA6 153 E2
Teddington Cl BA2 44 C4
Teesdale Cl BS22 49 D8
Teeside BA14 83 F4
Teign Ct BA16 156 D7
Teignmouth Rd BS21 6 E3
Telephone Ave BS1 227 A2
Telford Ho
Bath BA2 44 D3
Leigh Woods BS8 11 E7
Tellis Cross BA22 197 D8
Tellisford La BA2 81 F4
Tellis La BA3 114 D8
Temblett Gn TA6 208 C5
Templars Barton BA8 176 E1
Templars Ct
Long Sutton TA10 172 E1
1 Weston-Super-Mare BS22 49 D7
Templars Pl BA8 176 E1
Templars Way BS25 70 E7
Temple Back BS1 227 B2
Temple Back E BS1 227 C2
Temple Bridge Bsns Pk BS39 76 F7
Temple Circus Giratory BS1 227 C1
Templecombe La SP8 177 C3
Templecombe Sta BA8 176 E1
Temple Ct BS31 24 E5
Temple Field TA23 202 C6
Temple Gate BS1 227 B1
Temple Inf Sch BS31 24 F5
Temple Inn La BS39 58 E1
Temple La BA8 176 F1
Templeland Rd BS13 21 F5
Temple of Harmony* TA5 153 B5
Temple Prim Sch BS31 24 F6
Temple Rose St BS1 227 B2
Temple St
Bristol BS1 227 B2
Keynsham BS31 24 F5
Temple Way BS2 227 B2
Temple Way Underpass BS2 227 C3
Tenby Rd BS31 24 D4
Tengore La TA10 172 C6
Tennis Corner Dro BA11 102 D2
Tennis Court Ave BS39 77 D5
Tennis Court Rd BS39 77 D5
Tennyson Ave BS21 6 B2
Tennyson Cl BS31 24 F6
Tennyson Rd
Bath BA1 44 D7
Weston-Super-Mare BS23 49 A3
Tenterk Cl BS24 67 B6
Tents Hill BA11 118 B6
Terhill La TA4 151 F3
Termare Cl BA22 218 B6
Terrace The
Minehead TA24 201 A5
Shipham BS25 70 E7
Terrace View DT9 225 E5
Terrace Wlk BA1 228 C2
Terrell St BS2 227 A4
Terry Hill BA3 98 D8
Terry Ho BS1 226 C3
Tetbury Gdns BS48 9 A1
Tetton Cl TA6 208 B4
Teviot Rd BS31 25 A4
Tewkesbury BA21 218 D6
Tewther Rd BS13 22 D3
Teyfant Com Sch BS13 22 E4
Teyfant Rd BS13 22 E4
Teyfant Wlk BS13 22 E4
Thackeray Ave BS21 6 E4
Thackeray Ho BS23 49 A5
Thackeray Rd BS21 6 E4
Thames Dr TA1 213 D4
Thatcham Cl 2 BA21 218 F7
Thatcham Ct 1 BA21 218 F7
Thatcham Pk BA21 218 F7
Thatch Cotts TA20 194 E1
Thatcher Cl BS20 2 D4
Thatch The TA11 211 C4
Theaks Mews TA1 213 A3
Theatre Royal BS1 227 A2
Theillay Cl TA5 134 A3
There-and-Back-Again La BS1 226 C3
Theynes Croft BS41 11 B1
Thicket Mead BA3 78 A2
Thickthorn Cross TA19 183 C3
Thimble La DT9 217 D2
Third Ave
Bath BA2 44 D5
Bristol BS14 23 B7
Radstock BA3 97 D7
Thirlmere Rd BS23 49 A4
Thistledoo Vine TA7 136 F2
Thistle Pk TA6 209 B1
Thomas Cl BS29 51 A3
Thomas Ct BS1 227 B2
Thomas La BS1 227 B2
Thomas Lane Appartments BS1 227 B2
Thomas St
Bath BA1 228 C4
Bristol BS2 227 B4
Taunton TA2 212 F6
Thomas Way BA6 206 B4
Thomas Way Ind Est BA6 206 B4
Thompson Cl TA6 209 D6
Thompson Rd BS14 23 E6
Thomson Dr TA18 224 D5
Thong La TA10 184 D6
Thornash Cl TA2 213 F8
Thornbank Ct DT9 225 E4
Thornbank Pl BA2 228 A1
Thornbury Dr BS23 48 D2
Thornbury Rd BS23 48 C2
Thornbush Cross TA4 150 F3
Thorn Cl BS22 32 B2
Thorncombe Cres TA6 209 C5
Thorncombe Thorn TA20 199 B5
Thorndale BS8 226 A4
Thorndale Cl BS22 49 D8
Thorndale Mews BS8 226 A4

Thorndun Park Dr TA20 223 D6
Thorne Cross BA22 218 B7
Thorne Cross Way TA21 178 D8
Thorne Gdns BA21 218 C7
Thorne La
 Wheddon Cross TA24 147 C8
 Winsford TA24 147 C8
 Yeovil BA21 218 C8
Thorne Pk TA8 104 B5
Thorneymoor La TA10 172 A3
Thorney Rd TA12 185 B8
Thornhill Dro TA12 173 A1
Thornhill Rd DT10 190 B4
Thorn La TA3 169 D2
Thornton Rd BA21 218 D7
Thornwell La BA9 216 D3
Thornwell Way BA9 216 C3
Thorny La BA21 187 E8
Thornymarsh La BA7 175 B8
Three Ashes DT8 199 D7
Three Ashes La TA11 157 B4
Three Corner Mead BA21 218 C5
Three Gates Cross TA22 163 C6
Three Hill View BA6 206 E5
Three Horse Shoes Hill TA5 152 C4
Three Oaks Cross TA19 183 C4
Three Queens' La BS1 227 B2
Three Ways Sch Lime Grove Site BA2 45 B6
Threeways Sch Summerfield Site BA1 27 D1
Three Wells Rd BS13 21 F4
Thrift Cl DT10 190 C4
Throgmorton Rd BS4 22 F8
Throop Rd BA8 176 F1
Thrubwell La BS40 37 B4
Thrupe La BA5 114 A2
Thrush Cl 4 BS22 49 E8
Thumb La BA4 158 E7
Thurlbear CE Prim Sch TA3 182 C8
Thurlestone BS14 23 A6
Thurlocks BA22 186 B6
Thyme Cl BS20 2 F5
Thynne Cl BS27 90 B6
Tibbott Rd BS14 23 D5
Tibbott Wlk BS14 23 D5
Tichborne Rd BS23 30 E1
Tickenham CE Prim Sch BS21 7 F4
Tickenham Hill BS48 8 E4
Tickenham Rd BS21 7 A4
Tide Gr BS11 5 A8
Tides Reach TA24 125 C4
Tiffany Ct BS1 227 B1
Tiledown BS39 58 E1
Tiledown Cl BS39 58 F1
Tile Hill BA10 161 A7
Tile House Rd
 East Huntspill TA7 137 B8
 Mark TA9 106 C1
Tilery EX14 192 D3
Tilham St BA6 158 B6
Tilley Cl
 Farmborough BA2 60 A5
 Keynsham BS31 25 A2
Tilley La BA2 60 A5
Tilleys Dro BA5 138 F7
Tilsey La TA4 150 C5
Tilton Ct 5 DT9 225 D3
Timberscombe CE First Sch TA24 130 B5
Timberscombe Way TA6 208 B4
Timberscombe Wlk BS14 23 C5
Timbers The BA3 97 B7
Timberyard TA7 137 F1
Timewell Hill EX16 164 C4
Timsbury Rd
 Farmborough BA2 60 B5
 High Littleton BS39 59 D1
Timsbury Village Workshops BA2 59 F3
Tin Bridge Rdbt BA6 139 D3
Tinker's La
 Compton Martin BS40 74 B7
 Cucklington BA9 177 D7
 Halse TA4 167 C6
 Kilmersdon BA11 98 B1
Tinneys La DT9 225 E4
Tintagel Cl BS31 24 D4
Tintagel Rd BA21 218 D7
Tintern BA21 218 C6
Tintinhull Gdn* BA22 186 C6
Tintinhull Rd BA21 186 F5
Tipcote Hill 17 BA4 205 B6
Tipnoller Hill TA4 210 F7
Tippacott La EX35 122 A4
Tiptoft 3 TA14 185 F4
Tirley Way BS22 31 B2
Titan Barrow BA1 29 C2
Tithe Barn Cross EX15 179 D2
Tithe Ct BA20 218 D5
Tithe Mdw TA4 167 A7
Tithill La TA4 167 F7
Titlands La BA5 203 A7
Tiverton Gdns BS22 32 A2
Tiverton Rd
 Bampton EX16 164 C1
 2 Clevedon BS21 6 E1
Tivington Cross TA24 129 F8
Tivoli Ho BS23 48 E8
Tivoli La BS23 48 E8
Toghill La BS30 12 A8
Tolbury La BA10 215 D6
Tolbury Mill BA10 215 E6
Tolland BS24 49 A2
Tolland Cross TA4 150 E3
Toll Bridge Rd BA1 28 E3
Tolley's La TA20 194 C3
Toll Gate TA4 210 C4
Toll House Rd 1 TA5 135 B2
Toll Rd
 Porlock TA24 124 A3
 Weston-Super-Mare BS23 66 F8
Toms Cl TA20 223 B3
Tomtit's La TA11 211 C3
Tonedale Bsns Pk TA21 222 B7
Tonedale Ind Est TA21 222 B8
Tone Dr TA6 209 B3
Tone Gn TA4 167 E2
Tone Hill TA21 222 B8
Tone Rd BS21 6 D1
Toneway TA2 213 C6
Toose The BA21 218 C6
Top Hill BA4 142 F2
Top La
 Gasper BA12 161 E4
 Mells BA11 118 B6
Top Rd
 Charlton Adam TA11 173 F7
 Cheddar BS27 90 E5
 Shipham BS25 70 F7
 Westbury-sub-Mendip BA5 110 E6
Top St
 Kingsdon TA11 173 D5
 Pilton BA4 140 F3
Top Wood BA3 116 B7
Torbay Cl BA7 214 B5
Torbay Rd BA7 214 A5
Torbay Road Ind Est BA7 214 A5
Torbay Villas BA7 214 A5
Tor Cl BS22 32 A2
Torhill La BA5 203 F4
Torhole Bottom BA3 94 A4
Tormynton Rd BS22 31 E3
Torre Cider Farm* TA23 131 E3
Torre Rocks TA23 131 E2
Torre The BA21 218 C6
Torridge Mead TA1 213 D4
Torridge Rd BS31 25 A4
Torrington Ave BS4 22 F8
Torrington Cres BS22 32 A3
Tor St BA5 203 E4
Tor View
 Cheddar BS27 90 C7
 Woolavington TA7 136 E4
Tor View Ave BA6 206 D3
Tor Wood View BA5 203 E5
Totnes Cl BS22 32 A2
Totney Dro BS28 137 E8
Totshill Dr BS13 22 E4
Totshill Gr BS13 22 E4
Tottenham Pl BS8 226 B3
Totterdown La
 Pilton BA4 204 B1
 Weston-Super-Mare BS24 49 A1
Totterdown Rd BS23 48 F4
Touches La TA20 223 E5
Touches Mdw TA20 223 E5
Touching End La SN14 13 F8
Touch La TA10 156 C1
Touchstone Cl TA20 223 B4
Touchstone La TA20 223 B4
Tout Hill BA9 216 C3
Tout La BA22TA11 174 A6
Tovey Cl BS22 31 E4
Tower Cl
 Cheddar BS27 90 B6
 Stoke St Michael BA3 116 A3
Towerhead Rd BS29 51 D3
Tower Hill
 Bristol BS2 227 B3
 Bruton BA10 215 D6
 Holcombe Rogus TA21 178 D5
 Horsington BA8 176 E2
 Locking BS24 50 D4
 Stogursey TA5 134 B5
 Stoke St Michael BA3 116 A3
 Williton TA4 202 E2
Tower Hill Rd TA18 224 B5
Tower House La BS48 9 A4
Tower La
 Bristol BS1 227 A3
 Taunton TA1 212 E4
Towerleaze BS9 5 D3
Tower Rd
 Kilmington BA12 161 D6
 Portishead BS20 2 A4
 Stawell TA7 137 B1
 Yeovil BA21 219 C8
Tower St
 Bristol BS1 227 B2
 Taunton TA1 212 E4
Tower The BS1 227 B2
Tower View
 Frome BA11 119 F2
 South Cheriton BA8 176 D3
 Wanstrow BA4 142 E4
Tower Wlk BS23 30 D1
Town Barton BA2 81 F4
Town Cl
 North Curry TA3 170 B4
 Stogursey TA5 134 B6
Town End BA2 81 F4
Townend Villas TA14 185 F2
Town Farm TA3 170 B4
Townhall Bldgs BA5 203 E4
Town Hill EX36 162 C6
Town La BA4 205 C6
Town Marsh TA22 163 D7
Townrise 15 BA20 219 B4
Townsend
 East Harptree BS40 75 A5
Townsend *continued*
 Ilminster TA19 221 D3
 Marston Magna BA22 174 F1
 Middlezoy TA7 155 C3
 Montacute TA15 186 B3
 Shepton Mallet BA4 205 B5
 Westonzoyland TA7 154 F5
 Williton TA4 202 E3
Townsend Cl
 Bristol BS14 23 F5
 Bruton BA10 215 F7
Townsend Cotts TA24 147 C5
Townsend Gn 10 BA8 190 A6
Townsend La
 Chilton Polden TA7 137 B2
 Emborough BA3 95 B2
 Theale BS28 109 A2
Townsend Orch
 Merriott TA16 195 F8
 Street BA16 207 B5
Townsend Pk BA10 215 F7
Townsend Rd
 Bristol BS14 23 F5
 Minehead TA24 201 A6
Townsend Rise BA10 215 F7
Townshend Rd BS22 32 B5
Town St BA4 205 B6
Town Tree Farm Nature Trail* TA12 185 C8
Town Tree La TA10, TA12 185 D8
Tracey Cl TA7 209 E8
Trackfordmoor Cross TA22 163 B3
Tracy Cl BS14 22 F7
Trafalgar Rd BA1 27 B1
Traits La BA22 174 E4
Trajan's Way BA4 205 E5
Tramshed The BA1 228 C3
Transform Ind Est TA6 209 A6
Transom Ho BS1 227 B2
Transom Pl TA24 201 B7
Travers Cl BS4 22 D6
Trawden Cl BS23 31 A1
Treasure Ct TA8 85 A1
Treasurer's Ho* TA12 185 E6
Treborough Cl TA2 213 B8
Treefield Rd BS21 6 D2
Tregarth Rd BS3 11 F1
Tregelles Cl TA9 104 C4
Tregonwell Rd TA24 201 A7
Trelawn Cl BS22 32 D2
Trelissick Gdns 3 BS22 49 F8
Trellech Ct 3 BA21 218 C6
Tremes Cl SN14 13 F8
Tremlett Mews 3 BS22 32 B4
Trenchard Rd
 Locking BS24 50 D4
 Saltford BS31 25 D3
Trenchard St BS1 226 C3
Trendle La
 Bicknoller TA4 132 F2
 Stoney Stoke BA9 160 E3
Trendle Rd TA1 212 B1
Trendle St DT9 225 D3
Trendlewood Way BS48 9 A1
Trenleigh Dr BS22 32 A2
Trent Cl BA21 219 E8
Trent Ct TA1 213 D4
Trent Gr BS31 25 A4
Trent Mdw TA1 213 E4
Trent Path La DT9 225 A5
Trent Youngs CE Prim Sch DT9 187 F5
Tresco Spinney BA21 218 C6
Trescothick Cl BS31 24 E6
Trevanna Rd BS3 11 F1
Trevelyan Rd BS23 48 F7
Trevett Rd TA1 212 C2
Trevithick Cl BA11 120 C6
Trevor Rd TA6 209 C6
Trevor Smith Pl TA1 213 A3
Trewartha Cl BS23 48 F8
Trewartha Pk BS23 48 F8
Trewint Gdns BS4 22 F8
Triangle Ct 2 BA2 44 D5
Triangle Ctr The BS21 6 D3
Triangle E BA2 44 D5
Triangle N BA2 44 D5
Triangle S BS8 226 B3
Triangle The
 Castle Cary BA7 214 C5
 Clevedon BS21 6 D3
 North Curry TA3 170 A4
 Paulton BS39 77 E6
 Portishead BS20 2 B5
 Somerton TA11 211 D4
 Wrington BS40 35 D2
Triangle Villas 1 BA2 44 D5
Triangle W
 Bath BA2 44 D5
 Bristol BS8 226 B3
Tribunal & Lake Village Mus* BA6 206 D4
Trickey Warren La TA3 181 C1
Trim Bridge 3 BA1 228 B2
Trim St BA1 228 B2
Trinder Rd BS20 4 B4
Trindlewell La TA18 196 C4
Trinity Bsns Ctr TA1 213 A3
Trinity CE Fst Sch BA11 119 C4
Trinity Cl
 Bath BA1 228 B2
 Blackford BS28 107 D4
 Burnham-on-S TA8 85 A1
 Wellington TA21 222 C5
Trinity Coll BS9 5 E4
Trinity Ct
 Bridgwater TA6 208 F6
Trinity Ct *continued*
 Nailsea BS48 8 C1
 13 Yeovil BA20 219 B4
Trinity Gate TA1 213 A3
Trinity Mews 15 BS2 227 C3
Trinity Pl
 3 Bristol BS8 226 A2
 4 Weston-Super-Mare BS23 30 C1
Trinity Rd
 Bath BA2 45 B2
 Nailsea BS48 8 D1
 Taunton TA1 213 B3
 Weston-Super-Mare BS23 30 C1
Trinity Rise TA8 85 A1
Trinity Row
 Frome BA11 119 E5
 Wellington TA21 222 C5
Trinity St
 Bath BA1 228 B2
 Frome BA11 119 E5
 Taunton TA1 213 B3
Trinity Way
 Bridgwater TA6 208 E6
 Minehead TA24 201 B7
Trinity Wlk
 Bristol BS2 227 C3
 Frome BA11 119 E5
Trin Mills BS1 227 A1
Tripps Cnr BS49 34 D7
Tripps Dro BA5 139 A6
Tripps Row BS41 11 A1
Triscombe Ave TA6 208 D4
Triscombe Gate TA24 147 D8
Triscombe Ho TA4 151 D5
Triscombe Rd TA2 212 E8
Tristram Dr TA3 169 D4
Tropical Bird Gdn* TA8 47 F2
Tropiquaria Wildlife Pk* TA23 131 F4
Trossachs Dr BA2 45 D8
Trotts La TA19 183 B2
Trottsway Cross TA24 129 C2
Trowbridge Cl TA9 104 D4
Trowell La TA4 165 E4
Trow La BA12 144 C2
Truckwell La TA4 150 D4
Trull CE Prim Sch TA3 168 D1
Trull Green Dr TA3 168 D1
Trull Rd TA1 212 E2
Trumps Cross EX16 178 E3
Truro Cl TA8 104 C7
Truro Rd BS48 9 A1
Trym Bank BS9 5 D7
Trym Cross Rd BS9 5 C5
Trymleaze BS9 5 C5
Trym Side BS9 5 C5
Trymwood Par BS9 5 D6
Tucker's Cross DT9 188 A4
Tucker's La
 Baltonsborough BA6 157 F6
 Ubley BS40 73 E8
Tucker's Moor Cross EX16 162 F3
Tuckers La BA7 214 B7
Tucker St
 Bristol BS2 227 C3
 Wells BA5 203 C4
Tuckerton La TA7 153 F1
Tuckingmill La BS39 41 E5
Tuckmarsh La BA11 143 E7
Tuckmill BS21 6 B1
Tudballs TA24 128 D1
Tuddington Gdns BA5 203 B4
Tudor Ct
 Chard TA20 223 C6
 Yeovil BA20 219 A4
Tudor Rd
 Portishead BS20 2 E4
 Weston-Super-Mare BS22 32 A4
Tudor Way TA6 209 A1
Tudway Cl BA5 203 C4
Tufton Ave BS11 5 A8
Tugela Rd BS13 21 F7
Tuggy's La BA2 63 E1
Tulip Tree Rd TA6 209 E5
Tulse Hill BA12 161 F2
Tunbridge Cl BS40 39 B2
Tunbridge Rd BS40 39 B2
Tuncombe La TA18 195 D4
Tunley Hill BA2 60 E2
Tunley Rd BA2, BA3 61 D5
Tunnel La BA3 96 F5
Tunnell La 14 TA14 185 F4
Tunnel The TA24 128 B2
Tunscombe La BA4 142 D8
Tunstall Cl BS9 5 E4
Turkey Ct 5 TA1 212 E3
Turnbury Ave BS48 9 A1
Turnbury Cl BS22 31 F3
Turner's Barn La BA20 218 F2
Turner's Court La BA3 114 D8
Turner's La DT6 199 B2
Turner's Twr BA3 80 A1
Turner Cl
 Bridgwater TA6 209 A4
 Keynsham BS31 25 A5
Turner Ct
 Wells BA5 203 D3
 Weston-Super-Mare BS22 31 F3
Turner Rd TA2 212 E7
Turner Way BS21 6 B1
Turn Hill TA10 155 F2
Turnhill Rd TA10 156 A2
Turnpike
 Milverton TA4 167 A4
 Sampford Peverell EX16 178 C1
Turnpike Cl TA18 196 B3
Turnpike Cnr BA3 95 B8
Turnpike Cross TA14 185 E2
Turnpike Cvn Pk TA20 193 A4
Turnpike Gn TA18 196 B3
Turnpike La BA4 142 B6
Turnpike Rd
 Cross BS26 69 E1
 Shipham BS25 70 E8
Turstin Rd BA6 206 F6
Turtlegate Ave BS13 21 E4
Turtlegate Wlk BS13 21 E4
Tut Hill DT9 189 C1
Tutton Way BS21 6 D1
Tuttors Hill BS27 71 C1
Tuxwell La TA5 152 C8
Tweed Rd BS21 6 C1
Tweed Rd Ind Est 2 BS21 6 C1
Tweentown BS27 90 B8
Twelve Acre Post TA22 163 A4
Twerton Farm Cl 2 BA2 44 B6
Twerton Inf Sch BA2 44 A5
Twinell La TA5 152 D7
Twines Cl BA22 175 A5
Twinhoe La BA2 62 E2
Twistgates La EX14 192 A4
Twitchen Ball Cnr EX36 145 G3
Twitchens La BS27 90 F2
Two Acres Cvn Pk BS21 1 B1
Two Acres Rd BS14 23 A7
Two Ash Hill TA20 193 F1
Two Ash La TA20 194 A1
Two Elms BA21 187 E8
Two Tower La BA22 219 B2
Two Trees BS40 72 E8
Twyford Pl TA21 222 D5
Tydeman Rd BS20 2 F5
Tyler's La TA4 167 A7
Tyler Gn 2 BS22 32 B4
Tylers End TA9 104 F3
Tyler Way TA9 104 D3
Tyndall's Park Rd BS8 226 C4
Tyndall Ave BS8 226 C4
Tyndall Ho 5 BS2 227 C3
Tyndalls Park Mews BS2 226 C4
Tyne Gr BS20 2 F6
Tyne Pk TA1 213 D3
Tyning Cl BS14 23 A7
Tyning Cotts BA3 116 C7
Tyning End BA2 45 B5
Tyning Hill
 Hemington BA3 99 C8
 Radstock BA3 79 B3
Tyning La BA1 28 B1
Tyning Pl BA2 45 C2
Tyning Rd
 Bathampton BA2 28 F2
 Bath BA2 45 C2
 Peasedown St John BA2 79 D7
 Saltford BS31 25 E2
 Winsley BA15 64 E7
Tynings BS39 58 D3
Tynings La BA5 203 C8
Tynings Mews BS23 48 E4
Tynings Rd BA16 207 B4
Tynings The
 Clevedon BS21 6 A1
 Portishead BS20 1 F1
Tynings Way
 Clutton BS39 58 E3
 Westwood BA15 64 F3
Tyning Terr 15 BA1 28 A1
Tyning The
 Bath BA2 45 B5
 Freshford BA3 64 B4
Tynte Ave BS13 22 E3
Tynte Rd TA6 209 D6
Tyntesfield Rd BS13 22 A8
Tyrone Wlk BS4 22 E8
Tytherington La BA11 143 E8
Tythe St BA6 206 E3
Tythings Com Ctr The BA9 216 C3
Tythings Ct TA24 200 F7
Tything Way BA9 216 D3

U

Ubley CE Prim Sch BS40 55 D1
Ubley Dro BS40 73 B7
Ullcombe La EX14 191 F4
Ullswater Cl BS23 49 A4
Ullswater Dr BA1 28 A2
Uncombe Cl BS48 19 D7
Underbanks BS20 4 D4
Underdown BA21 219 F5
Underdown Ho BS1 227 A1
Underdown Hollow
 Bradford Abbas DT9 187 E2
 Yeovil BA21 219 F4
Underdown La DT9 225 F6
Underhill
 Gurney Slade BA3 114 E7
 Hambridge TA10 184 D8
 Penselwood BA9 161 D1
Underhill Ave BA3 77 F2
Underhill Cl BA16 207 B5
Underhill Dr BS23 48 D1
Underhill La
 Midsomer Norton BA3 77 F2
 Staple Fitzpaine TA3 182 B4
Underhill Rd BA16 207 B5
Under Knoll BA2 79 E8
Under La BS40 36 D1
Underleaf Way BA2 79 D7

Undertown BS40 .... 74 A7
Undertown La BS40 .... 74 A7
Under Way TA20 .... 193 D6
Underwood Ave BS22 .... 31 B1
Underwood Bsns Pk BA5 203 B6
Underwood End BS25 .... 52 A4
Underwood La TA10 .... 172 C8
Underwood Rd
Glastonbury BA6 .... 206 D6
Kingsdon TA11 .... 173 D5
Portishead BS20 .... 2 C3
Union Dro TA10 .... 172 B6
Union La TA4 .... 202 E4
Union Pas BA1 .... 228 C2
Union Pl BS23 .... 48 D7
Union St
Bath BA1 .... 228 C2
Bridgwater TA6 .... 209 B6
Bristol BS1 .... 227 B3
Cheddar BS27 .... 90 B7
Dulverton TA22 .... 163 D6
Nailsea BS48 .... 8 C1
Wells BA5 .... 203 D4
Weston-Super-Mare BS23 .. 48 D7
Yeovil BA20 .... 219 B4
Unite Ho BS1 .... 226 C2
Unity Ct BS31 .... 25 A5
Unity Rd BS31 .... 25 A6
Unity St BS1 .... 226 C2
University Cl BS9 .... 5 F4
University Rd BS8 .... 226 C3
University Wlk BS8 .... 226 C3
Univ of Bath BA2 .... 45 E5
Univ of Bristol BS8 .... 226 C3
Univ of Bristol Dept of Ed BS8 .... 226 C3
Univ of Bristol Dorothy Hodgkin Bldg BS1 .... 227 A4
Univ of Bristol Langford House Sch of Veterinary Science BS40 .... 53 B6
Univ of Bristol Sch of Veterinary Science BS2 .... 226 C4
Univ of the West of England BS3 .... 11 E4
Upcot Cres TA1 .... 212 B2
Upcott La
Bicknoller TA4 .... 132 F1
Winsford TA24 .... 147 D7
Upcott Rd TA1, TA4 .... 168 B3
Uphill Ct BS23 .... 48 D2
Uphill Dr BA1 .... 28 B2
Uphill Farm Cvn Pk BS23 .. 48 E1
Uphill Prim Sch BS23 .... 48 D2
Uphill Rd N BS23 .... 48 D4
Uphill Rd S BS23 .... 48 D2
Uphills BA10 .... 215 E7
Uphill Way BS23 .... 48 D1
Upjohn Cres BS13 .... 22 D3
Uplands
Bratton Seymour BA9 .... 176 B8
Mark TA9 .... 106 E4
Uplands Cl BA2 .... 63 F7
Uplands Dr BS31 .... 25 F2
Uplands Rd BS31 .... 25 F2
Uplands Terr BA22 .... 197 B8
Uplands The BS48 .... 18 C8
Uplowman CE Prim Sch EX16 .... 178 B2
Upottery Prim Sch EX14 .. 191 F2
Upper Belgrave Rd BS8 .... 5 F1
Upper Berkeley Pl BS8 .. 226 B3
Upper Bloomfield Rd BA2 44 D1
Upper Borough Walls BA1 .... 228 C2
Upper Breach BA5 .... 113 A2
Upper Bristol Rd
Bath BA1 .... 44 D7
Clutton BS39 .... 58 D3
Weston-Super-Mare BS22 .. 31 B1
Upper Byron Pl BS8 .... 226 B3
Upper Camden Pl BA1 .. 228 C4
Upper Church La
Bristol BS2 .... 226 C3
Hutton BS24 .... 49 D2
Upper Church Rd BS23 .... 30 D1
Upper Church St BA1 .... 228 B3
Upper Crannel Dro BA6 .. 139 C4
Upper East Hayes BA1 .... 28 B1
Upper Farm Cl BA2 .... 81 F4
Upper Flowerfield BA11 .. 143 B7
Upper Furlong BA2 .... 60 B3
Upper Green La BS40 .... 55 B7
Upper Hedgemead Rd BA1 .... 228 B4
Upper High St
Castle Cary BA7 .... 214 C5
Taunton TA1 .... 212 F3
Upper Holway Rd TA1 .. 213 C2
Upper Kewstoke Rd BS23 .. 30 B1
Upper Lambridge St BA1 .. 28 C2
Upper Lansdown Mews BA1 .... 27 F1
Upper Maudlin St BS2 .. 227 A3
Upper Merrifield BA3 .... 116 E8
Upper Merryfield BA3 .... 97 E1
Upper Mount Pleasant BA3 .... 64 A4
Upper Myrtle Hill BS20 .... 4 C4
Upper New Rd BS27 .... 90 A8
Upper North St BS27 .... 90 B8
Upper Oldfield Pk BA2 .. 228 A1
Upper Pitching BA3 .... 96 D5
Upper Rd BS39 .... 75 E6
Upper Stanton BS39 .... 40 A2
Upper Strode BS40 .... 55 F7
Upper Town La BS40 .... 37 C8
Upper Wells St BS1 .... 226 C2
Upper Whatcombe BA11 .. 119 E6
Upper Wood St TA1 .... 212 E4
Upper York St BS2 .... 227 B4
Upton BS24 .... 49 A2
Upton Cotts BS41 .... 38 F8
Upton La
Dundry BS41 .... 39 A8
Seavington St Michael TA19 .... 184 E2
Upton Noble CE Prim Sch BA4 .... 142 F2
Urchinwood La BS49 .... 34 F4

V

Vagg Hill BA22 .... 186 E5
Vagg La BA22 .... 186 F5
Vagg Pk BA22 .... 186 F5
Valda Rd BS22 .... 31 C2
Vale Cl TA18 .... 224 C4
Vale Cres BS22 .... 32 C2
Vale Ct BS8 .... 226 A4
Vale End BS48 .... 8 D1
Vale La BS3 .... 22 C8
Vale Mill Way BS24 .... 49 F8
Valentine Cl BS14 .... 23 B5
Valentines TA22 .... 163 E6
Vale Rd
Stalbridge DT10 .... 190 B4
Yeovil BA21 .... 219 E6
Valerian Cl BS11 .... 4 F6
Vale St BA8 .... 190 A6
Valetta Cl BS23 .... 48 F3
Valetta Pl TA6 .... 208 F5
Vale View
Aller TA10 .... 171 E8
Henstridge BA8 .... 190 A7
Radstock BA3 .... 79 A2
Wincanton BA9 .... 216 F5
Vale View Cotts TA4 .... 151 E4
Vale View Gdns BA9 .... 216 C2
Vale View Pl 16 BA1 .... 28 B1
Vale View Terr BA1 .... 28 F3
Valley Cl
6 Nailsea BS48 .... 8 E2
Wells BA5 .... 203 C4
Yeovil BA21 .... 219 B6
Valley Ct BS20 .... 1 E3
Valley Gdns BS48 .... 8 E2
Valley Line Ind Pk BS27 .. 90 A7
Valley Rd
Bristol, Bedminster Down BS13 .... 22 A8
Clevedon BS21 .... 6 F5
Crewkerne TA18 .... 224 C4
Leigh Woods BS8 .... 11 C7
Portishead BS20 .... 2 A2
Taunton TA1 .... 213 C5
Valley View
8 Axminster EX13 .... 198 A1
Chilcompton BA3 .... 96 D3
Clutton BS39 .... 58 E3
Frome BA11 .... 119 D6
Millmoor EX15 .... 179 E1
Morebath EX16 .... 164 B3
Valley View Cl BA1 .... 28 B3
Valley View Rd
Bath BA1 .... 28 C3
Paulton BS39 .... 77 E6
Valley Way Rd BS48 .... 8 E3
Valley Wlk BA3 .... 78 B2
Vallis Ct 7 BA11 .... 119 E5
Vallis Fst Sch BA11 .... 119 E5
Vallis Rd BA11 .... 119 D5
Vallis Trad Est BA11 .... 119 D5
Vallis Way BA11 .... 119 E5
Van Diemen's La BA1 .... 27 F2
Vandyck Ave BS31 .... 24 F6
Vane St BA2 .... 45 B7
Vanguard Ct BA22 .... 218 A5
Varsity Way BS24 .... 50 B6
Vaughan Ct BA5 .... 203 B4
Veales DT10 .... 189 F2
Veale The BS24 .... 67 C6
Veal La
Horrington BA5 .... 113 B2
Walton BA16 .... 156 E6
Vedal Dro TA10 .... 172 D4
Vee La BS40 .... 37 D8
Vellore La BA2 .... 45 C7
Vellow Rd TA4 .... 150 D8
Vellow Wood La TA4 .... 132 D1
Vemplett's Cross TA23 .. 131 E1
Venford Hill
East Anstey TA22 .... 162 E8
Hawkridge TA22 .... 146 D1
Venland Bsns Pk TA24 .... 201 B6
Venland Ind Pk TA24 .... 201 A6
Venn Cl TA4 .... 167 E6
Venn Cross TA4 .... 165 D3
Venn Hill DT6, TA20 .... 199 C6
Venniford Cross TA24 .... 129 F8
Vennland Way TA24 .... 201 A6
Venns Cl BS27 .... 90 B7
Venns Gate BS27 .... 71 A1
Venture 7 BA20 .... 218 C3
Venture 20 BA20 .... 218 C3
Venture Eleven The TA2 .. 213 B6
Venture Way TA2 .... 213 B6
Venus La BS39 .... 58 E3
Venus St BS49 .... 34 E2
Vera St TA2 .... 212 F7
Verbena Way BS22 .... 32 A1
Verdun Terr TA23 .... 131 E4
Vereland Rd BS24 .... 49 E3
Verlands BS49 .... 34 E5
Vernal La BA11 .... 119 D6
Vernalls Rd DT9 .... 225 D5
Vernham Gr BA2 .... 44 C1
Vernon Cl BS31 .... 25 D3
Vernon La BS26 .... 69 B3
Vernon Pk BA2 .... 44 C6
Vernon Terr BA2 .... 44 C6
Vernslade BA1 .... 27 A2
Verriers 10 TA6 .... 153 E3
Verrington Hospl BA9 .... 216 B4
Verrington La BA9 .... 216 B5
Verrington Park Rd BA9 .. 216 B4
Vesey's Hole Hill SP8 .... 177 E4
Vestry Cl BA16 .... 207 C5
Vestry Ct 1 BA16 .... 207 C5
Vestry Rd BA16 .... 207 C5
Vian End BS22 .... 31 F4
Vicar's Cl BA5 .... 203 E5
Vicar's La TA12 .... 184 F7
Vicarage Cl
Chard TA20 .... 223 C3
Coxley BA5 .... 139 E6
Creech St Michael TA3 .... 169 D4
8 Frome BA11 .... 119 F4
Stogursey TA5 .... 134 C6
Weston-Super-Mare BS22 .. 32 A3
Westonzoyland TA7 .... 154 F5
Vicarage Ct
Burnham-on-S TA8 .... 104 A7
Timberscombe TA24 .... 130 B5
Vicarage Gdns BA2 .... 79 B7
Vicarage Hill
Combe St Nicholas TA20 .. 193 D6
Dulverton TA22 .... 163 D6
Vicarage La
Barrow Gurney BS48 .... 20 C6
Compton Bishop BS26 .... 69 B3
Compton Dando BS39 .... 41 D6
Creech St Michael TA3 .... 169 D4
Draycott BS27 .... 90 F3
Mark TA9 .... 106 E5
Norton St Philip BA2 .... 81 E4
Pawlett TA6 .... 135 F5
Shapwick TA7 .... 137 F1
7 Wookey BA5 .... 139 D8
Vicarage Lawns TA3 .... 169 D4
Vicarage Rd
Bristol, Bishopsworth BS13 .... 22 A6
Carhampton TA24 .... 131 B5
Leigh Woods BS8 .... 11 D6
Minehead TA24 .... 200 F8
Stogursey TA5 .... 134 C6
Wookey BA5 .... 139 E8
Woolavington TA7 .... 136 E4
Vicarage St
Burnham-on-S TA8 .... 104 A7
Frome BA11 .... 119 F4
Tintinhull BA22 .... 186 C6
6 Yeovil BA20 .... 219 B4
Vicarage Wlk BA20 .... 219 B5
Vicars La TA6 .... 208 D5
Vickery Cl
Bridgwater TA6 .... 208 D3
Curry Rivel TA10 .... 171 D4
Victoria Art Gall The* BA2 .... 228 C2
Victoria Ave TA20 .... 223 D4
Victoria Bldgs
Bath BA2 .... 44 D6
Glastonbury BA6 .... 206 E4
Victoria Bridge Ct BA1 .. 228 A3
Victoria Bridge Rd BA1, BA2 .... 228 A2
Victoria Bsns Pk TA20 .. 223 D4
Victoria Cl
Bath BA2 .... 44 C5
Portishead BS20 .... 2 D5
Yeovil BA21 .... 219 D6
Victoria Cotts BA2 .... 62 F7
Victoria Ct
Castle Cary BA7 .... 214 B5
Chard TA20 .... 223 D4
Frome BA11 .... 120 A4
Ilminster TA19 .... 221 C4
Portishead BS20 .... 2 D5
Victoria Gate TA1 .... 213 B4
Victoria Gdns
Batheaston BA1 .... 28 F3
Castle Cary BA7 .... 214 B6
15 Henstridge BA8 .... 190 A6
Victoria Gr BA4 .... 205 D5
Victoria Ho
Bath BA1 .... 44 D8
Keynsham BS31 .... 24 F4
Victoria Hospl BA11 .... 119 E4
Victoria Jubilee Homes BS40 .... 53 C6
Victoria La BA4 .... 141 E1
Victoria Lodge BS22 .... 31 E2
Victoria Mews BA7 .... 214 B5
Victoria Park Bsns Ctr BA1 .... 44 D7
Victoria Pk
Castle Cary BA7 .... 214 B5
Weston-Super-Mare BS23 .. 30 D1
Victoria Pl
Bath, Combe Down BA2 .... 45 C1
2 Bath, Lambridge BA1 .... 28 C1
Chardstock EX13 .... 198 A7
Highbridge TA9 .... 104 D3
Paulton BS39 .... 77 D5
Weston-Super-Mare BS23 .. 48 D8
Victoria Quadrant BS23 .. 48 E8
Victoria Rd
Avonmouth BS11 .... 4 B7
Bath BA2 .... 44 D6
Bridgwater TA6 .... 208 E5
Castle Cary BA7 .... 214 B5
Clevedon BS21 .... 6 C3
Frome BA11 .... 120 A4
Minehead TA24 .... 201 A5
Saltford BS31 .... 25 D3
Yeovil BA21 .... 219 D6
Victoria Sh Mews TA18 .. 224 C6
Victoria Sq
Bristol BS8 .... 226 A3
Crewkerne TA18 .... 224 B6
Evercreech BA4 .... 141 E1
Portishead BS20 .... 2 D5
Weston-Super-Mare BS23 .. 48 D7
Victoria St
Bristol BS1 .... 227 B2
Burnham-on-S TA8 .... 104 A7
Taunton TA1 .... 213 B4
Wellington TA21 .... 222 D6
Victoria Terr
Bath BA2 .... 44 D6
14 Bristol, Clifton BS8 .... 11 F6
14 Henstridge BA8 .... 190 A6
Paulton BS39 .... 77 E6
Victoria Way TA5 .... 152 E7
Victory Rd TA2 .... 213 A7
Vigor Rd BS13 .... 22 B5
Viking Cl TA23 .... 202 D7
Vilberie Cl TA2 .... 212 A7
Village Rd TA3 .... 182 F6
Villa Rosa 16 BS23 .... 30 C1
Villes La TA24 .... 124 A4
Villice La BS40 .... 74 A7
Vincent Cl TA8 .... 104 C7
Vincent Pl BA20 .... 219 B5
Vincents Cl DT9 .... 189 A1
Vincent St 5 BA20 .... 219 B5
Vine Gdns
Frome BA11 .... 119 F6
Weston-Super-Mare BS22 .. 32 A2
Vine Gr BA8 .... 176 E1
Vine House Gdns TA20 .. 223 C3
Vinery The BS25 .... 70 A7
Vine St BA8 .... 176 E1
Viney's Yd BA10 .... 215 F6
Vineyards BA1 .... 228 C3
Viney La EX14 .... 191 F1
Viney St TA1 .... 213 B3
Vining's Hill BA4 .... 142 D1
Vinney La BA11 .... 143 F8
Violet La DT9 .... 176 A2
Virginia Cl 1 BA8 .... 190 A6
Virginia Orch TA3 .... 169 C3
Viscount Sq TA6 .... 208 E7
Vivary Ct TA1 .... 212 E3
Vivary Gate TA1 .... 212 F3
Vivary Hts TA1 .... 212 E2
Vivary Rd TA1 .... 212 E3
Vivien Ave BA3 .... 78 A2
Vixen Cl BA22 .... 174 A3
Vobster Cross BA3 .... 117 D7
Vobster Hill BA3 .... 117 D7
Vole Rd
Brent Knoll TA9 .... 86 D1
Mark TA9 .... 106 B7
Volis Cross TA5 .... 152 F1
Volis Hill TA2 .... 168 F8
Vowell Cl BS13 .... 22 B4
Vowles Cl BS48 .... 9 A3
Vulcan Ho BA2 .... 228 C3
Vulcan Rd TA24 .... 201 B6
Vynes Cl BS48 .... 9 A1
Vynes Ind Est BS48 .... 9 A3
Vynes Way BS48 .... 9 A1
Vyvyan Rd BS8 .... 226 A3
Vyvyan Terr BS8 .... 226 A3

W

Wadbrook Cross EX13 .. 198 C4
Wade Cl TA7 .... 154 E6
Wadeford Hill TA20 .... 193 D5
Wade St BS2 .... 227 C3
Wadham's Almshouses TA19 .... 183 E4
Wadham Cl
Bridgwater TA6 .... 209 D6
Ilminster TA19 .... 221 A4
Wadham Cross
Knowstone EX36 .... 162 A2
West Anstey EX36 .... 162 A4
Wadham Hill EX36 .... 162 A2
Wadham Sch TA18 .... 224 D7
Wadham St BS23 .... 48 D8
Wagg Dro TA10 .... 172 B5
Waggs Plot EX13 .... 198 B4
Wagon & Horses Hill BA4 .... 141 E8
Wagtail Gdns BS22 .... 49 E8
Wains Cl 3 BS21 .... 6 C2
Wainwright Cl 5 BS22 .... 32 B4
Wainwright Ct BA4 .... 205 B4
Wainwright Dr BA11 .... 120 C7
Waits Cl BS29 .... 50 F3
Wakedean Gdns BS49 .... 17 A1
Walcombe La BA5 .... 203 E6
Walcot Bldgs
Bath BA1 .... 45 B8
Bath BA1 .... 228 C4
Walcot CE Inf Sch BA1 .. 228 C4
Walcot Ct BA1 .... 228 C4
Walcot Gate BA1 .... 228 C4
Walcot Ho BA1 .... 228 C4
Walcot Par BA1 .... 228 C4
Walcot St BA1 .... 228 C3
Walcot Terr BA1 .... 228 C4
Waldegrave Rd BA1 .... 27 E1
Waldegrave Terr BA3 .... 79 A3
Walden Rd BS31 .... 25 A4
Waldock Barton TA13 .... 220 D4
Waldron's Cross TA21 .... 165 E1
Wales La BA22 .... 174 E3
Walford Ave BS22 .... 32 C3
Walford Cross Roads TA2 .... 169 D7
Walker Rd BA11 .... 120 A3
Walkers Dr BS24 .... 49 F7
Walkers Gate TA21 .... 222 D5
Walker St BS2 .... 226 C4
Walk La TA13 .... 184 F1
Wallace La BS40 .... 74 E3
Wallace Rd BA1 .... 28 B1
Wallace Wells Rd TA8 .. 104 D5
Wallbridge BA11 .... 120 B4
Wallbridge Ave BA11 .... 120 A4
Wallbridge Gdns BA11 .. 120 A4
Wallbridge Ho BA11 .... 120 A4
Wallbridge Ind Est BA11 .. 120 B4
Wall Ditch La TA16 .... 196 A8
Wallenge Cl BS39 .... 77 F6
Wallenge Dr BS39 .... 77 F6
Walley La BS40 .... 57 B7
Wall Gn BS26 .... 70 C1
Wallingford Rd BS4 .... 22 D7
Wallington Way BA11 .. 119 D6
Walliscote Grove Rd 11 BS23 .... 48 E7
Walliscote Prim Sch BS23 48 E7
Walliscote Rd BS23 .... 48 D6
Walliscote Rd S BS23 .... 48 D4
Walls La BS28 .... 108 B8
Walls The TA7 .... 137 C2
Wall The TA9 .... 106 D5
Wally Court Rd BS40 .... 56 E8
Walmsley Terr 4 BA1 .... 28 B1
Walnut Bldgs BA3 .... 79 A3
Walnut Cl
Axbridge BS26 .... 70 B1
Cheddar BS27 .... 90 B7
Easton-in-G BS20 .... 4 A3
Keynsham BS31 .... 24 C4
Nailsea BS48 .... 18 E8
Puriton TA7 .... 136 C4
Rode BA11 .... 101 E8
Taunton TA1 .... 212 B4
Weston-Super-Mare BS24 .. 49 B2
Walnut Dr
Bath BA2 .... 44 E4
Bridgwater TA6 .... 209 D3
Somerton TA11 .... 211 D4
Walnut Gr BA4 .... 205 C4
Walnut La TA7 .... 136 F3
Walnut Rd TA10 .... 172 A6
Walnuts The TA7 .... 137 B2
Walnut Tree Cl
Ubley BS40 .... 55 D1
Wells BA5 .... 203 C5
Walnut Tree Cnr TA23 .. 131 F4
Walnut Tree Ct BS49 .... 34 D4
Walnut Tree Dr TA24 .... 131 A5
Walnut Wlk
Bristol BS13 .... 22 A6
Frome BA11 .... 120 B7
Keynsham BS31 .... 24 C4
Walridge Cross TA4 .... 166 A4
Walrond's Pk TA3 .... 184 B7
Walrond Ct TA19 .... 221 B3
Walrow TA9 .... 104 E3
Walrow Ind Est TA9 .... 104 F2
Walrow Terr TA9 .... 104 E3
Walscombe Cl 1 TA14 .. 185 F4
Walsh Ave BS14 .... 23 A7
Walsh Cl BS24 .... 49 B2
Waltham End BS24 .... 50 A8
Walton BS24 .... 49 A2
Walton Bay House Park Homes BS21 .... 1 B1
Walton CE Prim Sch BA16 .... 156 E7
Walton Cl
Bridgwater TA6 .... 209 D5
Keynsham BS31 .... 24 D4
Walton Cres BS40 .... 37 F8
Walton Cross BS21 .... 7 B7
Walton Ct TA24 .... 201 A7
Walton Dro BA16 .... 156 D5
Walton Rd
Bristol BS11 .... 4 D6
Clevedon BS21 .... 6 F4
Walton St
Portishead BS21 .... 1 A1
Walton in G BS21 .... 7 A8
Walwyn Cl BA2 .... 44 A6
Walwyn Gdns BS13 .... 22 C3
Wambrook Cl TA1 .... 212 E1
Wansbeck Gn TA1 .... 213 D3
Wansbeck Rd BS31 .... 25 A4
Wansbrough Rd BS22 .... 32 B4
Wansdyke Bsns Ctr BA2 .. 44 D4
Wansdyke Ct BS14 .... 23 B5
Wansdyke Prim Sch BS14 .. 22 F4
Wansdyke Rd BA2 .... 44 D1
Wansdyke Sch BA2 .... 62 E8
Wansdyke Workshops
Keynsham BS31 .... 25 A6
Peasedown St John BA2 .. 79 D6
Wapping Rd BS1 .... 227 A1
Warden Rd TA24 .... 200 F6
Ward La TA7 .... 154 E8
Wardleworth Way TA21 .. 222 C7
Wardour Rd BS4 .... 22 D8
Wareham Cl BS48 .... 8 D1

Wareham Cross EX13 . . . . 198 E1
Wareham Rd EX13 . . . . 198 E2
Wares La TA6 . . . . 208 D6
Waring Ho BS1 . . . . 227 A1
Warleigh Cl BA11 . . . . 119 D4
Warleigh Dr BA1 . . . . 29 A3
Warleigh La BA1 . . . . 46 C5
Warleys La BS24 . . . . 32 C1
Warman Cl BS14 . . . . 23 F6
Warman Rd BS14 . . . . 23 F6
War Meml Hospl TA8 . . . . . 104 B7
Warmington Rd BS14 . . . . . 23 C8
Warminster Rd
Beckington BA11 . . . . 101 E4
Claverton BA2, BA3 . . . . 46 B5
Frome BA11 . . . . 120 B4
Warne Pk BS23 . . . . 49 A6
Warner Cl BS49 . . . . 35 A7
Warne Rd BS23 . . . . 49 A6
Warren's Cl BS27 . . . . 71 B1
Warren Cl
Bridgwater TA6 . . . . 208 F6
Bruton BA10 . . . . 215 E6
Charlton Horethorne DT9 . 176 A2
Hutton BS24 . . . . 49 D2
Warren Farm Cvn Pk & Camp Site TA8 . . . . 65 F5
Warren Gdns BS14 . . . . 23 F5
Warren La BS41 . . . . 20 E8
Warren Rd
Brean TA8 . . . . 65 F6
Minehead TA24 . . . . 201 B7
Warrens Hill BS27 . . . . 71 B1
Warrens Hill Rd BS27 . . . . . 71 D4
Warren St TA21 . . . . 222 A4
Warrens Way BA5 . . . . 113 A1
Warren The BA16 . . . . 207 A5
Warres Rd TA2 . . . . 213 C8
Warrilow Cl BS22 . . . . 32 B5
Warrior Ave BA22 . . . . 218 B6
Warry Cl BS48 . . . . 9 B2
Warth La BS22 . . . . 32 A8
Warwick Ave TA6 . . . . 209 C3
Warwick Cl BS22 . . . . 49 C8
Warwick Gdns
Burnham-on-S TA8 . . . . 85 B1
Clutton BS39 . . . . 58 D3
Taunton TA1 . . . . 213 C2
Warwick Rd
3 Bath BA1 . . . . 44 B7
Keynsham BS31 . . . . 24 D4
Taunton TA2 . . . . 213 A8
Washcross La TA19 . . . . . . 184 E3
Washford Cross TA23 . . . . 131 F3
Washford Hill TA23 . . . . . . 202 A5
Washford Sta TA23 . . . . 131 E4
Washingpool DT9 . . . . 188 E7
Washing Pound La
Bristol BS14 . . . . 23 B4
Nailsea BS48 . . . . 8 B4
Washington Gdns TA6 . . . 208 E5
Washington Terr TA20 . . . 223 B5
Wash La TA15 . . . . 186 B4
Washpool La BA2 . . . . 43 F2
Wassail Cl 5 TA24 . . . . 131 A5
Wassail View TA2 . . . . 168 B4
Watchet Boat Mus* TA23 . . . . 202 C7
Watchet Sta TA23 . . . . 202 C7
Watch House Pl BS20 . . . . . . 2 E7
Watch House Rd BS20 . . . . . 4 D4
Watchill Ave BS13 . . . . 21 F6
Watchill Cl BS13 . . . . 21 F6
Watchwell Dro BA6 . . . . . 157 D7
Waterbridge Rd BS13 . . . . . 21 F4
Watercombe Hts BA20 . . 218 D2
Watercombe La
Yeovil BA20 . . . . 218 C2
Yeovil, Preston Plucknett BA20 . . . . 218 D5
Watercombe Pk BA20 . . . 218 D3
Watercress Cl BS48 . . . . 9 B2
Waterfield Cl TA1 . . . . 212 B3
Waterfield Dr TA1 . . . . 212 B3
Waterford Beck BA14 . . . . . 83 F6
Waterford Cl TA6 . . . . 209 A2
Waterford Pk BA3 . . . . 78 E1
Waterfront Ho BA2 . . . . . . 228 B1
Water Hill TA4 . . . . 150 F7
Waterhouse La BA2 . . . . 63 F8
Water La
Bristol BS1 . . . . 227 B2
Butleigh BA6 . . . . 157 E4
Charlton Horethorne DT9 . 176 A2
Crowcombe TA4 . . . . 151 A7
Frome BA11 . . . . 119 E3
Horningsham BA12 . . . . . . 144 D4
Keenthorne TA5 . . . . 134 C1
Lopen TA13 . . . . 185 A1
Nether Stowey TA5 . . . . . . 134 A1
Paulton BA3, BS39 . . . . 78 A4
Pill BS20 . . . . 4 C4
Somerton TA11 . . . . 211 C3
Stogumber TA4 . . . . 150 F7
Waterlake DT10 . . . . 190 B4
Waterlake Rd TA20 . . . . . . 198 C8
Waterlands La TA18 . . . . . 224 C8
Waterleaze TA2 . . . . 213 D7
Waterlip BA4 . . . . 141 F7
Waterloo
Frome BA11 . . . . 119 F5
Puriton TA7 . . . . 136 C4
Waterloo Bldgs 4 BA2 . . . . 44 B6
Waterloo Cl TA7 . . . . 136 C4
Waterloo Cotts TA1 . . . . . 212 B4
Waterloo Cres DT9 . . . . . . 176 A1
Waterloo Ho BS20 . . . . 4 D5
Waterloo La
Stalbridge DT10 . . . . 190 A1
Yeovil BA20 . . . . 219 A4
Waterloo Pl 19 BS2 . . . . . 227 C3
Waterloo Rd
Bristol BS2 . . . . 227 C3
Radstock BA3 . . . . 79 A2
Shepton Mallet BA4 . . . . . . 205 B7
Wellington TA21 . . . . 222 C6
Waterloo St
Bristol BS2 . . . . 227 C3
9 Bristol, Clifton BS8 . . . . . . 11 F7
Weston-Super-Mare BS23 . . . 48 E8
Waterloo Terr DT9 . . . . . . 225 F4
Watermans Mdw TA6 . . . . 208 E6
Watermead TA20 . . . . 198 D8
Watermead Cl 9 BA1 . . . . 228 B2
Water Path TA21 . . . . 222 A5
Waters Edge BS20 . . . . 2 E7
Waterside Cres BA3 . . . . 78 D1
Waterside La BA3 . . . . 98 A6
Waterside Pk BS20 . . . . 1 D4
Waterside Rd
Radstock BA3 . . . . 78 D1
Wincanton BA9 . . . . 216 C4
Waterside Way BA3 . . . . 97 D8
Waters La BS27 . . . . 90 C8
Watersmeet Cl
Golsoncott TA23 . . . . 131 D1
Rooks Bridge BS26 . . . . 87 B5
Water St
Barrington TA19 . . . . 184 D5
Curry Rivel TA10 . . . . 171 C4
East Harptree BS40 . . . . 74 F4
East Lambrook TA13 . . . . . 220 C8
Hambridge TA10 . . . . 171 D1
Lopen TA13 . . . . 185 A1
Martock TA12 . . . . 185 D5
Seavington St Michael TA19 . . . . 184 E1
Watery Combe BA3 . . . . 94 E7
Watery La
Axminster EX13 . . . . 198 A3
Bath BA2 . . . . 44 A6
Broadway TA19 . . . . 194 B8
Charlton Horethorne DT9 . 176 C1
Clatworthy TA4 . . . . 149 C2
Coultings TA5 . . . . 134 E3
Doynton BS30 . . . . 12 A8
Halstock BA22 . . . . 197 D3
Hewish TA18 . . . . 195 D3
Langford Budville TA4, TA21 . . . . 166 C2
Minehead TA24 . . . . 200 F7
Nailsea BS48 . . . . 8 B2
North Petherton TA6 . . . . . 153 E4
Spaxton TA5 . . . . 152 F4
Stogursey TA5 . . . . 134 C5
Stratton-on-t F BA3 . . . . 97 A3
Williton TA4 . . . . 202 E4
Winford BS40 . . . . 38 B4
Wiveliscombe TA4 . . . . 210 C6
Watling St BA21 . . . . 218 D7
Watling Way BS11 . . . . 4 D7
Watsons La TA6 . . . . 209 A5
Watts's Quarry La TA10, TA11 . . . . 173 A5
Watts's Rd TA7 . . . . 137 D8
Watts La TA4 . . . . 151 E1
Waveney Rd BS31 . . . . 25 A3
Wavering Down Rise BS26 . . . . 70 A3
Waverley TA11 . . . . 211 C4
Waverley Cl
Frome BA11 . . . . 120 C6
Somerton TA11 . . . . 211 C4
Waverley Rd
Backwell BS48 . . . . 19 A7
Bridgwater TA6 . . . . 208 F6
Bristol, Shirehampton BS11 . . 4 E6
Weston-Super-Mare BS23 . . . 48 F4
Waverly Ct BS49 . . . . 34 D3
Waverney Cl TA1 . . . . 213 D3
Wayacre Dro BS24 . . . . 66 E6
Wayclose La BA9 . . . . 177 D5
Waycroft Prim Sch BS14 . . 23 E5
Waydown Cross TA24 . . . . 130 A4
Waydown La TA24 . . . . 130 A4
Wayfield Gdns BA1 . . . . 28 F4
Wayford Cl BS31 . . . . 25 A3
Wayford Hill TA18 . . . . 195 C1
Wayland Rd BS22 . . . . 31 E3
Waysdown La TA4 . . . . 149 D1
Wayside
Staplehay TA3 . . . . 181 D8
Weston-Super-Mare BS22 . . . 31 D2
Wayside Cl BA11 . . . . 120 C6
Wayside Dr BS21 . . . . 6 E5
WCA Ho BS1 . . . . 227 A2
Weacombe Rd
Bridgwater TA6 . . . . 209 C5
Taunton TA2 . . . . 212 F7
Weal Terr BA1 . . . . 27 B2
Weal The BA1 . . . . 27 C2
Weare CE Fst Sch BS26 . . . 88 D7
Weare Ct BS1 . . . . 226 A1
Weares La TA7 . . . . 137 D2
Weatherley Dr BS20 . . . . 1 F3
Weatherly Ave BA2 . . . . 44 D2
Weaver's Reach TA21 . . . . 222 B7
Weavers Cl
Crewkerne TA18 . . . . 224 D5
Shepton Mallet BA4 . . . . . . 205 D4
Weavers Ct BA11 . . . . 119 E3
Weavers Orch BA2 . . . . 62 D1
Weavers The BA11 . . . . 101 E4
Webb's Cl BA5 . . . . 203 D3
Webb's Hill BA11 . . . . 119 B5
Webber Rd BA4 . . . . 205 D4
Webbers TA4 . . . . 167 F7
Webbers CE Prim Sch TA21 . . . . 178 F5
Webbers Cl TA21 . . . . 222 E4
Webbers Way TA7 . . . . 136 B4
Webbington Rd BS26 . . . . . . 69 C3
Webbs Mead
Beckington BA11 . . . . 101 E4
Chew Stoke BS40 . . . . 56 D8
Wedgwood Cl BS14 . . . . 23 B5
Wedgwood Rd BA2 . . . . 44 A5
Wedlakes TA23 . . . . 202 C6
Wedlands TA2 . . . . 212 F7
Wedlock Way BS3 . . . . 11 F3
Wedmore Cl
Bath BA2 . . . . 44 A3
Burnham-on-S TA8 . . . . 104 C8
Frome BA11 . . . . 120 C7
Weston-Super-Mare BS23 . . . 48 F2
Wedmore Fst Sch BS28 . . 108 B4
Wedmore Pk BA2 . . . . 44 A3
Wedmore Rd
Cheddar BS27 . . . . 90 A7
Clevedon BS21 . . . . 6 B1
Nailsea BS48 . . . . 18 E8
Saltford BS31 . . . . 25 D4
Weekesley La BA2 . . . . 60 D1
Weekes Mdw TA21 . . . . 179 E6
Week La TA22 . . . . 147 D4
Weetwood Rd BS49 . . . . 34 E5
Weind The BS22 . . . . 31 D2
Weirfield Gn TA1 . . . . 212 D5
Weirfield Rd TA24 . . . . 201 A8
Weir Head Cotts TA22 . . . 163 D7
Weir La
Abbots Leigh BS8 . . . . 10 F5
Marshfield SN14 . . . . 13 F8
Pilton BA4 . . . . 140 E3
Yeovilton BA22 . . . . 174 A1
Weir Rd BS49 . . . . 34 E3
Welbeck Rd BA21 . . . . 219 E7
Welland Cl TA1 . . . . 213 D4
Welland Rd
Keynsham BS31 . . . . 24 F4
Yeovil BA21 . . . . 219 D7
Wellard Cl 1 BS22 . . . . 32 B4
Well Cl
Long Ashton BS41 . . . . 11 B1
Weston-Super-Mare BS24 . . . 49 B2
Winscombe BS25 . . . . 70 A8
Wellesley Ct TA1 . . . . 212 C1
Wellesley Gn BA10 . . . . 215 E6
Wellesley Park Prim Sch TA21 . . . . 222 E4
Wellesley Pk TA21 . . . . 222 D4
Wellesley St TA2 . . . . 212 F6
Wellesley Way TA3 . . . . . . 192 A7
Wellfield Hill DT6, EX13 . . . 199 B2
Well House Cl BS9 . . . . 5 E3
Wellhouse La BA6 . . . . 206 F4
Wellings Cl TA20 . . . . 198 C8
Wellington Bldgs BA1 . . . . . 27 B2
Wellington Cottage Hospl TA21 . . . . 222 D5
Wellington Ct BS21 . . . . 6 C5
Wellington Flats BA20 . . . 219 A4
Wellington Hill TA21 . . . . . 222 F2
Wellington Jun Sch TA21 . . . . 222 E5
Wellington Mews BS11 . . . . . 4 D5
Wellington Mus TA21 . . . . . 222 D6
Wellington New Rd TA1 . . 212 B3
Wellington Pl
Cheddar BS27 . . . . 90 B7
Weston-Super-Mare BS23 . . . 48 D7
Wellington Rd
Bridgwater TA6 . . . . 209 B5
Bristol BS2 . . . . 227 C4
Taunton TA1 . . . . 212 D4
Wellington Sch TA21 . . . . . 222 E5
Wellington Sq TA24 . . . . . . 200 F7
Wellington Terr
18 Bristol BS8 . . . . 11 F6
Clevedon BS21 . . . . 6 D5
Wiveliscombe TA4 . . . . 210 C5
Well La
Banwell BS29 . . . . 50 E3
Purse Caundle DT9 . . . . . . 189 D4
Timberscombe TA24 . . . . . . 130 A5
Yatton BS49 . . . . 34 C8
Wellow Brook Ct BA3 . . . . . 78 B3
Wellow Brook Mdw BA3 . . . 78 B2
Wellow Dr BA11 . . . . 120 C7
Wellow La
Hinton Charterhouse BA2 . . . 63 D1
Norton St Philip BA2 . . . . 81 D5
Peasedown St John BA2 . . . . 79 C6
Shoscombe BA2 . . . . 79 E6
Wellow Mead BA2 . . . . 79 B7
Wellow Rd BA2 . . . . 80 B8
Wellow Tyning BA2 . . . . 79 D7
Well Pk BS49 . . . . 34 E4
Wells Cathedral* BA5 . . . 203 E4
Wells Cathedral Jun Sch BA5 . . . . 203 E5
Wells Cathedral Sch BA5 . . . . 203 E5
Wells Central CE Jun Sch BA5 . . . . 203 C3
Wells Cl
Bristol BS14 . . . . 23 C5
Burnham-on-S TA8 . . . . 104 C7
Nailsea BS48 . . . . 9 B1
Taunton TA2 . . . . 213 A8
Wells & District Hospl BA5 . . . . 203 F5
Wellsea Gr BS23 . . . . 49 B7
Wellshead La TA24 . . . . . . 128 A3
Wells Mus* BA5 . . . . 203 E4
Wellsprings Prim Sch TA2 . . . . 212 F8
Wellsprings Rd TA2 . . . . . . 212 F7
Wells Rd
Bath BA2 . . . . 228 B1
Bristol BS14 . . . . 23 C7
Chilcompton BA3 . . . . 96 F4
Clevedon BS21 . . . . 6 D1
Corston BA2 . . . . 43 B7
Dundry BS40, BS41 . . . . 38 F7
Glastonbury BA6 . . . . 206 E6
Glastonbury, Southway BA5, BA6 . . . . 139 D4
Hallatrow BS39 . . . . 77 B7
Norton St Philip BA2, BA3 . . . 81 C3
Priddy BA5 . . . . 92 E2
Radstock BA3 . . . . 78 E2
Rodney Stoke BS27 . . . . 91 B1
Shepton Mallet BA4 . . . . 204 E6
Theale BS28 . . . . 109 B1
Westbury-sub-Mendip BA5 . 110 E6
Wookey Hole BA5 . . . . 203 A7
Yarley BA5 . . . . 139 C8
Wells Road Trad Est BA6 . 206 F7
Wells Sq BA3 . . . . 78 D1
Wellsway
Bath BA2 . . . . 44 F3
Keynsham BS31 . . . . 24 F3
Wells Way BS28 . . . . 107 F3
Wellsway Pk BA2 . . . . 62 D8
Wellsway Sec Sch BS31 . . . 25 A5
Well The TA21 . . . . 222 B5
Welsford Ave BA5 . . . . 203 C5
Welsford Cl BA5 . . . . 203 B5
Welsh Back BS1 . . . . 227 A2
Welsh Ct BA5 . . . . 203 B4
Welshmill La BA11 . . . . 119 F5
Welshmill Rd BA11 . . . . 119 F5
Welton Gr BA3 . . . . 78 B3
Welton Prim Sch BA3 . . . . . 78 C2
Welton Rd BA3 . . . . 78 E2
Welton Vale BA3 . . . . 78 B2
Wembdon Ct TA6 . . . . 208 E4
Wembdon Hill TA6 . . . . 208 C6
Wembdon Orch TA6 . . . . . . 208 C6
Wembdon Rd TA6 . . . . 208 E4
Wembdon St George's CE Prim Sch TA6 . . . . 208 C6
Wemberham Cres BS49 . . . 17 A1
Wemberham La BS49 . . . . . 33 E8
Wendick Dro TA10 . . . . 171 E3
Wentwood Dr BS24 . . . . 49 A1
Wentworth Cl BS22 . . . . 32 A3
Wentworth Rd BA21 . . . . . 219 E7
Werren Cl TA23 . . . . 202 B7
Wesley Ave BA3 . . . . 78 C1
Wesley Cl
Brean TA8 . . . . 65 F3
Frome BA11 . . . . 119 F4
Southwick BA14 . . . . 83 E2
Taunton TA1 . . . . 212 C1
Wanstrow BA4 . . . . 142 F4
Wesley Ct BS23 . . . . 48 F8
Wesley Dr BS22 . . . . 32 A3
Wesley La BA14 . . . . 83 E2
Wesley Mews BS27 . . . . 90 B7
Wesley Rd BA3 . . . . 78 D1
Wesley Slope 13 BA11 . . . . 119 F4
Wesley Villas
Coleford BA3 . . . . 116 F6
12 Frome BA11 . . . . 119 F4
Wessex Bldgs TA11 . . . . 211 B5
Wessex Bsns Ctr BS27 . . . . 90 A7
Wessex Cl
Bridgwater TA6 . . . . 209 C4
Chard TA20 . . . . 223 C2
Street BA16 . . . . 207 D6
Wessex Ct 4 DT9 . . . . 225 D3
Wessex Dr DT9 . . . . 187 E1
Wessex Fields BA11 . . . . . . 119 D2
Wessex Fields Ret Pk BA11 . . . . 119 D2
Wessex Ho 10 BS2 . . . . 227 C3
Wessex Pk TA11 . . . . 211 B5
Wessex Rd
Stalbridge DT10 . . . . 190 C4
Taunton TA1 . . . . 168 E1
Weston-Super-Mare BS24 . . . 49 B2
Yeovil BA21 . . . . 218 D8
Wessex Rise TA11 . . . . 211 E3
Wessex Way BA9 . . . . 216 B3
Westacre BA16 . . . . 207 A4
Westacre Cl BS27 . . . . 90 B8
Westacre Rd BS27 . . . . 90 B8
West Anstey School Cross EX36 . . . . 162 C5
West Approach Rd TA7 . . 136 D4
West Ave
Bath BA2 . . . . 44 C5
Highbridge TA9 . . . . 104 C4
Westaway Cl BS49 . . . . 34 C7
Westaway Pk BS49 . . . . 34 D7
West Bank BA5 . . . . 203 A8
Westbourne Ave
Clevedon BS21 . . . . 6 B2
Keynsham BS31 . . . . 24 E5
Westbourne Cl BA20 . . . . . 218 E5
Westbourne Cres BS21 . . . . . 6 B2
Westbourne Gr BA20 . . . . . 218 E5
Westbourne Ho BA2 . . . . . . 228 C2
Westbourne Pl BS8 . . . . 226 B3
West Bourton Rd SP8 . . . . . 177 E8
West Bower La TA5 . . . . . . 153 C7
West Bow Ho TA6 . . . . 208 E4
Westbridge Pk DT9 . . . . 225 B2
West Brook BA21 . . . . 218 D6
Westbrook Ct BA4 . . . . 141 E1
Westbrooke Ct BS1 . . . . . . 226 A1
Westbrook Pk BA1 . . . . 27 A2
Westbrook Rd
Bristol BS4 . . . . 23 D8
Evercreech BA4 . . . . 141 E1
Weston-Super-Mare BS22 . . . 31 D1
Westbrook Vale BA4 . . . . . . 141 E1
West Buckland Com Prim Sch TA21 . . . . 180 F7
West Buckland Rd TA21 . 180 D7
Westbury
Bradford Abbas DT9 . . . . . . 187 E1
Sherborne DT9 . . . . 225 D3
Westbury Court Rd BS9 . . . . 5 F7
Westbury Cres BS23 . . . . 48 F2
Westbury Gdns BA22 . . . . . 186 C2
Westbury La BS9 . . . . 5 C7
Westbury Terr
Dunkerton BA2 . . . . 61 E5
2 Sherborne DT9 . . . . 225 D3
Westbury View BA2 . . . . 79 E8
West Camel Farm BA22 . . 174 E3
West Camel Rd BA22 . . . . . 174 E3
West Charlton TA11 . . . . . . 173 E7
West Chinnock CE Prim Sch TA18 . . . . 196 B8
West Cl
Bath BA2 . . . . 44 A5
Dunster TA24 . . . . 201 D2
West Coker CE Prim Sch BA22 . . . . 197 A8
West Coker Rd BA20 . . . . . 218 E2
Westcombe BA8 . . . . 176 E1
Westcombe Hill BA4 . . . . . 142 C2
Westcombe Rd
Evercreech BA4 . . . . 141 F2
Westcombe BA4 . . . . 142 A2
Westcombes EX13 . . . . 198 B7
Westcombe Trad Est TA19 . . . . 183 E1
West Compton La BA4 . . . 204 E3
West Coombe
Bristol BS9 . . . . 5 D6
Yeovil BA21 . . . . 218 D6
West Coombe La TA4 . . . . 165 D8
West Cornmoor Dro TA9 . . . . 136 D7
Westcott Cl BA11 . . . . 120 C6
Westcott Cross TA23 . . . . . 130 D1
Westcott La TA4 . . . . 148 F2
West Cotts TA24 . . . . 127 A2
West Cres TA19 . . . . 221 B2
West Croft
Blagdon BS40 . . . . 54 E2
Clevedon BS21 . . . . 6 B2
West Ct
Horrington BA5 . . . . 112 F1
Portishead BS20 . . . . 2 D4
Templecombe BA8 . . . . 176 E1
West Dene BS9 . . . . 5 E6
West Dro TA7 . . . . 137 D4
West Dundry La BS41 . . . . . 21 E2
West End
Bristol BS3 . . . . 226 C1
Bristol, Kingsdown BS2 . . . 227 A4
Frome BA11 . . . . 119 F5
Lower Weare BS26 . . . . 88 D8
Marston Magna BA22 . . . . . 174 E1
Somerton TA11 . . . . 211 C4
Street BA16 . . . . 207 B5
Wedmore BS28 . . . . 108 C3
West End Cl
Somerton TA11 . . . . 211 C4
South Petherton TA13 . . . . . 220 B4
West End Ct
Chedzoy TA7 . . . . 136 D1
South Petherton TA13 . . . . . 220 B4
West End Farm Cvn Pk BS24 . . . . 49 E4
Westend La BA11 . . . . 143 C6
West End La BS48 . . . . 18 A8
West End Trad Est BS48 . . . . 8 B1
West End View
Barrington TA19 . . . . 184 C5
South Petherton TA13 . . . . . 220 B4
West End Way TA13 . . . . . . 220 B4
Westerkirk Gate TA2 . . . . . 212 C7
Westerleigh Rd
Bath BA2 . . . . 45 B1
Clevedon BS21 . . . . 6 B2
Westerly Ct TA19 . . . . 221 B4
Western Approaches BA22 . . . . 174 A2
Western Ave BA21 . . . . 218 B6
Western Ct
Clevedon BS21 . . . . 6 D3
Shepton Mallet BA4 . . . . 205 B6
Western Dr BS14 . . . . 22 E6
Western Gate TA10 . . . . 172 C7
Western La
Minehead TA24 . . . . 200 F7
Ridge BS40 . . . . 74 C3
Western Retreat BA5 . . . . . 203 B5
Western St DT9 . . . . 187 E4
Western Way
Bridgwater TA6 . . . . 208 F7
Winsham TA20 . . . . 194 E1
Westex Ho BS23 . . . . 49 B5
Westfield
Bruton BA10 . . . . 215 D5
Clevedon BS21 . . . . 16 D8
Curry Rivel TA10 . . . . 171 C3
Shepton Mallet BA4 . . . . 205 A6
Sherborne DT9 . . . . 225 B2

Westfield Ave BA21 ...... 218 E6
Westfield Cl
Backwell BS48 .... 19 A6
Bath BA2 .... 44 E3
Bridgwater TA6 .... 208 E4
Burnham-on-S TA8 .... 104 B8
Keynsham BS31 .... 24 C5
Weston-Super-Mare BS23 ... 48 D2
West Field Cl TA1 .... 212 A2
Westfield Com Sch BA21 218 E6
Westfield Cres
Banwell BS29 .... 51 A3
Yeovil BA21 .... 218 F6
Westfield Ct TA8 .... 104 B8
Westfield Dr
Backwell BS48 .... 19 A6
Burnham-on-S TA8 .... 104 B8
Westfield Est BA12 .... 161 F2
Westfield Gr BA21 .... 218 F6
Westfield Ho
Bath BA2 .... 44 E3
Bridgwater TA6 .... 208 E4
Westfield Ind & Trad Est
BA3 .... 97 C7
Westfield Inf Com Sch
BA21 .... 218 E6
Westfield La
Curry Rivel TA10 .... 171 C3
Draycott BS27 .... 90 E3
North Curry TA3 .... 170 C3
Rodney Stoke BS27 .... 110 C8
Street BA6, BA16 .... 207 E2
West Field Lawn TA8 ..... 104 B8
Westfield Pk BA1 .... 44 A7
Westfield Pk S BA1 .... 44 A7
Westfield Pl
Bristol BS8 .... 11 F7
Yeovil BA21 .... 218 E6
Westfield Prim Sch BA3 ... 97 C8
Westfield Rd
Backwell BS48 .... 19 A6
Banwell BS29 .... 51 A3
Burnham-on-S TA8 .... 104 B8
Frome BA11 .... 119 D3
Wells BA5 .... 203 C4
Weston-Super-Mare BS23 ... 48 D2
Yeovil BA21 .... 218 F6
Westfields TA19 .... 184 C5
Westfield Terr BA3 .... 78 D1
Westford Cl TA21 .... 222 A5
Westford Ct TA21 .... 222 A5
Westford Dr TA21 .... 222 A5
West Garston BS29 .... 51 A3
Westgate BS1 .... 226 B1
Westgate Bldgs BA1 ..... 228 B2
Westgate St
Bath BA1 .... 228 B2
4 Taunton TA1 .... 212 E3
Westhall Rd BA1 .... 44 D7
West Harptree Rd BS40 ... 74 F5
West Hatch La TA3 .... 182 F8
Westhaven Cl BS48 .... 19 A6
Westhaven Sch BS23 ...... 48 D2
Westhay Broad Dro TA7 .. 137 E6
Westhay Cross EX13 ...... 198 F3
Westhay Moor Dro BA5,
BA6 .... 138 D6
Westhay Rd BA6 .... 138 C4
West Hay Rd BS40 .... 35 C3
West Hendford BA20 ..... 218 F3
West Hill
Milborne Port DT9 .... 217 D2
Nailsea BS48 .... 9 A5
Portishead BS20 .... 2 B5
Wincanton BA9 .... 216 B4
West Hill Ct BS20 .... 2 C6
West Hill Gdns BS20 .... 2 C5
West Hill Gdns
Radstock BA3 .... 78 D1
Radstock BA3 .... 78 E1
Westhill La TA9 .... 105 C2
West Hill Rd BA3 .... 78 D1
Westholm Rd TA11 .... 211 B4
West Howetown La
TA24 .... 147 D5
West Huntspill Com Prim
Sch TA9 .... 104 C1
West La
Alhampton BA4 .... 159 C5
Alweston DT9 .... 189 A2
Barrington TA13 .... 184 F5
Croscombe BA5 .... 140 F8
Felton BS40 .... 37 C8
Lynford-on-F TA11 .... 158 D2
Sherborne DT9 .... 188 F1
Westlake Cl TA7 .... 155 C2
Westland Rd BA20 .... 218 F4
West Lea Rd BA1 .... 27 A1
West Leaze BA16 .... 207 B6
Westleigh Gdns BA4 ..... 205 A6
West Leigh Inf Sch BS48 .. 19 A6
Westleigh Pk BS14 .... 23 B8
Westleigh Rd TA1 .... 213 B3
West Links BS23 .... 48 D2
West Links Cl BS22 .... 31 B3
West Littleton Rd SN14 ... 13 F8
West Lodge BA4 .... 205 A5
West Lynne BS27 .... 90 B8
West Mall BS8 .... 11 F7
Westmans Est TA8 .... 104 C7
Westmarch Way BS22 ..... 32 A4
Westmead BA3 .... 96 D3
Westmead Gdns BA1 ...... 27 A2
West Mendip Com Hospl
BA6 .... 139 D3
Westmere Cres TA8 ..... 104 C8
West Mill La
Marnhull DT10 .... 190 D6
Sherborne DT9 .... 225 C2
Westminster BA21 .... 218 C7
Westminster Bldgs DT10 . 190 B4
Westminster Cotts DT10 .. 190 B4
Westminster St BA20 .... 219 A4
West Monkton CE Prim Sch
TA2 .... 213 F8
Westmoor Dro TA10,
TA12 .... 184 E7
Westmoor La TA10 ...... 184 D8
Westmoreland Dr BA2 .. 228 A2
Westmoreland Rd BA2 .. 228 A1
Westmoreland St BA2 ... 228 A2
Westmoreland Station Rd
BA2 .... 228 A1
Weston All Saints CE Prim
Sch BA1 .... 27 A2
Weston Bsns Pk BS24 ..... 49 E5
Weston Cl
Bristol BS9 .... 5 C7
East Chinnock BA22 ...... 196 E8
Weston Coll
Nailsea BS48 .... 8 E2
Weston-Super-Mare BS23 ... 48 D8
Weston Coll (Westcliff)
BS23 .... 30 B1
Weston Ct BS24 .... 49 B3
Weston Dro BS20 .... 7 F8
Weston Euro Pk BS24 ..... 49 B4
Weston Express Bsns Pk
BS22 .... 49 C6
Weston Farm La BA1 ...... 27 C2
Weston Gateway Tourist Pk
BS24 .... 32 C1
Weston General Hospl
BS23 .... 48 E2
Weston Hill SP8 .... 177 D3
Westonia BS22 .... 31 E2
Westonian Ct BS9 .... 5 C4
Weston Ind Est BS24 ...... 49 B2
Weston La
Bath BA1 .... 44 C8
Christon BS26 .... 68 C7
East Coker BA22 .... 197 E5
Halstock DT2 .... 196 F1
Weston Lock Ret BA2 ..... 44 C6
Weston Lodge BS23 .... 48 D8
Weston Milton Sta BS22 ... 49 C7
Weston Miniature Rly*
BS23 .... 48 D5
Weston Park Ct BA1 ...... 27 D1
Weston Park Prim Sch
BS11 .... 4 F8
Weston Pk BA1 .... 27 C1
Weston Pk E BA1 .... 27 D1
Weston Pk W BA1 .... 27 C1
Weston Rd
Bath BA1 .... 44 D8
Brean TA8 .... 66 A5
Congresbury BS49 .... 34 B5
East Brent BS24, TA9 ...... 86 D6
Failand BS8 .... 10 C3
Long Ashton BS41 .... 20 D8
Weston Ret Pk BS23 ...... 49 A6
Weston Sixth Form Coll
BS23 .... 48 F2
Weston St
Buckhorn Weston SP8 .... 177 D3
East Chinnock BA22 ...... 196 E8
Weston-Super-Mare Sta
BS23 .... 48 E7
Weston Town BA4 .... 141 E1
Weston Way BS24 .... 49 F2
Weston Wlk BA11 .... 119 C6
Weston Wood Rd BS20 ..... 2 C3
Westonzoyland Prim Sch
TA7 .... 154 F5
Westonzoyland Pumping
Sta* TA7 .... 154 D3
Westonzoyland Rd TA6,
TA7 .... 209 E4
Westover's Cnr BS28 .... 108 B4
Westover
Frome BA11 .... 119 D4
Nunney BA11 .... 143 B7
Westover Ct BA11 .... 119 D4
Westover Gdns BS9 .... 5 F8
Westover Gn TA6 .... 208 E4
Westover Green Com Sch
TA6 .... 208 E4
Westover La
Crewkerne TA18 .... 224 B7
Martock TA12 .... 185 F8
Westover Rd BS9 .... 5 F8
Westover Trad Est TA10 .. 171 F5
Westover View TA18 ..... 224 C7
Westowe Hill TA4 .... 151 A3
West Par BS9 .... 5 C7
West Park Cl TA24 .... 200 E7
West Pennard CE Prim Sch
BA6 .... 140 B1
West Pk
Bristol BS8 .... 226 B4
Butleigh BA6 .... 157 E4
Castle Cary BA7 .... 214 B6
Minehead TA24 .... 200 E7
Yeovil BA20 .... 218 F5
Westport La TA3, TA10 ... 184 B7
West Quay TA6 .... 208 F5
West Rd
East Brent BS24, TA9 ...... 86 B7
Lympsham BS24 .... 67 B1
Midsomer Norton BA3 ..... 78 A3
Wiveliscombe TA4 .... 210 B4
Yatton BS49 .... 34 B7
Westridge DT9 .... 225 C3
Westridge Way TA4 ...... 167 E7
West Rocke Ave BS9 .... 5 D6
West Rolstone Rd BS24 ... 33 A1
West Sedgemoor Nature
Reserve* TA3 .... 170 F3
West Sedgemoor Rd
TA3 .... 170 D3
West Shepton BA4 .... 205 A5
West Somerset Com Coll The
TA24 .... 201 B5
West Somerset Rly
Crowcombe TA4 .... 151 C4
Stogumber TA4 .... 150 F7
West Somerset Rural Life
Mus* TA24 .... 124 C4
West St
Ashcott TA7 .... 156 B8
Axbridge BS26 .... 70 B2
Bampton EX16 .... 164 B1
Banwell BS29 .... 51 A3
Banwell BS29 .... 51 B3
Bishops Lydeard TA4 ..... 167 E8
Bridgwater TA6 .... 208 E4
Bristol BS2 .... 227 C3
Carhampton TA24 .... 131 B4
Crewkerne TA18 .... 224 B6
Dunster TA24 .... 201 D1
Hinton St George TA17 ... 195 C7
Ilchester BA22 .... 173 E1
Ilminster TA19 .... 221 B4
Kington Magna SP8 ...... 177 E1
Martock TA12 .... 185 E8
Minehead TA24 .... 200 E6
Seavington St Mary TA19 .. 184 D1
Somerton TA11 .... 211 D4
South Petherton TA13 .... 220 B4
Stoke sub Hamdon TA14 .. 185 E3
Templecombe BA8 .... 189 E8
Watchet TA23 .... 202 B7
Wells BA5 .... 203 C3
Weston-Super-Mare BS23 ... 48 D8
Wiveliscombe TA4 .... 210 C4
Yarlington BA9 .... 175 F7
Yeovil BA20 .... 218 F4
West Terr BA2 .... 82 C1
West Town Gr BS4 .... 23 D8
West Town La
Baltonsborough BA6 ...... 157 F5
Bristol BS4, BS14 .... 23 C8
West Town Pk BS4 .... 23 D8
West Town Rd
Backwell BS48 .... 19 A5
Bristol BS11 .... 4 C7
West Tyning BA2 .... 42 B1
Westview BS39 .... 77 C5
West View
Creech St Michael TA3 .... 169 D5
Long Sutton TA10 .... 172 E4
Milborne Port DT9 .... 217 D3
Queen Camel BA22 .... 174 F4
South Cadbury BA22 ..... 175 D4
West Monkton TA2 .... 169 D8
West View Cl TA7 .... 155 B4
Westview Orch BA3 .... 64 B5
West View Rd
Batheaston BA1 .... 29 A3
Keynsham BS31 .... 24 E5
West Villas TA4 .... 167 F6
Westville BA21 .... 219 C5
Westward BS41 .... 11 B2
Westward Cl BS40 .... 35 D2
Westward Dr BS20 .... 4 C4
Westward Gdns BS41 ...... 11 B2
Westward Rd BS13 .... 21 F7
Westway
Nailsea BS48 .... 8 E2
Street BA16 .... 207 B6
West Way BS21 .... 6 C3
Westway Ctr BA11 .... 119 F5
Westway La BA4 .... 205 B4
West Ways BA22 .... 196 E8
West Well La BS28 .... 109 C1
West Wick BS24 .... 32 C1
West Wick Rdbt BS22,
BS24 .... 50 B8
Westwood BA2 .... 45 E6
Westwood Ave BS39 .... 59 C2
Westwood Cl 2 BS22 ...... 31 F2
Westwood Cotts BA8 ..... 176 E1
Westwood Dr BA11 ...... 119 C4
Westwood Dro TA11 ..... 158 C3
Westwood Rd
Bridgwater TA6 .... 209 D7
Bristol BS4 .... 23 D8
Westwoods BA1 .... 29 B3
Westwood with Iford Prim
Sch BA15 .... 64 F3
Wetherell Pl BS8 .... 226 B3
Wet La BS27 .... 90 F2
Wetlands La BS20 .... 2 C3
Wetlands & Willows Visitor
Ctr* TA3 .... 170 D5
Wetmoor La
Langport TA10 .... 172 C2
Westbury-sub-Mendip BA5 . 110 E1
Wexford Rd BS4 .... 22 D8
Weycroft Ave EX13 ...... 198 A2
Weylands BA11 .... 119 E6
Weymont Cl TA7 .... 155 B3
Weymouth Ct BA1 .... 45 B8
Weymouth Rd
Evercreech BA4 .... 141 E1
Frome BA11 .... 119 E4
Weymouth St BA1 .... 45 B8
Whaddon Hill BA10 ...... 160 C7
Wharf Cotts TA21 .... 222 B8
Wharf Ho TA19 .... 221 B4
Wharf La
Ilminster TA19 .... 221 B3
Portbury BS20 .... 3 B5
Wharfside BS24 .... 66 E3
Wharnecliffe Cl BS14 ..... 23 B5
Wharnecliffe Gdns BS14 .. 23 B5
Whatcombe Rd BA11 ..... 119 E6
Whatcombe Terr BA11 ... 119 E6
Whatley TA10 .... 171 F5
Whatley Cross TA20 ..... 194 C1
Whatley La
Buckland St Mary TA20 ... 192 D7
Langport TA10 .... 172 A5
Tatworth TA20 .... 194 C1
Winsham TA20 .... 199 A8
Whatley Mews TA10 ..... 171 F5
Whatley Vineyard & Herb
Gdn* BA11 .... 118 D4
Wheatfield Dr BS22 .... 32 A5
Wheatfield La BA3 .... 95 A6
Wheathill Cl
Keynsham BS31 .... 24 D5
Milborne Port DT9 .... 217 D2
Wheathill La DT9 .... 217 E3
Wheathill Way DT9 ..... 217 D2
Wheatleigh Cl TA1 ...... 212 E2
Wheatley Cres TA1 ...... 213 B5
Wheatstones 10 TA4 ..... 167 F8
Wheeler Gr BA5 .... 203 B4
Wheelers Cl BA3 .... 78 C2
Wheelers Dr BA3 .... 78 C2
Wheelers Rd BA3 .... 78 D2
Wheel House La TA20 .... 199 B7
Wheelwright & Gypsy Mus*
BS26 .... 68 D4
Whellers Mdw TA12 ..... 185 E7
Whetham Mill Cross
DT8 .... 199 F5
Whetham Mill La DT8 .... 199 F6
Whetstones Almshouses
TA19 .... 183 F4
Whippington Ct BS1 ..... 227 B3
Whirligg La 15 TA14 ..... 185 F4
Whirligig La TA1 .... 212 F4
Whirligig Pl 7 TA1 ...... 212 F4
Whistley La BS40 .... 74 F6
Whitbourne Moor BA12 .. 144 E8
Whitbourne Springs
BA12 .... 144 F7
Whitchey Dro TA9 .... 137 A5
Whitchurch District Ctr
BS14 .... 23 A5
Whitchurch La
Bristol, Bishopsworth
BS13 .... 22 B5
Bristol, Hartcliffe BS13 .... 22 C5
Bristol, Whitchurch BS14 ... 22 E5
Dundry BS41 .... 22 C1
Henstridge BA8 .... 190 A7
Yenston BA8 .... 189 F8
Whitchurch Prim Sch
BS14 .... 23 C4
Whitchurch Rd BS13 ...... 22 A6
Whitcombe Farm La
DT9 .... 175 D2
Whitcross 10 BA22 .... 197 F8
White's Dro BA5 .... 138 F7
White's La TA4 .... 133 A1
White Ash La TA20 ...... 193 A5
Whitebeam Cl TA6 .... 209 D5
Whitebrook La BA2 .... 79 A8
Whitebrook Terr TA21 ... 178 F5
White Cats Cotts BA8 .... 176 E3
Whitechapel La BA11 .... 101 C1
Whitecroft TA4 .... 202 E4
White Cross
Brent Knoll TA9 .... 105 C8
Exford TA24 .... 128 B1
Whitecross Ave BS14 ..... 23 C6
White Cross Gate BS39 ... 76 F6
Whitecross La
Banwell BS29 .... 51 A4
Minehead TA24 .... 200 E7
Whitecross Rd
East Harptree BS40 .... 74 F4
Weston-Super-Mare BS23 ... 48 E6
Whitecross Way TA24 ... 200 E7
Whitedown Cross EX15 .. 191 B4
Whitefield Cl BA1 .... 29 B4
Whitefield Cross EX36 .. 162 D3
Whitefield La TA19 ...... 184 D4
Whitefield Rocks TA4 .... 150 B1
Whitegate Cl
Bleadon BS24 .... 67 B6
Minehead TA24 .... 201 A6
Whitegate Rd TA24 ...... 201 A6
Whitegates Gdns TA24 ... 200 F6
Whitehall
Taunton TA1 .... 212 F5
Watchet TA23 .... 202 B7
Whitehall Cl TA13 .... 220 D4
Whitehall Ct TA18 .... 224 C7
White Hart La TA21 ..... 222 D6
White Hill
Langport TA10 .... 172 A7
Shoscombe BA2 .... 79 F6
White Hill Dro TA20 ..... 193 C5
Whitehole Hill BA3 ...... 116 E4
White Horse Dr BA11 .... 120 C6
White Horse La BS28 .... 138 D8
White Horse Rd BA15 ..... 64 E7
Whitehouse Ctr (PRU)
BS13 .... 22 C5
Whitehouse La
Litton BA3 .... 75 D3
Wraxall BS48 .... 9 A6
White House La
East Huntspill TA9 .... 136 E7
White House La *continued*
Loxton BS26 .... 68 A3
Whitehouse Rd BS49 ...... 34 F8
White House Rd TA5,
TA6 .... 135 D5
Whiteladies Rd BS8 ..... 226 B4
Whitelands Hill BA3 ...... 79 B3
Whiteleaze La
Thurloxton TA2 .... 153 C1
West Monkton TA2 .... 169 D8
White Lodge Pk BS20 ...... 2 D6
White Mead BA21 .... 218 D6
Whitemill La BA11 ...... 119 C3
Whitemoor Hill TA20 .... 194 C4
Whitemoor La TA4 .... 150 F3
Whitemore Ct BA1 .... 29 A4
Whiteoak Way BS48 .... 18 D8
White Oxmead La BA2 .... 61 E1
White Ox Mead La BA2 ... 61 F1
White Post
Midsomer Norton BA3 ..... 97 B6
Twitchen EX36 .... 145 K2
Whitepost Gate DT9 ..... 188 D6
Whites Cl TA6 .... 208 E2
Whitesfield Ct BS48 .... 8 D2
Whitesfield Rd BS48 ...... 8 D1
Whitesome's Dro BS27 .. 109 C6
White St
Bristol BS5 .... 227 C4
Creech St Michael TA3 ... 169 E4
Horningsham BA12 .... 144 E4
North Curry TA3 .... 170 C4
Whitestaunton Cross
TA20 .... 193 B5
Whitestone Rd BA11 .... 120 B6
Whitewall Cnr TA3 ...... 181 D2
Whiteway TA20 .... 193 E6
Whiteway Rd BA2 .... 44 A3
Whitewell Pl BA11 ...... 119 E3
Whitewell Rd BA11 ...... 119 E3
Whitewells Rd BA1 .... 28 A2
Whitewick La TA5 .... 134 F8
Whitfield Rd TA6 .... 209 D6
Whitford Hill
Corfe TA3 .... 182 A4
Pitminster TA3 .... 181 F5
Whitford La TA3 .... 182 A4
Whithys The BA16 .... 207 C7
Whiting Cl BA4 .... 205 C4
Whiting La 1 TA6 .... 153 E3
Whiting Rd
Bristol BS13 .... 22 A4
Glastonbury BA6 .... 206 F5
Whiting Way BA5 .... 203 D4
Whitland Ave BS13 .... 22 B5
Whitland Rd BS13 .... 22 B5
Whitley La BA16 .... 156 D7
Whitley Rd TA7, BA16 .... 156 C8
Whitling St BS40 .... 38 A2
Whitmead Gdns BS13 ..... 22 C4
Whitmore La TA2 .... 212 D8
Whitmore Rd TA2 .... 212 E8
Whitnage La EX16 .... 178 C2
Whitnell Cnr BA5 .... 113 F6
Whitnell La
Binegar BA3 .... 114 B8
Keenthorne TA5 .... 134 D2
Whitney Hill TA19 .... 193 F8
Whitson Ho 1 BS2 ...... 227 C3
Whitson St BS1 .... 227 A4
Whitstone BA4 .... 205 C5
Whitstone Cl BA4 .... 205 C6
Whitstone Cnr BA4 ...... 205 D1
Whitstone Ct BA4 .... 205 D5
Whitstone Hill BA4 ..... 204 C1
Whitstone La BA4 .... 205 E1
Whitstone Rd BA4 .... 205 D4
Whitstone Rise BA4 ..... 205 D4
Whitswood Steep TA24 .. 130 D4
Whittakers Ho 6 BA4 .... 205 B6
Whitting Rd BS23 .... 48 E4
Whittington Dr BS22 ..... 31 D2
Whittock Rd BS14 .... 23 D6
Whittock Sq BS14 .... 23 D7
Whittox La BA11 .... 119 E5
Whitwell Rd BS14 .... 23 B8
Whitworth Rd
Frome BA11 .... 119 F2
Minehead TA24 .... 200 D7
Wicketsbeer Rd BA22 .... 197 C6
Wickfield BS21 .... 6 C1
Wickham's Cross or Beggar's
Grave BA6 .... 157 C3
Wickham Ct BS21 .... 6 C3
Wickham Rise BA11 ..... 119 F6
Wickham Way
East Brent TA9 .... 86 D4
Shepton Mallet BA4 ...... 205 A6
Wick Hill
Charlton Horethorne
DT9 .... 176 A1
Milborne Port DT9 .... 217 B6
Wickhill Rd TA10 .... 171 D5
Wick Hollow BA6 .... 206 F5
Wick House Cl BS31 ...... 25 D3
Wick La
Burnham-on-S TA9 .... 85 E6
Glastonbury BA6 .... 139 E2
Lympsham BS24 .... 66 E1
Peasedown St John BA2,
BA3 .... 60 F1
Pensford BS39 .... 40 D3
Upton Cheyney BS30 ...... 26 A8
Wicklow Rd BS4 .... 22 E8
Wick Moor Dro TA5 ..... 134 C7
Wick Rd
Bishop Sutton BS39 .... 57 C3
Lympsham BS24 .... 66 D2

Wick Rd *continued*
Milborne Port DT9 217 C4
Wick St Lawrence BS22 32 B7
Widcombe BS14 23 A6
Widcombe CE Jun Sch
BA2 45 B5
Widcombe Cres BA2 45 B5
Widcombe Hill BA2 45 C4
Widcombe Inf Sch BA2 45 B5
Widcombe Par BA2 228 C1
Widcombe Rise BA2 45 B5
Widcombe Terr BA2 45 B5
Wideatts Rd BS27 90 A7
Widmore Gr BS13 22 B5
Wigeon Cl TA24 201 C5
Wight Row BS20 2 F6
Wigmore Gdns BS22 31 D2
Wiindsor Cres TA20 223 B3
Wilbye Gr BS4 22 D7
Wildcountry La BS48 20 E6
Wilde Cl TA8 104 C6
Wilder Ct BS2 227 B4
Wilderness Dro BA16 138 E2
Wilderness The 9 DT9 225 E4
Wilder St BS2 227 B4
Wildmoor La TA21 180 F6
Wild Oak Ho TA3 168 D1
Wild Oak La TA3 168 D1
Wilfred Rd TA1 213 A4
Wilfrid Rd BA16 207 D6
Wilkins Cl TA20 223 E4
Wilkins Rd TA6 209 D5
Willcocks Cl 6 TA21 222 D5
Willcox Cl BA6 206 E5
Willet's La BA3 94 D6
Willet Cl TA9 104 D3
Willett Hill Cross TA4 150 D5
Willey Rd TA3 170 E6
William Daw Cl BS29 50 F3
William Herschel Mus*
BA1 228 B2
William Reynolds Ho
BA16 207 D7
William St
Bath BA2 228 C3
Taunton TA2 212 F6
Williamstowe BA2 45 C1
Willie Gill Ct TA1 212 E4
Willinton Rd BS4 22 F8
Willis's La TA18 196 C4
Willis Hay DT9 225 D3
Williton Cres BS23 48 F3
Williton & District Hospl
TA4 202 D3
Williton Sta TA4 202 F4
Will La TA4 151 A3
Willmott Cl BS14 22 F3
Willmotts Cl TA7 137 B2
Willoughby Cl BS13 22 B7
Willoughby Pl TA20 223 D3
Willoughby Rd TA6 208 C4
Willowbank TA24 130 B4
Willow Cl
Bath BA2 62 E8
Clevedon BS21 6 E3
East Huntspill TA9 136 E7
Langport TA10 172 A6
Long Ashton BS41 10 F1
Portishead BS20 2 C4
Radstock BA3 78 E2
Taunton TA1 213 D1
Weston-Super-Mare, St Georges
BS22 32 D2
Weston-Super-Mare, Uphill
BS23 48 E2
Westonzoyland TA7 154 E5
Williton TA4 202 E3
Willow Ct TA6 209 D5
Willowdown BS22 31 E4
Willow Dr
Bleadon BS24 67 C6
Hutton BS24 49 E2
Shepton Mallet BA4 205 A6
Weston-Super-Mare BS24 49 E5
Willowfalls The BA1 28 E3
Willow Gdns BS22 32 D2
Willow Gn
Bath BA2 44 D4
Chedzoy TA7 154 D8
Willow Gr TA23 131 E4
Willow Ho BS13 22 D4
Willow La EX15 180 F2
Willow Rd
Street BA16 207 B3
Yeovil BA21 218 F6
Willows The
Brent Knoll TA9 86 A2
Nailsea BS48 8 F3
Willow The BA3 96 F2
Willow Tree Cl BA22 174 A4
Willow Vale BA11 119 F5
Willow Way TA18 224 D7
Willow Wlk
Bridgwater TA6 209 C4
Keynsham BS31 24 D4
Wills Ind Est TA6 209 A4
Wills Rd TA6 208 F1
Wills Way BS4 22 D6
Willway St BS2 227 C3
Wilmots Way BS20 4 D4
Wilsham Cross EX35 122 A5
Wilsham La EX35 122 A5
Wilson Pl BS2 227 C4
Wilsons Cl TA5 134 B2
Wilson St BS2 227 C4
Wilton Cl
Burnham-on-S TA8 104 C8
Street BA16 207 D5
Wilton Cl *continued*
Taunton TA1 212 E3
Wilton Ct BS23 48 D7
Wilton Gdns BS23 48 D7
Wilton Gr TA1 212 E3
Wilton Orch
Street BA16 207 D5
Taunton TA1 212 E2
Wilton Rd BA21 219 E8
Wiltons BS40 35 D2
Wilton St TA1 212 E3
Wiltown TA10 171 D3
Wiltown La EX15 180 F3
Wiltshire Cl TA1 212 C2
Wiltshire Ct TA1 212 C2
Wiltshires Barton 4
BA11 119 E5
Wiltshire Way BA1 28 A2
Wilway La TA22 163 C6
Wimblestone Rd BS25 51 F2
Wimborne Cl TA1 213 D3
Wimborough La BA22 196 F6
Winash Cl BS14 23 D7
Wincanton Bsns Pk BA9 216 B3
Wincanton Cl BS48 9 B1
Wincanton Prim Sch
BA9 216 C3
Wincanton Town Mus*
BA9 216 C4
Winchcombe Cl BS48 19 A8
Winchcombe Gr BS11 4 F5
Winchester Cotts TA19 184 E1
Winchester Gdns BA21 219 C7
Winchester Ho 2 TA1 213 A4
Winchester Rd
5 Bath BA2 44 D5
Burnham-on-S TA8 104 C7
Winchester St TA1 213 A4
Windball Hill TA22 163 B7
Windcliff Cres BS11 4 E7
Wind Down Cl TA6 208 C4
Windermere Ave BS23 48 F4
Windermere Cl BA20 218 F2
Windmill TA3 170 F5
Windmill Bsns Pk BS21 16 E8
Windmill Cl TA9 105 B7
Windmill Cotts TA15 186 C4
Windmill Cres TA7 136 E3
Windmill Hill
Hutton BS24 50 A2
Wrantage TA3 170 A2
Windmill Hill La
Ashill TA19 183 B3
Westbury-sub-Mendip
BA5 110 D4
Windmill Hill Rd BA6 206 E5
Windmill La
Langport TA10 172 C5
Montacute TA15 186 C4
West Pennard BA6 140 C1
Windmill Rd
Clevedon BS21 16 E8
High Ham TA10 156 A1
Windmill Rise TA18 224 C7
Windrush Cl BA2 43 F4
Windrush Gn BS31 25 A4
Windrush Rd BS31 25 A4
Windsbatch Hill BA11 101 C1
Windsbatch La BA11 101 B1
Windsor Ave BS31 24 E4
Windsor Bridge Rd BA1,
BA2 44 D7
Windsor Castle BA1 44 D7
Windsor Cl
Burnham-on-S TA8 85 B1
Clevedon BS21 6 D2
Minehead TA24 200 E6
Taunton TA1 212 C1
Windsor Cres BA11 120 A5
Windsor Ct
4 Bath BA1 44 C7
13 Bristol, Clifton BS8 11 F6
Windsor Dr
Bridgwater TA6 209 D7
Nailsea BS48 8 E2
Windsor Hill La BA4 141 B8
Windsor Ho TA6 209 C5
Windsor La TA14 186 A4
Windsor Pl
5 Bath BA1 44 C7
Bristol, Clifton BS8 11 F6
Windsor Rd
Bridgwater TA6 209 D7
Weston-Super-Mare BS22 31 C2
Windsor Terr
Bristol, Clifton BS8 11 F6
17 Henstridge BA8 190 A6
Paulton BS39 77 E5
Windsor Villas 3 BA1 44 C7
Windway Hill TA4 164 D6
Windwhistle Circ BS23 48 F4
Windwhistle La
Sticklepath TA4 149 F6
Weston-Super-Mare BS23 48 E3
Windwhistle Prim Sch
BS23 48 F3
Windwhistle Rd BS23 48 D3
Windy Ridge TA17 195 D7
Windyridge La TA11 211 B1
Wine St
Bath BA1 228 C2
Bristol BS1 227 A3
Frome BA11 119 E4
Yeovil BA20 219 B4
Winford CE Prim Sch
BS40 37 F7
Winford Cl BS20 2 E4
Winford Gr BS13 22 A8
Winford La BS41 21 C1
Winford Rd BS40 38 F3
Winford Rural Workshops
BA22 197 A2
Winford Terr
Bridgwater TA6 209 B6
Bristol BS41 21 C5
Wingard Cl BS23 48 D2
Wingard Ct 6 BS23 48 E5
Wingate Ave BA21 219 C7
Wingfield CE Prim Sch
BA14 83 C6
Wingfield Rd DT9 225 C3
Winifred's La BA1 27 E1
Winifred Cliff Ct 1 EX16 164 B1
Winkworth Way TA1, TA2 213 A5
Winnibrook La TA24 131 A5
Winnowing End BS25 52 A3
Winpenny La TA2 168 E8
Winsbeer La
Rockwell Green TA21 222 A6
Runnington TA21 179 F8
Winsbury View BA2 42 B1
Winscombe Cl BS31 24 D6
Winscombe Ct BA11 120 B5
Winscombe Dro
Shipham BS25 70 D6
Winscombe BS25 70 A5
Winscombe Hill BS25 69 F5
Winscombe Rd BS23 49 A7
Winscombe Woodborough
Prim Sch BS25 70 A8
Winsham Cl BS14 23 B5
Winsham Prim Sch TA20 194 E1
Winslade Cl TA2 213 B7
Winsley CE Prim Sch
BA15 64 E7
Winsley Hill BA3 64 B6
Winsley Rd BA15 64 F7
Winsors La TA24 131 A5
Winstitchen Cross TA24 127 C2
Winstitchen La TA24 127 C2
Winston Cl TA2 212 E6
Winston Dr BA21 218 F8
Winstone Ct BS2 226 C3
Winter's La TA4 150 C3
Winterfield TA18 196 B5
Winterfield Pk BS39 77 E4
Winterfield Rd BS39 77 E5
Winterhay La TA19 221 A5
Winter La DT9 188 C8
Winters Cross TA4 165 C8
Winters Field TA1 213 A5
Winters Hill La BA4 204 C3
Winters La BS40 36 D6
Winters Orch TA3 169 C1
Winterstoke Commercial Ctr
BS23 49 A6
Winterstoke Rd
Bristol BS3 11 F3
Weston-Super-Mare BS23,
BS24 49 B4
Winterstoke Underpass
BS3 11 F4
Winterwell La BA4 141 F4
Wint Hill BS29 51 B2
Winyards View TA18 224 D4
Wireworks Est The TA6 136 A2
Wirral Park Rd BA6 206 C3
Wirral Park Rdbt BA6 206 C3
Wishford Mews BA3 78 C2
Wisley Wlk BS22 49 F7
Wisteria Ave BS24 49 D2
Wisteria Cl BA22 218 B5
Wiston Cross EX36 162 D2
Witches Wlk TA6 208 E2
Witch Hazel Rd BS13 22 E3
Witcombe Dro TA12 172 F1
Witcombe La TA12 185 F8
Witham Cl TA1 213 D3
Witham Rd BS31 25 A3
Withey Cl E BS9 5 F6
Withey Cl W BS9 5 F5
Witheys The BS14 23 C4
Withial Hill BA4 158 D8
Withiel Dr TA5 135 B2
Withiel Hill TA24 148 F6
Withies La BA3 97 A8
Withies Pk BA3 96 F8
Withmoor Dro TA10 172 E4
Withybed La BA9 177 E6
Withy Cl BS48 8 F3
Withycombe Cross TA24 131 C4
Withycombe Hill TA5 135 A5
Withycombe Hill Gate
TA24 130 F4
Withycombe La TA24 131 B5
Withy Cotts BA3 115 C5
Withyditch La BA2 61 C4
Withy Gr TA9 136 C7
Withy Grove Cl TA6 209 D7
Withy Hays Rd 3 TA11 173 F7
Withy La
Barton St David TA11 158 A3
Clatworthy TA4 149 B2
Hemyock EX15 180 B1
Oakhill BA3 115 C5
Withypool Cross
Hawkridge TA22 146 C2
Twitchen EX36 145 J4
Withypool Gdns BS14 23 B5
Withy Rd TA9 136 C7
Withys The BS20 4 D4
Withywine La TA22 164 C5
Withywood Com Sch
BS13 22 A5
Withywood Gdns 1 BS13 21 F4
Withy Wood La BA4 142 C5
Withywood Rd BS13 21 F4
Witney Cl BS31 25 D3
Witney La
Chard TA20 223 B8
Tatworth TA20 193 F1
Wittey's La TA20 199 B6
Wiveliscombe Prim Sch
TA4 210 B5
Wivenhoe Ct BA11 120 C6
Woburn Rd BA21 219 E7
Wolfester Terr BA22 174 F4
Wollens Cl BA6 206 C4
Wolmer Cl TA6 208 E2
Wolsey Cl BA5 203 B3
Wolverlands BA22 175 A6
Wolvershill Ind Units
BS29 50 C6
Wolvershill Pk BS29 51 A3
Wolvershill Rd BS29 50 E6
Wonhouse Dro BS28 138 B6
Wood's Cross EX36 162 C5
Woodacre BS20 2 E7
Woodadvent La TA23 131 E1
Woodbarton TA4 166 F4
Woodbirds Hill La TA10 172 C8
Woodborough Cres BS25 70 A7
Woodborough Ct BS25 70 A8
Woodborough Dr BS25 70 A8
Woodborough Hill Cotts
BA2 79 C4
Woodborough La BA3 79 A4
Woodborough Rd
Radstock BA3 79 A3
Winscombe BS25 69 F8
Woodburn Cross EX16 162 F2
Woodburn Hill EX16 162 F2
Woodburn Water Cross
EX16 162 F1
Woodbury Ave BA5 203 F5
Woodbury Cl BA5 203 F5
Woodbury Rd TA6 208 D4
Wood Cl BA5 203 B4
Woodcliff Ave BS22 31 C1
Woodcliff Rd BS22 31 C1
Wood Close La TA17 195 A8
Woodcock St BA7 214 C5
Woodcock Way EX13 198 B7
Woodcombe Brake
TA24 200 D7
Woodcombe Cotts TA24 200 C8
Woodcombe La TA24 200 C8
Woodcote BA20 218 D2
Woodcroft BS39 57 C3
Woodcroft Mdws TA20 192 E7
Wooddene BS25 70 A8
Wood Dro TA10 171 E8
Wood End TA4 167 D6
Wood End Wlk BS9 5 C6
Wood Farm Cotts TA5 134 E4
Woodfield Cl TA8 104 C5
Woodford Cl BS48 9 A1
Woodford Cotts TA4 132 A1
Woodford Ct 2 BS23 48 E5
Woodford La
Coxley BA5 139 F6
Wells BA5 203 B1
Woodford Rd BA5 140 A6
Woodfords Gn BA7 214 B6
Woodhayes BA8 190 A6
Woodhayes Ct 19 BA8 190 A6
Woodhayes Ho 12 BA8 190 A6
Woodhayes Rd BA11 120 C6
Woodhenge BA22 218 B5
Woodhill BS49 34 E6
Woodhill Ave BS20 2 D6
Woodhill Ct BS20 2 D6
Wood Hill Pk BS20 2 D7
Woodhill Rd BS20 2 D6
Woodhill Terr TA3 170 F6
Woodhill Views BS48 8 F3
Woodhouse Cross SP8 177 F6
Woodhouse La
Axminster EX13 198 D1
Chard TA20 194 B6
Marston Magna BA22 175 B1
Montacute TA15 186 C3
Woodhouse Rd
Axminster EX13 198 D1
Bath BA2 44 A6
Woodhurst Rd BS23 49 A7
Woodington Rd BS21 6 C1
Wood Kilns The BS49 17 A1
Wood La
Axbridge BS26 70 D2
Blue Anchor TA24 131 C6
Butleigh BA6 157 C4
Carhampton TA24 131 B4
Chapmanslade BA13 121 D4
Clapton in G BS20 8 E8
Crowcombe TA4 151 C7
Drimpton DT8 199 E7
High Ham TA10 155 E1
Marnhull DT10 190 F2
Moorlinch TA7 155 E8
Rodney Stoke BS27 91 B1
South Cheriton BA8 176 C4
Stalbridge DT10 190 B4
Stawell TA7 137 A1
Stogumber TA4 150 D7
Weston-Super-Mare BS23 30 F1
Woodland Ave TA7 154 F5
Woodland Cl
6 Carhampton TA24 131 A5
Failand BS8 10 B4
Woodland Cotts BA3 64 D6
Woodland Ct BS9 5 C3
Woodland Glade BS21 6 E5
Woodland Gr
Bath, Bushey Norwood
BA2 45 E5
Bath, Weston Park BA1 27 C1
Bristol BS9 5 D6
Yeovil BA20 219 B4
Woodland Pl BA2 45 D5
Woodland Rd
Bristol BS8 226 C4
Frome BA11 119 F4
Nailsea BS48 8 E3
Taunton TA2 213 A7
Watchet TA23 202 C6
Weston-Super-Mare BS23 48 D4
Woodlands
Axbridge BS26 70 D2
Wellington TA21 222 F3
Weston-Super-Mare BS23 30 D1
Woodlands Bsns Pk
EX16 179 C3
Woodlands Ct BS11 4 E5
Woodlands Dr
Ruishton TA3 169 C3
Winsley BA3 64 B6
Woodlands La
Holcombe BA3 116 B7
Isle Abbotts TA3 183 E6
Woodlands Mead DT10 190 F6
Woodlands Pk BA1 28 C2
Woodlands Rd
Baltonsborough BA6 158 A8
Clevedon BS21 6 C4
Portishead BS20 2 D8
Woodlands The
Peasedown St John BA2 60 F3
Shepton Mallet BA4 205 D5
Woodland Way BS8 10 B4
Woodleaze BS9 5 B6
Woodleigh Gdns BS14 23 C6
Woodmarsh Cl BS14 23 A4
Woodmead Gdns BS13 22 C4
Woodmill BS49 17 A1
Woodmill Cl DT10 190 B5
Woodpecker Ave BA3 97 B8
Woodpecker Dr BS22 49 E8
Woodram La TA3 181 E5
Wood Rd
Ashill TA19 183 B4
High Ham TA10 172 A8
Woodridge Mead TA4 167 F8
Wood Rock EX36 162 C5
Woodrush Cl TA1 213 C1
Woods Batch BA16 207 B6
Woods Cnr TA11 173 E8
Woods Hill BA3 64 A6
Woodside
Bristol BS9 5 D3
Midsomer Norton BA3 77 E1
Woodside Ave BS24 49 B2
Woodside Cl TA24 200 D7
Woodside Ct BS23 49 A8
Woodside Gdns BS20 1 E5
Woodside Rd BS21 6 E5
Woodspring Ave BS22 31 B3
Woodspring Cres BS22 31 A3
Woodspring Mus* BS23 48 E8
Woodspring Priory*
BS22 14 C1
Woods Rd BA16 207 A6
Wood St
Bath BA1 228 B2
Bath, Beechen Cliff BA2 228 B1
Milverton TA4 166 F5
Taunton TA1 212 E4
Woodstock Rd
Taunton TA1 212 E5
Weston-Super-Mare BS22 49 B8
Yeovil BA21 219 C7
Woodview
Chilcompton BA3 96 E5
2 Clevedon BS21 6 F3
Paulton BS39 77 C5
Wells BA5 203 E5
Woodview Cl BS11 4 E7
Woodview Dr BS49 35 B8
Woodview Rd BS27 90 C7
Woodview Terr
Nailsea BS48 8 F2
Weston-Super-Mare BS23 49 A6
Wood Way EX35 122 D4
Woodwell Rd BS11 4 E5
Wookey Cl BS48 18 F8
Wookey Hole Cave*
BA5 111 E5
Wookey Hole Papermill &
Mus* BA5 203 A8
Wookey Hole Rd BA5 203 B5
Wookey Prim Sch BA5 139 D8
Woolavington Hill TA7 136 E3
Woolavington Rd TA7 136 D4
Woolavington Right Dro
TA7 154 D6
Woolavington Village Prim
Sch TA7 136 E4
Woolcott La SP8 161 E1
Wooler Rd BS23 48 E8
Wooley La TA19, TA20 194 C6
Woolhayes La TA20 223 A8
Woollard La
Bristol BS14, BS39 41 A7
Whitchurch BS14 23 E1
Woollen La BA22 174 F1
Woolley La BA1 28 A4
Woolley Rd BS14 23 E5
Woolpit La TA24 146 B7

Woolshed Cl TA24........**129** E1
Woolstone La TA5.........**134** F7
Woolston Rd BA22.......**175** E6
Woolvers Way BS24.......**50** B6
Wooton Hill BA6.........**157** C5
Wootton Cross EX13 ....**198** F1
Wootton Gr DT9 ....**225** E5
Wootton St BA6 ....**157** C6
Wootton Vineyard★ BA4. **140** C5
Worberry La BA3 ....**95** B7
Worcester Bldgs BA1....**28** B2
Worcester Cl BA2........**79** D7
Worcester Cres BS8.... **226** A4
Worcester Ct BS8....... **226** A4
Worcester Gdns BS48...**18** C8
Worcester Pk BA1 ......**28** B2
Worcester Pl BA1...... **226** A4
Worcester Rd BS8 ..... **226** A4
Worcester Terr
  Bath BA1..............**28** B2
  Bristol BS8.......... **226** A4
Wordsworth Ave TA6....**208** E6
Wordsworth Cl TA8 .....**85** B2
Wordsworth Dr TA1 ....**213** B3
Wordsworth Rd
  Clevedon BS21.........**6** C2
  Weston-Super-Mare BS23...**49** A3
World's End La BS31.....**25** C5
Worldwide Butterflies &
  Lullingstone Silk Farm★
  DT9 ....**187** F3
Worlebury CE Fst Sch
  BS22.................**31** B3
Worlebury Cl BS22......**31** B3
Worlebury Hill Rd BS22,
  BS23.................**31** B2
Worlebury Park Rd BS22 ..**31** A2
Worle Com Sch BS22 ....**31** E1
Worle Ct BS22...........**31** F3
Worle Ind Est BS22......**32** B2
Worle Moor Rd BS24....**49** E7
Worle Sta BS22.........**32** B1
Wormcliff La SN13......**29** F3
Worminster Batch BA4..**140** D5
Worston La TA8..........**104** C5
Worston Orch TA9 ......**104** E4
Worston Rd TA9 ....**104** E5
Worthings The BS24 .....**67** B1
Worthington Cl BS28....**108** D5
Worth La TA22, TA24 ....**146** C4
Worthy Cres BS24........**67** B1
Worthy La
  Creech St Michael TA3...**169** D5
  Pilton BA4............**140** F3
  5 Weston-Super-Mare
    BS23...............**48** E8
  West Pennard BA4, BA6...**140** D1
Worthy Pl **4** BS23......**48** E8
Worthy Toll Rd TA24....**123** D4
Wouldham Rd TA23 .....**202** D6

Wrangcombe La TA21... **180** A4
Wrangcombe Rd TA21... **180** A4
Wrangle Farm Gn BS21 ....**6** E2
Wrangle The **5** BS24 ....**49** F7
Wrangway Rd EX15 .....**180** A3
Wraxall CE Prim Sch BS48 .**9** B4
Wraxall Cross Rds BA4.. **159** A7
Wraxall Gr BS13 ....**22** A8
Wraxall Hill
  Ditcheat BA4.......... **159** A8
  Wraxall BS48...........**9** C5
Wraxall Rd BA4......... **159** B7
Wraxall Vineyard★ BA4.. **159** A7
Wraxhill Cl BA16........ **207** D5
Wraxhill Rd
  Street BA16........... **207** C5
  Yeovil BA20...........**218** E1
Wreath La TA20........**194** B3
Wren Cl
  Frome BA11...........**120** B6
  Taunton TA1 ....**212** C4
  Weston-Super-Mare BS22...**31** A1
Wrenmoor Cl TA6....... **209** C3
Wrington CE Prim Sch
  BS40.................**35** E2
Wrington Cres BS13 .....**22** A7
Wrington Hill BS40 .....**35** F5
Wrington La BS49 ....**34** E5
Wrington Mead BS49 ....**34** E5
Wrington Rd BS49 ......**34** F4
Wristland Rd TA23 .....**202** D7
Writhlington Ct BA3 ....**79** C2
Writhlington Sch BA3....**79** C1
Writh Rd DT9...........**189** B1
Wroughton Dr BS13......**22** D4
Wroughton Gdns BS13 ..**22** D4
Wry La TA4.............**149** F2
Wyatt's Cl BS48.........**8** D2
Wyatt Ave BS13.........**21** F5
Wyatt Cl BS13 ....**21** F5
Wyatts Ct TA17 ....**195** C7
Wyatts Field TA3........**168** D1
Wyatts Way TA19.......**183** C4
Wych Ct EX13 ....**198** E3
Wych Elm Rd BA11 .....**120** C6
Wydford Cl DT9.........**225** B3
Wydon La TA24 ....**124** F3
Wye Ave TA6............**209** D3
Wyedale Ave BS9 ....**5** C7
Wyke La
  Wyke ChampflowerBA10.. **215** A5
  Wyke Champflower BA10 . **215** A6
Wyke Rd
  Castle Cary BA7, BA10 ...**214** E7
  Wyke Champflower BA10 ..**215** C6
Wylds Rd TA6..........**209** A7
Wyllie Ct BS22..........**32** A5
Wymbush Cres BS13....**22** C5
Wymbush Gdns BS13....**22** C5
Wyndam Ct BS2 ....**227** B4
Wyndeats La TA5.......**134** B5
Wyndham's TA4.........**210** C4
Wyndham Cres BS20....**4** B4

Wyndham Ct BA21 ......**219** C5
Wyndham Rd
  Bridgwater TA6 .... **209** C6
  Taunton TA1...........**212** E7
  Watchet TA23.........**202** C6
Wyndham St BA20 ......**219** C5
Wyndham View BA21... **219** D5
Wyndham Way BS20.....**2** E5
Wyndham Way Ret Pk
  BS20...................**2** D5
Wynford Rd BA11.......**120** B5
Wynnes Cl DT9 ....**225** C3
Wynnes Rise DT9 ......**225** C3
Wynsome St BA14 ....**83** F3
Wynter Cl BS22.........**32** A3
Wyrral Cl BA6 ....**206** D3
Wytch Gn EX13 ....**198** E3
Wythburn Rd BA11..... **120** C5
Wyvern Cl
  Bruton BA11..........**215** F7
  Weston-Super-Mare BS23..**48** F7
  Yeovil BA20...........**218** C1
Wyvern Com Sch BS23 ...**48** F5
Wyvern Ct TA18.........**224** C6
Wyvern Mews **5** BS23...**48** F7
Wyvern Rd TA1 ....**168** E1
Wyville Rd BA11 ....**120** C6

Y

Yadley Cl BS25..........**70** A7
Yadley La BS25.........**70** A6
Yadley Way BS25.......**70** A7
Yallands Hill TA2......**213** E8
Yanel La BS25..........**52** B5
Yanhey Hill EX16.......**162** E4
Yanleigh Cl BS13........**21** D6
Yanley La BS41, BS13 ...**21** C7
Yarbury Way BS24 ......**32** B1
Yarde Pl TA1...........**212** F4
Yard La
  Marshwood DT6 ....**199** F3
  Wiveliscombe TA4 .....**210** C6
Yardleigh Cross EX13 ...**198** D4
Yard The BA11..........**143** C4
Yardwall Rd TA9 ....**106** A3
Yarley Cross BA5 ......**139** C8
Yarley Field La BA5 ....**139** B7
Yarley Hill BA5 ....**139** C7
Yarlington Cl TA2......**168** B4
Yarnbarton BA8.........**176** E1
Yarn Barton BA20......**219** A4
Yarrow Ct BS22.........**32** A5
Yarrow Rd TA9 ....**106** D3
Yatton Cl BS13..........**21** F8
Yatton Jun & Inf Schs
  BS49.................**34** C8
Yatton Sta BS49........**17** A1
Yeabsleys Way BA7 ....**214** C6
Yealscombe La TA24 ...**128** B2
Yeamen's Ho BS1.......**227** B1
Yeap's Dro BA5........**139** A7

Yearmoor La TA5.......**134** F8
Yearnor Mill La
  Oare TA24............**122** F5
  Porlock Weir TA24 ....**123** B5
Yeates Ct BS21..........**6** E3
Yeatman Cl BS39 ......**57** D4
Yeatman Hospl DT9....**225** D4
Yellingmill La BA4 .....**141** C8
Yellowcombe La TA24...**147** C5
Yellow Rose Cvn Pk
  TA20................ **193** D6
Yellow Way Rd
  Maiden Bradley BA11,
    BA12...............**144** A3
  Witham Friary BA11 ...**143** F3
Yellow Wood Cross TA4 . **132** D2
Yenston Hill BA8.......**189** F8
Yeo Bank La BS21 ......**15** F1
Yeo Cl
  Cheddar BS27.........**90** B6
  Weston-Super-Mare BS23...**49** A5
Yeo Ct
  Clevedon BS21.........**6** C2
  Congresbury BS49......**34** D4
Yeo La
  Bridgwater TA6 ....**209** B2
  Long Ashton BS41......**10** F1
Yeolands Dr BS21........**6** B1
Yeomanry Way BA4 ....**205** D5
Yeomans Cl BS9 ....**5** D5
Yeomanside Cl BS14 ....**23** C5
Yeomans Lodge BA11 ...**119** C4
Yeomans Orch BS40 ....**35** E3
Yeomead BS48..........**8** F3
Yeomeads BS41.........**10** F1
Yeo Mill Cross EX36....**162** C5
Yeo Moor BS21..........**6** E2
Yeo Moor Dro BS27,
  BS28.................**109** D3
Yeo Moor Inf Sch BS21....**6** E2
Yeo Moor Jun Sch BS21....**6** E2
Yeo Rd TA6............**209** B2
Yeo Valley **2** BA22....**197** F8
Yeo Valley Way BS48 ....**9** B2
Yeovil Bsns Ctr BA21....**219** F7
Yeovil Coll BA21 ....**219** A6
Yeovil District Hospl
  BA21.................**219** B5
Yeovil Junction Sta
  BA22.................**219** E1
Yeovil Marsh Pk BA21.. **187** A5
Yeovil Rd
  Crewkerne TA18.......**224** E7
  Halstock BA22........**197** D3
  Montacute TA15.......**186** B3
  Sherborne DT9 ....**225** C4
  Tintinhull BA22.......**186** C6
  Yeovil BA22..........**218** F1
Yeovil Small Bsns Ctr
  BA22................ **218** B6
Yeovil Trinity Foyer **7**
  BA20.................**219** B4
Yeoward Rd BS21........**6** E1

Yeo Way BS21 ....**6** B2
Yet Mead La BS27 .....**110** B7
Yewcroft Cl BS14 ....**23** A4
Yewtree Batch BS40 ....**37** A1
Yew Tree Cl
  Bishop Sutton BS39....**57** D4
  Lower Langford BS40 ...**53** E6
  Nailsea BS48...........**8** C1
  Yeovil BA20.......... **218** D4
Yew Tree Cotts BS40 ....**54** E3
Yew Tree Ct BS14 ....**23** B5
Yew Tree Dr BS22......**50** B8
Yew Tree Gdns
  Nailsea BS48...........**8** C1
  Pill BS20..............**4** C4
  Sandford BS25........**52** A4
Yew Tree La
  Compton Martin BS4 ...**74** A7
  Kingston Seymour BS21 .**16** B1
  Taunton TA2..........**213** E6
Yew Tree Pk BS49......**34** D3
Yomede Pk BA1 ....**44** A7
Yonder Dro TA10......**184** E8
Yonder Hill Cotts TA20 . **198** E2
Yonder Mead TA4......**167** F7
York's La BA3 ....**94** B6
York Bldgs TA6 ....**208** F5
York Cl
  Axminster EX13 ......**198** A1
  Weston-Super-Mare BS22...**32** A4
York Ct BS2 ....**227** B4
York Gdns BS8..........**11** F6
York Lodge **4** BA20... **219** A5
York Pl
  Bath BA1..............**45** B8
  Bristol, Brandon Hill BS1.. **226** C2
  Bristol, Victoria Park BS8 .**226** B3
  Yeovil BA20..........**219** A5
York Rd
  Bridgwater TA6 ....**208** F2
  Bristol BS2 ....**227** C1
  Taunton TA1..........**213** C5
York St
  Bath BA1..............**228** C2
  Bristol BS2...........**227** B4
  5 Frome BA11.......**119** E5
  Weston-Super-Mare BS23...**48** D7
Youngwood La BS48 ....**18** D7

Z

Zeals Rise BA12.........**161** F2
Zembard La TA20 ..... **223** C4
Zeta Cl TA7............**209** E8
Zig Zag BS21 ....**6** D4
Zion Hill
  Midsomer Norton BA3...**96** B7
  Oakhill BA3 .... **115** A3
  10 Shepton Mallet BA4 ..**205** B6

Any feature in this atlas can be given a unique reference to help you find the same feature on other Ordnance Survey maps of the area, or to help someone else locate you if they do not have a Street Atlas.

The grid squares in this atlas match the Ordnance Survey National Grid and are at 500 metre intervals. The small figures at the bottom and sides of every other grid line are the National Grid kilometre values (**00**°to°**99** km) and are repeated across the country every 100°km (see left).

To give a unique National Grid reference you need to locate where in the country you are. The country is divided into 100 km squares with each square given a unique two-letter reference. Use the administrative map to determine in which 100 km square a particular page of this atlas falls.

The bold letters and numbers between each grid line (**A**°to°**F**,°**1**°to°**8**) are for use within a specific Street Atlas only, and when used with the page number, are a convenient way of referencing these grid squares.

Example   *The railway bridge over DARLEY GREEN RD in grid square B1*

Step 1: Identify the two-letter reference, in this example the page is in **SP**

Step 2: Identify the 1 km square in which the railway bridge falls. Use the figures in the southwest corner of this square: Eastings **17**, Northings **74**. This gives a unique reference: **SP 17 74**, accurate to 1°km.

Step 3: To give a more precise reference accurate to 100 m you need to estimate how many tenths along and how many tenths up this 1 km square the feature is (to help with this the 1 km square is divided into four 500 m squares). This makes the bridge about **8** tenths along and about **1** tenth up from the southwest corner.

This gives a unique reference: **SP 178 741**, accurate to 100°m.

Eastings (read from left to right along the bottom) come before Northings (read from bottom to top). If you have trouble remembering say to yourself Along the hall, THEN up the stairs !

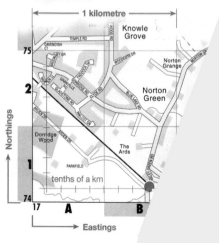

PHILIP'S MAPS

the Gold Standard for drivers

◆ **Philip's street atlases cover every county in England, Wales and much of Scotland**

◆ Every named street is shown, including alleys, lanes and walkways

◆ Thousands of additional features marked: stations, public buildings, car parks, places of interest

◆ Route-planning maps to get you close to your destination

◆ Postcodes on the maps and in the index

◆ Widely used by the emergency services, transport companies and local authorities

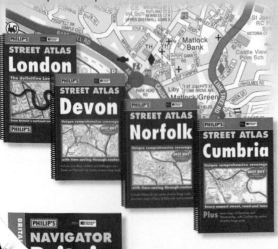

For national mapping, choose **Philip's Navigator Britain** the most detailed road atlas available of England, Wales and Scotland. Hailed by Auto Express as 'the ultimate road atlas', this is the only one-volume atlas to show every road and lane in Britain.

Street atlases currently available

England
Bedfordshire
Berkshire
Birmingham and West Midlands
Bristol and Bath
Buckinghamshire
Cambridgeshire
Cheshire
Cornwall
Cumbria
Derbyshire
Devon
Dorset
County Durham and Teesside
Essex
North Essex
South Essex
Gloucestershire
Hampshire
North Hampshire
South Hampshire
Herefordshire
Monmouthshire
Hertfordshire
Isle of Wight
Kent
East Kent
West Kent
Lancashire
Leicestershire and Rutland
Lincolnshire
London
Greater Manchester
Merseyside
Norfolk
Northamptonshire
Northumberland
Nottinghamshire
Oxfordshire
Shropshire
Somerset
Staffordshire
Suffolk
Surrey

East Sussex
West Sussex
Tyne and Wear
Warwickshire
Birmingham and West Midlands
Wiltshire and Swindon
Worcestershire
East Yorkshire
Northern Lincolnshire
North Yorkshire
South Yorkshire
West Yorkshire

Wales
Anglesey, Conwy and Gwynedd
Cardiff, Swansea and The Valleys
Carmarthenshire, Pembrokeshire and Swansea
Ceredigion and South Gwynedd
Denbighshire, Flintshire, Wrexham
Herefordshire Monmouthshire
Powys

Scotland
Aberdeenshire
Ayrshire
Dumfries and Galloway
Edinburgh and East Central Scotland
Fife and Tayside
Glasgow and West Central Scotland
Inverness and Moray
Lanarkshire
Scottish Borders

Northern Ireland*
County Armagh and County Down
Belfast
County Londonderry and County Antrim
County Tyrone and County Fermanagh

*Publishing autumn 2006

How to order Philip's maps and atlases are available from bookshops, motorway services and petrol stations. You can order direct from the publisher by phoning **01903 828503** or online at **www.philips-maps.co.uk** For bulk orders only, phone 020 7644 6940